KU-510-173

THE DRAWINGS OF
PONTORMO

TEXT

THE DRAWINGS OF
PONTORMO

Janet Cox Rearick

HARVARD UNIVERSITY PRESS

Cambridge, Massachusetts

1964

LIBRARY OF CONGRESS CATALOG CARD NUMBER 64–13427

PRINTED IN THE UNITED STATES OF AMERICA

DISTRIBUTED IN GREAT BRITAIN BY OXFORD UNIVERSITY PRESS, LONDON

PUBLICATION OF THIS BOOK HAS BEEN AIDED BY A GRANT FROM THE FORD FOUNDATION

To

S. J. FREEDBERG

PREFACE

The primary research for this book was supported by grants from the Fulbright Program and the American Association of University Women, while it was completed with the aid of a grant from the American Council of Learned Societies and a fellowship made possible by the Friends of the Fogg Art Museum. It is to these foundations that I owe my first thanks and I gratefully acknowledge their aid to my research. The period 1961–1962, during which this book was brought to completion, was made additionally productive by my association, as a Fellow, with the Harvard University Center for Italian Renaissance Culture, Villa I Tatti, Florence. I am grateful to the director, Prof. Kenneth Murdock, as well as to my colleagues, the Fellows, for their assistance and encouragement.

In addition to the staff of the Biblioteca Berenson, I Tatti, I wish to thank the staffs of the other libraries in which I have worked while preparing this book, most particularly, the library of the Fogg Art Museum, Harvard University, the Frick Art Reference Library, New York, and the Kunsthistorisches Institut, Florence.

I am grateful to the keepers and staffs of all the drawing collections in which I have studied Pontormo's drawings. For their cooperation and aid in procuring information and photographs, I should especially like to thank Mr. Keith Andrews, Mlle. Roseline Bacou, Dr. Egbert Begemann, Dr. Lidia Bianchi, Dr. Bernhard Degenhart, Miss Agnes Mongan, Mr. A. E. Popham, Mr. Philip Pouncey, Miss Felice Stampfle, and, among private owners of drawings, Mr. Janos Scholz and Count Antoine Seilern. Special thanks are due to Prof. Giulia Sinibaldi and Dr. Maria Fossi Todorow, who were exceptionally helpful during two extended periods of study at the Gabinetto Disegni e Stampe degli Uffizi, Florence (where the major portion of Pontormo's drawings are to be found), and who facilitated in every way possible my studies in that collection.

I am deeply indebted to those who have been kind enough to read the manuscript of this book during its preparation; it has been greatly enriched by their valuable suggestions and comments. I owe thanks to Prof. Jakob Rosenberg, Harvard University, with whom I first studied Renaissance drawings and whose criticisms in the early stages of this project were most helpful. I am extremely grateful to Mr. Philip Pouncey of the British Museum Print Room, who has given me the benefit of his unequalled knowledge of sixteenth-century drawings, and has made many illuminating suggestions, especially concerning the large body of material that has been associated with Pontormo. To Prof. Craig H. Smyth, Institute of Fine Arts of New York University, I wish to express special thanks for his sympathetic criticism of the manuscript and for his generosity with unpublished material on Bronzino and Bronzino's drawings, which I have quoted liberally.

My most particular thanks are to Prof. S. J. Freedberg for his encouragement and sustained interest in every phase of this work, his criticisms on matters both methodological and specific, and his contributions too numerous to acknowledge in every instance. It is to Professor Freedberg that I owe my orientation in Italian Renaissance painting — as well as the suggestion to undertake this book — and it is to him that I gratefully dedicate it.

I would also like to thank the many colleagues and friends who have contributed in various ways toward the completion of this book. Among them, Dr. Luciano Berti, Mr. Eugene Carroll, Mrs. Iris Cheney, Prof. John Coolidge, Dr. Gino Corti, Miss Elaine Johnson, Mrs. Kathleen Posner, Dr. Donald Posner, Mr. Michael Rinehart, Mr. Eric Schroeder, Dr. Walter Vitzthum, Prof. Rudolf Wittkower, and, particularly, Dr. Gertrude Bing, have made suggestions that have proved helpful. I am especially grateful to Mr. Edward Sanchez, who has generously called my attention to a number of documents concerned with Pontormo and has discussed their interpretation with me. Finally, to my husband, whose understanding help has extended far beyond that of any other colleague, I wish to express my deepest gratitude.

I Tatti, Florence
January 23, 1963 J. C. R.

Since the date of this preface I have benefited from the continuing interest and assistance of many of those mentioned above. In addition, I owe thanks to Dr. Walter Gernsheim, who most generously gave permission to reproduce the Pontormo photographs from his *Corpus Photographicum*, photographs that make up a large portion of the illustrations in this book. I am also grateful to Miss Ann Orlov, who has edited the manuscript with exemplary care, and to Mrs. Ann Leval, who was kind enough to assist in reading the proofs.

CONTENTS

THE DRAWINGS OF
PONTORMO

INTRODUCTION

. . . una cosa sola c'è che è nobile, che è
el suo fondamento, e questo si è el disegno . . .

PONTORMO'S response to the questionnaire sent by Benedetto Varchi to the leading artists of Florence on the relative merits of sculpture and painting is substantially contained in this passage from his answering letter.[1] His assertion of the supremacy of drawing is not surprising from a Florentine artist, to whom *disegno* — considered broadly to include invention as well as execution — was indeed the basis of art. Pontormo's words echo throughout Florentine Renaissance writings on art; from Ghiberti and Leonardo, with their concern for the instructional role of *disegno*, to Zuccaro, with his defense of the Mannerist concept of the *disegno interno*. However, there are few Florentine artists whose avowed preference was more substantiated by actual practice; few who drew with such continuous energy and creativity; and few who were innovators both in their graphic manner and in their expansion of the traditional Renaissance concept of *disegno*. To the average Florentine artist drawing was the basis of art in a somewhat academic sense. Indeed, this was the spirit of Varchi's investigation, itself reflecting an academic tendency of the mid-sixteenth century to justify in theory the style and practice of the *Maniera*. To Pontormo, out of sympathy with theoretical definitions of sculpture, painting, or *disegno* (as is evident from the tone of his letter), drawing was

[1] See B. Varchi, *Due Lezzioni di M. Benedetto Varchi* (Florence, 1549), 132–135. The context of the passage quoted from Pontormo's letter (spelling modernized by P. Barocchi, *Trattati d'Arte del Cinquecento*, Florence, 1960, I, 67) is as follows: "La cosa in sé è tanto difficile, che la non si può disputare e manco risolvere, perché una cosa sola c'è che è nobile, che è el suo fondamento, e questo si è el disegno, e tutte quante l'altre ragioni sono debole rispetto a questo (vedetelo che chiunche ha questo, fa l'una e l'altra bene); e se tutte l'altre arguizioni sono debole e meschine rispetto a questo, come si può ella disputare con questo solo, se non lassare stare questo da parte, non avendo simile a sé, et produrre altre ragioni più debole, senza fine o conclusione?"

not a matter for learned discussion, but the essence of his art. It was an investigative and creative activity, at once intellectual and intuitive, that was essential to the full expression of his artistic individuality. Without the evidence of the drawings themselves, the linear complexity and refinement of Pontormo's paintings would suggest this; after even the most cursory survey of them, their key role in Pontormo's art is beyond dispute. Furthermore, these drawings are not (as is so often the case) a mere appendage to Pontormo's paintings, sharpening or modifying the image of an artistic personality whose outlines and substance are already clear. Beyond this basic function Pontormo's drawings have an independent stylistic identity and development, a specifically graphic language of their own that extends significantly, and in often unpredictable directions, our understanding of his total artistic achievement.

Fortunately, the drawings survive in considerable numbers and are sufficiently varied in type and in date to provide a sound basis for general conclusions and to permit us to assess this achievement in some detail. Of the many drawings attributed to Pontormo, three hundred and eighty-three are here considered original.[2] In contrast to the wide range and constant experimental flux of graphic expression that we will find in Pontormo's drawings, their graphic mode is unusually limited. Pontormo was consistent throughout his career in his choice of working materials. His characteristic achievement as a draughtsman is the red or black chalk figure study on white to cream paper measuring about 400 x 250 mm.[3] His chalks were the *matita rossa* and *matita nera* that were in general use in Florence in the early sixteenth

[2] The recto and verso (where it exists) of 256 sheets are numbered separately and arranged in approximately chronological order in the Catalogue Raisonné. See pp. 347–356 for a discussion of the sketches in Pontormo's diary.

[3] The size varies, partly because most of the drawings have been irregularly cut down. However, with the exception of the considerably smaller sketchbook sheets (see note 7), most of Pontormo's drawings appear to have been executed on a standard size of paper measuring 450 x 315 mm. See Meder 1919, 174n1; C. M. Briquet, *Les Filigranes* (Leipzig, 1923), I, 3–4. About one third of the sheets bear watermarks, of which the following are specifically identifiable in Briquet: B. 50 (cat. 324, 340, 363); B. 613 (cat. 346); B. 4196 (cat. 275); B. 5536 (cat. 198); B. 5540 (cat. 321); B. 5543 (cat. 90, 200, 294, 349); B. 5641 (cat. 3, 12, 20, 28, 48, 51); B. 5927 (cat. 318, 354, 364); B. 5963 (cat. 165); B. 6086 (cat. 343); B. 6088 (cat. 371); B. 6305 (cat. 267); B. 6895 (cat. 373); B. 7106 (cat. 353); B. 7392 (cat. 37, 93, 188, 249, 263, 292); B. 7435 (cat. 143, 145, 155, 159, 160, 161, 162, 174, 178, 225); B. 7697 (cat. 313); B. 11663 (cat. 84); B. 12419 (cat. 101); B. 13899 (cat. 342). A watermark that occurs on cat. 135, 136, 151, 153, and 157 (all for Poggio a Caiano) has been identified by Mongan and Sachs 1940, W. 8. Three watermarks not identifiable in Briquet occur on a number of Pontormo drawings: a large eagle on cat. 8, 244, 279, 289, 298, and 327; a smaller eagle on cat. 74, 238, and 248; and a small crown on cat. 281, 286, 287, 288, and 317 (in the last group all but cat. 317 date from ca. 1527–1528). Two watermarks occur on the sheets from the Corsini sketchbook, but do not appear on other Pontormo drawings (see note 10 on p. 167).

century.[4] While both colors are found in his drawings until 1530, black chalk was increasingly favored after 1530 and apparently used almost exclusively after 1545. A small number of drawings in pen and bistre occur at irregular intervals before 1530 in Pontormo's *oeuvre*, but their appearance is quite incidental and the potential of this medium was never developed.[5] Pontormo seldom deviated from his favored white paper, using brown, grey, or blue papers only occasionally in the period before 1530.[6] However, at various times between about 1517 and 1550 he prepared the white paper of a sketchbook with a pink wash that becomes a luminous ground for red or black chalk.[7] Aside from white highlighting on a number of drawings,[8] this is the extent of Pontormo's variation in working materials. Such a purposeful limitation in media is closely related to the most characteristic feature of Pontormo's graphic expression: in his chalk drawings Pontormo relied to an uncommon extent on the simplest and most difficult of graphic means — line itself. There was no attempt to create pictorial effects, to imitate the language of painting through the exploitation of color and of combined media. Pontormo expressed in a singularly undistilled form the linear bias that is uniquely and characteristically Florentine.

The types of drawings that comprise Pontormo's *oeuvre* are not as clear-cut as those in the work of his High Renaissance predecessors or even some of

[4] See Meder 1919, 109–113, 119–126; J. Watrous, *The Craft of Old Master Drawings* (Madison, 1957), 92ff, 110ff. Pontormo's red chalk is of a light tonality that contrasts with the deeper tone sometimes used in the later sixteenth century. 194 of the drawings are in red chalk, while 139 are in black chalk, and 46 are in red and black chalk. In most cases red and black chalk are used in separate sketches on the same sheet, rather than being combined with a pictorial intention. At other times Pontormo began a drawing very lightly in one chalk (usually black) and then finished it in the other color. Brown chalk, which was unusual in Florence in the early sixteenth century (Meder 1919, 116), appears in only a single drawing (cat. 72).

[5] Pontormo's ink has the characteristic pale brown tonality of bistre and his washes are light and transparent. Cat. 1 is in pen with bistre wash. In cat. 40 pen is used with black chalk, and in cat. 131–132 pen and wash are used over very faint black chalk. In cat. 272 bistre wash has been added to a primarily black chalk compositional drawing. Cat. 101, 176, and 319 are chalk drawings but there are also small sketches in pen on the same sheet. In contrast to this very sparing use of pen and bistre in the authentic drawings, see the List of Attributed Drawings for the many pen studies wrongly given to Pontormo.

[6] Cat. 28, 39, 50, 61 and 82 are on brown paper; cat. 141, 170, 190, and 223, are on blue or blue-grey paper. Cat. 187 is on grey-green paper. Cat. 307, a compositional drawing of 1532–1534 unique for its large size, is executed on a heavy brown paper.

[7] There are 60 of these drawings, of which 36 are from the Corsini Sketchbook. See notes 10–12 on p. 167 for a discussion of this group. The uneven pink ground of these sheets, which could be created most readily by dampening red chalk, is found also in the drawings of Pontormo's contemporaries such as Correggio and Fra Bartolommeo.

[8] Of the 59 drawings in which white has been used, 11 are compositional studies. With the exception of the red chalk drawings heightened with white from the Corsini Sketchbook, they are black chalk figure studies.

his Mannerist contemporaries. There is a blurring of the conventional distinctions between *pensieri*, *studi*, and *modelli* that suggests a highly individual variant of the disciplining, dialectic preparatory process of the Renaissance.[9] Furthermore, Pontormo experimented with the free sketch and the finished drawing, two kinds of drawings whose potential had not been fully explored in the High Renaissance. These novelties, together with the overlapping of conventional types, make it difficult to categorize Pontormo's drawings. There are a handful of recognizable *pensieri*; quick, light, first sketches of compositional ideas, usually small in scale (cat. 29, 130, 212; figs. 37, 116, 204). However, the majority of Pontormo's drawings are individual figure studies, either nude or draped. These are usually, but not invariably, preparatory in function. There are numerous drawings that are clearly not connected with pictorial preparation, but are free sketches in the most modern sense (cat. 186, 253; figs. 165, 241). There are many other similar studies that are ultimately related to pictorial motives, but the relation is a tangential one. They are connected, not as links in a rational sequence, but as freely associated and purely graphic ideas that often led Pontormo far from the original or ultimate pictorial problem. Thus, a large number of Pontormo's preparatory drawings are actually independent sketches of a most private and spontaneous sort, quite unlimited by a preconceived scheme leading in a predictable and direct line to the final painted solution (cat. 144, 264; figs. 137, 248). While there are many preparatory studies of complete figures, there are few *studi* of details, such as those frequent among Andrea del Sarto's drawings. We find head studies, interesting to Pontormo because of their psychological content (cat. 36, 275; figs. 43, 262). However, studies of details such as drapery and hands, with their somewhat academic connotations, apparently held little interest for him. His few drawings of this type are not finished in execution and are far from academic (cat. 47, 273; figs. 50, 261). The same might be said of Pontormo's *modelli*, even when they are squared for enlargement. Many of the final studies for single figures or for entire compositions are finished in the sense of a fully developed idea but retain a spontaneity and fluidity of line and shape usually found only in a *primo pensiero* (cat. 104, 154, 192; figs. 114, 148, 181). After 1530 the *modello* became more precise, until, in the work of the later years, the distinction between the final study for a painting and an independent finished drawing is often unclear (cat. 321, 359; figs. 310, 345). Like the free sketch, but at the opposite pole from it, the finished drawing is an independent graphic statement possessing significance for the artist, and presumably for his con-

[9] See Tolnay 1943, 19–27, for a useful survey of the types of drawing in the Renaissance.

temporaries, beyond its connection with the preparatory process. As such, the finished type of drawing and the free sketch are each facets of Pontormo's expansion of the traditional concepts of *disegno*.

According to Vasari (V/M, VI, 288), there were "molti disegni, cartoni, e modelli di terra bellissimi" in Pontormo's house at his death.[10] Like any other fresco painter, Pontormo made cartoons, and we can find mention of the cartoons for the San Lorenzo choir in his diary.[11] However, since neither cartoons nor terracotta models have survived, the drawings remain the only evidence of Pontormo's working procedure in preparing for a panel or a fresco. A few of them show that Pontormo used the simple process of incising outlines in order to transfer the design to another sheet or to the panel.[12] However, when enlarging a drawing in preparation for the cartoon and its transfer to panel or plaster, Pontormo employed the usual device of squaring.[13] When enlarging for a fresco his scale was one square (less often two squares) to one *braccio*.[14] There are notes on the scale of enlargement on drawings for the Poggio a Caiano lunette and on studies for the upper-range San Lorenzo

[10] As cartoons generally were not preserved after their use in transferring a design to the wall, Vasari may have been referring in part to unused cartoons, such as those he notes elsewhere (V/M, VI, 276), which were owned by Lodovico Capponi. On the basis of Vasari's mention of terracotta models and his statement (*ibid.*, 287) that Pontormo made "modelli di terra" for San Lorenzo, there have been several unconvincing attempts to identify terracotta *bozzetti* as the work of Pontormo. See E. Tietze-Conrat, "Ein plastiches Modell des Pontormo," *ZBK* 63 (1929/30), 165–168; and Schlegel 1961, 28–38. Schlegel has connected cat. 15, 29, 35, 36, 44, 77, 80, 122, 250, 300, and 323 with a *bozzetto* of *Adam and Eve with Cain and Abel* (Berlin) that she wrongly identified as a Pontormo of 1512–1518.

[11] See pp. 352, 353, 356. July 22, 1555: "El dì apuntai quello cartone che Battista portò." October 26, 1555: "Sabato ordinai el cartone che gli va a lato." August 27, 1556: "Portai el cartone del Sancto Lorenzo a apicossi da poter lavorare."

[12] Cf. cat. 195, 206, 208, 224, 260, 321, 327, and 375, where the outlines are incised for transfer. In all these cases except cat. 195 the drawings are so much smaller than the painting that it is evident that the design was simply transferred to another sheet of paper. (This procedure was clearly used in cat. 224, where the reverse of the sheet is blackened and a figure traced onto cat. 227.) However, in cat. 195 for the *Victory and Baptism of the Ten Thousand Martyrs*, there is the possibility that this compositional drawing served as the actual *modello* for the Pitti and Uffizi panels.

[13] Cat. 192, 223, 271, 272, 287, 289, and 293 are drawings that were squared in preparation for panel pictures. Cat. 93, 152, 153, 160, 206, 211, 224?, 232?, 261, 266, 278, 279, 327?, 350, 354, 355, 357, 360, 366, 370, and 376 are drawings that were squared in preparation for frescoes.

[14] The Florentine *braccio* is given as 58.4 cm in the *Enciclopedia italiana* 7 (1930), 649. While the *braccio* varied during the years it was used as a measure and it varied in the sixteenth century from artist to artist, from painter to architect, several of Pontormo's squared studies indicate that his *braccio* was about 60 cm. If the 60 cm figure is used, the measurements in *braccia* written by Pontormo on cat. 131 and 132 for Poggio a Caiano agree with the actual size of the lunette. Another example, cat. 206, is squared in 10 vertical and 10 horizontal squares for a fresco field in the Certosa cloister measuring about 311 x 287 cm. The squares must then equal about 30 cm (or half a *braccio*) each. The outline of the left edge of the drawing is drawn within the last square to indicate the slightly smaller horizontal dimension of the fresco.

frescoes, but Pontormo was not generally given to making notations on his drawings: there are no color notes or indications of subject at all, and only a single date.[15]

As is suggested by Vasari's remark that there were many drawings left in his house when he died, the majority of Pontormo's drawings must have been dispersed only after his death. Although his pupils Bronzino and Naldini had access to his drawings and must have been given some of them, Pontormo did not found a *bottega* in which his drawings would have been used for instruction and thus scattered. Indeed, by his unusually systematic preservation of his drawings, Pontormo indicated his regard for them as more than mere working material subordinated to another end, as more than a means of instruction. If they were preserved for instructional purposes, it was solely for his own instruction. Evidence that he did use his old drawings is found in his unusually frequent reference back to earlier motives, in his habitual use of the verso of a sheet years — even as much as twenty years — later,[16] and to the reinterpretation of earlier motives in a later style on the same sheet.[17] Thus, the introverted and self-critical approach that is so marked in Pontormo's stylistic development is already clear in his working procedure. Especially in the late years, his artistic isolation is reflected not only in his dislike of assistants, his jealously secretive hiding of his work at Villa Castello and San Lorenzo, but also in the solitary activity that drawing became for him. An entry in his diary written a year before his death provides a glimpse of an isolated existence quite different from that of the communal *bottega* with which we often associate the Renaissance draughtsman: "Lunedì . . . non lavorai e insino a sabato stetti a casa a disegnare." [18]

[15] Measurements occur on cat. 131 and 132 for the Poggio a Caiano lunette, on cat. 350, 354, 357, 359, 360, 364, 366, 367, and 380 for the San Lorenzo choir. Pontormo notes the date on cat. 170, makes a correction on cat. 190, and evidently reminds himself to finish a composition on cat. 261. The notes are in the same medium as the drawing, except for cat. 354 and 367, where they are in ink. Pontormo's handwriting may be readily identified by comparison with the writing in his diary (see pp. 347–356).

[16] While it is not unusual for the recto and verso of Pontormo's drawings to date about 5 years apart, as in cat. 1 for the *Carro della Zecca* and cat. 43 for the Visdomini altar, or in cat. 141 for Poggio a Caiano and cat. 223 for the *Portrait of Ippolito de' Medici*, longer periods sometimes elapsed before Pontormo used the reverse of a sheet. See cat. 14 and 203, cat. 104 and 361, cat. 197 and 349, cat. 238 and 339, and cat. 334 and 377. Cat. 200 and 201 are the recto and verso of a sketchbook sheet with drawings for the Certosa of 1523–1524 on the left sides and drawings from ca. 1550 on the right sides, indicating that Pontormo used the same sketchbook at widely separated dates.

[17] See cat. 63, 66, 67, 69, 71, and 239. A figure from cat. 104 of ca. 1520 is reinterpreted on the verso, a sketch of ca. 1546–1550.

[18] See p. 353 (Pontormo's diary, September 8–14, 1555). Pontormo also mentions drawing in the diary on September 16, 1555: "Lunedì disegnai"; and on October 27–28, 1555: "Stetti que' duo dì in casa a disegnare." (See p. 353.)

Little is known of the fate of Pontormo's accumulation of drawings after his death and their passing with his estate to his nearest relative, Andrea Chiazzella.[19] There are only scattered references to their belonging to specific collectors in the later sixteenth century. Vasari says (V/M, VI, 276) that Lodovico Capponi owned some of Pontormo's cartoons for the unexecuted frescoes at Poggio a Caiano and, "in una carta, una storia d'ignudi che giuocano al calcio." This drawing is probably identifiable as the large *modello* now in the Uffizi (cat. 307; fig. 296). Somewhat later both Borghini and Bocchi note that Baccio Valori owned a study for the San Lorenzo *Resurrection of the Dead and Martyrdom of St. Lawrence*, a drawing in black chalk on white paper about three quarters of a *braccio* in size.[20] This drawing has not been identified, nor has the "modello . . . in piccolo" for the Carmignano *Visitation* that Cinelli later knew in the collection of Andrea Pitti.[21] During the seventeenth and eighteenth centuries, in contrast to the paintings — which were in churches and large private collections and continuously noted in the literature[22] — the drawings virtually disappeared from circulation and Pontormo's reputation as a draughtsman did not often elicit extensive comment.[23] Behind this situation lies the obvious fact that the drawings were not widely dispersed or known outside Florence. Since Pontormo had no school or even a group of close followers, his drawings had not been imitated during his lifetime. Even his two pupils, Bronzino and Naldini, developed their graphic manner in quite diverse directions after Pontormo's death. With the defection of his pupils, the general decline of his popularity in the period of the *Maniera* (in spite of a revival of interest among a few artists), and the widespread shift in taste after 1600, Pontormo's eclipse as a draughtsman may have been complete within a

[19] Clapp 1914, 28–29; and Clapp 1916, app. II, doc. 30, cited documentary evidence that the drawings went to Chiazzella. However, F. Baldinucci, *Notizie dei professori del Disegno da Cimabue in qua* (Florence, Manni, 1771), X, 160, asserted in his life of Naldini that Pontormo gave all his drawings to Naldini. It is certainly likely that during his association with Pontormo in the last years of the master's life Naldini was given a number of drawings, but there is no evidence that he received any of those that were in Pontormo's possession when he died.

[20] Borghini 1548, 485; Bocchi 1591, 183–184. (See note 33 on p. 325.) Three quarters of a *braccio* (40 cm) is exactly the height (or original height before cutting-down) of most of Pontormo's San Lorenzo compositional studies, all of which are in black chalk like this lost drawing.

[21] Cinelli 1677, 286.

[22] On the reputation of Pontormo's paintings, see L. Berti, "Fortuna del Pontormo," *Quaderni Pontormeschi* no. 2 (Empoli, 1956).

[23] Typical is Mariette's commentary on the Pontormo drawings in the Crozat collection. See *Description Sommaire des Dessins des Grands Maistres . . . du Cabinet de Feu M. Crozat* (Paris, 1741), 4. Pontormo is grouped with Rosso, Daniele da Volterra, Salviati, and Vasari, no drawing by him being separately listed. Mariette notes that "les commencements du Pontorme sont dignes d' André del Sarte; il faisoit ses Etudes avec un grand soin d'après nature, & ses figures d'Académies sont fort prisées."

relatively short time. Whereas the paintings continued to be noted — albeit in unflattering terms — it is possible that within seventy-five years of his death, knowledge of Pontormo's personal drawing style would have virtually died out. During this period the great majority of his drawings must have remained unnoticed in the hands of Florentine collectors,[24] coming eventually to the Uffizi about 1700 with the Medici collections.[25] While there are one hundred and eighty-six sheets in the Uffizi (including four Santarelli drawings), few drawings by Pontormo appear to have found their way into other major European drawing collections.[26] Even with the discovery of several unnoted Pontormo drawings in recent years, only seventy sheets, twenty-nine of them in Rome, the others widely scattered in twenty-seven different collections, are to be found today outside the Uffizi.

Precisely because of the small number of Pontormo's drawings in circulation and the consequent lack of knowledge of his style, many of the drawings outside Florence and a handful in the Uffizi formerly carried other attributions, such as Andrea del Sarto (cat. 3, 4, 15, 17, 18, 37, 64, 97, 190, 230, 231), Rosso (cat. 13, 194), Bronzino (cat. 357), Correggio (cat. 30, 84, 159), Beccafumi (cat. 13), Michelangelo (cat. 351, 365), Cavaliere d'Arpino (cat. 360), Ammanati (cat. 25), Fra Bartolommeo (cat. 124), Baroccio (cat. 272),

[24] There are numerous inscriptions on the drawings attributing them to Pontormo (many of which, however, are of eighteenth-century origin), but only a single collector's name appears. This name, followed by a number, is inscribed at the lower left in ink on the following drawings in the Uffizi: cat. 28, 61, 133, 135, 144, 156, 157, 164, 175, 197, 201, 226, 227, 238, 243, 250, 290, 302, 312, and 334. There has been a difference of opinion both on the reading of the name and on the date of this inscription. Clapp 1914, 29, and Cecchi 1956, 145, read it as "Fran[co] Rozi" and dated it in the late sixteenth century, while Marcucci, *MDM* 1954, 27, 30; and *MP* 1956, 67, 94, 97, 98, 105, and 106, read it as "Bardo Rosi" and dated it in the eighteenth century. I am indebted to Mr. Edward Sanchez for a correct reading of this inscription as "Fran[co] Rosi" and for identifying the collector as Francesco d'Antonio Rosi. Rosi is recorded as active as a goldsmith in 1636. (See A.S.F., Carte dell'Ancisa, EEa, car. 570.) He was buried January 7, 1638 [new style]. See in the Biblioteca Nazionale, Florence, the MS. Cirri, Necrologio Fiorentino XVI, Famiglia Rosi.

[25] The collection of Cardinal Leopoldo (1617–1675) formed the basis of the Medici collection of drawings. It contained sheets that had belonged to Vasari and Borghini, but there is no specific evidence that Pontormo was represented in these important late sixteenth-century Florentine collections. The Medici collection was augmented by Leopoldo's nephew, Cosimo III (1642–1732), who acquired drawings from collections such as those of Gaddi, Michelozzi, Hygford, and Mariette. See the introduction in Ferri 1881, and F. Lugt, *Les Marques de Collection de Dessins et d'Estampes* (Amsterdam, 1921), nos. 929–930. There are no collector's marks on the Uffizi drawings other than that of the Uffizi itself. (L. 929–930), which appears on all the drawings, and that of Santarelli (L. 907) on the drawings that he gave to the Uffizi in 1866 (cat. 84, 194, 261, and 365).

[26] The following drawings are among those formerly in important private collections: cat. 188 (Crozat); cat. 195, 314 (Harzen); cat. 124, 232, 254 (Lawrence); cat. 219, 220 (Mannheim); cat. 97, 171 (Mariette); cat. 232 (Ottley); cat. 159 (Pacetti); cat. 84, 172, 252 (Reynolds); cat. 172, 255, 272 (Richardson Sr.); cat. 155 (Royal French Collections); cat. 3 (Royal Saxon Collections); cat. 84, 194, 261, 365 (Santarelli); cat. 151, 190 (Vallardi).

Niccolò dell'Abate (cat. 261), Naldini (cat. 39, 232), Schiavone (cat. 170), Tintoretto (cat. 376), and Sebastiano del Piombo (cat. 195, 214). However, the number of past misattributions of authentic drawings is far exceeded by the number of drawings by other hands that have been and continue to be wrongly given to Pontormo.[27] Large blocks of these are old, traditional attributions such as those in the Uffizi (cat. A24–A198), or in the Baldinucci Collection of the Louvre (cat. A259–A319, A327–A333), but many are attributions that have been made in the last sixty years. Much of this irrelevant material has accrued to Pontormo's *oeuvre* because in the eighteenth and nineteenth centuries there was little coherent idea of how Pontormo's drawing style differed from that of his master, Andrea del Sarto; or his pupils, Bronzino and Naldini; or from certain draughtsmen of the later sixteenth century. Actually, it is essentially this lack of definition of Pontormo's personal style, rather than its overdefinition in the form of the copies and school drawings that swell the *oeuvres* of so many Renaissance draughtsmen, that accounts for the overextension of Pontormo's *oeuvre*.[28]

During the past sixty years, the number of drawings attributed to Pontormo in the literature has been cut in half. Berenson began this process in his monumental publication of 1903, *The Drawings of the Florentine Painters*, and it was continued by Clapp in his careful and comprehensive *Dessins de Pontormo* of 1914. Clapp's *catalogue raisonné* also included many drawings that he rejected as Pontormo's, often with helpful suggested attributions to other artists. Berenson's 1938 edition of his work carried the reduction of the *oeuvre* further, a tendency that will be evident in the present catalogue as well.

These changes have come about gradually as the result of a twofold investigation. The first aspect of this investigation has been the definition of Pontormo's artistic personality and limitations as a draughtsman. The second aspect has been the emergence of his contemporaries — from those still working

[27] See the List of Attributed Drawings. A group of drawings attributed to Pontormo is listed geographically and by museum inventory number as cat. A1–A378, the recto and verso bearing the same number. This list makes no claim to completeness. However, an attempt has been made to consider all the drawings given to Pontormo in the Uffizi, Florence, and in the Gabinetto Nazionale delle Stampe, Rome, among which are found most of the "borderline" cases. Included also (even where it was apparently redundant to do so) are all the attributions to Pontormo in Clapp's and Berenson's lists, as well as attributions appearing in the more recent literature and in collections we have examined.

[28] Copies make up a small percentage of the wrong attributions to Pontormo, but a larger one than has previously been recognized. The following drawings are certainly copies after Pontormo drawings or paintings: Cat. A1, A7, A33, A43, A88, A95, A106, A107, A120, A124, A126, A144, A151, A153, A157, A159, A167, A172, A193, A199, A200, A201, A208, A214, A216, A217, A226, A227, A234, A235, A237, A238, A239, A240, A248, A252, A259, A265, A327, A328, A329, A334, A336, A348, A354, A362, A370, and A377.

within the classical frame of reference of the first decade of the century, to those active at the very end of the century — as distinct individualities. Berenson has clarified much of the confusion between Pontormo and Andrea del Sarto, a task largely dependent on the recognition of the incipient individuality of Pontormo's youthful Sartesque red chalk studies.[29] However, many drawings, some also recognized by Berenson, should be assigned to less important draughtsmen of the early sixteenth century such as Sogliani,[30] Puligo,[31] and Bacchiacca.[32] These artists, strongly influenced in their graphic style by both Andrea and Pontormo, are responsible for a number of so-called early Pontormo chalk drawings. There has also been some overlapping in this area with Rosso, but his distinctive drawing style is not as easily confounded with Pontormo's early work. Pontormo's drawings of the later twenties are often confused with those of Bronzino, who emerged about 1525 as a draughtsman closely dependent on but temperamentally quite opposite from his master. Bronzino's graphic style, especially in its earlier phases, is still much less precisely defined than that of Andrea del Sarto or Pontormo himself. His known *oeuvre* is small and the details of his emergence as an individual from Pontormo's dominant manner of the late twenties are still problematic.[33]

Of the remaining drawings wrongly attributed to Pontormo that have definite interest for us, there are three distinct groups, all originating from

[29] Only six drawings by Andrea occur in the present listing (cat. A20, A27, A52, A215, A228, and A243) and all have been associated with him before. Cat. A198, A205, A210, and A221 are copies or probable copies after Andrea.

[30] Of the drawings attributed here to Sogliani, cat. A100, A123, and A325 have been ascribed to him by Berenson and Clapp. To these may be added cat. A99, A213, A358, and A359. For Sogliani as a draughtsman see Berenson 1938, 164–165, nos. 2009–2755C, figs. 405–408.

[31] Of the drawings suggested here as possibly by Puligo, cat. A335 has been ascribed to him by Berenson. To this drawing may be added cat. A25, A28, A58, and A149. Two drawings (cat. A191 and A353), similar in general type to those given to Sogliani and Puligo, are probably attributable to a draughtsman active slightly later under the influence of Pontormo and Andrea, Pier Francesco di Jacopo Foschi. For Puligo's drawings see Berenson 1938, 295–297, nos. 2370F–2382, figs. 926–929; and for Foschi's drawings see M. Pouncey, "Five Drawings by Pier Francesco di Jacopo di Domenico Toschi," *Burl.* 99 (1957), 159.

[32] The three drawings given here to Bacchiacca have all been ascribed to him before (cat. A29, A118, and A166). For Bacchiacca's drawings see Berenson 1938, 297–299, nos. 180–189, figs. 930–934.

[33] In this list cat. A16, A66, A75, A113, A121, A129, A134, and A260 have been associated with Bronzino before. To these we may add cat. A9, A125, and A147, all dating from before 1530, and cat. A108, possibly a Bronzino drawing from the midthirties. For Bronzino's drawings see Berenson 1938, 321, nos. 593A–605A, figs. 1000–1003; *MDM* 1954 (Marcucci), nos. 95–100; and Smyth 1955. Much larger than the number of drawings that can be attributed to Bronzino himself is a group of drawings that are strongly Bronzinesque and must come from his immediate circle: cat. A44, A55, A67, A68, A78, A89, A93, A96, A102, A146, A148, A188, A189, A242, and A333. To Allori, the primary exponent of the Bronzino tradition later in the century, may be attributed the following drawings, many of them copies after Pontormo: cat. A119?, A132, A139, A140, A141, A142?, A143?, A144?, A236, A237, A238, A239, A240, A259?, A355, A378.

after 1550. First, there is a group of drawings imitative of Pontormo's San Lorenzo manner, some of which are very close to his style and none of which can be definitely reassigned to another hand. They have very little individuality of graphic style and many must be copies.[34] Second, there is a sizable group of drawings that may be given to Naldini. Because of his close relation to Pontormo as his only pupil in the later years, he must have had access to Pontormo's drawings of diverse periods. He learned from all of them, and because of his chameleonlike artistic personality and his clever ability to ape his master's various styles, many of Naldini's drawings still pass as Pontormo's.[35] The last group is the most problematic, and the attributions are suggested only tentatively in the hope that there may be an occasional helpful signpost among them. These drawings generally date from the last quarter of the century and are indicative of a strong "Pontormo revival" at that time, a reaction against the decorative and facile formulae of the *Maniera*, the period in which these artists had received their training. All bear the stamp of the *Maniera*, but they also reveal a cognizance of the style of the first generation. Some of these drawings are by artists who worked in the *Studiolo* of Francesco I de' Medici, such as Cavalori, Maso da San Friano, and Macchietti. Others are attributable to a group of late sixteenth-century draughtsmen like Cigoli, Boscoli, Empoli, and Pocetti, who were active into the seventeenth century.[36]

[34] In this catalogue the following drawings are related closely to Pontormo's late style — to his studies for the loggia decorations of the thirties, the tapestries of the forties, and the choir of San Lorenzo of ca. 1546–1556: cat. A80, A82, A83, A87, A88, A90, A91, A97, A98, A103, A108, A110, A112, A114, A115, A120, A122, A126, A128, A151, A153 *verso*, A156, A170, A171, A172, A212, A220. Cat. A80, A97, A98, and A120 are evidently from the same hand. The other studies range from borderline cases like cat. A82, A91, A110, A156, A171, and A172, to weak copies or imitations like cat. A83, A88, A114, and A126.

[35] Battista Naldini (1537–1591) was adopted by Pontormo from the Innocenti in 1549 when he was twelve. After Pontormo's death he went to Rome, and later worked with Vasari in the Palazzo Vecchio (1565–1571) and in the *Studiolo* of Francesco I (1570–1572). From the same years as the *Studiolo* pictures are the three large altarpieces in S.M. Novella. See V/M, VI, 288–289, VII, 610–611; Borghini 1584, 613–619; F. Baldinucci, *Notizie dei professori del Disegno da Cimabue in qua* (Florence, Manni, 1771), X, 159–170. In his paintings Naldini's typically late *Maniera* style diverged sharply from Pontormo's, but in his drawings, many presumably dating from between 1549 and about 1565, he was strongly influenced by both Pontormo and Andrea del Sarto. Many of them are in red or black chalk and reveal his study of Andrea's chiaroscuro and Pontormo's linear shorthand, but they are readily identified as his by a characteristic scrubby outline, brittleness of form, and unarticulated hands and feet. In this listing cat. A4, A5, A6, A13, A64, A81, A158, and A168 have been ascribed to Naldini before, mainly by Berenson. To these we add several copies after Pontormo: cat. A33, A95, A327, A328, A329, and A330; and a number of other studies: cat. A3, A35, A42, A46, A48, A69, A86, A131, A162, A322, and A324.

[36] The following attributions may be suggested: Cavalori: cat. A37, A63, A79, A117, A150, and A157. Maso da San Friano: cat. A179?, A190, A361. Macchietti: cat. A173. Cigoli: cat. A204, A376.

The important groundwork of Berenson and Clapp in beginning to clarify Pontormo's *oeuvre* has been supplemented by articles on specific drawings, such as those by Gamba, Di Pietro, Goldschmidt, Giglioli, Sinibaldi, Popham, Delacre, Byam Shaw, Weihrauch, Bassi, Grassi, and Andrews. The most recent contributions specifically on the drawings have been made by Becherucci's brief essay in the *Disegni del Pontormo* of 1943, and by Marcucci's work on the Uffizi drawings exhibited in the *Mostra dei disegni manieristi* of 1954 and the *Mostra del Pontormo* of 1956. Nevertheless, Clapp's book of 1914 remains the only *catalogue raisonné* and Berenson's 1903 essay the only sustained attempt to characterize Pontormo's drawing style and to assess its historical importance. During the intervening years, interest in and knowledge of an artist's preparatory material and methods — in the process of artistic creation — have increased so that drawings are now increasingly regarded not only from a connoisseur's point of view as separate works of art, but as an integral part of a total artistic production. In this same period, the outlines of Pontormo's *oeuvre* have begun to clarify, as we have suggested above, and previously unknown works have been found; so that now even the chronology must be interpreted quite differently. Considering the subject more broadly, these years have also seen an intensive investigation of Pontormo's artistic milieu, of the phenomenon of Mannerism. As a result, his production must be seen in the perspective of the stylistic developments of an entire century; not, as Berenson chose to see it, as a diverting but final episode in the history of Florentine drawing. Finally, the special role of Pontormo's drawings (as distinct from the different though interrelated problems of the paintings) in the evolution of Mannerism must be considered. Therefore, in any reassessment of Pontormo's drawings, Pontormo's *oeuvre* and chronology must first be established, eliminating even borderline material into the "attributed" category, so that a coherent picture of his personality and development as a draughtsman may emerge.[37] Then, Pontormo's historical situation as an innovator — the significant transformation of style that he effected — must be considered both

Boscoli: cat. A7, A40, A43?, A45, A133, A252?, A354? Jacopo da Empoli: cat. A14, A23, A71, A178, A217, A258. Pocetti: cat. A250?, A346, A369. There is no general work on these draughtsman, but see L. Marcucci, "Appunti per Mirabello Cavalori disegnatore," *Riv. d'A.* 28 (1953), 77–98; L. Marcucci, "Girolamo Macchietti disegnatore," *Mitt. KHIF* 7 (1953), 121–132; G. Sinibaldi et al., *Mostra del Cigoli* (San Miniato, 1959); A. Forlani, *Mostra di Disegni di Andrea Boscoli*, Gabinetto Disegni e Stampe degli Uffizi (Florence, 1959); A. Forlani, *Mostra di Disegni di Jacopo da Empoli,* Gabinetto Disegni e Stampe degli Uffizi (Florence, 1962).

[37] Arguments on the attribution and dating of Pontormo's drawings as well as a discussion of other opinions will be found in the chronologically arranged Catalogue Raisonné, to which frequent references are made by catalogue number in the following introductory remarks.

in relation to the development of sixteenth-century Florentine drawing and to the evolution of Mannerism in Florence.

It has become a cliché to point out that drawings reveal a further dimension of an artistic personality, that they uncover immediate emotional responses that are distilled, masked, or conventionalized in paintings by the same artist. It is also more than evident that drawings document the creative process itself, the genesis of an artist's ideas, and that the type of drawings we find and their function within the total *oeuvre* can tell us something of the artist's notion of what a drawing is and what end it serves. The expected revelation of the total artistic personality and the importance of the role that drawings play in its expression is found in an investigation of Pontormo's drawings. That aspect of this study needs no further justification. However, beyond this definition of personal style, Pontormo's historical situation makes a study of his drawings yet more complex and fruitful. Pontormo was active as a draughtsman at a time when the very kind and degree of his personal stylistic individuality was to be crucial in creating the new historical style of Mannerism. Therefore, his drawings take on additional meaning in their relation to the dissolution of the Florentine High Renaissance and to the formulation of Mannerism, a style whose novelty depended so much on that complete expression of artistic individuality that is revealed in an artist's drawings. In quite different ways from his paintings, Pontormo's drawings show us in heightened relief and with pointed accuracy what it is that was new in Mannerism. The nature of Pontormo's novel graphic manner and of his expansion of the traditional concept of *disegno* is, in fact, central to our comprehension of the stylistic revolution that took place in Florence after 1515. More than in the High Renaissance, when the unique individuality that drawings reveal tended to be absorbed by and subordinated to other ideals, a study of drawings in the Mannerist period is important; a study of those by a major draughtsman, imperative.

In considering Pontormo's role as an innovator, we find that even without reference to the specific characteristics of his style, the nature of his experimental stylistic evolution marks him as an inventor of a new style. While there are certain broad divisions into which his drawings may be grouped (indicated in the Catalogue Raisonné by Parts I–VI), these divisions do not form the sort of pattern we might expect. Early, middle, and late periods do not exist in the traditional sense. Unlike the stylistic development of a typical Renaissance artist, Pontormo's style is not one that was stated in general outline early in his career and then enriched or refined in a consistent and predictable direction. In his early years the tendency toward a highly individualistic interpretation of the current stylistic vocabulary is immediately apparent, but the particular forms in which he would eventually express this individuality are not yet evident. His development toward a mature statement of his Mannerism is neither logical nor consistent. Instead of the elaboration and refinement of a style, Pontormo's development may be seen as a search for a style through constant experimentation, a search in which new factors were constantly being added. In the first years of activity (1514–1519; cat. 1–92), we are concerned with Pontormo's relation to tradition and to inherited late Quattrocento concepts of drawing. Only a few drawings in this group can properly be called *juvenilia* (cat. 1–8). In the period 1516–1518, Pontormo's drawings began to reveal his experimental mentality, often earlier than the paintings. They provide a most exact documentation of the genesis of certain Mannerist points of view, a foil to Andrea del Sarto's drawings of this period. In the works of no other draughtsman, in Florence or elsewhere, is there such a complete documentation of the beginnings of Mannerism and of its exact relation to its classical antecedents. The second period of Pontormo's evolution is a short phase of greatly accelerated development from which has survived an unusual concentration of almost one hundred drawings (1519–1521; cat. 93–191). At this time Pontormo's artistic perspective broadened to include the Roman High Renaissance. Partly as a consequence of this stimulus, he entered a newly intensive phase of graphic experimentation in the drawings for the Poggio a Caiano lunette, evolving a specifically Mannerist graphic mode and, as an important incident in his expansion of traditional concepts of *disegno*, a novel and explicitly Mannerist idea of the relation between preparation and painting. The third phase of activity involved an abrupt shift of direction that is typical of Pontormo (1522–1525; cat. 191–257). In the drawings for the Certosa cloister he moved suddenly into a phase of artistic and spiritual isolation, rejecting his own previous stylistic formulations and turning from his own graphic tradition to that of Dürer. The next period of Pontormo's development is generally considered to be his maturity (1525–1530; cat. 258–306). While any of Pontormo's drawings after about 1518 could be called mature in that they are coherent statements of a Mannerist point of view, only in the drawings of the late twenties did he achieve a synthesis of the disparate elements of his style, a resolution between Mannerist novelty and classical tradition. However, once this resolution was accomplished, its possibilities were exhausted within a few years. The element of restless individuality that could not be contained within the High Renaissance system had itself formulated a style that only generated further novelty. After

1530 Pontormo's evolution again became experimental. The long period until 1545 (cat. 307–346) was Pontormo's later maturity, but it is not characterized by the enrichment or refinement of a style already stated that we generally associate with this stage in an artist's evolution. In the drawings of this phase Pontormo became increasingly involved with the art of Michelangelo and his style became experimental within this frame of reference and in relation to the formulae of the *Maniera.* The final phase of Pontormo's development as a draughtsman was, once again, one of experimentation (1545–1556; cat. 347–383). It took the form of a reaction in isolation against the conventions of the *Maniera*, a response that paralleled Pontormo's own earlier revolt against the High Renaissance. The sheer creativity and novelty of the San Lorenzo drawings, the only works that survive from Pontormo's later years, equals that of any of his earlier work. These singular drawings, begun about the time of his letter to Varchi, are Pontormo's final and positive reaffirmation of his own words: "una cosa sola . . . è nobile . . . e questo si è el disegno."

Pontormo was born in 1494 in the small town of Pontorme, near Empoli. He was named Jacopo Carucci, but on his arrival in Florence, probably in 1507,[38] he was known as Pontormo after the place of his birth. Since a boy of thirteen would normally have begun his artistic training at this age as a pupil of a master painter, it can be assumed, as Vasari implies, that Pontormo was apprenticed shortly after his arrival.[39] Therefore, the year 1507 may be taken as the actual, if not yet the effectual, beginning of Pontormo's training as artist and draughtsman. The artistic climate that Pontormo found in Florence in 1507 must have been intensely active, filled with the aura of innovation accompanying the widespread initiation of the classical style of the High Renaissance. By 1507 the style of the new century, a style with an

[38] The exact date of Pontormo's arrival in Florence is not known. According to Vasari (V/M, VI, 246), he came to Florence at the age of 13. Since Vasari gives Pontormo's birthdate as 1493 (*ibid.*, 245), he may have meant that Pontormo arrived in 1506. However, since Pontormo was actually born May 24, 1494 (see Clapp 1916, 4n24), he was only 12 in 1506 and must, if we are to believe Vasari, have arrived in 1507 instead. This date seems credible in view of Vasari's statement that Pontormo was placed in the care of Pupilli and Clapp's documentary evidence that Pontormo came to Pupilli on January 24, 1508 [new style] (*ibid.*, app. II, doc. 11). In spite of this evidence, Clapp believed that Pontormo was in Florence and had already begun his apprenticeship in 1503 at the age of nine. Clapp (*ibid.*, doc. 10), based this conclusion on the mention of a Jacopo Carucci in a document of that year. However, even if this document does refer to Pontormo, he can hardly have had much substantial artistic training before about 1507 and it is probable that, in spite of its inconsistencies, Vasari's chronology is basically correct.

[39] V/M, VI, 246: "[Jacopo] non era stato molto mesi in Fiorenza, quando fu messo da Bernardo Vettori a stare con Lionardo da Vinci . . ." (See Clapp 1916, app. I, for a general discussion of Pontormo's apprenticeship.)

identity quite as marked in drawing as in painting, had been established in Florence by Michelangelo and Raphael, who based themselves in large measure on the precedent of Leonardo's precocious accomplishment. However, the conservative traditions of the late Quattrocento *botteghe* persisted into this first decade of the sixteenth century, perhaps even more in drawing than in painting. Retarding conventions and formulae of style may even be found in the drawings made before 1508 by the primary innovators of the classical style; they are conspicuous in the drawings by creators of lesser accomplishment like Fra Bartolommeo; and they account in major part for the drawing style of the older or minor masters of the period, such as Granacci, Albertinelli, Ridolfo Ghirlandaio, Bugiardini, or Piero di Cosimo, who even at this moment were making varying degrees of adjustment toward the modern manner. Furthermore, as late as the beginning of Pontormo's apprenticeship, a number of the long-lived creators of the now outmoded Quattrocento conventions of drawing, such as Lorenzo di Credi, Filippino Lippi, and Perugino, were still active and teaching young artists to draw in a manner and spirit often quite at variance with the new classical style. This strong hold of the older traditions on the draughtsmen of Florence at the time of Pontormo's arrival in the city was to become yet more marked during the first few years of his apprenticeship. The departure of Leonardo in 1507, Raphael and Michelangelo in 1508, and the temporary absence of Fra Bartolommeo in 1508 must have created a major hiatus in the artistic life of the city. Pontormo, just beginning his effective training in drawing about 1508, would have received at best a second-hand glimpse of the modern concepts of drawing to the extent that they were reflected in the work of those artists remaining in Florence. In fact, had it not been for the major developments in Fra Bartolommeo's manner after his return from Venice in 1509, there would not have been an important and authoritive draughtsman working in the classical style in Florence during Pontormo's formative years.

Because of the vital role of *disegno* as the basis of the training and artistic outlook of the Florentine artist, it is not surprising that older traditions would persist, in drawings especially, into the sixteenth century. In the later Quattrocento drawing was concerned mainly with instruction, not with inspiration, its practice being closely governed by conventions dictating the medium, manner, and subject of the drawing. These precepts as laid down by the master would normally form the base on which an apprentice's style was built. The art of *disegno* learned, it would then be utilized in making the various types of studies that comprised an artist's pictorial preparation:

pensieri, *studi*, and *modelli*. During this period the most common instruments were pen, typically used in compositional sketches and studies of figures; and silverpoint, which was more closely identified with the academic process of instruction, as in the characteristic late Quattrocento drapery studies on colored papers highlighted with white. We find only an occasional excursion into chalk, later to be the favored medium of the classical draughtsman and of Pontormo himself. When chalk was used, its potential for linear expressiveness and for the development of chiaroscuro effects was not realized; it was handled like pen.

This restrictive concept of the role of drawing, with its close association with instruction and preparation, its conventions, and its limited exploitation of media was certainly that of most Florentine draughtsmen of the first decade of the sixteenth century. The major personalities who emerged at this juncture did so in varying degrees dependent on their level of inventive accomplishment in the formulation of the new High Renaissance style. It was not, however, the role of even Leonardo, Michelangelo, Raphael, and Fra Bartolommeo to break totally away from convention in these years, investing the art of *disegno* with strikingly novel, private, and personally inventive meanings. Such was not the nature or the aim of the classical style; this radical break with convention was to be made only after 1515 by the postclassical generation. Rather, the accomplishment of these major draughtsmen during the first decade was to infuse the conventions learned in their own youth with the new energy, discipline, and ideality of the classical style. And it is against this background that Pontormo's style was initially formed.

Of these major figures Fra Bartolommeo deviated least from the established practice. His still Quattrocento-bound pen style derives from that taught in the *bottega* of Ghirlandaio and in that of Cosimo Roselli, where he had received his training in the late 1480's. On sheets of small scale Fra Bartolommeo's pen lightly outlines Madonnas and angels, whose forms are crosshatched too delicately to create an impression of substantial physical presence, and whose movements are ornamented by graceful calligraphic flourishes. Until his departure for Venice in 1508, Fra Bartolommeo had barely indicated the direction of his later development in drawing and merely succeeded in prolonging a quattrocentesque concept with considerable charm and skill. Like Fra Bartolommeo, and in precisely the same moment, Michelangelo emerged from a late Quattrocento *bottega*. However, in contrast to Fra Bartolommeo, Michelangelo had effected a change in the old manner well before 1508. His sculptor's transformation of his master's style of pen drawing had shaped Ghirlandaio's carefully crosshatched pen technique into something quite novel. Calligraphic flourishes are disciplined into form-building strokes and monumental, sculptural nudes replace sheets full of small, floating figures. Furthermore, his concept of drawing suggests an intellectual expansion. The nude studies of this period are informed by a creative relation to the antique that is positively novel and they are an important step in the emergence of drawing in the sixteenth century as a spontaneous creative activity rather than one that is limited by the requirements of self-instruction or pictorial preparation. However, there is little evidence that Michelangelo's developing High Renaissance style of drawing had any great influence in Florence before his departure for Rome in 1508 or that it played any role in the initial formation of Pontormo's style. Only later, toward the middle of the next decade, did Pontormo's prolonged and intense study of Michelangelo's style begin.

Raphael had also extended the limits of the Quattrocento manner of drawing by 1508, although not as profoundly as Michelangelo. His training in Perugino's *bottega* must have been just as doctrinaire as a contemporary Florentine education and his manner of drawing in these years clearly reflects his particular, provincial place of apprenticeship. In silverpoint and pen, less often in chalk, the drawings of the youthful Raphael do not break away from the Quattrocento concept and practice of drawing as decisively as do Michelangelo's, but they infuse the timid lines of Perugino with greater rotundity and life, breathing spaces appear between formerly continuous outlines, and lines are regrouped with a unique intuitive sense of graceful order and ideal form. Whereas it is the discipline of Michelangelo's early drawings that is significantly novel, it is the incipient vitality of Raphael's drawings that distinguishes them from his late Quattrocento tradition. Like Michelangelo, Raphael left Florence without having had widespread influence on his contemporaries as a draughtsman. What Florentine draughtsmen would eventually, after 1508, assimilate of his manner, they received by way of Fra Bartolommeo's response to it. However, Pontormo himself seems to have been singularly immune to this component in Fra Bartolommeo's style, and this basic antipathy may have been significant in his early turn to Andrea del Sarto's decisively less Raphaelesque manner.

The last of the major draughtsmen active in Florence before 1508 is, paradoxically, the first chronologically but the most revolutionary in his singularly personal graphic style. Leonardo was in Florence 1501 to 1507, but he had adumbrated well before 1500 many of the developments out of the Quattrocento that we have mentioned in the drawings of Michelangelo and

Raphael and had moved beyond their accomplishments in directions even less likely to be comprehended by the Ghirlandaio-trained Florentines than the innovations of his younger contemporaries. In his drawings more, perhaps, than in his paintings Leonardo saw beyond the High Renaissance, his freedom of approach to drawing (although not his graphic mode) anticipating that of a Mannerist draughtsman like Pontormo. The art of *disegno* became a separate world for Leonardo, governed by its own laws and free from the limitations of form and content imposed by Quattrocento convention. Drawing for Leonardo, as it eventually was to be for Pontormo, was not a public demonstration but a private creative act, a channel through which he freely expressed the range and depth of his artistic personality. Certainly, drawings in the conventional Quattrocento sense of instruction and preparation do exist, but they did not serve these ends exclusively. Nor are they, like the typical High Renaissance preparatory studies, predictable steps in the harmonious adjustment of reality towards a suprapersonal ideality of form and feeling, an ideality that does not obliterate but absorbs and elevates the personal manner of the draughtsman. Partly as a result of the personal expressiveness of his drawings, Leonardo expanded the limits of conventional Quattrocento media as neither Michelangelo nor Raphael had done. In addition to his richly varied use of pen and silverpoint, Leonardo was the first artist to exploit the linear and chiaroscuro possibilities of red chalk, anticipating its widespread use in the early sixteenth century in Florence, conspicuously by Andrea del Sarto and Pontormo. Leonardo also made black chalk an expressive tool for the creation of *sfumato* effects rather than using it as it was generally employed, as a convenient instrument for drawing cartoons. And in his late studies, his state of mind anticipated that which led both Michelangelo and Pontormo, half a century later, to use black chalk exclusively in their own latest drawings.

Pontormo was undoubtedly fortunate in his guardian's choice of Leonardo as his first teacher; the oldest artist active in Florence in 1507 was, profoundly, the most advanced. However, since Leonardo left in the same year and Pontormo was not yet fourteen, we can hardly suggest that he was a major formative influence. Nevertheless, given a precocious mind and hand and a more than fleeting stay with the master, Pontormo could have absorbed something of the most eloquent draughtsmanship of the time, possibly even a measure of Leonardo's freedom of approach to drawing and his employment of the chalk medium that was later to suit Pontormo's own graphic temperament so well. With Leonardo's departure Pontormo was of necessity passed on to another *bottega* to further his training. It seems likely that the close association between Piero di Cosimo and Leonardo would have made Piero the logical choice among those whom Vasari mentions as Pontormo's subsequent masters.[40] Although there may have been a deepening of the Leonardesque mode because of Piero's recent association with the master, it is certain that Pontormo was also exposed to a cross section of late Quattrocento practice, since Piero's pen and silverpoint technique were well formed in the traditional manner before he came under Leonardo's influence. In any case, the often noted similarity in the personalities of Piero di Cosimo and Pontormo, their mutual penchant for eccentricity of expression, must have made the association temperamentally satisfactory.

Piero may already have acted as a filter for Fra Bartolommeo's new manner in 1509, as his drawings of that time reveal the influence of the broader, black chalk style that Fra Bartolommeo practiced after his return from Venice. However, with his move to Albertinelli's shop, probably in 1509,[41] Pontormo would have been exposed more decisively to the softened pictorialism and the simplified outlines of Fra Bartolommeo's mature High Renaissance style. This manner was to be the major shaping influence in Pontormo's apprenticeship. As Fra Bartolommeo's close disciple, Albertinelli can be expected to have passed on to Pontormo something of his master's mode of drawing, although evidence for the draughtsmanship of Albertinelli himself (as distinguished from Albertinelli as a filter for Fra Bartolommeo) is scantier even than that for Piero di Cosimo and not as encouraging on a qualitative basis. That Piero was a consumate draughtsman is evident, but Albertinelli was apparently an indifferent one whose conservative pen style derived mainly from Fra Bartolommeo's pre-1508 manner.

[40] *Ibid.*: ". . . e poco dopo con Mariotto Albertinelli, con Piero di Cosimo, e finalmente l'anno 1512 con Andrea del Sarto . . ."

[41] If Pontormo went first to Piero di Cosimo, as we have noted as a possibility, his apprenticeship to Albertinelli would have occured later than has generally been supposed. (See Clapp 1916, 267, who believed that Pontormo was with Albertinelli from 1503 to about 1507.) Furthermore, it would make more credible Vasari's account of Pontormo's earliest picture. According to Vasari (V/M, VI, 246), Pontormo painted an *Annunciation* (now lost) while he was with Albertinelli. This remark presupposes that Pontormo was experienced enough to paint independently while he was in Albertinelli's *bottega*. Especially if he did not come to Florence until 1507, this can hardly have been before 1509 at the earliest, when he was fifteen. However, Vasari tells an anecdote about this picture (in line with his usual stories of early promise), saying that Raphael saw and praised it. This would place the work before September 1508, when Raphael left for Rome. Not only is 1508 a suspiciously early date for an impressive picture by the fourteen year old apprentice but it raises the question of why Vasari mentions no other works by Pontormo until the period of his apprenticeship to Andrea del Sarto, which did not begin until four years later in 1512. Therefore, it is likely that Vasari invented this tale, moving the picture — and by extension Pontormo's apprenticeship to Albertinelli — back to before 1508 in order to have a reliable witness to attest to Pontormo's precocious achievement.

Presumably in 1512, when Albertinelli gave up painting and closed his shop, Pontormo joined Andrea del Sarto, with whom he stayed until mid-1514.[42] Pontormo's senior by eight years, Andrea had practiced independently since 1508, showing the greatest individuality of any member of the younger generation. Like Pontormo, he had been a pupil of Piero di Cosimo and had been in partnership with Franciabigio, who had himself come from the *bottega* of Albertinelli. His manner of drawing, like Pontormo's, had been formed essentially on Fra Bartolommeo's classical black chalk style of post-1508. Thus, it is not surprising to find Bartolommesque reminiscences in Pontormo's drawings dating from his years with Andrea. While none of Pontormo's drawings can be dated before he joined Andrea in 1512, his earliest drawings of circa 1514 betray the unmistakable stamp of his primary training in the Bartolommesque mode. Two studies after sculptural motives reflect the practices of the Fra Bartolommeo circle in their media as well as in style. The study for the Carro della Zecca *St. John the Baptist* (cat. 1; fig. 2) is Pontormo's only pen sketch of these years, a drawing that may be the survivor of a whole group of juvenile preparatory studies. A study after Donatello's *David* (cat. 7; fig. 8) is in black chalk, a medium characteristic of the Bartolommeo circle but rarely used by Pontormo until some years later, and is reminiscent of Franciabigio's youthful approximations of Fra Bartolommeo's style. The simplified shapes of these marionettelike figures, the imprecise articulation of structure and surface, and the use of his facial type are evidence

[42] As is the case with Pontormo's apprenticeship to Albertinelli, the evidence for the year in which Pontormo came to Andrea del Sarto is contradictory: Vasari states (V/M, VI, 246) specifically that Pontormo went to Andrea in 1512, but he also says (*ibid.*, 247) that he moved to Andrea's shop "quando appunto egli avea fornito nel cortile de'Servi le storie di San Filippo." These frescoes were finished in 1510, but Andrea continued to work in the *cortile* of the Annunziata and there is no reason to take Vasari literally on Pontormo's having gone to Andrea "immediately" after the completion of the Benizzi frescoes, as Clapp 1916, 269, has done. Furthermore, if Pontormo came to Andrea in 1510 rather than 1512, his apprenticeship to Andrea would have lasted almost five years, a supposition that is contradicted by Vasari, who says (*ibid.*, 246) Pontormo spent little time with Andrea. There is other evidence in favor of the 1512 date; this was the year in which Albertinelli stopped painting and, therefore, a time when Pontormo would have been left without a master. This was also the year of Andrea's S. Gallo altar for which Pontormo painted the predella, the only work that Vasari specifies that Pontormo painted while Andrea's assistant (*ibid.*, 247). While still Andrea's apprentice Pontormo also began to accept commissions on his own (see note 2 on p. 99). He painted *carri* for the Medici for the carnival of 1513 and, after the election of Leo X, he was engaged on festival decorations and other works in honor of the Pope (*ibid.*, 247–255). Among these is the ruined *Faith and Charity* fresco (Florence, SS. Annunziata, formerly over the portal, 430 x 500 cm). This work is mentioned by Vasari (*ibid.*, 247–250), and described in detail by Bocchi 1591, 204–205. It is documented November 1513 to June 1514 (Clapp 1916, app. II, doc. 12). Since Vasari states that this was the last work that Pontormo painted while with Andrea, it would seem that his apprenticeship lasted less than two years — from 1512 to mid-1514.

of Pontormo's immature and tentative assimilation of the vocabulary of Fra Bartolommeo's drawings of about 1512. This Bartolommesque current persisted in Pontormo's drawings of these early years, but never again in such undiluted form, since Andrea's graphic manner soon became dominant. Andrea's drawings are immediately distinguishable from those of the Fra Bartolommeo circle by their freer and more animated handling of the chalk, the quick, sharp angularity of observed detail. There is never the impression — so strong in Fra Bartolommeo's drawings — that the draughtsman was operating solely within a flexible graphic convention. These tendencies of Andrea's early drawings are also evident in Pontormo's studies of 1514 for the S. Ruffillo altar, although there is no question of their still essentially Bartolommesque mode. The red chalk sheet in Dresden (cat. 3–4; figs. 4, 6) shows Pontormo's translation of Fra Bartolommeo's manner. The insecure articulation and the unrhythmical design of both nude and draped figures is typical of Pontormo's youthful drawing in chalk or in paint. Other evidence of his close study of Fra Bartolommeo's drawings is a landscape sketch (cat. 5; fig. 7) that is unique in Pontormo's *oeuvre*. However, an informal study of a boy (cat. 6; fig. 10), which is not as closely linked to pictorial preparation as the S. Ruffillo figure studies, is quicker and more angular in handling. It is as if Pontormo, like Andrea, were searching for a more sharply expressive manner of using his chalk. Furthermore, both artists showed at this early date an evident preference for red chalk that may possibly have come to each of them independently from Leonardo through Piero di Cosimo.

We may consider these drawings of circa 1514 as a youthful group in which the model of Fra Bartolommeo predominated without subduing Pontormo's incipient individuality of style or creating in him a disciple who would be immune to the greater potential of Andrea's developing manner. In the next years, 1515–1516, when Pontormo was painting in a Bartolommesque classical mode in the *Visitation* and the *St. Veronica*, he tended on occasion to look back to Fra Bartolommeo's drawings as the authoritative model of classical draughtsmanship in spite of his obvious preference for Andrea's more individualistic manner. Two studies for the *Visitation* (cat. 11–12; figs. 16–17) show Pontormo's conscious attempt to discipline his hand in accordance with Fra Bartolommeo's broad, slow outlines, spherical forms, and careful hatching. Angularities are minimized and smoothed-over and even facial types refer back to the S. Ruffillo drawings. With these exceptions, Pontormo never again made overt reference to Fra Bartolommeo's classical drawing style; further influence of his drawings came only about 1517 when Pontormo responded to his radically different latest drawings. In general, the drawings of the *Visitation* period show Pontormo's development in the direction of Andrea's red chalk manner, just as the paintings of this phase begin to display his awareness of Andrea's as well as Fra Bartolommeo's variant of the High Renaissance style. Now the drawings of both Andrea and Pontormo contrast decisively with the spherical generalization of form, bland regularity of touch, and the underlying sense of convention of the Bartolommesque style. Pontormo and Andrea not only saw with greater freedom, but they communicated their perceptions with a spontaneous vitality of line and *sfumato.* Lines vibrate with repetition rather than forming smooth, wide arcs, the edge of the chalk is used for accents sharper than Fra Bartolommeo had desired, and the forms never intend the same unequivocal rotundity. However, Pontormo's relation to Andrea was no more that of a disciple in the strictest sense than was his relation with his other masters. Andrea's individuality in the handling of red chalk did not prompt Pontormo to imitate him; rather, on Andrea's authority, he began to experiment toward his own highly personal red chalk manner. It is of primary significance for Pontormo's future development as a draughtsman that he shifted his allegiance at this time to Andrea. The potential for Pontormo's kind of drawing — and even for his Mannerism — did not lie in Fra Bartolommeo's style, doubly limited as it was by its grounding in the Quattrocento and its canonical adherence to the precepts of the High Renaissance.

A number of important Sartesque drawings survive from the years 1515–1516. These are to be distinguished from Pontormo's earlier Bartolommesque drawings principally by the increasingly rhythmic animation of line and shape, the newly dense *sfumato* that gives more weight and chromatic emphasis to the forms, and by the increasingly frequent appearance of details in handling that insistently announce the specific hand of Pontormo. The *Venus and Cupid* drawing (cat. 15; fig. 20), an elaborated red chalk study formerly given to Andrea, is an harmonious reworking of the Madonna and Child group of S. Ruffillo. Now the disruptive tensional accents of the earlier group are smoothed out and the figures are rhythmically interrelated, the theme interpreted in Andrea's harmoniously animate manner. The spontaneous red chalk *pensiero* for a *Madonna and Child with St. John* (cat. 14; fig. 18) is Pontormo's earliest surviving compositional drawing and shows an easy comprehension of the essentials of Andrea's style of about 1515. However, the basically harmonious design of rounded shapes is unexpectedly broken into and accented by a sudden squaring-off and pointing of forms; the intimate mood is brought unconventionally close to us by the oblique expression of the

Madonna and the outright stare of the St. John, his head cut off by the lower edge of the frame in an early instance of this familiar Mannerist device. Still other drawings of 1515–1516 show the animation that is characteristic of both Andrea and Pontormo in these years. In the brilliant, richly modelled red chalk sheet in Munich with studies for a *Visitation* (cat. 17; fig. 21) and a *St. John the Baptist* (cat. 18; fig. 22), Pontormo was concerned primarily with the development of a movemented sequence of forms. The Berlin study for a figure in the SS. Annunziata *Visitation* (cat. 13; fig. 15) is a variant of a turning motive that becomes a virtual cliché in the works of Andrea and Pontormo at this time. The figure in strong contrapposto, twisting with the arm pulled sharply across the body, must derive ultimately from Michelangelo's Doni tondo, but it was first used by Andrea in the putti of the Dresden altar, by Pontormo in the cramped action of the Child in the S. Ruffillo altar. Pontormo then explored this motive in the various drawings of 1515–1516 noted above (cat. 13, 14, 15, 17, 18), expanding it freely in the monumental *St. Veronica* of the Cappella del Papa. This motive is a key to the animate classicism to which both Pontormo and Andrea aspired, an ideal that constantly restrained the potentially unclassical disruptiveness of this motive and held it carefully in check — more so in the paintings than in the drawings. In the painted version of the figure studied on cat. 13 for the *Visitation*, the expansive action of the turning figure is suppressed; however, in much the same way as in Andrea's contemporary *Birth of the Virgin*, Pontormo allowed a more violent expression of this motive to enter the restrained, decorous, and Bartolommesque *Visitation* fresco only in the putti of the lunette above.

The period shortly after the *Visitation* was completed in 1516 is an important pivotal point in Pontormo's development. With Fra Bartolommeo's death in 1517, Andrea del Sarto assumed the position of foremost practitioner of the classical style in Florence, having demonstrated his capacity to fill this role in the SS. Annunziata and the first Scalzo frescoes. Pontormo, too, had shown his ability to excel in the classical style in the *Visitation*; while an intention to classicism had also been evident in his early drawings, most of which were quite consonant in style with his work in painting in spite of their incipient individuality. For all the sense of personality and sharp nuance in the pre-1516 drawings, there is no feeling in them of intentional deviation from a norm. Quite to the contrary, Pontormo evidently disciplined his hand in accord with the High Renaissance concept of *disegno*, in which drawing was not considered primarily as an end in itself or as an expression of personal individuality, but as a means to the achievement of a classical harmony and ideality that absorbed personal idiosyncracies of style. However, with the studies of 1516–1518 for the *Story of Joseph* panels and the Visdomini altarpiece, Pontormo's manner of drawing and his concept of drawing began to diverge sharply both from his own earlier norms and from those of the contemporary Andrea. A new freedom of graphic expressiveness precedes and exceeds Pontormo's radical tendencies in paint; there is a shift in the basic notion of what a drawing is and what ends it serves. Pontormo began to explore modes of formal and psychological expression not previously associated with drawings, investigations that were his first anticlassical experiments. Concurrent with these experiments — and perhaps necessary to them — there is a broadening and deepening of Pontormo's comprehension of the recently past and contemporary achievements in the High Renaissance style. Pontormo continued to be cognizant of Andrea's activities, becoming at the same time aware of the latest phase of Fra Bartolommeo's draughtsmanship. He also experienced the delayed impact of Michelangelo's *Cascina* cartoon, and there is evidence of his awareness of the developed Roman classicism of Raphael. It would seem that only now, with his own mastery of the classical idiom and his knowledge of its expression in the art of his contemporaries, did Pontormo begin with characteristic hypersensitivity and intellectual deliberation to work upon the classical tradition available to him, transforming the numerous drawings of this period into repeated assertions of his own unclassical individuality.

During the years 1516–1518 three major developments account for a change in the essential character of Pontormo's drawings from approximately classical to patently Mannerist. First, there is a shift away from a normative image of the human form that is evidently the consequence for Pontormo of a period of intense Michelangelo research. Secondly, there is an intensification of the inherent rhythmic animation of Pontormo's drawings (explored only tentatively before) that is stimulated to some extent by the example of Fra Bartolommeo's late drawing style of 1516–1517. Finally, Pontormo's will to communicate psychological sensation, certainly strengthened by the model of Andrea's communicative drawings, results in images of a novel kind of intensity and personal eccentricity that are quite unrelated to classical norms. This period, then, was essentially one of experimentation and exploration. And it is primarily, in some instances exclusively, in the drawings that we can discover the complexities of these investigations.

The first of these changes is connected with Pontormo's response to Michelangelo's *Cascina* cartoon, generally available since 1512, but not widely exploited in Florence until it effected a delayed reaction when it was broken up in 1516. Andrea was also influenced by the cartoon, as is evident in the Scalzo *Baptism of the Multitude* and the drawings for it, but his was a response more temporary and less profound. Andrea's ability to absorb foreign influences into his style, to reconcile opposites, and to reject the unsuitable served him well at this juncture. On the other hand, Pontormo neither reconciled nor rejected, but explored separately each of the paths opened to him with an intensity that led to deviation. He eventually and much later brought them into a synthesis, but this synthesis was no longer classical. Pontormo's study of Michelangelo's cartoon led him away from the schematized modelling and veiling *sfumato* of the preceding years, and led him to a newly bold use of black chalk, often heightened with white for a fuller plastic effect. He experimented with more specific physical description and with the possibilities of a graphic style that is more plastic than pictorial. However, at the same time — and this is typical of Pontormo's approach to a problem — the Sartesque *sfumato* was not abandoned but carried to a new extreme of intensity and used in a newly articulate manner; just as Pontormo's customary red chalk was now handled with greater richness and refinement than before.

A number of drawings of this period specifically recall *Cascina* motives, such as the seated nude (cat. 74; fig. 77), whose transformation into the St. John the Baptist of the Visdomini altar can be followed in a series of studies (cat. 37–42; figs. 44–49). The Visdomini Christ also derived from a *Cascina* cartoon figure (the central turning nude), but the intermediary stage is missing and only a series of putti studies in which the motive is already assimilated survives (cat. 34–35; figs. 40–41). Other drawings show the results of Pontormo's study of the anatomical and muscular description of Michelangelo's nudes rather than the adaptation of specific motives. The earliest instance of this new preoccupation is a black chalk sheet of studies for the figure of Joseph in the *Story of Joseph* (I) of 1516 (cat. 20; fig. 26) followed by studies of 1517 for the *Story of Joseph* (III) (cat. 25–26; figs. 34–35). For the first time in Pontormo's drawings, the interior modelling, especially that of the muscular torso, is specific rather than schematized, perceived with an intensity of seeing and set down with an intensity of transcription thus far not evident in Pontormo's drawings. In these studies, furthermore, it is clear that this investigation was unlimited by — indeed, even tangential to — the requirements of pictorial preparation. In the paintings of the *Story of Joseph* not only are these same figures clothed, but they are quite un-Michelangelesque, miniscule in scale, and totally unrelated in handling to the plastic mode of the drawings. These studies are the first symptoms of Pontormo's shift away from the idea that drawings are primarily instructional or preparatory in function, a premise that the High Renaissance draughtsman had, with some modification, accepted from the practice of the late Quattrocento. The drawing now became a means of private research into problems of graphic expression, and it was not necessarily connected directly with the painting to which it eventually related. For Pontormo drawings were now separate creative acts that link one to another as a solution was intellectually searched out, such as in the extraordinary series of red chalk nude studies for the Christ of the Dublin *Pietà* (cat. 62–67; figs. 66–71). The minute scale and summary manner in which this predella figure would be painted could not possibly have incorporated the results of Pontormo's detailed investigation of the theme of the muscular nude in drawings that transcend in anatomical exactness and subtlety of transcription the nude studies of any contemporary Florentine, with the exception of Michelangelo himself.

The pattern of response to and deviation from Michelangelo that was established at this early date was to be repeated in various guises throughout Pontormo's career as a draughtsman. The very energy of vision and transcription that he applied to his Michelangelo model led Pontormo to distortions of form and eccentricities of shape that could no longer be gathered up by the generalizing, disciplining contours of a classical drawing. Pontormo began to develop a separate vocabulary of form that belonged specifically to his drawings, a vocabulary whose syntax became increasingly incomprehensible in classical terms. While the consequences of Pontormo's Michelangelo researches were realized only partially in these years (the conclusion of this aspect of his early development came only in the studies for Poggio a Caiano), we are already dealing in 1516–1518 with Mannerist drawings. A red chalk study for the St. John of the Dublin *Pietà* (cat. 70; fig. 74), for example, is evolved from a more normative image of the same figure (cat. 69; fig. 73). In the second study the pressures of Pontormo's sharply pointed chalk break the contour of the back and legs into a sequence of angular fragments of line that pull the shapes of the figure from a normal into an eccentric relation with one another. A putto study of this same moment (cat. 84; fig. 79) is a patently unclassical image; the figure is set down in arbitrary linear shorthand in which some forms are dislocated forward, others suggested by line alone rather than modelled in the conventional sense. It would seem that these deviations from the classical style of an earlier putto drawing for the *Visitation* (cat. 12; fig. 17) are meaningful primarily in the light of Pontormo's intervening study and comprehension of the plastic and dynamic mode of the early Michelangelo. Even less normative, and inconceivable within the classical style, is a study for the head of the Visdomini altar Madonna (cat. 31; fig. 38), in which Pontormo evinced an arbitrary disregard for the High Renaissance ideal of a total integer of natural-seeming form. The normal, if extremely angular, drapery frames a face that is schematized and anormative in shape and expression. The very unnaturalness of this image is unclassical, but even more significant is the implied breakdown of a classical sense of totality in the way it is disjunctively seen. However, just as Pontormo's Michelangelo researches in anatomical transcription are not incorporated into the paintings of this date, so an image like this head does not appear in such radical form in its painted transformation in the Visdomini altar. At this stage, natural form in Pontormo's paintings still conformed more than in the drawings to a recognizable actuality. However, this dichotomy is in itself indicative of a Mannerist point of view, since the classical draughtsman would rarely admit into a drawing any element that was not implicit in his conception of the painting. Thus, Pontormo's anticlassical experiments began to break down not only the forms of the High Renaissance style but its very processes of creation.

As Pontormo investigated the problem of more precisely articulated physical description in these years, he simultaneously explored the possibilities of expressing movement in more cogent graphic terms than he and Andrea had developed about 1515. The function and nature of his line began to change under the pressure of a dynamic concept that shaped line differently than before, compelling it to move more swiftly, with a more broken rhythm, and finally to take an abstracting path. Just as a drawing (cat. 20; fig. 26) for the *Story of Joseph* (I) shows the first results of Pontormo's Michelangelo researches, another study for the picture gives us an initial glimpse of the rhythmic excitement and energy of line that would reach a climax in Pontormo's Poggio a Caiano drawings. The spotty, diagonal shading of the red chalk study for the kneeling figure to the left of the picture (cat. 21; fig. 27) is typical of both Andrea and Pontormo in these years, but the modelling has now been focussed by a continuous contour of back and leg that is more dynamic in its upward impulsion than any lines we have seen in Andrea's drawings or in those of Pontormo himself. Neither have we encountered the purely graphic excitement of the abbreviated windblown lines of the hair or the expressively vibrating *pentimenti* of the leg. These two studies of 1516 show clearly the poles of Pontormo's drawing style at this time: a plastic, Michelangelesque mode and a more rhythmic, pictorial manner that was closely related to but rapidly deviating from that of Andrea del Sarto.

These two lines of investigation persisted through 1518, sometimes occuring in separate studies, in other instances in the same drawing. The sketch for the man walking down the steps in the background of the *Story of Joseph* (II) of 1517 (cat. 24; fig. 29) is even more movemented than the study (cat. 21) for the *Story of Joseph* (I) and is an illuminating analogue to Andrea's drawing of a similar motive for the executioner in the Scalzo *Capture of St. John the Baptist* of the same year. Pontormo's altogether more dynamic response to the subject is translated into red chalk with a nervous immediacy of touch and urgency of repeated lines that is far from the more fluid and continuous movement of Andrea's figure. The studies of 1517–1518 for the predella designed for the Visdomini altar also show the coexistence of Pontormo's two modes of drawing at this time. On a sheet of ideas, probably for the *St. Francis* (cat. 71; fig. 75), the rapid evolution of the motive is exposed in the two successive versions of the figure, an act of creation that has a compulsive tenor quite incompatible with classical deliberation. The more developed figure is dynamically conceived in a swirling river of repeated lines whose energies are generated in the compressed forms of the legs, then suddenly discharged in the pointing hand and blown hair. Certain of the drawings for the Visdomini altar are also handled in this rhythmic mode, notably the nude studies in red or black chalk on pink-washed paper from Pontormo's sketchbook. Many of these are Michelangelesque muscled torsos, but others are linear abstractions of energized form. A study for the St. John the Baptist (cat. 41; fig. 48) employs a free-swinging red chalk line of unprecedented freedom; a drawing of muscled arms for the Evangelist (cat. 47; fig. 50) conveys an energy akin to the vibrations of the nervous system.

The energetic rhythms of these drawings may have been in part a response to the later style of Fra Bartolommeo, a dynamic manner of setting down compositional ideas in black chalk with white lights, often on colored papers, that is seen in his drawings of 1516 for an *Assumption of the Virgin.* Contact with these drawings is evident in Pontormo's only compositional study of this period, the *pensiero* for the Visdomini altar from his sketchbook (cat. 29; fig. 37). Pontormo's drawing shares an explosive linear activity with Fra Bartolommeo's, but the almost Baroque exuberance of his forms becomes, in Pontormo's composition, an unstable, nervous pattern of movement. Fra Bartolommeo handled black chalk softly, creating an atmospheric *sfumato* from which the figures emerge to move freely in space, while Pontormo used his black chalk in a more sharply angular, almost slashing manner, creating with the aid of white highlighting (new in his drawings at this time) a chiaroscuro that does not bind the forms together in a spatial continuum but makes an arbitrary pattern of flickering light and fragmented form.

Pontormo's new concept of line in these years emerged under the pressure of his desire to animate form, to infuse it with some measure of the intensity of his personal response. Line no longer contains and controls form as in classical drawings, but it is broken into active fragments, each energetic and movemented in itself. Besides fragmenting the classical totality of the form, Pontormo's line began to be overstressed at the expense of a sense of plastic form. Where these two factors were harmoniously interrelated in classical drawings, the volumes determining the shape and directions of the outlines, line separates itself from forms in Pontormo's drawings; it is no longer part of a classical synthesis but is developed independently for its aesthetic and emotive possibilities. It is this that makes Pontormo's line in 1516–1518 already unclassical. However, as in the case of Pontormo's other anticlassical experiments of these years, the consequences of this development were only partially realized. Only in the drawings of 1519–1520 did Pontormo begin to manipulate line with an aesthetic deliberation and precise grace; only in the Poggio a Caiano drawings did his line attain a completely unfettered expressiveness.

A final innovation in Pontormo's drawings of these years that may be called Mannerist is their personal expressiveness of content, which, like their graphic style, becomes more sharply formulated later in the Poggio a Caiano drawings. However, even before 1520 we find that Pontormo has evolved an unclassical psychological as well as formal vocabulary. Furthermore, in contrast to the classical draughtsman, whose aim was always to narrow rather than widen the gap caused by the difference in media and scale between drawing and painting, this new emotional mode has to do specifically and exclusively with drawings. As was the case with Pontormo's transcriptions of the nude, his ability to communicate psychological sensation became first more specific, then more personal and eccentric. It is the accentuation of the quality of personal eccentricity that places the drawings of 1516–1518 into a postclassical context. In the black chalk portrait bust of an old woman (cat. 28; fig. 33), which Pontormo used for the Pharaoh's wife in the *Story of Joseph* (III), he investigates, in a most precise transcription of reality, the realm of the unbeautiful and disturbed. In the red chalk head studies of Christ (cat. 36; fig. 43) and the St. Joseph (cat. 44; fig. 53) for the Visdomini altar he explores with heightened drama and in terms of minutely specific psychological response the rapturous states of these figures, the broken linear fragments and faceted light creating an analogous formal excitement.

In his drawings Pontormo now inhabited each of his creations with an intensity far in excess of the requirements of pictorial preparation, a personal involvement and commitment that becomes further intensified by the insistently communicative stares of the figures themselves. Before 1516 there was no such contact: faces were sometimes vaguely disturbed in mien, but specific contact was avoided by *sfumato*-veiled eyes and oblique glances. Now, in the earliest instance, the brusquely angular study for a background figure in the *Story of Joseph* (II) of 1517 (cat. 23; fig. 31), we are confronted by the startled awareness of our presence in the face of the boy. This unclassical image urgently insists, as no figure in a High Renaissance drawing had done, on our participation in his existence. Furthermore, this existence is evidently that of the artist himself. The aura of self-portraiture in this drawing is not accidental; increasingly the intensity of Pontormo's personal identification with the act of drawing led Pontormo to record his own features, to inhabit a variety of figures who play various roles. While there are outright self-portrait studies of no apparent further purpose (cat. 16; fig. 23), we find the same face in, among others, a drawing for the St. John of the Dublin *Pietà* (cat. 69; fig. 73). The very creation of this figure evidently exacted this degree of personal involvement, yet there is no trace of Pontormo's features in the more finished drawing for the figure (cat. 70; fig. 74). The communication that is established by the Pontormolike faces who stare out of his drawings with increasing frequency is that of the artist with himself, a dialogue in which we become immediately and inextricably involved. There may even be a deliberately ambiguous situation set up at times in which we (as the object of Pontormo's glance) become equated with the mirror into which the artist looks to record his image, and thus our reaction is identified with that of Pontormo himself. Such a complex network of subjective associations, linking the observer to the drawing, certainly places these studies outside the pale of the classical style, with its objectively clear separation between the subject and the object. Pontormo has removed, or at least confounded, the traditional Renaissance distinctions between the seer and the object seen. These more personal and singular of Pontormo's experiments of this period, these omnipresent self-images, rarely persist into paint. However, the intensity of Pontormo's involvement with the subjects of his art, documented so precisely in these drawings, does survive in the increasingly charged emotional climate of his paintings.

In a period of accelerated development that led into Pontormo's first artistic maturity at Poggio a Caiano, a new mode of drawing evolved. For a brief interlude, 1519–1520, the separate paths of Pontormo's investigations of the preceding years came together into a synthesis; or, more precisely, a plateau of control and discipline in which experiments ceased to exist separately and were brought into equilibrium with one another. Now Pontormo no longer probed the extreme consequences of his 1516–1518 experiments, but drew in a manner less drastically unclassical, less dependent on eccentric distortions than in the years just past. He no longer exploited his ambivalence between the *sfumato* manner of Andrea and Fra Bartolommeo and the plastic style of Michelangelo, but evolved out of his experiments a graphic mode of complete originality in which certain properties of classical draughtsmanship were transmuted by his own temperament. There is a sudden clarification and refinement. Line is disciplined, of a cursive flexibility and precise ornamental grace not previously evident; chiaroscuro is transparent, nonobscuring of form and only subtly accented. This graphic clarification is expressed exclusively in red chalk, a medium that is associated in Pontormo's development with moments of heightened clarity and rarefied sensation, while black chalk is generally found in experimental, investigative drawings. The possibilities of red chalk as an instrument are intimately linked with the definition of linear grace and luminous surface refinement that is characteristic of this phase and that of S. Felicita, the other period in which Pontormo used red chalk to achieve analogous effects, however different may be the kind of adjustment among the elements of his graphic style in 1526–1528. Now, as in the later twenties, the moment of equilibrium was brief; the shift in direction after 1520 depending on the nature of the commission for the Poggio a Caiano fresco. The particular challenge that this project made required Pontormo to redirect his graphic style in a newly experimental direction.

Pontormo's style of drawing in this interlude just before Poggio a Caiano is seen most clearly in the studies for the altarpiece painted for S. Michele in Pontorme and for the destroyed *St. Cecilia* lunette, his two most important works of circa 1519. Although anticipated on a small scale in the *Joseph in Egypt* of 1518–1519, the rhythmic elegance, the lighter and more brilliant surfaces, and the attenuated shapes that we find in the two S. Michele saints are evidence of a shift in style from the Visdomini altar that is a sudden and singular development. Further evidence of this change in style is found in the drawings for the altarpiece. The black chalk compositional studies for the St. John the Evangelist (cat. 98; fig. 101) and for the St. Michael (cat. 100; fig. 102) are still related to the chiaroscuro mode of the Visdomini drawings, although the figures are more elongated and eccentric in shape. The Evangelist recalls the similar figure in the background of the *Story of Joseph* (II) of 1516; painted at a time when Pontormo permitted such an emphatically distorted form only on a small scale and in a statue. The detail study for the legs of the St. Michael (cat. 101; fig. 100) takes us into another realm of sensation entirely. Each line has a wiry strength, yet the red chalk is handled with an unprecedented delicacy, a veil of chiaroscuro creating a translucent surface that suggests the most refined of possible substances. Shapes are, as in the painted figure, of a precise *grazia*; a quality that does not connote a slackening of Pontormo's control into prettiness and triviality of form, but rather his tightened discipline over his graphic style. This cursive mode is of a flexibility that makes it adaptable to the dramatic tableau of the *Pietà*, a plan for a lunette to surmount the S. Michele altar (cat. 103; fig. 105), as well as to the elegant *St. Michael*. By virtue of Pontormo's control over the red chalk, the tensile strength of his lines, and the evocative curvilinear patterns of the composition, the pathos of the subject is actually heightened. We can deduce from surviving evidence in drawings that the *St. Cecilia* lunette was created in a similar style and must have made something of the same impression of precious yet affecting elegance as the St. Michael. The stages of Pontormo's preparation for this fresco are similar to those for the S. Michele altar. A rather early blocking-out of the composition (cat. 93; fig. 92) is, like the drawings for the S. Michele saints, somewhat within the chiaroscuro mode of the Visdomini altar and altogether more dramatic and heroic in feeling that the more accessible and lyric figure that must finally have been painted. A late sixteenth-century copy after the fresco (cat. A354; fig. 95) certainly may exaggerate this aspect of the original, but Pontormo's study for the head (cat. 97; fig. 96) is a drawing whose charm and lightness of handling convinces us that Pontormo's invention is rather accurately reflected in the copy.

A number of other drawings for unexecuted or lost works from these years show a similar preoccupation with grace of form and feeling. Several studies for individual saints are of a refined pathos made even more sensible by Pontormo's intimate approach to the subjects: among them, a seated, praying saint (cat. 178; fig. 177), a *St. Christopher* twisting forward (cat. 168; fig. 157), and a *St. John the Baptist in the Wilderness* projecting his isolation urgently toward us (cat. 161; fig. 152). The quality of feeling in the yearning saint, which pulls him out of himself even more than the enraptured saints of the Visdomini altar, is more *raffiné* than theirs, and is expressed through a line that modulates from a thread of vibrating delicacy in the face to a flexible, strong, and almost continuous contour in the body. The St. John is related to the St. Michael of the S. Michele altar in the tensed torsion of his pose, the expansive yet sharply restricted movement of each limb, and the linear precision of the silhouette. They share the same ecstatic expression, verging on the fanatic in the St. John, bordering on the precious in the St. Michael. In this period even a portrait drawing (cat. 89; fig. 86) is unexpectedly refined in style, especially in the subtle luminosity of Pontormo's adjustment of values from the white of the paper to the few translucent red chalk shadows. If executed, the portrait of Piero de' Medici might have had the same stylistic relation to the pendant *Portrait of Cosimo il Vecchio* as the S. Michele altar has to the Visdomini altar.

In the study for a *Creation of Eve* of 1519–1520 (cat. 104; fig. 114) beauty of cursive line and transparent surface refinement are carried to an extreme. Possibly because it is so elaborately finished, this drawing strongly attests to Pontormo's intention to make ornamental beauty of form and feeling a primary factor in his drawing style. This study also points up the fact that the origin of this particular property of Pontormo's style was in the drawings of the High Renaissance itself. Ornamental beauty had been an important premise of the classical style in the sense that forms were transformed by idealization to accord with a preconceived standard of beauty that was expressed through lines of calculated grace. In the drawings of the Raphael tradition, especially, the lines and shapes that made up the idealized classical forms had a sensible beauty in themselves. However, no single aspect of the classical totality in the High Renaissance was so stressed as to be obtrusive or overemphatic at the expense of an harmonious whole. In Pontormo's drawings, on the contrary (as we have already seen in his manipulation and exaggeration of classical linear movement in 1516–1518), it is just such willful, disproportionate, and often unexpected stress that is characteristic. Chalk is manipulated with an extreme virtuosity and oversubtlety, creating surfaces of a febrile aliveness that the classical draughtsman would not have permitted. Lines are repeated for aesthetic effect, to stress a beautiful contour, not because a *pentimento* is genuinely required. Furthermore, as we have come to expect, the shapes that this stressed and evocative line makes are not classical ones and the quality of feeling that they impart is not normative but overrefined in the same sense as the forms. Thus, Pontormo has effected a characteristic abstraction from the synthesis of the classical style; an out-of-context exploitation of the property of *grazia* in the High Renaissance style that emphatically and permanently (within Pontormo's historical situation) changes its meaning from classical to Mannerist. There is here an anticipation of the kind of relation to the High Renaissance that we find later in the drawings of the Florentine *Maniera*, but the difference is decisive. The ideal of *grazia* in the *Maniera* has to do, among other things, with a deliberate classicizing by artists who were not trained originally in the classical style but at a time when there was no longer a consistent integer of classicism to violate. At this later moment there was none of the intellectual experimentation that was involved in Pontormo's first attempts to adjust the disparate elements of his style — the impulse to eccentric distortion and the desire to create a work of ornamental beauty — in order to create a valid new stylistic unity. The drawings of the phase just before Poggio a Caiano represent a significant — if brief — resolution of these factors. After 1520, the problem of this adjustment became a crucial one for Pontormo's entire career, to be continually resolved and re-resolved on different levels. The first shift occurred immediately with the Poggio a Caiano drawings themselves. In response to the nature of this commission, Pontormo re-created in a Mannerist context another property of style that was part of his heritage from the High Renaissance: adherence to visual reality. And it was precisely this concern that prompted him, during the course of the preparation of the Poggio a Caiano fresco, to abandon the solution he had reached in his drawings of 1519–1520 and to turn his attention to the recreation in actuality of Ovid's legendary characters.

Before defining the particular form that this investigation of visual reality took, we must consider an important event that profoundly affected it as well as Pontormo's entire artistic development in 1519–1520: his response to the art of Michelangelo and to variants of Raphael's classical style, probably as a result of a trip to Rome. The keystone of the prevailing Roman style in 1519, Raphael's achievement in the Vatican since his departure from Florence eleven years earlier, seems to have had limited appeal for Pontormo. However, the less authoritative, more personal brand of classicism practiced by Peruzzi, a fellow Tuscan in Rome, interested him considerably. Not only did the decorative illusionism of the Villa Farnesina provide a general model for the projected scheme of the Poggio a Caiano *Salone*, even to the Ovidian subjects, but the quotient of *grazia* that we have noted in Pontormo's style toward 1520 may have been augmented by Peruzzi's example. The design for the lunette overdoor of *St. Cecilia* (cat. 93; fig. 92) explicitly recalls the *trompe l'oeil* overdoors in the Sala delle Prospettive of 1515. Pontormo's half-draped girl surrounded by *amoretti* and looking out at us must have made an impression similar to that of Peruzzi's illusionistic scheme; and the poetic sweetness of Pontormo's drawing for her head (cat. 97; fig. 96) mirrors an unproblematic existence not unlike that of the Farnesina figures. Something of this appealing lightness of concept was eventually reflected in the reclining goddesses and playful putti of the Poggio a Caiano fresco, which may in fact refer back to Peruzzi's own ultimate source: Raphael's allegorical lunette in the Stanza della Segnatura. However, the *Vertumnus and Pomona* lunette is far from Raphael's and Peruzzi's classicism both in intention and in total effect; it is the end result of a long travail during which Pontormo involved himself with a number of other problems presented by contemporary Roman painting. Primary among these was an intensive renewal of his interest in Michelangelo's art that began about 1519 with updated variants of earlier Michelangelo motives that had interested him in the past. A study recalling the reclining figure in the *Cascina* cartoon is executed in the exquisitely transparent red chalk curvilinear manner of 1519–1520 (cat. 183; fig. 174). Here Pontormo no longer saw the motive as a virtuoso display of muscular nudity; his eyes opened to Michelangelo's own expansion of style, he projected it in terms of the monumental rhythms of the Sistine Ceiling nudes, the arm of his figure moving in the eloquent gesture of the Adam. Pontormo still found potential in the contrapposto of the Madonna in the Doni tondo, adapting the figure as the seated Mary in the lunette *Pietà* (cat. 103; fig. 103). Moreover, the Madonna motive is dramatically expanded by his vision of its descendent on the Sistine Ceiling, the Libyan Sibyl; while its specific context in the *Pietà* may well be a delayed response to Raphael's 1507 Borghese *Entombment*. Likewise, the *St. Cecilia* reflects the monumental form and breadth of movement of the Sibyls, but her illusionistic context refers to Peruzzi.

In 1520 Pontormo was provided with an opportunity to emulate Roman style on a larger scale in a commission that was unique in Florence at this time for its pretense to *Romanità*. The decoration of the great *Salone* at Poggio a Caiano was an unusual undertaking; not only in the antique subjects assigned to the artists at the direction of Cardinal Giulio de' Medici, but in the classicizing form in which, surely by common agreement, each attempted to present his subject. Whereas the more classically oriented Andrea del Sarto and Franciabigio succeeded in producing a credible facsimile — or at least a Florentine version — of the prevailing decorative style of the Raphael circle, the early drawings by Pontormo for his part in the decoration show his relation to the style of Rome to be more complex and difficult, permeated with contradiction, tension, and irresolution. This situation was due in large part to the additional problems that Pontormo created for himself by establishing a creative relation to the Sistine Ceiling. Furthermore, it was the struggle with the problems presented by this work that was the undoing of Pontormo's pretense to a Roman classical style and that ultimately freed him for the highly original creation of the Poggio a Caiano lunette.

The first drawing for Poggio a Caiano, a large red chalk study for an *Anointing of an Athlete* (cat. 124; fig. 117), explicitly demonstrates Pontormo's intention to explore two current and antithetic Roman styles: the Peruzzian and the Michelangelesque. It is a scheme of daring illusionism intended to be carried out on a monumental scale across the end wall of the room. The illusionistic idea is explicitly like that of the Sala delle Prospettive: an architectural framework of which the lower portion is intended as actual space, the upper as a fictive scheme of decoration within the already illusionistic setting. Such a characteristic Mannerist play on levels of reality may have been intended to be executed with the lower part in natural colors and the upper section in grisaille. The notion of dividing this upper portion into separate illusionistic niches containing *amoretti* and reclining figures also relates to the Peruzzi model; and the *Leda* lunette is merely an extension of Pontormo's earlier *St. Cecilia*. Peruzzi's concept, although a personal visual conceit, was not unacceptable within the broad limits of Roman classicism, but the accent that Pontormo has given his scheme is most unclassical. Pontormo's own by now well-established Mannerist intentions were compounded by a dislocating attempt to emulate Michelangelo's dynamic action of monumental forms, his *gran maniera*. Pontormo's figures move with a compulsive and nervous shuttling activity that is immediately constricted by the shallow space into which they have been set. They are not, like Peruzzi's figures, discretely few and scaled comfortably to the architecture, but numerous and (considering the scale of the projected fresco) of colossal proportions. Furthermore, the degree of generalization that is taken for granted in Roman classical illusionism was violated by Pontormo, just as it was by Giulio Romano in this same moment. Already in this drawing, the figures have a precisely specified physical presence that would surely have overstepped, in execution, the bounds of classical representation. It is as if the population of Peruzzi's Sala delle Prospettive frieze, greatly enlarged in scale, were to migrate downward and move with restless energy among the columns of his illusionistic architecture.

Clearly, if this design had been executed, the effect would have been overwhelming; even more so if it had been on the same wall with the lunette of *Vertumnus and Pomona* as first projected, and if it had been a pendant to the *Rape of the Sabines* that was probably planned for the opposite wall. A small red chalk *pensiero* for the *Rape of the Sabines* (cat. 130; fig. 116), like the

Athlete, is of friezelike proportions with the compositional energies concentrated in a central knot of forms, thinning out to the sides in pairs of figures who move restlessly in or out of the composition. The upper portion of the composition is barely suggested, but it must also have been intended as a fictive architectural setting for the action. Since this drawing was not brought to the same degree of finish as the *Athlete*, Pontormo's Romanizing intentions are not as easy to assess. However, he has treated a subject that had little Florentine precedent in the generally accepted Roman manner of handling scenes of conflict that had been evolved by Raphael and Giulio. Furthermore, details of his composition suggest study of the *Expulsion of Heliodorus* and certainly the *Battle of Ostia*.

The first drawing for the lunette itself (cat. 131; fig. 123), executed in an uncharacteristic pen and bistre technique, is at once the most extreme of Pontormo's Roman experiments and the terminus of this investigation. Sistine Ceiling motives hover in the background in the subsequent preparatory drawings for the fresco, but such a complete espousal of Michelangelo's monumental forms and dynamic movement within an essentially unMichelangelesque scheme of illusionistic decoration does not occur again. For this decorative assignment, a thirty-foot lunette pierced by a bull's-eye window, there was no real precedent in Florentine painting. Nor was there a prototype in the decorations of Raphael's circle, with the exception of the Stanza della Segnatura lunette, which we have mentioned may eventually have been recalled in Pontormo's fresco. However, at this stage, Pontormo turned most ambitiously to the Sistine Ceiling, in particular to the Ignudi. Michelangelo's nudes are transformed into illusionistic figures whose active muscularity is explained by the necessity of holding the sapling that is twisted around the window from its imminent uncoiling. Elaborate compositional tensions are generated by the rhythmic relations of the contours of these six decorative nudes, figures who are actually unable to move because of the spatial restrictions of the lunette, but whose forms are pressed forward into our space because of the very shallowness of the picture space. The design thus becomes a conceit in which powerless giants pretend to a functional role. Here there is also an analogy to the *Brazen Serpent* that anticipates a later wide-spread tendency to transmute certain Sistine Ceiling compositions into explicitly Mannerist terms. This analogy also exposes the wide gulf in basic intentions between Michelangelo and Pontormo. Michelangelo had invented a dramatically motivated composition of forms interwoven around a central void that contains the serpent — the cause of their action. In a caracteristically Mannerist fashion

Pontormo adapted the formal pattern of the action only, not its motivation, and used it in a purely decorative context. The central void is not the psychological focus of the composition, but a window looking into real — not pictorial — space. The movement of the figures is serpentine, but there is no serpent; the pattern that they make is purely aesthetic in meaning. While there is in the genesis of this drawing a certain analogy to contemporary Roman practice, this kind of response to Michelangelo was not characteristic of Pontormo's own Florentine Mannerism until after 1530. Such a rhetorical reduction of Michelangelo into a decorative scheme was not at all like Pontormo's usual response to High Renaissance art at this time and it is not surprising that he ultimately rejected the project.

These compositional drawings for Poggio a Caiano are Pontormo's first attempts to adapt a Roman style to a classical subject on a monumental scale, but they were not the only evidence at this time of a renewal of his interest in Michelangelo's art. In figure studies connected closely or tangentially to the preparation of the fresco, we find detailed documentation of this important phase in Pontormo's first artistic maturity. Two sheets especially provide us with evidence of Pontormo's immediate and untransmuted response to aspects of the Sistine Ceiling, the spontaneous juxtaposition of the images suggesting the actual presence of Michelangelo's work before his eyes. The first (cat. 133; fig. 125) contains sketches after Michelangelo's embracing putti, a motive that does not appear in any other drawings. On this sheet there is also a preliminary layout of the lunette in which Michelangelo's Bronze Nudes are adapted as standard-bearing figures above the window. These figures were transformed into Pontormo's own graphic language on the recto of this sheet (cat. 150; fig. 142) and in another red chalk study (cat. 151; fig. 143), in which there is an urgency of personal communication in the staring faces and a forward dislocation of the upper body that is Pontormo's alone. However, both the expressive intensity and assertive plasticity of these youths proved unsuitable to Pontormo's final conception of the lunette. Like the even more Romanizing compositional scheme (cat. 131), the Michelangelesque idea was abandoned and the figures were transformed through a series of studies (cat. 152–155; figs. 144–145, 148–149) into the smaller, lighter putti of the fresco.

The second sheet connected with the Sistine Ceiling (cat. 184; fig. 163) contains studies after the God Father of the *Creation of the Sun and Moon*, the Eve of the *Expulsion*, the Ignudi, and the *Haman*, all motives that appear in various guises now and later in Pontormo's drawings. The Eve and the God Father are evidence of Pontormo's close study of the central bays of the ceiling, a study which lies behind important inventions of 1520 such as the *Creation of Eve* (cat. 104; fig. 114). In this sheet of studies, as in many others of this phase, Michelangelo's example ultimately acted as a catalyst that released the energies — the cursively fluid refinement of touch — of Pontormo's personal graphic style. The sketches after two Ignudi reveal the impact on Pontormo of the immense virtuosity of Michelangelo's nudes. While reminiscences of Ignudi occur in various drawings, they never persisted into Pontormo's paintings except in a singularly piquant recollection: the garland-holding putti on the lower wall in the lunette are survivors of the original nudes who hold the sapling in the first compositional drawing (cat. 131), and thus distantly echo the functional pretext of Michelangelo's Ignudi. In a series of black chalk drawings for these putti (cat. 157–160; figs. 146–147, 150–151), Pontormo translated Michelangelo's heroic figures into forms so personally poetic, so light and childish, that their ultimate derivation is hardly sensible to us. The Ignudo theme is carried over to a study on the recto of this sheet (cat. 165; fig. 155), a red chalk drawing of a *St. John the Baptist in the Wilderness* that is clearly inspired by one of the nudes. However, Pontormo's graphic individuality is so marked and the figure has been so personalized, realized in terms of such a specific spiritual situation, that its original derivation is also veiled. The last sketch on the sheet is Pontormo's first response to Michelangelo's dramatic image of *Haman*. As with the *Brazen Serpent*, Pontormo was one of the first to explore the Mannerist implications of this figure, a motive that fascinated him and whose action he would reinterpret several times in later drawings. In the Certosa period he recalled the motive, possibly in connection with plans for a *Crucifixion* (cat. 213; fig. 206), and at about the same time drew himself in a variant of the pose in which his own mirrored image is the object of the outstretched, pointing hand (cat. 253; fig. 241). More immediate influence of the *Haman* can be found in many of the preparatory drawings for the Poggio a Caiano lunette, drawings in which the forward dislocation of the upper part of the body by energetic torsion effects a straining contact with the world of the spectator. Indeed, this torsion is their binding characteristic in contrast to the quieted action of the fresco. The Vertumnus bends urgently forward to shade his eyes (cat. 134; fig. 126); the goddess with the staff leans forward even in her position of repose (cat. 148; fig. 140); the youths above the window swing out their powerful muscular arms (cat. 151; fig. 143); and, even translated into the lighter forms of the putti (cat. 152; fig. 145), they still recall the *Haman* motive in their vigorous forward action. In contrast, the more self-contained figures in the fresco have relinquished this aggressive movement and direct attack on the spectator's consciousness: Vertumnus's action and glance are not specifically directed; the goddess gazes gently at us without challenge; and the putti sit quietly on the fragile remnants of the once powerful sapling.

The most extreme translation of the *Haman* motive is the drawing connected with the boy on the wall (cat. 143; fig. 136). In the drawing the figure gyrates aggressively toward us, led by his pointing hand, while in the fresco this action is inverted so that he leans back into the picture space. This drawing is a paradigm of nervous energy: the red chalk is handled with a sharp angularity extreme even for Pontormo and the lines of the background gravitate toward the figure like metal filings on a magnetic field. Here we find evidence of the persistence of a habit of mind that Pontormo had established as early as 1516: the idea that drawings can be private explorations of graphic problems not necessarily related to their function as preparatory studies. The *Haman* motive of corkscrew forward movement is used here, not in the limited context of preparation for the fresco figure (although it does serve this function as well), but as a part of Pontormo's intimate probing of the further limits of the breakdown of the normative relation between subject and object that had concerned him for several years. This boy does more than contemplate us; by pointing out toward us he implicates us in his action, extending his person and the space he controls forward into an unstable merger with ours. Thus, in an inversion of classical single-point perspective, we become the focus of the composition, and the notion of our measurable and objective distance from the drawing is broken down. Furthermore, we are implicated not only in the action of the boy but in his psychological motivation. Who but the spectator could be the stimulus for the otherwise inexplicable overreaction of this figure? By extension, we became involved with Pontormo's own psychological state — his own excitable overreactions, which are inseparable from those of the pointing boy. Eventually, in the uncommunicative action of the figure in the fresco, there is no trace of the radical and intimate extreme of Pontormo's drawing and even less of its original origin in the *Haman*. In this sense the drawing may be tangential to the preparation of the fresco figure, but it is also — in the light of Pontormo's expanded concept of the role of drawings — vital to it. While the degree of violent physical movement and psychological eccentricity of drawings such as this one do not persist into the painted figures, a residue of the sheer energy of their conception does survive to impart to the Poggio a Caiano fresco its extraordinarily controlled sense of interior animation.

The phase that produced the masterpiece of the Poggio a Caiano lunette was in every sense a crisis in Pontormo's development, a crisis that was precipitated by the challenge of Michelangelo, and resolved in the fresco itself. As we have seen, this challenge was anything but unmet. Pontormo became neither copyist nor facile adapter of Michelangelo's inventions; nor did he attempt to emulate Michelangelo's sculptural forms by changing his graphic manner toward Michelangelo's broad red chalk style or his closely hatched pen manner. Rather, Pontormo was stimulated by Michelangelo's example toward a rapid maturity of his own personal drawing style and he established — by taking a stand simultaneously of involvement and independence — a precedent for a later more profound and stylistically decisive probing of Michelangelo's art. The maturity of Pontormo's Mannerist style was achieved at Poggio a Caiano only after he had abandoned his difficult Romanizing intentions and discarded the original projects for the end wall (cat. 124) and the lunette (cat. 131). Beginning with the second lunette plan (cat. 132; fig. 124), Pontormo set about to adjust the *Vertumnus and Pomona*, not to Roman standards, but to Florentine and ultimately profoundly original ones. The subject was transformed into a poetic pastorale at once of an ideality more abstract and an actuality more communicative than any analogous work in the classical style, including the frescoes by Andrea del Sarto and Franciabigio in the same room. The documentation for this decisive formulation of Pontormo's style is found in the most extensive group of his drawings that survives for a single painting (cat. 131–160; figs. 123–151). In these studies Pontormo concentrated his energies entirely on the recreation in actuality — simultaneously contemporary and idyllic — of each character in the story.

The drawings for the individual figures of the Poggio a Caiano fresco reveal a novel process of pictorial preparation that was suggested in Pontormo's work before 1520, but emerged decisively only now. The High Renaissance preparatory procedure, like the style of the drawings themselves, had an harmonious inevitability and smooth rhythm, beginning with a *pensiero* of the whole composition; continuing with *studi* that perfected its predetermined parts in relation to the data of reality; and ending with the reassimilation of these parts into the whole in the *disegno* or *modello*. Pontormo destroyed this predictability, this creative rhythm; he inverted this a priori procedure by equating the whole with the sum of the individualized parts. (Because of Pontormo's conscious deviation from classical practice, his calculated exploitation of its tradition for his own Mannerist purposes, this process is not to be confounded with the additive method of the preclassical Quattrocento.)

As is apparent from a study of the sequences of drawings for the various lunette figures, the pose of each and even its final relation to the other figures was predetermined only in the most general sense. Thus, Pontormo allowed himself a range of inventive possibility in his preparatory studies that was unknown to the previous generation of draughtsmen. He demonstrated here for the first time on a wide scale that the function of a drawing varies according to the individual artist and is conditioned by his response to the subject; that the drawing can be free from the mechanical overtones or limitations sometimes associated with preparatory studies done according to the classical dialectic system. A corollary to this creative freedom that Pontormo won for himself at Poggio a Caiano was the liberty to adjust at will the components of reality and ideality (abstraction) in his drawings. Inherent in the classical procedure was the assumption that this adjustment was one of synthesis in which the data of reality were adjusted to a formal ideal, and the irrational, accidental, and personally eccentric were reduced to a minimum. In Pontormo's drawings, synthesis in this sense was not an aim; rather, the polarities of the classical style were exposed. Pontormo developed reality and ideality to separate extremes, making artistic capital, on one hand, of the accidental and eccentric; on the other, of a personal concept of abstract beauty. These properties of style are often found in the same drawing — not because Pontormo wished to eliminate extremes by synthesis, but because he wished to emphasize them by juxtaposition.

In spite of these radical innovations, or perhaps because of them, Pontormo's preparatory studies — understood in this newly flexible sense — have a spontaneously creative relation to the Poggio a Caiano fresco. He began with a rapid *pensiero* of each figure, usually in black chalk — his instrument of experimentation. Sketches from this early stage survive for most of the figures: the Vertumnus (cat. 134–135; figs. 126–127), the goddess on the wall (cat. 144; fig. 137), the goddess with the staff (cat. 147; fig. 139), and the putto above to the right (cat. 150–151; figs. 142–143). All but one of these were taken from the nude boy model and the attitudes have an accidental-seeming nonchalance that belies the existence of a predetermined pose or silhouette. The shapes themselves are experimental in the degree of abstraction that Pontormo's line creates. This eccentricity of shape is as tangential to the final meaning of the fresco as is the intensity of psychological communication of the figures. These aspects of Pontormo's drawings are functions of his energy of seeing and his personal involvement with the creation of the drawing. Pontormo worked from these primary sketches to a series of studies for each figure, drawings that do not always evolve logically from one another but are of equal value as variants on a theme. There is nothing analytical or predictable about this procedure: Pontormo would bring one of these sequences of studies to an apparent solution, usually signaled by a shift to red chalk and a more finished execution, only to abandon it and begin again. Such is the case with the Vertumnus (cat. 137; fig. 129), the goddess with the staff (cat. 146; fig. 134), and the boy on the wall (cat. 143; fig. 136). This erratic and unpredictable manner of preparing for a painting may account in part for Pontormo's alleged slowness and certainly bears out Vasari's exasperated account of the work on the Poggio a Caiano lunette (V/M, VI, 264): ". . . si mise con tanta diligenza a studiare, che fu troppa; perciocchè guastando e rifacendo oggi quello che aveva fatto ieri . . ."

Each of the actors in the scene went through several metamorphoses before his final appearance in the fresco. Pontormo rarely made *studi*, detailed drawings of parts of figures that presuppose the existence of a completed idea. In any case, only a few, such as the study for the arm of the youth with the basket (cat. 142; fig. 132), have survived in proportion to other kinds of drawings. It was more characteristic of Pontormo to consider the figure as a whole, making a miniscule sketch on the lower part of the sheet and then expanding upon it (cat. 135, 147, 150–151; figs. 127, 139, 142–143). The final studies for each figure are executed in black chalk in a more pictorial manner than the earlier sketches, some of them squared for enlargement. In these latest studies, such as the poignant study for the head of the youth with the basket (cat. 141; fig. 135), Pontormo's draughtsmanship is less spare: modelling in black chalk is softened by rubbing and white highlights are added to create a luminous *sfumato* that establishes the vibrant light and shade patterns of the fresco. Line is not as sharply abstracting as before, but multiple and softly curving in the putti studies (cat. 160; fig. 150); of a thinner delicacy in the drawings for the women (cat. 145, 148–149; figs. 138, 140–141), one of which has an almost Rococo lightness and grace that indicates a return to a more normative image after the most bizarre of the first *pensieri* (cat. 144; fig. 137). In these final drawings Pontormo evolved an enriched pictorial graphic mode of personal intimacy and trembling aliveness. It is a *sfumato* manner that is removed by a far greater distance from Pontormo's Sartesque style of 1515–1516 than the five years that separate them might suggest, a mature Mannerist style of drawing that his accelerated development of the years 1519–1520 had made possible.

Pontormo had investigated his theme at Poggio a Caiano in terms of a penetrating actuality, but this investigation was not limited to drawings specifically preparatory to the fresco. His preoccupation at this time with the data of visual reality is further documented by a large number of drawings (cat. 161–191; figs. 152–179), many of which were made with no evident pictorial purpose. A series of nude studies from the posed model represents one aspect of this investigation (cat. 171, 185, 188, 191; figs. 170–173). Pontormo's line has a sharp energy, deforming and abstracting each shape, yet retaining in the end a most precise, even heightened, sense of physical reality. This is a type of drawing that became an Academy with the more prosaic vision and less impassioned execution of the later sixteenth-century Florentine draughtsman. Another aspect of this investigation is Pontormo's concern with psychological reality, often projected in terms of eccentric extremes: a sheet of spectral heads (cat. 176; fig. 162), an intensely focussed evocation of the spiritual state of a *St. Jerome* (cat. 170; fig. 160) or a *St. Christopher* (cat. 167; fig. 159). In quite another direction and with a wide-ranging curiosity that set him apart from Renaissance and Mannerist draughtsmen alike, Pontormo made sketches of the *garzoni* in his *bottega* that are of an unprecedented informality, sharp and witty in characterization (cat. 172, 177, 186; figs. 164–166). All of these drawings are indicative of the artistic personality who sought to actualize Ovid's legend in contemporary terms at Poggio a Caiano, but who also investigated reality for its own sake.

The stylistic development from the bucolic actuality of the Poggio a Caiano lunette, finished late in 1521, to the ghostly unreality of the Certosa frescoes, begun early in 1523, is a complex network, the separate threads of which contrast with the closeknit fabric of Pontormo's style at Poggio a Caiano. The Mannerist synthesis of actuality and abstraction achieved at Poggio a Caiano was never to be completely undone by Pontormo, but its very precariousness and eccentricity permitted — indeed compelled — a personality like Pontormo to enter a new phase of experimentation. In the drawings of 1522–1525 we find both a realism more pervasive and an abstracting order more ideal than we have seen at Poggio a Caiano. In these drawings the possibilities of actuality and of ideality were investigated in experimental, often novel ways, but were never fused in the kind of resolution that occurred at Poggio a Caiano and, later, on quite another level, at S. Felicita.

We begin to be aware of the incipient change in Pontormo's style in the Hermitage *Holy Family*, the only surviving work in painting that is closely related in style to the Poggio a Caiano lunette. The richly elaborated black and white chalk squared study for this painting (cat. 192; fig. 181) is identical in its luminous *sfumato* mode to the later lunette drawings. The Madonna in this drawing could easily change places with the Pomona (cat. 149; fig. 141), the Child with a putto (cat. 160; fig. 150). However, the relation of the painting to the drawing is not like that of the lunette to its preparatory studies. In the Madonna and Child of the painting the vibrating physical presence and psychological intimacy of the drawing are overcast with a stronger measure of cool ideality than is found in the Poggio a Caiano fresco, while the head of Joseph is painted with a realistic conviction bordering on caricature that finds no parallel in the lunette. The element of novelty in the eventual juxtaposition of these figures in the painting is the deliberate exploitation of this contrast.

As the synthesis of the Poggio a Caiano style loosened during the next year, Pontormo pushed his investigation of visual reality to a new extreme in the direction anticipated by the St. Joseph. The Pitti *Adoration of the Magi* is conceived in a style so actual and contemporary as to be a virtual caricature of Pontormo's own earlier realism, retaining nothing of the poetic ideality that so carefully balanced it in the Poggio a Caiano lunette. (We might note that a parallel development occurred in Pontormo's only portrait of this phase: the *Two Men* of about 1522 bears a similar relation to the earlier *Portrait of a Musician*, its heightened realism and individuality untempered by the *grazia* of 1519.) The *Adoration* was Pontormo's first essay in small-scale decoration since the completion of the Borgherini *Story of Joseph* four years earlier. In this picture Pontormo looked back to a type of composition — specifically an anormative spatial image — that he had developed in the last of the series, the *Joseph in Egypt*. Like a thread temporarily dropped, this image was picked up and further developed, although in the *Adoration* it may have been modified by the requirements of an oblong panel, possibly for a *cassone*. However, in the *Adoration* Pontormo did not take as radical a step into novelty as in the contemporary drawings for two works that apparently were never executed, probably because of Pontormo's flight to the Certosa from the plague late in 1522. One is an elaborate red chalk study for an altarpiece with the *Adoration of the Magi* (cat. 194; fig. 186); the other is a finished *disegno* for a fresco commissioned by the Brotherhood of the Camaldoli Martyrs, depicting the *Victory and Baptism of the Ten Thousand Martyrs* (cat. 195; fig. 185). In both drawings the complex of active forms in an illogically rising space recalls the *Joseph in Egypt*. However, unlike the small Borgherini picture, these compositions were intended to be projected on a monumental scale like that of similar compositions in the Certosa cloister: the *Way to Golgotha* and *Christ Before Pilate.* In the drawing of the *Adoration* fully plastic forms move in an unprecedented pattern of violence hardly suggested by the normal requirements of the subject. The Holy Family group is convulsed in an ecstatic frenzy of centrifugal movement; a deliberate tension is created between the movemented forms and the restricted space; the *repoussoir* figures tilt precariously into our space, while the crowd presses forward from a nonexistent background space. In the drawing of the *Martyres* we find the even more activated forms suitable to a battlepiece, while the space is made only slightly elastic to accommodate a rush out of the background that is abruptly halted by the knot of fighting figures. Both drawings depict a world far removed from that of idyllic repose and comfortable spatial interval in the Poggio a Caiano lunette. But this world is also quite distinct from that of the Certosa frescoes, where movement is slowed until there is no sense of restriction; and figures, although crowded, have surrendered their weight and their ability to move with independent assertiveness. The important difference between these projects and the Certosa compositions is their persistent reference to a physical reality, in details of the composition if not in the whole. The phase just preceding the Certosa is thus one of heightened investigation of the individualization of form that was an element of style at Poggio a Caiano, together with radical experimentation in spatial and compositional novelties in the direction earlier indicated by the *Joseph in Egypt.* Except for the small-scale *Adoration,* this phase goes unrecorded in painting, but it is amply shown in these two drawings to be a period of extremely inventive anticlassicism in Pontormo's development. If executed, the *Adoration* would have been as radical as any Mannerist altarpiece yet painted, excepting Rosso's Volterra *Deposition* of 1521, with its analogous composition but quite different vocabulary of form. Likewise, when projected on a wall, the violent restricted movement of the *Martyrs* would have made an impression as acutely disquieting as Rosso's contemporary *Moses and the Daughters of Jethro.* Indeed, the fact that, as far as we know, Pontormo did not carry these ideas beyond the preparatory stage has obscured analogies between his Mannerism and that of his most advanced Florentine contemporary.

The period of the Certosa Passion Series is a difficult phase of eccentric investigation that intervened between the more accessible styles of Poggio a Caiano and S. Felicita. Essential to a comprehension of this phase is a consideration of Pontormo's relation to the art of his contemporaries and to his own achievement. At the Certosa for the first time in his career Pontormo turned his back on his past accomplishments and took an entirely new experimental path. His isolation from his own past was matched by a willed separation from the art of Andrea del Sarto and Michelangelo, influences that had been, in effect, a measure of classicizing balance to his Mannerist innovation. Now, however, in the removed and otherworldly monastic atmosphere of the cloister, the grip of the classical style loosened; Pontormo turned for inspiration outside his own tradition to Dürer; he became aware for the first time of the implications of Rosso's anticlassical experiments; and he pushed his own Mannerist style into previously uncharted territory. Significantly, it is at this point in his *Vita* that Vasari first begins to remark on the novelty of Pontormo's style (V/M, VI, 268): ". . . non avendo fermezza nel cervello andava sempre nuove cose ghiribizzando . . ."

Pontormo's change of style was not simply a matter of Dürer imitation, but was brought about by a unique combination of isolating factors that made Dürer's art take on an expanded meaning for him. In the period just before he went to the Certosa Pontormo had become involved with the art of Dürer to the point where it had a significant influence on his style. His already well-formulated perception of physical eccentricity was sharpened by his response to Dürer's prints, and the influence of the Northern "realistic" manner was in no small measure responsible for the accentuation of this property of Pontormo's style about 1522. There are Northern references in the Pitti *Adoration*, the original of the *Madonna and Child with St. John* (Corsini 141), and a lost *Pietà* (V/M, VI, 265), but the lack of drawings for these works makes it difficult to assess in further detail the relation of Pontormo's draughtsmanship to Dürer in the period before the Certosa. It is evident, however, that the initial phase of Pontormo's creative response to Dürer did not involve the extreme reaction against the quotient of reality in his own style that occurred in the Certosa drawings, but served rather to accentuate it. Thus, in turning to the drawings for the Passion Series, we must look beyond Dürer for a complete explanation of Pontormo's sudden shift to a dematerialized and abstract style.

Of primary importance in this respect is a newly specific relation to the art of Rosso, involving both a parallel development and the influence of Rosso on Pontormo. The artistic isolation that Pontormo created for himself at the Certosa is a phenomenon not unlike Rosso's basic artistic situation. Rosso's art was motivated by an eccentric spirituality that was not rooted in an intellectual adjustment between persistent classicism and Mannerist invention but in a totally aclassical point of view. His is an art at once preclassical and post classical in character and, as such, quite different from Pontormo's. In his isolation from the classical tradition, Rosso had earlier discovered a bond with Dürer; now Pontormo found in Dürer's Late Gothic art a stimulus to further remove himself from the classical tradition, but he was not uninfluenced by Rosso's previous formulations. In these complex circumstances, it is not easy to conclude how much of the analogy in form and feeling between Rosso and Pontormo of the Certosa phase is due to the direct influence of Rosso on Pontormo and how much to a common penchant for Dürer's art; apparently native to Rosso, generated more tardily in Pontormo only under the peculiar circumstances of isolation that we have suggested.

As was the case with the projects just preceding Pontormo's flight to the Certosa, the number of drawings that survive for the frescoes of the Passion Series is small (cat. 196–214; figs. 188, 190–204, 206–207). Although Pontormo may have kept his drawings, this eccentric phase did not appeal to his contemporaries or to the collectors of the late sixteenth century who would have been responsible for preserving them, and it is likely that they were ignored and lost. Many of the surviving studies are mere notations in a sketchbook, only a handful are carried to any degree of finish or show the evolution of a motive from one drawing to another. This paucity of material, combined with the damaged condition of the frescoes, makes it difficult to assess not only the crucial problem of Pontormo's relation to Dürer and Rosso in this period, but the general range of his drawing style and the relation of the drawings to the paintings. However, certain tendencies are clearly evident: there was above all a reaction against the physical actuality that was Pontormo's inheritance from the High Renaissance and that still played such a dominant role at Poggio a Caiano and shortly afterwards. Now, not unlike Rosso's ghost figures, forms are thin and dematerialized, lacking both in ponderation and in organically motivated action, moving in a private dream world. Feeling is equally distant from reality. A sense of malaise envelopes each figure and an air of psychological detachment veils even their direct stares. In two red chalk studies for the man who carries the end of the cross in the *Way to Golgotha* (cat. 197–198; figs. 191, 193), the body is totally unarticulated physically, showing only the spiritual strain of lifting the cross. A drawing for the *Nailing to the Cross* that does have a measure of physical conviction (cat. 208; fig. 200) is followed by a dematerialized version of the motive (cat. 209; fig. 201) in which the temper of movement has changed from swift directness to obscure complexity, the figure not so much moving as vibrating in several directions at once. The St. Veronica studies for the *Way to Golgotha* (cat. 200–201; fig. 190) have an indecisive linear rhythm whose energies are released in impulses rather than resolved in committed gesture. As in Rosso's drawings, figures are not elaborately modelled but drawn in a thin, sometimes brittle, linear manner that adds to the impression of elongated weightlessness. In the study for the *Pietà* (cat. 213; fig. 206) the Christ especially shows a tendency toward the thin elongation and squaring-off of forms that is reminiscent of the Christ in the Volterra *Deposition*. The contrast with the bravura red chalk manner of the Poggio a Caiano drawings is extreme. Pontormo's line no longer has the tensile strength, the sharp and unexpected accents of the line in the studies for the lunette, but is softer, unstressed, and unenergetic. While Pontormo's always more cursive graphic mode never approaches the fragmented, splintered line and cubic reduction of form of Rosso's drawings, his rejection of the manner that has solved so well the particular problems presented by the *Vertumnus and Pomona* brings Pontormo's drawing style at the Certosa closer to Rosso's than at any other time.

Pontormo's effort to eliminate a sense of physical actuality from his drawings in this period was closely linked to his attempt to avoid the ornamental consequences of his previous manner by removing all traces of *grazia*. It is in this connection that Dürer's influence seems most crucial. The role that Dürer's prints played in the change in Pontormo's drawing style at the Certosa goes beyond the somewhat superficial borrowing of *invenzioni* that had been common practice in Florence for almost a decade and had been especially evident in Pontormo's own fascination with Northern motives, types, and costumes. While this use of Northern inventions in a narrow sense persisted — even reached a climax — in the Certosa frescoes, Dürer now held an additional and more profound meaning for Pontormo. In contrast to his previous practice, Pontormo identified with the entire *gestalt* of Dürer's prints, endeavoring to create paintings of the same subjects in the same spirit. Vasari notes this intention (V/M, VI, 266): ". . . pensò Jacopo, avendo a fare ne' canti di que'chiostri istorie della Passione del Salvatore, di servirsi dell'invenzioni sopradette d'Alberto Duro, con ferma credenza d'avere non solo a sodisfare a se stesso, ma alla maggior parte degli artefici di Firenze . . ." It is also significant that the compositional borrowings at the Certosa are almost all from the *Small Passion* woodcuts. These relatively late works reflected Dürer's own espousal of Italian art and to some degree the suppression of his earlier Gothicisms. The simplified and clarified compositions and less contorted linear style of these woodcuts may have been — ironically — the very ingredients that made Dürer's style accessible and palatable to Pontormo. Nonetheless, Pontormo must have shared the current opinion, which comes to us through

Vasari (V/M, VI, 267–270), that Dürer's art, despite a certain intriguing *bellezza*, was completely foreign to the Italian tradition. The artist schooled in the *maniera italiana* saw in Dürer a novel and fascinating emphasis on the accidental and the eccentric, but this was offset by a stiffness, a lack of *dolcezza* and — above all — of *grazia*. From the Florentine point of view, a deficiency in *grazia* referred specifically to a deficiency in *disegno*, a failure to achieve that suave ordering of forms and ornamental beauty of line that may be in differing ways a property of both High Renaissance and Mannerist drawings.

It is precisely in connection with Pontormo's own stylistic reversal from the *grazia* as well as from the physical actuality of his earlier style that Dürer's woodcuts must have had some formative role in the new graphic mode of the Certosa drawings. In these studies Pontormo's line no longer reads rhythmically, but is straightened and discontinuous, as in the awkward stress he has given the cross-bearing figure (cat. 197; fig. 191) or the St. Veronica study (cat. 200; fig. 190) for the *Way to Golgotha*. In other drawings, such as those for the *Nailing to the Cross* (cat. 207, 210; figs. 199, 202), his line vibrates in irregular sequences and with such accidental-seeming impulses that the form does not "scan" in any recognizable rhythm. Dürer's woodcut line is reflected even more specifically in the involved convolutions of draperies of a study for the St. John in the *Agony in the Garden* (cat. 196; fig. 188), which is also a close adaptation of a Dürer motive. Nor do these analogies cease in the works of about 1525: in the black chalk studies for the *Supper at Emmaus* (cat. 218–221; figs. 212–215) the draperies are drawn with the hooked line ending in a pocket of black that recalls the graphic mode of a woodcut. In these studies as well as in the St. Jerome for the *Madonna Enthroned* (cat. 222; fig. 216) and in several Certosa drawings (cat. 212, 214; figs. 204, 207) Pontormo modelled form in parallel curved strokes whose unusual regularity suggests the slightly mechanical quality of the woodcut line. A number of drastically simplified and schematized faces are evidently derived from woodcuts, such as the face in a Düreresque red chalk study of a melancholic seated woman (cat. 252; fig. 242), while a clearly outlined, thick-featured facial type (cat. 205; fig. 194) seems also to have evolved at this time out of Pontormo's study of Dürer. Even beyond his exploitation of the linear style of Dürer's prints, Pontormo may also have been affected by the black and white abstraction of the woodcuts, by simplified areas of light and shade that may have suggested to him a flattening and patterning of forms. No drawing of this period more vividly recalls a woodcut in this sense than the little *pensiero* for the unexecuted *Deposition* (cat. 212; fig. 204). Here and elsewhere Pontormo adapted Dürer's lengthened figure type with its excessively long limbs and singularly disjointed character. His translation effects a decentralization of the figure, a diminution of its ponderation, substance, and physical energy so that the form itself as well as the lines that circumscribe it lacks both plasticity and grace. Thus, given an innate tendency in the direction of abstraction and given this particular juncture in his development, Pontormo could hardly have avoided, even in part unconsciously, assimilating something of Dürer's graphic abstraction into his own drawing style. In any case, whatever may have been the extent of Dürer's influence in reinforcing his tendencies to innovation, Pontormo's turn from the accomplishments of the High Renaissance and his rejection of the properties of ornamental beauty and reality in the Certosa drawings produced his most radically anticlassical drawings to date.

The Certosa drawings of 1523–1524 consistently emerge as an extreme reaction against the normative elements in Pontormo's drawing style. In contrast to the vibrant actuality of Poggio a Caiano, the dominating modes are the spiritual, the abstract, and the ideal. In the phase just following the completion of the Passion Series, which includes the drawings for the Capponi *Madonna and Child* (cat. 258; fig. 245) and the destroyed cupola of the Capponi Chapel (cat. 259–266; figs. 246–252), as well as those for the *Supper at Emmaus* (cat. 215–221; figs. 209–215), the *Madonna Enthroned* (cat. 222; fig. 216), and the lost *Portrait of Ippolito de' Medici* (cat. 223; fig. 219), there were a number of subtle shifts in Pontormo's style of drawing. While Düreresque elements — the straightened nonornamental line, flattened parallel shading, broad angular draperies — persisted, there was also a significant readmission of a degree of objective realism in the studies for these pictures. The thin, elongated, and weightless Certosa figures became more volumetric and broader in proportions, while there was a portraitlike approach to the model that was rare in the preceding phase. Because this swing away from an extreme level of abstraction was combined with a comparatively unenergetic, unassertive draughtsmanship, this phase may be regarded as a brief *détente* within Pontormo's development. His experience was translated into drawings with neither the tense overexcitement of Poggio a Caiano, the introverted spirituality of the Certosa, nor the calculated distillation of S. Felicita. Pontormo made radical experiments in the drawings of this period, but they were projected within a context of deceptive relaxation.

Primary among these experiments was the way in which realism itself was recalled. It is of a different sort than we have encountered before, so conditioned by the subjective focus of the anticlassical visions of the Certosa as to be unrecognizable as the actuality that Pontormo had perceived with such energetic sensibility at Poggio a Caiano. After his flight from the real world — both in the sense of the reality of nature and that of the classical tradition — Pontormo never returned to an unequivocal attitude toward reality. After the Certosa, aspects of actuality were readmitted into Pontormo's drawings on his own terms, but not out of any sense of total commitment to the world of reality such as we find in the drawings of Andrea del Sarto. Pontormo tended increasingly to see and to record disjunctively rather than synthetically: all relations were perceived subjectively and there was no intention of adjusting the real and the ideal; rather, they are left suspended in ambivalent, ambiguous irresolution. Primarily because of this basic ambivalence, the comparisons that are often made between Pontormo's works of this period and the Caravaggesque Baroque are based on an apparent similarity only. Pontormo's naturalism and his emphasis on light in this period are conditioned by a disjunctive view of reality that is quite opposite from the more consistent texture of the Baroque perception of reality.

In considering this point of view as it appears in the drawings of this phase, we must note with more than usual care the relation between the drawings and the paintings for which they prepare. Indeed, it is generally only in the painting that a precarious coexistence of reality and abstraction becomes clear as Pontormo's intention. All but one of the *Supper at Emmaus* studies are quite normative; while in the painting these same figures are submerged in a visionary context that compromises their reality. A portrait study of a monk (cat. 216; fig. 209) is of a most poignant naturalism; yet, seen in the mystic light of the picture at the periphery of a curving space, this monk takes on an apparitional quality. On the other hand, in the red chalk study for the two monks (cat. 215; fig. 210), Pontormo was already dealing with a subjectively perceived relation in the drawing. These two independently convincing fragments of reality are placed in a mysterious conjunction that anticipates the disoriented psychology of the painting. They relate to one another and to the central scene only by way of Pontormo's subjective focus, a point of view that refers ultimately only to his personal experience. However, like the extraordinary existence of the still life on the table, Pontormo's transfigured reality still half convinces us of its objective validity.

We can see something of this same kind of change in a comparison of the *Portrait of Alessandro de' Medici* and the drawing for its pendant *Portrait of Ippolito de' Medici* (cat. 223; fig. 219). The figure in the drawing is a consistently perceived, credible reality; its parts are normative in relation to one another, and the black chalk *sfumato* on blue paper creates a softly pictorial continuum. However, in the *Alessandro* painting — and presumably also in the lost *Ippolito* — this image of reality is disintegrated by jumps from specific to abstract, or distorted, handling that are evidence of real fissures in Pontormo's way of seeing. Even the relatively naturalistic studies for the Patriarchs of the S. Felicita cupola (cat. 262–266; figs. 248–252) may have been transformed into painted figures of an ambivalent reality, creating on the curved surface of the vault the impression of realism within apparition that is so notable in Pontormo's other works of about 1525. In any case, Vasari found it necessary to remark (V/M, VI, 271) that the cupola was executed in Pontormo's "maniera da prima," and was, therefore, different in style from the other works in the chapel.

In the drawings of this period there are two further lines of experimentation, which Pontormo had already begun within the Certosa period, that were to be of utmost importance in effecting the transformation of his style that occurred in the drawings of 1526–1528. Free as he was from the conventional vision of the recent past, and of an innate hypersensitivity of perception, Pontormo became fascinated with the mechanics of seeing. He began to experiment with the optical distortions that result from the arbitrary manipulation of his distance from various parts of his subject and of his intensity of focus. The relation between the draughtsman and the object that he drew thus became yet more subjective and variable as the artist literally acted upon the object, transforming it by his very experience in seeing it. Pontormo's chalk produces effects of distortion and oddly displaced accents that involve us even more intimately than before in the dynamics of his subjective visual experience. The most telling instance of this singular transformation of an allegedly naturalistic image is the extraordinary self-portrait drawing (cat. 253; fig. 241), the recto of the enigmatic monks for the *Supper at Emmaus*. We have already mentioned Pontormo's adaption of Michelangelo's *Haman* motive in the drawing of the pointing boy of about 1521 (cat. 143; fig. 136). Here the effect is even more startling because, within so apparently normal an image, the abrupt displacement of the compositional accent by the pointing hand forces the eye of the spectator to jump forward. The whole focus of the drawing becomes unaccountably subjective: since the pointing man is Pontormo himself, his gesture and stare make a sharp thrust into our consciousness by placing us in the equivocal situation of being the object of this artist's own intense stare into his mirror. Such a transformation of a normal optical experience by an isolated or displaced accent also occurs in a Certosa drawing for the figure to the left in the *Nailing to the Cross.* In this drawing (cat. 209; fig. 201) the raised hand is expressively enlarged as if Pontormo had mentally magnified this portion of the body by the very stress of his perception of it. This hand makes a poignant effect as it vibrates toward the small head that seems in contrast to recede into the distance. Motives like the upraised arm, thus enlarged to become the unexpected psychological focus of the drawing, held special and privately expressive meanings for Pontormo at this time. Other figures of this period, such as the Christ in the *Supper at Emmaus* (cat. 221; fig. 215), the Patriarchs (cat. 264–265; figs. 248, 251) and the God Father (cat. 261; fig. 246) of S. Felicita, also move enlarged hands toward us in dreamlike, uncompleted gestures. Only subsequently in the drawings of 1526–1528 would these emotive fragments be gathered up into a rhythmic relation to one another, their effectiveness heightened by the crystallization and refinement of Pontormo's graphic means at S. Felicita.

Pontormo also experimented at this time with light, a *luminismo* that at first simply revealed and emphasized the fissures in his disjunctive world, but eventually in 1526–1528 became a luminous binding substance. Beginning with certain Certosa drawings, Pontormo's light has an abstracting and singular effect. If the frescoes themselves were in better condition, we might be able to see the handling of light that so impressed Vasari (V/M, VI, 267): "Fece . . . Cristo nell'orto, fingendo l'oscurità della notte illuminata dal lume della luna tanto bene, che par quasi di giorno . . ." Other evidence of Pontormo's light experiments in these years is a Certosa work now lost, of which Vasari says (V/M, VI, 269): "Fece . . . la Natività di Cristo, fingendo che Giuseppo nelle tenebre di quella notte faccia lume a Gesù Cristo con una lanterna . . ." In the only surviving compositional drawing for the Certosa, a black chalk study heightened with white for a *Nailing to the Cross* (cat. 206; fig. 198), there is a supernatural light that seems to radiate from the body of Christ, as it does in the *Resurrection* fresco. In the detail study for this figure (cat. 207; fig. 199) Christ's body is transfigured by a phosphorescent light that is suggested by the liberal use of white chalk over black. The only other drawing of this period that has such a luminous effect is the verso of a study for the same fresco (cat. 240; fig. 229). Here, probably in imitation of the bronze surface of a statue, Pontormo has created a gleaming surface of reflected lights in red chalk alone. In the study for the *Madonna Enthroned* (cat. 222; fig. 216) and in drawings for the *Supper at Emmaus* (cat. 216; fig. 209) Pontormo was also concerned with luminosity. A strong and directional, but not consistent light that transforms and flattens the figures is a primary factor in effecting their ambiguous naturalism. Finally, in the cupola studies, *luminismo* is exaggerated as Pontormo approached the refined concept of light of the S. Felicita drawings. In one Patriarch study (cat. 264; fig. 248) the figure is strongly and irregularly lit from below, suggestive of an apparition suddenly revealed by the flickering, uneven light of a candle. Drawings such as this one indicate that Pontormo may have intended to exploit the existence of the natural light that would have illuminated the cupola from below, just as he later used the light from the window in the *Annunciation* of the same chapel. Again, however, it must be stressed that this "illusionism" is quite unrelated to Baroque illusionism: it is founded on a ambiguous relation between real and created light rather than on their harmonious interpenetration.

At no time since 1516–1518, when Pontormo first began to diverge from Andrea del Sarto, was the contrast with Andrea's draughtsmanship more telling than in this period of increased naturalism that brought Pontormo's red chalk style superficially close to that of the contemporary Andrea. This point of contact only emphasizes their actual divergence — the distance that both Pontormo's concept of drawings and his graphic mode had come from the style of his former master. Andrea's adherence to a classical manner of drawing in the midtwenties (as in his studies for the *Pietà* and *Assumption* 191 in the Pitti, or the *Madonna del Sacco*) was such that optical reality held a meaning for him quite different from that of Pontormo's experimental reality of these years. Andrea's world was still all in one piece, not disintegrated by the stresses and shifting viewpoints of Pontormo's visual experience. In his red chalk drawings Andrea recreated an ordinary, though heightened, experience of reality in a style of animate naturalism that makes this experience immediately accessible, almost tangible. There are no subjective foci, no warping distortions or transforming light to make equivocal otherwise normative forms. Andrea's figures adhere to the idea of a consistent plastic substance, and their emotions are likewise consistent, expressive of ordinary states of being. The impassable barrier that now separated Andrea from Pontormo is indicative of the intellectual and emotional intensity with which Pontormo had pursued, since 1516, the problems presented by the dissolution of the classical style. Now, a decade later, in his mature works at S. Felicita, it became clear that Pontormo's point of view and that of his former master would never again coincide.

The period of S. Felicita, which includes the drawings for the *Deposi-*

tion (cat. 267–277; figs. 254–264) and *Annunciation* (cat. 278–279; figs. 266, 268) of the Capponi Chapel, the studies for the Uffizi *Madonna and Child with St. John* (cat. 280–282; figs. 270–272), the *St. Jerome in the Wilderness* (cat. 283–287; figs. 274–277), the *Portrait of a Halberdier* (cat. 288; fig. 279), and the Carmignano *Visitation* (cat. 289; fig. 281), is generally considered to be the fully mature phase of Pontormo's Mannerist style. It was a period of synthesis and harmonious resolution in which a residual classicism was once more brought into equilibrium with Mannerist invention. The nature of this equilibrium is partly a result of Pontormo's disjunctive view of reality in the Certosa period. The tensions that had been set up between elements of realism and abstraction were now resolved, but not in a synthesis like that of Poggio a Caiano. Rather, Pontormo made an adjustment or interpretation of realism and abstraction so subtle that each began to partake of the qualities of the other. Behind this adjustment lay the graphic experimentation of the preceding years: Pontormo's investigation of the mechanics of seeing, of optical effects that ostensibly belonged to the realm of reality, resulted in a reality so transformed as to be an abberation — the distorted but heightened realism of a vision. Pontormo's investigation of light, another property of the real world, produced a mystical *luminismo* that began in precise observation but ended in an abstract transfiguration of the real world. Thus, by 1526 and the drawings for S. Felicita, it is no longer feasible to speak of "realism" and "abstraction" as properties of Pontormo's style susceptible to independent definition.

The binding factor in this harmonious interpenetration of two worlds, without which it could not have been achieved, was a resurgence of the impulse to rhythmic ornamentalism of line and to the beauty of gleaming light-filled surfaces. Together these qualities account for the newly refined *grazia* that is a primary characteristic of Pontormo's mature style. In Pontormo's drawings of 1519–1520 this same quality was related to the High Renaissance; its reappearance in 1526–1528 (also after a phase of experimentation in isolated individuality) may be taken as evidence of Pontormo's reasserted concern with the achievements of the classical style. Both linear grace and tangible beauty of surface involved something of a concession to classical draughtsmanship and, by extension, to the classical style in general. Thus, at this time there was a positive readmission into Pontormo's drawings of influences from Michelangelo, Raphael, and Leonardo. Pontormo's yielding adjustment to them was the habit of mind that set his phase apart from the Certosa period, when the classical tradition had been abruptly rejected in favor of a style based entirely on eccentric novelty. The result of this new synthesis was a personal style of drawing, not made any less original by the revitalization of certain properties of the High Renaissance within it. Indeed, what we have termed an adjustment to the classical style was at the same time Pontormo's exploitation in the most general sense of his historical situation in relation to the High Renaissance: the very fact that he chose to relate his achievement so closely to that of the past only makes more pointed his essentially unclassical and Mannerist style. Thus, not even at this time do Pontormo's basic intentions have any connection with the total integer of the classical style to which Leonardo and Michelangelo — at opposite ends of the High Renaissance — aspired.

What has been said of the drawings from 1519–1520 applies equally to those of 1526–1528; but the stylistic plateau of the later period was loftier and more sustained. With even more consistency than in the earlier period, the drawings are in red chalk, Pontormo's preferred instrument of refinement; only now there is no sense of the problematic or self-consciously novel. Disruptive eccentric sensation recedes before a binding ornamental contour that maintains a harmonious ideality and unity — albeit an unclassical one — of form. Line is now a finespun red chalk filament slowly pulled out with a precise grace and without interruptive accent or undue stress. There is no trace of either the shorthand angularity that distorted shapes with sharp brilliance in the Poggio a Caiano drawings or of the laconic thinness of line that dematerialized them in the Certosa drawings. Forms are anormative by virtue of Pontormo's own experiments of the past decade, but these attenuated and warped shapes do not seem to be, as before, discovered at the moment of seeing. Rather, they exist as a priori rhythmic patterns that imperceptibly but with exact calculation absorb natural form. In these S. Felicita studies we witness the birth of the *disegno interno* in Pontormo's drawings and the shift in creative procedure that this concept implies.

Each of the figures in these drawings is reformed by a continuous, warping contour whose direction and shape are dictated by an abstract and abstracting rhythmic ideal. The *affilatura* of this line, the slow rhythm of the pulled-out contours that circumscribe the figures may, in fact, be the first reflection in Pontormo's art of the languorous grace of the Medici *Allegories*. This fluent, faintly tensed line emerges first in the study for the St. John of the *Deposition* (cat. 268; fig. 257), where it still has overtones of actual physical energy. It becomes more subtly refined in the later studies for the *Annunciation* (cat. 278–279, figs. 266, 268), where the illogical relation of the parts of the figure precludes any sensation of an energy other than the aesthetic vitality generated by the line itself. This is true even in a portrait drawing for the *Halberdier* (cat. 288; fig. 279), where Pontormo subjected natural form to the pressures of an abstract concept of elongated curving shapes. This total rhythmic organization of form was the binding principle of this period and the way it was made to work can be seen in detail in the series of studies for the *St. Jerome*. In the first study (cat. 283; fig. 274) the figure is mapped out in flowing sinuous contours whose upward moving rhythms deny any sense of physical weight. In the finished squared drawing (cat. 287; fig. 277) the process of distillation and refinement of shape has been carried out in accord with demands of an abstract pattern — the *figura serpentinata*, of which natural form finally becomes an indissoluble part. We also see the crystallization of a motive in a sheet for the *Deposition* with two studies of the same head (cat. 274; fig. 259), one so poignantly perceived from nature, the other delicately transformed in accord with the *disegno interno*. In the drawing for the head of Christ (cat. 276; fig. 264) line becomes so exquisitely refined and controlled as to suggest not rhythmic movement alone but the most unwordly of substances, ideal in its beauty. In studies such as these heads, the isolated fragment is more evocative than similar details in Pontormo's previous drawings essentially because of the newly expressive handling of line. Although relatively few of these detail studies survive, it is evident that each smallest portion of painted surface must have been prepared by similar drawings, each fragment of reality distilled in accord with the ideal of the *disegno interno*. Like the line itself, Pontormo's process of preparation in the years 1526–1528 became more calculated and perfectionist.

The other dominant quality in Pontormo's drawings of the S. Felicita period is their radiant chiaroscuro. Pontormo had experimented with effects of luminosity in the preceding period; but now, rather than illuminating forms of a specific reality, light enhances surfaces of a polished but immaterial beauty, making only faintly ambiguous their degree of substance. In the delineation of these effects Pontormo's media suddenly take on a new dimension of expressiveness: red chalk is handled with a more subtle perception of values, and pink-washed paper for the first time seems light-filled. The forms in all of the studies of this period are modelled by a transparent veil of chiaroscuro that is far from the covering *sfumato* of Pontormo's earlier drawings. This new richness of surface often suggests precedents in sculpture. The precisely modelled sculptural form of the Dead Christ study for the

Deposition (cat. 267; fig. 255) indicates that its relation to Michelangelo's early *Pietà* was more than one of motive alone, and the subtly differentiated reflected lights of the *St. Jerome* (cat. 287) give the figure an alabaster transluscence.

The only precedent for the chiaroscuro as well as for the sheer linear finesse of Pontormo's S. Felicita studies is provided by Raphael's and especially Leonardo's drawings, the delicacy of Pontormo's line and the refinement of his shading suggesting Leonardo's silverpoint head studies more than any intervening phenomenon. It hardly seems likely that Pontormo was not consciously recalling — without in any sense imitating — certain kinds of Renaissance drawings, especially since there is evidence in his paintings of the period of his renewed awareness of the achievement of these High Renaissance artists. Certainly nothing of this sort occurred in Pontormo's immediate milieu. Indeed, Pontormo had invented a mode of drawing unrelated in any specific sense to the graphic manner of his Florentine contemporaries, a kind of drawing that existed not quite in a vacuum, but in a rarefied atmosphere incapable of sustaining any but his dematerialized beings.

The quality of Pontormo's experience that is transmuted in these drawings is as rarefied and hypersensitive as their technique; but it is also as controlled and essentially harmonious. In the years 1526–1528 the introspective mood of the Certosa was never quite lost; emotional response was invariably veiled and distilled, with none of the sudden perceptions and excitable overreactions of Pontormo's earlier drawings. The two *St. Jerome* figures, separated by half a decade, belong to different worlds of feeling; the earlier (cat. 170; fig. 160) vibrating with physical and emotional response; the later (cat. 287) transfixed and immobile, withdrawn even though his forms curve out toward us. The range of emotion that we find in these drawings is at once narrowed and more subtle in its gradations, just as the already narrow value range of Pontormo's red chalk is broken down into the smallest modulations. Although maintaining a harmonious unity of feeling, the emotional states of the *Deposition* figures as seen in the preparatory drawings range from mute outcry (cat. 271; fig. 258), to yielding sympathy (cat. 268; fig. 257), to paralyzed inaction (cat. 269; fig. 256). Perhaps the exquisitely pained participation of Pontormo himself (cat. 277; fig. 263) and the searching communication of the youth looking out at us (cat. 275; fig. 262) convey most specifically the essence of Pontormo's spirituality in this period. These are the heads in the painting that relate most directly to the spectator, a function that is already specified in these red chalk studies. The youth becomes our entrance into the painting, a Mannerist device that is handled here by Pontormo with singular effect. He regards us with a dazed but knowing glance whose self-consciousness is a key to Pontormo's delicate manipulation of the emotional tenor of the scene. This figure is quite aware of the effect of his reaction; he is both artful actor and involved participant, commenting on his role without losing his effectiveness in it. The self-portrait head is our only possible exit from the *Deposition.* In giving his own likeness this key role as a link between the observer and the picture, Pontormo confounds the identity of artist and spectator, making both active participants in the action. Yet, unlike the earlier pointing self-portrait drawing (cat. 253; fig. 241), there is no desire to invade the spectator's consciousness by shock or attack, or to set up a disturbing ambivalence between our world and that of the *Deposition.* Pontormo has transformed his likeness into a head of curvilinear beauty suspended in a spaceless *ambiente*, hovering without commitment between the real and unreal, but also without upsetting the precarious harmony between them that is the central achievement of his mature style of drawing.

The synthesis of Pontormo's S. Felicita style maintained in careful balance certain elements that were to be isolated or accentuated in his drawings after 1530. Furthermore, their graphic refinement and ornamentalism was the basis not only of an aspect of Pontormo's own post-1530 style, but may even have anticipated to some extent Michelangelo's development in this direction in drawings like those for Cavalieri. These S. Felicita studies also contained the potential for radical formal ambiguities that were not exploited by Pontormo at this time because of his intention to harmony. We find here, for example, the inception of a characteristic of the *Maniera*: the contradiction between an overly precise surface and weightless, abstracted volumes. While Pontormo himself made little — even minimized — such contradictions, this duality was to form the basis of Bronzino's style. Thus, it is not surprising to find that these were precisely the years during which Bronzino was active as Pontormo's assistant and executant. Some of Bronzino's drawings of the late twenties, attributed wrongly to Pontormo (cat. A9, A66, A75, A125), begin to show exactly this direction of development, anticipating his own Mannerist formulation of the thirties.

About 1528, certainly by 1529, perceptible changes of emphasis appeared within Pontormo's S. Felicita drawing style. The very essence of the equilibrium of Pontormo's style at S. Felicita was a series of precarious adjustments between the classical and anticlassical, between reality and abstraction, each so delicately balanced that the slightest shift or displaced stress could destroy

Pontormo's tenuous harmony of form and feeling. Pontormo had actually evolved a style that was limited by its own premises, a style that was a plateau of accomplishment, but was also a dead end beyond which it was impossible to progress without a shift in intention and direction. If such shifts had not taken place, Pontormo's drawings would have become meaningless abstractions, caricatures of their S. Felicita prototypes, mannered as well as Mannerist. Linear refinement would lead to overrefinement; abstracting rhythms would crystallize into rigid patterns, the faintest hint of which would destroy the rarefied lightness of Pontormo's forms; the loss of subtle expressive content that comes with repetition would leave compositions of vacancy and lassitude. Such extreme consequences were almost immediately avoided by the renewed experimentation so characteristic of Pontormo's development, but for a brief moment toward 1530 there were evident fissures in the unity of Pontormo's S. Felicita style.

As early as 1528 there were signs of a crystallizing overrefinement. In the elaborately worked out red chalk final study for the Virgin of the S. Felicita *Annunciation* (cat. 278; fig. 268) there is a slight fussiness of detail and a concern with intricacy of shape for its own sake that detracts from the larger rhythms of the figure. The sudden stress in the convolutions of the drapery to the lower left and the complex movement of the feet anticipate the knotty involvements of form in the slightly later Pitti *Martyrdom* of 1529–1530. However, balance is regained in the fresco figure, whose serene eurhythmy of style is consonant with that of the *Deposition*. The Carmignano *Visitation*, also of about 1528, is well within the S. Felicita style, but there are signs of another aspect of Pontormo's incipient stylistic dissolution in the preparatory drawing, an instance in which the juxtaposition of drawing and painting illuminates the complexities of a moment in Pontormo's development. In comparison with the compositional study for the *Deposition* (cat. 272; fig. 254), there is a certain lassitude of line and a less energetic rhythmic unity in the black chalk drawing for the *Visitation* (cat. 289; fig. 281). The floating, interwoven forms of the painting are grounded, their movement halted rather than momentarily transfixed. Although the point at which incipient dissolution becomes actual is elusive, this drawing seems to anticipate such a development in the Louvre *Madonna and Saints* of the next year, a picture for which no drawings survive. In the Louvre altar binding rhythmic unity is no longer operative, line has become lax without losing its quality of precise calculation, and light undermines substance rather than maintaining the pale, phosphorescent consistency of the *Deposition*. There is also a certain psychological discontinuity in the picture, especially notable in the St. Benedict, who leads us into the painting. Pontormo placed him conventionally — almost anachronistically — to the side, abandoning the daring solution of the *Deposition*, in which this linking figure was also the pivot of the composition. St. Benedict's glance and gesture do not carry the same emotional charge as those of the *Deposition* youth because he is involved neither psychologically nor formally with the action. In her disturbed but uninvolving stare and in the flattened, comparatively meaningless shape of her silhouette, the attendant to the left of the *Visitation* drawing anticipates both the psychological and compositional roles of the St. Benedict. However, in the Carmignano painting, as contrasted with the Louvre altar, a series of subtle adjustments brings this figure into focus. Another aspect of the loosening of Pontormo's stylstic unity is found in the *Birthplate* of circa 1529 and the single drawing for it (cat. 290; fig. 283). The overrefinement and weightlessness of form in the Louvre altar are exaggerated here by the small scale treatment and adherence to the decorative requirements of furniture painting. Delicate sequences of rhythm create zig-zag patterns and the sharp illumination of a nervously flickering light cuts deep gashes of shadow into forms that seem bound together only by the circular shape of the plate, not by a cohesive rhythmic organization. The unexplained agitation of movement and complication of pose, especially the torsion of the woman and child, is also evident in the nervous intensity of the drawing for these figures. An eccentricity of form and feeling that is quite tangential to the requirements of such a tranquil scene makes this study reminiscent of Pontormo's earlier extemporizing in the Poggio a Caiano drawings, a habit of mind that was totally absent from the calculated creative process of distillation at S. Felicita. Furthermore, the drawing is executed in black chalk and with a rapid excitability in the hooked strokes and *pentimenti* that we have not seen in the decade since Poggio a Caiano.

The moment when the various changes in Pontormo's graphic manner ceased to be aspects of a threatened dissolution of style and began to shape a direction of renewed experimentation is difficult to pinpoint because of the rapid sequence — even simultaneity — of events and the paucity of the evidence: only one drawing for the Pitti *Martyrdom*, one for *Pygmalion and Galatea*, two for the lost *Portrait of Francesco Guardi*. Yet, we can isolate two positive novelties of style that emerged about 1530, both related to a new response to Michelangelo and both essential aspects of Pontormo's reformed drawing style of the thirties. The first was the reassertion of plastic, often eccentric form to the extent where it was incompatible with the rhythmic organization or the concept of *grazia* of S. Felicita. In drawings and paintings alike there is an ultrarefined precision of modelling and a more exact plasticity of detail than before. The second was an alteration in Pontormo's linear organization that involved both an extension of the rhythmic ideal of S. Felicita and a certain adjustment necessary to accommodate the new plastic irregularity of form. For the eurhythmic grace of 1526–1528 was substituted an unpredictable, often awkward rhythm that embodies the tensions of self-conscious experimentation, yet suggests a curious diminution of energy.

The drawing for the *Pygmalion and Galatea* (cat. 291; fig. 285) is evidence of Pontormo's new interest in plastic form; it is a specifically Michelangelesque nude study in which there is a concern with the heavy musculature of the back, with bulging and swelling forms that earlier would have been smoothed over by the demands of Pontormo's rhythmic organization. The figure in the painting, although clothed, has this same insistent plasticity, as does the precise and eccentric anatomy of the Galatea. Although the *Portrait of Francesco Guardi* is lost, it presumably resembled the *Pygmalion* in style, a manner of hardened precision that may be seen in a drawing probably for it (cat. 292; fig. 286). While in the preliminary sketch for the *Guardi* (cat. 293; fig. 287) the pose is set down in loose, rhythmic lines of somewhat aimless direction that suggest an unanchored weightless form, in this finished study rhythmic organization is suppressed in favor of a rigid alignment of forms of considerable plastic substance. There is a marked stylistic contrast with the drawing for the *Halberdier* (cat. 288; fig. 279), made only two years before at the apogee of the S. Felicita style. There Pontormo was concerned with the abstract quality of *grazia* that he could extract from and impose on his subject; he reformed the figure completely in accord with the characteristic curvilinear organization of the S. Felicita period, observing only the minimal requirements of adherence to physical actuality. However, in the *Guardi* drawing, forms are isolated from one another by a hardening line of much less conscious beauty, descriptively precise but of no yielding rhythm. That this is not a unique instance is seen in a self-portrait drawing (cat. 306; fig. 295) that is a telling signal of Pontormo's shift in style, especially when compared to the *Deposition* self-portrait study (cat. 277; fig. 263). In the later head a concern with reality is evident in the normal point of view, the exactness of unwarped physical description, and the sense of objective detachment. The graphic manner still has the lucid refinement of the *Deposition* head, but the forms are faintly chilled by a cooler precision of modelling and the plastic accents of the face are stressed by an increased pressure of the chalk, making contrasts that were absent from the narrow range of paleness of the S. Felicita study.

The Pitti *Martyrdom*, with its single drawing, is a pivotal work of about 1530 that seems to be a paradigm of stylistic dissolution, yet it also anticipates various elements in Pontormo's style of the thirties. The formal and psychological discontinuity of the picture is partially due to the reuse of a composition (cat. 195; fig. 185) of circa 1522 for the battle scene in the background, while newly invented figures have been inserted in the foreground. This willingness to recall an earlier invention as a unit in a new composition is in itself evidence of a shift in Pontormo's artistic point of view toward that of the thirties. Furthermore, the use of the *Martyrs* composition — an earlier moment of Michelangelism — is indicative of Pontormo's renewal of interest in Michelangelo at this time. However, the separate foreground group of the Pitti picture has quite a different stylistic accent, referring to Pontormo's study of the most recent of Michelangelo's works in sculpture: the *Allegories* and portrait statues of the Medici Chapel and the *Victory*. While there were specific references to the contemporary Michelangelo in the later twenties, such as that to the Medici *Madonna* in the Louvre altar and the *Birthplate*, this picture and its drawing are the first works that can be called Michelangelesque; the first overt demonstration of Pontormo's awareness of the contemporary Michelangelo and specifically of the aspects of his style that were novel about 1530. In addition to providing motives, Michelangelo's works suggested a principle of movement that became for Pontormo a metamorphosis of his own earlier concepts of rhythmic organization. The sculptures are dominated by the slow, swelling torsion and sinuous flow of multidirectional rhythmic impulses that do not depend on the inner constructive logic of the figure but on the will of the artist. This is not too dissimilar from what Pontormo himself had accomplished at S. Felicita (possibly stimulated in part by Michelangelo's example), but now these properties of style are more explicitly referable to Michelangelo because they shape forms that are explicitly Michelangelesque. However, these forms still bear Pontormo's personal stamp: whereas in Michelangelo's figures the rhythms are contained within a totality of plastic form and restrained by the actual substance of the stone, they become exaggerated when translated into Pontormo's more two-dimensional linear style. Line and form become endlessly pliable, subject to no logical controls, creating figures of a vague and directionless temper of movement that does not codify into a precise rhythmic pattern, yet is not energetic enough to be called restless. The black chalk drawing for the foreground figure in the *Martyrdom* (cat. 294; fig. 290) is on a sheet of Michelangelesque studies: one head is after the *Aurora*, another is suggestive of a personalized *Victory* head, while the nude itself is related in pose to the *Victory* but has a langour of movement that suggests a Medici Tomb *Allegory* turned vertically. This nude is a heavily muscled but flaccid figure of elongated proportions that seem even more attenuated than in Pontormo's earlier drawings because of the singular elasticity of the line and shape. Movement is slowly vertical in a pronounced serpentine path, more languidly dreamlike even than that of the S. Felicita figures, and the vague gesture of the raised arm announces a complete surrender of will.

The aspect of Michelangelo's style to which Pontormo was most sensitive in the drawings of the later twenties is more novel and less easily imitable than his heroic sculptural form in its totality. Pontormo's particular response to Michelangelo stems from his innate preference for a rhythmical organization of forms, his tendency to extract a rhythmic impulse from its total context (in this case sculptural) and to use it in a more abstract and essentially two-dimensional composition. This response to Michelangelo echoes Pontormo's transformation of classical rhythmic animation into a Mannerist's more irregular and unpredictable rhythmic vocabulary a decade earlier. However, although this basic creative process remains constant, the mechanics of response and transmutation into Pontormo's personal style became immeasurably more complex after 1530. In identifying with the contemporary Michelangelo, Pontormo exposed himself to an art that was itself grounded in the classical style in a most complicated way. Unlike the art of the High Renaissance — indeed, unlike Michelangelo's own earlier style — it was no longer normative, no longer to be equated with the classical idealized though essentially natural concept of form. The qualities of Michelangelo's style to which Pontormo responded — the elongated complexities of posture and movement, the arbitrary abstraction of certain forms, and the heightened perception of spiritual existence — were themselves a reflection in Michelangelo's art of the accomplishments of Mannerists like Pontormo, as well as an authority for future Mannerist development. Furthermore, in coming so close to Mannerism in their own style, Michelangelo's works of this period made him infinitely more accessible to a Mannerist personality such as Pontormo. The sculpture of the Medici Chapel, the *Victory*, the drawings for Cavalieri, the lost *Leda*, and the *Venus and Cupid* became the successors to Michelangelo's own earlier *Cascina* cartoon and Sistine Ceiling as the prototypes for Mannerist elaboration. Therefore, in his relation to the later Michelangelo as well as in his tendency to recall his own past works, Pontormo was, in the period initiated in 1530, further removed from the classical style than before, though not nearly so *anti*-classical in intention. Between his work after 1530 and any direct reference to the High Renaissance stood the formidable double barrier of Michelangelo's contemporary art (so complex in its own transformation of the classical style) and his own Mannerist achievement of the twenties. It is by virtue of developments such as this that we may isolate a second phase of Pontormo's Mannerism and of his draughtsmanship corresponding to a general stylistic phenomenon in Florence: the *Maniera.*

The year 1530 marked the beginning of a new phase in Pontormo's development. The caesura has been placed at this point with good reason, for it signifies a shift in artistic circumstances in Florence and the emergence of the style of the *Maniera* as well as changes in the personal evolution of Pontormo himself. In 1530 the siege of Florence was over, the exiled Medici were restored in the person of Duke Alessandro in 1532, and from this juncture the cultural life of Florence revolved increasingly around the ducal court. The four years of Alessandro's rule were marked by a revival of Medici commissions. Pontormo, along with the younger artists, was drawn into this narrowing circle of patronage and was awarded the important commissions for the decoration of the Medici villas at Poggio a Caiano in 1532 and Careggi in 1535. His position just after 1530 was that of foremost painter in the city, endorsed even by Michelangelo himself, who at this time sought out Pontormo as an executant for two of his cartoons. Pontormo's only competition, Andrea del Sarto, was dead; his future competitors, his former pupil Bronzino and the still younger Vasari and Salviati, had not yet reached their artistic maturity. The pattern thus established under Alessandro, Pontormo continued to function in the role of decorator, with Bronzino as his principal assistant, in Duke Cosimo's more elaborately organized program for the embellishment of Medici buildings. He took a major part in the decoration of the Villa Castello from 1537 to 1543 and about 1546 was awarded the most important Florentine church commission of the entire period: the frescoes of the choir of San Lorenzo.

While Pontormo was an important painter to Cosimo as far as domestic commissions were concerned, it is significant that he was not employed in secular projects of a more public and official nature, such as the extensive program of decoration in the Palazzo Vecchio. His one venture into such a work, the tapestry cartoons for the Sala de' Dugento done with Bronzino and Salviati in the forties, was reported by Vasari (V/M, VI, 284) to be a failure: ". . . non piacquero nè al duca nè a que' maestri che gli avevano a mettere in opera, parendo loro cosa strana . . ." It is evident that the component of personal eccentricity in Pontormo's style prevented him from adapting himself to the complex allegorical subjects and to the formalizations and conventions of style of those who did work at the Palazzo. His extremely slow working methods and his dislike of assistants were also quite at odds with the practice of a painter such as Vasari, who worked with a rapid facility and supervised a large *bottega*. This alleged deficiency was deplored by Pontormo's patrons (and reported by Vasari) on more than one occasion. In addition to his major work in fresco for the Medici, Pontormo painted a few devotional pictures that have not survived, but it is significant that there is no record of his having executed any large altarpieces of the type that abounded in the period of the *Maniera*. It was Bronzino's rather than Pontormo's example that was taken for this type of picture during the second half of the century. Of greater importance was Pontormo's role as a leading Medici portraitist in the thirties, when he painted Duke Alessandro, Duke Cosimo, and Cosimo's mother, Maria Salviati. However, in the forties, his eminence began to be seriously challenged as a portraitist as well as a decorator: the formal style of Bronzino accommodated itself more readily to the developed taste of the ducal court. Thus, for the last decade of his life, Pontormo was occupied solely with the San Lorenzo frescoes; but, shortly after his death, even these were to be regarded by Vasari as a relic of an eccentric and incomprehensible style, long outdated.

It would be difficult to formulate any clear idea of Pontormo's style in this period from the paintings that survive. Nor could we discover in them any hint of his importance as a decorator for the Medici, or of his vital role in the development of the *Maniera*, or of his final rejection of its ideals. The second set of Poggio a Caiano frescoes never progressed beyond the cartoon stage, while those at Careggi and Castello, along with the cycle at San Lorenzo, have been totally destroyed. Two of Pontormo's tapestries can be identified, but they provide a distorted record of Pontormo's compositions, surely Flemicized by the Northern weavers. Of the two *Madonna* pictures that Vasari says Pontormo painted, copies of only one survive. A fragmentary group of portraits remains from what must have been a much larger production. Thus, in this later period — the last twenty-five years — of Pontormo's activity, drawings assume an importance beyond their own intrinsic interest as evidence of the style of these destroyed or lost works in painting. However, the diminution in the number of paintings in this period is unfortunately all but equalled by the small number of surviving drawings: from the years 1530–1556, exclusive of a sizable group of studies for San Lorenzo, there are a mere forty-three drawings, of which only twenty-five can be associated with specific works: cat. 307–311 (figs. 296–300) for Poggio a Caiano, cat. 312–320 (figs. 301–307) for the Careggi loggia, cat. 336–344 (figs. 316–323) for the Castello loggia, and cat. 345–346 (figs. 329, 331) for the Giovanni della Casa and Maria Salviati portraits. This pattern of survival obviously precludes the year-to-year examination of Pontormo's evolution that was indicated for the earlier years. Furthermore, since this was a more homogeneous phase in which Pontormo was occupied with certain stylistic problems over a number of years, his later drawings may be profitably studied more as a unit than the earlier works.

While the gradual shift in style in Florence after 1530 was in part an internal development of Mannerism itself, it was also closely connected with the new circumstances of Medici patronage, with the demand for a more formalized and facile decorative style; a demand that had been made upon artists a decade earlier in Rome, only now tardily in Florence. This second phase of Mannerism, anticipated in some respects in Pontormo's own works from about 1529, became firmly established with the emergence to maturity of Bronzino, then, about 1540, of Vasari and Salviati. The style of the *Maniera* was unconnected — except by deliberate recollection — with the classical roots from which Pontormo's style had grown; rather it was an outgrowth of Pontormo's own earlier Mannerism. However, more than Pontormo's style of the twenties, it was strongly conditioned by Michelangelo, who had been intermittently in Florence in the twenties and until 1534 — the very years of the apprenticeship of the leading midcentury artists. This Michelangelizing crystallization and codification of the *primo manierismo* dominated the artistic environment of Florence during Pontormo's later maturity. It was nurtured by the taste of Duke Cosimo and, after 1539, of Duchess Eleonora, under whom it bacame a court art of marked decorative character.

Considering the private and eccentric nature of Pontormo's art, he eventually made an extraordinarily flexible adjustment in the midthirties to the requirements of the new era. This was due in major part to the coincidence of the inception of this period with a moment of personal crisis for Pontormo: the breaking up of the unity of the S. Felicita style and the intense study of Michelangelo. Instead of being responsible for the destruction of Pontormo's stylistic unity as has aften been asserted, it would seem, as we have already suggested, that Michelangelo is to be connected with the positive aspects of this phase, with Pontormo's newly experimental orientation about 1530. From the two years just after 1530 no important drawings have survived, but this must have been a crucial period of personal association with Michelangelo. Pontormo was chosen to execute two pictures from his cartoons, the *Noli me Tangere* in 1531, and the *Venus and Cupid* in 1532. Although the former did not seem to interest Pontormo at all, the *Venus* was to play a vital role in his drawings. Like the lost *Leda* of 1530, it is a mannerizing variant on the theme of the reclining nude that Michelangelo had explored in the Medici *Allegories*. At this time Pontormo must also have seen the drawings for Cavalieri, as his own drawings show that he was especially responsive to the *Tityus*, a reversed male version of the *Venus*. These personal contacts generated a phase of most intense Michelangelism, different in kind and degree of surrender to Michelangelo's style from Pontormo's subsequent adjustment and more directly imitative of Michelangelo than at any moment of his activity. In the period 1532–1534 Pontormo attempted to assimilate the essence of Michelangelo's forms, forcing a departure from his S. Felicita style that was more emphatic than in the works of the later twenties. We have already found hints of this development, not in drawings, but in the knotty involvement of muscular form in the Pitti *Martyrdom*.

Two studies of 1532–1534 are virtual copies of Michelangelo; one after the *Tityus* (cat. 308; fig. 299), the other after the *Venus* (cat. 329; fig. 315). In neither of these figures is there a trace of Pontormo's customary *grazia* or curvilinear organization of forms. On the authority of Michelangelo's mannerizing deformation of proportions, Pontormo has made forms stretch, swell, and shrink without regard even for the rarefied concept of beauty that formerly had shaped his *disegno interno*. With some modifications, this canon of proportions was to become standard for Pontormo's later drawings. Individual and eccentric shapes that no longer yield to a rhythmic curving organization are described in a manner that is imitative of Michelangelo's precisely modelled sculptural forms. Furthermore, these minutely characterized luminous surfaces are executed in a graphic technique that is, for the first time in Pontormo's career, directly imitative of Michelangelo. Individual strokes are no longer evident but are rubbed to a *sfumato* or broken into a stippled pattern suggesting a granular surface. Chiaroscuro does not follow the natural roundness of the forms but is forced to the edges into a band of shading that is then strengthened by an outline. The line is now thin and edgy, somewhat pinched, and has little independent energy. In this technique there is a radical departure from the linear beauty and vitality that had been an almost constant property of Pontormo's style.

Pontormo's wholesale imitation of Michelangelo's technique is additionally significant in connection with the simultaneous appearance of the finished drawing in the work of Michelangelo and Pontormo. While none of Pontormo's surviving drawings are with certainty "presentation drawings" like those for Cavalieri (however, we have no documentation for Pontormo's drawings comparable to that for Michelangelo's), he emulates the evenness and precision of finish of Michelangelo's drawings of this type. Even in preparatory studies that were not brought to completion this manner prevails, so that there is the effect of a finished drawing even when the drawing was not intended as such. In fact, Pontormo's drawings after 1530 are clearly and unmistakably set apart from his entire earlier *oeuvre* by this characteristic technique. In these drawings, as in Michelangelo's and those of many of his followers, there is an extreme selfconsciousness in the virtuoso display of technique and in the knowledge that a drawing, like a painting, can be an end in itself, intended for public appreciation. For Pontormo, this idea was a final step in one direction away from the older notion of drawings primarily as stages in a preparatory process, as a means toward an end. The final step in the other — diametrically opposed — direction he had long since taken in his extremely personal and anti-public Mannerist sketches dating from as early as 1517.

The *Tityus* drawing and another similar study of two nudes in red chalk (cat. 311; fig. 300) were preparatory studies for Pontormo's first commission from the Medici after 1530: the completion of the Poggio a Caiano *Salone* where Pontormo had painted the *Vertumnus and Pomona* a decade before. On one of the end walls was to be a fresco of *Nudes Playing Calcio*, for which a large compositional study survives (cat. 307; fig. 296). The fresco was projected as a multifigured pyrotechnical display of a recently acquired Michelangelism quite unlike either the vibrant actuality of Pontormo's earlier lunette or the disciplined refinement of his villa decorations later in the thirties. Individually, the figures resemble the *Tityus* study, each in his own manner overresponding to the stimulus of the game in a contorted pose of willful complexity. Collectively, their movement is that twisted involvement of not quite overlapping forms that was first suggested in Pontormo's work in the two foreground figures of the Pitti *Martyrdom*. We are reminded of another Michelangelesque project for Poggio a Caiano (cat. 131; fig. 123) that also marked a moment of ambitious response to Michelangelo's style. The earlier design was incongruously Michelangelesque and was ultimately discarded; like it, this project was not carried to completion. Pontormo did not execute this fascinating and eccentric conceit, this grotesque ballet for ball players; but it was probably because of his own awareness of the impossibility of this extreme surrender to Michelangelo as a solution to his stylistic dilemma, not — as Vasari would have us believe — because of his assistant Bronzino's absence in Pesaro.

The precisely finished red chalk drawing for a *Three Graces* (cat. 321; fig. 310) of the midthirties may be taken as representative of Pontormo's resolution of this stylistic dilemma. It is the epitome of the disciplined and decorative manner that Pontormo evolved in the Careggi and Castello decorations, evoking comparison with the most refined and sophisticated conceptions of any draughtsman of the period. Compared to a group of Michelangelesque figures such as the three players from the right of the *Calcio* drawing, these enigmatic females are a novel breed, designed in a new manner. The relation of spatial interval to precisely silhouetted eccentric form generates a vitality and sense of *respiro* that are reminiscent of the Poggio a Caiano lunette, although the forms themselves are quite different in shape from the normative physical beings of the earlier mythological scene. Surface intervals between the forms are made even more meaningful by the avoidance of overlapping planes; only the intertwined arms give an illusory sense of spatiality. This gentle separation of the forms, together with the reduction of bulging muscularity, makes the *Three Graces* a less assertively physical and plastic integer of form than the *Nudes Playing Calcio*. Instead of a knotty involvement of crowding forms, there is an elegant and precious rhythmic interrelation that creates a visual sensation analogous to — but not precisely descriptive of — the floating movements of the figures themselves.

Out of the crisis of his temporary surrender to Michelangelo Pontormo had evolved a new style of decorative refinement. Unlike his S. Felicita manner, it was capable of being sustained over a decade; even then, of being revitalized in the extraordinary coda of the San Lorenzo drawings. This turn of events was possible because the problems of the later period were not those with which Pontormo had struggled before 1530. The kind of precarious synthesis between conflicting classical and anticlassical tendencies, between reality and abstraction, that S. Felicita represented, was no longer an operative aim. In this later period, Pontormo's preoccupation with decorative, rhythmic organization was strongly reasserted; yet, at the same time, there is in these drawings a quite unabstract accent on plastic form, on precisely modelled surfaces. The resultant ambiguities were exploited more than previously: in these drawings there is neither a consistent sense of plastic substance nor a consistent reduction to pure abstraction. No drawing of Pontormo's is more arbitrarily organized according to a preconceived design than the *Three Graces*, but no drawing is at once more subtly characterized in the modulation of surfaces. This dualism, these shifts between an abstract and specific vocabulary of form that are never resolved, connects Pontormo intimately with the other artists of the Florentine *Maniera*. However, Pontormo's refinement of seeing, the understated vitality of his transcriptions, and their singularly emotive character effectively separate his drawings from those of his contemporaries. Bronzino's allegorical females of the forties are certainly related to the *Three Graces* in their proportions and in their patterns of posture. However, in Bronzino's less personal figures, Pontormo's mobile shapes and yielding rhythms become frozen forms of hardened substance; Pontormo's subtly play between abstract and real in both form and feeling is pushed from the realm of the enigmatic to that of enforced ambiguity.

The *Three Graces*, as characteristic of Pontormo's style of the late thirties to middle forties, is also notable for a different approach to the art of Michelangelo than we have found in either the *Nudes Playing Calcio* or in the Michelangelism of Pontormo's contemporaries. Some draughtsman of the *Maniera* habitually reduced Michelangelo's types and compositions to facile linear abstractions that made no pretense to an understanding of the meaning of Michelangelo's art. Others attempted to capture something of Michelangelo's *terribilità*, or at least his *Romanità*, in a virtuoso emulation of his heroic forms. After his extreme surrender to Michelangelo in the early thirties, Pontormo avoided either of these typical responses, and thus his drawings cannot be placed in quite the same category with those of any of his contemporaries. As previously in 1519–1520, his obsession with Michelangelo ultimately led him to be more fully himself, to realize more completely his own artistic individuality. By the time of the *Three Graces* Pontormo had evolved his own highly original and ingenious transmutation of Michelangelo's style in which there was a profound understanding of aspects of Michelangelo's art beyond the obvious, but at the same time a realization of the impossibility of competition. Vasari's remark (V/M, VI, 285) in connection with San Lorenzo on Pontormo's desire to surpass all artists "e forse, per quel che si disse, Michelangelo," may more accurately reflect Vasari's own ambitions than Pontormo's. The note of personal intimacy in Pontormo's later work (even, we surmise, that on a large scale), denies the impression that his intention was in any way competitive. Michelangelo's types and motives were completely transformed in a context of sophisticated ambiguity, the unequivocally decorative context of Pontormo's secular fresco schemes. His innate rhythmic organization dominated and subsumed whatever he had assimilated from Michelangelo, and we never sense his intention to emulate directly the essentially Roman monumentality of Michelangelo's forms. Indeed, the decorative figures of this period are utterly unmonumental, personal, and Florentine in style. Although their elegance and knowing awareness of their effect on us marks the *Three Graces* as belonging to a new era, they are — no less than the goddesses of the Poggio a Caiano lunette — singularly Pontormesque images, eminently suitable as decoration for a Florentine country villa.

In contrast to his earlier pattern of development, the refined manner of the *Three Graces* was quite uniform throughout Pontormo's entire *Maniera* phase. Most of the drawings of this period center around the two major commissions for the *logge* of the Medici villas of Careggi and Castello. Many of these are nude studies, similar in style to the *Three Graces*, for the female allegories of the lunettes and pendentives of the *logge*. They are drawn in a finished manner without *pentimenti* or other evidence of a spontaneously evolving idea. Even in the lightest sketch (cat. 341; fig. 319) the graphic assurance is such that the placement and rhythm of the lines seem instantaneously predetermined. Line is of utmost calculation, slow and continuous; modelling sometimes resembles the powdery surfaces of the *Calcio* drawings (cat. 314; fig. 305), but in other drawings (cat. 343; fig. 323) it becomes a silken *sfumato*. The studies for the flying *amoretti* of the vaults, notably those for Castello (cat. 336–337; figs. 316–317), are drawn with a similar delicate but calculated touch, the unimpeded linear flow giving an effect of suspension rather than flying that forecasts the floating images of San Lorenzo. The exception is a black chalk and pen sketch (cat. 319; fig. 301), freshly immediate in conception and sharply accented in line, that must have been the very first idea for the Careggi vault. Black and red chalk appear interchangeably in this group of drawings, often on the small, pink-washed sketchbook paper that Pontormo had not used since S. Felicita. The similarity in handling of both red and black chalk suggests a (possibly conscious) obliteration of the distinctions that Pontormo had formerly made between them. Rather than exploiting the disparate effects that each could produce, Pontormo reduced the possibility of such extremes by a disciplining limitation of his draughtsmanship to a consistent manner that was sustained in both media for over a decade.

Pontormo's style in general during this period shows a tendency to limit rather than to experiment. Instead of developing in the irregular, experimental pattern that characterized the earlier years, Pontormo narrowed down to a handful of key images that held for him particular emotive, formal, and ultimately decorative meanings. He rarely concerned himself in a drawing with more than a single figure; when he did, the two interlocked forms were treated as one. In the graphic preparation for the villa decorations of the thirties Pontormo returned to a problem that he had explored and solved years before in the Poggio a Caiano lunette drawings: that of the individual figure in isolation as a unit of fresco decoration. Now, of course, the quotient of reality that was essential to the decorative synthesis of Poggio a Caiano and that gave it its special poignance is no longer present; the singularly emotive impression of these drawings depends on more distilled and subtle sensations. Here, as earlier at Poggio a Caiano, Pontormo was concerned with the adjustment of shapes within the single figure, with the special quality of its silhouette, and only ultimately in the fresco itself with the relation of one figure to another through spatial interval. Thus, in these middle years, Pontormo's way of composing was quite opposite from the rhythmic continuum of S. Felicita and from its ultimate extension at San Lorenzo; just as his intention was not primarily spiritual expression but effective — and affective — decoration.

While Pontormo's key images in these years show the important role that Michelangelo continued to play in his later work, they also reveal the force of an artistic individuality that made unique each variant on a theme. Just as in earlier drawings of a less calculated and precious content, Pontormo's visual experience was always transmuted into a graphic language of utmost individuality; and the concentration on a few basic motives does not in the least diminish the sigular eccentricity of each drawing. Pontormo was always conscious of the overpowering vision of Michelangelo's prototypes, but his inventiveness was not essentially hampered by them. Never do we sense that the possibilities for variation were limited by Michelangelo, for the genesis of Pontormo's images was also rooted in a most complex way in his own past achievement. When studying a motive for the Careggi *Justice*, a figure that is clearly related to the Medici *Allegories* in its final form (cat. 316; fig. 306), Pontormo first drew from a rather differently posed model with a subtle refinement of observation that belies the notion that he had substituted Michelangelo's sculpture for his own direct experience (cat. 317; fig. 307). The intervention of a Michelangelo prototype appears in sketches below on the same sheet that are directly related to the Medici Tomb figures. A *Madonna and Child* drawing of the midthirties (cat. 333; fig. 312) must also reflect the intervention of a Michelangelo prototype, yet the motive of the sleeping child is linked unmistakably with a re-analysis of an earlier model study of a sleeping youth (cat. 239; fig. 233). Such is the complex layering of Michelangelo influence, self-criticism, and new invention that is typical of Pontormo's later drawings.

Although both had appeared in Pontormo's drawings before, the images that dominated now were the reclining figure and the *figura serpentinata* — the characteristic poses of the Florentine *Maniera.* After 1530 both motives began to take on a new meaning and specific identity in Pontormo's drawings because of their close relation to Michelangelo; the former to the *Venus-Tityus*, the *Leda*, and the Medici *Allegories*; the latter to the *Victory* and the Medici *Madonna.* It is significant that neither of the key images in Pontormo's formulation of a *Maniera* decorative style was expressive of overt energy; both these passive poses epitomize the surrender of the will of the figure to that of the artist. The langorous reclining pose requires no muscular control (except with tensional results in the *Venus-Tityus* variant), and the forms can be manipulated at will; while the vertical serpentine figure, whose pose should give evidence of inner control but does not, makes its effect through this violation of plausibility. Both of these types of figure were made to respond without organic logic or internal energy to Pontormo's decorative arrangements as he twisted their malleable anatomies into flattened arabesques, pulling out one side of the body into a long, elastic line, contracting the other into a sequence of smaller rhythms. The forms are lax more than before, without the muscular tensions that give evidence of a consistent organic existence. Likewise, the line that describes them is less tensed than before, not as vibrant and immediate a transcription of Pontormo's visual experience.

The reclining *Venus-Tityus* motive was a persistent image in Pontormo's later drawings, paralleling its continued appearance in Michelangelo's own late work. It is a precarious image typical of the *Maniera*, its appeal seemingly based on the uneasy combination of a languid, reclining posture and the tension of the opposing rhythms necessary to sustain it. In Pontormo's first variations of this motive in 1532–1534 (cat. 308, 329; figs. 299, 315), the complications of this tensely unnatural pose were exploited even more than in Michelangelo's design: the silhouette was made more irregular, the limbs displayed in a more explosive pattern, and the proportions more distorted. In the later thirties, Pontormo handled the motive with a less aggressive plasticity and a more suavely rhythmic coherence. The *Venus and Cupid* became a bizarre *Madonna and Child* (cat. 325; fig. 311), the larger figure containing the smaller in a disciplined integer of form whose silhouette is without the wide jumps and intervals of the earlier versions. The *Venus and Cupid* appears once again in a very faint sketch (cat. 383) of the San Lorenzo period, a dreamlike reminiscence of the motive that has only a tenuous relation to Michelangelo in its vaguely undulating shapes and rhythmically imprecise line.

The lunette fields of the Castello loggia must naturally have suggested the use of reclining figures there, but Pontormo used this motive for the astrological groups of the vaulting as well. Two studies for the lunette nudes (cat. 343–344; figs. 323, 321) have the extremely refined linear design and subtle modelling as well as sophistication of content that we have noted in the *Three Graces*. Like the *Graces*, these weightless arabesques of ambiguous sex undulate in and out of space by virtue of the calculated linear manipulation of their limbs, achieving thereby a kind of tenuous harmony. Unreal in form, yet of a disturbing aliveness and regarding us with intimately provoking appraisal, these inscrutable nudes make a total effect that is one of Pontormo's most personal inventions; an impression made still more singular by our awareness of the eventual link with the Medici *Allegories*. For the astrological subjects of the vaulting — the gods and their associated zodiacal signs — Pontormo invented a visual image in which the two forms were treated as a single unit based on the reclining figure. The *Mercury with the Sign of Gemini* (cat. 342; fig. 320) recalls the *Venus and Cupid* and is also related to Pontormo's own late *Venus and Cupid* (cat. 383). In the *Mars with the Sign of Leo* (cat. 341; fig. 319), and especially in the *Saturn with the Sign of Capricorn* (cat. 336, 340; figs. 316, 318), there is a recollection of the *Leda*, the most stylistically accessible prototype for the complex, rhythmic interweaving of human and animal forms that was Pontormo's as well as Michelangelo's intention.

In contrast to Castello, Pontormo's decoration of the Careggi loggia was built around isolated serpentine figures in pendentives, the obvious solution for an artist predisposed to a motive that perfectly fills the inverted triangle space available. Several of the surviving drawings give a clear impression of a decorative scheme that was based on the Farnesina Loggia di Psiche in some aspects, notably in the monumental half-draped figures and foliate borders of the pendentives (cat. 312; fig. 302), and in the *amoretti* holding animals flying above (cat. 319; fig. 301). However, in contrast to the Roman High Renaissance decoration, it is typical of Pontormo's *Maniera* scheme that only single more decoratively displayed figures were used in each pendentive and that there was no intention of creating an illusion that the *Allegories* inhabited an actual space behind the foliate framework. The drawings for these figures show Pontormo's transformation of Michelangelo's sculptural prototypes into ornamental serpentine figures. The *Justice* (cat. 316; fig. 306) is clearly related to the Medici *Allegories* in her monumental proportions and facial type, as well as in her pose — an arbitrary turning of Michelangelo's horizontal figure into a vertical position. Yet, in a drawing for the *Prudence* (cat. 314; fig. 305), any awareness of a sculptural prototype recedes before its transmutation into a serpentine form of patterned elegance that could hardly be called Michelangelesque. Plastic forms are flattened by a continuous contour that tends to pinch and squeeze the flesh into a predetermined sequence of oval shapes balanced around the wavering curve of the vertical axis. Both the pattern of the shapes and the untenable pose itself effect an extremely precarious balance. These serpentine figures are additionally unsettling as visual images because of the inherent three-dimensionality of the serpentine idea, a basically sculptural concept of form that required several views to take in the changing aspects of the twisting figure; or at least the possibility of such spatial involvement had to be suggested by a consistently plastic and organic form in a painting or a drawing. However, in Pontormo's *figura serpentinata*, as in that of his *Maniera* contemporaries, the contradiction between the expected spatial movement and its actual suppression creates a kind of formal tension and ambiguity that is characteristic of this second phase of his Mannerism.

The serpentine figure was the basis for a new development in Pontormo's drawings after 1545: the reassertion of interest in a complex, eurhythmic composition in which the *figura serpentinata* played a key role. While the cycle of drawings for San Lorenzo was the major achievement of Pontormo's last decade of activity as a draughtsman, there are several works in drawing and painting that are a prelude to Pontormo's latest style, even though they have none of the transcendent spirituality of the San Lorenzo drawings. The tapestry cartoons forecast the compositional schemes of San Lorenzo: serpentine figures are hung like the decorative garlands of the tapestry borders along a curving vertical axis set within an abruptly narrowed format. The *figura serpentinata*, often derived from an earlier invention, provides the exclusive basis for these compositions by its repetition and variation in terms of ornamental curve and countercurve. The three surviving drawings for the decorations are all for the *Benjamin at the Court of the Pharoah*. These show a change in Pontormo's graphic style from the subtle restraint of the Castello drawings to a more strenuous, tensed manner reminiscent of the Michelangelesque mode of the early thirties. The heavy, curving musculature of the drawing for Benjamin's leg (cat. 349; fig. 335) recalls the eccentric muscularity of the fallen *calcio* player (cat. 308; fig. 299), while the two back studies (cat. 347–348; figs. 333–334) are like the accentuated anatomies of the *Nudes Playing Calcio* or the Pitti *Martyrdom.* However, the patterning of the muscles and the simultaneous flattening and twisting of the forms is far more arbitrary and extreme than in the earlier nudes. Although they are separable in their greater fluidity from Bronzino's and Salviati's designs, the tapestries and their studies are Pontormo's most extreme surrender to the decorative style of Cosimo's court, his closest approach to a patently formalistic art. There are no other drawings from these years, but a certain concession to Bronzino's style and a renewed Michelangelism are also found in two paintings related to the tapestries and to their preparatory drawings. The Uffizi *Isaac Blessing Jacob* is monumentalizing in a Michelangelesque sense, using a River God motive, but its particular swelling giantism of form and full-featured faces bring it closer to Bronzino than Pontormo usually came. The insistent plasticity of the *Madonna and Child* is surely exaggerated in the copies that record this lost work, but there is also a close connection with the tapestries and even with Bronzino in the serpentine forms, with their simultaneous affectation and monumentality.

Pontormo's activity as a portraitist was another important aspect of his style between 1530 and 1545. Several drawings have survived that supplement our conception of Pontormo as a portrait painter, reveal stylistic changes from his earlier period that strikingly parallel and confirm those we have already noted, and help to clarify the relation of Pontormo and Bronzino as portraitists. To the period of the work at Poggio a Caiano belongs the last of the series of self-portrait drawings, this one a revealing document of that moment of crisis (cat. 331; fig. 325). The calculated pose of the three-quarter length seated figure is that usual for the commissioned portrait, only Pontormo's artisan's clothing revealing his position. In contrast to his earlier self-images, where he had cast himself in a spectator's role in a painting (cat. 277; fig. 263) or studied himself in a pose hardly intended for the public eye (cat. 253; fig. 241), Pontormo portrayed himself here in the early thirties in the role of the Artist, newly conscious of his position. His pose is rigid and his gaze self-consciously averted; he takes a newly objective view of himself rather than, as before, involving us so intimately in the stresses of his existence. We can trace the graphic style of this drawing back to the *Francesco Guardi* study (cat. 292; fig. 286) of a few years earlier, but its extremely even and meticulous finish is a new factor that surely indicates the influence of Michelangelo's finished manner, here utilized in a portrait study. Also new is a vitality and tension in the image that belongs to the phase of the early thirties. The unenergetic silhouette of the *Guardi* is now complex and movemented, but it is an activity that is simultaneously frozen. In this taut rigidity of the shapes and in the incisiveness of detail, there is a parallel to the *Nudes Playing Calcio* drawings, especially such a study as the fallen player (cat. 308; fig. 299).

Pontormo's self-portrait drawing was immensely influential among his immediate circle and may actually have been the first example of a mode of portrait representation that was shortly to become a *Maniera* formula, especially for Bronzino. Bronzino's Uffizi *Man with the Lute* is certainly derived from this image, while the stressed verticality, restless but contrained shapes, and expressions of thinly veiled distress of the Martelli and Panciatichi portraits surely owe something to Pontormo's invention. We do not know whether Pontormo himself developed this conception in the same direction; however, it would appear that he did not because his next portrait shows a shift in style. Although there are no studies for the *Alessandro de' Medici* of 1534–1535, a red chalk portrait study of a boy (cat. 324; fig. 324) of about the same date reflects the change seen in the Alessandro painting toward the less tensional and erratic concept of form that we have noted elsewhere as characteristic of the midthirties. In portraiture this change is manifested in a greater literalness of representation, a stable pyramid composition that is not broken by nervous irregularities but emphasized by straight-hanging drapery, a pose that is rigid but not tense, and a nonaggressive gaze. This altered concept of form is expressed through a graphic manner of lessened sharpness and vitality, of a greater blandness of touch. Bronzino's careful study for the *Man with the Lute* (cat. A9) betrays knowledge of this quieter mode, which was more suited to his own graphic temperament, as does an anonymous copy (cat. A1) after a lost Pontormo study for the Alessandro portrait. Among Pontormo's other portrait drawings of the midthirties, a striking parallel to the refined graphic style of the Careggi and Castello drawings is found in two portrait studies that may be connected with Pontormo's lost portraits of Duke Cosimo and of Maria Salviati from about 1537. The unusual profile view of Cosimo (cat. 334; fig. 326) specifically recalls Pontormo's draughtsmanship at Careggi in the spare modelling and the continuous accentuated contour that pinches and flattens the form onto a single plane. In this instance, the rigid immobility of line in the profile is directly expressive of the unyielding character of the subject himself and the summary treatment of the rest of the head only serves to accentuate the almost hyper-reality of the features. The bust-length portrait of Maria (cat. 335; fig. 327) is drawn without these cruel accents in a delicate and meticulously dry line and pale precision of modelling that recalls the Castello drawings. Even more than in the earlier portrait drawing of a boy (cat. 324) her silhouette is smooth and regular, the shoulders sloping unnaturally to accentuate further the verticality of the image.

In these drawings of the thirties the personality of Pontormo's sitters became denatured and uncommunicative. In the portrait drawing of Maria especially, the personality began to be enclosed by and to recede behind the forms that contain it, and the forms themselves refer more than before to a specific abstract ideal of eccentric beauty. However, in the slightly later drawings of the early forties for the *Portrait of Maria Salviati* and the *Portrait of Giovanni della Casa* (cat. 345–346; figs. 329, 331), the images have an intimate aliveness that is intensified by the vitality and subtle nuances of Pontormo's red chalk style. While we must base our conclusions on two drawings only, the style of these latest portrait studies indicates a sharp break with Bronzino that parallels to some extent Pontormo's change in this direction in the San Lorenzo drawings. While Bronzino continued to exploit the dichotomy between the rigidity of the image and the specific detail that it contains, and to concentrate on the public personalities of his sitters, Pontormo increasingly emphasized the hallucinatory unreality of portraits that are at the same time informed with a high degree of spiritual aliveness. Unlike the portrait drawings of the period before 1540, the studies for the *Maria Salviati* and the *Giovanni della Casa* are evidently preparatory sketches, experimental in pose and not brought to any degree of independent finish. In both drawings the statuary quality of solid substance and the hardened, ornamentalizing line of the preceding works is diminished; form is created entirely by a soft, unaccented line and a *sfumato* of rubbed red chalk. The dematerialization and ghostly apparitional effect is stressed by the cutting-off of these standing figures in such a way that their spatial situation is made uncertain, and by the elliptical shapes into which the forms are drawn. These slender, slope-shouldered figures are too slight for heads that stare out at us with poignant immediacy, each an intimate record of the spirit rather than the social or clerical façade of the sitter. While this humanity is not entirely preserved in the paintings, the sense of hallucination does persist: these typical late Pontormo images, like those of the San Lorenzo compositions, emerge from an indefinite distance to float toward us — essentially ungraspable.

Shortly after these portraits were painted, and in the same years that he was working on the tapestry cartoons for Duke Cosimo, Pontormo was awarded the commission to fresco the choir of the Medici church of San Lorenzo. It is not known who determined the program of the decoration, but it was a complex one that suggests a smaller scaled emulation of the Sistine Chapel. A cycle of seven scenes from the Old Testament and one from the New Testament was projected for the high fields that are separated by narrow windows in the upper zone of Brunelleschi's choir. The darker and larger square fields of the lower zone were to be filled with the great cosmic events of catastrophe: the *Deluge* and the *Resurrection of the Dead*, with a *Martyrdom of St. Lawrence* on the lower rear wall. Over the altar in the upper zone the beginning and the end were symbolically linked in the *Christ in Glory with the Creation of Eve*. These frescoes, a solitary and prolonged endeavor that recalls Michelangelo's struggles with the Sistine Ceiling, occupied Pontormo from about 1546 until his death ten years later. However, unlike the young Michelangelo's labor, which brought into being and then transcended a High Renaissance synthesis, Pontormo's work was the final effort of old age to make a monumental statement out of the antithetic elements of a personal Mannerist style. The result, as we understand it from the drawings, was a typical late work, isolated and singular both in the absolute sense and within its particular historical context.

Since the San Lorenzo frescoes were destroyed in the eighteenth century, Pontormo's late style becomes, for us, entirely a late drawing style. A remarkably complete series of thirty-two preparatory studies has survived, making possible a reconstruction of the placement of the various scenes in the choir as well as a detailed analysis of Pontormo's late style of drawing. Even the sheets themselves suggest the complete isolation of this phase of Pontormo's development. All but two of the drawings are, contrary to Pontormo's frequent practice, on sheets that he had not previously used. Also unusual in this phase is the consistency with which Pontormo used black chalk. In this choice there is a certain analogy to the latest drawings of Leonardo and Michelangelo. Pontormo's state of mind was, like theirs, more attuned to the abstracting effects that black chalk, but not the more vibrant red chalk, could produce. Finally, the high proportion of surviving compositional studies, many squared for transfer, also sets these drawings apart. Left in Pontormo's house on his death, these drawings must soon have passed as a group to a collector, thence to the Medici collections, and finally to the Uffizi, where all but four are found today. In these drawings there is a clear stylistic division into two groups that correspond to the preparation for the upper and lower ranges of frescoes. The earlier studies (cat. 350–372; figs. 338–356) are for the upper range and were probably completed by about 1551, certainly by 1554 when we know from Pontormo's diary that he was working on the lower range, which was left uncompleted at his death.

The changes in Pontormo's vocabulary of form and graphic language from the drawings of 1535–1545 to those for the upper range of San Lorenzo frescoes are quite subtle. Between the Castello studies, with their refined *sfumato* and delicate linear effects, and the upper-zone drawings had intervened Pontormo's presumed reexposure to the art of Michelangelo, which was partly responsible for the newly exaggerated patterning of forms and musculature in the tapestry drawings. This same graphic style is found in some of the individual studies for the upper frescoes, such as that for the Moses (cat. 356; fig. 352), but in general it is the less accentuated surfaces and slacker line of the Castello drawings that predominate in these black chalk studies. The tendency to accentuate the nonorganic aspects of the figure, to stress the flaccidity of the flesh, to dominate the physical form by the slowly pulled-out line, persists in studies such as the one for the Eve of the *Expulsion* (cat. 358; fig. 346). However, there is a new spirituality of content in these drawings that makes them novel and imparts to them a monumentality not found, or intended, in the studies for the decorations of the thirties and forties. In contrast to the purely aesthetic, even sensual, meaning of the Castello nudes, the same graphic qualities connote — with no lessening of their ornamental character — the helplessness of the physical and spiritual situation of the fleeing Eve.

The drawings for the upper range of frescoes record the compositions of all but two of the scenes. These compositions represent a departure from the mode of figural decoration that had prevailed at Careggi and Castello, a change that had already been suggested in the complex tapestry compositions. Like the contemporary tapestries, the first San Lorenzo designs utilized the serpentine motives of the thirties and forties in newly rhythmic combinations that are indicative of Pontormo's reassertion of interest in a mode of composition that he had for some time abandoned. However, unlike the tapestries, where there was a certain surrender of individuality to the cause of a decorative manner held in common with Bronzino and Salviati, the element of personal individuality in Pontormo's style was reasserted in the San Lorenzo conceptions. Pontormo now infused both the serpentine and the reclining motives of his secular villa decorations with new and personally expressive meanings. Like the eurhythmy and precarious harmony of his compositions, the rehabitation of his forms with spiritual significance recalls the style of S. Felicita — adjusted to his artistic achievement of the intervening twenty years. Thus, the texture of Pontormo's graphic style in this period of summation — its interweaving of self-recollection, continual awareness of Michelangelo, and novelty — is yet more complex than before, especially since each familiar motive is now so unexpectedly and singularly charged with meaning.

Several of the compositions of the upper range are very closely related to the tapestry cartoons in their elongated oval shapes and their serpentine forms, which balance one against the other in an upward rhythmic movement. The *Cain and Abel* (cat. 350; fig. 338) is a reworking of motives from the lower figures of both tapestry designs, and the curved forms of the *Labor of Adam and Eve* (cat. 370; fig. 356) are placed in alternating directions so that they both oppose and interlock like the forms in the *Lamentation of Jacob.* The Eve of this composition is also reminiscent of the semiseated serpentine females of the Careggi pendentives. The interweaving of the *Four Evangelists* (cat. 364; fig. 350) is even more complex than that of the tapestries: the tightly woven cone of floating form that precariously balances on the putto's foot recalls the compositional scheme of S. Felicita. The vertical upward spiraling of figures is carried to an extreme in the *Sacrifice of Isaac* (cat. 366; fig. 351), where the Isaac and the angel are linked by the serpentine figure of Abraham, the arrangement of the three forms recalling the gyrating sculptural groups of the *Maniera.* In contrast, the composition of the *Moses Receiving the Tables of the Law* (cat. 354; fig. 339) does not depend on interlocking rhythms but on the tension generated by the opposition of two groups, the Moses below and the God Father with angels above. Both are recollections of the earlier Michelangelo: the Moses turning with the large book of the Law recalls the Libyan Sibyl; and the God Father with the putti refers to the archtypes of the Sistine Ceiling. The last of the narrow compositions, the *Expulsion* (cat. 357; fig. 342), is quite without precedent in Pontormo's *oeuvre*, the faintly awkward temper of movement in the two figures and the singular paralleling of the limbs giving it an inexplicably Bronzinesque character.

The most complex of the compositions is the *Christ in Glory with the Creation of Eve* (cat. 359; fig. 345), the wider scene in the center of the end wall that holds the key to the synthetic meaning of the cycle as well. Its roots in Pontormo's past and in the art of Michelangelo are as complex and involved as the drawing itself. The composition is a reevocation of the interlace of forms of the S. Felicita *Deposition.* However, in view of the historical situation of Pontormo's late style, there is in the rhythmic organization and vocabulary of forms of the *Christ in Glory* a more direct connection with the norms of the *Maniera*. Where the *Deposition* depended on a tenuous harmony between reality and abstraction, delicately and movingly joined, the *Christ in Glory* makes its formal and emotive appeal purely in terms of the rhythmic patterns of the *Maniera*. As in the *Deposition*, the slow-tempered movement is generated below and winds upward in a curvilinear design that subsumes the separate identity of the forms. Even more than in the *Deposition*, this movement has no final destination or resolution but compells the eye to retrace its path or to move in contracting curves into the knotted details of the image. However, where the S. Felicita composition was rotary in movement, as a whole and in its parts, the spatial implications of the rhythmic movement are drastically reduced at San Lorenzo. This is a change that reflects Pontormo's absorption at this point in a *Maniera* style, and it is achieved by loosening the density of the composition so that surface intervals emerge and the serpentine central figure of Christ is isolated, floating almost free from the others. This rhythmic pattern is not only flatter but more regular than before, relating only to the *disegno interno*, not to natural movement. The rising rhythms originate in the symmetrically crossed figures of Adam and Eve to become the interlaced forms of the angel-*mandorla*, a regular oval shape that is heraldic in its flattened symmetry. The hypnotic, almost Byzantine appeal of the Christ, whose direct stare fixes the spectator, adds to the stylized effect of the composition. However, in spite of this emphasis, the image is far from rigid. Each figure is restlessly movemented and of a vibrant luminosity of surface and a soft pliable construction that suggests a whole gamut of subtle shifts. The image is only temporarily in focus, its peculiar fascination stemming from mobile shapes that disturbingly suggest change, while the abstract precision of the pattern that controls them denies any such possibility. The simultaneous fixity and fluidity of the composition is made more ambivalent by a most subjectively projected spatial image, an essentially spaceless composition that nevertheless has a subtle warping in its construction. Pontormo has projected an aspect of a private world of rarefied sensation, the nuances of which are recreated by the spectator as he perceives it. Something of this effect had been achieved in the *Three Graces* (cat. 321; fig. 310), where a sense of curving and fluid space emerged from the subtle manipulation of line and overlapping forms. Here there is the suggestion that Christ is suspended in the center of a spherical space, yet there are frequent counterassertions that the image is two-dimensional, the space nonexistent. The angel-*mandorla* is tipped forward at the top, back at the bottom, yet an apparently flat Christ touches both ends. The Creation group is arranged so that it does not overlap the Christ, thus it tends to recede when we focus on the central figure; however, from another point of view, it is joined to the Christ by the continuous rhythmic pattern of the contours. The precise nature of form and space are compromised still further by the subtle manipulation of light and atmosphere. The supernatural luminosity does not shine through rarefied air as at S. Felicita, but flickers dimly through an opaque mist that seems to be heavier than air because the forms are suspended in it. Both figures and atmosphere approach a common light-filled texture suggesting a mirage that has just taken shape.

The complex interaction in Pontormo's late style of his own earlier ideas and certain motives from Michelangelo is seen especially in the Christ and in the Adam of the *Christ in Glory*, figures that are based respectively on the serpentine and reclining prototypes of the thirties and forties. In the Christ Pontormo carried to an extreme the flattening of an originally sculptural image until all weight-support relations and spatial implications are denied. In this instance the figure is specifically related also to a Michelangelo precedent: the *Pietà* for Vittoria Colonna, which Pontormo could have seen in Rome or known by way of copies. Pontormo's entire scheme for the *Christ in Glory* has the same approximate symmetry and lateral display of forms as the *Pietà* and is a further instance of his reasserted interest in Michelangelo in the late forties. The Christ is similar to Michelangelo's in the finished graphic manner and even in the proportions, although Pontormo's innate rhythmic predilection imparts a wavering lightness to Michelangelo's more solid forms. The relation of Pontormo's composition to Michelangelo's *Pietà* also underscores the double role of Pontormo's Christ as the Christ of the Passion as well as the *Last Judgment*, a meaning that is emphasized in the drawing by the angels carrying the instruments of the Passion.

Not only did Pontormo look to recent works of Michelangelo but he recalled several Sistine Ceiling motives at San Lorenzo, giving the strong impression that he may have seen the ceiling itself again. The sleeping figure of Adam is a reinterpretation of the Adam from Pontormo's *Creation of Eve* drawing (cat. 104; fig. 114), a work that marked his first response to the Sistine Ceiling. While the Adam of the earlier drawing has the angular vitality of form, the sharp and brilliant handling of red chalk typical of Pontormo's drawings of about 1520, the later figure, whose evolution we can trace through three additional studies (cat. 361–363; figs. 343–344), reflects Pontormo's increased comprehension of Michelangelo's art. In the undulating arabesques of limp form Pontormo achieved something of the sense of passive power that inhabits Michelangelo's sleeping Adam; only it is a power tempered by the rhythmic grace of Pontormo's *disegno interno*. The crossed motive of Adam and Eve is also a characteristic Pontormo invention. Even more than in Michelangelo's composition, the crossing involvement of these two forms accentuates the contrast between the inert Adam and the rising energy of the Eve; it is a formal device that enhances rather than diminishes the meaning of the subject.

While the drawings for the upper range of frescoes owe their monumentality and spiritual intensity to Pontormo's manipulation of an already well-developed graphic style and vocabulary of form, an emphatic shift of direction occurred in the drawings for the lower frescoes. Pontormo carried certain properties of his *Maniera* style to an exaggerated conclusion and eliminated others completely. In general, the figures of the upper range are consistently ornamentalizing in their construction and they maintain their identity as arbitrary — if not organic — forms. However, even in the upper-zone drawings, the forms of the *Maniera* were infused with new meanings that placed stresses on their rhythmic organization, at times compromising their beauty and *grazia*. This conflict is evident in the Moses study (cat. 356; fig. 352), where the figure is deformed even by Pontormo's elastic standards, awkward in its nonrhythmic organization, anticipating the figures of the *Deluge* with their shrunken heads and withered limbs. In the drawings for the *Resurrection of the Dead* we find, not yet the very latest development in Pontormo's drawings, but a final extension of certain premises of the *Maniera*. Compared with its direct ancestors, the Castello nudes, a languid reclining figure probably for the *Resurrection of the Dead* (cat. 381; fig. 364) is the ultimate in substanceless form, a soul from the judgment scene that has barely assumed human guise. The body is of a morbid softness, its malleable substance held together by a line of rhythmic lassitude unparalleled in earlier drawings. Unlike the Castello nudes with their insinuating glances, this figure is uncommunicative, staring through us at the scene of the *Deluge* on the opposite wall of the choir. Two studies for the *Resurrection of the Dead*, a small *concetto* (cat. 377; fig. 363) that is loose in style, and the more precisely ordered study of a knot of forms (cat. 378; fig. 361), reveal the same tendency toward a reduction of formal tensions, a laxity of line, and will-less surrender of amorphous shapes to an unpredictable sequence of ideas. How these various knots of form were related in the painting can only be deduced from the scant evidence of a copy after a portion of the fresco (cat. A216; fig. 371), in which aspects of the arrangement are similar to Michelangelo's *Last Judgment*. Gigantic but powerless forms are suspended, many floating upward, dependent on a dynamic force outside themselves. However, it is impossible to tell whether Pontormo's scene in its entirety reflected Michelangelo's great rotary scheme.

In the drawings for the *Resurrection of the Dead*, and to a much greater extent those for the *Deluge*, Pontormo's graphic style underwent a final metamorphosis brought on by the pressures of an increasingly private and eccentric point of view. The subjects of the frescoes of the lower range must have suggested to Pontormo an expressionistic interpretation that could not be achieved within the present formulation of his style, a new departure that was influenced by Michelangelo's *Last Judgment* and paralleled by his even later works. Thus, about 1551, Pontormo entered a final period of eccentric analysis, more radically anticlassical than before, a phase in which he discarded the ornamental precision of form and content that had been in varying degrees important during his entire maturity and even persisted in the drawings for the upper range of frescoes. Although we know that Pontormo painted simultaneously on both the *Deluge* and the *Resurrection of the Dead*, the drawings for the *Deluge* (cat. 373–375; figs. 357–359) must be representative of a final stage of his graphic development. In these studies Pontormo operated quite outside the realm of the *Maniera* — both in the literal and historical sense — in a visionary distance of most private invention and meaning. Now it is no longer possible to discuss a specific graphic mode or a stylistic language of forms. Black chalk lines do not read rhythmically or suggest a precisely limited form; blurred modelling eludes any implication of a consistent plastic substance. In these knotted convolutions of shapes, the individual figure cannot be distinguished and it has no recognizable identity. The break with the *Maniera* ideal of *grazia* is complete. For it is substituted a vague formlessness and a macabre giantism of swollen forms. Bodies are stretched and distended, heads and limbs are shrunken in accord with no evident canon and have no precise relation to any norm of appearance. Furthermore, Pontormo has ignored still another property of the *Maniera* style in his withdrawal from any concern with the spectator. These figures are as inaccessible in human terms as they are indecipherable formally, having no specific — or even enigmatic — human meaning. No figure looks out at the spectator in these drawings, and back views are insistently repeated. The total impression of the *Deluge* drawings is not calculated and rhythmic as in the *Christ in Glory* or even in the studies for the *Resurrection of the Dead.* The intertwined forms of the *Deluge* are nebulous complexes at different stages of dissolution into the nothingness around them. They are the complete antithesis of *Maniera* decoration.

Pontormo's power to revitalize his style in these latest drawings can be attributed essentially to a reassertion of the constant reality of his artistic existence: his anticlassical experimental individuality. In the context of his late style, this reassertion may be seen in two related aspects. The first is a repetition of the sequence of Michelangelo-induced crisis and subsequent new invention that we have seen at other turning points in Pontormo's career. Now, as before, the eventual results of this contact are highly inventive and quite different from the intentions of Michelangelo himself. If we recall that Pontormo's study of the *Cascina* cartoon produced the first Mannerist drawings; that the impact of the Sistine Ceiling led Pontormo to the eccentric actuality of the Poggio a Caiano studies; and that his exposure to the Medici *Allegories* contributed to his unmonumental and rhythmic variant of the *Maniera*, it is not surprising that Pontormo's ultimate personal expressionism in the San Lorenzo drawings should be related to Michelangelo's *Last Judgment*, but be quite different from Michelangelo's powerfully articulated and more awesome, yet more humanly accessible concept.

While Pontormo's renewed study of Michelangelo and his personal transmutation of Michelangelo's *Last Judgment* style contributed to the particular form of his late drawings, there is also in them a reaction against the formalism, schematization, and overtones of academicism that the *Maniera* style had begun to take on after 1550, anticipating its real devitalization in the late sixteenth century. This reaction was a virtual repudiation by Pontormo of his own not insignificant role in the formation of the *Maniera* and a reassertion of the spiritual expressiveness that had marked his pre-1530 Mannerist style. It involved a self-imposed isolation from contemporary artistic developments. Pontormo's closing himself up in the San Lorenzo choir for ten years was not just the capricious and jealously secretive action of an eccentric; it signified the genuine spiritual isolation of the artist as well. Such an abrupt shift into an isolated phase of subjective experimentation recalls the stylistic reversal of the Certosa drawings thirty years before. Now, as then, having achieved a workable stylistic formulation, Pontormo threw it over before the challenge of a new project that suggested the possibility of further private experimentation. It is significant that it was at these two junctures, when Pontormo had deserted a successful solution to the problems of a decorative style, that he found himself most sharply criticized. His repudiation of the *Maniera* meant sacrificing the approval of a *Maniera* critic like Vasari, who said (V/M, VI, 286–287) the San Lorenzo frescoes were without "ordine . . . misura . . . regola . . . proporzione" and, especially, that they lacked "bontà" and "grazia." The underlying criticism is aimed at the same faults that Vasari had found in Pontormo's frescoes at the Certosa; only now they could not be blamed on Dürer.

In their reassertion of Pontormo's experimental individuality the San Lorenzo drawings (especially those for the lower frescoes) may also be seen as a kind of parallel to Pontormo's own earlier anticlassical revolt against the formalisms of the High Renaissance style. The classical style, like the *Maniera*, had tended to suppress the individuality of the artist. Pontormo's revolt against the normative and objective, the restraining and balancing equilibriums of the High Renaissance had induced his radical Mannerist experiments and produced a newly personal kind of drawing. However, in 1550, such a revolt could not be accomplished in terms of the Mannerist vocabulary that Pontormo had invented years before. That stylistic language itself had been crystallized into the formulae of the midsixteenth century, partly by artists such as Bronzino who had followed the lead of Pontormo. Pontormo's final revolt could be achieved only by eliminating the very elements of the classical style that he had retained — in whatever personal transmutation — within the context of his *Maniera* style: ornamental beauty of line and shape, the complex ideal of *grazia*. (In contrast, it was precisely these qualities that were increasingly stressed after 1550 by the members of the younger generation in their consciously classicizing variant of Mannerism.) As a corollary to his denial of the formal values of the *Maniera*, Pontormo withdrew from a concern that had always been that of the sixteenth-century artist: the consideration of the effect of the work of art on the spectator. In the High Renaissance this relation had been a complementary and harmonious one; in Pontormo's earlier Mannerism it had been a disturbed and ambivalent one; but in the San Lorenzo drawings it is nonexistent. Although we do not know what the frescoes actually looked like, it was certainly this quality of inaccessibility in Pontormo's floating compositions, just as much as their eccentric form, that was responsible for the almost total lack of comprehension of them in the later sixteenth and in the seventeenth centuries.

The repudiation of the formal and decorative ideals of the *Maniera* that won for Pontormo the unfavorable verdict of his critics parallels in kind, although not in all details of its realization, the expressionism of Michelangelo's latest work. It is for different reasons that these two artists are represented in their latest phase so largely by drawings, but it is for essentially the same reasons that these drawings are "late works" in the special, restricted sense that leads us to make analogies between the works produced in old age by Titian, Rembrandt, and Goya. Indeed, with the exception of Michelangelo, Pontormo would appear to be the earliest draughtsman to develop a genuine "late style" in drawings. Such a phenomenon had occurred in sculpture and in painting, but only in the context of the rapid and significant expansion of the concept of *disegno* in the sixteenth century — a development with which Pontormo was intimately involved — was it possible for an artist to reach a point where such a final revelation of his artistic personality could be made in graphic terms.

This last phase of Pontormo's experimental evolution detaches itself from and elevates itself above the long period of his maturity. In these drawings there is the total isolation of old age that is characteristic of the *spätwerk.* Even the minimal observance of the public requirements of art that Pontormo had previously made now disappeared. Although these drawings were connected with a specific commission, this did not mean (as we have seen throughout his entire career) that Pontormo's creative activity as a draughtsman was limited by its demands. In fact, the radical form and eccentric content of these drawings were more than before in direct defiance of the requirements of the commission. In the San Lorenzo drawings (and presumably in the frescoes) Pontormo was concerned solely with the projection of a personal point of view in an expressionistic style of a most uncompromisingly private character. The enigmatic spirituality of his religious subjects is suggested by a manipulation of black chalk that is different from the virtuoso technique of the *Maniera.* While Pontormo never abandoned precision of touch and ornamentalism of line to quite the same extent as did the late Michelangelo, the chalk is now rubbed to a soft *sfumato* that envelops rather than limits the figure, suggesting its spiritual reality rather than its physical presence. Furthermore, as in Michelangelo's drawings, the notion of spatiality is completely abandoned. There is a cosmic nothingness, a kind of limbo, in which these images are suspended or move, dreamlike, in a continuous flux. We can only imagine what must have been the singular — even disturbing — effect of these pale floating forms against the pristine rationality of Brunelleschi's architecture.

Like their form, the content of these last works cannot be measured against any norms, even those of Pontormo's own earlier achievement. Even more than in his past work, the content of the San Lorenzo drawings is sensible to us only through the subjective focus of Pontormo's experience; and that experience itself had now become enigmatic. Because of this quality, Pontormo's last drawings, unlike Michelangelo's, do not retain a forceful profundity of human content. The multiple vibrations of Michelangelo's line and the still heroic dimensions of his forms evoke a profound level of spiritual existence, but Pontormo's figures are not informed with the same heroic pessimism. Rather, they represent Pontormo's final retreat into isolated subjectivity, in which both refined eccentricity of feeling and exact control over abstract form are intensified. In these last drawings Pontormo affectingly projects a mystic spirituality that is at once painfully intimate and hauntingly inaccessible: the ultimate paradox of his singular artistic personality.

CATALOGUE RAISONNÉ

PART I · 1514–1519

Catalogue entries 1–92

NOTE ON PROCEDURE AND LIST OF ABBREVIATIONS

The chronological scheme of this Catalogue Raisonné is defined by the numbers assigned to the drawings, a sequence that represents our understanding of Pontormo's development as a draughtsman. In most cases it has been possible to place the drawings after the paintings with which they are associated; where the drawings are not related to paintings, they have been grouped by approximate date at intervals in the catalogue. The way in which the preparatory drawings are arranged varies considerably: if the order of execution of a group of preparatory studies can be determined, this sequence has been used; however, in some cases, it has seemed more illuminating to arrange the drawings as groups of studies for individual figures; and in instances where there is not enough evidence for either approach, the drawings have simply been listed by museum inventory number. In the case of preparatory studies for a painting the date given for the painting applies to each study and is not repeated.

The following material is included at the beginning of each drawing entry: catalogue number; museum and inventory number; painting for which the drawing is a study or the date of the drawing; brief description; subject and catalogue number of the recto (or verso) of the sheet; dimensions (in millimeters from the left and lower edges of the sheet, or the maximum if the drawing is cut irregularly); medium and paper (white to cream unless otherwise noted); watermark (reference to Briquet cited where possible); inscriptions (quoted if eighteenth-century or earlier; for the inscription "Franco Rosi" see p. 10, n. 24); collections (collector's marks noted and Lugt numbers cited except in the case of the Gabinetto Disegni e Stampe degli Uffizi, L. 929–930, a stamp that appears on each sheet but has not been recorded in each entry); bibliography (abbreviated references to the chronologically arranged bibliography are listed through 1961; the 1961 edition of Berenson's *Drawings of the Florentine Painters* is cited only when there has been a change or a new number added since the 1938 edition); photograph (source given if the drawing is not reproduced here or elsewhere).

The unusually close relation between Pontormo's drawings and paintings, together with the chronological arrangement of this catalogue, has made necessary a somewhat more detailed consideration of the paintings than might otherwise be required in a study devoted mainly to the drawings. Therefore, a note on each picture for which preparatory drawings have survived — and this is the majority but by no means all of Pontormo's paintings — has been inserted at the appropriate chronological place in the catalogue. Problems of attribution and date are discussed, but only insofar as is necessary to establish the place of a given work in the *oeuvre*. The Roman numerals I, II, and III have been used to summarize the nature and reliability of the external evidence for the attribution of the picture to Pontormo. Paintings of category I are those for which there is documentary evidence within the sixteenth century. Such works do not require supporting arguments for their attribution but often a discussion of their date is necessary. Pictures of category II are those for which the external evidence is in some measure incomplete or unreliable and which may be attributed to Pontormo only after evaluation of this evidence. Pictures of category III are those for which there is no external evidence and which must be attributed to Pontormo on the basis of stylistic comparison with works from categories I and II. These entries do not pretend to completeness; they are intended merely as a frame of reference that serves to place Pontormo's drawings in the perspective of his total artistic production.

The following abbreviations are used in the Catalogue Raisonné and the List of Attributed Drawings:

AB	*The Art Bulletin*
B.	C. M. Briquet, *Les Filigranes, Dictionnaire historique des marques du papier, dans leur apparition vers 1282 jusqu'en 1600*, Leipzig, 1923
Bar.	A. von Bartsch, *Le Peintre-Graveur*, Vienna, 1803–1821
Boll. d'A.	*Bollettino d'Arte*
Burl.	*Burlington Magazine*
Crit. d'A.	*La Critica d'Arte*
EMI	*Het Eerste Manierisme in Italië, 1500–1540*, Rijksmuseum, Amsterdam, 1954
G.	Walter Gernsheim, *Corpus Photographicum*, London
GNS	Gabinetto Nazionale delle Stampe, Rome
JPK	*Jahrbuch der preuszischen Kunstsammlungen*
L.	F. Lugt, *Les Marques de Collection de Dessins et d'Estampes*, Amsterdam, 1921; *Supplément, The Hague*, 1956
MC	*Mostra del Cinquecento Toscano*, Palazzo Strozzi, Florence, 1940
MDF	*Mostra di Disegni Fiorentini del Cinquecento*, Gabinetto Disegni e Stampe degli Uffizi, Florence, 1939
MDM	*Mostra di Disegni dei Primi Manieristi italiani*, Gabinetto Disegni e Stampe degli Uffizi, Florence, 1954
MF	*Fontainebleau e la Maniera italiana*, Palazzo dell' Arte, Naples, 1952
MM	*Mostra Medicea*, Palazzo Medici, Florence, 1939
MP	*Mostra del Pontormo e del Primo Manierismo Fiorentino*, Palazzo Strozzi, Florence, 1956
MPA	*Mostra dei Disegni di Andrea del Sarto e del Pontormo*, Gabinetto Disegni e Stampe degli Uffizi, Florence, 1910
Mitt. KHIF	*Mitteilungen des Kunsthistorischen Institutes in Florenz*
OMD	*Old Master Drawings*
Rep. KW	*Repertorium für Kunstwissenschaft*
Riv. d'A.	*Rivista d'Arte*
Sop.	Soprintendenza alle Gallerie, Florence
V/M	G. Vasari, *Le Vite de più eccellenti pittori, scultori ed architettori* [1568], G. Milanesi, ed., 9 vols., Florence, 1878–1885
VS	*Vasari Society for the Reproduction of Drawings by Old Masters*, first series, 1905–1915, second series, 1920–1935
W.	Watermark
ZBK	*Zeitschrift für Bildende Kunst*

PART I · 1514–1519

Early 1514. CARRO DELLA ZECCA: *Putti Wrestling*; *Putti Treading Grapes*; *Putti with a Goose*; *Putti with a Cat (?)*; *Baptism of Christ*; *Visitation*; *St. Matthew*; *St. Zenobius*; *St. John the Evangelist*; and *St. John the Baptist*. Florence, Palazzo Vecchio. I. Panels, the putti 32 x 44 cm; the others 69 x 45 cm. Fig. 1.

Bibliography: Clapp 1916, 14–15, 136–139; Gamba 1921, 4; Fraenckel 1933, 151–152; Becherucci 1944, 12; *MP* 1956 (Berti), nos. 2–11, figs. 2–3; Gamba 1956, 8, fig. 2.

These panels are mentioned by Vasari as painted by Pontormo for the *Carro della Zecca* for the procession of the Feast of San Giovanni.[1] They are also noted by Borghini 1584, 481. According to Milanesi (V/M, VI, 257n1), there were eighteen panels when the *Carro* was dismantled in 1810. There were four of over two *braccia* in length representing the *Life of the Baptist*, six of half that size, and six small panels with "baccanali di putti." The four largest panels do not belong with the Pontormo series and are probably by a seventeenth-century hand. The six smaller panels are the *Baptism* and the *Visitation*, and four saints by Pontormo. The last six panels with the "baccanali di putti" are by Pontormo and two later hands. The *Putti with a Flaming Jar* and the *Putti with a Hoop and a Ball* probably date from the later sixteenth century, while the *Putti with a Baptist's Cross* is evidently from the eighteenth century. Completing Milanesi's group of eighteen are two more panels of *Putti with the Medici Arms* (each 28 x 56 cm), which, judging from their style and the form of the arms, date from the seventeenth century. While all the panels that decorated the *Carro della Zecca* may have been by Pontormo, they must have been damaged by use and by exposure to the weather. Those by Pontormo that survive are heavily repainted and the others are evidently replacements. However, when the *Carro* was finally dismantled, all the panels, including the later additions, were attributed to Pontormo.

Clapp apparently accepted all of the panels as Pontormo's, dating them 1515–1516. Berti dated them 1514, evidently considering all of them to be by Pontormo, although only those listed here were exhibited at the 1956 *Mostra del Pontormo*, the others having been omitted because of their repainted condition. Berti based his dating on three drawings that he thought were stylistically analogous, but which are not accepted here as Pontormo (cat. A25, A28, and A50). However, there are indications that the work was done in 1514. Vasari (V/M, VI, 256) places the *Carro* at about the same time as the commission for the SS. Annunziata *Visitation*, but before Pontormo had begun painting it. Since the payments for the *Visitation* begin in late 1514, this would indicate 1514 as the year of the *Carro della Zecca*. Furthermore, Vasari mentions the *Carro della Zecca* after Pontormo's *carri* for the Medici[2] and after decorative works, such

[1] V/M, VI, 256–257: "In questo medesimo tempo dipinse alcuni quadri e storiette a olio per i maestri di zecca nel carro della Moneta, che va ogni anno per San Giovanni a processione . . ."

[2] *Ibid.*, 250–255. After discussing Pontormo's *Faith and Charity* and other works honoring the new pope, Leo X, Vasari says that for "il carnevale del medesimo anno" Pontormo painted *carri*

as the SS. Annunziata *Faith and Charity*, that were done following the elevation of Leo X to the papacy (March 11, 1513). Thus, it is probable that the commission for the *Carro della Zecca* was given on the basis of Pontormo's success in these works and that it was finished shortly before June 24, 1514, the Feast of San Giovanni, in time for the annual celebration.

What one can discern of the style of these ruined panels is well in accord with the style of Pontormo's only surviving works of ca. 1514: the *Ospedale di San Matteo* [3] and the S. Ruffillo altar. However, in contrast to these frescoes, it is evident that the panels for the *Carro della Zecca* were executed hurriedly and that they are unabashedly derivative. Pontormo's varied sources are superficially observed rather than adapted to his personal style, and the borrowings seem to have been more a convenience than a part of a conscious historical investigation. His major source is, not unexpectedly, the tradition of his master, Albertinelli. The *Visitation* is copied directly from Albertinelli's of 1503 (Uffizi), and the stance of the Evangelist from his *Annunciation* of 1510 (Accademia). The *St. Matthew*, the head somewhat awkwardly changed, derives from the St. Bartholomew of Fra Bartolommeo's altar of 1512 (Accademia). However, Pontormo has looked beyond the classical style of the preceding decade. The head of the Evangelist depends on Donatello's *Abraham and Isaac* from the east façade of the Campanile, while the putti making wine are taken from similar scenes on the base of Donatello's *Judith*. Finally, the composition of the *Baptism* is unusual in showing the St. John with his back turned. This figure does not derive from Sansovino's *Baptism* as Berti has suggested, but from Dürer's woodcut of the *Beheading of the Baptist* (1510, Bar. 125), which Andrea del Sarto later used in the Scalzo fresco of the same subject. This is the first instance of Pontormo's borrowing from

for the Medici. Since he states that these decorations were in honor of Leo X, they have always been placed after March 1513. See Clapp 1916, 13–14, 253–254, who dated them 1514–1515. However, J. Shearman, "Pontormo and Andrea del Sarto, 1513," *Burl.* 104 (1962), 478, has recently shown that these works were done for the carnival of 1513, and thus date before rather than after the election of Leo X. According to Vasari and other descriptions of the carnival decorations cited by Shearman, Pontormo painted three cars for the *Compagnia del Diamante*, led by Giuliano de' Medici, and seven cars for the *Compagnia del Broncone*, led by Lorenzo de' Medici. The *carri* for the *Diamante* were decorated with *chiaroscuri* of the *Transformations of the Gods.* According to Shearman, 479–483, figs. 1–2, two pictures from the Kress Collection representing the story of *Apollo and Daphne* (canvas, 60.5 x 46.5 cm, 61 x 46.5 cm) are part of Pontormo's series of the *Transformations of the Gods.* If these pictures are Pontormo's, they would be his earliest surviving works; however, not having seen the paintings themselves, it is impossible to express an opinion on this interesting attribution. For these works see also Berenson 1909, 109 (as Bacchiacca); T. Borenius, *A Catalogue of Paintings in the Collection of Sir Frederick Cook, Bt.*, London, 1913, I, 40 (as Franciabigio); *The Samuel H. Kress Study Collection at Bucknell University*, 1961, 16 (*Apollo and Cupid*, as School of Andrea del Sarto, with Longhi's opinion cited that the pictures may reflect works by Andrea of ca. 1510–1515 by a late Mannerist such as Macchietti or Cristofano Allori) and *The Walker Art Museum Bulletin* (Bowdoin College) 1 (Fall 1961), 8 (*Apollo and Daphne*, as Andrea del Sarto).

[3] Florence, Accademia 9385 (detached fresco, 91 x 150 cm). This small fresco was formerly attributed to Andrea del Sarto but was recognized as Pontormo by Gamba 1904, 18. It is closely associable in style with the *Carro della Zecca* (cf. especially the *Visitation*) and the S. Ruffillo altar. As pointed out by Freedberg 1961, 244, the derivation of details of the composition from Andrea del Sarto's *Birth of the Virgin* of 1514 precludes a date of before that year for this work. Berti, *MP* 1956, no. 13, fig. 4, also dated it 1514; but Clapp 1916, 6, 115, fig. 1, placed it 1513; and Fraenckel 1933, 15, 162, dated it 1512.

Dürer, whose prints were well known in the circle of his master, Andrea del Sarto.[4]

Only a single drawing has survived (cat. 1) for the ten panels of the *Carro della Zecca*. However, a sheet of studies in the Uffizi by Naldini contains two sketches that are likely to be copies after lost Pontormo drawings for the head of the *St. Matthew*.[5]

STUDY FOR THE CARRO DELLA ZECCA

1 · Florence, Uffizi 6581F *verso*: Study for the *St. John the Baptist* of the *Carro della Zecca*. Standing nude seen to the knees with the right arm raised and the left holding a staff. (*Recto*: Study for the Visdomini altar, cat. 43.) 175 x 127, pen and bistre wash. Fig. 2.

Bibliography: Clapp 1914, 166–167; Clapp 1916, 15, fig. 8; Berenson 1938, no. 2081; *MDM* 1954 (Marcucci), no. 39; *EMI* 1954, no. 57; Gamba 1956, 8, fig. 1; *MP* 1956 (Berti), 10; Berenson 1961, no. 2081, fig. 885.

Clapp recognized this sketch as a study for the *St. John*, but dated it 1515–1517. Marcucci, however, considered it reworked and reserved judgment as to its authenticity. There is little reason to doubt the authorship of this drawing, nor does it appear to be worked over. It is a slight, unelaborated sketch executed in a fresh and offhand manner for a panel that was itself of minor importance. However, the medium is somewhat unusual for Pontormo at this date, cat. 40 for the St. John the Baptist of the Visdomini altar being the only other example of Pontormo's use of pen before 1520.

Berti thought this figure was close to Sansovino's *Bacchus* (Bargello), while Clapp considered its source to be an antique Antinous. While there is little relation to the Sansovino, it is evident that Pontormo has adapted the pose of an antique statue, probably a Bacchus, for this figure.[6] The same motive appears elsewhere in Pontormo's early works, most conspicuously in the statues in *Joseph* (I) of 1515–1516 and in *Joseph in Egypt* of 1518–1519, where the figure appears in its least disguised form.

[4] We know from Vasari (V/M, V, 405) that Dürer prints had been available in Italy from about 1507. About 1514 the influence of the *Small Passion* in particular began to appear in the work of Andrea del Sarto. According to Vasari (*ibid.*, 22), while Andrea was at work on the Scalzo *Caritas*, *Justizia*, *Preaching of St. John*, and *St. John Baptising*, "uscirono fuori alcune stampe intagliate in rame d'Alberto Duro, e che egli se ne servì e ne cavò alcune figure . . ." Motives from Dürer's *Christ Before the People* (Bar. 10, 1512) and the *Birth of the Virgin* (Bar. 80, ca. 1506) appear in the *Preaching of St. John* of 1515, while Andrea also used Dürer's woodcuts as sources for his own *Birth of the Virgin* of 1514 and for the lost *Pietà* engraved by Agostino Veneziano in 1516 (see Bar. 14 and 122). Pontormo's only other borrowing from Dürer in this period is the *St. Veronica* of 1515.

[5] Uffizi 311F (red chalk, 411 x 253). On the recto of the sheet is a copy after Andrea del Sarto, another version of the figure Naldini copied on cat. A64. On the verso is a seated nude study, possibly after a Pontormo drawing of ca. 1514 (cf. cat. 2), and two studies of the head of a bearded man that are copies after preparatory studies for the St. Matthew head.

[6] See S. Reinach, *Répertoire de la Statuaire Grecque et Romaine* (Paris, 1930), I, 138, fig. 3, for an example that is particularly close in pose to Pontormo's figure.

Ca. 1514. S. RUFFILLO ALTAR: *Madonna and Child with Sts. Agnes, Lucy, Zachary, and Michael.* Florence, SS. Annunziata, Cappella di S. Luca; formerly S. Ruffillo. I. Fresco, 185 x 171 cm. Fig. 3.

Bibliography: Goldschmidt 1911, 44; Clapp 1916, 7–8, 117, fig. 2; Gamba 1921, 5, fig. 2; Venturi 1932, 92–94, fig. 43; Fraenckel 1933, 153-156; Berenson 1936, 401; Toesca 1943, 6, 8, fig. 1; Becherucci 1944, 13, fig. 4; Paatz 1952/55, I, 118, V, 32; *MP* 1956 (Marcucci), 62; *MP* Supplement 1956 (Berti); Freedberg 1961, I, 245–247, II, fig. 324.

This fresco is described by Vasari as painted by Pontormo in a chapel in the church of S. Ruffillo.[7] Vasari also mentions a lunette of *God the Father and Angels* that was painted above. When the painting was transferred to its present location in 1823, this part of the fresco, as well as the top and sides of the *Madonna and Child with Saints*, was destroyed. The fresco is also mentioned as in S. Ruffillo by Borghini 1584, 481; Cinelli 1677, 214; Del Migliore 1684, 155; and Richa 1754/62, IV, 146, who noted it in the first chapel on the right side of the church.

Vasari does not give a precise date for the S. Ruffillo altar, but he places it at the same time as the *St. Veronica* and before the SS. Annunziata *Visitation*. Stylistic comparison with the datable *St. Veronica* of 1515 and the documented *Visitation* of late 1514–1516 indicates a date of ca. 1514 for the S. Ruffillo fresco. Comparison with these two works makes clear Pontormo's tentative, immature formulation of both the composition and the forms in the S. Ruffillo altar, his partial assimilation of the tenets of the High Renaissance in his conscious attempt to work within the classical style. There is a combination of literal dependence on available models and a precocious independence of spirit and inventiveness. The Madonna is the stock figure who had already appeared in the *Carro della Zecca* as St. John the Evangelist. She derives in general from the Madonnas of Fra Bartolommeo, as well as from such figures as the Virgin in Albertinelli's *Annunciation* (Accademia, 1510) or Andrea del Sarto's *Annunciation* (Pitti, 1512). This figure is combined with an unusually energetic child (very like the St. John the Baptist in Andrea's Dresden altar of the year before), and with quite original inventions such as the kneeling St. Agnes or the unclassical St. Lucy, who stares urgently out of the picture. These diverse figures are pushed together in a space that has not been defined in the classical sense; and their attempted movements are constricted, so that the result is a series of twistings rather than the suave contrapposto of Pontormo's Bartolommesque models. In this first essay in monumental fresco painting Pontormo achieved neither the relaxation nor the discipline of the High Renaissance style as exemplified in the works of his masters. Therefore, it is difficult to accept the later dating of Berenson and Becherucci, who would place this fresco in 1516 at a time when Pontormo had completed the *Visitation* — a most explicitly classical work. On the other hand, while Marcucci has rightly noted that the picture dates not after 1514 and Freedberg has dated it 1514, Clapp's date of 1512–1513 and Berti's of 1513 tend to place this work unnecessarily early, still within the period of Pontormo's apprenticeship to Andrea del Sarto. Cat. A106 is a copy after the central part of this fresco.

[7] V/M, VI, 256: "Dipinse poi . . . nella chiesa di San Ruffello in una cappella in fresco la Nostra Donna col figliuolo in braccio in mezzo a San Michelagnolo e Santa Lucia e due altri Santi inginocchioni, e nel mezzo tondo della cappella un Dio Padre con alcuni serafini intorno."

STUDIES FOR THE S. RUFFILLO ALTAR

2 · Florence, Uffizi 6676F *verso*: Study for the Madonna, S. Ruffillo altar. Standing nude leaning back on the right arm; below, the head and shoulders studied twice. (*Recto*: Nude study, cat. 8.) 398 x 255, red chalk. Fig. 5.

Bibliography: Berenson 1903, no. 2161; Clapp 1911, 5; Clapp 1914, 226–227; Clapp 1916, 9, fig. 4; Berenson 1938, no. 2161; *MP* 1956 (Marcucci), no. 90, fig. 124b; Sinibaldi 1960, no. 46.

As Clapp has noted, this drawing is a study for the Madonna, although he dated it toward 1514 and the painting 1512–1513. Marcucci has dated the drawing not after 1514, noting that this study is advanced in style over the recto, and that here Pontormo has moved away from Fra Bartolommeo toward Michelangelo. This drawing is a preliminary model study for the Madonna, less carefully academic than the recto, which certainly precedes it, but still well within the orbit of Fra Bartolommeo. In the painting the action of the figure is shifted: with the removal of the supporting ledge on which the nude leans in the drawing, the pose becomes more ideally self-sufficient and self-contained. In the painted figure the head is turned further in profile, a change that Pontormo was perhaps considering in the two quick sketches of the head below. These sketches are not, as Clapp thought, for the St. Lucy (whom he called St. Claire).

3 · Dresden, Kupferstichkabinett C80 *recto*: Study for St. Zachary, S. Ruffillo altar. Draped man kneeling in profile to the left. (*Verso*: Study for the S. Ruffillo altar, cat. 4.) 342 x 227, red chalk; W: Latin Cross (B. 5641). Fig. 4.

Collection: Royal collection of Saxony, stamp recto (L. 486); acquired by the museum in 1738.

Bibliography: Woermann 1896/98, no. 200, pl. 10; Berenson 1903, no. 1959; Clapp 1911, 5; Clapp 1914, 83–84; Clapp 1916, 8, fig. 3; Byam Shaw 1929/30, 24; Berenson 1938, no. 1959.

Formerly attributed to Andrea del Sarto, this drawing was first given to Pontormo by Berenson, who dated it in Pontormo's earlier middle period. Clapp associated it with the St. Zachary, dating it 1513. As a final study for the saint in the painting differing only in minor details from the painted figure, this is the earliest elaborated study for a pictorial motive as well as the earliest drapery study by Pontormo that has survived. Cat. 6 of ca. 1514 and cat. 19 for *Joseph* (I) of 1515–1516 are other early studies of draped figures in a similar style. As Clapp has remarked, there is a point of departure for Naldini in Pontormo's youthful drawings of this type. In a number of his drawings that are imitative of the early Pontormo we find an exaggeration of the slashing, dry angularity of Pontormo's lines and of the way in which they are often repeated to the point of obscuring the clarity of the form (cf. cat. A81).

4 · Dresden, Kupferstichkabinett C80 *verso*: Study for St. Michael, S. Ruffillo altar. Nude standing turned toward the left with the right arm raised and the left studied twice holding a staff. (*Recto*: Study for the S. Ruffillo altar, cat. 3.) 342 x 227, red chalk. Fig. 6.

Bibliography: Berenson 1903, no. 1959; Clapp 1914, 84; Byam Shaw 1929/30, 24–25, fig. 7; Berenson 1938, no. 1959.

Formerly attributed to Andrea del Sarto, this drawing was given to Pontormo by Berenson, who dated it with the recto in Pontormo's earlier middle period. While Clapp connected the recto with the S. Ruffillo altar, only Byam Shaw has noticed that this drawing is a model study from the nude for the pose of the St. Michael in the same fresco. This study shows the left arm and hand of the saint, which were destroyed when the fresco was transferred. Cat. 5 is another detail study of the left hand, which is studied twice here.

5 · Florence, Uffizi 6556F *verso*: Study for St. Michael, S. Ruffillo altar, and other studies. Two hands, one holding a stick; a draped bust; above, a hilly landscape with trees and buildings. (*Recto*: Study for *Joseph* (II), cat. 22.) 240 x 337, black chalk, the landscape in red chalk. Fig. 7.

Bibliography: Berenson 1903, no. 2057; Clapp 1914, 151–152; Berenson 1938, no. 2057.

Berenson connected the hand holding the stick with the old woman to the left in the SS. Annunziata *Visitation*, noting that the motive is reversed in the painting, and the other hand possibly with the Virgin. He did not connect the draped bust with the woman to the left of the *Visitation*, as Clapp thought, but referred to the drapery study on the verso of the sheet. Clapp associated this draped bust with the *Visitation*, apparently with the kneeling saint to the left of the Virgin. The hands he connected with the Visdomini altar, the one with the stick with the St. John the Baptist, the other with the Virgin. These sketches may certainly be dated ca. 1514–1515, but the only one that may be identified precisely is the hand with the stick, which is a study for the left hand of St. Michael. This hand is cut off in the fresco, but is studied twice on cat. 4, the preparatory drawing for the figure. The other hand might possibly have been a study for the St. Michael's right hand in a slightly different position from the one in the painting.

Neither Berenson nor Clapp made particular mention of the landscape. This red chalk study is the only landscape drawing in Pontormo's *oeuvre*. It is very similar in the arrangement of hills, trees, and buildings to the landscape in the center background of *Joseph* (I) of 1515–1516, the earliest landscape in Pontormo's paintings. If this drawing was not actually preparatory to the picture, it is at least generically associated with it in its precise, geometric, and rather timid style, which recalls that of Bacchiacca in these same years and which was modelled ultimately on the landscape drawings of Fra Bartolommeo.

MISCELLANEOUS DRAWINGS CA. 1514

6 · Florence, Uffizi 6564F *recto*: Ca. 1514. Draped boy seated on a stool turned to the right; another figure slightly indicated behind. (*Verso*: Nude study, cat. 7.) 331 x 191, red chalk; piece of right side of the sheet replaced; inscribed in ink in an eighteenth-century hand: *Jac.º da Pontormo*. Fig. 10.

Bibliography: Berenson 1903, no. 2065; *MPA* 1910, 31; Clapp 1914, 156–157; Berenson 1938, no. 2065; *MP* 1956 (Marcucci), no. 89, pl. 123a; Marcucci 1956, 8, fig. 3.

Clapp dated this study 1513, comparing it with cat. 3 for the S. Ruffillo altar, cat. 19 for *Joseph* (I), and cat. A31. Berenson dated it "early," and Marcucci placed it 1513–1514. The drapery in this study and in cat. 3 is of the same hastily angular type that will still be found in a study of 1515–1516 such as cat. 19. However, there is no connection with cat. A31, a pen and bistre drawing not by Pontormo. This drawing belongs to the period of the S. Ruffillo altar or just slightly before. It is probable that we have here one of the earliest surviving sheets by Pontormo (see also the early style of the verso), done very close to the time of his apprenticeship in the shop of Andrea del Sarto. However, it is not so much the influence of Andrea that is found here as a parallel development in the way in which both younger draughtsmen deviated from the style of Fra Bartolommeo. In spite of his advantage of eight years over Pontormo, Andrea's drawing style was at this time almost equally immature. He vacillated from an angular, jagged manner similar to Pontormo's here (Uffizi 6435F) to a broader style of heavier, curving forms (Uffizi 273F). It was this second way of drawing that Pontormo would experiment with himself in drawings of ca. 1515 such as cat. 15 and 18. Marcucci saw the influence of the late Albertinelli in this drawing and compared it with a drawing for an *Annunciation* (Uffizi 308F). However, that drawing seems to be an isolated one in the *oeuvre* of a draughtsman who generally did not work in chalk, and its puffy draperies and timid forms bear little relation to the bolder, more angular manner of Pontormo's drawing. If Pontormo executed earlier drawings closer to Albertinelli's style — as indeed he may have when he was with Albertinelli ca. 1510–1512 — they have not survived.

7 · Florence, Uffizi 6564F *verso*: Ca. 1514. Standing nude boy seen to the ankles, his left hand on his hip; to the right cut off by the edge of the sheet, fragmentary profile of a figure. (*Recto*: Figure study, cat. 6.) 331 x 191, black chalk, figure to the right in red chalk. Fig. 8.

Bibliography: *MP* 1956 (Marcucci), no. 89, fig. 123b.

Marcucci remarked only on the Leonardesque quality of the profile to the right, which she believed resembled some in the *Story of Joseph* panels. This slight sketch is one of the earliest surviving Pontormo drawings. The abbreviated shorthand rendering of the facial features is very characteristic of Pontormo's studies of this very early period (cf. cat. 1 and cat. 11) and it is also found on occasion in Andrea del Sarto's early studies, such as Uffizi 6435F of 1511. In the proportions of the nude, and in its awkward articulation, this study is associable with cat. 1 for the *Carro della Zecca* of 1514; and, like cat. 1, it was inspired after a sculptural model. Pontormo's source here was Donatello's *David*, then in the courtyard of the Palazzo Vecchio.[8]

8 · Florence, Uffizi 6676F *recto*: Ca. 1514. Seated nude turned to the right and holding a staff. (*Verso*: Study for the S. Ruffillo altar, cat. 2.) 398 x 255, red chalk; W: Eagle. Fig. 9.

Bibliography: Berenson 1903, no. 2161; *MPA* 1910, 31; Clapp 1914, 226; Berenson 1938, no. 2161; *MP* 1956 (Marcucci), no. 90, fig. 124a; Sinibaldi 1960, no. 46.

Clapp dated this drawing 1515–1516, Marcucci 1514–1516. Sinibaldi placed it 1514, suggesting that it might have been intended as a study for a spectator in the SS. Annunziata *Visitation* or in the first panel of the *Story of Joseph*, which she dated 1516–1517. This model study is not convincingly associable with any painting, but should be placed 1514, probably predating its verso for the S. Ruffillo altar. This nude study is one of the most tentative we know from Pontormo's hand, especially when compared with the assured, although immature, handling of chalk and articulation of forms on the verso.

[8] See H. W. Janson, *Donatello* (Princeton, 1957), II, 4.

Late 1515. DECORATION OF THE CAPPELLA DEL PAPA: *St. Veronica*; *God the Father*; *Putti with the Instruments of the Passion*; *Putti with the Arms of Leo X.* Florence, Convent of S. M. Novella; now Collegio Militare. I. Frescoes on the wall and ceiling: *St. Veronica* lunette, 307 x 413 cm; *God the Father* medallion, 120 cm diameter; four *Putti* medallions, 60 cm diameter; four *Putti* squares, 75 x 75 cm. Fig. 11.

Bibliography: Goldschmidt 1911, 4, 45, pl. 3; Clapp 1916, 11–12, 123–125; Voss 1920, 163; Bodmer 1931, 355; Venturi 1932, 98, fig. 45; Fraenckel 1933, 156–160; Berenson 1936, 401; Berenson 1938, 302; Toesca 1943, 8–9; Becherucci 1944, 12, fig. 1; Paatz 1952/55, III, 730; *MP* Supplement 1956 (Berti); Freedberg 1961, I, 508–509, II, figs. 641–642; Thiem 1961, 13–15, fig. 16.

Pontormo's work in the Cappella del Papa is mentioned by Vasari (V/M, VI, 255–256, 541) and Borghini 1584, 481. Vasari specifies (*ibid.*, 256) that Pontormo painted in the chapel "un Dio Padre con molti putti, ed una Veronica che nel sudario aveva l'effigie di Gesù Cristo." According to Vasari, Ridolfo Ghirlandaio was already busy decorating rooms in the Palazzo Vecchio in 1514, and he evidently gave part of the work in the Cappella del Papa to Pontormo at the last minute. Vasari says (*ibid.*) that Pontormo did his frescoes "in tanta strettezza di tempo." Thus, Pontormo's work is securely datable within a short time before the Pope's arrival in Florence November 30, 1515.

Along with the *Visitation* of late 1514–1516, this precisely datable work is valuable as a secure point of reference for undocumented paintings and drawings that can be placed in these years. Pontormo's style here is still predominantly Sartesque, recalling the Dresden altar of 1513 and the upper part of the *Birth of the Virgin* of 1514 (cf. the rich chiaroscuro, the angels, and the curtain motive in the *Veronica* with the Dresden altar). However, Pontormo also shows an awareness of both Dürer and Michelangelo and, as was to be characteristic in his later works as well, impressions from these diverse sources overlap and lose their identity as quotations. Berenson has remarked that the Veronica's facial type is distinctly Michelangelesque; however, her powerful contrapposto is quite different from that of any figure in Pontormo's works to this date and specifically recalls that of the Madonna in Michelangelo's Doni tondo. Simultaneously, her actual pose derives from Dürer, perhaps through the intermediary of Andrea del Sarto.[9]

STUDIES FOR THE CAPPELLA DEL PAPA

9 · Florence, Uffizi 6688F *recto*: Study for the *Putti with the Arms of Leo X*, Cappella del Papa. Seated putto turned to the right. (*Verso*: Study for the same figures, cat. 10.) 129 x 109, red chalk. Fig. 12.

Bibliography: Berenson 1903, no. 2173; Clapp 1914, 234; Berenson 1938, no. 2173.

Clapp doubted the authenticity of this sheet without giving any reasons, while Berenson believed it to be an early study for a *St. John the Baptist*. Unlike the putto on the verso, this study cannot be specifically connected with one of the putti on the ceiling of the Cappella del Papa. However, it is close enough in pose and in type to these putti to be identified as a preparatory study for one of them. The putti in

[9] The St. Veronica recalls the angel in Dürer's *Birth of the Virgin* (Bar. 80, ca. 1506), a figure that also appears in Andrea's SS. Annunziata *Birth of the Virgin* of 1514. Cf. also Dürer's *Two Angels with the Sudarium* (Bar. 25, 1513).

these two sketches cannot be mistaken for those of any other period in Pontormo's work. They derive essentially from the putti in Andrea del Sarto's paintings of 1513–1514, notably the Dresden altar and the *Birth of the Virgin.* In both Andrea's and Pontormo's putti, the figure is plump with short, very rounded arms, tiny feet and hands, a mass of light hair falling over the face, darkened eyes and a half-smile, and is characteristically crouched, looking out from behind a hunched shoulder. These putti also occur in a *chiaroscuro* painted ca. 1515 by Pontormo, probably for a decoration in honor of Leo X.[10] In its draughtsmanship, notably in the patchy diagonal shading and the feathery contours made up of short curved strokes, this sheet is close to cat. 11 for the *Visitation* and cat. 15 for a *Venus and Cupid.*

[10] See O. Giglioli, "Chiaroscuri inediti di Andrea del Sarto di un suo aiuto e del Pontormo" *L'Arte* 29 (1926), 261–266, fig. 4. Pontormo's *chiaroscuro, Two Crouched Amoretti, One Playing a Flute* (Uffizi, Gabinetto dei Disegni 91460; canvas, 52 x 80 cm), may have been made for a frieze of an arch or for some other decoration in honor of the entrance of Leo X into Florence, the same occasion for which the Cappella del Papa was decorated. Vasari (V/M, VI, 255, 602), mentions Pontormo among the artists who participated in the decorative projects for this event. Giglioli also associated three *chiaroscuri* by Andrea del Sarto with Pontormo's putti and the 1515 festival, but Shearman (see n2) has shown that Andrea's works belong with the Medici decorations for the carnival of 1513. Shearman rightly pointed out that Pontormo's canvas belongs neither with the Andrea series nor to the year 1513, but in 1515, where we have placed it.

10 · Florence, Uffizi 6688F *verso*: Study for the *Putti with the Arms of Leo X*, Cappella del Papa. Seated putto leaning to the right. (*Recto*: Study for the same figures, cat. 9.) 129 x 109, red chalk.
Fig. 13.

Bibliography: Berenson 1903, no. 2173; Clapp 1914, 234; Berenson 1938, no. 2173.

See the recto for the style of this drawing. It is a study for the putto to the right in the *Putti with the Arms of Leo X* on the right side of the ceiling nearest to the far wall of the chapel.

Late 1514–1516. VISITATION. Florence, SS. Annunziata, Atrium. I. Fresco, 392 x 337 cm.
Fig. 14.

Bibliography: Goldschmidt 1911, 4, 44; Clapp 1916, 15–16, 117–119, fig. 5; Voss 1920, 163–164; Friedlaender 1925, 60, fig. 1; Venturi 1932, 94–98, fig. 44; Fraenckel 1933, 160; Berenson 1936, 401; Toesca 1943, 9, fig. 3; Becherucci 1944, 12–13, figs. 2–3; Nicco Fasola 1947, 28, fig. 1; Paatz 1952/55, I, 93; *MP* Supplement 1956 (Berti); Marcucci 1956, 9, fig. 6; Gamba 1956, 9; Baldini and Berti 1958, 80; Procacci 1958, 30, pl. 19; Freedberg 1961, I, 504–508, II, figs. 639–640.

Clapp 1916, app. II, doc. 13, has published documents that show payments to Pontormo for the *Visitation* from December 1514 to May 1516. It is described by Vasari (V/M, VI, 257–258), who says that it was completed in 1516; Borghini 1584, 481; Bocchi 1591, 211; Del Migliore 1684, 270; and Richa 1754/62, VIII, 60. This fresco may be regarded as the culmination of Pontormo's early period of activity, in the sense that it is a document of his full mastery of the High Renaissance style as developed in Florence by Fra Bartolommeo and Andrea del Sarto. The spacious architectural setting, the movement around a central axis, the contrapuntal balancing of one figure or motion against another, and the heavy, slowly moving forms show a development on the monumental altars of Fra Bartolommeo (Louvre, 1511; Accademia, 1512; S. Marco, 1512). To a lesser extent this picture is dependent on the example of the not-so-architectonically minded Andrea of the Dresden altar (cf. the putti in the lunette above Pontormo's scene) and the *Birth of the Virgin* in another corner of the SS. Annunziata courtyard. The placing of the figures in the architecture, the arch framing the protagonists, and the putto sprawling to the right on the steps also suggest that Pontormo might have been aware (through copies) of Raphael's *School of Athens*. And, as has been pointed out by Gamba, the diagonal relation of the main figures may reflect yet another painting by Raphael, the *Madonna dell' Impannata*, imported into Florence in 1514. (see V/M, IV, 351).

STUDIES FOR THE VISITATION

11 · Florence, Uffizi 6533F *recto*: Study for the woman and child, *Visitation*. Bust of a nude holding a child. (*Verso*: Undecipherable black chalk sketch, not catalogued.) 153 x 144, red chalk; inscribed in ink in a late sixteenth-century (?) hand: *Jacopo da Pont°*. Fig. 16.

Bibliography: Berenson 1903, no. 2036; Clapp 1914, 136; Berenson 1938, no. 2036.

This drawing is a preliminary idea for the woman and child to the left of the Virgin, belonging with cat. 12 early in the preparation for the fresco while compositional details were still to be changed. In the fresco the child is shifted to the other side. Berenson believed that this study might be a reminiscence of the *Sistine Madonna*. Considering Pontormo's classicizing intentions in the *Visitation* and his probable awareness of Raphael in other aspects of its composition, it is not impossible that Raphael's monumental development of the Madonna and Child subject in 1514 (note also the similarities to the *Madonna della Sedia* of the same date) might have had some formative effect on Pontormo's evolution of this group. However, Pontormo's immediate source — or his intermediary from Raphael — was Fra Bartolommeo, with whom he was in much more direct contact (cf. Fra Bartolommeo's *Madonna* of 1514 in S. Marco). This same motive, with the child to the left as in the fresco, and this time as a Madonna and Child, also appears in another Pontormo drawing of these years that is probably just subsequent to this one (cat. 14).

Clapp doubted the attribution of this drawing to Pontormo on the basis of the drawing of the eyes, but assigned to it a date of 1520–1530. The eyes, on the contrary, are particularly characteristic of certain early Pontormo studies, such as cat. 6 and 7 of ca. 1514, cat. 14 and 15 of ca. 1515, and cat. 24 of ca. 1516.

12 · Florence, Uffizi 6542F *recto*: Study for the boy on the steps, *Visitation*. Nude boy seated with legs apart looking to the right. (*Verso*: Study for *Joseph* (I), cat. 21.) 359 x 264, red chalk; W: Latin Cross (B. 5641). Fig. 17.

Bibliography: Berenson 1903, no. 2045; *MPA* 1910, 31; Clapp 1911, 7; Clapp 1914, 142; Clapp 1916, 16, fig. 7; Fraenckel 1933, 177n24; Berenson 1938, no. 2045; *MF* 1952, 61; *MP* 1956 (Marcucci), no. 91, fig. 125a; Berenson 1961, no. 2045, fig. 888.

Berenson originally connected this drawing with Poggio a Caiano, while Fraenckel did not accept it as Pontormo at all, suggesting that it might be by the assistant who was responsible for the putti in the Cappella del Papa. However, this drawing is of high quality, dates from a period when Pontormo is not known to have had assistants, and is, as Clapp has seen, a preparatory study for the boy on the steps in the SS. Annunziata fresco. In style it is similar to cat. 11, also for the *Visitation*, and to its verso for *Joseph* (I) of 1515–1516. While there is the possibility that a figure disposed in such a way on steps in front of the main action of the scene was suggested by the figure in Raphael's *School of Athens*, a more immediate source for the boy as it is drawn here is the angel above the bed in Andrea del Sarto's *Birth of the Virgin*, a fresco near Pontormo's in the courtyard that was finished the year Pontormo began the *Visitation*. In the painted figure, where the left arm is no longer across the body and the legs are more widely spread out, this connection is less evident.

The study that intervened between this one and the fresco exists but has been published too late for inclusion in this catalogue. The black chalk drawing in Budapest[11] shows the putto exactly as he appears in the fresco.

13 · Berlin-Dahlem, Kupferstichkabinett 4195: Study for the kneeling woman to the left, *Visitation*. Draped hooded woman kneeling and pointing to the right, but looking left. 328 x 194, red chalk; inscribed in darker red chalk: *Micarino*. Fig. 15.

Collection: Berlin, Kupferstichkabinett der Staatlichen Museen, stamp recto (L. 1632).

Bibliography: Berenson 1903, no. 2392; Kusenberg 1931, 138, pl. 66, fig. 1; Berenson 1938, no. 1954B; Barocchi 1950, 200.

As can be seen by the inscription, this drawing was once considered to be by Beccafumi. Both Berenson and Kusenberg gave this drawing to Rosso, Kusenberg dating it before 1517. However, Berenson later (1938) gave it to Pontormo, placing it at the time of the *Visitation*. Barocchi also attributed it to Pontormo, but associated it somewhat unconvincingly with Uffizi 6488F and Berlin-Dahlem 4196, both of which she attributed to Rosso. The connection between this drawing and the third figure from the left in the *Visitation* has not been noted. When it is seen that the woman is the counterpart of the kneeling man on the right, it becomes clear that this is a study for the kneeling woman. As such, it is valuable evidence of the style of the more finished preparatory drawings for the fresco. It is more advanced in style than cat. 11 and 12, which are still related to studies for the S. Ruffillo altar like cat. 2. However, it is closely linked with drawings we have dated ca. 1515 such as cat. 14–15 and cat. 17–18.

[11] No. 2181, 244 x 311. See I. Fenyö, "Sur Quelques Dessins Italiens du XVIe Siècle," *Bulletin du Musée National Hongrois des Beaux-Arts* 19 (1961), 59–60, fig. 45.

STUDY FOR A MADONNA AND CHILD WITH ST. JOHN CA. 1515

14 · Rome, GNS F.N. 2943 *recto*: Compositional study for a *Madonna and Child with St. John*, ca. 1515. Within a frame, the three-quarter length Madonna is turned to the right holding the Child to the left; below right, the bust-length St. John. (*Verso*: Study for the Certosa, cat. 203.) 341 x 257, red chalk. Fig. 18.

Bibliography: Grassi 1946, 42, fig. 9; Grassi 1947, 122, pl. 24; *MP* 1956 (Berti), 12; Berenson 1961, no. 2368A–1.

Grassi first attributed this study to Pontormo and dated it 1525–1530 as close in style to S. Felicita. Berenson dated it in Pontormo's "early middle period" with doubts as to the attribution. Berti placed it about 1514. This compositional study for a painting of a *Madonna and Child with St. John* is a striking example of Pontormo's drawing style of ca. 1515 and belongs with a group of stylistically identical studies: cat. 11 and 13 for the *Visitation*, cat. 15, 17, and 18. In all these studies we find the familiar Pontormesque figure with pointed facial features, shadowed eyes, and oblique glance; the high round bust, tapering extremities, and trailing fingers. This female type also occurs in the *St. Veronica* of 1515, but is considerably modified in the more classically normative figures of the *Visitation* fresco, finished in 1516.

This drawing is closely linked in motive to the woman and child to the left of the Virgin in the *Visitation* and to the preparatory study for this group, in which the child is held on the other side (cat. 11). The *Visitation* group is the most classical version of this mother and child motive, a tightly knit and stable pair of figures in which the movement of the child is contained by both arms of the woman, his glance is direct rather than oblique, and the tension created by the third figure of the St. John is removed. As was mentioned in discussing the *Visitation* group and cat. 11, this motive leads us back to a Bartolommesque (and ultimately Raphaelesque) prototype: Fra Bartolommeo's *Madonna* of 1514 in S. Marco. Furthermore, it would seem that the addition of the full-face, bust-length St. John to the composition in this drawing also recalls a Fra Bartolommeo design, a composition of a *Madonna and Child with St. John* current in his shop about 1511–1512 that would surely have been known to Pontormo during his association with Albertinelli.[12] However, in contrast to his model, Pontormo emphasizes the cut-off spatial situation of the St. John, his aggressive full-face contact with the spectator, and his ambiguous relation to the other figures in such a way that the motive is taken out of a classical context and placed in an incipiently unclassical and unharmonious one.

A painting corresponding to this drawing was first exhibited in 1956 at the *Mostra del Pontormo* (fig. 19).[13] While the attribution to Pontormo has remained unquestioned, there is much in this small picture that suggests an adaptation of Pontormo's composition by another hand. Especially telling are changes from the drawing — or possibly from Pontormo's lost original picture — that indicate a more conventional mentality: the Madonna's posture is more erect, her head less heavily draped, her arm not boldly extended but curving back into the composition. The St. John, in Pontormo's drawing placed as an intermediary between the spectator and the Madonna and Child, has been turned in profile to look up at the Christ Child. Furthermore, the Pontormesque eccentricities of content in the drawing — the nervously animated smile of the Madonna, the half-hidden face of the Child, and the transfixed expression of the St. John — are methodically suppressed in the painting. Nor do the morphological details of the forms bear out the attribution to Pontormo. The weak structure of the heads, the rigid regularity of the drapery folds, and the turgid heaviness of the surface are reminiscent of other derivative pictures such as the *Madonna and Child* in the Frascione Collection.[14]

MISCELLANEOUS DRAWINGS CA. 1515

15 · Florence, Uffizi 341F: Ca. 1515. Study for a *Venus and Cupid*. Partially draped woman with a putto at her left side who is balanced on a sphere. 393 x 180, red chalk; laid down. Fig. 20.

Bibliography: Ferri 1890, 138; Jacobsen 1898, 277; Berenson 1903, no. 1963; *MPA*

[12] Cf. the version in the Corsini Gallery, Florence, no. 160, dated 1511.

[13] Florence, Uffizi (panel, 64 x 50 cm). See Berti *MP* 1956, no. 14, fig. 6 (dated 1514); Baldini 1956, 1, fig. 1 (dated 1514); Marcucci 1956, 7, fig. 1 (dated 1512–1515); Sanminiatelli 1956, 242, fig. 25 (dated ca. 1515). The picture was also accepted as Pontormo by R. Oertel, "Pontormo und der Florentiner Frühmanierismus," *Kunstchronik* 9 (1956), 214, fig. 1.

[14] See *MP* 1956 (Berti), no. 15, fig. 7, where it is dated 1515.

1910, 36; Clapp 1914, 88–89; Berenson 1938, 276, no. 1963, fig. 937; Marcucci 1955, 250, fig. 19; Schlegel 1961, 32n30, fig. 14.

This drawing was attributed by Ferri and Jacobsen to Andrea del Sarto as a study for the Scalzo *Caritas*. Clapp ascribed it to an Andrea del Sarto assistant of the period 1513–1525 such as Pier Francesco di Jacopo (Foschi) or Antonio di Giovanni Solosmeo. Berenson gave this drawing to Pontormo, dating it 1512–1513. Marcucci also accepted it as Pontormo, dating it 1511–1512 and grouping it with cat. A25, A28, and A50, none of which are accepted here as Pontormo. This study is securely attributable to Pontormo, but it may date a little later than Berenson and Marcucci have placed it. The full, rounded forms, accented by rich chiaroscuro and an emphatic outline, are like those of cat. 12 for the *Visitation*, while the movement of the Venus and the shape of her arm and hand are analogous to cat. 13, also for the *Visitation*. There are also close parallels with the Cappella del Papa frescoes: cf. the Venus and the St. Veronica, especially the faces; cf. the putto and those holding the Medici arms, as well as the sketches for them (cat. 9, 10). To the drawings already noted may be added cat. 14 and cat. 17 of ca. 1515, both of which are virtually identical in the handling of the red chalk to this study.

As Berenson has remarked, the composition of this *Venus and Cupid* group and the types of the two figures are dependent on Andrea's Scalzo *Caritas* (ca. 1513–1514). The putto is close to the one held in the arms of Andrea's figure, while the rounded forms and the dynamic movement of both figures attest to a close community of style between Andrea and Pontormo in these years. A *Caritas* with four figures, also dependent on the Scalzo group, appears in Pontormo's slightly later *Joseph* (II) of ca. 1516, but this drawing does not seem to be related to it. However, it is possible, in view of the subject and the date of this drawing, that it might have been connected with the decorations in honor of Leo X in 1515, a project in which we know Pontormo participated (V/M, VI, 255).

According to Schlegel, who connected this drawing with the Eve in a *bozzetto* wrongly identified as a Pontormo of 1513–1518, Bronzino used this drawing for the *Pygmalion and Galatea* of 1529–1530. However, it was Pontormo himself who reinterpreted this Venus Pudique motive later for the statue of Galatea.

16 · Florence, Uffizi 6719F *recto*: Ca. 1515. Self-portrait study. Bust of a nude looking over his right shoulder. (*Verso*: Undecipherable fragment of a red chalk sketch, not catalogued.) 114 x 71, red chalk. Fig. 23.

Bibliography: Berenson 1903, no. 2202; Clapp 1914, 255; Berenson 1938, no. 2202.

Clapp dated this drawing toward 1516, while Berenson dated it "fairly early" and noted that it was a portrait study. Comparison with the self-portrait in Pontormo's *Adoration of the Magi* of ca. 1522,[15] suggests that this drawing is also a self-portrait. As such, it is the earliest

[15] E. Schaeffer, *Das Florentiner Bildnis* (Munich, 1904), 147, first noted the self-portrait of Pontormo to the far left of the Pitti *Adoration*. This identification was rejected by Clapp 1916, 23–24, but nevertheless has generally been accepted. In this picture as in the later S. Felicita *Deposition*, Pontormo has placed himself as an observer to a sacred event and has altered his features in accord with the diverse styles of these two pictures. The face in the *Deposition* has been cast in a mold of curved, curly-haired transparent beauty, the dazed immobility of the expression reflecting that of the figures who are more intimately involved; while in the *Adoration*, Pontormo has almost caricatured his features in a way quite in keeping with the analytical sharpness of the entire picture.

surviving likeness of Pontormo.[16] The pose, the expression, and the beard are so similar to those of the figure in the *Adoration* that one would be tempted to call this a study for it, were it not for the obviously early style of the drawing and the presence of certain awkwardnesses in the articulation of the forms that are no longer found in Pontormo's drawings after Poggio a Caiano. Clapp compared this study with cat. 77, which is similar in style, but perhaps dates a year or so later. The feathery contours and patchy diagonal shading of this study link it to cat. 9 and 10 for the Cappella del Papa and to other drawings of ca. 1515 such as cat. 15.

[16] The subject of the likenesses of Pontormo by himself and by others has been systematically investigated by Berti in his booklet "Sembianze del Pontormo" (Empoli, 1956). Our list agrees substantially with his, but there are a few additions. The following are portraits of Pontormo by other artists: (1) The head in Bronzino's *Christ in Limbo*, Museo di S. Croce, 1552 (Berti, 7, fig. 4). (2) The head in Allori's *Christ with the Doctors*, SS. Annunziata, 1560 (Berti, 6, fig. 3). (3) The head in Bronzino's *Martyrdom of St. Lawrence*, San Lorenzo, 1567–1569 (Berti, 7, fig. 12). (4) The woodcut in Vasari's second edition of the *Vite*, 1568, VI, 474 (Berti, 6, fig. 8). (5) The painting in the Uffizi, Giovio Collection, anonymous late sixteenth century? (Berti, 6, fig. 2). (6) The painting in the Uffizi similar to the last and, like it, probably derived from the frontispiece in Vasari (Berti, 5, fig. 1). The following are certain or probable self-portraits by Pontormo: (1) Drawing, cat. 16 of ca. 1515. (2) The man to the left in the Pitti *Adoration* of ca. 1522 (Berti, 11, fig. 9). (3) The man who carries the end of the cross in the Certosa *Way to Golgotha* of 1523–1524. (4) Drawing, cat. 253 of ca. 1525. (5) The man to the right in the S. Felicita *Deposition* of 1526–1527 (Berti, 12, fig. 10). (6) Drawing, cat. 277, for the *Deposition* head. (7) Drawing, cat. 306 of ca. 1528–1530. (8) Painting, Contini-Bonacossi Collection, Florence, of ca. 1530–1532? (Berti, 12, fig. 11, as possibly a Naldini of after 1550). (9) Drawing, cat. 331 of ca. 1533–1534 (Berti, 8, fig. 5, as by Bronzino, 1535–1540). Berti, 9, figs. 6–7, added to this list drawings cat. 242–243 as self-portraits of Pontormo, while Tietze 1953, 365–366, fig. 2, published a painting in Detroit as a self-portrait of the artist. However, these last examples are not convincing as likenesses of Pontormo.

17 · Munich, Staatliche Graphische Sammlung 14042 *recto*: Ca. 1515. Study for a *Visitation*. Two draped women standing close together. (*Verso*: Study for a *St. John the Baptist*, cat. 18.) 394 x 263, red chalk. Fig. 21.

Collection: Staatliche Graphische Sammlung, stamp recto (L. 1615); acquired in 1822.

Bibliography: Degenhart 1958, no. 46, pl. 46.

An old inventory (no. 8262) gives an attribution to Andrea del Sarto for this sheet, but it has more recently been catalogued as "sixteenth-century Florentine school." However, it has been recognized as a Pontormo by Degenhart, who suggested a date of ca. 1513–1514 and associated the sheet in style with the *Carro della Zecca*. While there is still some connection with the figure types of the *Carro della Zecca* panels (cf. especially the *Visitation*), this drawing seems decidedly more mature and coherent in style than the one study that we know for the *Carro* (cat. 1), or even those for the S. Ruffillo altar of the same date (cat. 2–5). The full, curving proportions of the Virgin, her bold stance, the form-revealing angular folds of the drapery, and the set of the head bring this figure close to the *St. Veronica* of 1515, a conception in which Pontormo has moved far beyond the timid and derivative figures of the *Carro della Zecca*. Furthermore, the handling of red chalk in this drawing is identical to that of cat. 13 for the *Visitation*, and to cat. 14 and 15 of ca. 1515. It is not known whether this drawing was connected with the preparation for a painting, but it is a somewhat less conventional variant on a theme that Pontormo painted twice in the years 1514–1516 (cf. *Carro della Zecca* and SS. Annunziata).

18 · Munich, Staatliche Graphische Sammlung 14042 *verso*: Ca. 1515. Study for a *St. John the Baptist.* Standing draped figure of a boy with a staff. (*Recto*: Study for a *Visitation*, cat. 17.) 394 x 263, red chalk. Fig. 22.

Like the recto of this sheet, this unpublished study was recognized as Pontormo's by Degenhart. Particularly to be noted in the St. John study on this side of the sheet is the fullness of the forms and the extremely rich chiaroscuro, suggesting a general community of style with the drawings of Andrea del Sarto and his circle. As is characteristic of Pontormo's drawings of ca. 1515, the figure is not precisely articulated with regard to the anatomical structure of the forms, but is generalized according to a piquant and highly individual concept of form. Similar figures are found in Pontormo's small-scale pictures of this date such as *Joseph* (I) (but not in the monumental *Visitation*) and in the putti on the ceiling of the Cappella del Papa, which are very close to this figure in their proportions, their faces and hair, and their tapering limbs with tiny extremities.

1515–1516. STORY OF JOSEPH (I): *Joseph Revealing Himself to His Brothers.* Henfield, Lady Salmond Collection. II. 35 x 142 cm. Fig. 25.

Bibliography: Waagen 1854, 11; Crowe and Cavalcaselle 1914, 202; Clapp 1916, 21–23, 162–164, fig. 26; Fraenckel 1933, 177n24; Berenson 1936, 402; Becherucci 1944, 13, fig. 5a; Wischnitzer 1953, 165–166, fig. 13; *MP* 1956 (Berti), no. 24, figs. 13–15; Freedberg 1961, I, 510–512, II, fig. 643.

Pontormo's pictures from the *Story of Joseph* are mentioned by Vasari (V/M, V, 26, 342–343; VI, 261–263) and by Borghini 1584, 482.[17] Besides Pontormo and Baccio d'Agnolo, who did the furnishings of the room (V/M, V, 26, 352), the artists who contributed to the decoration were: Andrea del Sarto,[18] Bacchiacca,[19] and Gra-

[17] For the relevant passages from Vasari see the following notes, 18, 20, and 21. The first three panels from the Borgherini *Story of Joseph* were formerly in the collection of Lady Desborough, Panshanger. They will be discussed together here and will be called *Story of Joseph* (I), *Story of Joseph* (II), and *Story of Joseph* (III) in this catalogue. For the later picture of the same series see *Story of Joseph* (IV): *Joseph in Egypt* of ca. 1518–1519.

[18] V/M, V, 26–27: "Aveva a punto allora Pier Francesco Borgherini fatto fare a Baccio d'Agnolo di legnami intagliati spalliere, cassoni, sederi, e letto di noce, molto belli, per fornimento d'una camera; onde, perchè corrispondessero le pitture all'eccellenza degli altri lavori, fece in quelli fare una parte delle storie da Andrea in figure non molto grandi, de'fatti di Giuseppo figliuolo di Jacob, a concorrenza d'alcune che n'aveva fatte il Granaccio e Jacopo da Pontormo, che sono molto belle. Andrea dunque si sforzò, con mettere in quel lavoro diligenza e tempo straordinario, di far sì che gli riuscissero più perfette che quelle degli altri sopradetti; il che gli venne fatto benissimo, avendo egli, nella varietà delle cose che accaggiono in quelle storie, mostro quanto egli valesse nell'arte della pittura." Andrea's two pictures, *The Selling of Joseph* and *The Dream of the Pharoah* (Florence, Pitti nos. 87 and 88, each 99 x 135 cm), were bought by Francesco de' Medici from Niccolò di Giovanni Borgherini in 1584. See *MP* 1956 (Baldini), nos. 142, 146, figs. 84–85. According to Freedberg 1961, 498–499, figs. 618–619, 625, these panels were executed with the assistance of Puligo, who was also responsible for another version of the *Selling of Joseph* (Borghese no. 463) that is not part of the Borgherini series but dates ca. 1520. See *MP* 1956 (Baldini), no. 144, fig. 86, where it is attributed to Bacchiacca as part of the *Story of Joseph.*

[19] V/M, V, 342–343, VI, 455: "Nella camera

nacci.[20] According to Vasari (V/M, VI, 263), Salvi Borgherini commissioned the decoration of a room in a house in Borgo SS. Apostoli on the occasion of the marriage of his son Pier Francesco and Margherita Acciaiuoli. In this room were two *cassoni* with scenes from the *Story of Joseph* by Pontormo and on the wall to the left of the entrance was a picture of *Joseph in Egypt* by Pontormo, in which his pupil Bronzino was portrayed sitting on the steps.[21] While the Borgherini marriage took place in 1515,[22] Vasari's discussion of much of the work in the bridal chamber implies a later date, closer to 1518–1519. Furthermore, Bronzino, who was born in 1503, did not come to Pontormo as an apprentice until 1518 at the earliest.[23] Since the *Joseph in Egypt* in which he appears is datable ca. 1518–1519 on the basis of its style as well, we must conclude that the decoration of the bridal chamber was by no means completed in the year of the marriage or even shortly afterward, but extended over a period of

---

di Pier Francesco Borgherini . . . fece il Bachiacca, in compagnia degli altri, molte figurine ne' cassoni e nelle spalliere, che alla maniera sono conosciute, come differenti dall' altre." Bacchiacca's six panels are, as Vasari noted, different in style from the others, Bacchiacca having made little attempt to adapt his individual style to that which had been established for the decoration by Pontormo and Andrea, and to some extent, Granacci. The two long panels in London (National Gallery nos. 1218 and 1219, each 35 x 150 cm), *The Brothers with Gifts and the Brothers Leaving* and *Joseph Receiving his Brothers*, are similar in size to Pontormo's *Joseph* (I) and may also have been part of a *cassone*. The four square panels in Rome (Borghese nos. 425, 427, 440, 442, each 26 x 14 cm) were undoubtedly used also as furniture decoration. All of Bacchiacca's panels probably date ca. 1516–1518. See *MP* 1956 (Baldini), nos. 143, 147, 149, 150, figs. 88–89; Freedberg 1961, 501–502, figs. 629–632.

[20] V/M, V, 342–343: ". . . tutti se ne tornarono a Fiorenza; dove dipinse il Granacci a Pierfrancesco Borgherini, nella sua casa di borgo Santo Apostolo in Fiorenza, in una camera (dove Jacopo da Puntormo, Andrea del Sarto e Francesco Ubertini avevano fatto molte storie della vita di Joseffo) sopra un lettuccio una storia a olio de' fatti del medesimo, in figure piccole fatte con pulitissima diligenza e con vago e bel colorito, ed una prospettiva, dove fece Giuseppo che serve Faraone, che non può essere più bella in tutte le parti." Granacci's two pictures, *The Arrest of Joseph* and *Joseph Presenting Jacob to the Pharoah* (Uffizi 2150, 2152; 99 x 135 cm, 95 x 224 cm) were bought by Francesco de' Medici from the Borgherini family with Andrea's panels in 1584. See *MP* 1956 (Baldini), nos. 145, 151, figs. 87, 90. As Freedberg 1961, 494, figs. 608–609, has indicated, these pictures are highly derivative and must be placed ca. 1517–1518, not at the beginning of the project as Vasari implies in another context (V/M, V, 26).

[21] V/M, VI, 261: "Lavorò anco Jacopo nell' ornamento di legname che già fu magnificamente fatto, come si è detto altra volta, in alcune stanze di Pierfrancesco Borgherini, a concorrenza d'altri maestri; ed in particolare vi dipinse di sua mano in due cassoni alcune storie de'fatti di Joseffo in figure piccole, veramente bellissime. Ma chi vuol veder quanto egli facesse di meglio nella sua vita, per considerare l'ingegno e la virtù di Jacopo nella vivacità delle teste, nel compartimento delle figure, nella varietà dell' attitudini e nella bellezza dell'invenzione, guardi in questa camera di Borgherini, gentiluomo di Firenze, all'entrare della porta nel canto a man manca, un'istoria assai grande pur di figure piccole; nella quale è quando Josef in Egitto, quasi re e principe, riceve Jacob suo padre con tutti i suoi fratelli, e figliuoli di esso Jacob, con amorevolezze incredibili: fra le quali figure ritrasse, a piedi della storia, a sedere sopra certe scale, Bronzino allora fanciullo e suo discepolo, con una sporta; che è una figura viva e bella a maraviglia."

[22] See P. Litta, *Famiglie Celebri Italiane* (Florence, 1844), I, pl. 6. Margherita Acciaiuoli was born July 15, 1495 and married to Piero [Pier Francesco] Borgherini in 1515.

[23] For a discussion of Bronzino's apprenticeship to Pontormo, see Smyth 1949, 207–209, who believed Bronzino came to Pontormo no earlier than 1518 and preferred a slightly later date of 1519–1520.

at least four years. However, the commission and the beginning of the work on the project presumably coincided with the date of the marriage. While Vasari's discussion of Pontormo's pictures gives no clue as to when he might have started to work, his notice on Andrea del Sarto's pictures (V/M, V, 26–27) implies a date of shortly after 1515. Apparently Andrea started his part of the decoration soon after the inception of the project, but after Pontormo and Granacci were already at work. Since some latitude should be allowed for the completion of Baccio d'Agnolo's furnishings for the room, the first pictures might not have been painted until 1516. In any event, if Vasari is correct in saying that Pontormo had already started to work when Andrea was employed, which of Pontormo's panels can have been executed before Andrea began? Pontormo's *Joseph Revealing Himself to his Brothers*, by its shape identifiable as one of his *cassone* pictures, is certainly the earliest in style and must be placed first: 1515–1516.

This first panel was traditionally attributed to Andrea del Sarto, but it was given to Pontormo by Clapp, who dated it 1517–1518, followed by Berenson (1517) and Becherucci. Berti and Freedberg, however, have rightly placed it 1515–1516. This panel has not been unanimously attributed to Pontormo. Fraenckel considered it a workshop picture and Wischnitzer believed that it was painted in Andrea's shop ca. 1513 with Pontormo's assistance. She identified it, as Milanesi (V/M, V, 17n4), had done, with a *Story of Joseph* that Vasari says Andrea painted for Zanobi Girolami. One of her reasons for rejecting it was a detail in its iconography that she believed placed it outside the series.[24] However, there is no cause to remove this panel from the series, and much positive evidence for retaining it. Those who rejected it knew of only one drawing for it (cat. 19) and were able to explain this one away, Wischnitzer allowing that the figure might have been painted by Pontormo and Fraenckel attributing the drawing to Naldini. However, two more drawings (cat. 20 and 21) may be associated with the picture, making it virtually certain that Pontormo was the author of the painting. Furthermore, there is no evident difference in hand between this panel and the other two panels in Lady Salmond's collection, and the color scheme of the three pictures is identical. This panel is more atmospheric in effect than the other, almost airless, pictures, and there is a softening *sfumato* in the modelling that is absent from the other panels. In addition, the more rational spatial construction of this picture has none of the crowding and ambiguity of the space in the two square panels, and the figures are less acutely characterized. However, these elements do not indicate that the picture is by another hand, but establish it more securely as a work of not later than 1515–1516, earlier than the others of the series. This panel parallels the classical style of Pontormo's *Visitation* of late 1514–1516 on a smaller scale and with the necessary adjustments to the special demands of *cassone* decoration. Analogies may also be found in the panels of the *Carro della*

[24] She called *Joseph* (I) "Benjamin Brought to Joseph" (Genesis 43: 16ff.), identifying the child to the far right as Benjamin. There is little reason to call this figure, who has no part in the central action, Benjamin, and the picture is more convincingly titled *Joseph Revealing Himself to His Brothers* (Genesis 45: 1–15). Wischnitzer retitled *Joseph* (II) "Benjamin Accompanying his Brothers to Egypt," finding a discrepancy between the "adolescent" leaving in *Joseph* (II) and the "child" arriving in *Joseph* (I), and concluding that *Joseph* (I) was therefore not by Pontormo. However, *Joseph* (II) illustrates Genesis 37:36 and 39:1, *Joseph Sold to Potiphar*, while the subject *Benjamin Accompanying his Brothers to Egypt* is included in Bacchiacca's London (1218) panel.

Zecca, a slightly earlier work executed in a similar scale. The boy to the far right in *Joseph* (I) may be compared with the putto who supports St. John the Evangelist's book; the niche statue with the *St. John the Baptist*, and the boy walking down the steps with the Christ in the *Baptism*.

Pontormo's *Joseph Sold to Potiphar* was also traditionally attributed to Andrea del Sarto and was first given to Pontormo by Crowe and Cavalcaselle. Goldschmidt and Voss dated it 1520; Gamba 1518–1519; Becherucci 1518; Clapp and Toesca 1517–1518; Berti 1516–1517; Wischnitzer and Freedberg 1516. This second of Pontormo's panels must be placed ca. 1516, directly after the first picture. It is advanced in style over *Joseph* (I) and shares several motives with Andrea del Sarto's first panel, the *Selling of Joseph*: cf. the group of Joseph and two men to the right of Pontormo's composition with the same group in Andrea's; cf. the pose of Andrea's Joseph with that of the figure to the left with his back turned in the Pontormo panel. The common vocabulary of these two works makes it difficult to determine which was executed first, but their interrelationship indicates that they belong close together, preceded in the Joseph Series only by Pontormo's *Joseph* (I).

Pontormo's first two *Story of Joseph* panels are further linked by their references to Ghiberti's *Story of Joseph* relief from the *Porta del Paradiso*.[25] In *Joseph* (I) the grain-carrying figure (also adapted by Pontormo in the contemporary *Visitation*), the kneeling man with his head in his hands, and the circular grainhouse all indicate Pontormo's close study of the relief. In *Joseph* (II) Pontormo's borrowings are more extensive still: the square format of the panel now approximates that of the relief, as does the juxtaposition of the large figures in the foreground with the figures of sharply reduced scale at the upper right (left in the relief). The figures themselves are now more gracefully elongated and some of them are quite closely adapted from Ghiberti, such as the man with his back turned, or the slender figure of Joseph with his straight-hanging garment. Furthermore, the head looking out of the round window in the right distance is surely a reflection of Ghiberti's prophet heads, one of which is just to the upper right of this relief. Although Ghiberti's representation of the subject would have been an easily accessible and reasonably obvious model, it is interesting — considering Pontormo's incipient unclassical tendencies — that he chose at this point to study one of the most important examples of the International Style in Florence.

Pontormo's *The Baker Taken to Execution and the Butler Restored to Office* was, like the first two panels, traditionally attributed to Andrea del Sarto. It was given to Pontormo by Crowe and Cavalcaselle, dated 1520 by Goldschmidt and Voss. Gamba dated it 1518–1519; Becherucci 1518; Clapp 1517–1518; Berenson and Freedberg 1517; Berti and Wischnitzer 1516. A date of 1517 is indicated for this third picture in the series. It approaches the explicitly Mannerist style of the Visdomini altar of 1517–1518 and the *Joseph in Egypt* of 1518–1519, which we have placed last in the series. In this picture Pontormo has turned away from the classically clear spatial order of *Joseph* (I) in a direction already indicated in *Joseph* (II) towards an anticlassical spatial image of arbitrarily arranged groups, separately conceived. Both this change and the shift to a system of continuous narrative in which both the butler and the baker appear twice, link *Joseph* (III) to *Joseph in Egypt*. Finally, in contrast to the studies for *Joseph* (I) and *Joseph* (II), the draw-

[25] Aspects of Pontormo's study of Ghiberti were suggested by S. McKillop, "The Decorative Scheme for the Borgherini Bridal Chamber" (unpub. paper, Dept. of Fine Arts, Harvard Univ., Cambridge, 1958).

ings for this third panel (cat. 25–28) are close to the style of the studies for the Visdomini altar of 1518.

This third panel is apparently contemporary with Andrea's second panel, *The Dream of the Pharaoh*. Andrea's picture must be dated before May 1518, when he left for France, but was probably painted in 1517. It is related to Pontormo's third panel in the same way that Andrea's first picture was related to Pontormo's second panel: the coincidence in motives between the two works (cf. the group on the stairs in both pictures, the man with his arm flung out on the right with the man in the center foreground of the Andrea) is such that it is impossible to be certain which picture was painted first. However, in this instance the exact chronological precedence of one picture over another is less significant than is the conscious community of style achieved by the two painters, in which there is an effort on the part of both (not shared by Bacchiacca or Granacci) to establish a continuity of style between the successive illustrations of the Joseph story.

STUDIES FOR THE STORY OF JOSEPH (I)

19 · Florence, Uffizi 6692F *recto*: Study for the figure on the steps, *Joseph* (I). Draped boy walking down a step to the right, holding a staff in the left hand and looking down to the left. (*Verso*: Study for *Joseph* (II), cat. 23.) 402 x 250, red chalk. Fig. 24.

Bibliography: Berenson 1903, no. 2176; *MPA* 1910, 31; Clapp 1914, 239; Clapp 1916, 23, fig. 25; Fraenckel 1933, 177n24; Berenson 1938, no. 2176; Becherucci 1943, 6, pl. 1; Wischnitzer 1953, 165.

Clapp identified this drawing with the figure walking down the steps in *Joseph* (I), but dated it 1517–1518, followed by Becherucci. In accord with her very early dating of the panel, Wischnitzer placed this drawing ca. 1513 as executed in an early, Sartesque moment. Berenson remarked on the similarity of the draughtsmanship to Naldini's, while Fraenckel actually attributed this study to Pontormo's pupil. While it is true that in his imitative moments Naldini took Pontormo's early drawing style as a point of departure, this sheet is unquestionably authentic. The motive is explicitly that of the figure in the picture, except that the painted figure supports a sack of grain over his shoulders with the left arm, while in the sketch he carries a staff. The style of this drawing suggests a date of not later than 1516, supporting our early dating of the panel itself. It is closely tied to Pontormo's earliest studies, such as cat. 3, for the S. Ruffillo altar, where the weightless, sketchy drapery, and the summary indication of the limbs are points in common. However, here and in cat. 21 for another figure in *Joseph* (I), the movement of the figure is more freely expressed than in the S. Ruffillo drawings, and brings these studies closer to cat. 12 for the *Visitation*.

20 · Florence, Uffizi 6601F *recto*: Studies for Joseph and the kneeling man to the left, *Joseph* (I). Nude seated on three steps in profile right with his left arm raised; below, the torso restudied; sideways on the sheet, kneeling nude; in reverse direction on the sheet, two nude busts and a head. (*Verso*: Study for the Dublin predella, cat. 71.) 390 x 264, black chalk, sketches sideways and in reverse in red chalk; W: Latin Cross (B. 5641). Fig. 26.

Bibliography: Berenson 1903, no. 2100; Clapp 1914, 178; Fraenckel 1933, 166, 168–169; Berenson 1938, no. 2100.

Berenson thought that this sheet was "fairly early" and that the nudes were studies for cat. A42 (probably Naldini). Fraenckel noted a connection in motive with the figure on the steps in the background of Andrea del Sarto's S. Gallo *Annunciation* (ca. 1512), a figure that she attributed to the young Pontormo. However, she also seemed to connect it with a group of early Pontormo drawings (cat. 21, 76, 77, 78, and 83) that she dated ca. 1515. Clapp dated the sheet 1516–1518.

It has not been noted that the black chalk nudes are studies for the seated figure of Joseph in *Joseph* (I). The upper study is very close to the painted figure except that in the painting his head is in profile and both legs are on the second step of the throne. Across the sheet in red chalk is a preliminary study for the kneeling man to the left of the seated Joseph, a figure who is studied more elaborately on cat. 21. The two busts may be ideas for the head of the boy who looks out of the picture at the extreme left. More than in the other studies for this panel and in those for the *Visitation*, this drawing announces the shift in Pontormo's drawing style that would take place during the next two years, culminating in the drawings for the Visdomini altar and the Dublin predella of 1517–1518. At this time Pontormo's draughtsmanship shifted from a manner dependent for its effect on bold, curving contours and spotty, schematic diagonal shading, to a manner in which variations of surface are sharply observed and elaborated, often in the form of emphatic patterning of muscles, and often at the expense of the outline.

21 · Florence, Uffizi 6542F *verso*: Study for the kneeling man to the left, *Joseph* (I). Nude kneeling turned to the right with his hands clasped. (*Recto*: Study for the *Visitation*, cat. 12.) 359 x 264, red chalk. Fig. 27.

Bibliography: Berenson 1903, no. 2045; Clapp 1911, 5–6; Clapp 1914, 142–143; Clapp 1916, 23, fig. 28; Fraenckel 1933, 166, 169; Berenson 1938, no. 2045; *MP* 1956 (Marcucci), no. 91, fig. 125b; Berenson 1961, no. 2045, fig. 894.

As Clapp has noted, this is a study for the kneeling figure to the far left of *Joseph* (I). Clapp dated it 1518 and Marcucci placed it 1514–1515, also as a study for the figure in the first Borgherini panel. This is an action study from the nude for the figure whose pose was first lightly sketched on cat. 20. There are close parallels between this study and works securely datable 1515. If doubt remains as to the early dating of *Joseph* (I), this drawing should be compared with its recto, a study for the *Visitation* of late 1514–1516. In both red chalk nude studies there is the same vigorous movement suggested by the emphasized curving outlines, and the same somewhat schematic modelling. Precisely this style occurs in painting in 1515 in the angels who kneel to either side of the St. Veronica. Indeed, the proportions and action of the angel to the left are so close to those of this figure that Clapp at first (1911) identified this drawing as a study for the angel, an association that was repeated by Fraenckel.

Ca. 1516. STORY OF JOSEPH (II): *Joseph Sold to Potiphar*. Henfield, Lady Salmond Collection. II. Panel, 58 x 50 cm. Fig. 28.

Bibliography: Waagen 1854, 12; Goldschmidt 1911, 5, 30; Crowe and Cavalcaselle 1914, 202; Clapp 1916, 21–23, 165–166, fig. 30; Voss 1920, 166; Gamba 1921, 7, fig. 12; Venturi 1932, 116, fig. 63; Berenson 1936, 402; Toesca 1943, 10, fig. 5; Becherucci 1944, 13, fig. 7; Wischnitzer 1953, 162–163, fig. 9; *MP* 1956 (Berti), no. 26, fig. 17; Freedberg 1961, I, 512–513, II, fig. 644.

See discussion under *Story of Joseph* (I).

STUDIES FOR THE STORY OF JOSEPH (II)

22 · Florence, Uffizi 6556F *recto*: Study for the man on the steps, *Joseph* (II). Draped figure seen from the waist down stepping down to the left. (*Verso*: Study for the S. Ruffillo altar, cat. 5.) 337 x 240, black chalk; lunette and circle marked out in red chalk. Fig. 30.

Bibliography: Berenson 1903, no. 2057; Clapp 1911, 7; Clapp 1914, 151; Clapp 1916, 23, fig. 31; Berenson 1938, no. 2057.

Berenson connected this study with the woman with the basket on her head in the *Visitation*, considering that she was originally intended to walk in from the right. Clapp first associated it with another figure in the *Visitation*, the saint to the extreme right, but later (1916) identified it as a study for the small figure in the background of *Joseph* (II). The action, direction of the movement, and fall of the draperies are identical to this figure, and there is no connection at all with the *Visitation* fresco. In this drapery study we find the same rather dry and sketchy style that was evident in Pontormo's earliest drapery studies, cat. 3 and cat. 19. However, here the weightlessness of the figure and the brittle fragmentation of the drapery folds approximates the diminished sense of plastic form and the smaller rhythmic sequences of the *Joseph* (II) panel.

23 · Florence, Uffizi 6692F *verso*: Study for the figure in a cloak behind the wall, *Joseph* (II). Standing draped man looking over his right shoulder. (*Recto*: Study for *Joseph* (I), cat. 19.) 402 x 250, red chalk. Fig. 31.

Bibliography: Berenson 1903, no. 2176; Clapp 1914, 239; Clapp 1916, 23, fig. 32; Berenson 1938, no. 2176.

Clapp connected this drawing with the figure in the background of *Joseph* (II) and dated it 1517–1518. The style of this study is close to that of cat. 22, a drawing for another of the little figures in the upper right corner of the picture that is also the verso of a slightly earlier study. Although this drawing is bolder in conception than cat. 22, both are still basically in the manner of the recto of this sheet, for *Joseph* (I), and cat. 3, for the S. Ruffillo altar, and thus cannot logically be placed later than 1516. Both Berenson and Clapp have remarked on the similarity to Naldini's style in this group of studies of draped figures. It is, of course, Pontormo's pupil who found in his master's early drawings a point of departure for his own chalk drawing style.

24 · Paris, Ecole des Beaux-Arts 3337 *recto*: Study for the figure in the background walking to the left, *Joseph* (II). Partially draped man walking down a step to the left with his right arm extended; sideways on the sheet, seated nude boy turned to the right. (*Verso*: Studies for the Visdomini altar, cat. 72.) 265 x 395, red chalk; inscribed in ink: *Jacopo d. Pontormo . . . voir au dos . . . Collection Cornu.* Fig. 29.

Collection: Cornu; Ecole des Beaux-Arts, stamp recto (L. 803).

Bibliography: Lavallée 1935, 30 (as the verso); Berenson 1938, no. 2336A; *MP* 1956 (Marcucci), no. 102, fig. 137 (as 5337 verso); *Paris Exhib.* 1958, no. 34.

Berenson called this sheet an early work connected with the *Story of Joseph* or the Visdomini altar. Marcucci, however, has rightly noted that the man walking is a study for a small figure in the right background of *Joseph* (II), dating it 1515–1516. Thus, the three studies that have survived for this second panel in the series are for the figures who stand on three sides of the *Caritas* statue in the right distance, figures who are sharply reduced in scale from the main actors of the story in the foreground. However, in its style, this sketch is a little different from the drawings for the other two figures, cat. 22 and 23. Pontormo's use of a heavy, repeated outline informs this figure with a more vigorous physical energy and forward movement than was evident in the gracefully restrained step of the figure in cat. 22. In this respect, this figure approaches in style such drawings of ca. 1517 as cat. 25 for *Joseph* (III) and even more cat. 71, for the *St. Francis* of the Dublin predella. The seated nude is not specifically associable with a pictorial motive, but it is close in type to the kneeling nude on the verso, a study for the *St. Francis* of the Dublin predella, and may have been connected with Pontormo's preparation for that figure.

Ca. 1517. STORY OF JOSEPH (III): *The Baker Taken to Execution and the Butler Restored to Office*. Henfield, Lady Salmond Collection. II. Panel, 58 x 50 cm. Fig. 32.

Bibliography: Waagen 1854, 12; Goldschmidt 1911, 5, 30; Crowe and Cavalcaselle 1914, 202; Clapp 1916, 21–23, 165–166, fig. 27; Voss 1920, 166; Gamba 1921, 7, fig. 11; Venturi 1932, 116, fig. 62; Berenson 1936, 402; Becherucci 1944, 13, fig. 6; Wischnitzer 1953, 163–165, fig. 11; *MP* 1956 (Berti), no. 27, fig. 16; Freedberg 1961, I, 513–516, II, fig. 645.

See discussion under *Story of Joseph* (I).

STUDIES FOR THE
STORY OF JOSEPH (III)

25 · Lille, Musée des Beaux-Arts 162 *recto*: Studies for the uppermost figure on the stairs, *Joseph* (III). Nude walking to the left studied in three successive poses. (*Verso*: Study for the Visdomini altar, cat. 45.) 410 x 270, red chalk. Fig. 34.

Bibliography: Gonse 1877, 555 (as no. 1429); Pluchart 1889, 36; Delacre 1931, 139, illustrated; Berenson 1938, no. 2252B; Bacou 1957, 62, illustrated p. 26.

This study was attributed to Ammanati by Gonse, but was already listed by Pluchart as Pontormo. Bacou dated it 1516–1520. An exact copy after this drawing (cat. A33) was called "early" by Berenson and dated 1516–1520 by Clapp, but neither the copy nor the original has been connected with *Joseph* (III). In this powerful series of studies for the movement of the figure on the stairs, the final pose is approached through three overlapping trial poses, the third being close to cat. 26, the final nude study for the figure. New directions in Pontormo's style that were announced in earlier *Story of Joseph* studies here become explicit. Here and in cat. 24 for *Joseph* (II) we find the first real indication of the energetic, movemented forms of Pontormo's later drawings. In this drawing and in cat. 26 the elaborate articulation of muscles through a rich and varied chiaroscuro that was hinted earlier in cat. 20 contrasts with the emphatic curving contours and schematic modelling of Pontormo's previous drawings. The style of this study and cat. 26 is precisely that of many of Pontormo's studies of 1517–1518 for the Visdomini altar and predella, while there is a close connection in motive between the central figure in this drawing and the studies for the putto on the right in the altar (cf. especially cat. 60). These connections with studies for works of 1517–1518 make more secure our dating of *Joseph* (III) as late as 1517.

26 · Florence, Uffizi 6690F *recto*: Study

for the uppermost figure on the stairs, *Joseph* (III). Nude walking down steps to the left leaning on a staff. (*Verso*: Study for the Dublin *Pietà*, cat. 66.) 396 x 253, red chalk. Fig. 35.

Bibliography: Berenson 1903, no. 2175; *MPA* 1910, 32; Clapp 1911, 14; Clapp 1914, 236–237; Clapp 1916, 23, fig. 29; Fraenckel 1933, 172–173; Berenson 1938, no. 2175.

Clapp identified the motive in *Joseph* (III) and dated this study 1518–1519, comparing it with cat. 8, a drawing of ca. 1514. Fraenckel dated it 1518 as for the figure in the picture, comparing it was cat. 280, a drawing of the late twenties. Berenson did not connect this study with *Joseph* (III), but thought it was done for an *Adoration of the Shepherds*, comparing it rightly with a very similar drawing of the same date, cat. 83. This drawing is the definitive study for the figure whose pose is seen in flux in cat. 25. Like cat. 25, it has close parallels among the studies of ca. 1517–1518 for the Dublin predella, such as its own verso and cat. 63, both for the Dead Christ.

27 · Rome, GNS F.C. 123: Study for the Pharaoh's wife, *Joseph* (III). Page from a sketchbook: Draped bust of a woman, the head inclined to the left, the lightly indicated right arm raised. 217 x 155, red chalk heightened with white on pink prepared paper; laid down; W: Cross with two circles and three triangles.

Collection: Corsini; R. Accademia dei Lincei, stamp verso (L. 1683).

Bibliography: Clapp 1914, 341; Clapp 1916, 42; Berenson 1938, no. 2362A; *MP* 1956 (Marcucci), no. 120, fig. 152b.

This drawing is a rapid sketch for the bust of the Pharaoh's wife, whose head is studied in portraitlike detail on cat. 28. Clapp thought this drawing was for the woman in the left background of the Certosa *Pietà*, while Marcucci connected it with the uppermost figure in the S. Felicita *Deposition* and dated it ca. 1525. The *Deposition* figure is similar in pose, but not in the sharp, angular drapery, and this drawing bears little resemblance to the other drapery studies for the picture. The figure in the Certosa *Pietà* is also similar in pose, but Clapp mistook the angular handling of drapery in this drawing as a sign of a date in the Certosa period. Actually, this drapery is to be associated with Pontormo's primary rather than his later Dürer impressions. Cat. 31 and 32, two studies for the head of the Visdomini Madonna, are close in style to this drawing, and aid in pinpointing Pontormo's earliest susceptibility to the Northern style (not merely Northern motives) in about 1517.

This drawing is a page from the Corsini Sketchbook, most of which consists of sketches not specifically associable with pictorial motives (cf. cat. 105–123). However, this drawing, those of the same date for the Visdomini altar (cat. 29, 41, 42, 46, 47, 53, 54, 55, 56, 59), that for *Joseph in Egypt* (cat. 92), and those for Poggio a Caiano (cat. 125–129) have been discussed separately from the sketchbook with the paintings for which they are preparatory. The association of this study with a picture datable as early as 1517 may indicate the date at which the sketchbook was begun.

28 · Florence, Uffizi 451F: Study for the Pharaoh's wife, *Joseph* (III). Bust-length portrait study of an old woman with a mantle over her head and shoulders. 405 x 295, black chalk heightened with white on brown prepared paper; W: Latin Cross (B. 5641); inscribed *Franco Rosi 220*. Fig. 33.

Bibliography: Ferri 1890, 116; Berenson 1903, no. 2008; *MPA* 1910, 23; Gamba 1912, no. 13, pl. 13; Clapp 1914, 97–98; *Paris Exhib.* 1935, no. 650; Berenson 1938, 319, no. 1974B, fig. 988; *MDF* 1939, 25;

MC 1940, 46; Becherucci 1943, 9, pl. 14; Becherucci 1944, 17, fig. 24; *MF* 1952, 63; *MDM* 1954 (Marcucci), no. 40, fig. 9; *EMI* 1954, no. 59, fig. 11.

Clapp dated this portrait study a little before 1532. Gamba considered it to be for one of the women in the Certosa frescoes or for the St. Anne of the Louvre altar (ca. 1529), which he dated ca. 1524. Becherucci identified the drawing as a study for one of the mourning women in the Certosa *Pietà*. Marcucci thought it was a portrait study of 1518–1522 that Pontormo referred to later in his paintings, noting that this type of old woman occurs in the Certosa *Pietà*, the Louvre altar, the Uffizi *Birthplate*, and the Pitti *Martyrdom*. While the connection with the latter picture is not evident, it is certainly true that Pontormo repeated this and other types frequently in the twenties. However, it has not been noted that this woman first appears as the Pharaoh's wife in *Joseph* (III) of ca. 1517. The head, which is very close to the head in the painting except for the tilt to the left, is perceived with the same sense of actuality — emphasized so as to be almost in the realm of caricature — that we find in the *Cosimo il Vecchio* and the portrait study of 1518–1519 for its pendant (cat. 89). The approach to portraiture in this drawing is quite different from the easier, more fluid naturalism of Pontormo's later study of an old man's head for Poggio a Caiano (cat. 138); and it has no connection with his portrait drawings of the twenties.

The draughtsmanship clearly indicates a date of ca. 1517 for this study rather than any later moment. The brittle, angular handling of the flattened drapery folds is similar to that of other drapery studies for the *Story of Joseph* (II) (cat. 22 and 23), while the high, round, Germanic headdress is the same as in the quick sketch for the pose of the figure (cat. 27). Furthermore, the years 1517–1518 mark the beginning of an experimental shift in Pontormo's technique, of which this appears to be the first example. While drawings in red chalk continue in the years of the Visdomini altar, there is a change from Pontormo's usual medium (almost all the drawings of 1514–1517 are in red chalk) to black chalk, usually heightened with white, often on brown paper (cf. cat. 35, 39, 44, 45, 48, 49, 50, 51, 58, 61). Many other drawings of this period are in black and red chalk together and, as was noted in discussing the other study for this head, this is the period when richly coloristic drawings in black or red chalk on pink prepared paper also begin to appear.

1517?–1518. VISDOMINI ALTAR: *Madonna and Child with Sts. Joseph, John the Evangelist, Francis, James, and John the Baptist.* Florence, S. Michele Visdomini. I. Paper glued on panel, 218 x 189 cm. Dated M·D·xviii on the Evangelist's book. Fig. 36.

Bibliography: Goldschmidt 1911, 5, 45; Clapp 1916, 18–20, 125–128, fig. 13; Voss 1920, 165, fig. 47 (Doetsch copy); Friedlaender 1925, 60–63, fig. 2; Venturi 1932, 100, fig. 46; Berenson 1936, 401; *MC* 1940, 39–40; Toesca 1943, 9, fig. 4; Becherucci 1944, 14, fig. 10; Nicco Fasola 1947, 28–29, fig. 2; Paatz 1952/55, IV, 198; *MP* 1956 (Berti), no. 29, fig. 21; Marcucci 1956, 8–10, fig. 7; Freedberg 1961, I, 517–523, II, fig. 646.

The Visdomini altar is described by Vasari (V/M, VI, 258) and is mentioned by Borghini 1584, 481–482; Bocchi 1591, 201; and Del Migliore 1684, 366. According to Vasari, it was commissioned by Francesco Pucci (d. 1518) for his family chapel in S. Michele Visdomini. Richa

(1754/62, VII, 23), noted that the chapel was the second on the right side of the church, where the picture is to be found today. The suggestion, made by Goldschmidt and Voss, that the picture formerly in the Doetsch collection is the original and that the altar in the church is a copy has been satisfactorily discredited by Clapp.[26]

Since Pontormo's monumental works of 1514–1516 had all been in fresco, this altarpiece is his first large-scale painting in oil. It is also his first major essay in a now explicitly Mannerist style, a style that is all the more striking in its novelty because of its simultaneous dependence upon and independence from the classical Florentine *Sacra Conversazione* as it had been developed by Fra Bartolommeo in the previous decade. In Pontormo's own paintings, the new style of the Visdomini altar had been anticipated in certain respects by the *cassone* pictures of 1516–1517. The preparation for the large altarpiece probably followed closely, or may even have overlapped that of *Joseph* (III) of ca. 1517, whose preparatory studies (cat. 25–28) are closely linked in style to many of those for the altar and its projected predella (cat. 29–72). However, as the date indicates, the altar was completed sometime during the following year.

STUDIES FOR THE VISDOMINI ALTAR

29 · Rome, GNS F.C. 147 *recto*: Compositional study for the Visdomini altar. Page from a sketchbook: The Madonna is seated to the left; below her, St. Joseph holds the Christ Child; to the right, St. John the Evangelist seated turned to the right; above him, St. Francis kneeling to the left and looking at the Holy Family with his right hand held up; to the far right, St. James studied twice; above in the center, a flying putto. (*Verso*: Nude studies, cat. 120.) 218 x 160, black chalk heightened with white on pink prepared paper; W: Cross with two circles and three triangles. Fig. 37.

Bibliography: Berenson 1903, no. 2356; Rusconi 1907, 271, illustrated; Clapp 1911, 5; Clapp 1914, 335; Clapp 1916, 127; Berenson 1938, no. 2337B; *EMI* 1954 (Bianchi), no. 53; *MP* 1956 (Marcucci), no. 92, fig. 127a; Schlegel 1961, 34.

Although Berenson had given this drawing to Pontormo, dating it ca. 1530, it was attributed by Rusconi to Filippino Lippi. Clapp restored it to Pontormo with a date of 1515–1518, suggesting that it might have been a first idea for the Visdomini altar, but noting that the pose of the Madonna and Child was identical to the group in the S. Ruffillo altar. (However, the Child in this drawing is held by St. Joseph and the Madonna is seated, not standing.) Both Bianchi and Marcucci have preferred to connect it with the S. Ruffillo fresco, Bianchi dating it 1514–1516. Marcucci dated it 1514, comparing it in style with the large red chalk study for the St. Zachary (cat. 3), a drawing whose style is not notably close to the complex draughtsmanship of this evidently later drawing.

Clapp's tentative suggestion, which has not met with any approval, is certainly the right association for this drawing. It is of great interest to find in this study some indication of the genesis of the Visdomini altar, a painting whose compositional innovations otherwise seem to appear out of a vacuum. While the exact relation of the Madonna and the four saints of the altar is still undecided here and the St. John the Baptist has not yet appeared (or is obscured in the *pentimenti* of this sketch), several of the major motives of the composition have been established: the group with the Madonna seated above and the St. Joseph below holding the Child; the

[26] See Clapp 1916, 126–127, 244. The copy of the Visdomini altar from the Doetsch Collection, Brussels (canvas, 86 x 73 ½ in.) was sold at Christie's on June 22, 1895, no. 107.

seated St. John the Evangelist (further to the right in the drawing); the St. Francis and the St. James (studied twice) on the right side of the composition. In the altar Pontormo reverted to a more ostensibly central composition, replacing the flying angel with the putti who hold back the curtains and moving the Evangelist to the left side of the picture so that there are two saints on either side of the Madonna and the children. However, the basic aspects of Pontormo's invention — the angular zig-zags of the figures, the dislocating shift of the major accent of the composition to the left, and the piling up of energies vertically toward the Madonna rather than around her in space, are all present in this preliminary idea. Most of the detail studies for the figures in the picture refer more explicitly to the final version of the composition, but in cat. 30 for the Madonna and in cat. 45 for the Evangelist, we find vestiges of this original design.

While the Visdomini altar in its final painted form refers in its composition and in its chiaroscuro to the altars of Fra Bartolommeo, such as the 1512 *Marriage of St. Catherine*, it is significant to discover in this drawing that the specific source for the major motive of the composition was Raphael's *Madonna dell' Impannata*, which had been in Florence since 1514 (V/M, IV, 351) and was possibly already known to Pontormo in 1515–1516 (cf. the SS. Annunziata *Visitation*). In the painting the close derivation of the Madonna and Child and St. Joseph from Raphael's composition is masked by the submergence of the diagonal grouping of these three figures into the more symmetrical arrangement of the whole composition. However, in this drawing the diagonal motive is more prominent, occupying the entire left side of the composition. Furthermore, in the painting and possibly in cat. 72 but not yet in this drawing, the diagonal juxtaposition of the Christ and the St. John the Baptist, and even the general notion of their poses, is suggestive of the two children in the *Impannata*. Even the specific motive of the Christ, who turns smiling away from the Virgin, apparently had its origin in Raphael's picture. However, comparing Pontormo's study for this head (cat. 36) with Raphael's Child, we find that Pontormo has individualized the form and externalized the emotions of Raphael's restrained Child, transforming quiet pleasure into a mood of ecstatic unconstraint.

Aside from its association with the Visdomini altar, the style of this study is of considerable interest. There is a connection with Fra Bartolommeo's drawings that aids in placing this study later than has generally been thought. Before 1517–1518 Pontormo's drawings were almost invariably large-scale red chalk studies on white paper. In this example and in other studies of 1517–1521 from the Corsini Sketchbook (cf. cat. 105–123 as well as the studies for the *Story of Joseph* and for the Visdomini altar), the sheet is half the usual size, prepared with pink, and the drawing is in black chalk. Fra Bartolommeo had been experimenting in about 1516 with precisely this combination of media in small drawings[27] whose vitality and spontaneity are not far removed from the manner of this drawing; although Fra Bartolommeo's compositions, however movemented and even explosive, are always less fragmented and dislocated than Pontormo's drawings. Since there is no other precedent in Pontormo's circle for this type of drawing, it may be concluded that Pontormo was influenced from about 1517 by the latest drawings of the recently dead master.

This study is also important as one of the two surviving compositional studies

[27] Cf., for example, the compositional study for an *Assumption of the Virgin* (Albertina S.R. 115; Berenson 1938, no. 510) and two studies for the same subject in Munich (nos. 2158 and 2159; Berenson 1938, nos. 456–457).

by Pontormo from before 1520. This drawing and cat. 14 of ca. 1515 are very similar to later compositional studies by Andrea del Sarto [28] in their very small scale, the marking-out of the format of the picture, and the summary, angular outline indications of the figures. No compositional studies by Andrea himself survive from the period between about 1515 and 1520, but on the basis of these similarities, we may conclude that this sort of compositional *pensiero* was probably common to both draughtsmen in these years.

30 · Florence, Uffizi 8976S *verso*: Studies for the Madonna, Visdomini altar. Seated nude boy leaning to the left; above, the figure lightly restudied cut off at the shoulders. (*Recto*: Putto study, cat. 84.) 335 x 195, red and black chalk. Fig. 39.

Bibliography: Santarelli 1870, 608; Di Pietro 1912, 86, fig. 8; Clapp 1914, 283; Clapp 1916, 32; Berenson 1938, no. 2248C; *MP* 1956 (Marcucci), no. 103, fig. 138b.

This drawing was attributed to Correggio in Santarelli's catalogue, but it was recognized as a Pontormo by Di Pietro, who connected it with cat. 150 for Poggio a Caiano, which he considered to be for a figure below on the wall leaning against the window. Clapp and Marcucci also believed that it was a discarded idea for the putto on the wall to the right of the window. A series of studies for this figure (cat. 157–159) would seem to exclude this association, while cat. 150 is not for this figure but for the putto above the window on the right.

Not only are the connections in motive with the Poggio a Caiano putti very tenuous, but the style of this drawing has no relation to that of Pontormo's studies for the lunette putti (cat. 150–160). The mixture of red and black chalk, the heavily accented yet unclear outline with its numerous *pentimenti*, and the schematic accents of the facial features can be found in studies for the Visdomini altar such as cat. 39, 41, and 61. If this drawing is compared to the compositional sketch for the altar (cat. 29), it is evident that these are studies for the seated Madonna, the lower study being close to the figure in cat. 29, the upper an alternate idea. In the painting the strong projection of the legs is suppressed, since they are turned to the right parallel to the picture plane, and the contrapposto of the figure with the left arm pulled across the body is discarded in favor of a more erect posture with the pointing right hand, by which the Virgin indicates the direction of the high altar, the external focal point toward which many of the figures in the painting turn.

31 · Florence, Uffizi 6551F *verso*: Study for the Madonna, Visdomini altar. Draped head. (*Recto*: Study for the Visdomini altar, cat. 58.) 249 x 182, red chalk. Fig. 38.

Bibliography: Berenson 1903, no. 2053; Clapp 1914, 148; Clapp 1916, fig. 17; Berenson 1938, no. 2053.

Berenson identified this study with the Visdomini Madonna. It is a study for her draped head, probably preliminary to cat. 32, where the folds are worked out in greater detail. The face in this drawing is one of the first examples of an abstracted facial type with very rounded, flattened forms that appears in Pontormo's drawings ca. 1518–1519 (cf. cat. 56 and 96), but which is not evident in the paintings until the twenties.

32 · Florence, Uffizi 6520F *verso*: Study for the Madonna, Visdomini altar. Draped head. (*Recto*: Studies for the Visdomini altar, cat. 33.) 265 x 341, red chalk; in-

[28] Cf. the study for the Pitti *Deposition* of 1524 (Florence, Horne Foundation 5543) or the drawing for the *Madonna del Sacco* of 1525 (British Museum 1912–12–14–2; Berenson 1938, no. 140).

scribed in ink in a seventeenth-century (?) hand: *Jacopo di Pontorno.*

Bibliography: Berenson 1903, no. 2025; Clapp 1914, 129; Berenson 1938, no. 2025. (Photo G.)

Clapp connected this draped head with the Visdomini Madonna, dating it 1517–1519. This type of complicated Madonna's headdress does not appear in Pontormo's paintings until after 1521 (cf. the Hermitage *Holy Family*), although a similar headdress occurs on a small scale in the Pharaoh's wife in *Joseph* (III) of ca. 1517. In Pontormo's paintings of the Certosa period, these high, rounded, and folded headdresses are generally considered as a sign of the German influence in Pontormo's works of the early twenties. However, this study and cat. 27 for the figure in *Joseph* (III) indicates that as early as 1517 Pontormo was aware of Dürer's tightly twisted drapery patterns, such as he could have seen in figures like the Magdalen of the *Entombment* (*Large Passion*, Bar. 13, ca. 1498). However, at this early date these draperies are not so unequivocally Düreresque as in the Certosa period. Significantly, this headdress does not survive in the altarpiece, but is replaced by a more conventional heavy mantle.

33 · Florence, Uffizi 6520F *recto*: Studies for the Christ, Visdomini altar. Seated putto leaning and pointing to the right studied three times. (*Verso*: Studies for the Visdomini altar, cat. 32.) 265 x 341, red chalk. Fig. 42.

Bibliography: Jacobsen 1898, 281; Berenson 1903, no. 2025; *MPA* 1910, 35; Clapp 1914, 128–129; Berenson 1938, 309, no. 2025; *Brussels Exhib.* 1954, no. 117.

Jacobsen identified these studies as for the Christ in the Visdomini altar. In this sheet of experimental poses the exact position of the figure has not yet been established, but the head of the putto on the right anticipates the pose and expression of the detail study for the head of the Christ, cat. 36. In this drawing the center sketch is especially close to the earliest surviving idea for the Christ and the St. John the Baptist (cat. 72), a sheet that also contains a study for the predella. Cat. 72 shows that Pontormo originally conceived the Christ and the St. John as embracing. The sequence of three studies on this sheet may be seen as a stage between the discarding of the embracing motive and the evolution of the self-sufficient pose of the figure in cat. 34 (identical in style to this sheet), cat. 35, and in the painting.

34 · Florence, Uffizi 6554F *recto*: Study for the Christ, Visdomini altar. Seated putto pointing to the right. (*Verso*: Nude study, cat. 79.) 289 x 205, red and black chalk. Fig. 40.

Bibliography: Ferri 1890, 118; Jacobsen 1898, 281; Berenson 1903, no. 1994; *MPA* 1910, 35; Di Pietro 1912, 80–81, fig. 3; Clapp 1914, 149–150; Berenson 1938, 309, no. 2055A, fig. 944; *MP* 1956 (Marcucci), no. 99, fig. 133a.

Jacobsen, Berenson, Di Pietro, and Clapp have all associated this drawing with the St. John the Baptist of the Visdomini altar, Clapp dating it 1517–1519. Marcucci did not connect it with the altar, but dated it 1518–1519 as approaching the style of the studies for Poggio a Caiano. She also pointed out the similarity between this figure and the Christ of the Varramista *Madonna and Child with St. John*, which she considered to be a Pontormo of 1518–1519.[29]

[29] Panel, 100 x 65 cm. This picture has generally been considered to date from the period of the Visdomini altar. See Clapp 1916, 128; Becherucci 1944, 14; Gamba 1956, 9, fig. 6; Sanminiatelli 1956, 242, fig. 30; *MP* 1956 (Berti), no. 28, fig. 19. In this pastiche the Christ and the head of the St. John are certainly derived from the children of the Visdomini altar and the pose of the

This study is for the Christ of the Visdomini altar, directly following the sketch to the left of cat. 33, which is identical to this drawing except for the pose of the left leg. Jacobsen considered this study to be related to the Sistine Ceiling Ignudi. However, its source is an earlier work by Michelangelo: the *Cascina* cartoon, a work that Pontormo studied closely in these years and from which he also derived the pose of the Visdomini St. John the Baptist.[30] The pose of this child, except for the head, is taken from the seated figure in the center foreground of Michelangelo's composition.

35 · Florence, Uffizi 6744F *verso*: Study for the Christ, Visdomini altar. Putto seated with his legs apart and pointing to the right. (*Recto*: Study for the Visdomini altar, cat. 48.) 367 x 253, black chalk heightened with white. Fig. 41.

Bibliography: Ferri 1890, 118 (as 6644 verso); Berenson 1903, no. 2004; Clapp 1914, 273–274; Clapp 1916, fig. 19; Berenson 1938, no. 2225A; Schlegel 1961, 33.

Ferri listed this drawing as for the Christ, Clapp as for the Christ or the St. John the Baptist, Berenson as for the St. John. This is the last of the three studies for the pose of the Christ Child, virtually identical in pose to cat. 34, except that instead of sitting independently, the Child is now conceived in relation to the rest of the composition. He is shown as if seated on the knees of St. Joseph and his head is now turned sharply to the left, but his half-standing posture in the picture with the left leg almost straight has not yet been worked out. Pontormo's concern with the light and shade patterns of the painting is evident in the shading of much of the right side of the figure, indicating that he planned the Child to be illuminated sharply from the left. The draughtsmanship of this study is identical to that of several other drawings for figures in the altar: cat. 39 for the St. John, cat. 48 for the St. Francis, cat. 51 for the St. James, and cat. 61 for the putto on the right. These drawings are among Pontormo's first experiments in black chalk heightened with white, a combination of chalks that are manipulated to create strong contrasts in chiaroscuro analogous to those of the painting, although not, in these preliminary studies, as refined. These studies are a departure from the sensitive and assured red chalk style of most of Pontormo's drawings of this date, such as those for the Visdomini predella (cat. 62–72), and their experimental nature is evident in the numerous *pentimenti*, the bulky and sometimes awkward forms, and the absence of a consistent system of modelling.

36 · Florence, Uffizi 654E *recto*: Study for the Christ, Visdomini altar. Head of a laughing child looking to the left. (*Verso*: Drapery study, cat. 73.) 215 x 168, black chalk. Fig. 43.

Christ is similar to that drawn in cat. 34, but the bland and conventional figure of the Madonna is quite unrelated to Pontormo's style in 1518.

[30] Michelangelo's *Battle of the Cascina* of 1504 was in the Sala del Papa at S.M. Novella from about 1512, but was taken to the Palazzo Medici during the illness of Giuliano de' Medici (August 1515–March 1516). Here it was copied by many artists, among whom Vasari mentions Pontormo, and eventually divided into pieces that became scattered. See V/M, VI, 137–138; VII, 161; and C. Tolnay, *Michelangelo* I (Princeton, 1943), 209–219, figs. 232–235, 274–275, on the *Cascina* cartoon and its early history. Considering the availability of the *Cascina* cartoon in its entirety as late as 1516, possibly in fragments after that, it is not surprising that its influence is found in Pontormo's drawings of ca. 1517–1518. Clapp 1911, 20, brought together a group of studies that he considered definitely derived from the cartoon (cat. 77, 78, 80, 81, 166, 183). In this catalogue the following drawings are cited as notably influenced by cartoon motives: cat. 34, 39, 74, 80, 166, 183.

Bibliography: Ferri 1881, 39; Ferri 1890, 117; Jacobsen 1898, 281; Berenson 1903, no. 1985; *MPA* 1910, 34; Gamba 1912, no. 5, pl. 5; Clapp 1914, 109; Clapp 1916, fig. 20; Berenson 1938, no. 1959D; *Paris Exhib.* 1950, no. 423; Schlegel 1961, 33, fig. 17.

This final study for the head of the Christ Child was traditionally called Andrea del Sarto and was listed under this attribution by Ferri. However, Ferri later (1890) recognized it as Pontormo's study for the Christ in the Visdomini altar. Like cat. 44 and 49, black chalk studies for other heads in the altarpiece, this drawing is an example of the fully elaborated chiaroscuro manner of the final studies for the painting, a style that is directly analogous to the painterly chiaroscuro of the altar. On cat. 44 there is a preliminary sketch for this head and for the left hand of the Christ.

37 · Rotterdam, Museum Boymans-Van Beuningen I285 *recto*: Study for St. John the Baptist, Visdomini altar. Nude boy seated on a step with his legs apart and the left arm pointing across his body; above to the right, the lower torso and legs to the knees restudied; below, the left leg restudied; below the figure, the right foot studied. (*Verso*: Studies for the Dublin *Pietà*, cat. 64.) 375 x 255, red chalk; left lower corner of the sheet missing; W: Fruit (B. 7392). Fig. 44.

Collection: Gigoux, stamp recto (L. 1164); Legros; Koenigs, stamp verso (L. 1023a).

Bibliography: Byam Shaw 1929/30, 23–25, pl. 27; V. R. Altena 1934, 156, no. 620; Fraenckel 1935, 195; Juynboll 1938, 19; Berenson 1938, no. 1761D; Freedberg and Rearick 1961, 8, fig. 21.

This drawing was formerly attributed to Andrea del Sarto, but it was given to the early Pontormo by Byam Shaw. This attribution has been accepted by the other authors cited, except by Berenson, who gave it to Naldini. The old attribution to Andrea is understandable in view of the Sartesque motive [31] as well as the somewhat Sartesque draughtsmanship. However, the ascription to Naldini (often suggested for drawings that have been called both Andrea and Pontormo) is not acceptable. Not only does this drawing evidently date from before 1520 because of its similarities to Andrea's and Pontormo's red chalk drawings of ca. 1515–1520, but it shows none of Naldini's mannerisms.

This drawing is a study for the St. John immediately following cat. 72, where he is shown in this same pose, but as embracing the Christ. After the preliminary sketches on cat. 72 Pontormo apparently decided to separate the two children and to place the St. John on a step below the Christ pointing up at him. The series of studies in which Pontormo worked out the details of this new arrangement begins with this drawing. Here the pose is still far from the final solution. The contrapposto of the boy is projected as a freely turning movement in space, while in later studies and in the painting the limbs are arranged in accordance with a more planar design, each parallel to the picture plane. In this drawing the upward twisting movement of the figure is still thought of in terms of a direct relation with the Christ — a vestige of the embracing motive — while in cat. 39–42 and in the painting, the St. John sits still rather than leaning to the left and his glance off to the right arrests any sensation of real movement in the direction of the other child.

38 · London, G. Fenwick Owen Collection (formerly?). *Verso*: Study for St.

[31] Both the motive and the figure type (cf. especially the legs) of Pontormo's putto recall the boy on the right on the steps in the *Dream of the Pharaoh* of 1517, the putto in the Scalzo *Baptism* of the same year, and the putto in the foreground of the Louvre *Caritas* of 1518.

John the Baptist, Visdomini altar. Nude boy seated turned to the left, holding a staff in both hands and looking upwards. (*Recto*: Study for the Visdomini altar, cat. 60.) 380 x 235, red chalk. Fig. 45.

Bibliography: Popham 1931, no. 230; Berenson 1938, no. 2256.

Although it is attributed to Pontormo, this drawing has not been dated or connected with the Visdomini altar. It is the second in a series of studies for the St. John in which the motive is developed directly from its Sartesque beginnings in cat. 37. The St. John points up at the Christ in cat. 37, but here Pontormo has experimented with having him hold a staff in both hands. The arm is still pulled across the body to the left as in cat. 37, but it is placed lower and there is less sense of a real turning movement to the left. Also contributing to the more static impression of this figure is the way in which the torso and legs have been turned in profile, the legs close together rather than in the wide apart pose of cat. 37. The extended right leg of the boy in cat. 37, which suggested the vigorous activity of the child, has been drawn here twice: the first time extended as in cat. 37, the second time bent back in profile, a *pentimento* that indicates clearly the evolution of this drawing from the preceding study. The red chalk style and the particular figure type of this nude occurs in other studies for the altar, such as the recto of this sheet or cat. 57, and in studies for the predella, such as cat. 65 and 66.

39 · Florence, Uffizi 7452F *recto*: Study for the St. John the Baptist, Visdomini altar. Nude boy seated in profile left with the right leg raised; sideways on the sheet, outline sketch for a *Madonna and Child with St. John*. (*Verso*: Studies for the Visdomini altar, cat. 50.) 309 x 192, black chalk, outline sketch in red chalk, on brown paper. Fig. 46.

Bibliography: Clapp 1911, 6; Clapp 1914, 281–282; Berenson 1938, no. 2240B.

This drawing was formerly attributed to Naldini, but it was given to Pontormo as for the St. John by Clapp, who thought the other sketch might be a preliminary idea for the composition of the altar. The compositional idea does not seem to be related to the altar, but this drawing belongs to the series of studies for the St. John. This is the first drawing for the figure in which the pose of the legs is the same as in the painting, a change that may have been a result of Pontormo's study of Michelangelo's *Cascina* cartoon. We know that Pontormo was drawing after the cartoon in these years: cat. 34 for the Christ of the Visdomini altar is related to the seated, turning figure in the center, and the nude to the right in cat. 74 is derived from the figure who pulls on his stockings. This study for the St. John is closely related to the nude on cat. 74, and it is quite evident that it too refers ultimately, if indirectly, to Michelangelo's figure. However, in the final studies for the St. John and in the painted figure the childish forms and the specific gesture and expression of an infant St. John all but mask over the original source of the pose. Much the same transformation of a Michelangelo motive occurred later in Pontormo's studies for the putti above the window in the Poggio a Caiano lunette, where the early drawings (cat. 150–151) were after young boys and clearly related to the Sistine Ceiling, while the putti of the final studies (cat. 152–155) would never suggest the actual source. In style, this St. John study is characteristic of the black chalk studies for the altar such as cat. 35, 51, and 61.

40 · Florence, Uffizi 6545F: Study for St. John the Baptist, Visdomini altar. Seated putto turned to the left with the right leg raised, looking up to the right. 114 x 65, pen and bistre over black chalk;

inscribed in ink in a sixteenth-century (?) hand: *Jacopo da Pontormo.* Fig. 47.

Bibliography: Berenson 1903, no. 2048; Clapp 1914, 145; Clapp 1916, 20, fig. 18; Berenson 1938, 309, no. 2048; Wallis 1939, 280, fig. 7; Berenson 1961, no. 2048, fig. 896.

As Berenson has noted, this is a study for the St. John, identical in pose to the figure in the painting except for the position of the arms. Allowing for the difference in media and scale, this small sketch is comparable in style to cat. 33 and 34 for the Christ, and to cat. 84, a putto study contemporary in date with the Visdomini altar studies. With the exception of the study for the *St. John the Baptist* of the *Carro della Zecca* of 1514 (cat. 1), this is Pontormo's only drawing in pen before 1520. In this drawing, like the earlier one, the pen seems to be an unfamiliar instrument to Pontormo. It is used, much as the black chalk is employed in cat. 35, to emphasize certain parts of the contours, not to model the forms in light and shade.[32]

41 · Rome, GNS F.C. 149 *recto*: Study for St. John the Baptist, Visdomini altar. Page from a sketchbook: Seated putto turned profile left with the right leg raised. (*Verso*: Traces of black chalk, not catalogued.) 217 x 155, black chalk heightened with white over red chalk on pink prepared paper. Fig. 48.

Collection: Corsini; R. Accademia dei Lincei, stamp verso (L. 1683).

Bibliography: Clapp 1911, 6; Clapp 1914, 336; Berenson 1938, no. 2338A; *EMI* 1954 (Bianchi), no. 56; *MP* 1956 (Marcucci), no. 98, fig. 127b.

Clapp identified this study with the St. John of the Visdomini altar. It is one of the studies from the Corsini Sketchbook (cat. 105–123) that can be associated with the Visdomini altar. Here and in cat. 42, the pose of the figure is almost identical to that of the figure in the painting. Yet, the *pentimento* of the head (studied twice, once looking up as in the painting, once looking straight forward) and the very tentative indication of the raised right arm indicate that Pontormo was still undecided as to the final details of the pose. As Marcucci has remarked, and as we noted in connection with cat. 29 (also for the altar and from the Corsini Sketchbook) this rapid sketch recalls the drawings of Fra Bartolommeo.

42 · Rome, GNS F.C. 127: Study for St. John the Baptist, Visdomini altar. Page from a sketchbook: Seated putto turned profile left with right leg and arm raised, the left leg seen only to the knee. 216 x 153, red chalk heightened with white on pink prepared paper; laid down. Fig. 49.

Bibliography: Berenson 1903, no. 2345; Clapp 1911, 6; Clapp 1914, 342; Clapp 1916, fig. 15; Berenson 1938, no. 2363A.

Clapp identified this study with the St. John of the Visdomini altar. Like cat. 41, it is one of the studies from the Corsini Sketchbook (cat. 105–123) that can be associated with the Visdomini altar. This study is a variant of cat. 41 in which the raised right arm is drawn as it was to be in the painting. These two sketches are the latest surviving drawings for the St. John, there being no finished studies of the type that are preparatory to other figures in the altar.

43 · Florence, Uffizi 6581F *recto*: Study for St. Joseph, Visdomini altar. Head of a

[32] The way Pontormo used pen in this drawing and in his few other pen studies: cat. 101, 176, 319, and (with wash) 1, 131, 132, is totally different from the Michelangelo-inspired elaborate cross-hatching and tightly defined forms of the pen drawings that are erroneously ascribed to him (cf. cat. A3, A42, A46, A48, A131).

bearded man looking upward. (*Verso*: Study for the *Carro della Zecca*, cat. 1.) 175 x 127, red chalk. Fig. 52.

Bibliography: Berenson 1903, no. 2081; *MPA* 1910, 34; Clapp 1914, 166; Clapp 1916, fig. 22; Tinti 1925, fig. 10; Berenson 1938, no. 2081; Becherucci 1944, 14; *MDM* 1954 (Marcucci), no. 39; *EMI* 1954, no. 57; Berenson 1961, no. 2081, fig. 895.

Berenson recognized this drawing as for the head of St. Joseph and observed that it was inspired by the *Laocoön*. This head occurs several times ca. 1516–1519 in works by Andrea del Sarto and Pontormo, and it is likely that a copy of the sculpture became available to them in Florence in these years.[33] The curious faceting of the surface and the extreme plasticity of the head in this first study for the St. Joseph would suggest a sculptural precedent even if none were known. Clapp found the style of this drawing close to Andrea del Sarto. However, it is not so similar to Andrea's style as it is an extreme exaggeration of his chiaroscuro mode of drawing. The light and shade models the forms with a violence that nearly shatters them, and the head is observed with an almost destructive intensity of perception that is never found in Andrea's more normative drawings. Cat. 74 of this same date, which is taken after a sculptural (if not sculptured) Michelangelo model, is a close parallel among Pontormo's studies to the very individual manner of this drawing.

[33] The head appears as Jacob in Andrea's *Selling of Joseph* of ca. 1516 and in Pontormo's *Joseph in Egypt* of ca. 1518–1519. The *Laocoön* was excavated in 1506 and was generally accessible at this time in the Belvedere, where it had been installed by Julius II. While Marco Dente's engraving (Bar. 353) had been made of it, it seems likely that Andrea and Pontormo knew a sculptured copy as well. However, it is not certain which of the many copies was available in Florence as early as 1516. Before his death in 1514, Bramante directed that a number of copies be made of the work, one of which was to be cast in bronze. Probably one of these or another early sculptured copy appeared in Florence by 1516. See V/M, VII, 489, and A. Venturi, "Il Gruppo del Laocoonte e Raffaello," *Archivio Storico dell'Arte* II (1889), 97–112.

44 · Florence, Uffizi 92201F *recto*: Studies for St. Joseph and the Christ, Visdomini altar. Head of a bearded old man looking up to the left; below, head of a child looking up; to the right, hand holding a stick. (*Verso*: Study for the Visdomini altar, cat. 49.) 329 x 219, black chalk, the child's head and the hand in red chalk; sheet mended across the center and upper left corner replaced. Fig. 53.

Bibliography: *MP* 1956 (Marcucci), no. 96, fig. 132a; Berenson 1961, no. 2248A–1; Schlegel 1961, 31, fig. 5.

This powerful drawing is the final study for the head of St. Joseph, following cat. 43, and a preliminary sketch for the head and left hand of the Christ, preceding cat. 36. The parallel in form and expression between the heads of St. Joseph and Christ in the altarpiece is already evident in this drawing, in which the two heads are juxtaposed almost as if one had evolved out of the other. The *Laocoön*-inspired face of the old man and the smiling face of the Child both show Pontormo's tendency at this time to animate and intensify facial expression by crowding the features into a small triangular area in the center of the face.

Marcucci, who has also recognized this study as for the Visdomini altar, found this drawing and its verso the closest to Andrea del Sarto of all Pontormo's drawings, notably in the structure of the forms and the handling of the chiaroscuro. However, in this study and to a lesser degree the other head studies for the altar (cat. 36 and 49), the chiaroscuro breaks up the surface into flickering patterns of light and shade, barely contained by the irregular contours, that anticipate the violent chiaroscuro of the painting. Furthermore, the highly characterized — quite un-Sartesque — emotional states of the figures in the painting are already evident in the charged content of these head studies.

45 · Lille, Musée des Beaux-Arts 163 *verso*: Study for the Evangelist, Visdomini altar. Seated draped figure turned to the right holding a large book; to the right, a drapery study. (*Recto*: Study for *Joseph* (III), cat. 25.) 410 x 270, black chalk. Fig. 51.

Bibliography: Pluchart 1889, 37; Delacre 1931, 139; Berenson 1938, no. 2252B.

The existence of this study on the verso of cat. 25 has been noted, but the drawing has not been discussed. It is a preparatory study for the St. John the Evangelist that must follow the compositional sketch (cat. 29) very closely, since the Evangelist appears there in just this position, looking to the right in profile, and holding the book in both hands. The drapery study to the right might have been connected with the figures to the right of the Evangelist in cat. 29.

In this study we see that Pontormo originally conceived the relation of the Evangelist to the other figures in the altar quite differently. When he moved the Evangelist to the far left in his final version of the composition, Pontormo made several changes in the pose of the figure that have the effect of separating him compositionally and emotionally from the rest of the group. In cat. 47 and in the painting his right arm is pulled back to the left rather than leading diagonally inward toward the other saints. As can be seen from the *pentimenti* in this study, Pontormo was already undecided here about the position of the Evangelist's head. In the painting, instead of looking to the right in the direction of the Madonna and Child as he does in this drawing, the Evangelist is unaware of them, turning his head to the left, straining to look out of the picture in the direction of the high altar of the church.

46 · Rome, GNS F.C. 117 *verso*: Study for the Evangelist, Visdomini altar. Page from a sketchbook: Right arm studied twice. (*Recto*: Studies for Poggio a Caiano, cat. 125.) 215 x 152, red chalk, the arm on the right in black chalk, on pink prepared paper.

Bibliography: Berenson 1903, no. 2357; Clapp 1914, 337; Berenson 1938, no. 2338C. (Photo museum)

Clapp dated this drawing 1517–1521. These studies for the bare right arm of the Evangelist are among the drawings from the Corsini Sketchbook (cat. 105–123) that may be associated with the Visdomini altar. This study is identical in style to cat. 47, also for the Evangelist's arm, but must precede it because here the arm is placed diagonally to support the edge of the book as in cat. 45.

47 · Rome, GNS F.C. 139 *recto*: Study for the Evangelist, Visdomini altar. Page from a sketchbook: Right arm studied three times. (*Verso*: Nude study, cat. 117.) 215 x 153, red chalk heightened with white on pink prepared paper; W: Fleur-de-lis. Fig. 50.

Collection: Corsini; R. Accademia dei Lincei, stamp verso (L. 2187).

Bibliography: Berenson 1903, no. 2358; Clapp 1914, 337; Berenson 1938, no. 2358.

Clapp dated this drawing 1518–1521. These are Pontormo's final studies for the Evangelist's arm, following cat. 46. Like cat. 46, this sheet is from the Corsini Sketchbook (cat. 105–123) and it is executed in the same rapid, unelaborated style. The arm is drawn here as it is in the painting, in an almost vertical position with the hand resting on the rock rather than holding the edge of the book as in the earlier studies.

48 · Florence, Uffizi 6744F *recto*: Study for St. Francis, Visdomini altar. Nude kneeling profile left in an attitude of prayer. (*Verso*: Study for the Visdomini altar, cat. 35.) 367 x 253, black chalk heightened with white; W: Latin Cross (B. 5641). Fig. 54.

Bibliography: Ferri 1890, 118 (as 6644); Jacobsen 1898, 381 (as 6444); Berenson 1903, no. 2004; *MPA* 1910, 35; Clapp 1914, 273; Clapp 1916, fig. 23; Fraenckel 1933, 170, 172–173; Berenson 1938, no. 2225A; Becherucci 1944, 14, fig. 11; Berenson 1961, no. 2225A, fig. 899.

Jacobsen connected this drawing with the St. Francis of the Visdomini altar. This is a model study from the nude for the pose of the figure just as he is in the painting. As Berenson has pointed out, this same motive occurs more than a decade later in the kneeling Pygmalion of Pontormo's *Pygmalion and Galatea*. However, this drawing cannot be a study for that figure as Berenson suggested. Cat. 291, which Berenson would associate with the St. Francis, is the study for the Pygmalion. This drawing is associable in style with several other studies for Visdomini altar figures in black chalk heightened with white: cat. 35 for the Christ, cat. 51 for the St. James, and cat. 61 for the putto on the right. It is the most elaborated of this group of figure studies, pointing to the smoother chiaroscuro of the final studies for the head of the Christ (cat. 36) and the St. Francis (cat. 49).

49 · Florence, Uffizi 92201F *verso*: Study for St. Francis, Visdomini altar. Head of a man looking up in profile left. (*Recto*: Studies for the Visdomini altar, cat. 44.) 329 x 219, black chalk heightened with white. Fig. 55.

Bibliography: *MP* 1956 (Marcucci), no. 96, fig. 132b; Berenson 1961, no. 2248A–1.

This drawing is a final study for the head of St. Francis, as has also been noted by Marcucci. It is similar in style to cat. 36 for the head of Christ, and to some extent to its recto for the St. Joseph, although it is more carefully finished. Marcucci considered that in this sheet Pontormo turned in his drawing style from the "tutto tondo" of Fra Bartolommeo to the "alto rilievo" of Andrea del Sarto. When compared with the graphic eccentricity and excitement of the recto, this study appears relatively Sartesque in the more normative handling of the forms and in the unagitated expression of the head, which does not yet have the exaggerated thinness of shape and rapt, open-mouthed expression of the head in the altar. However, in no drawing of Andrea's do we find quite such an angular and broken silhouette as Pontormo has made of this profile, nor such a sacrifice of the plastic rotundity of the head for the sake of the complex luminosity of its surface. (For a contemporary drawing analogous in subject, cf. Uffizi 669E, Andrea's study for the profile of St. Peter in the *Disputà*.)

50 · Florence, Uffizi 7452F *verso*: Study for St. James, Visdomini altar. Two superimposed studies with many *pentimenti* of a nude seen to the knees. (*Recto*: Studies for the Visdomini altar, cat. 39.) 310 x 200, black chalk on brown paper.

Bibliography: Clapp 1914, 282; Berenson 1938, no. 2240B. (Photo G.)

Clapp dated this sketch 1516–1518 as a first idea for the St. James. Like the St. Francis, the St. James appears to the right in the compositional study for the altar, cat. 29. However, unlike the St. Francis, whose kneeling pose was established from the beginning, the pose of the St. James was undecided in cat. 29. There is a faint indication of the figure standing looking out of the picture, but he also seems to be studied kneeling below. Here in this tentative sketch we see again Pontormo's indecision as to the pose of this figure. The St. James is drawn once full face with his arm resting on a staff to the right, and once moving in profile to the left as he does in the painting.

51 · Florence, Uffizi 6525F *recto*: Study for St. James, Visdomini altar. Nude standing holding a staff to the right and looking up to the left. (*Verso*: Nude study, cat. 76.) 400 x 110, black chalk heightened with white, top of the sheet cut in an arch; W: Latin Cross (B. 5641); inscribed in ink: *Jac º da Pontormo.*
Fig. 56.

Bibliography: Berenson 1903, no. 2028; Clapp 1914, 131; Berenson 1938, no. 2028.

Clapp dated this drawing toward 1517, comparing it in style with cat. 48 for the St. Francis of the Visdomini altar. In cat. 50 there was some indecision as to whether the St. James was to stand in profile or frontally, and this drawing may be Pontormo's unsuccessful experiment with a frontal pose. In spite of its obvious weaknesses (perhaps partially due to the difficulties with the pose), this drawing is closely linked in style with other studies for the Visdomini altar in black chalk heightened with white, such as cat. 35, 39, 48, and 61.

52 · Naples, Galleria Nazionale Capodimonte 0242: Study for St. James, Visdomini altar. Left arm draped above the elbow; underneath, figure walking to the left looking back to the right. 240 x 111, red chalk; laid down. Fig. 57.

Bibliography: Berenson 1938, no. 2256E.

Berenson thought that this drawing was "much gone over," but it did not appear so to the author. This drawing is a study for the half-draped left arm of the St. James, and is like the arm in the painting in every detail. The light sketch underneath the arm may be a tentative idea for the action of the whole figure.

53 · Rome, GNS F.C. 119: Study for the putto on the left, Visdomini altar. Page from a sketchbook: Nude torso turned right with the right arm raised. 219 x 156, red chalk on pink prepared paper; laid down; illegible inscription to the lower left.

Bibliography: Berenson 1903, no. 2348; Clapp 1914, 342; Berenson 1938, no. 2363B. (Photo Museum)

Clapp dated this study 1516–1520 and Berenson placed it ten years later at the time of S. Felicita. This drawing and cat. 54–56 and 59 are studies from the Corsini Sketchbook (cat. 105–123) for the putti of the Visdomini altar. This sketch and cat. 54–58 are studies for the putto who holds back the curtain on the left of the altar. Here very little of the final pose is indicated except that the figure will walk to the right with his left leg forward and his right arm will be raised. In these drawings, as was the case with the St. John the Baptist studies for the altar (cat. 37–38) or the studies for the putti of Poggio a Caiano (cat. 150–151), Pontormo first studied the poses of figures that were eventually to be putti from muscular youths.

54 · Rome, GNS F.C. 120 *recto*: Study for the putto on the left, Visdomini altar. Page from a sketchbook: Three-quarter length nude in profile right with the right arm raised, looking over his shoulder (*Verso*: Study for the same figure, cat. 55.) 216 x 154, red chalk on pink prepared paper; W: Fleur-de-lis. Fig. 58.

Collection: Corsini; R. Accademia dei Lincei, stamp verso (L. 2187).

Bibliography: Berenson 1903, no. 2360; Clapp 1914, 338; Berenson 1938, no. 2360.

See cat. 53. This second in the series

of studies for the putto on the left and its variant (cat. 55) were dated 1517–1520 by Clapp, "early" as perhaps connected with the *Story of Joseph* by Berenson. Here and in cat. 55 the torso of the figure has been turned completely in profile and the weight has been shifted forward as it will be in the painted figure. Also established in this sketch is the notion that the putto will look forward out of the picture.

55 · Rome, GNS F.C. 120 *verso*: Study for the putto on the left, Visdomini altar. Page from a sketchbook: Nude torso turned to the right. (*Recto*: Study for the same figure, cat. 54.) 216 x 154, red chalk on pink prepared paper.

Bibliography: Berenson 1903, no. 2360; Clapp 1914, 339; Berenson 1938, no. 2360. (Photo museum)

See cat. 54, of which this study is a less elaborated variant.

56 · Rome, GNS F.C. 148 *verso*: Study for the putto on the left, Visdomini altar. Page from a sketchbook: Bust of a nude turned to the right with his right arm raised and head tipped back. (*Recto*: Nude study, cat. 121.) 215 x 144, red chalk on pink prepared paper.

Bibliography: Berenson 1903, no. 2359; Clapp 1914, 338; Berenson 1938, no. 2359; *EMI* 1954 (Bianchi), no. 74. (Photo museum)

See cat. 53. This drawing was dated 1525–1530 by Clapp. In this fourth study for the putto on the left, the greater impetuosity of movement of the painted figure is suggested for the first time. In the painting the motive of the violently raised arm is retained, but the relation of head to arm is reversed so that the arm is higher than the head. The bold and rhythmic style of this study is much like that of cat. 41–42 and cat. 46–47, also from the Corsini Sketchbook and for the Visdomini altar.

57 · Florence, Uffizi 6691F *verso*: Study for the putto on the left, Visdomini altar. Nude boy walking down a step to the right with his right arm raised, looking over his shoulder. (*Recto*: Study for the Dublin *Pietà*, cat. 63.) 408 x 266, red chalk. Fig. 60.

Bibliography: Berenson 1903, no. 2001; Clapp 1914, 238–239; Berenson 1938, no. 2175A; Freedberg and Rearick 1961, 8, fig. 18.

Clapp dated this study 1519. This is the only full-length drawing for the putto on the left. It is taken, like the sketchbook studies for the same figure, from a boy model rather than a child. Aside from the translation into the rounder forms of a putto, the pose of the putto in the painting is rather different from that of the figure in this drawing. In the painted figure the walking action is somewhat arrested, while the spiraling of the forms that culminates in the raised arm is made more pronounced. In this way Pontormo transformed the naturalistic model study of this drawing in accord with the design of twisting and rising forms that dominates the composition of the picture. Cat. 60, a drawing in red chalk on the same scale and probably from the same model, is the pendant to this drawing for the putto on the right side of the altar. Clapp mentioned Uffizi 7439F (attributed to Naldini) as related to this drawing, but the motive is only vaguely similar.

58 · Florence, Uffizi 6551F *recto*: Study for the putto on the left and for St. John the Baptist, Visdomini altar. Head of a putto; sideways on the sheet, left leg bent at the knee and the knee restudied. (*Verso*: Study for the Visdomini altar, cat. 31.) 249 x 182, black chalk; the legs in red chalk.

Bibliography: Berenson 1903, no. 2053; Clapp 1914, 148; Clapp 1916, fig. 16; Berenson 1938, no. 2053.

Berenson noted that the putto head was for the child on the left and that the leg was for the St. John the Baptist. This head is the latest surviving study for the putto, the only one that is drawn from a child model and the only one in which the final relation of the head to the raised arm is indicated (see the blank space at the left where the arm is to cross over the side of the head in the painting).

59 · Rome, GNS F. C. 138 *recto*: Study for the putto on the right, Visdomini altar. Page from a sketchbook: Nude torso in profile left with his left arm raised. (*Verso*: Study for Poggio a Caiano, cat. 129.) 216 x 153, red chalk on pink prepared paper; W: Fleur-de-lis. Fig. 59.

Collection: Corsini; R. Accademia dei Lincei, stamp verso (L. 2187).

Bibliography: Berenson 1903, no. 2351; Clapp 1914, 339; Berenson, 1938, no. 2361A.

Clapp dated this sketch 1516–1520, while Berenson called it "early." Four studies from the Corsini Sketchbook (cat. 53–56) have survived for the putto on the left, but this is the only sketchbook drawing for the putto on the right. It is identical, but reversed, to cat. 54. Here and in cat. 60 we find an early version of the pose of the putto on the right from a moment when Pontormo evidently thought of the putti as pendant figures almost identical in pose.

60 · London, G. Fenwick Owen Collection (formerly?). *Recto*: Study for the putto on the right, Visdomini altar. Nude boy walking to the left with his left arm raised; sideways on the sheet, bust of a nude in profile left with arm raised and head down. (*Verso*: Study for the Visdomini altar, cat. 38.) 380 x 235, red chalk. Fig. 61.

Collection: Geiger (sold Sotheby, December 9, 1920; cat. no. 243, pl. 243).

Bibliography: Popham 1931, no. 230, pl. 194; Berenson 1938, no. 2256.

Popham identified this drawing as a study for the putto on the right of the altar. This drawing is a pendant to cat. 57 for the putto on the left and shows that Pontormo at first thought of the two putti as striding forward toward the center of the composition looking out over a raised arm. The style of this study and of cat. 57 is very close to that of the drawings for the Dublin *Pietà*, of which one is the recto of cat. 57, and to cat. 25 for *Joseph* (III), in which the central figure is identical in motive to this nude. The other sketch on this sheet is not for a reclining figure as Berenson thought, but is probably an alternate idea for the head and arm of the boy, suggestive of the final pose of the putto on the other side.

61 · Florence, Uffizi 6662F *recto*: Study for the putto on the right, Visdomini altar. Putto standing with left arm raised, the right across the body, the legs apart; to the right, the figure restudied; across the sheet, two bits of drapery. (*Verso*: Nude study, cat. 82.) 401 x 263, black chalk heightened with white on brown paper; the right lower corner replaced; inscribed [Fran]co *Rosi 235*. Fig. 62.

Bibliography: Berenson 1903, no. 2153; Clapp 1914, 214–215; Clapp 1916, fig. 21; Berenson 1938, no. 2153; *MP* 1956 (Marcucci), no. 97, fig. 131a; Berenson 1961, no. 2153, fig. 898.

Berenson identified these studies as for the putto on the right. Other drawings must have intervened between the preliminary drawings for the putto and the final pose as set down in this definitive study, the only drawing for this figure in which Pontormo used a child rather than a boy as a model. At some stage in the evolution of the composition Pontormo changed his original concept of the putti as identical in their action, a change that contributes to the compositional irregularity of the altarpiece. In their final form the putti who hold back the curtains are no longer reminiscent, as were the figures of the preliminary studies, of their more conventional prototypes in Pontormo's SS. Annunziata *Visitation* and Andrea del Sarto's Dresden altar. Instead of acting as mirror images, enhancing the equilibrium of the composition, these putti call attention to the active imbalance of the altar by willfully pulling and turning as they please. In style, this black chalk study is the same type that we have seen in cat. 35, 39, 48, and 51, other studies for figures in the altarpiece.

1517–1518ff. DUBLIN PREDELLA: *Pietà with St. Bartholomew, St. Lawrence, St. Francis, and St. Peter* (on the left); *St. Benedict, St. Zenobius, St. Jerome, and St. Apollonia* (on the right). Dublin, National Gallery 103–104, the *St. Bartholomew* and *St. Zenobius*, Warwick Castle, Earl of Warwick Collection. Panels: *Pietà* 19.5 x 47.8 cm; *St. Bartholomew* 19 x 18 cm; *St. Lawrence* 19.5 x 17.7 cm; *St. Francis* 19.7 x 18.1 cm; *St. Peter* 19.5 x 18.9 cm; *St. Benedict* 19 x 18.7 cm; *St. Zenobius* 19.3 x 17.2 cm; *St. Jerome* 19.2 x 17.9 cm; *St. Apollonia* 19.2 x 18.2 cm.[34] (Executed by an anonymous hand in part after Pontormo's drawings?) Figs. 63–65.

Bibliography: *Dublin Cat.* 1867, 95; Crowe and Cavalcaselle 1914, 204; Sinibaldi 1925, 153–158, figs. 1–7; Venturi 1932, 109–112, figs. 52–58; Fraenckel 1933, 116, 173n3; Fraenckel 1935, 239n96; Berenson 1936, 401; Becherucci 1944, 12; *MDM* 1954 (Marcucci), 26; Marcucci 1955, 252; *MP* 1956 (Berti), nos. 16–22, figs. 8–11; Sanminiatelli 1956, 242; *Dublin Cat.* 1956, 63–64; Freedberg and Rearick 1961, 7–8, figs. 7-16; Freedberg 1961, I, 523–525, II, figs. 647–649.

The Dublin panels were acquired in Rome in 1864–1865 as Andrea del Sarto and were listed under this attribution in the 1867 catalogue and by Crowe and Cavalcaselle. They came from the Menichini collection in Perugia, the same source from which the two Warwick panels were bought in 1867. Sinibaldi first suggested the attribution of the predella to Pontormo, connecting the series of drawings in the Uffizi with it (cat. 62–63, 65–71). Sinibaldi and Venturi, who accepted the attribution to Pontormo, did not discuss the question of date, but (according to Berti) Lányi identified these panels with the lost predella that Vasari says (V/M,

[34] This predella consisted originally of three panels: the central *Pietà* and the two side panels, each with four saints. The side panels have each been sawed into four pieces. Their combined width is 72 cm on the right side and 72.7 cm on the left side. Examination of the sawed edges of the panels and the planing of their backs indicates the order of the panels as they are listed above. The inside edges of the two panels flanking the *Pietà* have 7 mm (*St. Peter*) and 5 mm (*St. Benedict*) unpainted strips, indicating that they were the original ends of the side panels and confirming, as the horizon line indicates, that they belong next to the *Pietà*. The *St. Bartholomew*, *St. Lawrence*, and *St. Francis* should be arranged on the left as the horizon lines indicate, but a change should be made in our former order for the three remaining panels of the right side (see Freedberg and Rearick 1961, fig. 1). The *St. Jerome* and *St. Benedict* do not match, while the right edge of the *St. Apollonia* shows that she belongs at the end. Thus, the *St. Zenobius* should be placed between the *St. Jerome* and the *St. Benedict* rather than on the end. The 19.5 cm height of the *Pietà*, which agrees with the height of the rest of the predella, has been increased by the addition of a 20 mm strip at the top and a 7 mm strip at the bottom, these additions accounting for the 21 cm vertical measurement usually cited for this panel.

VI, 247) Pontormo and Rosso painted for Andrea del Sarto's S. Gallo *Annunciation* of ca. 1512. Fraenckel denied the attribution of the predella to either Andrea del Sarto or Pontormo, considering it a work of ca. 1530 by a Sarto pupil or follower influenced by both Andrea and Pontormo. Otherwise, the attribution of this predella to Pontormo has been affirmed, and the identification with the S. Gallo predella of ca. 1512 has been accepted by Becherucci, Marcucci, and Sanminiatelli. However, such an early dating for the predella presented problems in the dating of the preparatory drawings, which are evidently later than ca. 1512, or even 1514, the latest date at which Pontormo could have participated in the execution of the predella to Andrea's altar. Consequently, both Berenson and Marcucci separated the drawings from the predella, Berenson dating them ca. 1520, Marcucci 1516–1518. On the other hand, Berti has rightly maintained that the predella and the drawings belong together. He placed the project 1515–1516, between the S. Ruffillo altar and the SS. Annunziata *Visitation*, and denied any association with the S. Gallo predella. It certainly seems advisable to disassociate this work from the predella of the S. Gallo *Annunciation*, which according to Vasari was not similar in subject or composition to the Dublin panels.[35] However, Berti's dating still seems somewhat early for the paintings and for drawings whose style clearly indicates 1517 as the earliest year in which the predella could have been designed.

It was first suggested by Freedberg that the predella was designed for Pontormo's Visdomini altar, finished in 1518. The Visdomini *Madonna and Saints* is the only altar by Pontormo that could have had a predella of this type and size;[36] and, if there once existed another altarpiece of comparable scale for which this predella was intended, some mention of it would surely have been made by Vasari. As noted by Freedberg, there are stylistic analogies between the predella and the altar, and there is a close coincidence in style between the drawings for the altar and those for the predella. Furthermore, three drawings for the predella occur on the same sheets as drawings for the altar. On cat. 72 there is a sketch for the St. Francis of the predella together with ideas for the Christ and the St. John of the altar. Two studies for the Dead Christ of the predella (cat. 63 and 64) have studies for the altar in an identical style on the reverse of the sheet.

It seems a reasonable hypothesis that the series of drawings for the Christ (cat. 62–67) and the St. John (cat. 68–70) of the *Pietà*, the *St. Lawrence* (cat. 68), and the *St. Francis* (cat. 71–72) was made for the predella to the Visdomini altar and that the corresponding panels in Dublin derive from these drawings. However, since the predella is not now with the altar and since no notice of the Visdomini altar refers to such a predella, it is evident that it was not executed or not completed by 1518, was never delivered, or was shortly afterwards removed from the altar. While we formerly believed that the predella was executed at least partially by Pontormo ca. 1517–1518, even though it was apparently

[35] V/M, VI, 247: "... vi fece un Cristo morto con due angioletti che gli fanno lume con due torce, e lo piangono; e dalle bande in due tondi due Profeti ..."

[36] The lateral measurement of the Visdomini altar is 189 cm and the combined width of the predella panels in 192 cm. Thus, there is certainly no objection to their association on the basis of size. When the three panels of the predella were framed, probably in such a way as to carry out the painted balustrade motive where it is lacking (such as to the sides of the *Pietà*), the predella may have been slightly wider than the altar, a relation wherein the predella forms a wider base for the altarpiece, not uncommon in this period.

never set up with the altar, further examination of the Dublin and Warwick panels now suggests that the predella may have been executed later than the Visdomini altar by another hand, and only partially after Pontormo's drawings of 1517–1518.

The execution of the predella has presented a problem to all those who have written about it. Following Vasari's remark on the joint execution of the S. Gallo predella, it has been divided between Pontormo and Rosso: Becherucci gave only the *Pietà*, the *St. Francis*, and the *St. Lawrence* to Pontormo. Marcucci gave the entire predella to Pontormo with the exception of the *St. Apollonia*, the Virgin and the Magdalen of the *Pietà*. With Rosso's participation no longer an issue, Freedberg considered the *Pietà* and the *St. Lawrence* to be certainly by Pontormo, the *St. Francis* fairly surely by him, and the *St. Apollonia* possibly by him. The other Dublin saints he suggested were by an anonymous helper of the Sarto school, the Warwick panels by still a third, possibly later, hand. Evidently, since these panels have been so variously attributed to different hands (not to mention the variable dating of the predella), there are elements in this predella that strongly suggest a lack of stylistic unity. However, we would propose that the discrepancies in the predella are due not to differences in execution so much as to differences in design. Indeed, the hand appears to be the same in all the panels. The brilliant colors and the extremely opaque, granular, and often thready application of paint are characteristic of each panel and we are unable to detect more than a single hand in their execution. However, the handling of paint in these panels is quite different from the transparent surface quality of Pontormo's panel pictures. His colors, although clear, are somewhat muted by the very transparency of his application of paint and do not resemble the rather harsh tones of these panels. There is also little evidence in this predella of the delicate fragmentation of each shape, the linear complexity of silhouette and of draperies that is so characteristic of Pontormo's panel pictures of comparable scale and date, such as the three later *Story of Joseph* pictures.

While there may be a unity in the execution, there is a considerable variety in design and in morphological details among the panels of the predella, variations that are the logical result of the artist's heterogeneous sources. It has generally been agreed that the *Pietà*, the *St. Lawrence*, and the *St. Francis* are the most Pontormesque of the group. The composition of the *Pietà* is one that was quite familiar in Florence about 1517, especially in the circle of Fra Bartolommeo.[37] This design is consonant with Pontormo's personal style at that time as well as with general developments in Florentine painting in the middle of the second decade of the century. The extensive series of drawings for the Dead Christ (cat. 62–67) and the studies for the St. John (cat. 68–70) indicate that Pontormo carried the design of at least these figures to an advanced stage and, therefore, certainly, the general design of the *Pietà* composition as a whole. One wonders, however, if a Pontormo drawing ever existed behind the rather uncharacteristic Magdalen, which is copied almost directly (and in the process misunderstood

[37] The most conspicuous example is Fra Bartolommeo's own Pitti *Pietà*, finished in 1517 by Bugiardini. However, the composition had appeared earlier in Fra Bartolommeo's drawings and often in the late fifteenth century, sometimes without the Magdalen. (Cf. Raffaellino del Garbo, Munich; Filippino Lippi, unexecuted but intended for the Certosa di Pavia in 1495; Piero di Cosimo, Perugia, etc.) Closer to Pontormo is Raphael's predella panel of ca. 1505 (Gardner Museum, Boston) and Andrea's predella panel of ca. 1508 (Borghese). In both of these pictures the *Pietà* is set into the landscape in a way similar to the Dublin panel.

in pose) from the figure in Raphael's *Pietà* predella (Boston, Gardner Museum). While no finished drawings survive for the *St. Francis* and *St. Lawrence*, cat. 68, 71, and 72 are sketches for these figures, and it is likely that more completed designs once existed for them. In contrast to the other lateral saints, the *St. Francis* and *St. Lawrence* are decidedly Pontormesque in their tensed and complex postures, attitudes that reflect the angular tensions of the saints in the Visdomini altarpiece. These two saints are also the most explicitly Pontormesque in facial type and expression, characteristically looking out of the picture as does the St. James of the altar itself. Close analogies in type, although not in execution, may also be found between such heads as that of the baker to the right of *Joseph* (III) and that of *St. Lawrence*. Compared with the *St. Francis* and *St. Lawrence*, the *St. Peter*, *St. Benedict*, *St. Bartholomew*, and *St. Zenobius* are not conspicuously Pontormesque. They are more conventional in design than the *St. Francis* and *St. Lawrence* and somewhat unvaried in their poses (cf. the *St. Peter* and the *St. Bartholomew*). These four saints suggest in a general way Sartesque rather than Pontormesque precedents, but they may well have been the inventions of the anonymous executant of the predella himself. As Fraenckel has pointed out, the remaining two panels are specifically Sartesque, the *St. Apollonia* having been derived explicitly from the St. Catherine of the Berlin altarpiece of 1528, and the *St. Jerome* from the Pisa altarpiece of 1530. Thus, unless these panels are considered as executed later than the others — a supposition that is contradicted by the unity of execution — the predella must then have been painted ca. 1530, in part after Pontormo's drawings of 1517–1518 and in part after figures from the altarpieces of the late Andrea del Sarto.

STUDIES FOR THE DUBLIN PREDELLA

62 · Florence, Uffizi 6670F *verso*: Study for the Dead Christ, Dublin *Pietà*. Nude lying on drapery across to the left with the right arm extended; in reverse direction, same figure lightly indicated. (*Recto*: Study for the same figure, cat. 65.) 280 x 396, red chalk, the reverse sketch with some black chalk. Fig. 66.

Bibliography: Ferri 1890, 119; Berenson 1903, no. 2159; Clapp 1914, 222; Clapp 1916, 16; Sinibaldi 1925, 156; Berenson 1938, no. 2159; Berenson 1961, no. 2159, fig. 925.

Clapp, who did not know the Dublin *Pietà*, dated this drawing and part of the following series (cat. 63, 65, 66, 67) between 1516 and 1520 as perhaps for Pontormo's now destroyed *Pietà* fresco at S. Gallo.[38] Berenson dated the same series of Dead Christ studies, in addition to cat. 68, 69, and 70 for St. John the Evangelist, about 1520. He connected them with a lost *Pietà* of that date, possibly the one for which cat. 103 was the compositional study. Sinibaldi was the first to identify all these drawings (cat. 62–63, 65–70) with the Dublin *Pietà*, adding cat. 71 to the

[38] V/M, VI, 260–261: "In testa all'orto e vigna de'frati di San Gallo, fuor della porta che si chiama dal detto santo, fece in una cappella che era a dirittura dell'entrata, nel mezzo un Cristo morto, una Nostra Donna che piagneva, e duo putti in aria; uno de'quali teneva il calice della Passione in mano, e l'altro sosteneva la testa del Cristo cadente. Dalle bande erano da un lato San Giovanni Evangelista lacrimoso, e con le braccia aperte, e dall'altro Santo Agostino in abito episcopale, il quale, appoggiatosi con la man manca al pastorale, si stava in atto veramente mesto e contemplante la morte del Salvatore." Vasari is not precise, but the date implied for this work is ca. 1517–1519. From Vasari's description the composition of this *Pietà* must have been very like Pontormo's later tabernacle of the *Crucifixion* with two flanking saints, formerly at Boldrone.

series. Berenson (1938) did not agree with Sinibaldi's association of the drawings with the Dublin predella, arguing that so important a series of studies would not have been done for such a small work and that they were probably for a larger composition that is now lost. However, we know that Pontormo often executed elaborate studies (cf. cat. 22, 23, 25, 26) for figures of less importance than this Dead Christ; which, it should be noted, is the central figure of a predella that measures almost two meters in width. Thus, Berenson's objection does not seem sufficient cause to disassociate these drawings from the figures of the Dublin predella, to which they correspond so closely.

We have added cat. 64 and 72 to Sinibaldi's series, making a total of eleven drawings for the predella. These red chalk drawings are on eight sheets of similar size and are an unusually homogeneous group stylistically, requiring little argument in favor of their close association with one another. Even the drawings on these sheets that are not for the predella are for works of the same years in which Pontormo must have designed the predella: the verso of cat. 63 and the recto of cat. 64 are studies for the Visdomini altarpiece, with which we have associated the predella; the recto of cat. 66 is for *Joseph* (III) of 1517; the verso of cat. 72 is for *Joseph* (II) of ca. 1516; and cat. 72 itself has studies for the Visdomini altar together with the predella study.

Sinibaldi has worked out a chronological sequence for the studies for the Dead Christ that includes cat. 66, 65, and 67 as three stages in the development of that figure. However, this drawing, noted by Sinibaldi but not considered in her sequence, seems to mark the earliest stage of Pontormo's idea. Here the figure is rapidly set down with very little interior modelling of the torso, and with much indecision, especially as to the position of the head, marked by numerous *pentimenti.*

63 · Florence, Uffizi 6691F *recto*: Study for the Dead Christ, Dublin *Pietà.* Nude lying on a drapery across to the left with the right arm extended back, the left across the body; below, two small reclining nudes. (*Verso*: Study for the Visdomini altar, cat. 57.) 266 x 408, red chalk, the small studies in black chalk. Fig. 67.

Bibliography: Ferri 1890, 119; Berenson 1903, no. 2001; *MPA* 1910, 33; Clapp 1914, 237; Clapp 1916, 16; Sinibaldi 1925, 156, fig. 11; Berenson 1938, 315, no. 2175A, fig. 967; Freedberg and Rearick 1961, 8, fig. 20.

See cat. 62. Ferri connected this study with cat. 103 as for the Certosa *Pietà.* This drawing is second in the series of studies for the Christ. It is a more elaborated version of the pose tentatively sketched on cat. 62, this time drawn carefully — almost academically — from the model. The upright position of the head, still undecided in cat. 62, has been worked out in detail here. The two smaller sketches in black chalk below the figure are later additions to this sheet similar to those on other studies for the predella (cat. 66, 67, 69, and 71). As Clapp has noted, these sketches date from the mid-thirties and are reinterpretations of the pose of the Dead Christ influenced by Michelangelo's Medici Tomb *Allegories.*

64 · Rotterdam, Museum Boymans-Van Beuningen I285 *verso*: Studies for the Dead Christ, Dublin *Pietà.* Nude lying across to the left with the right leg bent and the right arm extended back; above, the torso and head restudied with the right arm across the body; above sideways on the sheet, lightly sketched leg. (*Recto*: Study for the Visdomini altar, cat. 37.) 257 x 370, red chalk. Fig. 68.

Bibliography: Byam Shaw 1929/30, 23–25, fig. 6; V. R. Altena 1934, no. 620; Fraenckel 1935, 195; Berenson 1938, no. 1761D; Freedberg and Rearick 1961, 8, fig. 19.

Formerly attributed to Andrea del Sarto, this drawing was given to the early Pontormo by Byam Shaw. This attribution was accepted by V. R. Altena and Fraenckel, but not by Berenson, who ascribed it to Naldini. Like its recto, this study is rather Sartesque, but its high quality excludes an attribution to Naldini, whose most Pontormesque drawings are more schematic in modelling and less decisive in contours than this drawing. This study is closely related stylistically to cat. 63, is almost surely taken from the same model, and may be placed right after it in our series. In the sketch above the head is upright as in cat. 63, but an indication that this was not to be Pontormo's final solution is seen in the lower figure, where the thrown back head is lightly sketched. A peculiarity of this drawing not found in any of the others is the sharply bent right leg, which eventually appears in this position in the painting.

65 · Florence, Uffizi 6670F *recto*: Study for the Dead Christ, Dublin *Pietà*. Nude lying across to the left with the right arm extended; below, the head and shoulders restudied. (*Verso*: Study for the same figure, cat. 62.) 280 x 396, red chalk. Fig. 69.

Bibliography: Ferri 1890, 119; Berenson 1903, no. 2159; *MPA* 1910, 33; Clapp 1914, 221–222; Clapp 1916, 16; Sinibaldi 1925, 156, fig. 9; Berenson 1938, 315, no. 2159, fig. 948.

See cat. 62. This study was the second in Sinibaldi's series for the Dead Christ, but it seems rather to be the fourth of the surviving studies. In the lower sketch of cat. 64 there was a suggestion of the more reclining pose with the head tilted back that we see developed here. It was the position of the head that was Pontormo's major concern in this drawing. Below, the head is restudied in a position more parallel to the plane of the body, as it would be in the painting.

66 · Florence, Uffizi 6690F *verso*: Study for the Dead Christ, Dublin *Pietà*. Nude lying across to the left with the right arm extended back; below, torso and legs. (*Recto*: Study for *Joseph* (III), cat. 26.) 253 x 396, red chalk, the sketches below in black chalk. Fig. 70.

Bibliography: Berenson 1903, no. 2175; Clapp 1914, 237; Clapp 1916, 16, fig. 9; Sinibaldi 1925, 156, fig. 8; Berenson 1938, 315, no. 2175.

See cat. 62. Sinibaldi thought this was Pontormo's first study for the Christ because it is relatively unelaborated. However, it is closer to the final pose of the Christ than the preceding three studies. It is a development on the pose of the figure in cat. 65 in which the position of the head and torso was the central concern, the rest of the figure being only lightly indicated. The head is now placed forward parallel to the line of the body, as was suggested in the restudying of the head in cat. 65. The torso, too, is turned in a more frontal position that forces the left shoulder forward and reintroduces the left arm across the body. As Clapp has noted, the sketches in black chalk below are of the thirties, like those on cat. 63, 67, 69, and 71, and show evidence of Pontormo's study of Michelangelo's Medici Tomb *Allegories*.

67 · Florence, Uffizi 6689F *recto*: Studies for the Dead Christ, Dublin *Pietà*. Nude lying across to the left with the right arm extended, the left across the body; above, the head restudied; to the right, the left foot restudied; below, the right hand restudied three times and on a smaller scale, the figure restudied twice. (*Verso*: Studies for the Dublin *Pietà*, cat. 69.) 280 x 404, red chalk; the small studies in black chalk. Fig. 71.

Bibliography: Berenson 1903, no. 2174; Clapp 1911, 14; Clapp 1914, 234–235; Clapp 1916, 16; Sinibaldi 1925, 156, fig. 10; Berenson 1938, 309, 315, no. 2174, fig. 966.

See cat. 62. As Sinibaldi has noted, this is the latest sheet of studies for the Dead Christ. In this drawing the body, head, and left arm are drawn much as they were in cat. 66 and as they would be in the *Pietà*, but the right arm is drawn in a series of experimental poses. This is the first drawing of the series to be dominated by a concern with the composition as a whole. The hand of the Virgin appears under the right arm of the Christ, and the repeated studies of this right arm are evidently attempts to lower it in order to make room for the kneeling St. John. In the painted figure the arm has been shifted still further in a vertical position, a change that must reflect a final study that has not survived. As Clapp has noted, the two small variations of the figure below are possibly inspired by Michelangelo's Medici Tomb *Allegories*. (Cf. also in this series cat. 63, 66, 69, and 71.)

68 · Florence, Uffizi 6693F *verso*: Studies for St. John and for the *St. Lawrence* (?), Dublin *Pietà*. Nude kneeling turned to the right and looking down; above, bust of a young saint with a martyr's palm. (*Recto*: Study for the Dublin *Pietà*, cat. 70.) 392 x 261, red chalk, the sketch above in black. Fig. 72.

Bibliography: Berenson 1903, no. 2177; Clapp 1914, 240; Sinibaldi 1925, 158; Fraenckel 1933, 170; Berenson 1938, no. 2177; *MDM* 1954 (Marcucci), no. 38; *EMI* 1954, no. 54.

See cat. 62. Clapp dated this study 1516–1518, but did not connect it with the other drawings from the *Pietà* series. Fraenckel dated it a little before 1518 as connected with cat. 69 and 70 but not as related to the Dublin *Pietà*. Marcucci placed this drawing 1515–1518 as connected with the *Pietà* series, but not as for the Dublin predella, which she considered to be earlier and identifiable with the predella to the S. Gallo *Annunciation*. The kneeling figure is the first study for the St. John. It corresponds in Pontormo's development of the composition to cat. 65 and 66 for the Christ, drawings for the figure in a pose that would have permitted the St. John to be in this position. While Sinibaldi identified the kneeling nude with the St. John, no mention has been made of the sketch above, except that Berenson called it a young Baptist. It is most likely to have been a first jotting for the *St. Lawrence* of the predella, the only one of the saints who holds the martyr's palm. In draughtsmanship this study is extremely reminiscent of the contemporary portrait sketches by Andrea del Sarto, such as Uffizi 301F and 661E.

69 · Florence, Uffizi 6689F *verso*: Studies for St. John, Dublin *Pietà*. Nude kneeling turned right, looking out at the spectator; to the right, the figure restudied bent over, the arms and legs restudied; in the center, two small nudes. (*Recto*: Studies for the Dublin *Pietà*, cat. 67.) 280 x 404, red chalk, small sketches in black chalk. Fig. 73.

Bibliography: Berenson 1903, no. 2174; Clapp 1914, 235–236; Sinibaldi 1925, 158; Fraenckel 1933, 170; Berenson 1938, no. 2174.

See cat. 62. Clapp dated this drawing 1516–1517 but did not specifically connect it with the other drawings from the *Pietà* series. Fraenckel connected it with cat. 68 and 70 as datable shortly before

1518, but did not relate them to the *Pietà* or its other studies. Sinibaldi associated this sheet with the Dublin predella, but thought it more likely to be for one of the flanking saints than for the St. John. The studies on this sheet belong at an early stage in the development of the composition before the final position of the Christ had been established. In the subsequent study for the St. John, his right arm is moved forward to hold Christ's right arm, with the consequent shift in his weight and in the position of his legs. The small nude in the center of the sheet is a later reinterpretation of the pose, probably dating from the thirties like the later sketches on cat. 63, 66, 67, and 71.

70 · Florence, Uffizi 6693F *recto*: Study for St. John, Dublin *Pietà*. Kneeling nude turned to the right with the right hand extended, looking over his shoulder. (*Verso*: Study for the same figure, cat. 68.) 392 x 262, red chalk. Fig. 74.

Bibliography: Berenson 1903, no. 2177; *MPA* 1910, 32; Clapp 1914, 240; Sinibaldi 1925, 158, fig. 12; Fraenckel 1933, 170; Berenson 1938, no. 2177; *MDM* 1954 (Marcucci), no. 38; *EMI* 1954, no. 54; Sanminiatelli 1955, 96.

See cat. 62. Clapp dated this study ca. 1518 but did not associate it with the other drawings for the St. John or with the other *Pietà* studies. Fraenckel dated it a little before 1518 as connected with cat. 68 and 69 but not as related to the Dublin *Pietà*. Marcucci placed this drawing 1515–1518 and Sanminatelli dated it not before 1515 as connected with the *Pietà* series, but not with the Dublin predella, which they considered to be earlier and identifiable with the predella of the S. Gallo *Annunciation*. It is difficult to understand how this drawing could be separated from the St. John of the Dublin *Pietà*, but only Sinibaldi has made the connection. In this final nude study for the figure, the St. John is posed exactly as he is in the *Pietà* with the right arm extended to hold Christ's arm. As Fraenckel has noted, this exact figure appears as a putto in a *Madonna della Carità* (Florence, Ospedale degli Innocenti), a pastiche attributed to Pontormo in which a putto from cat. 244 also occurs.

71 · Florence, Uffizi 6601F *verso*: Studies for the *St. Francis*, Dublin *Pietà*. Kneeling nude turned to the right pointing to the right and looking at the spectator; to the right, the figure restudied; to the left, lightly sketched nude turned left; to the extreme right, small seated nude. (*Recto*: Study for *Joseph* (I), cat. 20.) 390 x 264, red chalk, the small nude in black chalk. Fig. 75.

Bibliography: Berenson 1903, no. 2100; Clapp 1911, 13; Clapp 1914, 178–179; Sinibaldi 1925, 158; Berenson 1938, no. 2100.

See cat. 62. Berenson dated this study "fairly early," while Clapp placed it not later than 1518, although he originally connected it with the figure who supports Christ's shoulders in the S. Felicita *Deposition*. As Sinibaldi has suggested, these are studies for one of the kneeling saints of the predella. The *St. Francis*, a figure which is also studied on cat. 72 in a pose very close to that of the kneeling figure in the painting, is the most probable. The small nude study to the right dates from the thirties like the other later sketches on studies for the Dublin predella (cf. cat. 63, 66, 67, 69), and was probably done after Michelangelo's *Lorenzo de' Medici* seen from the side.

72 · Paris, Ecole des Beaux-Arts 3337 *verso*: Study for the *St. Francis*, Dublin *Pietà*, and for the Christ and St. John the Baptist, Visdomini altar. Kneeling nude pointing to the right and looking at the spectator; to the right, seated nude turned left cut off at the legs; to the left, two kneeling embracing putti. (*Recto*: Studies for *Joseph* (II), cat. 24.) 265 x 395, red chalk; the figure to the right in black chalk and the putti in black and brown chalk; inscribed in ink: *Palma Collection Cornu.* Fig. 76.

Bibliography: Lavallée 1935, 30; Berenson 1938, no. 2336A; *MP* 1956 (Marcucci), no. 102, fig. 136; *Paris Exhib.* 1958, no. 34; Freedberg and Rearick 1961, 8, fig. 17; Schlegel 1961, 33.

See cat. 62. Berenson connected this sheet with the Visdomini altar or the *Story of Joseph*, but did not specify any particular figures. Marcucci dated it ca. 1520 on the basis of the embracing putto motive, which she found similar to cat. 133 for Poggio a Caiano, but she dated the kneeling figure ca. 1516–1517. The style of this sheet is quite consistent and it is a key link between the Visdomini altar and the Dublin *Pietà*, containing studies for both the altar and the predella. The central figure in red chalk is a nude study for the *St. Francis* of the predella in a pose almost identical to that of the figure in the painting. The putti have no relation to the embracing putti of the Poggio a Caiano drawing cited by Marcucci, which are derived from the Sistine Ceiling, but are first ideas for the Christ and the St. John of the Visdomini altar. The St. John alone is sketched lightly to the right of the sheet. The notion of these embracing figures must have been abandoned by Pontormo shortly after this drawing, since in the subsequent studies (cat. 33–42) the Christ and the St. John are conceived as separate from one another, even though their poses, especially that of the Christ, remain very close to those sketched here.

The motive of the embracing Christ and St. John was a not unusual one in the circle of Fra Bartolommeo, occurring most notably in the *Holy Family* of 1516 (Rome, Galleria Nazionale). However, even if they derive ultimately from this source, the Pontormo children are less Raphaelesque in their postures and considerably more impetuous in their embrace than Fra Bartolommeo's. Possible evidence for the existence of a more finished drawing by Pontormo for these children is a Pontormesque painting formerly in the Spinelli Collection, Florence,[39] in which the embracing children are posed very much as they are here. Schlegel has connected these children with a *bozzetto* in which a similar motive, perhaps derived from Pontormo, occurs. However, the work is not a Pontormo sculpture of 1513–1518 as Schlegel asserts.

MISCELLANEOUS DRAWINGS CA. 1517–1518

73 · Florence, Uffizi 654E *verso*: Ca. 1517–1518. Cast of drapery. (*Recto*: Study for the Visdomini altar, cat. 36.) 218 x 170, red chalk.

Bibliography: Clapp 1914, 109; Berenson 1938, no. 1959D. (Photo G.)

Clapp dated this study ca. 1518. The style of this drapery is the same as that of cat. 75, another drapery study of this date, and cat. 31, for the draped head of the Visdomini altar Madonna. This study is probably connected with the draperies of a figure in the Visdomini altar or with the curtain held back by the putti, but the folds cannot be precisely identified.

74 · Florence, Uffizi 675E *recto*: Ca. 1517. Three seated nudes. (*Verso*: Drapery study, cat. 75.) 204 x 254, red chalk; W: Small eagle. Fig. 77.

Bibliography: Ferri 1881, 40; Ferri 1890, 115; Berenson 1903, no. 1988; *MPA* 1910,

[39] *Madonna and Child with St. Elizabeth and St. John* (panel, 124 x 95 cm). This painting is attributed to Pontormo in the catalogue of the sale of the collection, *La Raccolta Severino Spinelli di Firenze*, Galleria Pesaro, Milan, 1928, no. 25, fig. 4; and by Venturi 1932, 120n1, fig. 64, who dated it 1515–1518.

27; Clapp 1914, 111–112; Berenson 1938, no. 1959G; *MP* 1956 (Marcucci), no. 100, fig. 134a; Marcucci 1956, 11, fig. 10.

Berenson (1903) dated this sheet 1530, while Clapp dated it 1518, Marcucci 1518–1520. This study belongs in the period of the Visdomini altar. The way the forms are broken up, especially in the two heads to the right, is reminiscent of Pontormo's study influenced by the *Laocoön* (cat. 43), which he used for the St. Joseph of the altarpiece. Ferri first noted that the nude to the right was inspired by the figure who pulls on his stockings in Michelangelo's *Cascina* cartoon. Several other drawings of the years 1517–1518 are related to motives from the cartoon (cf. cat. 34). The studies for the Visdomini altar St. John the Baptist (cat. 39–42) and another drawing (cat. 80) are derived from the same figure that was the source for this nude. In the St. John studies the motive has already been transformed, but here and in cat. 80 there is a direct relation to Michelangelo in the heavy proportions and emphatic musculature of the nude. The crouched nude to the left appears in cat. 77 and 78 of this same date.

75 · Florence, Uffizi 675E *verso*: Ca. 1517–1518. Cast of drapery. (*Recto*: Nude studies, cat. 74.) 204 x 254, red chalk.

Bibliography: Giglioli 1926, 786–787; Berenson 1938, no. 1959G; *MP* 1956 (Marcucci), no. 100, fig. 134b. (Photo G.)

Giglioli noted that this drapery study was Düreresque and dated it 1525–1530. Marcucci dated it 1518–1520 and connected it with the woman nearest the window on the lower wall of the Poggio a Caiano fresco. Neither of these later dates is convincing for this study, which is similar in style to drapery studies for the Visdomini altar (cat. 31, 45, 52) and should be dated with its recto at that time.

76 · Florence, Uffizi 6525F *verso*: Ca. 1517–1518. Seated nude boy leaning to the right. (*Recto*: Study for the Visdomini altar, cat. 51.) 400 x 110, red chalk; bottom of the sheet cut in an oval.

Bibliography: Berenson 1903, no. 2028; Clapp 1914, 131; Fraenckel 1933, 167, 169; Berenson 1938, no. 2028. (Photo G.)

Berenson connected this study with Poggio a Caiano, while Fraenckel associated it with the *Putti with the Arms of Leo X* of the Cappella del Papa of 1515. Clapp rightly dated it 1517–1518. He considered it as possibly for the Christ of the Visdomini altar, but this drawing is not related to the series of studies (cat. 33–35) for that figure. It is very close in style to such Visdomini altar studies as cat. 30 for the Madonna, and must be dated contemporary with its recto, a study for the St. James of the altar.

77 · Florence, Uffizi 6543F *recto*: Ca. 1517–1518. Nude seated with his arms around his left knee looking at the spectator; to the right above, nude kneeling turned left looking down with his right arm extended. (*Verso*: Nude studies, cat. 78.) 394 x 266, red chalk. Fig. 80.

Bibliography: Berenson 1903, no. 2046; *MPA* 1910, 28; Clapp 1914, 143, pl. 2; Fraenckel 1933, 166–168; Berenson 1938, 311, no. 2046; Schlegel 1961, 31, fig. 10.

Berenson thought these nudes were done in connection with Poggio a Caiano. Fraenckel placed this drawing 1514–1515 as related to the seated figure in the background of Andrea del Sarto's S. Gallo *Annunciation*, a figure that she believed was painted by Pontormo. Clapp dated this sheet 1515–1516, noting the connection in the pose of the seated nude with the figure on the left of cat. 74 and with the crouched figures on the verso, and the connection in the pose of the kneeling nude with another study for the figure on the verso, and with an almost identical figure on cat. 83. The kneeling figure, drawn more elaborately on cat. 83, might have been an idea for a figure in an *Adoration*. Except that he looks down rather than up, the pose is not far from that of the St. Francis in the first sketch for the Visdomini altar (cat. 29). This drawing and its verso are also very close in style to the series of studies for the Dead Christ of the Dublin *Pietà* (cf. especially cat. 67), and the sheet should be dated not before 1517.

78 · Florence, Uffizi 6543F *verso*: Ca. 1517–1518. Reclining nude seen from behind; below, a crouching nude studied twice; over these studies, a kneeling figure turned to the left lightly indicated. (*Recto*: Nude studies, cat. 77.) 394 x 266, red chalk. Fig. 78.

Bibliography: Berenson 1903, no. 2046; Clapp 1914, 143; Fraenckel 1933, 166–168; Berenson 1938, 311, no. 2046.

See the recto. This drawing was rightly dated ca. 1517 by Clapp. Berenson thought the crouched figures were for the Vertumnus of the Poggio a Caiano lunette. Fraenckel dated the drawing 1514–1515, connecting the crouched figures with the *Putti with the Arms of Leo X* in the Cappella del Papa, and the reclining figure with the female figures in the *chiaroscuri* (Uffizi 91461 and 91464) by Andrea del Sarto, which she considered were painted with the assistance of Pontormo.

79 · Florence, Uffizi 6554F *verso*: Ca. 1517–1518. Nude boy seen from behind. (*Recto*: Study for the Visdomini altar, cat. 34.) 289 x 205, red chalk over faint black chalk; inscribed in ink: *Jacopo di Pontormo*.

Bibliography: Clapp 1914, 150; *MP* 1956 (Marcucci), cat. 99, fig. 133b; Berenson 1961, no. 2055A.

Clapp rejected this study as a Pontormo, apparently because of the poor construction of the right leg. It was not mentioned by Berenson. Marcucci called it a study in deformity, comparing it with cat. 322. This nude study is identical in style to its recto for the Christ of the Visdomini altar and may be dated at the same time.

80 · Florence, Uffizi 6594F *recto*: Ca. 1517–1518. Nude seated with back turned looking over his left shoulder; below in reverse direction, torso in profile left and a left arm. (*Verso*: Nude studies, cat. 81.) 399 x 257, red chalk.

Bibliography: Berenson 1903, no. 2093; *MPA* 1910, 31; Clapp 1914, 173–174; Berenson 1938, no. 2093; Schlegel 1961, 30, fig. 10.

Berenson connected these studies with Poggio a Caiano. Clapp dated this sheet 1516–1517, noting rightly that the proportions and modelling of the figures were influenced by Pontormo's study of Michelangelo's *Cascina* cartoon. The style of this drawing is close to cat. 74 and 77 of this same date, while similar heavily muscled torsos occur in a number of drawings from the Corsini Sketchbook, such as cat. 114. The nude with his back turned is not specifically derived from the cartoon, but the torso in profile is identical to the figure on the right in cat. 74 and both are derived from the figure who pulls on his stockings in the *Cascina* cartoon.

81 · Florence, Uffizi 6594F *verso*: Ca. 1517–1518. Seated nude leaning to the left; sideways on the sheet, seated figure in profile right with a child. (*Recto*: Nude studies, cat. 80.) 399 x 257, red chalk.

Bibliography: Berenson 1903, no. 2093; Clapp 1914, 174; Berenson 1938, no. 2093. (Photo G.)

Berenson connected these studies with Poggio a Caiano. Clapp dated the drawing toward 1518 and related the seated figure to the *Cascina* cartoon. The nude is stylistically similar to drawings that are after Michelangelo's cartoon (cat. 74 and the recto), but it is not specifically related to it in motive. This figure is connected in style, in the figure type with the very long and heavy torso, and in some aspects of the pose, with cat. 38, a study for the St. John the Baptist of the Visdomini altar, and it must be very close to it in date. The sketch above is probably an idea for a Madonna and Child and is similar in composition to the outline sketch for a Madonna group on cat. 39 of this same period.

82 · Florence, Uffizi 6662F *verso*: Ca. 1517–1518. Seated nude with legs to the left and the right arm raised; left below sideways on the sheet, a head. (*Recto*: Studies for the Visdomini altar, cat. 61.) 401 x 263, black chalk heightened with white on brown paper.

Bibliography: Berenson 1903, no. 2153; Clapp 1911, 8; Clapp 1914, 215; Clapp 1916, 32, fig. 62; Berenson 1938, no. 2153; *MP* 1956 (Marcucci), no. 97, fig. 131b.

Berenson thought this drawing was possibly for the St. John the Baptist of the Visdomini altar, while Clapp believed it was a study for the Pomona of the Poggio a Caiano lunette, comparing it in style with cat. A70 and A77. Clapp dated the drawing 1518–1519, and considered that it marked a transition between the style of the Visdomini altar and Poggio a Caiano. This drawing has no connection with Poggio a Caiano. None of the figures in the preparatory studies for the lunette are so indecisive in the modelling, so unclear in the contours, or so rounded — almost lumpy — in proportions. This study is identical in style to its recto, cat. 35, 39, and 51, all for the Visdomini altar, and must be dated no later than 1518.

83 · Florence, Uffizi 6677F *recto*: Ca. 1517–1518. Kneeling nude turned to the left looking down and holding a staff; below, smaller nude reclining to the left. (*Verso*: Nude studies, cat. 183.) 405 x 272, red chalk. Fig. 81.

Bibliography: Ferri 1890, 119; Berenson 1903, no. 2162; Clapp 1914, 227; Fraenckel 1933, 168; Berenson 1938, no. 2162; *MC* 1940, 50.

Berenson dated this drawing 1520, rightly connecting it in style with drawings for the Dublin *Pietà* (cat. 65 and 67) and for *Joseph* (III) (cat. 26), all of which, however, should be dated ca. 1517. Like cat. 77 and 78, to which these studies are related in motive, this sheet is very close to the drawings for the Dublin *Pietà* and should be dated at the same time. Clapp placed it a little earlier, 1516, and connected the figure below with the reclining figure to the far right of Michelangelo's *Cascina* cartoon. This nude is related to a sketch on cat. 78, to cat. 81 (a more seated variant of the pose), and to the verso of this sheet. However, only the verso, a later study of ca. 1519–1520, has any specific connection with the cartoon figure. The kneeling nude above is a more elaborated version of the figure that is studied on cat. 77 and 78. As Clapp has noted, it may have been drawn for an *Adoration*. The pose is very like that of the St. Francis as he appears in the compositional study for the Visdomini altar (cat. 29), and it is not impossible that there was some connection with that figure. Fraenckel, who dated the sheet 1514–1515, believed this figure was used for the kneeling Isaac in the SS. Annunziata *Visitation*. Cat. A79 is a copy after this figure.

84 · Florence, Uffizi 8976S *recto*: Ca. 1517–1518. Putto seated with the right leg drawn up, blowing a pipe. (*Verso*: Studies for the Visdomini altar, cat. 30.) 335 x

195, red chalk; W: Mountains (cf. B. 11663); inscribed in ink: *Coregio 49.*
Fig. 79.

Collection: Reynolds, stamp recto (L. 2364); Santarelli, given to the Uffizi in 1866, stamp recto (L. 907).

Bibliography: Santarelli 1870, 608; Di Pietro 1912, 78, fig. 2; Clapp 1914, 282–283; Clapp 1916, 32; Berenson 1938, no. 2248C; Becherucci 1943, 7, pl. 5; Toesca 1943, 13; Parigi 1951, no. 929; *MP* 1956 (Marcucci), no. 103, fig. 138a; Berenson 1961, no. 2248C, fig. 909.

This sheet was attributed to Correggio in Santarelli's catalogue, but it was recognized as a Pontormo by Di Pietro. This putto study has been unanimously connected with the putti of the Poggio a Caiano lunette, but not without considerable disagreement as to which figure: Di Pietro thought it was for the putto to the left above the window, Clapp and Marcucci connected it with the putto on the wall to the right, and Becherucci with the putto above the window to the right. There is very little stylistic connection between this drawing and the studies for the Poggio a Caiano putti (cat. 150–160), nor (except for the legs of the putto on the wall to the right) is there any specific relation in motive. This study belongs earlier in the period of the Visdomini altar and is identical in style to several studies for that picture, such as its verso for the Madonna, cat. 33 and 34 for the Christ, cat. 40 for the St. John, and cat. 58 for the putto on the left. In this group of drawings, most of them also in red chalk, there are the same puffy forms, uneven contours, exaggerated roundness of the head, and deeply shadowed eyes that are evident in this study. The pose is so similar to that of the St. John the Baptist that it would be tempting to connect it with that figure, but the action and mood of the putto, who is probably intended to be playing a musical instrument, make this association rather unlikely.

1518–1519. PORTRAIT OF COSIMO IL VECCHIO. Florence, Uffizi 3574. I. Panel, 86 x 65 cm.
Fig. 83.

Bibliography: Trapesnikoff 1909, 20, pl. 9; Clapp 1916, 21–22, 147–152, fig. 42; Voss 1920, 176, fig. 54; Venturi 1932, 122–126, fig. 66; *Paris Exhib.* 1935, no. 382; Berenson 1936, 401; *MM* 1939, 91; Toesca 1943, 22, fig. 43; Becherucci 1944, 14, fig. 9; Nicco Fasola 1947, illus. pp. 57–58; Alazard 1948, 144–147, fig. 42; *Brussels Exhib.* 1954, no. 57, fig. 15; *MP* 1956 (Berti), no. 37, fig. 28; Marcucci 1956, 10, fig. 8; Freedberg 1961, I, 529–530, II, fig. 651.

This painting is mentioned by Vasari (V/M, VI, 264), who says that a portrait of "Cosimo vecchio de' Medici dalle ginocchia in su" was ordered by Goro da Pistoia, secretary to the Medici. Lorenzino de' Medici, Duke of Urbino, presumably ordered the picture of his famous ancestor through his secretary, Goro Gheri.[40] Lorenzino's death in May 1519

[40] Lorenzino was descended from Cosimo il Vecchio in a direct line through Piero il Gottoso, Lorenzo il Magnifico, and his father, Piero. The laurel branch at the left of the painting is the Medici *broncone*, its flourishing right side representing the line of the family then in power, the other side signifying the side of the family who no longer ruled. In describing the carnival decorations of 1513, Vasari notes (V/M, VI, 250–251) that Giuliano de' Medici was head of the *Compagnia del Diamante* because the diamond was the device of his father Lorenzo il Magnifico: ". . . e dell'altra, che aveva per nome e per insegna il Broncone, era capo il Signor Lorenzo

thus provides a *terminus ante quem* for the commission. When Vasari wrote, the picture was still owned by the Medici and hung in the house of Ottaviano de' Medici in the possession of his son Alessandro. It is likely that Pontormo planned a portrait of Piero de' Medici as a pendant to the *Cosimo il Vecchio*, but that it was never executed. For this projected pendant five studies have survived (cat. 85–89).

The date 1518–1519 that is indicated by the circumstances of the commission has been generally accepted for this picture, except by Toesca, who dated it 1523. The portrait is closely related in style to the *Joseph in Egypt* of the same date and to the Visdomini altar of 1518, especially to such figures as the St. Francis. Since Cosimo died in 1465, Pontormo's likeness is of course based on Quattrocento representations of Cosimo, probably on a medal (see Clapp for a list of these).

STUDIES FOR A PORTRAIT OF PIERO DE' MEDICI 1518–1519

85 · Rome, GNS F.C. 137 *recto*: Compositional study for a portrait of Piero de' Medici (for a pendant to the *Cosimo il Vecchio*?), 1518–1519. Three-quarter length figure seated in a chair almost in profile right holding a paper in front of him in his left hand. (*Verso*: Study for the same figure, cat. 86.) 278 x 191, red chalk. Fig. 82.

Collection: Corsini; R. Accademia dei Lincei, stamp verso (L. 2187).

Bibliography: Berenson 1903, no. 2349; Clapp 1914, 334; Berenson 1938, no. 2336G; Toesca 1943, fig. 14; *MP* 1956 (Marcucci), no. 131, fig. 151; *MP* 1956 (Berti), 50–51; Gamba 1956, 11, fig. 13; Berenson 1961, no. 2336G, fig. 962; Freedberg 1961, I, 529, II, fig. 652.

This portrait study was connected with other studies from the same model (cat. 86, 87, and 89) by Berenson, Clapp, Berti, and Marcucci, and with cat. 86 and 89 by Gamba, who dated it in the Certosa period. Clapp dated the project 1525–1530, while Marcucci placed it ca. 1530, Berti ca. 1534–1535. It is difficult to see either the delicately refined draughtsmanship of the twenties (cf. red chalk drawings, cat. 236 and 288) or the dry and meticulous style of the thirties (cf. the tightly disciplined line and rigid forms of cat. 331) in these vigorous studies. The style of this drawing and of cat. 86–89 points instead to a date of ca. 1518–1519. The open and spontaneous handling of line, the subdued chiaroscuro and light diagonal shading is to be found in the red chalk studies for the S. Michele altar of ca. 1519, especially cat. 99, 101, and 103. The nervous animation in the drawing of the hands and the pointed shape of the fingers is specifically characteristic of Pontormo's drawings until about 1521, but never after that date. The composition of this portrait relates it not only to the *Cosimo il Vecchio* (in reverse) but to the *Portrait of a Musician*, Pontormo's only other portrait of this period.[41] (Cf. the placement of the figure in the chair, the role of the hands, the folds and silhouette of the draperies, etc.)

Before the 1956 *Mostra del Pontormo* no suggestions had been made as to the

---

figliuolo di Piero de' Medici; il quale, dico, aveva per impresa un broncone, ciò è un tronco di lauro secco che rinverdiva le foglie, quasi per mostrare che rinfrescava e risurgeva il nome dell'avolo." In describing Lorenzino's car representing the *Golden Age*, Vasari mentions (*ibid.*, 254) a dried branch putting forth new leaves as representing a new golden age of the Pope, although he remarks "alcuni dicessero che la cosa del broncone alludeva a Lorenzo de' Medici, che fu duca d'Urbino."

[41] Uffizi 743 (panel, 88 x 67 cm). Gamba 1921, 6, fig. 10, first attributed the *Portrait of a Musician* (Francesco dell'Ajolle?) to Pontormo, dating it 1518. See *MP* 1956 (Berti), no. 36, fig. 27, dated 1516–1520; Freedberg 1961, 530–531, fig. 653, dated ca. 1519.

identity of the sitter in these drawings or their possible connection with Pontormo paintings. Those made on the occasion of the exhibition did not offer any easy solution to this problem, especially since the early date of these studies had not been recognized. Marcucci and Berti tentatively connected this study and cat. 86, 87, and 89 with the *Portrait of a Man* attributed to Pontormo in the Pitti[42] and with the *Portrait of a Man* formerly in Bordeaux (fig. 84),[43] which they agreed was of dubious authenticity. Gamba thought this drawing, cat. 86, and cat. 89 were studies for the ex-Bordeaux portrait, which he considered to be a Pontormo from the Certosa period. He suggested further that this picture was a Medici portrait similar to the *Cosimo il Vecchio*, probably representing Giovanni di Bicci. Gamba has dated these studies too late, the ex-Bordeaux picture is almost certainly a copy,

[42] No. 249. See *MP* 1956 (Berti), no. 79, fig. 72. Not only is there little basis for the attribution of this bust-length, profile portrait to Pontormo, but the present group of studies for a seated figure in three-quarter view are certainly not connected with it, in spite of a certain very general resemblance in facial type between the two sitters.

[43] This portrait was listed by Berenson 1936, 401, as a Pontormo in the collection of Pierre Chapannan, Bordeaux. It was also given to Pontormo by Nicco Fasola 1947, 58, fig. 41, and Gamba 1956, 11, the latter dating it in the Certosa period. Berti, *MP* 1956, 51, and Marcucci, *MP* 1956, 100–101, have noted it with doubts as to its authenticity. I am indebted to J. G. Lemoine of the Musée des Beaux-Arts, Bordeaux, for the information that the picture belonged to William Pierre Chabanneau, who bought it about 1925. It passed to his niece on his death, was sold in Paris in 1932–1933, and its present location is unknown. The portrait measured 100 x 80 cm, a little larger than the *Cosimo il Vecchio*, and the figure was dressed in red robes, as is the Cosimo. Although our conclusions must be drawn on the basis of a photograph, this picture appears to be a copy based on Pontormo's invention of 1518–1519.

and his association with Giovanni di Bicci is not convincing.[44] However, as Freedberg has suggested, this series of drawings might be Pontormo's preparation ca. 1518–1519 for an historical Medici portrait, a picture that was intended as a pendant to the *Cosimo il Vecchio*.

Not only does the style of these drawings point to a date contemporary with the Cosimo, but certain peculiarities suggest that they were drawn for its pendant. This is the only three-quarter length portrait composition by Pontormo in which the subject looks almost in profile to the right. (The *Musician* is seated to the right, but his head is nearly full-face.) This departure from the more normal direction alone would suggest that the composition was intended to complement one in which the figure faces left. The format of the composition is the same as the *Cosimo*, the pose of the figure seated in the chair is that of the *Cosimo* in reverse, and the archaic robe and hat are similar to Cosimo's costume. Furthermore, there is a vagueness of characterization and a lack of precision in the notation of the profile, suggesting that Pontormo was working not from a living model but from an inanimate painted or sculptured source. In these drawings as in the *Cosimo*, Pontormo compensated for the lack of vitality in the expression of the face by emphasizing the nervous activity of the hands. Pontormo drew the hands of this subject in at least three different positions (cat. 86, 88), while the head is always drawn from the same angle and with the same expression. Also, as in the *Cosimo*, Pontormo tried to place the near profile of the head onto a less archaic three-quarter view of the body, even attempting in one drawing (cat. 87) to turn the body into a frontal position.

These drawings strongly suggest that

[44] The face does not resemble the known likenesses of Giovanni de' Medici. See *MM* 1939, 40, 48, 88, 89.

Pontormo planned another posthumous portrait as a pendant to the *Cosimo*. However, the important question remains: who was this portrait to represent? It must have been a Medici, and we can be sure that Lorenzino would have commissioned a portrait of another in the direct line of Medici rulers from Giovanni di Bicci to himself. As a pendant to the portrait of the *Pater Patriae*, only a portrait of a Medici of equal stature would have been suitable. This reduces the possibilities to Giovanni di Bicci (1360–1429), Cosimo's father; Piero il Gottoso (1416–1469), Cosimo's son; and Lorenzo il Magnifico (1449–1492), Lorenzino's grandfather. As we have noted, it is not Giovanni di Bicci, nor is it the well known face of Lorenzo il Magnifico. There is, however, positive evidence that the person represented in these drawings is Piero il Gottoso.

The earliest likeness of Piero is the marble bust in the Bargello by Mino da Fiesole, which is dated 1453 and shows Piero aged thirty-seven.[45] Piero appears about six years later in Benozzo Gozzoli's *Adoration of the Magi* of 1459–1460 in the Palazzo Medici.[46] He rides in profile at the head of the group behind the Magi. The likeness is very close to Mino's except that Piero wears a hat that hides most of his hair, while the sagging jowls and downturned mouth indicate his more advanced age. From the years just before Piero's death in 1469 there is a medal that shows him in profile and as conspicuously older than in either of the previous portraits.[47] Piero is shown kneeling in the center of Botticelli's *Adoration of the Magi* of 1475 (Uffizi), but this posthumous portrait is idealized, depicting him as more youthful than in the medal.

Although Pontormo must have known Mino's bust, it is clear that he wished to represent Piero as an older man, an intention that is explicit in cat. 89, a study for the head of the figure. The features and apparent age of Piero in Pontormo's drawings correspond more closely to those in the Gozzoli fresco and in the medal. However, these are both profile views, while the more nearly three-quarter view in Pontormo's drawings suggests that he also knew a three-quarter view of Piero. The only such representation known to us is in fact the Mino bust, but the upright angle of the head with the chin thrust out is quite different from that in Pontormo's drawings. In these studies the head is tilted down at the same angle as the head in the *Cosimo il Vecchio*. Therefore, unless Pontormo used a model that has not survived, it is probable that his *Piero*, like his *Cosimo*, was a synthesis of the available material, and that the exact pose of the head as well as that of the body was invented by Pontormo himself.

There is little evidence that this projected pendant was ever executed by Pontormo. However, the ex-Bordeaux portrait gives us some idea of how Pontormo's ideas would have looked in painted form. This picture, which probably does not date before the forties, is based on Pontormo's drawings (cat. 85–86, 89) or on a finished drawing that has not survived. The figure is seated in the same position as in cat. 85, but the position of the hands is that of cat. 86, while the head and expression of the face are similar to cat. 89.

[45] For the bust and portraits derived from it, such as the Bronzinesque picture in London, see Trapesnikoff 1909, pl. 12, fig. 2 and pl. 13, fig. 1. Vasari notes (V/M, IV, 123) that the bust was in the Palazzo Medici in a lunette over a door in Piero's room.

[46] See Trapesnikoff 1909, pl. 12, fig. 3; and E. Toesca, *Benozzo Gozzoli* (Milan, 1958), pl. 5.

[47] See Trapesnikoff 1909, pl. 12, fig. 1; and G. F. Hill, *A Corpus of Italian Medals of the Renaissance before Cellini* (London, 1930), I, no. 908, II, pl. 146. There are miniatures copied from this medal in a manuscript of 1469 dedicated to Piero (Biblioteca Laurenziana). See *MM* 1939, nos. 96 and 99.

However, compared to Pontormo's study, the features of the face have been youthfully idealized. If a painting that was the model for the ex-Bordeaux picture was executed by Pontormo at the same time as the *Cosimo*, Vasari would surely have mentioned it. While he was not in Florence when Pontormo painted the *Cosimo*, he knew the exact whereabouts of the picture at the time of his writing and would presumably have known its pendant. Therefore, it is most likely that the death of Lorenzino in 1519 interrupted the work after the first part of the commission, the *Cosimo il Vecchio*, had been completed. There remains the possibility that Pontormo executed a pendant later, using these early drawings. Ottaviano de' Medici, who owned the *Cosimo*, could have given such a commission at any time until his death in 1546. However, Vasari reports much of Ottaviano's activity as a kind of artistic overseer for the Medici,[48] and no mention is made of such a commission. A further possible argument against Pontormo's later execution of the Piero portrait is another picture that may have been painted as the pendant to the *Cosimo il Vecchio*: Vasari's own *Portrait of Lorenzo il Magnifico*, painted for Alessandro in 1533 (V/M, VII, 657) is almost exactly the same dimensions (90 x 72 cm) as the *Cosimo*, the figure is three-quarter length, and it faces to the right. Furthermore, like the *Cosimo il Vecchio*, this picture was in the house of Ottaviano at the time of Vasari's writing, a circumstance suggesting that then (as today in the Uffizi) they hung as pendants.

[48] Ottaviano seems to have been in charge of Medici commissions from about 1520. In relation to Pontormo in particular, he commissioned the work at Poggio a Caiano in 1520–1521 (V/M, VI, 264) and in 1532–1534 (*ibid.*, 275); he was connected with Pontormo's portraits of Alessandro and Ippolito about 1525 (*ibid.*, 273); he asked Pontormo to paint a picture that was never executed in the thirties (*ibid.*, 279); and he bought from Rossino the mason three pictures that Pontormo had given him.

86 · Rome, GNS F.C. 137 *verso*: Study for a portrait of Piero de' Medici (cat. 85). Three-quarter length figure lacking the head seated in a chair almost in profile right holding a paper in front of him in his left hand. (*Recto*: Study for the same figure, cat. 85.) 278 x 191, red chalk; damaged inscription in ink in a sixteenth-century(?) hand: *Jac°. de Pontorno.* Fig. 85.

Bibliography: Berenson 1903, no. 2349; Clapp 1914, 334; Berenson 1938, no. 2336G; *MP* 1956 (Marcucci), no. 131, fig. 152b.

See cat. 85. This drawing is Pontormo's model study for the drapery and hands of a portrait of Piero de' Medici. To this body he added, as on the recto, the head of Piero studied from an earlier portrait. The hands in this drawing were the source for the hands in the ex-Bordeaux portrait painted after Pontormo's studies for the Piero de' Medici.

87 · Rome, GNS F.C. 133 *recto*: Study for a portrait of Piero de' Medici (cat. 85). Bust of a man in a hat looking to the right. (*Verso*: Study for the same figure, cat. 88.) 111 diameter, red chalk; sheet cut in a circle. Fig. 87.

Collection: Corsini, R. Accademia dei Lincei, stamp verso (L. 2187).

Bibliography: Berenson 1903, no. 2354; Clapp 1914, 346; Berenson 1938, no. 2368A; *MP* 1956 (Marcucci), 99.

See cat. 85. In this small sketch Pontormo experimented with the pose of the Piero de' Medici, placing the nearly profile head on a frontal body with rather awkward results. This position was evidently not developed further, since the more finished drawings (cat. 85–86) show the body in three-quarter view, as does the ex-Bordeaux portrait, which may have been painted after Pontormo's final *modello* for the portrait.

88 · Rome, GNS F.C. 133 *verso*: Study for a portrait of Piero de' Medici (cat. 85). Hands grasping the arm of a chair. (*Recto*: Study for the same figure, cat. 87.) 111 diameter, red chalk; sheet cut in a circle; mount inscribed in ink in a seventeenth-century (?) hand: *di mano di Jacopo da Puntormo.* Fig. 88.

Bibliography: Berenson 1903, no. 2354; Clapp 1914, 347; Berenson 1938, no. 2368A.

See cat. 85. This study of hands for a portrait of Piero de' Medici has not been connected with the other drawings in the series by Clapp and Berenson. The position of the hands sketched here was changed in cat. 85 and 86, where the right hand rests on the arm of the chair and the left hand holds a folded piece of paper.

89 · Florence, Uffizi 440F: Study for a portrait of Piero de' Medici (cat. 85). Portrait bust of a man in a hat turned to the right. 157 x 198, red chalk. Fig. 86.

Bibliography: Ferri 1890, 116; Berenson 1903, no. 1967; *MPA* 1910, 23; Clapp 1914, 91, pl. 6; Berenson 1938, no. 1967; Toesca 1943, fig. 56; *MP* 1956 (Marcucci), no. 130, fig. 150a; *MP* 1956 (Berti), 50; Gamba 1956, 11, fig. 14.

See cat. 85. This is the most carefully finished drawing of the series for a portrait of Piero de' Medici, and the only one in which the features are really articulated in any detail. The conspicuously aged face in this study confirms the idea that Pontormo intended to depict Piero as a middle-aged man, just as he had painted Cosimo, while in the ex-Bordeaux portrait derived from these drawings he appears much more youthful. In this study, in contrast to the others for the figure, we find a real analogy with the rich chiaroscuro and strong plasticity of the *Cosimo.* This drawing style, with the transparent and yet firm red chalk modelling and the liberal use of the white of the paper for highlights, is very close to that of cat. 99 and 101 for the S. Michele altar of ca. 1519.

Ca. 1518–1519. STORY OF JOSEPH (IV): *Joseph in Egypt.* London, National Gallery 1131. I. Panel, 96 x 109 cm. Fig. 89.

Bibliography: Goldschmidt 1911, 5, 30; Schubring 1915, 174, 404; Clapp 1916, 21–22, 156–159; Voss 1920, 166; Venturi 1932, 116–120, fig. 61; Berenson 1936, 402; Toesca 1943, 10, figs. 6–7; Becherucci 1944, 13, fig. 5b; Nicco Fasola 1947, 29–31, fig. 3; Wischnitzer 1953, 145–161, figs. 1–3, 6, 8b; *MP* 1956 (Berti), 16; Nicco Fasola 1956, 18, fig. 8; Gamba 1956, 10; Freedberg 1961, I, 525–529, II, fig. 650.

See the *Story of Joseph* (I). Clapp dated this last picture in the series 1518–1519 on the basis of the apparent age of Bronzino, whom Vasari tells us (V/M, VI, 261) is the boy seated on the steps in the foreground and whom we know came to Pontormo as a pupil at about this time. Goldschmidt and Voss dated the picture 1520 on the basis of Vasari's remark; however, it seems unlikely that the boy Pontormo painted was as old as seventeen. Freedberg dated it 1518; otherwise, this painting has been dated inexplicably early: Berenson placed it 1517; Wischnitzer and Berti dated it 1516, believing that a delay of one year from the date of the Borgherini marriage was possible but not three; and Becherucci dated it ca. 1515.

The style of this picture is quite different from that of the other three panels, even considering its larger scale and the fact that, unlike the first three of the series, it is not a *cassone* picture. The extreme spatial illogic, the sophisticated manipulation of the narrative, and the individualization of the types beyond even those of *Joseph* (III) are characteristic of a more advanced moment in Pontormo's development than 1515 or even 1517. In addition, there are figures that are clearly dependent on the Visdomini altar (cf. the dying Jacob with the St. Joseph, the old woman on the steps with the St. Francis, the putti with the Christ and the St. John, etc.) and the *Cosimo il Vecchio* (cf. the men to the left by the doorway), indicating a date contemporary with or even slightly later than these works. There is, furthermore, a novel factor in this picture that separates it from the others. It is the first of Pontormo's paintings in which Northern art, in the form of the prints of Lucas van Leyden as well as those of Dürer, played an important formative role.[49]

[49] Pontormo's exploitation of Northern prints before this date had been limited to the borrowing of an occasional motive from Dürer (see ns. 4 and 9). The *Joseph in Egypt* is the first picture in which Pontormo showed an interest in Lucas van Leyden as well as Dürer and an awareness of the Northern style in general, rather than merely of isolated motives. While the results of his earlier borrowings (like all those of Andrea del Sarto) are not the least Düreresque, this picture is decidedly Germanic in some of its episodes, anticipating Pontormo's more extensive investigation of Northern style in the early twenties. Cf. the layout of the composition, the little knots of figures, and the caricaturing of the types, with Lucas' *Return of the Prodigal Son* (Bar. 78, ca. 1510). The landscape is distinctly Northern in character, the rocks and little pointed roofs, towers, and dormer windows replacing the calm horizontal accents of the Italian landscape setting of *Joseph* (I). The model for this landscape might have been Lucas' *Ecce Homo* (Bar. 71, 1510) or his *Susanna in the Bath* (Bar. 33, ca. 1508). Andrea had also discovered the prints of Lucas van Leyden at this time, in particular the *Ecce Homo*, as can be seen in his *Dream of the Pharaoh* of ca. 1517. Since Pontormo's *Joseph in Egypt* closely follows Andrea's picture in date and the two artists were working together on the *Story of Joseph*, it is likely that Andrea introduced him to these Lucas prints.

STUDIES FOR THE STORY OF JOSEPH (IV)

90 · Florence, Uffizi 6735F *recto*: Study for the man to the lower left, *Joseph in Egypt*. Page from a sketchbook: Three-quarter length nude in profile right with the head turned away and hair blowing. (*Verso*: Study for *Joseph in Egypt*, cat. 91.) 219 x 135, black chalk heightened with white on pink prepared paper; W: Greek Cross in a circle (B. 5543). Fig. 90.

Bibliography: Berenson 1903, no. 2217; Clapp 1914, 266; Berenson 1938, no. 2217; *MP* 1956 (Marcucci), no. 124, fig. 154a.

Clapp thought that this figure was a study for the woman to the left behind Christ in the S. Felicita *Deposition*, dating it ca. 1526. Marcucci also dated it at the time of S. Felicita. This study has little in common with the refined style of Pontormo's drawings for the *Deposition*. Pontormo also used pink prepared sketchbook paper in some of the *Deposition* studies (cat. 271, 274, 275, 277), but they are all in red chalk and more delicate and ornamental in style. This sheet is so similar in style, in paper, medium, and dimensions to the drawings from the Corsini Sketchbook (cat. 105–123, as well as the studies for *Joseph* (III), *Joseph* (IV), and the Visdomini altar), that it must belong to the same period and may even originally have been part of the sketchbook. Since this nude is close in motive to the man to the extreme lower left of *Joseph in Egypt*, and its verso, as well as cat. 92 from the Corsini Sketchbook, is a study for the picture, this drawing is most likely to have been a study for the action of that figure.

91 · Florence, Uffizi 6735F *verso*: Study for the statue of a woman, *Joseph in Egypt*. Page from a sketchbook: Nude woman in profile left; to the left, faint sketch of an arm. (*Recto*: Study for *Joseph in Egypt*, cat. 90.) 219 x 135, red chalk, the arm in black chalk, on pink prepared paper.

Bibliography: Berenson 1903, no. 2217; Clapp 1914, 266; Berenson 1938, no. 2217; *MP* 1956 (Marcucci), no. 124, fig. 154b.

See the recto. Clapp and Marcucci both dated this drawing much later than they placed the recto, ca. 1535–1540. Clapp had reservations about the attribution to Pontormo. This sketch is somewhat unusual in character because it has been copied from an antique Venus torso, to which Pontormo has added one arm and the legs.[50] Pontormo used this figure, with the addition of the raised right arm and with a slight shift in the position of the feet, for the female statue in the background of *Joseph in Egypt*. The statue of the man at the left, for which there is also a sketchbook study (cat. 92) is also derived from an antique prototype.

92 · Rome, GNS F.C. 122 *recto*: Study for the statue of a man, *Joseph in Egypt*. Page from a sketchbook: Three-quarter length nude with right arm raised above his head; head and arm partly cut off. (*Verso*: Nude study, cat. 108.) 218 x 152, red chalk heightened with white on pink prepared paper. Fig. 91.

Bibliography: Berenson 1903, no. 2366; Clapp 1914, 344; Berenson 1938, no. 2366.

Clapp dated this study 1516–1518. It is one of the drawings from the Corsini Sketchbook (cat. 105–123) that can be associated with a definite pictorial motive. In this study for the upper part of the statue of a man to the left of the picture Pontormo used a familiar motive, probably derived from an antique Bacchus, that he had used as early as the *Carro della Zecca* of 1514 (cf. cat. 1).

[50] This Venus of the Medici Venus type was often copied in Florence in the sixteenth century. Cf. Fra Bartolommeo's drawing (Uffizi 1159E; Berenson 1938, no. 278); Michelangelo's drawing (Chantilly no. 29; Berenson 1938, no. 1397), and Pontormo's own *Venus and Cupid* (cat. 15) of ca. 1515 or *Pygmalion and Galatea* of 1529–1530. For other contemporary adaptations of this Venus type, see S. J. Freedberg, *Parmigianino* (Cambridge, 1950), pt. II, n. 45.

PART II · 1519–1521

Catalogue entries 93–191

PART II · 1519–1521

Ca. 1519. ST. CECILIA. Fiesole, Compagnia di Santa Cecilia. Lunette fresco over a doorway (destroyed).

Bibliography: Clapp 1916, 17, 255.

This fresco is described by Vasari[1] and mentioned by Borghini 1584, 481. By 1730 it had already been destroyed in the building of a new door (see Borghini, ed. Bottari, 1730, 393). Our identification of the preparatory studies for this fresco is based in part on an early eighteenth-century inscription on one of them (cat. 96): "Sta Cecilia che è a Fiesole." Further evidence for the appearance of this lost work is a black chalk drawing of the late sixteenth century (cat. A354; fig. 95), which is a copy after the lunette or after Pontormo's *modello* for it. It shows the figure fully draped, with the roses mentioned by Vasari in her hand, but without the putti indicated in one of Pontormo's studies (cat. 93).

Marcucci accepted the early dating for the *St. Cecilia* implied by Vasari (who mentioned it after the *Carro della Zecca*), placing it 1515–1516, while Clapp and Toesca dated it 1517–1518. However, in view of the similarity of the preparatory studies not only to the drawings for the Visdomini altar but especially to those for the S. Michele altar of 1519, it seems advisable to place the project ca. 1519 rather than earlier.

[1] V/M, VI, 257: ". . . ed in sul poggio di Fiesole, sopra la porta della Compagnia della Cecilia, una Santa Cecilia colorita in fresco con alcune rose in mano, tanto bella e tanto bene in quel luogo accomodata, che, per quanto ell'è, è delle buone opere che si possano vedere in fresco."

STUDIES FOR ST. CECILIA

93 · Rome, GNS F.C. 146 *recto*: Compositional study for *St. Cecilia*. In a lunette a crouching partially draped woman leaning to the right with the left hand extended holding a flower; behind her, three winged putti. (*Verso*: Study for the same figure, cat. 94.) 230 x 400, red chalk squared; St. Cecilia's face stained; sheet cut in lunette shape; W: Fruit (B. 7392). Fig. 92.

Collection: Corsini; R. Accademia dei Lincei, stamp verso (L. 2187).

Bibliography: Berenson 1903, no. 2355; Rusconi 1907, 270, illustrated; Clapp 1911, 6; Clapp 1914, 333; Clapp 1916, 17, fig. 11; Berenson 1938, no. 2336F; Toesca 1943, 10, illustrated; Becherucci 1943, 7, pl. 2; Becherucci 1944, 14; *EMI* 1954 (Bianchi), no. 55; *MP* 1956 (Marcucci), no. 93, fig. 126; Berenson 1961, no. 2336F, fig. 890.

Clapp first identified this drawing as Pontormo's compositional study for the *St. Cecilia*. It was dated 1515–1516 by Marcucci as close to the studies for the *Visitation* and anticipating the drawings for the Visdomini altar. Clapp and Bianchi placed it 1516–1518, Toesca 1517–1518. Since it closely parallels in style the drawings of 1518–1519, this drawing provides the best evidence that the *St. Cecilia* cannot have been painted before 1518 and more probably belongs in the year 1519. A chiaroscuro that is even richer and more intense than that of the Visdomini studies, together with details such as the angularity of the hand and the stiffened, free-standing draperies brings this drawing close to cat. 98 and 100, compositional studies for the S. Michele altar of ca. 1519. The bold, cursive design of the lunette and the increased tension in the composition are also akin to the S. Michele altar and to the related *Pietà* drawing (cat. 103). Furthermore, the St. Cecilia is, formally at least, a cousin to the putto under St. Michael's feet.

Additional reason for placing this drawing in 1519 is the connection with Pontormo's study of Michelangelo and with his probable trip to Rome at that time. (Cf. cat. 104 for a discussion of this problem.) Michelangelo's monumental Sibyls with putti behind them are certainly the general prototypes for Pontormo's composition, while the specific relation between the *St. Cecilia* and the Delphic Sibyl is particularly striking. In Pontormo's paintings of this date a very close parallel to the *St. Cecilia* may be found in the crouched, prophetlike *St. Anthony*, himself recalling the Prophets of the Sistine Ceiling.[2]

94 · Rome, GNS F.C. 146 *verso*: Study for *St. Cecilia*. Nude seen almost from behind turned to the right looking over the right shoulder; to the left, the right leg restudied. (*Recto*: Study for the same figure, cat. 93.) 400 x 230, red chalk.
Fig. 93.

Bibliography: Berenson 1903, no. 2355; Clapp 1914, 333–334; Berenson 1938, no. 2336F; *EMI* 1954 (Bianchi), no. 55; *MP* 1956 (Marcucci), no. 93, fig. 128a.

[2] Florence, Uffizi 8379 (canvas, 78 x 66 cm). Although Gamba 1921, 6, dated this picture ca. 1518 it has generally been called a late work; Clapp 1916, 132–133, dating it 1540–1545, and Berti, *MP* 1956, no. 72, fig. 65, dating it 1535–1545. It is datable ca. 1519 on the basis of its close stylistic rapport with the Visdomini altar and with the St. John the Evangelist of the S. Michele altar.

As Marcucci has seen, this drawing is probably a very first jotting for the figure of St. Cecilia, which is studied in final form on the recto of the sheet. The sparse, angular style of the drawing is similar to cat. 33 and 34 for the Visdomini altar of 1517–1518.

95 · Florence, Uffizi 6694F *verso*: Study for *St. Cecilia*. Nude seen almost from behind turned to the right, the head and lower legs cut off. (*Recto*: Study for the same figure, cat. 96.) 209 x 215, red chalk.
Fig. 94.

This unpublished sketch is a very early idea for the figure of St. Cecilia, similar to cat. 94 except that here the figure stands in a more upright position. The sharp, angular conception of the forms links this sketch with cat. 103, the *Pietà* study of ca. 1519. Furthermore, the motive of this figure is almost identical to that of the nude to the left of the *Pietà* drawing.

96 · Florence, Uffizi 6694F *recto*: Study for *St. Cecilia*. Half-length draped figure of a woman leaning to the right and looking out at the spectator. (*Verso*: Study for the same figure, cat. 95.) 209 x 215, red chalk; inscribed in ink in an early eighteenth-century hand: *Sta Cecilia che è a Fiesole*.
Fig. 97.

Bibliography: Ferri 1890, 119; Berenson 1903, no. 2178; Clapp 1911, 6; Clapp 1914, 240–241; Clapp 1916, 17, fig. 12; Berenson 1938, no. 2178; *MP* 1956 (Marcucci), 65.

Ferri connected this study with the lost *St. Cecilia* on the basis of the inscription. It is a study for the drapery of the figure in the same angular style as the verso. Here the drapery is similar to that in the copy after the fresco (cat. A354), but rather different from the less conventional half-draped figure in the compositional study, cat. 93. Both the handling of the drapery and the abbreviated drawing of the face are close to the studies for the head of the Madonna of the Visdomini altar, cat. 31 and 32.

97 · Paris, Louvre, Cabinet des Dessins R.F. 496: Study for *St. Cecilia.* Head of a smiling young woman looking over her right shoulder. 175 x 130, red chalk; laid down; badly foxed. Fig. 96.

Collection: Mariette, stamp recto (L. 1852); Dupan, stamp recto (L. 1440); His de la Salle, stamp recto (L. 1333); acquired by the Louvre in 1878, stamp recto (L. 1886).

Bibliography: De Tauzia 1881, 82, no. 105; Berenson 1903, no. 2334; Clapp 1914, 332 (as no. 105); Berenson 1938, no. 2334; Bacou 1955, no. 68.

This study was ascribed to Andrea del Sarto until it was attributed to Pontormo by Berenson, but without comment as to date or purpose. The recent appearance of a copy after the fresco (cat. A354) corroborates our identification of the subject as St. Cecilia. The features and expression of this head are the same in the copy, whose affected sweetness is a late *maniera* transcription of the fresh directness and naturalism of Pontormo's study from life.[3] This must have been the latest stage in the preparation for the fresco and this head was probably identical with the painted version. The delicacy in handling the red chalk is very close to cat. 101, the study for the legs of the *St. Michael* of ca. 1519.

[3] A *Sibyl* attributed to Pontormo in the Loeser Collection, Palazzo Vecchio, Florence (panel, 66 x 52 cm) is evidently related to Pontormo's *St. Cecilia* and must reflect a lost original of the same moment. The facial type and expression are similar to cat. 97, while the composition of the figure and the costume are close to the St. Cecilia as she appears in the later drawing after the fresco. Gamba 1956, 10, considered the Loeser *Sibyl* an original contemporary with the *Story of Joseph,* while Berti, *MP* 1956, no. 27, fig. 18, thought it possibly a copy of an original of ca. 1516–1517.

Ca. 1519. S. MICHELE ALTAR: *St. John the Evangelist and St. Michael.* Empoli, Museo della Collegiata; formerly Pontorme, S. Michele. I. Panels, each 173 x 59 (min.) 96 (max.) cm; the inside edges cut in a curve to fit around a shrine. Figs. 98–99.

Bibliography: Berenson 1896, 127; Gigliolí 1905, 146–151; Goldschmidt 1911, 47; Clapp 1916, 24–25, 177–179, figs. 35–36; Gamba 1921, 6, figs. 5–6; *Mostra Sacra* 1933, 117; Berenson 1936, 401; Toesca 1943, 10; Baldini 1955, nos. 12–13; *MP* 1956 (Berti), nos. 31–32, figs. 17–18; *MP* 1956 (Marcucci), 66; Baldini, *Empoli Cat.* 1956, 11–12, figs. 6–7; Baldini 1956, 8, figs. 2–3; Freedberg 1961, I, 531–533, II, figs. 655–656.

This altarpiece is mentioned by Vasari as executed shortly after the Visdomini altar for the Madonna chapel of S. Michele at Pontorme.[4] It was moved after restoration in 1955 to the museum at Empoli.

Giglioli placed the S. Michele altar merely "after 1516," while Goldschmidt and Clapp dated it correctly 1518–1519, following Vasari's implied date. With the exception of Gamba and Marcucci, who placed it no later than 1517, there has been general agreement on this dating. The altarpiece is surely datable ca. 1519, not only after the Visdomini altar, but after the *Cosimo il Vecchio* and the *Joseph in*

[4] V/M, IV, 259: ". . . fece Jacopo agli uomini di Puntormo una tavola che fu posta in Sant'Agnolo, lor chiesa principale, alla cappella della Madonna, nella quale sono un San Michelagnolo ed un San Giovanni Evangelista."

Egypt as well. The striking rhythmic vitality of Pontormo's post-Visdomini style in this altar is especially close to that of the last Borgherini panel, although on a more monumental scale. Furthermore, the Evangelist's face may be compared with that of the dying Jacob, the St. Michael with the elongated statues, his face with the highly characterized faces in the crowd, and the putto under his feet with the children pulling the chariot.

There is evidence of Pontormo's preoccupation with Michelangelo in the years 1519–1520 in both the saints. The Evangelist suggests the *St. Matthew*, although the figure has been greatly attenuated in accordance with Pontormo's new canon of form. The St. Michael may be a recollection of certain figures in Michelangelo's *Julius Tomb* projects of 1505 and 1513. Certainly the concept of the Victory Group as seen in these early projects must stand behind Pontormo's unusual arrangement of the St. Michael and the putto, while the attitude of the St. Michael recalls those of the bound slaves, especially the *Rebellious Slave* of ca. 1513.[5]

STUDIES FOR THE S. MICHELE ALTAR

98 · Florence, Uffizi 6571F *recto*: Study for the St. John and for the hands of St. Michael, S. Michele altar. Amply draped bearded man standing turned right writing on a tablet and looking at the spectator; the figure is framed within a rectangular field that is extended to the upper right; to the right below, two grasping hands. (*Verso*: Figure study, cat. 179.) 406 x 251, black chalk heightened with white; the hands in red chalk. Fig. 101.

Bibliography: Berenson 1903, no. 2071; Giglioli 1905, 150, illustrated; Gamba 1912, no. 1, pl. 1; Clapp 1914, 161; Clapp 1916, 24, fig. 37; Berenson 1938, 308–309, no. 2071, fig. 935; *MP* 1956 (Marcucci), no. 95, fig. 130a; Freedberg 1961, I, 532, II, fig. 654.

This compositional study for the Evangelist was first associated with the altar by Berenson. While Clapp placed it 1517–1518, and Freedberg ca. 1519, Gamba has dated it 1512–1515 and Marcucci no later than 1517. A dating of even as early as 1517 is difficult to justify in view of the evidently more mature style of the whole project as well as of this drawing. As would be expected in a drawing for the altarpiece following the Visdomini altar, stylistic tendencies of the Visdomini drawings are found here. The bold exaggeration of Andrea del Sarto's chiaroscuro manner that is evident in cat. 44 and 45 for the Visdomini Evangelist is still seen here; only now a new monumentality and clarity of form begins to emerge through the chiaroscuro. In this respect, the Evangelist study, its pendant for the St. Michael (cat. 100), and the *St. Cecilia* drawing (cat. 93) could be regarded as Pontormo's final extension of his Sartesque style of the years 1516–1518, in which there is at the same time a clear indication of the next stage of his development.

99 · Lille, Musée des Beaux-Arts 569 *verso*: Studies for the putto, S. Michele altar. Seated putto, cut off through the head and at the thigh, turned to the right with the right leg bent, the right arm pointing back, the left arm on his right leg; to the right, the figure restudied with the right arm at his side, the legs cut off. (*Recto*: Study for the S. Michele altar, cat. 100.) 158 x 385, red chalk; remains of

[5] No statues were executed for the 1505 project, but two drawings related to lost Michelangelo originals (Louvre 694 and 712) should be compared with the pose of St. Michael. Pontormo may not have seen any of the actual slave statues, as there is some doubt as to whether Michelangelo brought them back to Florence in 1518. See C. Tolnay, *Michelangelo* IV (Princeton, 1954), 46.

old mount and border to each side of the sheet. Fig. 103.

Bibliography: Pluchart 1889, 135, no. 569.

This drawing and its recto, the compositional study for the St. Michael, have been mentioned in the literature only under the old erroneous attribution to Timoteo Viti. However, the sheet has been recognized as Pontormo's by A. E. Popham and by Philip Pouncey, who called it to the author's attention. These model studies are trial poses for the putto before the final motive, as seen on the recto, was established. Pontormo's red chalk manner of the period just before Poggio a Caiano is strikingly in evidence here: the incisive linear treatment of the contours and the delicate, very transparent red chalk modelling is found in many other drawings of this precise moment, such as cat. 101 and 103 for the altar; cat. 104 for a *Creation of Eve;* cat. 89 for a portrait of Piero de' Medici; as well as in model studies, especially cat. 165, 178, and 183.

100 · Lille, Musée des Beaux-Arts 568 *recto*: Study for St. Michael, S. Michele altar. Draped figure standing turned slightly to the right with the left arm raised to his shoulder holding the scales, the right arm, seen only to the wrist, raised above his head; his right leg is bent, the foot resting on the shoulder of a putto who is crouched at his feet. (*Verso*: Study for the S. Michele altar, cat. 99.) 385 x 158, black chalk. Fig. 102.

Bibliography: Pluchart 1889, 135, no. 568.

This important compositional study was recognized as Pontormo's by A. E. Popham and by Philip Pouncey, who called it to the author's attention. It is the pendant drawing to cat. 98 for the Evangelist, identical in style, also in black chalk, and with the figure drawn in the same scale. Although the details of the pose have been worked out, this is not a final, finished drawing for the panel. It was probably followed by a number of studies for parts of the figure, of which only the one for the legs survives (cat. 101).

101 · Florence, Uffizi 6506F *recto*: Study for St. Michael, S. Michele altar. Figure seen from the waist down, the torso lightly draped, the weight on the left leg, the right leg bent and resting on a sphere; to the right in reverse direction, the right foot restudied; below, on a smaller scale, another foot. (*Verso*: Nude study, cat. A57.) 393 x 260, red chalk, small foot in ink; W: Fish in a circle (cf. B. 12419). Fig. 100.

Bibliography: Berenson 1903, no. 2014; Giglioli 1905, 151, illustrated; Clapp 1914, 117–118; Clapp 1916, 24, fig. 40; Berenson 1938, 310, no. 2014, fig. 945; Becherucci 1944, 14; *MP* 1956 (Berti), 20.

This drawing was first recognized by Giglioli as a study for the legs of St. Michael. Clapp had some misgivings due to the extremely delicate style of modelling and the similarity of the pose to that of the Galatea in the *Pygmalion and Galatea* of 1529–1530, but dated it 1517. Gamba dated the drawing 1512–1515 as for this picture, finding it quattrocentesque. Berenson, on the other hand, placed it 1520–1530 and thought that it was from a female model and may have been used for both pictures. The drawing is unquestionably from a male model and for the St. Michael rather than the Galatea, whose pose is actually quite different although her proportions are somewhat similar. In contrast to cat. 98 and 100, the compositional studies for the two saints, which are executed in a dramatic black chalk chiaroscuro manner, there is here a clarity of shape and substance suggested by an elegant, finespun contour line and a translucent modelling in red chalk. This high-keyed delicacy of surface, in which the white of the paper is used for highlights, is a new tendency of this date in Pontormo's studies, which we also see in such a diverse drawing as cat. 89 for a portrait of Piero de' Medici.

102 · Empoli, Museo della Collegiata, drawings on the reverse of the S. Michele altar: On the Evangelist panel a sketch for a *Pietà*: the Christ lies to the left with his legs bent at the knee; to the right, a crouched figure; to the left, a figure supporting Christ's shoulders; in the center, a figure leaning forward from behind. On the St. Michael panel: a left profile, part of a torso, a seated nude turned left, and a standing putto. Red chalk, the first sketch on the St. Michael panel in black chalk. Fig. 104 (detail).

Bibliography: Baldini 1955, 28; *MP* 1956 (Berti), 20; Baldini, *Empoli Cat.*, 1956, 12, fig. 17.

When the S. Michele altarpiece was brought to Florence for restoration of war damages, these sketches were discovered on the reverse of the two panels. Berti pointed out the similarity in composition between no. 103, a compositional drawing for a lunette of a *Pietà*, and the sketch on the back of the Evangelist panel. It is tempting to conclude that Pontormo actually planned a lunette to surmount the altarpiece, that he made a notation of its composition on the reverse of one of the panels, and then worked it out in detail in the compositional study (cf. cat. 103).

103 · Florence, Uffizi 300F *recto*: Compositional study for a *Pietà* lunette (for the S. Michele altar?). The Dead Christ lies across to the left, his head and shoulders supported by St. John; further to the left, a kneeling figure holding a torch; to the right, the three Marys. (*Verso*: Figure study, cat. 173.) 167 x 333, red chalk; sheet cut in lunette shape. Fig. 105.

Bibliography: Ferri 1890, 115; Berenson 1903, no. 1962; *MPA* 1910, 36; Gamba 1912, no. 2, pl. 2; Clapp 1914, 87; Clapp 1916, 29, fig. 39; Berenson 1938, 315, no. 1962, fig. 970; Becherucci 1943, 7, fig. 3; Becherucci 1944, 14; *MF* 1952, 61; *MP* 1956 (Marcucci), no. 101, fig. 135a; Marcucci 1956, 10, fig. 9; Freedberg 1961, I, 533–534, II, fig. 657.

Ferri thought this study was for the Certosa *Pietà*, Gamba placed it in Pontormo's "periodo andreesco," while Berenson (1903) dated it 1530. However, Clapp dated it correctly ca. 1520, followed by Marcucci, both of whom connected it with the lost *Pietà* at S. Gallo mentioned by Vasari (V/M, VI, 260). Becherucci has dated the drawing 1518–1521, noting the close affinity with the *St. Cecilia* compositional drawing (cat. 93). Not only are these two drawings close in their red chalk style and in their monumentality of conception, but both are experimental solutions to the problem of lunette composition, preceding by a year the first ideas for the Poggio a Caiano lunette (cat. 131 and 132).

Like other works of ca. 1519 this composition shows evidence of Pontormo's intensive study of Michelangelo at that time. The motive of the turning woman supporting the Virgin recalls the contrapposto of the Doni tondo Madonna. Even more explicitly — and in a manner that can hardly be coincidental — the woman is reminiscent of Raphael's earlier adaptation of Michelangelo's invention in his Borghese *Entombment*, where the figure is placed in an identical context. As Marcucci has remarked, there is also a close affinity with Rosso here. The extreme angularity of the forms, the dramatic violence of the conception, and even the composition of figures around a central void, is enough to indicate that this is a point at which Pontormo and Rosso in, for example, the Volterra *Deposition* came together in both intention and in stylistic vocabulary.

With the aid of the sketches on the back of the S. Michele altar (cat. 102) Freedberg has been able to identify this drawing as a compositional study for a lunette that was probably intended to surmount the altarpiece, but was for some reason never executed. The design of the lunette, conceived as if seen from below, would have had a close compositional and stylistic rapport with the panels of the saints. The extended figure of Christ provides the horizontal balance to the unrelieved verticality of the lower panels and extends the cursive arabesque of the St. Michael; the diagonal accents of the figures below are echoed above, notably in the extension of the Evangelist's arm in the torch; the *Pietà* is set on the same narrow ledge as are the figures below; the massed draperies of the Marys on the right above are balanced by those of the Evangelist on the left below, while the partial nudity of St. Michael and the putto is echoed in the Christ and the legs of the other two figures on the left above. Cat. A235 is a late sixteenth-century copy of this drawing.

Ca. 1519–1520. EXPULSION OF ADAM AND EVE. Florence, Uffizi 1517. III. Panel, 43 x 31 cm. Fig. 115.

Bibliography: Goldschmidt 1911, 46; Clapp 1916, 207–208; Venturi 1932, 183–184, fig. 110; Berenson 1936, 401; *MP* 1956 (Berti), no. 71, fig. 64.

According to Berti, this panel was in the collection of Don Antonio de' Medici in 1632 as a Pontormo, but was later given to Salviati, then returned to Pontormo in 1825. Clapp rejected the attribution to Pontormo and Berti also doubted its authenticity on the basis of quality. This picture may be a copy, but it is probably authentic. Damage and repaint coupled with heavy varnish account for the murky effect of the whole and the reduced effectiveness of the original contours of the figures. In any case, it is certainly a Pontormo invention and the question of its date has not been satisfactorily answered. It has generally been thought to be a late rather than an early work, Berti dating it ca. 1530–1535. The difficulty lies partly in an erroneous late dating of the *Creation of Eve* drawing (cat. 104), to which Berti has also suggested this panel might be related. The drawing does not belong in the San Lorenzo period, or even in the thirties, but should be dated ca. 1520. It then becomes clear that this painting and cat. 104 are very closely associated indeed, probably belonging to a projected series of scenes from the *Story of Adam and Eve*. Besides the obvious narrative connection, there is a strong similarity in types and setting in these works, and they are further linked by a common dependence for certain motives on Dürer prints [6] and on the Sistine Ceiling.[7] Furthermore, this panel

[6] The settings of these scenes with the narrow ledge of space and the background consisting only of multiple-trunked trees may have been derived from Dürer prints such as the *Adam and Eve* (Bar. 1, 1504) or the *Adam and Eve* and the *Expulsion* from the *Small Passion* (Bar. 17–18, 1509–1511). This same kind of background appears in cat. 161 for a St. John the Baptist, a compositional drawing close in style to cat. 104 and also dating ca. 1520.

[7] The Adam and Eve of the *Expulsion* are freely adapted from Michelangelo's and reversed, while the angel may have been derived from the God Father in the *Creation of the Sun and Moon*. The sketch after the Eve of the *Expulsion* on cat. 184 of this same date may be connected with the Eve of this picture. The composition of the *Creation of Eve* is not as Michelangelesque as the *Expulsion*, although the relation of the three figures recalls Michelangelo's fresco.

and cat. 104 are almost precisely the same size. This suggests that the drawing was a final study for another picture in the series and that this panel, if not original, was at least based on a Pontormo drawing similar to cat. 104.

In addition to its close connection with the *Creation of Eve* drawing, there are parallels between this picture and other authentic works of the 1519–1520 period. The heavy chiaroscuro and somber tonality of the picture are found in the Uffizi *St. Anthony*. The figures, with their stocky proportions and bulging muscles, who move parallel to the picture plane are precisely those of the compositional studies for the wall frescoes at Poggio a Caiano (cat. 124 and 130). While none can be said to be explicitly for this picture, a number of the nude studies from the Corsini Sketchbook have a suggestive similarity to the Adam. Cat. 122 especially shows the same kind of heavily muscled torso in profile, the raised shoulder, extended arm, and head thrown up and back.

STUDY FOR A CREATION OF EVE
CA. 1519–1520

104 · Florence, Uffizi 465F *recto*: Compositional study for a *Creation of Eve* (for a pendant to the *Expulsion of Adam and Eve*?), ca. 1519–1520. Adam lies asleep in the foreground across to the left; behind him Eve kneels beside God the Father, who stands holding her hands with his left hand and points into the background with his right hand; behind the figures, trees. (*Verso*: Study for San Lorenzo, cat. 361.) 423 x 315, red chalk.
Fig. 114.

Bibliography: Ferri 1890, 117; Berenson 1903, no. 1983; *MPA* 1910, 38; Clapp 1911, 20; Clapp 1914, 107; Berenson 1938, no. 1983; Toesca 1943, 20, fig. 36; *MF* 1952, 61; *MDM* 1954 (Marcucci), no. 61; *EMI* 1954, no. 82.

There has been a considerable variety of opinion on the subject of this drawing. Ferri, Toesca, and Marcucci considered it to be a study for the San Lorenzo *Christ in Glory with the Creation of Eve* (cat. 359). Berenson, however, thought it was "not yet in Pontormo's latest manner, but may have been nevertheless used for S. Lorenzo." Marcucci believed that the drawing could not date before 1539 because Pontormo allegedly did not go to Rome until that year.[8] Clapp dated it 1535. The idea that this drawing was for San Lorenzo derives from the similarity in subject and motive to cat. 359, not from any stylistic resemblance to Pontormo's San Lorenzo drawings. However, even the motive is considerably changed in the bona fide drawings for the San Lorenzo version of the subject (cat. 359–363). The sketch for the Adam of the San Lorenzo composition on the verso of this sheet, unrecognized as such by the authors cited in favor of the late dating, only confirms the early dating of the recto by the contrast in style. It is one of those instances in Pontormo's later years when he went back to an early sheet and reworked the pose of a figure in preparation for a painting. Aside from the many objections to this drawing as a late work, there is plentiful evidence in favor of a date towards 1520. The draughtsmanship is exactly that brilliant red chalk chiaroscuro combined with a bold, cursive linearism that we find in cat. 99 and 103 for the S. Michele altar, and in cat. 137 for Poggio a Caiano, among many studies from this period in this manner. The type of the God Father is very close both to the St. John of the S. Michele altar and the *St. Anthony* of ca. 1519–1520.

In considering the *Expulsion* and the *Creation of Eve*, other works of ca. 1519–1520 such as the *St. Cecilia* and the *St.*

[8] As Clapp has shown, there is no evidence for a trip to Rome in 1539. See note 37 on p. 333.

Anthony, as well as many of the preparatory studies for Poggio a Caiano, the question of Pontormo's relation to the Sistine Ceiling becomes crucial. There is not the slightest doubt that Pontormo was profoundly affected by Michelangelo's frescoes about 1519–1520. However, lacking documentary evidence for a Roman trip at this time, it is not easy to determine whether he had first-hand knowledge of them, and such an assumption must remain an hypothesis only. Clapp believed that Pontormo had access only to drawings.[9] There is certainly the possibility that Pontormo knew finished drawings for the ceiling that Michelangelo might have brought back from Rome in 1518. However, Pontormo's own drawings, such as cat. 131, 133, and 184, give a strong impression of his response to the totality of the ceiling. In cat. 133 and 184 especially there is a juxtaposition of motives from different parts of the ceiling that speaks strongly in favor of Pontormo's presence in the Sistine Chapel. Furthermore, in many of the drawings of this period, such as some of those in the Corsini Sketchbook, there is an exaggeration in shape and in modelling of the nude that would naturally have occurred as Pontormo attempted to grasp the essence of Michelangelo's canon of form. It is difficult to believe that small-scale copies of parts of the ceiling, or even Michelangelo's own drawings, would have made such a powerful impact.

DRAWINGS FROM THE CORSINI SKETCHBOOK CA. 1517–1520

105 · Rome, GNS F.C. 118 *recto*: Page from a sketchbook, ca. 1517–1520. Bust of a nude turned left; to the right, lower torso and thigh in profile right. (*Verso*: Nude study, cat. 106.) 214 x 153, red chalk heightened with white on pink prepared paper. Fig. 106.

Collection: Corsini; R. Accademia dei Lincei, stamp verso (L. 2187).

Bibliography: Clapp 1914, 342–343; Berenson 1938, no. 2363C.

This drawing is one of a group that came to the Gabinetto Nazionale delle Stampe from the Corsini Collection.[10] The drawings from this homogeneous group have been dated variously from 1513 to 1530, as well as being confused with other, later sketchbook studies.[11] However, these sketchbook drawings may definitely be dated 1517–1520. Certain of the drawings are preparatory to paintings from these years: cat. 27 for *Joseph* (III) of 1517; cat. 29, 41, 42, 46, 47, 53, 54, 55, 56, and 59 for the Visdomini altar of 1517–1518; cat. 92 for *Joseph in Egypt* of 1518–1519; cat. 125–129 for the Poggio a Caiano wall project.[12] The remaining drawings (cat. 105–

[9] Clapp 1911, 20, brought together a group of studies that he considered derived from the Sistine Ceiling via Michelangelo's drawings: cat. 104, 162, 165, 181, 184, 213, 305, A92, A110, A157.

[10] These thirty-six drawings all came from volume 157 G/I and there is every indication that they were once part of a sketchbook. Although they were cut to an approximately uniform 215 x 155 when they were mounted, the drawings were evidently the same size originally as well. The paper is a light-weight white and prepared with a pink wash. Two watermarks appear on these sheets (neither specifically identifiable in Briquet): a cross with two circles and three triangles on cat. 27, 29, 115, 123; a fleur-de-lis on cat. 46, 54, 59, 107, 121, 125. Twenty-eight of these drawings are in red chalk, four in black chalk, and four in red and black chalk.

[11] Later sketchbook studies, also on small sized pink-washed paper, form several distinct groups: cat. 196, 197, 200, 201 and 205 for the Certosa frescoes, and cat. 242–243 of the same period; cat. 271, 274, 275 and 277 for the S. Felicita *Deposition*; cat. 312–313 for the Careggi loggia; and cat. 348–349 for the tapestry cartoons.

[12] There are two sheets in the Uffizi (cat. 90–91 for *Joseph in Egypt* and cat. 163–164 for a St. John the Baptist that may originally

123) are for the most part nude model studies that often relate to more than one painting or compositional drawing from these years. Pontormo's penchant for repeating motives is such that, in addition to the paintings already noted above, we find echoes of these drawings in the Uffizi *Expulsion* of ca. 1519–1520 and in compositional studies for a *St. John the Baptist* (cat. 164) and a *St. Christopher* (cat. 167) of these same years. Thus, we have placed these sketchbook drawings together as a group under the date 1517–1520.

Clapp dated this particular sketch 1517–1519. Like many of the Corsini Sketchbook drawings, the exaggerated treatment of the muscles betrays Pontormo's study of the Sistine Ceiling Ignudi (cf. the Ignudo to the right above the Persian Sibyl). The pose and proportions of this nude also suggest those of the kneeling anointer in cat. 124 for Poggio a Caiano.

106 · Rome, GNS F.C. 118 *verso*: Page from a sketchbook, ca. 1517–1520. Fragments of two nude torsos turned to the right. (*Recto*: Nude studies, cat. 105.) 214 x 153, red chalk on pink prepared paper.

Bibliography: Clapp 1914, 343; Berenson 1938, no. 2363C.

These slight sketches are associable in motive and style with the study on the recto of the sheet.

107 · Rome, GNS F.C. 121 *recto*: Page from a sketchbook, ca. 1517–1520. Study for an allegorical figure (*Fortune*?). Nude woman standing with the left foot raised and placed on a sphere, the right arm raised above her head holding a drapery behind her. (*Verso*: Study for Poggio a Caiano, cat. 126.) 216 x 154, red chalk heightened with white on pink prepared paper; W: Fleur-de-lis. Fig. 107.

Collection: Corsini; R. Accademia dei Lincei.

Bibliography: Berenson 1903, no. 2362; Clapp 1914, 340; Berenson 1938, no. 2362; *MP* 1956 (Marcucci), no. 94, fig. 129a.

Clapp dated this study 1518–1521. Both Clapp and Berenson connected the pose with Pontormo's later *Pygmalion and Galatea*. However, this figure resembles the Galatea only superficially and her balance is quite different. Galatea's left leg is not raised and actively projected outward, but is turned parallel to the picture plane, thus prohibiting the kind of easy movement found in this nude. Clapp also noted the connection with cat. 101 for the S. Michele altar, a comparison more relevant to the early style of this drawing. In cat. 101 for the legs of the St. Michael we find the same attenuation of shape and rhythmic movement, but this drawing is certainly not related specifically to the St. Michael. Marcucci mentioned a possible connection with the statues in the *Story of Joseph*, dating the drawing 1516–1517. While it is unlikely to be connected with the earlier panels, it might possibly have been a discarded idea for a statue in the *Joseph in Egypt* of 1518–1519, or, more probably, for another allegorical figure of the same date.

108 · Rome, GNS F.C. 122 *verso*: Page from a sketchbook, ca. 1517–1520. Nude torso turned left. (*Recto*: Study for *Joseph in Egypt*, cat. 92.) 218 x 152, red chalk heightened with white on pink prepared paper; triangular tear repaired lower center.

Bibliography: Berenson 1903, no. 2366; Clapp 1914, 344; Berenson 1938, no. 2366. (Photo Museum)

Clapp rightly dated this variant of cat. 114 ca. 1517.

have belonged to the Corsini Sketchbook. These sheets are the same size as those in Rome, the paper is pink-washed, and the style of the drawings indicates a date of ca. 1518–1520.

109 · Rome, GNS F.C. 124 *verso*: Page from a sketchbook, ca. 1517–1520. Nude woman seen to the knees seated turned right with her arms extended to the right. (*Recto*: Study for Poggio a Caiano, cat. 127.) 215 x 154, red chalk on pink prepared paper. Fig. 108.

Bibliography: Berenson 1903, no. 2363; Clapp 1911, 8; Clapp 1914, 342; Clapp 1916, 32; Berenson 1938, no. 2363.

Clapp dated this drawing 1518 and associated it with the Pomona of the Poggio a Caiano lunette. It is certainly not for that figure, but may possibly be connected with the figure of Leda in cat. 124 for Poggio a Caiano. In style, this drawing is identical with its recto, a study for Leda's children in the same composition.

110 · Rome, GNS F.C. 125 *verso*: Page from a sketchbook, ca. 1517–1520. Nude torso seen almost from behind turned right with right arm extended. (*Recto*: Study for Poggio a Caiano, cat. 128.) 213 x 152, red chalk with a little black chalk on pink prepared paper.

Bibliography: Berenson 1903, no. 2361; Clapp 1914, 339; Berenson 1938, no. 2361. (Photo Museum)

Clapp dated this study 1516–1520. It is similar in style to the other Corsini Sketchbook torso studies, some of which are for the Visdomini altar (cat. 53–55, 59).

111 · Rome, GNS F.C. 126: Page from a sketchbook, ca. 1517–1520. Study for a St. John the Baptist. Seated putto with legs apart and right arm raised. 217 x 153, red chalk on pink prepared paper; laid down. Fig. 109.

Collection: Corsini; R. Accademia dei Lincei.

Bibliography: Berenson 1903, no. 2361; Clapp 1911, 9; Clapp 1914, 340; Clapp 1916, 33; Berenson 1938, no. 2361B.

Clapp thought this drawing was a study for the putto above the window to the right in the Poggio a Caiano lunette, while Berenson dated it 1515–1518 as a St. John. In style this sketch is identical to cat. 41 and 42 from the Corsini Sketchbook, studies for the St. John the Baptist of the Visdomini altar. However, the pose does not fit into the sequence of the drawings that are surely for the St. John (cat. 37–42), and this drawing could only have been connected very loosely with Pontormo's evolution of the Visdomini figure.

112 · Rome, GNS F.C. 128: Page from a sketchbook, ca. 1517–1520. Bust of a nude turned to the right with his head thrown back. 113 x 153, red chalk on pink prepared paper; laid down.

Collection: Corsini; R. Accademia dei Lincei.

Bibliography: Berenson 1903, no. 2338; Clapp 1911, 13; Clapp 1914, 336; Berenson 1938, no. 2338. (Photo Museum)

Clapp believed that this study was for the figure who supports Christ in the S. Felicita *Deposition*. However, it clearly dates earlier and is a variant of cat. 122 from the Corsini Sketchbook.

113 · Rome, GNS F.C. 129: Page from a sketchbook, ca. 1517–1520. Crossed legs; underneath, a right leg. 217 x 157, red chalk, the right leg in black chalk, on pink prepared paper; laid down.

Collection: Corsini; R. Accademia dei Lincei.

Bibliography: Berenson 1903, no. 2340; Clapp 1914, 344; Berenson 1938, no. 2366A. (Photo Museum)

Clapp dated this study 1518–1521. It is possibly connected in motive with cat. 162, a study for a *St. John the Baptist in the Wilderness* of ca. 1520.

114 · Rome, GNS F.C. 130: Page from a sketchbook, ca. 1517–1520. Nude torso turned to the left seen from behind. 217 x 157, red chalk on pink prepared paper; laid down; large triangular repair lower center.

Collection: Corsini; R. Accademia dei Lincei, stamp verso (L. 1683).

Bibliography: Berenson 1903, no. 2344; Clapp 1914, 335; Berenson 1938, no. 2337A. (Photo Museum)

Clapp dated this sketch 1517–1521. Cat. 108 is an identical study also in the Corsini Sketchbook. The motive of the muscled backstudy is related to several figures in Pontormo's works of toward 1520, and even looks back to drawings of ca. 1517 such as cat. 25.

115 · Rome, GNS F.C. 132 *recto*: Page from a sketchbook, ca. 1517–1520. Right side of a nude bust with the head looking up to the right, the arm extended to the left. (*Verso*: Arm, cat. 116.) 218 x 159, red chalk on pink prepared paper; W: Cross with two circles and three triangles. Fig. 110.

Collection: Corsini; R. Accademia dei Lincei, stamp verso (L. 2187).

Bibliography: Berenson 1903, no. 2365; Clapp 1914, 343; Berenson 1938, no. 2365.

Clapp dated this sketch ca. 1519. The style of the drawing as well as the motive recall the figure who runs in from the left in cat. 124 for Poggio a Caiano. In that nude the handling of the chin and neck muscles and the highlighting of the side of the face are very close to the manner of this drawing.

116 · Rome, GNS F.C. 132 *verso*: Page from a sketchbook, ca. 1517–1520. Right arm draped at the elbow. (*Recto*: Nude study, cat. 115.) 218 x 159, black chalk on pink prepared paper.

Bibliography: Berenson 1903, no. 2365; Clapp 1914, 344; Berenson 1938, no. 2365. (Photo Museum)

This motive is possibly connected with the St. James of the Visdomini altar. Cat. 119 is a similar study from the Corsini Sketchbook.

117 · Rome, GNS F.C. 139 *verso*: Page from a sketchbook, ca. 1517–1520. Bust of a nude turned to the right seen from behind (*Recto*: Study for the Visdomini altar, cat. 47.) 215 x 153, red chalk heightened with white on pink prepared paper.

Bibliography: Berenson 1903, no. 2358; Clapp 1914, 237–238; Berenson 1938, no. 2358. (Photo Museum)

Clapp dated this study 1518–1521. It is related in style to the other Corsini Sketchbook drawings, but is not identifiable with any pictorial motive, except possibly the nude to the far left of cat. 124 for Poggio a Caiano.

118 · Rome, GNS F.C. 140 *recto*: Page from a sketchbook, ca. 1517–1520. Outline sketch of a seated putto (?). (*Verso*: Arm, cat. 119.) 219 x 154, black chalk on pink prepared paper.

Collection: Corsini; R. Accademia dei Lincei, stamp verso (L. 1683).

Bibliography: Berenson 1903, no. 2364; Clapp 1914, 343; Berenson 1938, no. 2364.

This very slight sketch cannot be associated in motive with any other drawings by Pontormo.

119 · Rome, GNS F.C. 140 *verso*: Page from a sketchbook, ca. 1517–1520. Right arm with drapery above the elbow. (*Recto*: Figure study, cat. 118.) 219 x 154, black chalk on pink prepared paper.

Bibliography: Berenson 1903, no. 2364; Clapp 1914, 343; Berenson 1938, no. 2364.

Clapp dated this sketch ca. 1527. It is possibly associable with the St. James of the Visdomini altar. Cat. 116 is a similar arm study also from the Corsini Sketchbook, while cat. 46 and 47 are Sketchbook studies for the Evangelist's arm in the Visdomini altar.

120 · Rome, GNS F.C. 147 *verso*: Page from a sketchbook, ca. 1517–1520. Bust of a nude with head thrown back and arms extended downward; above, the bust restudied without the head. (*Recto*: Study for the Visdomini altar, cat. 29.) 218 x 160, red chalk on pink prepared paper. Fig. 111.

Bibliography: Berenson 1903, no. 2356; Clapp 1911, 13; Clapp 1914, 335; Clapp 1916, 48; Berenson 1938, no. 2337B; *EMI* 1954 (Bianchi), no. 53; *MP* 1956 (Marcucci), no. 92, fig. 128b.

Clapp thought this study was for the figure who supports the shoulders of Christ in the S. Felicita *Deposition* of 1526–1528, while Marcucci called it a study for the St. Agnes in the S. Ruffillo altar of 1514, and Berenson connected it with the Visdomini altar of 1518. This drawing is not specifically connected with any pictorial motive, but it is related in motive to the group of studies for a *St. Christopher* (cat. 167–169) of ca. 1519–1521, and to cat. 112 and 122 in the Corsini Sketchbook. The inscription that Clapp noted on this drawing is no longer visible.

121 · Rome, GNS F.C. 148 *recto*: Page from a sketchbook, ca. 1517–1520. Nude seen to the knees turned right with his right arm bent up to the left shoulder. (*Verso*: Study for the Visdomini altar, cat. 56.) 215 x 144, red chalk on pink prepared paper; W: Fleur-de-lis. Fig. 112.

Collection: Corsini; R. Accademia dei Lincei.

Bibliography: Berenson 1903, no. 2359; Clapp 1914, 338; Berenson 1938, no. 2359; *EMI* 1954 (Bianchi), no. 74.

Clapp dated this sketch 1527–1530 and associated it with the figure to the left of the angel in the baptising group in the Pitti *Martyrdom* of 1529–1530. However, this drawing dates at the same time as the other Corsini Sketchbook studies and should be compared with the nude to the left of the athlete in cat. 124 for Poggio a Caiano.

122 · Rome, GNS F.C. 150: Page from a sketchbook, ca. 1517–1520. Nude torso turned to the right with head thrown back; below, the head and shoulders restudied. 218 x 156, red chalk heightened with white on pink prepared paper. Fig. 113.

Collection: Corsini; R. Accademia dei Lincei, stamp verso (L. 1683).

Bibliography: Berenson 1903, no. 2347; Clapp 1911, 13; Clapp 1914, 336; Clapp 1916, 48, fig. 96; Berenson 1938, no. 2337C; *EMI* 1954 (Bianchi), no. 58; *MP* 1956 (Marcucci), no. 123, fig. 155a; Schlegel 1961, 32, fig. 8.

Clapp dated this study 1517–1521, but also (1911 and 1916) connected it with the figure who supports Christ in the S. Felicita *Deposition*. Berenson and Marcucci also made this association, Marcucci associating this drawing with cat. 90, which she wrongly considered for the *Deposition*. Only Bianchi thought the drawing might date before Poggio a Caiano. The direct emotionalism of the figures, the violent chiaroscuro, and the boldly accented line of this drawing are far removed from the *raffiné* feeling and delicate handling of the S. Felicita drawings, while there are numerous connections with works of 1519–1520. It is identical in style to cat. 90, a drawing in the Uffizi for *Joseph in Egypt* that may originally have been part of the Corsini Sketchbook. It is also connected closely in motive with studies of ca. 1519–1521 for a *St. Christopher* (cat. 167–169) and with cat. 112 and 120 in the Sketchbook. Finally, this figure was used in reverse for the Adam in the *Expulsion* of ca. 1519–1520. The motive may have been inspired by one of the Sistine Ceiling Ignudi, such as the one to the left above the Erithrean Sibyl.

123 · Rome, GNS F.C. 151: Page from a sketchbook, ca. 1517–1520. Muscular neck and head looking up. 216 x 154, red chalk on pink prepared paper; W: Cross with two circles and three triangles.

Collection: Corsini; R. Accademia dei Lincei, stamp verso (L. 1683).

Bibliography: Berenson 1903, no. 2342; Clapp 1914, 336–337; Berenson 1938, no. 2338B; *MP* 1956 (Marcucci), no. 127, fig. 157a.

This sketch was dated 1517–1521 by Clapp and ca. 1527–1530 by Marcucci, who connected it with cat. A147. Because of the vigorous and exaggerated treatment of the muscles, this study must date ca. 1519–1520. It is similar in style to cat. 90 for *Joseph in Egypt* of 1518–1519 and to cat. 122, also in the Corsini Sketchbook.

1520–1521. VERTUMNUS AND POMONA. Environs of Florence, Villa Poggio a Caiano. I. Lunette fresco, 461 x 990 cm; round window in the center 320 cm. diameter. Fig. 122.

Bibliography: Goldschmidt 1911, 6, 48, pl. 1; Di Pietro 1912, 80–89, figs. 1, 7, 10–11; Clapp 1916, 28–36, 173–177, figs. 50–52; Voss 1920, 166–167; Friedlaender 1925, 63–65, fig. 3; Venturi 1932, 128–130, figs. 70–71; Berenson 1936, 402; Berenson 1938, 304–308; Steinbart 1939, 6, illustrated; Toesca 1943, 10–12, figs. 8–13; Becherucci 1944, 15, figs. 16–18; Nicco Fasola 1947, 31–34, figs. 4–6; *MP* Supplement 1956 (Berti); Marcucci, 1956, 11–12, fig. 13; Freedberg 1961, I, 563–566, II, figs. 678–679.

Pontormo's lunette is discussed in detail by Vasari (V/M, VI, 264–265) and mentioned by Borghini 1584, 482. Vasari also notes Andrea del Sarto's (*ibid.*, V, 35) and Franciabigio's (*ibid.*, 195–196) part in the decorations of the *Salone*. Vasari's account is our major source of information on the most important sixteenth-century Medici commission in Florence before Duke Alessandro came to power in 1531. The idea originated with Leo X, who wanted the villa decorated with antique subjects in memory of his father, Lorenzo il Magnifico.[13] Cardinal Giulio de' Medici was ordered to have the decoration done; Ottaviano de' Medici was put in charge of the work and of the payments to the artists. A third was given to Andrea, a third to Franciabigio, and the rest to Pontormo (*ibid.*, 35), and they each received thirty *scudi* a month (*ibid.*, 196). Franciabigio and Andrea di Cosimo Feltrini were employed to gild the vaulting (*ibid.*, 195, 209). According to Vasari, the subjects of the frescoes were assigned by the historian Paolo Giovio, Bishop of Nocera, who was in Florence with Cardinal Giulio. Andrea was commissioned to paint *Caesar Receiving Tribute* on one of the side walls, while Franciabigio was to paint the *Triumph of Cicero* on the other.[14] Pontormo was given

[13] V/M, V, 195. The villa was designed by Giuliano da Sangallo for Lorenzo il Magnifico and begun in 1480. See G. Marchini, *Giuliano da Sangallo* (Florence, 1942), 16–20, 85–86.

[14] ". . . quando a Cesere sono presentati i tributi di tutti gli animali . . ." (V/M, V, 35–36); ". . . quando Cicerone dai cittadini romani è portato per gloria sua . . ." (*ibid.*, 195). Milanesi (*ibid.*, 35n2) notes that the *Caesar Receiv-*

the two end walls, "dove sono gli occhi che danno lume (cioè le finestre) dalla volta infino al pavimento"; in one of the lunettes he was to paint *Vertumnus and Pomona*.[15]

Because of the death of Leo X (December 1, 1521) the project at Poggio a Caiano was abandoned uncompleted. Pontormo finished only one lunette, and neither Franciabigio nor Andrea had completed their work, although Andrea's fresco is signed 1521.[16] Thus a *terminus ante quem* is securely established for the frescoes. The time of the commission is somewhat less certain. We may safely deduce 1520 as the date, although Clapp has placed it as early as 1518.[17] If Vasari is correct in saying that Cardinal Giulio gave the commission, then he was unlikely to have done so until he came to power after the death of Lorenzino in May 1519. Even if the idea had been projected immediately afterward, Andrea del Sarto, at least, could not have begun work until he returned from France, probably not before the autumn of 1519 (*ibid.*, 29n1). Then the gilding of the ceiling had to be completed before the frescoes could be started. In view of these circumstances — and considering how little had been done by late 1521 — it is reasonable to suppose that

ing Tribute referred to an event in 1487 when Lorenzo il Magnifico received a gift of animals from the Sultan of Egypt. The *Triumph of Cicero* must have been an allusion to the literary activities of Lorenzo. Both subjects were clearly intended to glorify the Medici by implicitly connecting them with the great figures from Roman history.

[15] Vasari (V/M, VI, 264–265) continues: "Onde avendo a fare un Vertunno con i suoi agricultori, fece un villano che siede con un pennato in mano, tanto bello e ben fatto, che è cosa rarissima; come anco sono certi putti che vi sono, oltre ogni credenza vivi e naturali. Dall' altra banda facendo Pomona e Diana con altre Dee, le avviluppò di panni forse troppo pienamente: nondimeno tutta l'opera è bella è molto lodata." This subject is taken from Ovid, *Metamorphoses*, xiv, 623–697. Pontormo's treatment of it is quite different from the traditional interpretations such as that in the *Hypnerotomachia Polophili* of Francesco Colonna (1467), in which the Vertumnus and Pomona ride conventionally in triumphal cars. Here, the story of Pomona, the wood nymph of Latium who ruled over orchards and gardens, and Vertumnus, the Italian god of husbandry, becomes an eminently suitable subject for a fresco in a country villa. Pomona is seated to the right on the wall with two of her companions below. Vasari calls one of these Diana, but since the figures lack attributes, it is not possible to confirm this identification. However, while Diana does not occur in the Pomona and Vertumnus story, she is linked with Pomona as another woodland goddess. The wall and the separation of the men from these goddesses (for which purpose Pontormo has effectively utilized the round window) refer to Ovid's narrative, where it is related that Pomona shut herself in her domain away from all men. The old man seated to the far left is identifiable as Vertumnus, who affected many disguises in order to win Pomona; among them, a reaper with a basket of grain.

[16] Andrea's fresco is also signed 1582 by Allori, who enlarged it and Franciabigio's fresco. He also restored Pontormo's lunette. See "I Ricordi di Alessandro Allori," ed. I. B. Supino, *Biblioteca della Rivista d'Arte* (Florence, 1908), 28ff. He painted a second lunette at the opposite end of the hall and decorated both end walls below the lunettes with fictive architectural motives and figures. In connection with this completion of the *Salone*, cf. Uffizi 10/orn. a drawing that shows Allori's plans for the enlargement of the existing work as well as his own new decorations.

[17] Partly in consequence of his citation of Lorenzino's death as in 1518, Clapp has given Pontormo's work at Poggio a Caiano a broader dating than we have allowed for it, considering the commission to date at the latest 1519, possibly in 1518. He has dated preparatory studies for the lunette from 1518 to 1521, while only in the later two years is it certain that Pontormo was working on the project. This difference of opinion will not be repeated in the entries for each of the sixty-four studies for Poggio a Caiano.

the work was probably not begun until early 1520.

In 1532 Giulio de' Medici (then Pope Clement VII) tried with no success to persuade Pontormo to finish the decoration of the *Salone*. Pontormo made the cartoons but did not execute the frescoes.[18] Vasari (*ibid.*, 36) reports that Duke Alessandro wanted Pontormo to complete Andrea's work as well as his own, but "non ebbe forza di far sì che vi mettessi mano."

STUDIES FOR POGGIO A CAIANO

124 · London, British Museum 1860–6–16–106–107: Compositional study for the wall below the lunette, Poggio a Caiano. Composition with an architectural setting divided into two major fields by a cornice, the upper field half as large as the lower. Below, the scene of the *Anointing of the Athlete*: a nude with four attending nudes stands in the center; two nudes enter the doorway to the right and a nude enters from the left while another nude leaves; in the left foreground, a pot inscribed *OL/-VNG/VM*. Above in the center, lunette of *Leda and the Swan;* over the doorways, smaller lunettes with busts, the one to the right of a bearded man; above the lunettes, putti holding shields with Medici arms. 475 x 500, red chalk; six sheets are mounted together; laid down. Fig. 117.

Collection: Lawrence; Woodburn (sold Christie's, June 4–16, 1860).

Bibliography: Wickhoff 1899, 214; Berenson 1903, no. 2255; *VS* 1905/06, I, no. 22, pl. 22; Clapp 1914, 291–292; Meder 1919, 326, fig. 120; Berenson 1938, no. 2255; Popham 1939, 29; Gamba 1956, 9–10, fig. 8; Berenson 1961, no. 2255, fig. 921; Freedberg 1961, I, 558–559, II, fig. 674.

This study was formerly attributed to Fra Bartolommeo, but was given by Wickhoff to Pontormo. Berenson suggested that this ambitious compositional project was intended for one of the end walls at Poggio a Caiano, but was never executed because the death of Leo X stopped the work after Pontormo had finished only the *Vertumnus and Pomona*. While this association has generally been accepted, Gamba suggested that this drawing was meant for the decoration of a nymphaeum in a palace by Giuliano da Sangallo (d. 1516) that was to be built for the Medici between via Laura and the city walls. The style of this drawing certainly precludes a dating before 1520 and we do not know of any connection with this Sangallo project.[19]

Vasari's account (V/M, VI, 264) of Pontormo's work at Poggio a Caiano specifies that he was assigned the entire end walls, not just the lunettes. The area below the lunettes is a rectangular space above two windows and a door, which are recessed in squared niches of equal size. In the right lower corner of this drawing can be seen the outline of the upper part of one of the niches and to the left is a line that may have been meant as the inner edge of another. The *pentimento* in the figure below the athlete may indicate that his pose was changed in order to bring the entire figure within a narrower compositional field than Pontormo had at first laid out. The oil jar to the left would presumably also have been shifted upward, since the niche around the window to the left would have projected into this space. When the drawing is compared with the wall of the *Salone*, it becomes clear that it has been cut at the sides. The doorways lack their outer frames, those of the small lunettes above are incomplete, and the small space that would have corresponded to the area between the window niches and the corners of the room is missing.

[18] For an account of this later project see V/M, V, 196 and VI, 275–276. Cat. 307–311 are Pontormo's studies for one of the frescoes.

[19] See Marchini, *Sangallo,* 77, 101.

The addition of about four centimeters on either side of the drawing would bring it up to the exact proportions of the area to be painted. When Allori did paint this space, his fictive architecture followed the articulation of the wall just as Pontormo had apparently planned to do, the false windows being placed on a line with the actual ones below. It is possible that Pontormo might even have begun this wall, at least to the extent of indicating the divisions of the major fields, before the work was discontinued.

There is some disagreement about the subject represented in the lower part of the drawing. Berenson thought it was *Seneca in his Bath*, a Roman subject appropriate to those of Andrea and Franciabigio, but it has more generally been interpreted as the *Anointing of an Athlete.* This subject seems sufficiently "antique" to comply with the papal wish that the villa be decorated with "storie antiche" (V/M, V, 195) and it is a more convincing interpretation of the action of these nudes.[20]

In style this drawing is a link between the post-Visdomini drawings of ca. 1519 and the radical innovations of draughtsmanship in Pontormo's studies for the Poggio a Caiano lunette itself. It is still somewhat Sartesque — even Bartolommesque — in its chiaroscuro, but there is a new intensity of movement and an increasingly insistent angularity of shape. Spatial contradictions are introduced that deny adequate space for these figures or for their activity. The architectural divisions do not project the composition into space, but are on the same plane as the figures, causing a contradictory flattening effect that immediately deprives the architecture of its ostensibly illusionistic and supporting function. The composition of the *Leda* above is related to Pontormo's lunette compositions of ca. 1519, cat. 93 for the *St. Cecilia* and cat. 103 for a *Pietà*; yet there is now an ambiguity in the spatial relations that did not exist earlier. Cat. 125–129 from the Corsini Sketchbook are studies for Leda's children. There are no studies that can be definitely connected with the *Anointing of the Athlete*, although cat. 105, 109, 115, 117 and 121 from the Sketchbook suggest figures in this drawing, and cat. 53–55 and 59, which have been connected with the putti of the Visdomini altar, have a curious similarity to the nudes who rush in from the sides of this composition.

[20] The central group recalls the figures in the upper left corner of a drawing attributed to Bacchiacca (Uffizi 476F) that represents several groups of athletes. See Barocchi 1950, 199, fig. 169, where it is given to Rosso. The Uffizi drawing and Pontormo's may depend on the same original, possibly a Michelangelo study connected with the *Cascina* cartoon.

125 · Rome, GNS F.C. 117 *recto*: Page from a sketchbook: Study for *Leda and the Swan* (cat. 124), Poggio a Caiano. Two putti reclining to the left, one winged. (*Verso*: Studies for the Visdomini altar, cat. 46.) 215 x 152, red chalk heightened with white on pink prepared paper; W: Fleur-de-lis. Fig. 118.

Collection: Corsini; R. Accademia dei Lincei, stamp verso (L. 2187).

Bibliography: Berenson 1903, no. 2357; Clapp 1914, 337; Berenson 1938, no. 2338C.

Clapp dated this drawing and the four following (cat. 126–129) 1518–1521 and noted the connection with the *Leda* lunette in cat. 124. This particular sheet is probably a study for the putto in the center or the one to the right. These studies for the putti with Leda must date 1520, at the very beginning of Pontormo's work at Poggio a Caiano. As Berenson has suggested, there is evidence of Pontormo's lingering point of contact with Fra Bartolommeo's chalk drawings, such as the two putti studies in

Munich (2169 and 2174; Berenson 1938, nos. 442–443).

126 · Rome, GNS F.C. 121 *verso*: Page from a sketchbook: Study for *Leda and the Swan* (cat. 124), Poggio a Caiano. Putto seated turned to the right seen almost from behind; above, putto reclining to the right with back turned. (*Recto*: Nude study, cat. 107.) 216 x 154, red chalk on pink prepared paper.

Bibliography: Berenson 1903, no. 2362; Clapp 1914, 340–341; Berenson 1938, no. 2362; *MP* 1956 (Marcucci), no. 94, fig. 129a.

See cat. 125. These putti may be connected with the putto to the left of the *Leda* lunette. Marcucci has dated this drawing 1516–1517 as stylistically connected with putti in the *Story of Joseph* and the SS. Annunziata *Visitation*. These motives are not to be found in the Borgherini panels or in the fresco. Furthermore, these putti are quite different in style from the Sartesque putti in Pontormo's drawings of five years earlier, such as cat. 9 and 10.

127 · Rome, GNS F.C. 124 *recto*: Page from a sketchbook: Study for *Leda and the Swan* (cat. 124), Poggio a Caiano. Two winged putti reclining to the left. (*Verso*: Nude study, cat. 109.) 215 x 154, red chalk heightened with white on pink prepared paper. Fig. 119.

Collection: Corsini; R. Accademia dei Lincei, stamp verso (L. 2187).

Bibliography: Berenson 1903, no. 2363; Clapp 1914, 341; Berenson 1938, no. 2363.

See cat. 125. These sketches are probably studies for the putto on the right or the one in the center of the *Leda* composition. They are very close in pose to the putti of cat. 125.

128 · Rome, GNS F.C. 125 *recto*: Page from a sketchbook: Study for *Leda and the Swan* (cat. 124), Poggio a Caiano. Seated putto looking to the left. (*Verso*: Nude study, cat. 110.) 213 x 152, red chalk heightened with white on pink prepared paper; upper right corner replaced. Fig. 120.

Collection: Corsini; R. Accademia dei Lincei, stamp recto (L. 2187).

Bibliography: Berenson 1903, no. 2361; Clapp 1914, 339; Berenson 1938, no. 2361.

See cat. 125. This drawing is probably a sketch for the putto to the right in the *Leda* lunette and is identical to the figure in the compositional drawing.

129 · Rome, GNS F.C. 138 *verso*: Page from a sketchbook: Study for *Leda and the Swan* (cat. 124), Poggio a Caiano. Putto seen from behind reclining to the right. (*Recto*: Study for the Visdomini altar, cat. 59.) 216 x 154, red chalk on pink prepared paper. Fig. 121.

Bibliography: Berenson 1903, no. 2351; Clapp 1914, 339–340; Berenson 1938, no. 2361A.

See cat. 125. This sketch is for the putto to the left of the *Leda* and exactly corresponds to the figure in the compositional study.

130 · Florence, Uffizi 6672F: Compositional study for the wall below the lunette, Poggio a Caiano. *The Rape of the Sabines*: large group of fighting and struggling figures enclosed below by a frame; above, indications of an architectural setting. 173 x 285, red chalk; two sheets joined together; W: unidentified object in a circle. Fig. 116.

Bibliography: Ferri 1890, 119; Berenson 1903, no. 1998; *MPA* 1910, 27; Clapp 1914, 223; Berenson 1938, no. 2159B; Grassi 1946, 40, fig. 1.

This study was placed "quite early" by Berenson and dated 1516 by Grassi. However, as Clapp has seen, it must be dated closer to 1520. In contrast to the brittle angularity of an earlier compositional *pensiero* such as cat. 29 for the Visdomini altar, the rich chiaroscuro and the complex interaction of forms set forward on a narrow stage bring this drawing close to cat. 124, the elaborate compositional drawing for the wall at Poggio a Caiano. The figure types, with their legs that diminish to a point, round heads, and blacked-out eyes, are the same in the two drawings. If cat. 124 was intended for the wall space below one of the lunettes, then this composition was surely conceived as a pendant for the opposite wall. The proportions of the rectangular area that is marked out are the same as those of the lower level of cat. 124, which has been cut at the sides and is therefore slightly more square. A lunette arrangement similar to that of cat. 124 was probably planned above the *Rape of the Sabines* scene. The architectural divisions that are tentatively marked out above are like those of cat. 124: a central space the size of the two side areas together. Thus, like cat. 124, the composition would have followed the already existing articulation of the wall.

Since the subject of this drawing is also from Roman history, it would have fit appropriately with the Roman subjects assigned to Franciabigio and Andrea del Sarto. Furthermore, there is some indication that Pontormo, like Franciabigio, had seen and absorbed such contemporary Roman prototypes for scenes of conflict as Raphael's *Expulsion of Heliodorus* and *Battle of Ostia* from the Vatican *Stanze*. (Cf. the figure in the center with the fallen Heliodorus; the paralleling of movements in various figures with the right side of the *Battle of Ostia*.) As in cat. 124 and in cat. 131, the first project for the lunette, there is evidently a conscious attempt to achieve a Romanizing style in this composition.

131 · Florence, Uffizi 454F: Compositional study for the lunette, Poggio a Caiano. Six partially draped figures reclining on two walls around a circular window; the two uppermost figures hold down the branches of a tree trunk coiled around the window. 198 x 380, pen and bistre wash over faint black chalk; sheet cut in lunette shape; written in ink in Pontormo's hand to the left below: *b^a 5 e ½*;[21] and in the center of the window: *Fog^li 62 . . . pezzi 137*. Fig. 123.

Bibliography: Ferri 1890, 116; Berenson 1903, no. 1977, pl. 152; *MPA* 1910, 26; Goldschmidt 1911, 9–10, pl. 1; Di Pietro 1912, 85, fig. 5; Clapp 1914, 98–99; Clapp 1916, 34–35, fig. 73; Friedlaender 1925, 63–65, fig. 4; Berenson 1938, 306–307, no. 1977, fig. 941; Toesca 1943, 11; Becherucci 1944, 15, fig. 15; Grassi 1946, 40, fig. 3; Marcucci 1951, no. 39; *MF* 1952, 62; *MDM* 1954 (Marcucci), no. 41; *EMI* 1954, no. 60; Marcucci 1956, 11, fig. 11; Freedberg 1961, I, 559–560, II, fig. 675.

Berenson (followed by Goldschmidt, Friedlaender, and Toesca) considered this drawing as a preparatory study for the second lunette at Poggio a Caiano that Pontormo planned when he was commissioned to finish the decoration of the *Salone* (1532–1534). Pontormo's complete filling of the lunette space, his anticlassical composition, mannered draughtsmanship, and Michelangelism are among the arguments advanced in favor of this later dating. However, the other writers on the subject, following Ferri, have dated this drawing correctly as the first project for the *Vertumnus and Pomona* lunette. As Clapp pointed out, the woman on the wall

[21] The first notation "five and one half *braccia*" (330 cm) refers to the width of the fresco along the bottom from the window to the left edge. The second notation probably was connected with the number of sheets required for the cartoon. See cat. 380 for another notation related to a cartoon.

to the right is clearly an early idea for the Pomona, while the nude to the left of the window is a prototype for the youth with the basket. More important still, the style of this drawing has no connection with the suave, calculated curvilinear manner of Pontormo's drawings of 1532–1534 for the second lunette (cf. cat. 307–311). Indeed, each of the reasons given for a later dating of the drawing can with greater accuracy be utilized in an argument for a date of 1520. The composition is an experimental essay by Pontormo in a "gran maniera" version of his Mannerist style. It is more Roman than Florentine, an ambitious response to the stimulus of the Sistine Ceiling.[22] The monumental heaviness of this drawing was not only unsuitable to the pastoral subject to be represented, but it was antithetic to the direction in which Pontormo's own Mannerist inventions had been leading him. It is not surprising that he rejected it. However, it is tied stylistically to several other drawings of this date. There is an illusionistic intention comparable to that of cat. 124 for the wall below the lunette. There is no rearward extension and the figures are not contained within the space, but seem to fall out of it. This effect is only intensified by the giantism and plasticity of the forms. As in the *Rape of the Sabines* (cat. 130) and the *Leda* lunette (cat. 124), the entire space is filled with these bulky figures. Even the window is exploited illusionistically, the coiling of the heavy sapling making it appear to be set behind the plane of the picture.

Dating this drawing on the basis of its draughtsmanship is complicated by the fact that it is executed in pen and bistre wash, a medium rarely used by Pontormo. However, analogies with chalk drawings of ca. 1520 are numerous: the drawing of the tree, which has bulging, often broken contours like those of the figures, and the regular horizontal lines of the background are close to cat. 104, for a *Creation of Eve*. Among morphological details, the distortion of the lower arm (mentioned by Berenson as a sign of later date) is found in the figures of cat. 104 as well as in many figure studies for the lunette (cat. 151, 158, 160, etc.). The reclining figures below are comparable in concept of form to the Christ of cat. 103 for a *Pietà*, and to the *Leda* (cat. 124), where there is a similar illusionistic projection of one of the putti in front of the picture plane.

[22] See cat. 104 for a discussion of Pontormo's probable Roman trip in 1519. Besides the general exploitation of the *Brazen Serpent* spandrel in the composition and the imitation of the pretext of function of the Ignudi in the figures (noted by Freedberg 1961, I, 559), there are a number of specific motives that refer to the ceiling: the three men on the lower step recall the Adam of the *Creation of Adam*; the serpentlike sapling and the women reaching up suggest the Eve of the *Temptation*; the figure on the upper wall to the left is taken after the Ignudo to the right above the Daniel; and the woman below on the far right is related to the Bronze Nudes above the *Jesse* spandrel.

132 · Florence, Uffizi 455F: Compositional study for the lunette, Poggio a Caiano. Eight draped figures standing and sitting on two walls around a circular window that is encircled by a tree trunk; below the window, Medici arms in a cartouche. 185 x 381, pen and bistre wash over black chalk; sheet cut in lunette shape; written in ink in Pontormo's hand to the left on the wall: *b^a 4*;[23] and in red chalk on the verso: *mezo*. Fig. 124.

Bibliography: Ferri 1890, 116; Berenson 1903, no. 1976; *MPA* 1910, 26; Di Pietro 1912, 85, fig. 4; Clapp 1914, 100–101; Clapp 1916, 34–35, fig. 74; Berenson 1938, 306, 311, no. 1976 (as Uffizi 453F), fig. 940; Toesca 1943, 11; Becherucci 1944, 15, fig.

[23] The notation "four *braccia*" (240 cm) refers to the width of the wall on the left side of the window.

15; Parigi 1951, no. 931; *MF* 1952, 62; *MDM* 1954 (Marcucci), no. 42; *EMI* 1954, no. 61; Marcucci 1956, 11, fig. 12; Freedberg 1961, I, 560–562, II, fig. 676.

Generally grouped with cat. 131, this drawing was considered by Berenson to be later for the unexecuted second lunette; by Ferri, Clapp, Di Pietro, Becherucci, Marcucci, Freedberg, and Toesca (who separated the two drawings) to be for the *Vertumnus and Pomona*. This study is an interesting record of an intermediary step in the evolution of Pontormo's compositional idea for the Poggio a Caiano fresco. The composition as an active, rhythmic interconnection of figures was still a major concern in cat. 131, but here spatial tensions are eased and figures are in freer isolation, not as rhythmically interwoven. The shapes of the lunette and of the window are now less of a consideration; figures begin to move counter to the direction of the window and the composition becomes more independent of the shape of the lunette. The emergence of the horizontal accent of the two walls gives the design a conservative stability that was not present in cat. 131. The illusionistic intention of cat. 131 is weakened in this drawing, since the figures are turned more parallel to the picture plane and the effect of physical projection is less acute. The figures are smaller, overlap less, and are not so assertively plastic; the sapling around the window is flatter and now lies almost in the same plane as the window. In the fresco the forms do not overlap at all, they are even smaller in relation to the space, and the window is not emphasized as having any spatial situation. Therefore, in the final painted version of the composition there is a complete reversion from the original Michelangelesque conception to a scheme that may be in part a reminiscence of Raphael's lunette in the Stanza della Segnatura.[24]

Although the boys with the violas are the prototypes for the putti that Pontormo used in the fresco, none of the other figures were retained. This difference in characters, together with the presence of musical accessories in this drawing, suggests that the subject of this drawing may not be *Vertumnus and Pomona*. Indeed, there is the possibility that it was actually a project for the unexecuted second lunette planned for the other end of the room, which clearly would have been similar in composition to the *Vertumnus and Pomona*, but of a different subject. Whichever the case, the stylistic position of this drawing between the Michelangelism of cat. 131 and the pastoral mode of the fresco would remain the same.

133 · Florence, Uffizi 6660F *verso*: Compositional study for the lunette, Poggio a Caiano. Mapping out of a lunette with a round window; above the window, two seated figures holding standards with a cartouche between them; below, indications of two figures; outside the lunette, to the left, two embracing putti, the heads restudied; outside the lunette, to the right in reverse direction, pair of putti standing on a pedestal. (*Recto*: Study for Poggio a Caiano, cat. 150.) 269 x 420, red chalk, the window and cartouche in black chalk; inscribed: *Fran^co^ Rosi 238*; inscribed in ink in a seventeenth-century (?) hand: *Jacopo da Pontormo*. Fig. 125.

Bibliography: Berenson 1903, no. 2151; Di Pietro 1912, 85, fig. 6; Clapp 1914, 212–

[24] Pontormo had shown awareness of the *Stanze* in a drawing for Poggio a Caiano (cat. 130) and, possibly, as early as 1516 in the SS. Annunziata *Visitation*. The general scheme of his final solution for the *Vertumnus and Pomona*, with the single wall, the spacious background of sky, and the playing putti contrasted with the draped figures of the goddesses, certainly recalls — but without overt reference to its classical style — Raphael's *Virtues of Justice*. This connection was suggested (verbally) by C. H. Shell.

214; Clapp 1916, 30, 36, fig. 53; Berenson 1938, 306, 310, no. 2151, fig. 939; Toesca 1943, 11; Grassi 1946, 40, fig. 2; *MDM* 1954 (Marcucci), no. 43; *EMI* 1954, no. 62.

As Berenson has noted, this sheet contains a mapping out of the Poggio a Caiano lunette. It is a third stage in the evolution of the composition and shows a marked change in concept from cat. 131 and 132. The center wall has been placed lower than in the first studies, thus making room for a third level, which is now occupied by the two standard-bearing figures. With three levels, the figures on the lower two walls would have overlapped one another considerably. The large standard-bearing figures at the top of the lunette would also have maintained the space-filled effect of cat. 131 and 132, in contrast to the airy openness that results when putti are substituted for them in the fresco. However, with the change to three levels in this drawing, the forms necessarily become less colossal and the direction toward the smaller figures of the fresco is established.

Aside from the scheme of the lunette itself, this sheet has its starting point in motives from the Sistine Ceiling. The figures who lean against the upper curve of the window are modelled directly on the Bronze Nudes in the areas above each spandrel of the ceiling. (Cf. those above the *Zorobabel* for the exact motive.) However, Pontormo has transformed Michelangelo's inert, dreamy figures into his own idiom, making them strain forward and stare out at the spectator, and he carries this tendency even further in the nude studies for these youths, cat. 150 and 151. The embracing putti outside the lunette scheme also derive from the Sistine Ceiling, as Berenson has noted. They are particularly close to those to the right and left of the Prophet Zachary, although, like the standard-bearing youths, they are not direct copies.

134 · Florence, Uffizi 6685F *verso*: Studies for Vertumnus, Poggio a Caiano. Two studies with many *pentimenti* of a nude seated crosslegged on the ground; sideways on the sheet, profile of a man. (*Recto*: Study for the same figure, cat. 136.) 265 x 403, black chalk heightened with white. Fig. 126.

Bibliography: Berenson 1903, no. 2170; Clapp 1914, 233; Berenson 1938, no. 2170; *MDM* 1954 (Marcucci), no. 45; *EMI* 1954, no. 64.

Berenson first connected these studies with the Vertumnus. These very first ideas for the figure have an evident rapport with cat. 133, where the standard-bearing figures lean forward with an urgency typical of Pontormo's early studies for the various figures in the fresco. The pose of the figure on the right may be a carryover from that of the figures who reach up and hold down the branches on the lower level of cat. 131. When the *raison d'être* of this gesture was removed, it was the motive of the figure on the left instead that was developed further in the later studies, cat. 135–137. Marcucci connected other drawings with the development of this figure, which in our opinion have no relation to the lunette (cf. cat. 77, 264–266). The caricaturelike profile drawn under the Vertumnus studies is, as Clapp has remarked, reminiscent of Leonardo.

135 · Florence, Uffizi 6515F *recto*: Study for Vertumnus, Poggio a Caiano. Nude seated crosslegged shading his eyes with his right hand; below, two sketches of his right knee and one of his right foot; on a smaller scale below, sketch of the whole figure; above in reverse direction, small seated nude leaning back. (*Verso*: Study for Poggio a Caiano, cat. 147.) 432 x 265, black chalk; W: Scales in a circle and a crown (cf. Mongan and Sachs W. 8); inscribed: *Fran*[co] *Rosi 242.* Fig. 127.

Bibliography: Ferri 1890, 117; Berenson 1903, no. 2020; *MPA* 1910, 27; Clapp 1914, 124–125; Clapp 1916, 33–34; Berenson 1938, 311–312, no. 2020, fig. 953; *MDF* 1939, 28; *MC* 1940, 47; *MF* 1952, 62; *MDM* 1954 (Marcucci), no. 44; *EMI* 1954, no. 63; Sinibaldi (*Uffizi Exhib.*) 1960, no. 92.

Berenson first connected these studies with the Vertumnus. While this idea has been accepted, Sinibaldi would associate the knee studies with the boy next to Vertumnus in the lunette. The drawing has generally been placed first in the series of Vertumnus studies. However, it should probably be placed second because cat. 134 is so tentative in form and so closely connected with the early compositional ideas. Here the forms are set down in the schematic, extremely angular style depending on a minimum of interior modelling that is characteristic of other preliminary sketches for the lunette figures such as cat. 144 and 150.

Berenson and Marcucci believed that the small nude was for the boy on the wall above the Vertumnus, but Clapp (1914) dated it ca. 1535. There are studies of the thirties on earlier sheets that are similar to this one, such as cat. 63, 66, 67, 69, and 71; however, this sketch may well date as late as the fifties. There is a sketch of identical motive in Pontormo's diary (p. 4), a motive that also appears on cat. A208 and A216, copies after the San Lorenzo *Resurrection of the Dead.*

136 · Florence, Uffizi 6685F *recto*: Study for Vertumnus, Poggio a Caiano. Nude seated crosslegged on the ground shading his eyes with the right hand. (*Verso*: Studies for the same figure, cat. 134.) 403 x 265, black chalk; W: Scales in a circle and a crown (cf. Mongan and Sachs W. 8). Fig. 128.

Bibliography: Berenson 1903, no. 2170; *MPA* 1910, 27; Gamba 1912, no. 8, pl. 8; Clapp 1914, 232–233; Clapp 1916, 34, fig. 71; Berenson 1938, 311, no. 2170, fig. 951; Becherucci 1943, 7–8, pl. 7; Becherucci 1944, 15, fig. 19; *MF* 1952, 62; *MDM* 1954 (Marcucci), no. 45, fig. 10; *EMI* 1954, no. 64, fig. 12.

This study was first connected with the Vertumnus by Berenson. Here, as in cat. 135 and 137, but in contrast to the verso of this sheet, the pose of the old man is studied from a youthful model. The draughtsmanship is a linear manner of extreme sureness and flexibility that is characteristic of other of the preliminary studies for the fresco, such as cat. 143 and 151. Clapp saw the pose as derived from the spandrel figure of Jesse from the Sistine Ceiling, but the connection seems a little remote.

137 · Florence, Uffizi 6599F *recto*: Study for Vertumnus, Poggio a Caiano. Nude seated on the ground shading his eyes with the right hand; in reverse direction, bust of the same figure lightly sketched. (*Verso*: Nude study, cat. 182.) 390 x 276, red chalk over black chalk; the bust in black. Fig. 129.

Bibliography: Ferri 1890, 118; Jacobsen 1898, 282; Berenson 1903, no. 2098; Clapp 1914, 177; Clapp 1916, 34; Berenson 1938, 311, no. 2098, fig. 952; Grassi 1946, 41, fig. 8.

Berenson first associated this study with the Vertumnus. The drawing is the last of the series of studies for the figure. However, the final pose of the Vertumnus as he appears in the fresco was still to be evolved and we lack the definitive study for the whole figure. The graphic manner of this drawing is slightly different from that of most of the other Poggio a Caiano drawings, except perhaps cat. 146. However, the same meticulous cross-hatching and ornamentalizing intention in the cursive contours occurs in cat. 104, for a *Creation of Eve.*

138 · Florence, Uffizi 6579F *recto*: Study for Vertumnus, Poggio a Caiano. Head of an old man looking to the right. (*Verso*: Nude study, cat. 180.) 177 x 109, red chalk. Fig. 130.

Bibliography: Berenson 1903, no. 2079; *MPA* 1910, 22; Clapp 1911, 9; Clapp 1914, 165; Clapp 1916, 34, fig. 72; Berenson 1938, no. 2079; Grassi 1946, 41, fig. 4; *MDM* 1954 (Marcucci), 31; *MP* 1956 (Marcucci), no. 105, fig. 140a; Berenson 1961, no. 2079, fig. 918.

Identified by Clapp as a study from nature for the head of Vertumnus, this is the only later study for the figure that survives. In contrast to the other drawings for Vertumnus, it is close in form and feeling to the head in the fresco, the softened contours and modelling approximating the effect of the painted head.

139 · Cambridge (Mass.), Fogg Art Museum 1932.342 *verso*: Study for the youth with the basket, Poggio a Caiano. Two profile heads of men and a small nude seen from behind; sideways on the sheet, seated figure turned to the right. (*Recto*: Study for Poggio a Caiano, cat. 151.) 290 x 440, black and red chalk. Fig. 131.

Bibliography: Berenson 1903, no. 2249A; Clapp 1914, 85; Berenson 1938, no. 1955A; Mongan and Sachs 1940, I, 83.

Clapp believed this drawing to be in Pontormo's latest manner. The vaguely indicated seated figure is a link with the compositional drawing cat. 131, in which the man to the left on the wall near the window is placed in a similar pose. In the fresco figure the left leg is pulled up on the parapet, a change calculated to decrease the illusion of physical reality; and all vestiges of the tree motive, still evident here in the raised arms, are removed. The profiles may also have been ideas for the figure when he was still conceived as looking up to the right, as in cat. 131. In these Michelangelesque heads, Pontormo has translated Michelangelo's manner of cross-hatching in pen into red chalk. (Cf. a Michelangelo sheet in Oxford, Ashmolean Museum no. 291.) This drawing and cat. 176, where we find similar heads, are the only surviving examples of Pontormo's imitation of Michelangelo's draughtsmanship before 1530.

140 · Florence, Uffizi 6514F *verso*: Study for the youth with the basket, Poggio a Caiano. Head of a man looking to the left. (*Recto*: Study for Poggio a Caiano, cat. 146.) 342 x 365, black chalk. Fig. 133.

Bibliography: Ferri 1890, 117; Berenson 1903, no. 2019; Clapp 1914, 123–124; Berenson 1938, no. 2019.

Clapp dated this study 1519–1521, but it has not yet been identified as the first study from nature for the head of the youth with the basket. In the sequence of studies for this figure, it may be placed after cat. 139, when the pose was still undecided, but before the exact angle of the head was established. The head is set down here in angular contours and clear diagonal shading rather than in the softened freely curving line and *sfumato* of the final study, cat. 141.

141 · Florence, Uffizi 452F *verso*: Study for the youth with the basket, Poggio a Caiano. Head of a man in a hat looking up almost in profile left. (*Recto*: Study for the *Portrait of Ippolito de' Medici*, cat. 223.) 332 x 211, black chalk on bluish prepared paper. Fig. 135.

Bibliography: Giglioli 1926, 777, illustrated; Berenson 1938, 311, no. 1975; Becherucci 1943, 7, pl. 6; Berenson 1961, no. 1975, fig. 919.

Published by Giglioli as a finished study for the head of the youth, this is the second of the two drawings for this expressive head and is an excellent example of the softened handling of black chalk in the later studies for the lunette figures. It is close in style to the final drawings for the women (cat. 145, 148–149) and especially to cat. 154–155, for the putti above the window.

142 · Florence, Uffizi 6559F *recto*: Study for the youth with the basket, Poggio a Caiano. Left arm draped at the elbow, the hand grasping the handle of a basket. (*Verso*: Study for Poggio a Caiano, cat. 156.) 257 x 192, red chalk. Fig. 132.

Bibliography: Berenson 1903, no. 2060; Clapp 1911, 9; Clapp 1914, 154; Clapp 1916, 33, fig. 70; Berenson 1938, no. 2060.

As has been noted by Clapp, this study is for the left arm holding the basket and is identical to the arm of the youth in the fresco. It is close in style to cat. 138, also a red chalk final study for a figure in the lunette.

143 · Florence, Uffizi 6727F: Study for the boy on the wall, Poggio a Caiano. Nude boy seated pointing toward the spectator with his right arm and leaning back on his left arm. 405 x 262, red chalk over faint black chalk; W: Acorn (B. 7435); inscribed in ink in a seventeenth-century hand: *jacopo da puntormo*. Fig. 136.

Bibliography: Ferri 1890, 120; Berenson 1903, no. 2210; *MPA* 1910, 30; Clapp 1914, 261, pl. 3; Clapp 1916, 35, fig. 75; Berenson 1938, 310, no. 2210, fig. 947; *MDF* 1939, 31; *MC* 1940, 51; Becherucci 1943, 8, pl. 8; *MF* 1952, 62.

Berenson connected this study with Poggio a Caiano but did not specify which figure. Clapp thought that the frightened expression of the face was not in keeping with the spirit of the fresco, but dated the sheet 1519–1521. Clapp's objection does not seem justified since many of the studies for the lunette are informed with an air of frantic intensity that is diminished in the more placid fresco figures. (Cf. cat. 134, 135, 137, 145, 148, 151, etc.) This preliminary study for the boy is connected with compositional study cat. 132, in which we find the same pose of the legs in the boy to the right on the wall. This pose will be retained in the fresco figure, but the upper part of the body will be changed so that it recalls the action of the Prophet Jonah of the Sistine Ceiling. The aggressive gesture of the upper part of the figure in this drawing reflects a stage in Pontormo's planning of the lunette in which a number of illusionistic motives were projected, such as placing the legs of the figures on the lower wall in front of the wall, e.g., the picture plane. The draughtsmanship of this study is among the most brilliant of the Poggio a Caiano group in its intensity, expressive angularity, and buoyancy of line, an explosive linear activity that is extended even to the dynamic shading of the background.

144 · Florence, Uffizi 6557F: Study for the woman with her back turned, Poggio a Caiano. Nude boy lying on his right side; on a smaller scale, a nude seated straddling a wall with the head turned away. 281 x 402, black chalk; inscribed: [Franco Ro] *si 243*. Fig. 137.

Bibliography: Jacobsen 1898, 282; Berenson 1903, no. 2058; Clapp 1911, 8; Gamba 1912, no. 9, pl. 9; Clapp 1914, 152–153; Clapp 1916, 30, 32, fig. 54; Berenson 1938, 309, 311, no. 2058, fig. 950; *MDF* 1939, 28; *MC* 1940, 45; Becherucci 1943, 8, fig. 9; *MF* 1952, 63.

Berenson connected this study with Poggio a Caiano, while Clapp first specifically identified it as a study for the woman with her back turned. Clapp thought that Pontormo at first planned a single high wall placed back far enough to allow for this figure. However, in a composition such as this lunette where forms are not located precisely in depth but in terms of spatial interval on the surface, such considerations of the rearward extension of space are unnecessary. This figure is flattened so completely that it takes up no more space than does the fresco figure, in spite of the apparent extension of the pose. Furthermore, there is no indication in any of the other drawings that Pontormo originally planned a more spacious arrangement (cf. cat. 131). Clapp thought the smaller nude to the right was an idea for the Pomona. However, her pose was already established in cat. 131 much as it is in the fresco. This sketch is not precisely identifiable with any of the figures, but might have been connected with the putto on the wall to the right at a time when the motive of holding down the branches was still a major theme of the composition. The extremely angular and spare linear manner of this drawing is also found in several other preliminary studies for the lunette figures, such as cat. 135, 136, 143, and 150.

145 · Florence, Uffizi 6673F *recto*: Study for the woman with her back turned, Poggio a Caiano. Draped woman reclining to the right with back turned, looking over her left shoulder. (*Verso*: Study for Poggio a Caiano, cat. 148.) 237 x 350, black chalk heightened with white; W: Acorn (B. 7435). Fig. 138.

Bibliography: Ferri 1890, 119; Berenson 1903, no. 1999; *MPA* 1910, 25; Clapp 1914, 223–224; Clapp 1916, 30, fig. 55; Berenson 1938, 309, 312, no. 2159C, fig. 957; *MDF* 1939, 29; *MC* 1940, 50; Becherucci 1944, 15, fig. 20; *MDM* 1954 (Marcucci), no. 46; *EMI* 1954, no. 65.

As was first observed by Ferri, this is the final study for the woman with her back turned. It is identical to the figure in the fresco except that the curves of the drapery over the wall and behind her left arm are somewhat more timid in the drawing. The intensity that was characteristic of the preliminary studies for the fresco is replaced here by a lighter and more playful mood that is the antithesis of the tension and strain of Pontormo's first idea for the lunette, cat. 131. The soft and vibrant handling of black chalk with white lights is akin to that of the other final studies for the woman (cat. 148–149) and to the latest putti studies (cat. 152–155, 157–160).

146 · Florence, Uffizi 6514F *recto*: Study for the woman with a staff, Poggio a Caiano. Nude reclining to the right on a wall with a staff in his right hand. (*Verso*: Study for Poggio a Caiano, cat. 140.) 342 x 365, red chalk; inscribed in ink in a sixteenth-century hand: *iacopodapuntornofaciebatP* . . . Fig. 134.

Bibliography: Ferri 1890, 117; Jacobsen 1898, 282; Berenson 1903, no. 2019; *MPA* 1910, 26; Clapp 1914, 123; Clapp 1916, 31, fig. 56; Berenson 1938, 310, no. 2019, fig. 949; *MDF* 1939, 31; Sinibaldi 1960, no. 47.

Berenson noted that this study from a boy model was the first idea for the woman with the staff, in which all but the pose of the legs had been established. (The legs in this drawing would later be used in reverse for the Pomona.) At this point in the development of the composition, Pontormo projected a more illusionistic scheme in which the leg of this figure and the leg of the boy with the basket on the other side would hang over the parapet into our space, an idea that was already set down in the compositional study, cat. 131. The vertical accents of these legs were later shifted up to the figures seated on the wall (cf. the putti, Pomona, the boy), while only drapery was finally allowed to hang over the lower parapet. The rather finished, curvilinear manner of this drawing is close to that of cat. 137 for the Vertumnus, also a solution for a pose that was later discarded.

147 · Florence, Uffizi 6515F *verso*: Study for the woman with the staff, Poggio a Caiano. Draped boy reclining to the right holding a staff in his right hand; below, the figure on a smaller scale; above, a leg from the knee down. (*Recto*: Study for Poggio a Caiano, cat. 135.) 432 x 265, black chalk. Fig. 139.

Bibliography: Ferri 1890, 117; Berenson 1903, no. 2020; Clapp 1914, 125; Clapp 1916, 31, fig. 57; Stscherbatscheva 1934/36, 181; Berenson 1938, no. 2020; *MDM* 1954 (Marcucci), no. 44; *EMI* 1954, no. 63.

As was noted first by Berenson, this sketch is a second idea for the woman with the staff, also using a boy model. Here, the definitive reclining pose of the figure has been established and the left leg no longer hangs over the parapet as in the first study, cat. 146. Pomona's right leg appears in this drawing much in the same position as it will be in the fresco, except that here it actually overlaps the leg of the reclining figure. This is most likely to indicate an intermediary stage in Pontormo's ideas about the scale of the figures in relation to the lunette space; these figures may still have been conceived as larger than they eventually were in the fresco and therefore overlap in a way that recalls the original design, cat. 131. Clapp and Marcucci would associate cat. 251 with this leg, but actually it dates from the middle twenties. The angular manner of this drawing as well as the urgent contact with the spectator in the staring face of the boy connect this sheet with other ideas for lunette figures, such as cat. 135 and 150.

148 · Florence, Uffizi 6673F *verso*: Study for the woman with the staff, Poggio a Caiano. Draped woman reclining to the right holding a staff in her right hand and looking out at the spectator. (*Recto*: Study for Poggio a Caiano, cat. 145.) 237 x 350, black chalk heightened with white. Fig. 140.

Bibliography: Ferri 1890, 119; Berenson 1903, no. 1999; Clapp 1914, 224; Clapp 1916, 31, fig. 58; Stscherbatscheva 1934/36, 181, fig. 200; Berenson 1938, 312, no. 2159C, fig. 956; Becherucci 1943, 8, pl. 10; *MDM* 1954 (Marcucci), no. 46; *EMI* 1954, no. 65; Marcucci 1956, 12, fig. 14.

Ferri recognized this drawing as a final study for the woman with the staff, a pendant to cat. 145 for the woman with her back turned. In the fresco figure the drapery folds over the parapet are bolder in design and the figure lies more in one plane because the upper part of the body is not dislocated forward. The more relaxed posture of the figure in the fresco is matched by a placid facial expression that contrasts with the cross-eyed frenzy of this face. The study is comparable in style to its recto for the other woman, to cat. 149 for the Pomona, and to the later putti studies in black chalk. Berenson, Clapp, and Marcucci have connected cat. A70 and A77 with the evolution of this figure, drawings that have only a superficial connection in motive with Pontormo's invention.

149 · Florence, Uffizi 6530F *verso* and 6531F: Study for Pomona, Poggio a Caiano. Draped figure of a woman seated on a wall with her left hand held up and right leg extended down in front of the wall. (*Recto* of 6530F: Figure study, cat. 177.) The original sheet has been cut in half so that the upper part of the figure is 6531F, measuring 170 x 223, and the lower part of the figure is 6530F *verso*, measuring 214 x 277. When the two halves of the sheet are joined, about 2 cm are missing from the drawing. Black chalk heightened with white; inscribed in ink on 6530F *verso*: *Jacopo da Ponto . . .* Fig. 141.

Bibliography: Ferri 1890, 117 (6531F); Berenson 1903, nos. 2033–2034; *MPA* 1910,

24–25; Clapp 1914, 135–136; Clapp 1916, 32, fig. 63 (6531F); Stscherbatscheva 1934/36, 181; Berenson 1938, 312, nos. 2033–2034, fig. 958 (6531F).

Berenson connected these two drawings with the Pomona, but only Clapp has noted that they were originally a single large drawing. As a final study for the Pomona, this drawing is identical in style to cat. 145 and 148 for the other women, and to all the later studies for the putti. The soft handling of the black chalk, the multiple vibrations of the line, and the *sfumato* that envelops the figure contrast with the urgently sharp linearism of the preliminary studies for the fresco figures.

150 · Florence, Uffizi 6660F *recto*: Studies for the figure to the right above the window, Poggio a Caiano. Nude boy leaning against a curved surface to the left; below, the figure studied again to the knees with his right arm raised; above, the right bust and shoulder restudied; below left, the figure sketched on a smaller scale. (*Verso*: Study for Poggio a Caiano, cat. 133.) 420 x 269, black chalk. Fig. 142.

Bibliography: Berenson 1903, no. 2151; Di Pietro 1912, 85, fig. 9; Clapp 1914, 211–212; Clapp 1916, 36; Berenson 1938, 306, 310, no. 2151, fig. 942; *MDM* 1954 (Marcucci), no. 43; *EMI* 1954, no. 62.

The connection of these nudes with the pose of the putto above the window to the right was first noted by Berenson. Clapp pointed out the possible derivation of the motive in the Bronze Nudes above the *Zorobabel* spandrel of the Sistine Ceiling. Since the standard-bearing motive has not yet been worked out in this sheet of experimental poses, this drawing should be placed before the verso, where the lunette plan including figures on either side above the window is sketched. Here and in cat. 151 it can be seen even more clearly than on the verso that if these elongated figures had been used instead of putti, the lunette would have been top-heavy and crowded, closer to Pontormo's first Michelangelesque scheme, cat. 131. In style this sheet belongs with other of the earlier preliminary sketches for figures in the lunette, such as cat. 135, 144, and 147, as well as with the studies for the same figures, cat. 133 and 151.

151 · Cambridge (Mass.), Fogg Art Museum 1932.342 *recto*: Studies for the figure to the right above the window, Poggio a Caiano. Two studies of a nude boy leaning against a curved surface to the left with legs crossed and holding a staff out to the right. (*Verso*: Studies for Poggio a Caiano, cat. 139.) 440 x 290, black chalk; W: Scales in a circle and a crown (cf. Mongan and Sachs W.8). Fig. 143.

Collection: Vallardi, stamp recto and verso (L. 1223); Pacini, stamp verso (L. 2011); Prayer, stamp recto and verso (L. 2044); Loeser, given to the museum in 1932.

Bibliography: Berenson 1903, no. 2249A; Clapp 1914, 84; Berenson 1938, no. 1955A; Mongan and Sachs 1940, I, 83, II, fig. 83; Tolnay 1943, 120, no. 95; *Indianapolis Exhib.* 1954, no. 9, fig. 9; *Baltimore Exhib.* 1961, no. 63, fig. 63.

Clapp dated this sheet in Pontormo's last period, but Mongan and Sachs recognized the connection with the figures above the window in the lunette. There is a hint of the pose of the main figure in the upper corner of cat. 150, but it seems likely that the compositional sketch (cat. 133), in which the figure leans forward as he does here, has intervened between the two drawings. This drawing is typical of the preliminary studies for the lunette figures not only in its spare, linear manner, but in the urgency of contact with the spectator's world, expressed here by the straining forward of the nude. Also characteristic of these early sketches is Pontormo's way of sketching the motive in a small trial drawing, and then enlarging it (cf. cat. 135, 147, and 150). In this case, the pose of the small drawing is actually closer to the final solution in the fresco than are the larger sketches.

152 · Florence, Uffizi 6511F *recto*: Study for the figure to the left above the window, Poggio a Caiano. Putto seated astride foliage with his left arm raised and the right holding a staff. (*Verso*: Head of a woman in black chalk by another hand on a paper used to repair the damaged corner of the drawing, not catalogued.) 227 x 100, black chalk squared. Fig. 145.

Bibliography: Ferri 1890, 117; Jacobsen 1898, 282; Berenson 1903, no. 1992; *MPA* 1910, 25; Clapp 1914, 121; Berenson 1938, 309, 312, no. 2017A; *MDF* 1939, 27; *MC* 1940, 50.

Late in the evolution of the lunette composition Pontormo substituted small putti supported by delicate foliage for the large heavy nudes and thick, coiling tree trunk that he had originally planned around the window. Thus, the muscular youths of cat. 150 and 151 (cf. also compositional study cat. 133), were changed into the putti that are studied on this sheet and on cat. 153–155.

Although there is no evident difference in style or motive between this sketch and cat. 153, another study for the same putto, Berenson thought that this drawing and cat. 158 (for the putto below to the right) were for the second lunette that Pontormo planned a decade later. On the other hand, Clapp connected it rightly with the *Vertumnus and Pomona*. Indeed, the vigorous drawing and the spirited exaggeration of the forms, especially bulging arms and legs, are seen in all the later studies for the executed lunette. The final drawings for the women (cat. 145, 148, 149) and the other putto drawings are in this same black chalk style. In each of these drawings the forms press actively out toward the spectator, contrasting with the more reticent movements of the figures in the fresco.

153 · Florence, Uffizi 6661F: Study for the figure to the left above the window, Poggio a Caiano. Putto seated astride foliage with his left arm raised and the right holding a staff; to the right, the edge of the circular window. 216 x 155, black chalk heightened with white squared; W: Scales in a circle and a crown (cf. Mongan and Sachs W. 8). Fig. 144.

Bibliography: Berenson 1903, no. 2152; *MPA* 1910, 25; Clapp 1914, 214; Clapp 1916, 33, fig. 66; Berenson 1938, no. 2152; *MP* 1956 (Marcucci), no. 104, fig. 139b; Marcucci 1956, 12, fig. 15.

This drawing was connected with Poggio a Caiano by Berenson, with this particular figure by Clapp. As Marcucci has remarked, this version of the figure certainly should be placed after cat. 152. In cat. 152 the pose was worked out, but in this drawing the figure is placed in relation to the curve of the window. In this respect it is a pendant to cat. 157 for the putto below to the right of the window, which is drawn in the same scale and also with the window indicated. The *sfumato* and the vibrant contours of this figure are found in the final studies for the women (cat. 145, 148, 149) as well as in the other studies for the putti.

154 · Paris, Louvre, Cabinet des Dessins 2903 *verso*: Study for the figure to the left above the window, Poggio a Caiano. Nude boy seated with left leg pulled up and right arm extended. (*Recto*: Study for Poggio a Caiano, cat. 155.) 407 x 257, black chalk heightened with white. Fig. 148.

Bibliography: Bacou 1955, no. 71.

This drawing is the latest of the surviving studies for the putto to the left above the window. It must have been part of the very last phase of Pontormo's preparation for the lunette, for it is identical to the figure in the fresco except for its somewhat more elongated forms. In style, especially in the soft, luminous interior modelling, this drawing and its pendant (cat. 155) are close to other of the definitive studies for the lunette figures, such as cat. 141 for the head of the youth with the basket, cat. 145 and 148 for the reclining women.

155 · Paris, Louvre, Cabinet des Dessins 2903 *recto*: Study for the figure to the right above the window, Poggio a Caiano. Nude boy seated with right leg drawn up and right arm extended across his body. (*Verso*: Study for Poggio a Caiano, cat. 154.) 407 x 257, black chalk heightened with white; W: Acorn (B. 7435). Fig. 149.

Collection: Unidentified initials in ink recto and verso (L. 2961); initials of A. Coypel in ink recto (L. 478); Louvre stamps recto and verso (L. 1899, 2207).

Bibliography: Bacou 1955, no. 71.

This drawing is the definitive study for the putto above to the right and the only drawing that survives for that figure after Pontormo had changed the nude youth (cf. cat. 150–151) into a putto. Now the figure has little connection with its Michelangelo prototype, although it should be noted that the small sketch on cat. 151 does anticipate the final pose as it is seen here. In the fresco the putto will hold a standard in his left hand, while his left leg will be flattened down against the edge of the window rather than projecting as boldly as it does here. The verso of this drawing, for the putto to the left above the window, is identical in style.

156 · Florence, Uffizi 6559F *verso*: Studies for the figures above the window, Poggio a Caiano. Two studies of knees; below, faint indication of a hand. (*Recto*: Study for Poggio a Caiano, cat. 142.) 257 x 192, black chalk; inscribed: *Franco Rosi 181*.

Bibliography: Berenson 1903, no. 2060; Clapp 1911, 9; Clapp 1914, 154–155; Berenson 1938, no. 2060. (Photo G.)

The study of the left of this minor sheet is for the right knee of the putto on the left of the window. The study on the right is for the left leg of the putto on the right side of the window.

157 · Florence, Uffizi 6646F: Study for the putto below the window to the right, Poggio a Caiano. Putto seated on a wall with right arm raised and left leg tucked under him; to the left, the edge of the circular window. 237 x 160, black chalk heightened with white; W: Scales in a circle and a crown (cf. Mongan and Sachs W. 8); inscribed: [Franco] *Rosi 177*; inscribed verso in ink in a seventeenth-century hand: *di Jacopo*. Fig. 147.

Bibliography: Berenson 1903, no. 2138; *MPA* 1910, 25; Clapp 1914, 202–203; Clapp 1916, 32, fig. 65; Berenson 1938, 309, 312, no. 2138.

Berenson first recognized this drawing as for the putto on the wall. When Pontormo removed the coiled sapling from around the window, reduced the scale of his major figures, and changed the youths above the window to putti, there was then room on either side of the window for putti to complement those above. This idea might already have been developing in cat. 133, where there are vague indications of figures next to the window. However, at that stage the effect would have been quite different, since those figures would have touched if not overlapped the feet of the large figures above. The pose of the putto in this drawing and in the succeeding sketch is not yet the definitive one. Pontormo was still undecided about the position of the legs and the upraised arm is a vestige of the original conceit in which all the figures reached up to hold down the branches of the sapling (cf. cat. 131–132). In the subsequent studies and in the fresco the putti hold the ends of a garland that curves under the window, a curious reversion to the action of Michelangelo's Ignudi. This study is a pendant to cat. 153 for the putto to the left above the window. They are on the same paper, in the same scale, and in each the position of the figure in relation to the window is considered. In this latter respect, these two drawings are unique among the studies for the lunette.

158 · Florence, Uffizi 6512F: Study for the putto below the window to the right, Poggio a Caiano. Putto seated on a wall with the right arm raised, the right leg drawn up. 207 x 107, black chalk; the lower part of the sheet from the leg to the left edge replaced. Fig. 146.

Bibliography: Ferri 1890, 117; Jacobsen 1898, 282; Berenson 1903, no. 1993; *MPA* 1910, 25; Clapp 1914, 121–122; Berenson 1938, 309, 312, no. 2017B, fig. 960; *MDF* 1939, 28; *MC* 1940, 49.

Ferri connected this study with the lunette, but Clapp specified this figure and placed the drawing before cat. 157. As in cat. 157, the putto's arm is raised as if to hold down branches from above, but his facial expression and the inclination of the head (lost in *pentimenti* in cat. 157) are close to those of the putto in the fresco. The position of the left leg, which was only faintly suggested in cat. 157, is also that of the painted figure. Berenson believed that this study and cat. 152 might have been for the second lunette planned for Poggio a Caiano a decade later because of their "mannered draughtsmanship."

159 · Berlin-Dahlem, Kupferstichkabinett 465 *verso*: Study for the putto below the window to the right, Poggio a Caiano. Putto seen to the shoulders seated on a wall with his right leg pulled up and his hands extended downward to hold the end of the garland. (*Recto*: Nude study, cat. A3.) 405 x 215, black chalk; ink outlines of the drawing on the verso visible; mount inscribed in ink: *Correggio;* W: Acorn (B. 7435). Fig. 151 (detail).

Collection: Pacetti, stamp recto (L. 2057); Bruch; Berlin, Kupferstichkabinett, stamp verso (L. 1632).

Bibliography: Goldschmidt 1915, 88, fig. 33; Berenson 1938, no. 1954A; *Wiesbaden Exhib.* 1946, 24.

Goldschmidt identified this study as for the putto, but mistakenly connected it with cat. 156, for the putti above the window, and with cat. A73. In contrast to the preceding studies, this drawing shows the figure as it will be in the fresco, holding one end of the garland that extends under the window. This drawing is a quick setting down of the pose and is related more to the sharp linear draughtsmanship of the earlier studies for the fresco than to the softened manner of the elaborated putti studies.

160 · Florence, Uffizi 6651F: Study for the putto below the window to the left, Poggio a Caiano. Putto seated on a wall with the left leg bent behind him, the left arm holding the end of a garland. 275 x 182, black chalk heightened with white squared in red; W: Acorn (B. 7435); inscribed in ink in a sixteenth-century hand: *Jacobi de pont . . .* Fig. 150.

Bibliography: Berenson 1903, no. 2143; *MPA* 1910, 25; Clapp 1914, 206–207; Clapp 1916, 33, fig. 69; Popham 1931, no. 229, pl. 193; Berenson 1938, 312, no. 2143, fig. 954; Grassi 1946, 41, fig. 5; *Paris Exhib.*

1950, no. 424; Berenson 1954, pl. 48; Freedberg 1961, I, 562–563, II, fig. 677.

Berenson related this drawing in general to the lunette putti, while Clapp connected it with this specific figure. This is the only surviving drawing for the putto to the left of the lunette and shows the figure just as it is in the fresco. Cat. A265 is probably a copy after an earlier idea for the figure. It confirms Berenson's idea that these putti were originally inspired by the Sistine Ceiling Ignudi. Except for the exact position of the extended arm, the pose of the putto in the copy is the same as that of the Ignudo to the left of the Erithrean Sibyl. In style this drawing is similar to the other putti studies, and perhaps even further from the sharp, spare style of the preliminary drawings for the lunette. Here, the shadows are softly indicated, contours are blurred, and all the angularity of the earlier studies has disappeared.

STUDIES FOR A ST. JOHN THE BAPTIST IN THE WILDERNESS CA. 1519–1521

161 · Florence, Uffizi 6597F: Compositional study for a *St. John the Baptist in the Wilderness*, ca. 1519–1521. Nude seated on a rock, his right hand resting on the branch of a tree and his left hand holding a bowl to his lips. 393 x 271, red chalk; cut irregularly around edges; W: Acorn (B. 7435). Fig. 152.

Bibliography: Ferri 1890, 118; Berenson 1903, no. 2096; *MPA* 1910, 30; Clapp 1914, 175–176; Clapp 1916, 35, fig. 76; Berenson 1938, no. 2096; *MP* 1956 (Marcucci), no. 118, fig. 157b.

Berenson and Clapp dated this study ca. 1520, but Marcucci placed it ca. 1525 as close to S. Felicita drawings like cat. 268. This drawing is the most elaborated of a series of studies and was probably intended for a small altarpiece or devotional picture that was never executed or has been lost. Cf. cat. 162–166 for the other drawings in this group.[25] The woodland setting in this composition is close to that of the *Expulsion* and the *Creation of Eve* (cat. 104) of ca. 1519–1520, while the head of the saint recalls that of the St. Michael, also of ca. 1519. This study is also related in style to works of this period, such as cat. 104, and cat. 101 for the S. Michele altar, where we find the same complex but transparent red chalk chiaroscuro combined with the new ornamental clarity of linear structure that is typical of many figure studies of about 1520.

162 · Florence, Uffizi 6595F: Study for a *St. John the Baptist in the Wilderness* (cat. 161). Nude seated on a step with his legs crossed. 387 x 237, red chalk; cut irregularly; W: Acorn (B. 7435); inscribed verso in ink: *Pontormo.* Fig. 153.

Bibliography: Berenson 1903, no. 2094; *MPA* 1910, 28; Clapp 1914, 175; Berenson 1938, no. 2094.

Berenson thought this drawing was for Poggio a Caiano, while Clapp dated it 1520 as possibly connected with the lunette. It seems rather to be related to the series of St. John the Baptist studies, perhaps as a trial version of the pose from the same model as cat. 161. Clapp thought the pose derived from that of the Ignudo to the left above the Delphic Sibyl (cf. the engraving by Ghisi) or the one to the right which is approximately the same pose in reverse, but there seems to be only a very general connection with Michelangelo's figures.

163 · Florence, Uffizi 6645F *recto*: Study for a *St. John the Baptist in the Wilderness* (cat. 161). Page from a sketchbook:

[25] A drawing in the Musée des Beaux-Arts, Lille no. 2256 (black chalk, 358 x 268), wrongly attributed to Francesco Salviati, is apparently a copy of still another variant of the St. John's pose, reflecting a lost original of the series.

Seated nude seen to the knees turned to the left drinking from a bowl held in his left hand. (*Verso*: Study for the same figure, cat. 164.) 218 x 153, red chalk on pink prepared paper. Fig. 154.

Bibliography: Berenson 1903, no. 2137; Clapp 1911, 6; Clapp 1914, 202, pl. 1; Clapp 1916, 35; Berenson 1938, no. 2137.

This drawing was dated 1519–1521 by Clapp, who considered it "peut-être le dessin le plus spontané et le plus beau de Pontormo." The motive of drinking from the bowl seen here was first sketched at the bottom of cat. 165, which must precede this drawing, and then elaborated in the final drawing, cat. 161. However, in the final study, the right arm is not placed as here, but is moved back to rest on the tree trunk. Unlike the other drawings of the St. John the Baptist series, this drawing is on a small sheet of pink-washed paper, corresponding exactly with the paper of the Corsini Sketchbook (cat. 105–123). Since the style of the drawing is also similar to that of the Sketchbook, it is possible that this sheet was originally part of it. However, this is not necessarily the case, since Pontormo continued to use the same type of sketchbook paper in later years.

164 · Florence, Uffizi 6645F *verso*: Study for a *St. John the Baptist in the Wilderness* (cat. 161). Page from a sketchbook: Bust of a nude turned to the left. (*Recto*: Study for the same figure, cat. 163.) 218 x 153, red chalk on pink prepared paper; inscribed: [Fra]*nco* *Rosi 236*.

Bibliography: Clapp 1914, 202. (Photo G.)

This study is a slight sketch for the head of the St. John the Baptist who is studied on the recto, but it is more closely related in pose to the motive as first sketched on cat. 165 and thus may have preceded the recto.

165 · Florence, Uffizi 6726F *recto*: Study for a *St. John the Baptist in the Wilderness* (cat. 161). Nude seated leaning forward and holding a staff in his left hand; below, the bust repeated with the left hand raised. (*Verso*: Sheet of sketches, cat. 184.) 405 x 286, red chalk; W: Hammer and anvil (B. 5963). Fig. 155.

Bibliography: Berenson 1903, no. 2209; *MPA* 1910, 28; Clapp 1911, 20; Clapp 1914, 259–260; Berenson 1938, no. 2209; *MP* 1956 (Marcucci), no. 116, pl. 156a.

Clapp dated this study 1517–1521 and Berenson placed it at the time of Poggio a Caiano. It is closely associated in style with the Poggio a Caiano drawings, especially cat. 135, 143, and 146. The delicate modelling, the drawing of the face, and details such as the trailing fingers also recall the Adam in the *Creation of Eve* drawing of ca. 1520 (cat. 104). In this drawing Pontormo has established the general pose of the St. John but the motive of drinking from the bowl that was to be used in the final version of the composition (cat. 161) appears only in the light sketch below. Clapp and Marcucci both thought the seated pose to be derived from the Sistine Ceiling Ignudi. The closest in pose is the Ignudo above to the right of the Delphic Sibyl, which was cited in connection with cat. 162 of this same series. However, the pose is not identical and by the time this drawing was executed and the *St. John the Baptist in the Wilderness* motive had evolved, Pontormo was well beyond his first response to Michelangelo's nudes, having completely transformed his source into his own idiom.

166 · Florence, Uffizi 6740F *verso*: Studies for a *St. John the Baptist in the Wilderness* (cat. 161). Three superimposed studies of a seated figure turned to the left with left leg bent back, shoulders hunched, and right leg extended; to the right, seated partially draped figure leaning forward with his left hand touching the ground. (*Recto*: Nude study, cat. A157.)

286 x 410, black chalk over red chalk; figure to the right in red chalk. Fig. 156.

Bibliography: Ferri 1890, 120; Berenson 1903, no. 2222; Clapp 1911, 20; Clapp 1914, 269; Berenson 1938, no. 2222; Grassi 1946, 42, fig. 10.

Clapp thought the study on the left was for a *Madonna and Child* of 1516 and Gamba connected it with the Madonna of the Pitti *Adoration*. However, as Berenson has noted, it is not for a *Madonna and Child* but for a *St. John the Baptist*. Of the three trial poses on the left side of the sheet, one is developed in the drawing to the right, where the St. John leans down to pick up his bowl. Since this motive is quite different from that finally evolved, this sheet of experimental poses may precede the rest of the group of studies. The pose of this St. John may derive ultimately from the figure who leans down toward the water in the Michelangelo *Cascina* cartoon, a connection that is supported by another drawing of this same moment (cat. 183), which is explicitly taken from a figure in the cartoon. In style these drawings are, like the other St. John studies, very close to the Poggio a Caiano studies. The vigorous contours and the excitement generated by the swirling lines around the figure on the right of this sheet recall especially cat. 143.

STUDIES FOR A ST. CHRISTOPHER CA. 1519–1521

167 · Rome, GNS F.C. 135 *recto*: Compositional study for a *St. Christopher*, ca. 1519–1521. Partially draped figure walks to the right holding a staff in the left hand and looking up at the Christ Child, who is seated in profile right on his shoulders. (*Verso*: The Child has been traced in black chalk by a later hand, not catalogued.) 409 x 261, red chalk. Fig. 159.

Collection: Corsini; R. Accademia dei Lincei, stamp verso (L. 1683).

Bibliography: Berenson 1903, no. 2352; Clapp 1914, 344–345; Berenson 1938, no. 2366B; *MP* 1956 (Marcucci), no. 106, fig. 139a.

Clapp dated this drawing 1517–1521, Marcucci 1520–1521, while Berenson placed it at the time of the Certosa. It is a quite elaborated study for a picture of the Poggio a Caiano period that was not executed or has been lost. Cat. 168–169 are other St. Christopher studies related to this project. The type and proportions of the saint, as well as the vigorous forward thrust of his arm, recall the St. Michael of the S. Michele altar of ca. 1519, while the movement of the figure is very close to that of the Adam in the *Expulsion* of ca. 1519–1520. As Marcucci has pointed out, the Child is related in pose to the Christ in cat. 192 for the Hermitage *Holy Family* of ca. 1522. However, the identical type of putto had appeared already in the S. Michele altar of several years earlier.

168 · Florence, Uffizi 6612F: Study for a *St. Christopher* (cat. 167). Nude seen to the knees walking toward the spectator holding a staff to the right and looking up. 278 x 162, red chalk; several holes in the paper and a major loss at the top of the sheet. Fig. 157.

Bibliography: Berenson 1903, no. 2111; *MPA* 1910, 32; Clapp 1914, 185; Berenson 1938, no. 2111.

Berenson and Clapp dated this study ca. 1521, Berenson suggesting that it was either for Poggio a Caiano or for a *St. Christopher*. Here, in contrast to the two subsequent studies (cat. 167 and 169), the saint does not walk to the right, but twists violently out toward the spectator. This drawing is essentially an action study for the figure, without drapery and without the Christ Child. Several sketches from the Corsini Sketchbook (cat. 112, 120, and 122) are closely related to the action of the figure in this drawing, which may be an example of the way Pontormo elaborated the ideas that he set down so quickly in the Sketchbook. The style of this drawing is typical of a large group of red chalk studies of ca. 1519–1520, drawings in which the chiaroscuro is brilliant but transparent and the line strongly accented and flexible (cf. cat. 99, 104, 161, 165, 178, and 183).

169 · Florence, Uffizi 6625F: Study for a *St. Christopher* (cat. 167). Partially draped figure walking to the right holding a staff in the left hand and looking up at the Christ Child seated in profile right on his shoulders. 98 x 60, red chalk; verso scrawl in red chalk and inscription in ink in an eighteenth-century (?) hand: *Pontormo*. Fig. 158.

Bibliography: Berenson 1903, no. 2121; *MPA* 1910, 36; Clapp 1914, 192–193; Berenson 1938, no. 2121.

Clapp dated this sketch 1517–1521, while Berenson noted the connection with cat. 167. This drawing is a first idea for the figure that is studied on a much larger scale on cat. 167, and is identical in pose except for the position of the right arm. This drawing is unique in Pontormo's *oeuvre* for its small scale, a circumstance which suggests that it was once part of a larger drawing; possibly a sheet such as cat. 150 for Poggio a Caiano, where the motive is drawn on a small scale and then enlarged. A parallel to the handling of red chalk on this scale is found in the figures in the *Rape of the Sabines* drawing for Poggio a Caiano (cat. 130).

STUDY FOR A ST. JEROME IN THE WILDERNESS CA. 1521

170 · Rome, GNS F.C. 754: Compositional study for a *St. Jerome in the Wilderness*, ca. 1521. Partially draped nude kneeling on a rock in profile left reading a book held close to his face in both hands; to the left, the cardinal's hat. 430 x 279, red chalk heightened with white on bluish prepared paper; laid down; written lower left in Pontormo's hand: *a di 29 dagosto*, followed by two illegible lines. Fig. 160.

Collection: Corsini; R. Accademia dei Lincei.

Bibliography: Berenson 1903, no. 2367; Clapp 1914, 345; Berenson 1938, no. 2367.

Although it has been ascribed to Pontormo by Berenson, followed by Clapp, this important study for a *St. Jerome* has gone virtually unnoticed and is still catalogued under the unlikely name of Schiavone. The drawing does not belong in the forties, as Clapp dated it, but to the period of Poggio a Caiano. The extreme nervous energy of these contours occurs at no other time in Pontormo's development, certainly not in the forties. The forms are insistently connected in an upward-moving rhythmic pattern whose energies culminate in the intense involvement of profile and hands. The spiritual intensity of the figure and the rhythmic uncoiling of the composition recall the *St. Anthony* of ca. 1519–1520, as well as other compositions of single saints that survive only in drawings, such as cat. 161–166 for a *St. John the Baptist* and cat. 167–169 for a *St. Christopher*. The emphasis on the muscular back is reminiscent of the many torso studies in the Corsini Sketchbook from the period just before Poggio a Caiano. However, the curvilinear richness and the singular individuality of the shapes in this drawing are based on the experiments in the lunette drawings, and place this study at the end of the Poggio a Caiano period rather than at the beginning. The style of the *St. Jerome* even points to studies that we have dated ca. 1522. It is close in draughtsmanship to cat. 251 and to cat. 194 for an *Adoration of the Magi*. The St. Jerome is very similar in physical type and expression to the St. Joseph of the Hermitage *Holy Family*, also of ca. 1522. Finally, the pose and action of the figure connect it with Pontormo's study of Michelangelo's works in the Poggio a Caiano period. The St. Jerome's attitude recalls not so much the traditional iconography for this subject as it does the monumental and introspective Libyan and Persian Sibyls of the Sistine Ceiling.

There are two paintings that derive from Pontormo's *St. Jerome* drawing. The first, a small panel (55 x 42 cm) in the Capponi Collection, Florence, was copied, probably after the drawing, in the later sixteenth century. The setting and accessories follow Pontormo's indications in the drawing and the figure of the saint is almost exactly the same size. The other picture presents more complex problems. The *St. Jerome*, formerly in the Guicciardini Collection, Florence (fig. 161), is generally attributed to Rosso and has never been associated with the Pontormo drawing.[26] However, in spite of certain changes in the setting and accessories, it is based on Pontormo's drawing and has no connection with Rosso at all. Indeed, as early as 1606 the picture was recorded in the possession of the Guicciardini family as a Pontormo.[27] The changes that have been made from the drawing, as well as the evident differences in hand in the execution, suggest that this picture may have been begun by Pontormo and then, sometime before 1606, completed by another hand. The figure of the saint himself is very close to Pontormo, except that the brilliant differentiation of light and shade is somewhat more extreme than is usual in Pontormo's paintings after the Visdomini altar. (This is surely one of the reasons why the attribution to Rosso has been suggested. The angular contours of the figure, which make it stand out sharply against the background, and the exaggeration of light and shade contrasts suggest his schematic and abstracted forms.) However, it must be considered that the figure is quite out of context in the non-Pontormo surroundings and tends to look exaggerated merely because of the difference in handling. Whatever the equivocal relation of the figure to Pontormo, the background and accessories are certainly not by his hand. They are heavy-handed in execution, have none of the vibrant quality of Pontormo's painted forms, and deprive the figure of much of its power. The upward impetus of the figure is lost in the literal-minded multiplication of accessories. The balanced vertical accents of the crucifix and the hat weaken the serpentine rhythm of the figure, whose precarious balance loses meaning because of the weighting of the composition to the lower left. The planar disposition of the forms in the drawing has been changed by the opening out of the space to the left, a movement into depth that is emphasized by the displacement of the saint to the right side of the composition. Thus, while the figure

[26] Panel, 139 x 95 cm. Venturi 1932, 206. fig. 116; Becherucci 1944, 26, fig. 67; and *Amsterdam Exhib.* 1955, no. 103, attributed it to Rosso as dating ca. 1518. Barocchi 1950, 92–94, 250, fig. 65; and Baldini, *MP* 1956, no. 159, fig. 98, rightly rejected the Rosso attribution and dated it in the later sixteenth century. R. Longhi, "Il Rosso Fiorentino," *Paragone* 13 (1951), 59, suggested Paladino or Lilio. A drawing in the Albertina (inv. 22374; red chalk, 195 x 146), attributed wrongly to Agostino Caracci, is a seventeenth-century copy after Pontormo's composition, probably taken from this painting. See A. Stix and A. Spitzmüller, *Katalog der Handzeichnungen in der Albertina* (Vienna, 1941), no. 85, fig. 85.

[27] Lib. 159, c. 124t, April 15, 1606. Gualterotto di Angnolo Guicciardini received 250 ducats "per ritratto di un quadro di San Girolamo del Puntormo vendato al Sig. Piero Guicciardini per detto prezzo, quale Sig. Piero me ne volle pagare detta somma dicendo voler mandarlo fuori di Firenze per cosa che gli importava." This document was brought to my attention by S. J. Freedberg.

may have been begun by Pontormo after his compositional drawing, the picture as it was completed bears very little relation to his style.

MISCELLANEOUS DRAWINGS
CA. 1519–1521

171 · Berlin-Dahlem, Kupferstichkabinett 4626 *recto*: Ca. 1520. Nude standing turned to the right with his right arm extended across his body to the right and holding on to a post; to the left, light sketch of a shoulder. (*Verso*: Nude study, cat. A4.) 402 x 265, red and black chalk partly gone over in ink. Fig. 170.

Collection: Mariette, stamp recto (L. 1852).

Bibliography: Voss 1928, 45, pl. 6; Berenson 1938, no. 1754A.

This drawing was first attributed to Pontormo by Voss. Berenson, however, thought it was a Naldini inspired by a Pontormo like cat. 191. While this drawing has been partly worked over by the artist who did the drawing on the verso (probably Naldini), the chalk study underneath is a Pontormo drawing for a pendant figure to the one on cat. 191. The modelling of the torso and the right hand have been left untouched by the later artist, who has also ignored the beginning of a raised left arm and instead drawn the hand on the hip in ink. In addition to cat. 191, this drawing is associable in style with other model studies, cat. 183, 185, and 188.

172 · Budapest, Szépmüvészeti Múzeum: Ca. 1521. Four boys in contemporary costume seated on stools singing from a book held by the central figure. 237 x 288, red chalk; sheet cut in lunette shape. Fig. 164.

Collection: Reynolds, stamp recto (L. 2364); Richardson, stamp recto (L. 2183); Barnard; Poggi; Esterhazy, stamp recto (L. 1965); acquired by the museum in 1927.

Bibliography: Schönbrunner and Meder 1896, pl. 473; Berenson 1903, no. 1955; Clapp 1914, 80; Hoffmann 1930, no. 64; Berenson 1938, no. 1955; Gamba 1956, 9, fig. 7; Vayer 1956, no. 45, pl. 45; *Budapest Exhib.* 1956, no. 54; Berenson 1961, no. 1955, fig. 923.

Formerly ascribed to Andrea del Sarto, this drawing was attributed to Pontormo by Meder. While it was dated rightly 1518–1522 by Clapp, Gamba suggested that it should be placed "quando Jacopo lavorava nella bottega di Andrea." As Pontormo was not with Andrea del Sarto after 1514 (V/M, VI, 248), this characteristic drawing of the Poggio a Caiano period could not possibly have been executed while he was a pupil of Andrea. The angular manner of this drawing is closely related to such red chalk studies for Poggio a Caiano as cat. 143. However, it is more closely associated in type and purpose with cat. 177 and 186, which are also drawn after boy models in contemporary dress. There is a sense of urgent individuality — an individuality that is the result of Pontormo's graphic experiments at Poggio a Caiano — in all the figures in these drawings. Their unique shapes and specific psychological states are more sharply characterized than in any earlier drawings. This attitude, which borders on caricature, and the penchant for accentuating the eccentricities of stylish dress of the moment (cf. the figure on the left), is also evident in Pontormo's Pitti *Adoration* of 1522. For later drawings of this same type cf. cat. 255 and 256, both of the middle twenties.

173 · Florence, Uffizi 300F *verso*: Ca. 1519–1520. Right side of a seated draped figure cut off at the shoulders and legs. (*Recto*: Study for a *Pietà*, cat. 103.) 333 x 167, red chalk.

Bibliography: Giglioli 1926, 780; Berenson 1938, no. 1962; *MP* 1956 (Marcucci), no. 101, fig. 135b.

Giglioli published this slight sketch as a first idea for the Pomona of the Poggio a Caiano lunette, an association with which Berenson and Marcucci concurred. While there may be a connection with the Pomona, the motive is not that of the fresco figure or its preparatory study (cat. 149), nor is it clear that the figure is a woman. However, the style of the drawing is certainly that of the Poggio a Caiano period, and it may be dated with its recto at that time.

174 · Florence, Uffizi 672E *recto*: Ca. 1520. Nude boy seated leaning on his hands to the left; behind him, a standing nude examining his legs; further behind, bust of a nude; below to the left, a pair of crossed legs. (*Verso*: Two of the figures traced in pencil by a later hand, not catalogued.) 375 x 283, red chalk; W: Acorn (B. 7435). Fig. 175.

Bibliography: Ferri 1881, 40; Ferri 1890, 115; Berenson 1903, no. 1987; *MPA* 1910, 30; Gamba 1912, no. 4, pl. 4; Clapp 1914, 110–111; Clapp 1916, fig. 43; *Paris Exhib.* 1935, no. 652; Berenson 1938, no. 1959F, fig. 943; *MF* 1952, 62.

Gamba dated this sheet 1516, associating it with Pontormo's study of Michelangelo's *Cascina* cartoon. Clapp dated it 1517, but later (1916) placed it 1519–1521. This study is more like those for Poggio a Caiano than it is like the drawings of the Visdomini altar period. The studies of 1516–1517 connected with the *Cascina* cartoon tend toward a richer, more Sartesque chiaroscuro, and a less spare and linear concept of form (cf. cat. 74). However, the angularity and insistent pull of these contours is closely linked to the experiments in linear expression at Poggio a Caiano. There are close parallels between these nudes and the red chalk drawings for the lunette figures, such as cat. 143 and 146.

175 · Florence, Uffizi 6504F *recto*: Ca. 1520–1521. Nude lying face down with the right arm covering his face and the right leg drawn up. (*Verso*: Studies of heads, cat. 176.) 270 x 423, black chalk; the ink lines of the verso show through at the left; inscribed: *Franco Rosi 225*. Fig. 179.

Bibliography: Berenson 1903, no. 2012; *MPA* 1910, 33; Clapp 1914, 116; Clapp 1916, fig. 46; Berenson 1938, 311, no. 2012; *MDF* 1939, 28; *MC* 1940, 45; Becherucci 1943, 8, pl. 11; Becherucci 1944, 15, fig. 21; *MF* 1952, 63.

Clapp has dated this study ca. 1520, but he mistook the heads that show through from the verso for studies on this side of the sheet. The fluidity of contour and the spare handling of line in a detail such as the foot connect this drawing in style with Poggio a Caiano studies such as cat. 135. Cat. 182, from the same model in a similar pose, is closely connected with this drawing.

176 · Florence, Uffizi 6504F *verso*: Ca. 1519–1521. Four studies of heads of old men; above, two curly-haired boys' heads; sideways on the sheet, head of an old man and a bald-headed youth looking up to the right; in the lower left corner, small nude seated profile right. (*Recto*: Nude study, cat. 175.) 423 x 270, black chalk heightened with white, two heads below and the nude in brown ink. Fig. 162.

Bibliography: Berenson 1903, no. 2012; Clapp 1914, 116; Berenson 1938, no. 2012.

This interesting sheet of studies records Pontormo's many-faceted researches of the years 1519–1521; his intense investigation into eccentricities of form and content. Some of the studies give evidence of Pontormo's study of Michelangelo at this time. The little nude recalls the Sistine Ceiling Ignudi, while the two bearded heads below are Michelangelesque in draughtsmanship as well as in type. They are, with the heads on cat. 139, the only surviving examples of Pontormo's imitation of Michelangelo's technique before 1530. These heads are close to that of St. Joseph in the Pitti *Adoration* of ca. 1522 and may very well have been used when Pontormo was making preparatory studies for that figure. In the two heads of curly-haired boys above Pontormo achieves a round-eyed, disturbed contact with the spectator similar to that of the St. Michael drawing of ca. 1519 (cat. 100), and to many of the Poggio a Caiano figures, such as cat. 148. The spectral head sideways on the sheet resembles that of Vertumnus in the Poggio a Caiano fresco, but is almost shattered as a solid form by the light and shade patterns and broken contours (cf. the somewhat different effect in the cubistic heads of cat. 228). The head to the right is of a type that is found in several of Pontormo's studies of ca. 1520, such as cat. 178. A complete contrast to the others on the sheet, it is an example of Pontormo's continuous underlying preoccupation with an ornamentalizing and delicate linear style.

177 · Florence, Uffizi 6530F *recto*: Ca. 1520. Draped man seated backwards on a chair turned to the right, his arms extended forward, the hands resting on the back of the chair. (*Verso*: Study for Poggio a Caiano, cat. 149.) 277 x 214, red chalk. Fig. 166.

Bibliography: Berenson 1903, no. 2033; Clapp 1914, 135; Berenson 1938, no. 2033.

Berenson and Clapp both considered this drawing to be a study for the Vertumnus of Poggio a Caiano, but it has nothing to do with the evolution of that figure. It was probably not even made with a pictorial purpose in mind, but simply as a sketch of one of *garzoni* of the studio in his work clothes. Cat. 172 and 186 of this same period are drawn after similar models.

178 · Florence, Uffizi 6541F: Ca. 1519–1520. Nude seated on a bit of drapery looking up to the left, his hands held up to the right as if in prayer. 392 x 250, red chalk; W: Acorn (B. 7435). Fig. 177.

Bibliography: Ferri 1890, 118; Berenson 1903, no. 2044; *MPA* 1910, 29; Clapp 1914, 141; Berenson 1938, no. 2044.

Berenson and Clapp dated this drawing ca. 1520, Berenson suggesting logically that it was intended for a saint to the right of an altarpiece. The delicate red chalk modelling of the forms and the decisive, insistent contour recalls the cursive ornamentalism of cat. 101 and 103 for the S. Michele altar, and cat. 104 for a *Creation of Eve*. The head of this saint and the head of Adam in cat. 104 are especially close, both in form and in the refinement of expression.

179 · Florence, Uffizi 6571F *verso*: Ca. 1519. Standing partially draped youth turned slightly to the right. (*Recto*: Study for the S. Michele altar, cat. 98.) 406 x 251, red chalk. Fig. 167.

Bibliography: Berenson 1903, no. 2071; Clapp 1914, 161–162; Clapp 1916, fig. 45; Berenson 1938, no. 2071; *MP* 1956 (Marcucci), no. 95, fig. 130b.

Marcucci dated this drawing not after 1517 and Clapp placed it 1519. This study is intimately associated with the drawings for the S. Michele altar of ca. 1519, especially cat. 101, which is identical in style and apparently from the same model. This extremely refined red chalk manner is also found in numerous studies of this time, such as cat. 165, 168, 178, and 183.

180 · Florence, Uffizi 6579F *verso*: Ca. 1519–1520. Study with many *pentimenti* of a nude cut off at the shoulders and ankles with his left hand on his hip, the right resting on a staff. (*Recto*: Study for Poggio a Caiano, cat. 138.) 177 x 109, black chalk heightened with white.

Bibliography: Clapp 1914, 165; *MP* 1956 (Marcucci), no. 105, fig. 140b.

Clapp thought this drawing might be a study for the St. James of the Visdomini altar, but the relation to that figure is not particularly close. As Marcucci has seen, the style of the drawing is that of the Poggio a Caiano studies (cf. cat. 134), and it may be dated with its recto at that time.

181 · Florence, Uffizi, 6596F: Ca. 1519–1520. Nude seated in profile right with his head turned away and holding a staff in the right hand. 395 x 272, red chalk; cut irregularly. Fig. 168.

Bibliography: Berenson 1903, no. 2095; *MPA* 1910, 31; Clapp 1914, 175; Berenson 1938, no. 2095.

Clapp dated this study 1520, but Berenson's suggestion that it might have been done in connection with Poggio a Caiano is not convincing. While it does not seem to be specifically connected with the *St. John the Baptist in the Wilderness* project of ca. 1519–1521, it is from the same model and in the same red chalk style as cat. 161 and 162 for a St. John. Like those drawings, it bears the impression of Pontormo's study of the Sistine Ceiling Ignudi (cf. the one above to the right of the Persian Sibyl). The exaggerated, Michelangelesque musculature of Pontormo's back-studies from the Corsini Sketchbook (cf. cat. 108 and 114) is accompanied here by the new emphasis on contours characteristic of the Poggio a Caiano period.

182 · Florence, Uffizi 6599F *verso*: Ca. 1520–1521. Nude seen to the waist lying face down. (*Recto*: Study for Poggio a Caiano, cat. 137.) 390 x 276, black chalk.

Bibliography: Ferri 1890, 118; Berenson 1903, no. 2098; Clapp 1914, 177; Berenson 1938, no. 2098. (Photo G.)

Clapp noted only that this nude was later than the drawing on the recto. However, it is similar in style to the black chalk Poggio a Caiano drawings as well as being a variant of cat. 175, a drawing that certainly dates ca. 1520–1521.

183 · Florence, Uffizi 6677F *verso*: Ca. 1519–1520. Nude reclining to the left and pointing back to the right; behind him, two reclining nudes. (*Recto*: Nude studies, cat. 83.) 272 x 405, red chalk. Fig. 174.

Bibliography: Ferri 1890, 119; Berenson 1903, no. 2162; *MPA* 1910, 34, Clapp 1911, 6; Gamba 1912, no. 3, pl. 3; Clapp 1914, 227–228; Clapp 1916, 35, fig. 78; Fraenckel 1933, 177; Berenson 1938, no. 2162.

Gamba dated this drawing ca. 1516, Fraenckel dated it later than she placed the recto (1514–1515), and Clapp dated it 1518–1522. The central figure, which may be related to the small nude on the earlier recto, is derived from the reclining figure to the right in Michelangelo's *Cascina* cartoon and is one of the many examples of Pontormo's study of Michelangelo ca. 1519–1520. The sensitive manipulation of a rich but no longer exaggerated chiaroscuro and the flexible, expressive line is Pontormo's graphic style of 1519–1520 par excellence. Among many similar drawings, cf. cat. 104 for a *Creation of Eve*, where the central figure of this study is repeated with some changes in the Adam; cat. 99 and 103 for the S. Michele altar; cat. 165, 168, and 178.

184 · Florence, Uffizi 6726F *verso*: Ca. 1519–1520. Sheet of studies: (a) standing nude who moves toward the spectator with his left arm outstretched; (b) two seated nudes; (c) on a larger scale, nude seen to the knees walking to the left with both hands to his head; (d) sideways on the sheet, seated (?) figure looking down with the left arm extended. (*Recto*: Study for a St. John the Baptist, cat. 165.) 405 x 286, red chalk; inscribed in ink in a seventeenth-century (?) hand: *Jacopo.º da Punt. 30*; in an eighteenth-century (?) hand: *di Jacopo da Pontormo*. Fig. 163.

Bibliography: Berenson 1903, no. 2209; Clapp 1911, 20; Clapp 1914, 259–260; Berenson 1938, no. 2209; *MP* 1956 (Marcucci), no. 116, fig. 156b; Sinibaldi 1960, no. 48.

A sheet of extreme interest, these sketches document Pontormo's study of the Sistine Ceiling ca. 1519–1520. (See cat. 104 for a discussion of Pontormo's probable trip to Rome.) As Clapp first pointed out, sketch (a) was inspired by the lunette figure of *Haman*. Pontormo never used this motive in a painting, but he sketched it again on a sheet connected with the Certosa *Pietà* of 1524 (cat. 213). Clapp thought that this later drawing was intended for the Certosa *Resurrection* or unexecuted *Crucifixion* and that the study on this sheet was a first idea for the Christ, although he dated it ca. 1520, at least two years before the Certosa commission. Clapp has noted that sketch (b) was drawn after the Ignudo to the right above the Jeremiah. The nude on the right is very close to Michelangelo's figure, while the nude on the left is a variant on the pose. It should be remarked that this particular Ignudo is the closest to the *Haman* lunette and that both figures could have been seen by Pontormo at the same time if he were actually drawing after the ceiling itself. This motive was not used by Pontormo again, except perhaps as a starting point for the legs of the putto below the window to the left in the Poggio a Caiano lunettte. The larger outline sketch (c) was taken in reverse from the Eve of the *Expulsion*, with the arms raised a little higher. Although Pontormo did not use this identical motive in his own *Expulsion* of the same date, his figures also move to the left. Marcucci connected this sketch with the woman on the left of the *Deluge*. Sketch (d) was probably inspired by the various God the Father figures in the last three bays of the ceiling. Marcucci, however, associated it with the *Drunkenness of Noah*.

Berenson dated this sheet rightly in the Poggio a Caiano period. Clapp considered sketches (a) and (b) of that date, but placed sketches (c) and (d) ca. 1524. Marcucci dated the entire sheet at the time of the Certosa. Sinibaldi also tended to place the drawing in the Certosa period, although she felt the style was still linked to the Poggio a Caiano drawings. However, she also suggested a connection with a possible trip to Rome in the thirties. A date of 1519–1520, which coincides with Pontormo's other studies related to the Sistine Ceiling, certainly seems indicated for this sheet. The vigorous style of these sketches has nothing in common with the more delicately handled Certosa drawings, but is very close indeed to various Poggio a Caiano drawings that reflect Pontormo's study of Michelangelo (cf. cat. 131, 139, 150 and 151).

185 · Florence, Uffizi 6741F *recto*: Ca. 1520–1521. Nude seen from behind looking down to the left and holding back a curtain with his left hand. (*Verso*: Figure study, cat. 186.) 402 x 280, red chalk. Fig. 173.

Bibliography: Ferri 1890, 120; Berenson 1903, no. 2223; *MPA* 1910, 32; Clapp 1914, 270; Berenson 1938, 310, no. 2223; *MDF* 1939, 30; *MC* 1940, 51; *Brussels Exhib.* 1954, no. 118, fig. 71.

Clapp dated this study 1520–1521. Berenson connected it with Poggio a Caiano and thought that Pontormo planned a divided window curtain that was held in place by figures standing on the parapet. However, there is no trace of such a motive in any of the drawings that are definitely for the fresco. The same model holding the curtain appears in profile in cat. 191. It is likely that these two drawings are simply model studies, unconnected with a pictorial motive. Cat. 171, 183, and 188 are nude studies of this same type also from the Poggio a Caiano period.

186 · Florence, Uffizi 6741F *verso*: Ca. 1521. Draped figure of a boy reclining on steps, his head on a pillow. (*Recto*: Nude study, cat. 185.) 280 x 402, red chalk. Fig. 165.

Bibliography: Ferri 1890, 120; Berenson 1903, no. 2223; Clapp 1914, 270; Berenson 1938, no. 2223; Berenson 1961, no. 2223, fig. 916.

This drawing was dated in the Poggio a Caiano period by Berenson and Clapp. Like cat. 177, this study does not seem to have any definite pictorial purpose, but is a casual study after one of the youths in Pontormo's *bottega*. The extremely angular, almost masklike distortions of the face occur in Poggio a Caiano drawings like cat. 143 and 148, and also link this study to the drawing of four boys singing (cat. 172). Cat. 172 is not only drawn after the same kind of model, but the face of the uppermost figure is identical to this one. As may be seen in the Pitti *Adoration of the Magi* and in cat. 194, this caricaturizing tendency is a facet of Pontormo's intense investigation of the eccentricities of form and content of the individual figure during and just after his work at Poggio a Caiano.

187 · Frankfurt a/M., Städelsches Kunstinstitut 4288: Ca. 1519. Two nudes sitting with their heads close together looking into a mirror; below to the left, a putto with his right leg drawn up looking over his hunched shoulder. 422 x 271, black chalk heightened with white on gray-green prepared paper; inscribed verso in an eighteenth-century hand: *No. 5/No. 85/ Giacomo Carrucci da Pontormo.* Fig. 176.

Bibliography: Berenson 1903, no. 2250; Clapp 1914, 289–290; Clapp 1916, 35, fig. 77; Schrey, 1927, pl. 80; Berenson 1938, no. 2250; *Wiesbaden Exhib.* 1946, 24.

Clapp's date of 1521 for these model studies is certainly a terminal date because of the close relation with works of the years 1519–1520. The putto is of a type that first appears in the S. Michele altar of ca. 1519 (cf. cat. 100), then in the *Leda* lunette for Poggio a Caiano (cat. 124), and in the putti studies for it (cat. 125–129). Slightly later a child of almost identical pose and proportions is found in the *Adoration of the Magi* drawing, cat. 194. The two nudes are similar to those in cat. 103 for the S. Michele altar and in cat. 124 for Poggio a Caiano. The head of the man on the right is especially close to that of the St. Michael in cat. 100.

188 · New York, Pierpont Morgan Library 1954.4 *recto*: Ca. 1520–1521. Nude standing with back turned, left arm on his hip and right arm extended; behind him, two seated nudes, one turned to the right and the other crouched over to the left. (*Verso*: Nude study, cat. 189.) 406 x 225, red chalk heightened with white; W: Fruit (B. 7392); inscribed in ink: *Jacopo da Pontormo.* Fig. 172.

Collection: Crozat, mark in ink recto and verso (L. 2951) and inscription recto: *334*, verso: *335*; Reitlinger (sold Sotheby, December 9, 1953, no. 84).

Bibliography: *Royal Acad. Exhib.* 1953, no. 55; Scharf 1953, 352, fig. 3; Gamba 1956, 11, fig. 12; *Morgan Lib. Exhib.* 1957, no. 86; *Columbia Exhib.* 1959, 20–21, pl. 11; Berenson 1961, no. 2256H, fig. 905.

It has generally been assumed that this

study of nudes is connected with Poggio a Caiano. However, as noted in the 1957 exhibition, it has more the character of a sheet of model studies that are not connected with specific pictorial motives. It may be associated with a group of red chalk nude studies from the Poggio a Caiano period (cat. 171, 183, 185, and 191), none of which are associable with any pictorial project. This group of drawings, while far from academic, tends to have fewer of the exaggerations of contour and distortions of form that are so notable in the studies for specific figures in the fresco. Cat. A330 is a copy after this drawing.

189 · New York, Pierpont Morgan Library 1954.4 *verso*: Ca. 1520–1521. Nude seen from behind walking to the right with his arms raised above his head. (*Recto*: Nude studies, cat. 188.) 406 x 225, black over red chalk heightened with white. Fig. 178.

Bibliography: Berenson 1961, no. 2256H.

Berenson associated this drawing with Poggio a Caiano. It certainly belongs to the same period as the recto, although it does not have the same clear articulation of form or economy of line that was so striking in the recto. In its stress on the modelling of the muscular back it is similar to cat. 181 of these same years. We have no clear indication of the purpose of this study, although the pose of the figure might suggest a study for a *Flagellation*. Cat. A328 is a copy after this drawing.

190 · Paris, Ecole des Beaux-Arts 10907: Ca. 1519–1520. Three-quarter length seated nude turned to the right with the right arm raised and the head lightly indicated. 235 x 135, red chalk heightened with white on grey paper; laid down; written in red chalk in Pontormo's hand to the right: *tropo*; inscribed in ink: *Jacopo*. Fig. 169.

Collection: Vallardi, stamp recto (L. 1223); Gasc, stamp recto (L. 1131); Gigoux; Ecole des Beaux-Arts, stamp recto (L. 832).

Bibliography: Lavallée 1935, 31; Berenson 1938, no. 2336B; *Paris Exhib.* 1958, no. 35.

Formerly attributed to Andrea del Sarto, this drawing was first published as Pontormo by Lavallée, who placed it in Pontormo's late period. Berenson suggested that it might be a first idea for the Christ of the S. Felicita *Deposition*. The strongly curving contours and exaggerated light and shade patterns of the modelling would place this drawing in an earlier period. While it is difficult to associate it with any specific work, there is a certain analogy with the nude torsos from the Corsini Sketchbook, although this torso is more elongated in proportions. Among the studies for Poggio a Caiano, there are several similar figures in the *Rape of the Sabines* drawing (cat. 130) and, in a different context, there are analogous motives in the branch-holding figures of the lunette project, cat. 131. In cat. 150 for the figure above the window, the sketch of a youth to the left is quite similar to this figure, although less elaborated.

191 · Rennes, Musée des Beaux-Arts 38–1: Ca. 1520–1521. Nude standing in profile left with his right arm raised, the left at his side holding a curtain. 400 x 230, red chalk; inscribed in ink in a seventeenth-century hand: *Jac° da Potormo*, and in an eighteenth-century hand: *12°33 . . . Pontorm . . .* Fig. 171.

Bibliography: Jan 1884, 156; Delacre 1931, 139–140 illustrated; Berenson 1938, no. 2336E.

This drawing is still listed by the museum as "late sixteenth-century Florentine school," although it was published as Pontormo by Delacre. The drawing dates from the time of Poggio a Caiano and is connected in motive as well as in style with cat. 185, in which the same turbaned figure holds back a curtain. Cat. 171, which Berenson thought was copied from a drawing like this one, is a study from the same model for a pendant figure in reversed position. Cat. 183 and 188 also belong to this group of model studies.

PART III · 1522–1525

Catalogue entries 192–257

PART III · 1522–1525

Ca. 1522. HOLY FAMILY WITH ST. JOHN. Leningrad, Hermitage 5527. III. Panel, 120 x 98 cm. Fig. 180.

Bibliography: Stscherbatscheva 1934/36, 179–184, fig. 196; Becherucci 1944, 18; Smyth 1949, 201–202; Gamba 1956, 13, fig. 26; *Hermitage Cat.* 1958, 154, fig. 86.

According to the museum, this picture was acquired in 1922 from a Russian private collection. Stscherbatscheva first published this painting as a Pontormo, connecting it with the preparatory study (cat. 192) and dating it 1521–1522. Becherucci and Gamba dated it ca. 1527. Smyth, however, suggested that the picture might be a Bronzino contemporary with his Washington *Holy Family*, which he dated ca. 1525–1526. According to Smyth, Bronzino would have used Pontormo's drawing (cat. 192) as a model for the picture, just as he had used cat. 251, the verso of cat. 192, for the St. Elizabeth in the *Holy Family*. Smyth also pointed out certain stylistic qualities that suggested the young Bronzino, such as the rigidity and verticality of the Madonna, the stiffened contours, and the flattened areas of drapery. However, since Smyth wrote, the picture has been cleaned and it appears now (on the basis of a good photograph) to be the work of Pontormo. Areas such as the faces of the Madonna, the Child, and the Madonna's draperies, formerly repainted, now have a surface transparency and a flexible linear structure that is characteristic of Pontormo. The relation to Bronzino's *Holy Family* noted by Smyth remains valid, but may be restated as the dependence of the pupil's work of ca. 1527–1528 on an earlier painting by the master.

A date of ca. 1522 — between Poggio a Caiano and the Certosa — is strongly suggested for this work. Such a date is supported primarily by its stylistic affinities with the lunette. The Madonna is an idealized version of the women in the fresco and her ample draperies are arranged in the same broad areas. The Child is a variant of the putto above to the right and the St. John is identical to the putto above to the left in the lunette. St. Joseph — a slightly caricatured head — finds his exact counterpart in the Pitti *Adoration of the Magi*, painted just after Poggio a Caiano, ca. 1522. Indeed, he may have been inserted into the composition after Pontormo's work on that picture had begun. In any case, as can be seen in the preparatory study (cat. 192), he was not part of the original conception. As Stscherbatscheva has remarked, this conception was evidently based on Andrea del Sarto's *Madonna di Porta a Pinti* of ca. 1521.[1] This tabernacle, which Andrea must have painted while he and Pontormo were working together at Poggio a Caiano, made a strong impression on his former pupil,

[1] This destroyed work is known only in copies, such as the one attributed to Jacopo da Empoli (Florence, San Salvi). While Andrea's *Madonna* in any case predates Pontormo's Hermitage *Holy Family*, the traditional dating close to 1520 cited here has been shifted back to ca. 1515 by C. Ragghianti, "Andrea del Sarto a Cortona," *Crit. d'A.* VIII (1949), 113–124; and J. Shearman, "Andrea del Sarto's Two Paintings of the Assumption," *Burl.* 101 (1959), 124n2. Andrea's drawing for the head of the St. John survives (Melbourne; see Berenson 1938, no. 141B) and it is evident that the St. John of the Hermitage picture was closely based on Andrea's figure.

for its influence appears in at least two other *Madonna and Child with St. John* compositions of ca. 1522–1523 (see ns. 2 and 4). Here Pontormo has borrowed the bust of St. John with little change. However, he has exaggerated the pose of Andrea's Madonna into a decided "S" curve, and his Child, instead of standing as in Andrea's composition, repeats the serpentine curve of the Madonna. Furthermore, here and in other adaptions of the Pinti *Madonna*, Pontormo has cut off the lower part of the composition so that the forms become unanchored and unstable, seeming to rise into the picture from our space. This device, and the resulting apparitional effect, suggests the compositions of the Certosa frescoes, begun early in 1523.

STUDY FOR THE HOLY FAMILY WITH ST. JOHN

192 · Florence, Uffizi 6729F *recto*: Compositional study for the *Holy Family with St. John*. The heavily draped seated Madonna is seen to the knees with her legs shifted slightly to the left; the Child is held in profile right but looks out at the spectator, holding a bird in both hands. (*Verso*: Head studies, cat. 251.) 255 x 189, black chalk heightened with white, squared in red chalk. Fig. 181.

Bibliography: Ferri 1890, 120; Berenson 1903, no. 2003; *MPA* 1910, 37; Clapp 1914, 262–263; Clapp 1916, 20, fig. 24; Stscherbatscheva 1934/36, 180, fig. 197; Berenson 1938, no. 2211A; Becherucci 1944, 18; Smyth 1949, 201–202; *MDM* 1954 (Marcucci), no. 47; *EMI* 1954, no. 66; Gamba 1956, 13, fig. 27; Emiliani 1960, 61; Berenson 1961, no. 2211A, fig. 956.

As was noted by Stscherbatscheva, this drawing is the final squared study for the Hermitage picture. The St. John is indicated by a shadow, but the balancing head of St. Joseph had not yet been inserted into the composition, indicating quite clearly Pontormo's debt to Andrea's Pinti *Madonna* in his initial conception of the picture as a three-figured composition. In style this drawing is related to the later Poggio a Caiano drawings, but only Stscherbatscheva, Smyth, and Marcucci have placed it at that time. Ferri dated it 1529 as for the Louvre altar, Becherucci and Gamba placed it ca. 1527, while Clapp dated it 1516–1520 as possibly for the lost *drappelloni* that Vasari says (V/M, VI, 260) Pontormo painted for the funeral of Bartolommeo Ginori. However, even when it has been rightly dated, a clear distinction between this type of drawing and those of 1524–1525 has not been made. Marcucci associated it with cat. 236, a drawing of ca. 1524 whose calculated linear refinement is quite different from the energetic vibrating lines of this study. Stscherbatscheva cited cat. 258 as a study for the Christ Child. This study is for Pontormo's Capponi *Madonna and Child* of ca. 1525 and betrays its later date by the flattened forms and regular diagonal shading. More convincing are comparisons with any of the studies for the Poggio a Caiano women or putti. The Child, with his mass of curly hair and his soft multiple contours, is exactly the type seen in putti drawings such as cat. 160. As has been remarked by Stscherbatscheva, the Madonna is similar to cat. 148 and 149 for the Poggio women, especially in the clear oval of her face and the rich light and shade contrasts of her drapery. Smyth compared this drawing to cat. 223, a compositional study that cannot date before 1524. While this drawing is more energetic in line, sharper and more vibrant in its modelling, it is related to cat. 223, as well as to such later compositional drawings as cat. 272 for S. Felicita, as the first example of a type of compositional study in black chalk heightened with white that was to occur frequently in Pontormo's drawings of the twenties.

A problematic composition that survives in several versions, none of them original, is related to this drawing. The *Madonna and Child with St. John* in the Corsini Gallery, Florence,[2] has long been attributed to Pontormo, but it has not been connected with this drawing and the Hermitage picture. While it is so overpainted that it is impossible to tell whether it is a copy or whether there is an unfinished original beneath, the composition of this picture is undoubtedly attributable to Pontormo. It shares with cat. 192 a dependence on the Pinti *Madonna*, although the Child has been shifted to the right side and the St. John moved into a spatially ambiguous position in front of the Madonna. This composition, removed a step further from the classical balance of Andrea's picture than cat. 192, may be dated just after the Hermitage *Holy Family*, into the period of the Certosa frescoes. The spatial ambiguities of the composition recall the Certosa frescoes, the Child has a compelling verticality not unlike that of the Christ in the *Resurrection*, while the Düreresque landscape was a feature of Pontormo's works of precisely this date.[3] There are two variants of this painting in which the St. John is changed to an angel and another angel is added to the left.[4]

[2] Panel, 87 x 67 cm. See U. Medici, *Catalogo della Galleria dei Principi Corsini in Firenze* (Florence, 1880), no. 141, as Rosso. This picture was given to Pontormo by Berenson 1896, 127, and has been generally accepted as his: see Goldschmidt 1911, 45; Voss 1920, 170; and Venturi 1932, 150. Clapp 1916, 52, 129, fig. 103, dated it 1528–1529. Gamba 1921, 10; Becherucci 1944, 17; and Berti, *MP* 1956, no. 51, fig. 55, dated it 1522–1525.

[3] Cf. the Pitti *Adoration* of ca. 1522 and the Certosa *Agony in the Garden* of ca. 1523. Vasari mentions (V/M, VI, 265) a *Pietà* that Pontormo painted after Poggio a Caiano in which there was "un bellissimo paese, tolto per la maggior parte da una stampa d'Alberto Duro."

[4] The one with the landscape is in the Pucci Collection, Florence. See *MP* 1956 (Berti), 32, where it is mentioned as a variant of the Corsini picture. The other (panel, 102 x 79 cm) is in the Kress Collection. It is accepted as an original of 1523 by Longhi and by W. Suida, *The Samuel H. Kress Collection*, M. H. De Young Memorial Museum, San Francisco, 1955, 52. Berti, *MP* 1956, no. 52, fig. 44, considered it a replica of the Corsini picture. While these two paintings are partial replicas of the Corsini *Madonna*, they suggest Vasari's description (V/M, VI, 265) of a *Madonna and Child with Putti* that Pontormo painted just after Poggio a Caiano: "Fece similmente un quadro di Nostra Donna col Figliuolo in collo e con alcuni putti intorno. . . ." See also Borghini 1584, 482. It is not impossible that the original on which these copies depend was the painting that Vasari notes and that it dated ca. 1522–1523.

Ca. 1522. PORTRAIT OF TWO MEN. Venice, Conte Cini Collection. I. Panel, 95 x 75 cm. Fig. 182.

Bibliography: Gamba 1921, 11, fig. 16; Giglioli 1926, 777; Venturi 1932, 101–104, fig. 48; *MC* 1940, 42, fig. 26; Toesca 1943, 22, fig. 40; Becherucci 1944, 17, fig. 12; Nicco Fasola 1947, 58, figs. 42–43; Alazard 1948, 144, fig. 41; *MDM* 1954 (Marcucci), 32; *MP* 1956 (Berti), no. 39, fig. 30; Baldini 1956, 9.

Vasari describes a portrait in which Pontormo painted "in uno stesso quadro due suoi amicissimi: l'uno fu il genero di Becuccio Bicchieraio, ed un altro, del quale parimente non so il nome . . ." (V/M, VI, 260). Since there are no other double portraits by Pontormo, it is most likely that this is the portrait mentioned by Vasari. This picture, formerly in the Guicciardini Collection, Florence, was first published by Gamba, who dated it 1515–1520. Alazard and Toesca also took the Vasari passage, which is near his discussion of the Visdomini altar, as indicative of a date before 1520 for this portrait. However, Giglioli, Becherucci, Marcucci, and Berti have placed it between 1520 and 1525 on the basis of stylistic qualities that strongly indicate a date closer to the period of the Certosa frescoes. The unique individuals of this portrait are portrayed with an intensity of characterization that did not occur in Pontormo's work before Poggio a Caiano and that first appears in the Pitti *Adoration of the Magi* of ca. 1522. Comparisons with Pontormo's earlier portraits, the *Cosimo il Vecchio* and the *Portrait of a Musician*, especially the more nearly comparable *Musician*, reveal a degree of psychological penetration and specific physical observation that was not germane to Pontormo's style before 1520. Nor can this picture be dated after 1525, the time of the *Portrait of Alessandro de' Medici*, a portrait in which there is a new elegance and formality, an elongated canon of proportions, and a mask of restraint imposed on the personality by the broad rigidity of the composition and the impassive expression of the face. Pontormo's friends are more at home in the Certosa period. Many of the faces looking out of the frescoes with expressions of thinly veiled distress bear a distinct resemblance to these slightly haunted young men. They also have something in common with the monk portraits in the *Supper at Emmaus* of 1525, heads that are placed in a similar tangential relation to one another. However, because of their semivisionary context, the monks are not projected so intensely as psychological realities as are the *Two Men*.

STUDY FOR THE PORTRAIT OF TWO MEN

193 · Florence, Uffizi 449F *verso*: Study for the *Portrait of Two Men*. Left hand holding a piece of paper. (*Recto*: Figure study, cat. 236.) 247 x 148, red chalk. Fig. 184 (detail).

Bibliography: Giglioli 1926, 777, illustrated; Berenson 1938, no. 1974; *MC* 1940, 35; Becherucci 1944, 17; *MDM* 1954 (Marcucci), no. 48; *EMI* 1954, no. 67.

This study for the hand that holds the paper in the portrait was identified by Giglioli and dated 1522–1524.

STUDY FOR AN ADORATION OF THE MAGI CA. 1522

194 · Florence, Uffizi 436S: Compositional study for an altarpiece of the *Adoration of the Magi*, ca. 1522. Within an arched frame with a double moulding, a scene on two levels: above under a shed, the Madonna holds the Child at arm's length; below her to the left, St. Joseph and St. John the Baptist; to the right, St. Elizabeth and a kneeling King; to the right and below, a crowd with another King and two attendants in the center foreground.[5] 475 x 314, red chalk; laid down; mount decorated by a former owner (late sixteenth century?) with a blue ground and stars in the upper corners; below, with a blue ground and a decorative frame inscribed in ink: *Guarda la Vergin ch' humilmente stassi in piccola capanna, e'l figlio accanto, col' fido sposo da'l ciel vinti, et lassi.* Fig. 186.

Collection: Santarelli, given to the Uffizi in 1866, stamp recto (L. 907).

Bibliography: Santarelli 1870, 39; Berenson, 1903, no. 2249; *MPA* 1910, 29; Clapp

[5] The subject of this drawing has been interpreted variously: Clapp saw the lower half of the composition as the Madonna standing with the Child adored by the three Magi, while a shepherd kneels at the feet of the Christ Child above. Berenson thought that all the figures on the first level were Magi, that St. Anne was with the Madonna above, and that the St. John was "addressing the crowd below."

1914, 90–91; Berenson 1938, no. 2249; Gamba 1956, 10, fig. 10.

Attributed to Rosso in Santarelli's catalogue, this drawing was given to Pontormo by Berenson. He dated it 1528, but later agreed with Clapp in placing it ca. 1520. With cat. 192, 195, and the Pitti *Adoration of the Magi*,[6] this composition belongs in Pontormo's development between Poggio a Caiano and the Certosa frescoes, in the year 1522. In establishing the stylistic position of this study at the beginning of the Certosa period, the closest term of comparison is the Pitti *Adoration*, which undoubtedly just precedes it. In this drawing the two sides of the oblong composition of the painting have been placed one on top of the other to form a novel kind of composition. The Holy Family group with the kneeling King, the figure leaning into the picture from the far left, the grimacing crowd, and the shed setting are similar elements that are combined differently in the two works. This drawing may be considered as an important turning point in Pontormo's development and a link to the style of the Certosa frescoes. The way in which the crowd is piled up vertically suggests not only the use of this same device in the *Martyrs* drawing (cat. 195), but also the composition of the *Agony in the Garden*. The double-tiered composition, filled to the top of the arched field with activity and without any supporting architectural framework, is precisely the scheme of the *Way to Golgotha* and the *Nailing to the Cross* (cat. 206), although the extreme spatial ambiguities of the Certosa compositions are not yet in evidence here. Clapp and Berenson both noted that this unusual composition looks forward to the schemes of the later sixteenth century, Berenson mentioning Tintoretto in the Scuola di San Rocco. There is no precedent for this kind of composition in Florentine painting, excepting those pictures in which there is an architectural or supernatural justification for it, such as a conjunction between heavenly and earthly spheres. Therefore, it is quite possible that Pontormo (perhaps inspired by a Northern example?) was an inventor of a type of Mannerist composition that was to become common in the mid- and late sixteenth-century altarpiece. Judging from the monumental and ambitious nature of the composition, this drawing was probably intended for a large altarpiece, not for a tabernacle, as Gamba believed. Designs for tabernacles were generally of a less complex, more purely devotional type, as in Pontormo's own later tabernacle at Boldrone.

Clapp suggested cat. 124 for the unexecuted *Anointing of the Athlete* as a close parallel in draughtsmanship to this drawing. However, although it dates only two years later, the style of this drawing is quite different from the Poggio a Caiano compositional study and is much closer to cat. 195. The concept of form is dependent on the vigorous and precisely specified individuality of the later Poggio

[6] Florence, Pitti 379 (panel, 85 x 191 cm). This picture is mentioned by Vasari (V/M, V, 196, 209; VI, 263–264) as part of the decoration for the *anticamera* of Giovanni Maria Benintendi, to which Franciabigio (*David and Bathsheba*, Dresden) and Bacchiacca (*Legend of the Dead King*, Dresden, and *Baptism*, Berlin) also contributed. Following Vasari's association of it in date with the *Story of Joseph* pictures, the *Adoration* has generally been dated ca. 1518–1519. See Clapp 1916, 23–24, 135–136, fig. 33; Venturi 1932, 126, figs. 68–69; Becherucci 1944, 14–15, fig. 14. However, Marcucci, *MDM* 1954, 33, has noted that it belongs with Franciabigio's panel, which is dated 1523, and Berti, *MP* 1956, no. 40, figs. 31–32 has dated it 1520–1522. This important work, for which no studies have survived, belongs to the moment just preceding the Certosa frescoes, begun early in 1523, and is a major document of Pontormo's susceptibility to the prints of Dürer and Lucas van Leyden at that time. As has been generally agreed, the head to the far left is a self-portrait. See note 15 on p. 777.

a Caiano drawings. The line is infinitely more differentiated, more nervous and variable than the less developed linear style of cat. 124, which still contains echoes of Andrea del Sarto and Fra Bartolommeo.

STUDY FOR A VICTORY AND BAPTISM OF THE TEN THOUSAND MARTYRS CA. 1522

195 · Hamburg, Kunsthalle 21253: Compositional study for a *Victory and Baptism of the Ten Thousand Martyrs*, ca. 1522. Within an arched picture space, a battle scene with nudes and horses; in the middle distance, soldiers with spears approach from behind a hill, two of them carrying banners; in the distance, a group of nudes being baptised by an angel; above them, three flying putti with arrows; at the top, the triplefaced sign of the Trinity. 420 x 367, red chalk; outlines incised for transfer; sheet cut to an arched shape and laid down; inscribed in ink: *del Piombo* and *Vasari Fra Sebastiano*. Fig. 185.

Collection: Harzen; unidentified stamp recto (L. 2798); unidentified eighteenth-century stamp recto (L. 1976).

Bibliography: Berenson 1903, no. 2252, pl. 172; Clapp 1914, 290; Clapp 1916, 54, fig. 108; Berenson 1938, 315, no. 2252, fig. 963; *MF* 1952, 62, fig. 99; *MP* 1956 (Berti), 40; *Hamburg Exhib.* 1957, no. 90, fig. 16.

Berenson connected this compositional study with the Uffizi version of the *Legend of the Ten Thousand Martyrs* (fig. 183), and Clapp dated it 1527–1530 as for a lost variant of the same picture.[7] In discussing this drawing in relation to the Pitti *Martyrdom* of 1529–1530 and its partial replica in the Uffizi, Berti suggested that in this drawing Pontormo might also have thought of a fresco lunette of the same subject. The connections between this drawing and the two *Martyrdom* paintings are complex; it is the invention from which both the Pitti and the Uffizi versions derive, yet it is not identical in format or composition with either and thus must have been planned for still a third version. In both paintings the original arched composition is adapted to the rectangular shape of a panel picture. In the Uffizi version the simple expedient is used of separating the angels from the baptising group in order to fill the upper half of the panel. In the Pitti picture a more sophisticated solution involves the insertion of Michelangelesque figures who condemn the martyrs in the foreground, thus displacing the original battle scene into the middle distance to the left, and the addition of the crucified martyrs in the right distance. Whereas the Pitti *Martyrdom* is essentially a new composition that makes use of this drawing for its major episode, the Uffizi version is merely a rearrangement of the parts of the original design with a corner of the crucifixion scene taken from the Pitti composition. The relations among these three versions of the subject are further complicated by the fact that the painting closest to the drawing is the one in the Uffizi, a picture that is probably by Bronzino rather than Pontormo.[8] It is likely that when there was a demand for a replica of Pontormo's com-

[7] Florence, Uffizi 1187 (panel, 64 x 43 cm). Since the differences between this picture and the one in the Pitti are those mentioned by Vasari, this picture has been identified as the varied replica of the Pitti *Martyrdom* that Vasari says (V/M, VI, 275) Pontormo made for Carlo Neroni: "Un altro quadro simile al sopradetto fece a Carlo Neroni, ma con la battaglia de' Martiri sola, e l'Angelo che gli battezza. . . ." See Clapp 1916, 54–55, 139–140; Berenson 1936, 401; Becherucci 1944, 20; Berti, *MP* 1956, no. 66, fig. 59.

[8] The Uffizi picture does not fit comfortably into Pontormo's *oeuvre*, either at the time of the drawing (cat. 195) or at the time of the Pitti *Martyrdom*. However, as Smyth 1955, 107–109, has noted there is a strong case for Bronzino's execution of the replica. He was working with Pontormo until he went to Pesaro in 1530. He certainly knew Pontormo's drawing, since he used the motive of the two fighting men in the foreground in his *Apollo and Marsyas* (Hermitage), painted in Pesaro. Furthermore, the execu-

position, Bronzino used Pontormo's drawing for it, painting the Uffizi panel ca. 1530. The contours of the drawing are incised for transfer, and the parts of Pontormo's drawing and Bronzino's panel that correspond in composition are almost exacly the same size. Since this is also true of Pontormo's own panel, it is probable that the drawing served both artists as the actual *modello* for the battle scene.

In spite of its close connections with the *Martyrdom* pictures, it is unlikely that this drawing was directly preparatory even to Pontormo's version. While it has always been dated at the same time as the paintings, the style of this drawing suggests that it actually preceded them by some years. There is no trace of the strained rigidity that informs the figures in the Pitti painting, or any evidence of the kind of Michelangelism that came into Pontormo's draughtsmanship toward 1530, such as in the study for the foreground figure in the Pitti picture (cat. 294). Nor is there any suggestion of the diminished plasticity of the Certosa drawings or of the rarefied delicacy of those from the S. Felicita period. Rather, the vigorous and complex chiaroscuro and the strongly accented, flexible line recall the drawings of ca. 1521–1522. The red chalk draughtsmanship is generally similar, although more lucid and finished, to that of the *Adoration of the Magi* drawing of ca. 1522 (cat. 194). The composition is also characteristic of the period just before Pontormo went to the Certosa. The agitation of the composition, the strong movement that rushes out of the background and turns abruptly across the front plane, and the squat, vigorous figures all occur in the Pitti *Adoration of the Magi* and in the *Adoration* drawing noted above. There is also evidence here of the spatial experimentation that occurs in Pontormo's works at this time. This experimentation was a reassertion of Pontormo's earlier radical experiments in spatial illogic that was to come to a climax in the Certosa compositions of 1523–1524, such as cat. 206 for the *Nailing to the Cross*. As in the *Joseph in Egypt* of 1518–1519, the rational spatial image in this drawing is negated by the rising sequences of forms and by knots of figures that seem to expand and contract the space around them at will. (Cf. the crowd of soldiers in the center with the crowd pushing forward in the *Joseph in Egypt*, or the baptism group with the scene of the dying Jacob in the earlier picture.)

There is some evidence that Pontormo made this drawing for a specific commission in 1522. The *Legend of the Ten Thousand Martyrs* was also the subject of a commission that was given to Perino del Vaga by the Brotherhood of the Camaldoli Martyrs when he was in Florence in 1523. Perino was unable to complete the project because the plague broke out in Florence and he left the city, arriving back in Rome by the fall of 1524.[9] However, Perino's

tion suggests his hand; it is considerably less precise and rhythmic in line than Pontormo's *Martyrdom* and it differs sharply in color from it. Details such as the heads of the fighting men are explicitly Bronzinesque, while the landscape is similar to that in the *Pygmalion and Galatea*, also probably executed by Bronzino at about this time.

[9] Vasari (V/M, V, 602–609) says that Perino left Rome and came to Florence because of an outbreak of the plague in 1523. Vasari also mentions the circumstances of Perino's departure in his life of Lappoli (*ibid.*, VI, 8).

Perino's subsequent departure from Florence is also recounted by Vasari (*ibid.*, V, 608–609): "Intanto la peste cominciata . . . in Foirenza . . . Partendo dunque di Firenze Perino, lasciò in abbandono l'opera de' Martiri . . ." Vasari (*ibid.*, VI, 9–10) notes that Rosso, Lappoli, Parmigianino, and Perino all returned to Rome after the last outbreak of the plague in that city in the summer of 1524. Vasari's account is supported by frequent references to the outbreaks of the plague in 1522–1524 from other sources, among them: B. Cellini, *La Vita Scritta da lui medesimo*, ed. F. Tassi (Florence, 1829), 109; A. Lapini, *Diario Fiorentino dal 252 al 1596*, ed. G. Corazzini (Florence, 1900), 93. See also S. Ammirato, study for the fresco survives and is so similar to Pontormo's drawing in composition and format that both drawings must have been done for the same commission.[10] The possibility of a competition for this commission is not to be ruled out, especially in the light of Vasari's emphasis on Perino's fame as a practitioner of the "maniera di Roma" and his willingness to display his art in a competitive spirit (V/M, V, 603–606). However, unless Perino came to Florence before February 1523 — and this is not impossible since the plague in Rome began in 1522 — Pontormo may already have begun work at the Certosa before Perino arrived in Florence. If this was the case, it is more likely that the sequence of events was as follows: Pontormo was given the commission for the fresco in 1522 but, because of an outbreak of the plague in Florence, he fled to the Certosa late in the year leaving it unexecuted.[11] Perino arrived from Rome in 1523 and was awarded the commission,[12] but he too was forced to leave without executing it.

It is likely that Perino knew Pontormo's composition, for there are similarities that go beyond the identity in format, but he transformed it into a Roman scheme with the major emphasis on the foreground group — a tableau set in front of the actual martyrdom scene consisting of Raphaelesque figures seated in graceful contrapposto. According to Vasari, when Perino left Florence, his cartoon remained with Giovanni di Goro, passing later to Piloto, who "mostrandolo volentieri a ogni persona d'ingegno, come cosa rarissima . . ." (*ibid.*, 609). It was undoubtedly this cartoon that influenced Pontormo's reinterpretation of his original invention in the Pitti *Martyrdom* of 1529–1530, where monumental figures have been inserted on a stage in front of the battle and baptism scenes and the crucified martrys are depicted at the upper left of the composition.[13]

Istorie Fiorentine (Florence, 1849), pt. II, 6, 68–69; and F. Guicciardini, *La Storia d'Italia* (Milan, 1830), bks. XIV, XV.

[10] Vienna, Albertina Inv. 2933. See also the version in the Fogg Art Museum 1932.265 (Mongan and Sachs 1940, no. 191, fig. 101). The possibility of a connection between Pontormo's drawing and Perino's drawings was briefly noted by A. E. Popham, "On Some Works by Perino del Vaga," *Burl.* 88 (1945), 59n3.

[11] Vasari (V/M, VI, 266) says that Pontormo left for the Certosa in 1522. The first document of payment to him is February 4, 1523 [new style]. See Clapp 1916, app. II, doc. 16.

[12] Vasari implies in his life of Perino (V/M, V, 606) that this was not the first attempt of the Camaldoli to have this fresco painted: ". . . i quali avevano avuto voglia più volte di far dipignere una facciata che era in quella, drentovi la storia di essi Martiri . . ."

[13] In an article, "The Legend of St. Achatius: Bachiacca, Perino, Pontormo," *AB* 45 (1963), 258–263, that was published too late for detailed consideration in this study, H. S. Merritt clarifies the iconographic connections between Pontormo's drawing, Perino's drawing, and the two later paintings in the Pitti and Uffizi. He points out that the drawings depict two different episodes in the *Legend of St. Achatius and the Ten Thousand Martyrs*: Pontormo's, the victory and baptism; Perino's, the condemnation and martyrdom. Thus, according to Merritt, the drawings must be projects for pendant frescoes rather than two ideas for a single fresco. Merritt opts for a competition between the two artists and believes that the subject of Pontormo's drawing is understandable only as a complement to Perino's. Merritt supports this hypothesis by pointing out that when Pontormo later painted the subject in the Pitti picture, he made the legend complete and the narrative self sufficient by adding the episodes of the condemnation and martyrdom, and that the completion of the story is at least suggested in the Uffizi version by the inclusion of a fragment of the crucified martyrs scene.

1523–1524. CERTOSA PASSION SERIES: *Agony in the Garden*, *Christ before Pilate*, *Resurrection*, *Way to Golgotha*, *Pietà*. Galluzzo, Certosa di Val d'Ema. I. Detached frescoes, 311 x 287 cm; the *Resurrection*, 253 x 287 cm (without the painted frames).

Bibliography: Goldschmidt 1911, 6–8, 44, pl. 3; Clapp 1911, 10–12; Clapp 1916, 39–41, 107–114, figs. 79–81; Voss 1920, 167–168; Friedlaender 1925, 65–70, figs. 5–6; Venturi 1932, 132–141, figs. 72–82; Berenson 1936, 401; Steinbart 1939, 8; Toesca 1943, 12–14, figs. 16–18; Becherucci 1944, 16–17, figs. 26–33; Nicco Fasola 1946, 37–48; Nicco Fasola 1947, 34–44, figs. 7–17; *MP* 1956 (Berti), nos. 45–49, figs. 37–41; Baldini 1956, 9–11, figs. 7–11; Nicco Fasola 1956, 14–17, figs. 4, 6–7; Marcucci 1956, 13–15; Lavin 1957, 113–118, fig. 1.

The Passion Series is discussed in detail by Vasari (V/M, VI, 266–269), is mentioned by Borghini 1584, 482–483, and later by Moreni 1791/95, II, 153–154. Clapp has published a document that records payments to Pontormo for his paintings in the cloister from February 4, 1522 to April 10, 1524 (Clapp 1916, app. II, doc. 16). However, Clapp did not consider the Florentine calendar in interpreting the entries in this account book. The date of the first payment should be read as February 4, 1523 [new style]. Vasari states that Pontormo went to the Certosa to avoid an outbreak of the plague in 1522 (V/M, VI, 266). Thus, since the first payment is recorded in February 1523, it is likely that Pontormo went to the Certosa in the winter of 1522–1523 and that his actual work in the cloister began early in 1523, not early in 1522, as has always been assumed. The terminal date for the work is also satisfactorily established by the document cited as April 10, 1524, even though payments to Pontormo in the account books of the Certosa continue until 1527 (see Clapp 1916, app. II, doc. 16). Pontormo apparently continued to work for the monks for several more years, even after he had returned to Florence, painting the *Supper at Emmaus*, which is dated 1525, and several other works noted by Vasari (V/M, VI, 269–270) that have not survived. Vasari also mentions the Certosa frescoes in his life of Bronzino (V/M, VII, 605). He says that he met his friend Bronzino there in 1524, ". . . allora che lavorava alla Certosa col Pontormo, l'opere del quale andava io giovinetto a disegnare in quel luogo."

The frescoes were detached from their places in the cloister for the *Mostra del Pontormo* in 1956 and are now in the museum of the monastery. With them are displayed small (126 x 115 cm) copies on canvas by Jacopo da Empoli.[14] Except for the *Resurrection* the compositions are faithfully copied. Since the size of the field to be painted was smaller, this fresco is not as high as the others. Therefore, Empoli has added a strip to the bottom of his copy to make its proportions more nearly square.[15] Because of the damaged condition of the originals these copies are a useful guide to the details of Pontormo's compositions and three of them

[14] Milanesi (V/M, VI, 269n2), first noted them. See also Clapp 1916, 41; and *MP* 1956 (Berti), 29.

[15] According to Nicco Fasola 1956, 14–17, Empoli's copy shows that Pontormo's fresco originally extended some 60 cm further down, but was reduced in size when the door below it was put in. Not only does Pontormo's composition become awkward and illogical with the addition in Empoli's copy, but the door does not appear to be later than the others in the cloister and the painted frame along the lower edge of the fresco is identical with the rest of Pontormo's frame. Furthermore, three late sixteenth-century copies after the fresco (cat. A7, A252, A326) show the composition without any addition below the figures.

are here reproduced (figs. 187, 189, 205).

Since the date of Pontormo's work in the cloister is well established as 1523–1524, the only problem remaining is the order of execution of the frescoes. While this question will be clarified in the discussions of the individual frescoes, the general scheme may be indicated here: to the left of the entrance door in the corner was the *Agony in the Garden*, and on the adjoining side wall was the *Christ Before Pilate*. These are the first two scenes in the narrative sequence and also the first mentioned by Vasari.[16] On the right side wall in the corner was the *Way to Golgotha*.[17] There was to have been a *Nailing to the Cross* in the adjacent space on the entrance wall, but it was never executed. This subject is not mentioned by Vasari, but the compositional drawing for it (cat. 206) is unmistakably for this space and it is close in style to the *Way to Golgotha*. Continuing in the far right corner of the cloister, the *Pietà* occupied the space on the side wall. For this space Pontormo was in doubt as to whether to paint a *Pietà* or a *Deposition*.[18] A preliminary compositional drawing for a *Deposition* survives (cat. 212), showing the door that is to the left of the space where the *Pietà* was actually painted. The space next to the *Pietà* on the end wall remained empty. Here, according to Vasari (see n. 18) Pontormo intended to paint a *Crucifixion*, but never executed it. Continuing to the far left corner of the cloister, the *Resurrection* occupied a space on the far wall over a door, and was therefore smaller in size than the other frescoes.[19] Thus, Pontormo followed the narrative order of events in pairs of scenes around the cloister, ending with the *Resurrection* in isolation.

Agony in the Garden: In its style as well as in the narrative order and in Vasari's listing, this fresco is the first of the series. Like the Pitti *Adoration* of ca. 1522 the composition is somewhat additive, the space is broken into quite distinct sections, and a group of isolated figures is balanced against a tightly wedged crowd that emerges abruptly from the depth. Also like the *Adoration* and unlike the other Certosa frescoes, landscape plays an important part in this composition.[20] The grouping of the foreground figures and the figure of Christ are adapted freely from Dürer's woodcut of the same sub-

[16] V/M, VI, 267. Since Vasari was at the Certosa in 1524 (*ibid.*, VII, 605), he may have known the order in which Pontormo's frescoes were executed and have listed them in that sequence. However, he does not (as Clapp says) state specifically that his order is chronological.

[17] V/M, VI, 268. After noting the first pair of frescoes (the *Agony in the Garden* and the *Christ Before Pilate*) and the *Resurrection*, Vasari continues: "Seguitando poi in uno degli altri canti le storie della Passione, fece Cristo che va con la croce in spalla al monte Calvario . . ."

[18] V/M, VI, 269: "Aveva dopo queste [the *Resurrection* and the *Way to Golgotha*] a seguitare negli altri canti la Crucifissione e Deposizione di Croce; ma lasciandole per allora con animo di farle in ultimo, fece al suo luogo Cristo deposto di Croce, usando la medesima maniera . . ."

[19] See n15. Vasari departs from both the narrative sequence and the order of the frescoes around the cloister in mentioning the *Resurrection* third rather than last. After noting the *Christ Before Pilate*, he continues (V/M, VI, 268): "Avendo a far poi in uno degli altri cantoni la Resurrezione di Cristo . . . " This departure from the normal sequence most likely indicates the actual order in which the frescoes were executed.

[20] Düreresque landscapes are common in Pontormo's paintings of these years. The dominant role of the landscape in the *Agony in the Garden* is not evident in the fresco, where scarcely more than the skyline remains, but the hilly countryside with Düreresque houses and towers is clear in Empoli's copy. A similar background occurs in the Pontormesque *Madonna and Child with St. John* in the Corsini Gallery (no. 141), Florence. A lost *Pietà* mentioned by Vasari (V/M, VI, 265) as notable for its landscape after Dürer must also have belonged to this group of works of ca. 1522–1523 in which Northern influence was very marked.

ject (*Small Passion*, 1509–1511, Bar. 26).[21]

Christ Before Pilate: This fresco belongs second in the series in style as well as in the narrative order and in Vasari's listing. In contrast to the *Agony in the Garden*, there is a much more bold experimentation with space and with the establishment of several levels of reality. Strongly emphasized verticality of composition appears here for the first time in Pontormo's paintings, an effect that is intensified by the removal of the horizontal base of the composition and the substitution for it of apparitional figures that rise into the picture. These qualities connect the *Christ Before Pilate* with the *Resurrection*, and the two frescoes may be grouped as a second phase of Pontormo's work at the Certosa. The *Adoration* drawing (cat. 194) and the Hermitage *Holy Family*, both dating ca. 1522, anticipate in some respects the stylistic premises of these two frescoes.

Pontormo's adaptions from Dürer in this fresco are more complex and stylistically decisive than was the case with the *Agony in the Garden*.[22] The Pilate with his extended hand, the crowding of the soldiers, the gesturing toward the left that creates a tensional pull against the central axis, the slender figure of Christ, and even the sense of void below the figures all derive from Dürer's woodcut of *Christ Before Herod* (*Small Passion*, 1509, Bar. 32), while the Pilate may also be related in motive to the king in the *Martyrdom of St. John the Evangelist* (1498, Bar. 61). The half-length soldiers have generally been thought to derive from Dürer's woodcut *The Bathing House* (ca. 1496, Bar. 128). However, while Dürer's figures are cut off, they are illusionistically placed in relation to a logically developed space limited by a firm horizontal wall. They are quite different from Pontormo's figures, who seem to float into the picture as if from a bottomless void. As has been pointed out by Lavin, a more likely source for this motive as well as for certain other elements in the composition that are unexplained by Dürer, is Donatello's pulpit relief of the same subject, which Pontormo could have seen in San Lorenzo.[23] However, Pontormo has disguised his adaptations from Donatello by translating the sculptor's Renaissance idiom into German, filtering out all that is classical in Donatello's scene by adapting it, with Dürer's aid, to his own anticlassical conception of the subject.

Resurrection: Although it is the last in narrative sequence, this fresco is mentioned third by Vasari and stylistic evidence supports this order. The style of the *Resur-*

[21] Although we have made certain deletions and ammendments to his findings, these and other derivations from Dürer in the Certosa frescoes were first brought together by Clapp 1911, 10–12. Vasari thought (V/M, VI, 267) that Pontormo had completely abandoned "la maniera italiana" in this fresco. He found that the main figures were painted in a "maniera tanto simile a quella del Duro" and that "non lungi è Giuda che conduce i Giudei, di viso così strano anch' egli, sì come sono le cere di tutte que' soldati fatti alla tedesca con arie straveganti. . . ."

[22] Vasari seems to have realized this, remarking that if one did not know that Pontormo painted the fresco, one would think it executed by a Northerner (V/M, VI, 267). As in the case of the *Agony in the Garden*, he found the soldiers especially Germanic in costume and expression; however, perhaps because of its isolated clarity and carefully balanced contrapposto, the figure on the steps was thought to retain something of Pontormo's "vecchia maniera" (*ibid.*, 268).

[23] In Donatello's relief the soldiers appear in a similar floating context, although Pontormo has intensified this effect by turning their backs. The figure of Pilate in Pontormo's fresco is also closely related to the relief and, as Lavin has indicated, the somewhat unusual presence of Pilate's wife confirms Pontormo's close study of the relief. Furthermore, the balustrade with the small figures is reminiscent of Donatello's setting and the figure on the stairs surely derives from the winged boy on the pedestal to the right of Donatello's scene.

rection is close to that of the *Christ Before Pilate*, with which it may be grouped. Verticalism of composition is here even more strongly asserted, with the central vertical of the Christ dominating the jagged diagonals and dislocated forms of the sleeping figures. The Christ floats as an apparition that belongs to another reality, yet the soldiers are compositionally dependent on him as the central axis of the picture. The composition, especially the Christ and the soldiers to the right, is freely derived from Dürer's woodcut of the same subject (*Large Passion*, 1510, Bar. 15), while the soldier on the left is taken directly from the woodcut in the *Small Passion* (1509–1511, Bar. 45).[24]

Way to Golgotha: The next fresco in the narrative sequence and Vasari's order (discounting the *Resurrection*) is the *Way to Golgotha*. This work is strikingly different from the *Agony in the Garden*, the *Christ Before Pilate*, and the *Resurrection*, and it may be paired with the unexecuted *Nailing to the Cross* composition (cat. 206), which was intended for the adjacent space, as a third phase of the work in the cloister. In these two compositions the vertical constructions of the *Christ Before Pilate* and the *Resurrection* have been exchanged for a design whose vertical rhythms are independent of any stabilizing axis at all. Furthermore, somewhat as in the *Adoration* drawing of ca. 1522 (cat. 194), the action takes place close to the picture plane, there is no rearward extension of space at all, and the figures completely fill the arched picture surface. In this sense the compositions of the *Way to Golgotha* and the *Nailing to the Cross* are Düreresque in a more profound way than those of the preceding frescoes. Here, the analogy is not with the *Small Passion*, from which Pontormo continued to take ideas for figures and poses, but with Dürer's more emphatically Late Gothic style of a dozen years earlier in the *Large Passion* and the *Apocalypse*.[25]

Pietà: Vasari's implication that this was the last fresco to be executed is supported by its style. There is nothing in Pontormo's work at the Certosa that could logically be placed after the *Pietà*. Like cat. 212, the study for a *Deposition* that was initially planned for this space, this fresco is evidence of a relaxation and simplification after the stylistic complexities of the *Way to Golgotha* and the *Nailing to the Cross*. There is a marked shift from the self-conscious experimentation that is evident in the broken forms and calculated spatial inversions of the earlier compositions. A new continuity of previously shattered outlines and a new rhythmic unity in the composition anticipate the emergence of Pontormo's S. Felicita style. Even while it was still based in motive on Dürer, Pontormo developed in this last Certosa fresco a rhythmic style that — as would become evident at S. Felicita — was to be the complete antithesis of Dürer's style. The specific connections with Dürer in this last phase of Pontormo's work at the Certosa are quite consistent with these changes. In his radically anticlassical experiments in the earlier frescoes Pontormo found the Late Gothic Dürer of the early prints most compatible even though he used compositional motives from the later *Small Passion* woodcuts.

[24] Vasari mentions (V/M, VI, 268) the German manner of this fresco, but seems to have been more struck by the change in Pontormo's palette to a coloring "tanto dolce e tanto buono." In the present condition of the frescoes, this distinction in color is not notable.

[25] Cf. especially Bar. 10, 12 from the *Large Passion* (1498); Bar. 67 from the *Apocalypse* (1498). The following motives derive from the *Small Passion* (1509–1511): the group of weeping women from the *Nailing to the Cross* (Bar. 39), the Veronica, the man with his head through the ladder, and the man with the beard to the right between the two crosses from the *Way to Golgotha* (Bar. 37). For unspecified reasons, Vasari preferred this fresco as less Germanic than the others (V/M, VI, 268).

However, in the *Deposition* drawing (cat. 212) and in the *Pietà* fresco, as well as in the *Supper at Emmaus*, he drew exclusively from the simplified compositions of larger, quieter figures of the *Small Passion*.[26]

Considering the magnitude of Pontormo's work at the Certosa, very few drawings for the frescoes have survived: there are compositional studies only for the two subjects that were not executed, the *Nailing to the Cross* (cat. 206) and the *Deposition* (cat. 212); there is but a single study for the *Agony in the Garden*; and there are none at all for the *Christ Before Pilate* and the *Resurrection*.

STUDY FOR THE AGONY IN THE GARDEN

196 · Florence, Uffizi 6682F *recto*: Study for St. John, *Agony in the Garden*. Page from a sketchbook: Seated heavily-draped man asleep with his right leg raised and his head leaning on his right hand. (*Verso*: Leg, cat. 247.) 199 x 158, red chalk on pink prepared paper. Fig. 188.

Bibliography: Berenson 1903, no. 2167; *MPA* 1910, 22; Clapp 1914, 230–231; Clapp 1916, 35, 84, fig. 49; Giglioli 1926, 781; Berenson 1938, no. 2167; *MP* 1956 (Marcucci), no. 107, fig. 141a.

Clapp dated this drawing 1521 and Giglioli thought it was for the Vertumnus of Poggio a Caiano. As Marcucci has also concluded, it is a study for the St. John. The figure is identical in every detail to the sleeping Evangelist in the fresco, a figure who can be seen more clearly in Empoli's copy (fig. 187). As this is the only surviving study for this fresco and there are none for the *Christ Before Pilate* and the *Resurrection*, it becomes an important document for the first phase of Pontormo's work at the Certosa. As in the studies for the *Way to Golgotha*, the style is a soft, simplified outline manner, which nevertheless does not stress the contours as such. Also, like cat. 197, 200, 201, and 205 for the *Way to Golgotha*, it is in red chalk on pink prepared paper, probably from a sketchbook. We may suppose that this was the general mode of the earlier Certosa drawings, while in some of the later studies there was a shift away from this understated style toward a more complex manner. The transition from the richly elaborated and vigorous draughtsmanship of the Poggio a Caiano drawings to the quiet, delicate handling of the red chalk in this study was apparently quite abrupt. There was certainly no hint in the drawings of 1521–1522 of an incipient shift to an unassertive and introverted style that is completely without the technical bravura of the Poggio a Caiano studies. We cannot doubt that Pontormo's study of Dürer's woodcuts had some influence on the formation of his new graphic manner and that drawings such as this one were the result of conscious experimentation. The regular curves of the left leg, for example, could have been suggested by the lines of a woodcut, while the uncharacteristic expression of the face was surely an attempt to emulate something Düreresque. The new kind of draughtsmanship in this and other similar Certosa drawings is part of one of the most important experimental shifts of direction in Pontormo's development: the turn from the physical excitement of the Poggio a Caiano lunette, where the basis of his style was still physical reality, to the unreal and fantastic world of the Certosa frescoes.

STUDIES FOR THE WAY TO GOLGOTHA

197 · Florence, Uffizi 6643F *verso*: Study for the man carrying the end of the cross,

[26] The setting and the figure of the Magdalen are taken from the *Lamentation* (Bar. 43), the head of the woman at the upper left from the *Entombment* (Bar. 44), and the Joseph of Arimathea from the old man on the right in the *Descent from the Cross* (Bar. 42).

Way to Golgotha. Page from a sketchbook: Nude seen to the knees bending over to the left with his arms extended downward. (*Recto*: Study for a tapestry, cat. 349.) 218 x 153, red chalk on pink prepared paper; inscribed: [Fran]*co* *Rosi 189*, and in ink in a seventeenth-century hand: *Jacopo da Pontormo*. Fig. 191.

Bibliography: Berenson 1903, no. 2135; Clapp 1914, 201; Clapp 1916, 42; Berenson 1938, 313, no. 2135.

As Clapp has noted, this nude is a study for the man who carries the end of the cross. Like cat. 196 for the *Agony in the Garden*, it is executed in a soft red chalk on pink-washed paper in a manner of utmost simplicity and understatement.

198 · Florence, Uffizi 6529F *recto*: Study for the man carrying the end of the cross, *Way to Golgotha*. Nude seen to the knees turned and leaning over to the left, with his arms extended downward; to the left, nude reclining on his right side with his legs extended to the right and leaning on his right arm. (*Verso*: Study for the Certosa, cat. 202.) 243 x 361, red chalk; W: Greek Cross (cf. B. 5536); inscribed in ink: *Puntormo*. Fig. 193.

Bibliography: Berenson 1903, no. 2032; Clapp 1914, 134; Berenson 1938, no. 2032.

Clapp has identified the figure to the right as a study for the man who carries the end of the cross. It is drawn in the same unassertive style as cat. 197, the first sketch for the figure, but shows the final version of the pose with the head raised and looking out at the spectator as in the fresco. Of this drawing Clapp remarked perceptively: "On croirait surprendre dans ce dessin l'effort d'un artiste qui essaie de changer sa manière de dessiner." Certainly the change in such a brief period from the style of the Poggio a Caiano drawings to this kind of drawing must have been the result of a real shift in purpose and a self-imposed experimentation with new stylistic premises that required a change in draughtsmanship.

The other figure in this drawing has not been discussed in the literature, but is of singular interest. The motive occurs nowhere in the Certosa frescoes, but is identical to Bronzino's *St. Lawrence*, a lunette fresco over an entrance door to the cloister, that Bronzino painted in 1523–1524 while he was working there with Pontormo.[27] This sketch and another on the verso were probably the master's indications to the pupil as to how the *St. Lawrence* should be done, instructions that were no doubt necessary as Vasari says that the young Bronzino painted the fresco "senza aver mai più veduto colorire a olio" (V/M, VI, 270). This supposition is supported by a comparison with Bronzino's own drawing for the figure, in which we see the pupil's weaker attempt to work out the pose for himself (cat. A121). The influence of Pontormo's ascetic reclining figure, with his slender, elongated proportions, his long arms, and small bald head, also occurs later in Bronzino's work in his *St. Benedict* fresco (Badia) of ca. 1525–1526.

199 · Florence, Uffizi 6578F: Study for the man carrying the end of the cross, *Way to Golgotha*. Head of a man full face. 80 x 66, red chalk; cut irregularly. Fig. 192.

Bibliography: Berenson 1903, no. 2078; Clapp 1914, 165; Berenson 1938, no. 2078.

Clapp rightly connected this head with that of the man carrying the end of the cross, but dated it 1520–1525. This small study is undoubtedly a fragment of a larger drawing for the entire figure and was probably not intended as a detail

[27] Vasari reports (V/M, VI, 270) that Bronzino painted "sopra un arco, un San Lorenzo ignudo in sulla grata." See McComb 1928, 51; and Smyth 1949, 186–188, fig. 1.

study for the head alone. The articulation of the features is not as precise as in most of Pontormo's head studies. Furthermore, the head in the fresco is a self-portrait of Pontormo, while this head does not bear any particular resemblance to his features.[28] The final detail study for the self-portrait head has not survived. In this drawing, as in cat. 196 for the *Agony in the Garden*, the unusually regular and parallel curved lines of the modelling seem to indicate Pontormo's attempt to translate Dürer's woodcut technique into chalk.

200 · Florence, Uffizi 6548F *recto*: Studies for St. Veronica, *Way to Golgotha*, and later studies. Two pages from a sketchbook: On the left page, kneeling nude turned to the right with arms extended studied twice. On the right page, nude reclining on the right side of an arch; below, the figure restudied on a smaller scale; above in reverse direction, small figure with raised arms. (*Verso*: Studies for the same figure, cat. 201.) 215 x 303, red chalk on pink prepared paper, the right page in black chalk; W: Greek Cross in a circle (B. 5543). Fig. 190.

Bibliography: Berenson 1903, no. 2051; *MPA* 1910, 36; Clapp 1914, 146; Berenson 1938, no. 2051; *MP* 1956 (Marcucci), no. 138, fig. 166a.

Clapp thought the sketches on the left page were for the *Creation of Eve* (cat. 104), which he wrongly dated 1535. Berenson and Marcucci associated these studies with the San Lorenzo version of the same subject (cat. 359), Marcucci connecting them also with cat. 104 and dating all three drawings 1545–1546. This drawing has no connection with either cat. 104 of ca. 1520 or with cat. 359 of ca. 1546–1551, but is explicitly for the St. Veronica and is identical in style to other Certosa drawings. This soft, unornamental handling of red chalk occurs in no San Lorenzo drawing (the San Lorenzo studies are, with the exception of one for the *Resurrection of the Dead*, in black chalk and on a larger scale), but is precisely the style of cat. 196, 197, 203, and 205 for the Certosa frescoes. In the larger sketch Pontormo has worked out the general pose of the St. Veronica, but was still in doubt as to the position of the arms, which he drew in the smaller sketch and on the verso as they are in the fresco figure.

Clapp dated the sketches on the right page ca. 1535, while Marcucci connected them with San Lorenzo as for the *Deluge* (cat. 373) or for one of the figures above to the right in the *Christ in Glory* (cat. 359). Berenson also dated the right page at the same time as the left page, apparently about 1535. However, the two sides of this sheet are not necessarily contemporary in date. We have here an example of a sheet that was once folded and sewn at the center (the marks can still be seen) as part of a sketchbook. While the two left pages of the folded sheet were used by Pontormo for the St. Veronica sketches (cf. cat. 201, left page), the two right pages were not used until much later (cf. cat. 201, right page). As Berenson has pointed out, the reclining figure is derived from Michelangelo's Medici *Allegories* (cf. especially the *Aurora*) and, if we are correct in associating the left page with the Certosa, could not possibly have been contemporary with it. Furthermore, there are stylistic similarities with later drawings, such as cat. 342 for the Castello vault of ca. 1537–1543, although these sketches may be closer to 1550 in date. However, in spite of certain analogies in motive with the San Lorenzo drawings mentioned by Marcucci, this drawing probably was not connected with the choir frescoes. It is clearly a secular decorative motive, perhaps an idea for an allegorical spandrel figure.

[28] For a list of portraits of Pontormo see note 16 on p. 112.

201 · Florence, Uffizi 6548F *verso*: Studies for the St. Veronica, *Way to Golgotha*, and later studies. Two pages from a sketchbook: On the left page, kneeling nude turned to the right studied three times. On the right page, upper half of a woman turned to the right; sideways on the sheet, bust of a figure with arms extended; in reverse direction, the same bust on a smaller scale. (*Recto*: Studies for the same figure, cat. 200.) 215 x 303, red and black chalk on pink prepared paper, the right page in black chalk; inscribed: *Franco Rosi 173.*

Bibliography: Berenson 1903, no. 2051; Clapp 1914, 146–147; Berenson 1938, no. 2051; *MP* 1956 (Marcucci), no. 138, fig. 166b.

The sketches on the left page are studies for the St. Veronica following those on the recto. In the upper, final sketch the figure is posed exactly as it is in the fresco. See the discussion of the recto for the opinions of Berenson, Clapp, and Marcucci.

Clapp and Marcucci both connected the sketches on the right page with cat. A128, a sheet of copies after the San Lorenzo *Resurrection of the Dead*, although Clapp dated the sheet ca. 1535. This side of the sheet is of the San Lorenzo period like the right side of the recto. It may have been connected with the *Resurrection of the Dead*, since a similar motive appears in one of the studies for the fresco, cat. 379.

202 · Florence, Uffizi 6529F *verso*: Studies for the *Way to Golgotha*. Nude seen to the knees and almost from behind turned to the right studied twice; in reverse direction, smaller nude reclining on his right arm with his legs extended to the right. (*Recto*: Study for the Certosa, cat. 198.) 243 x 361, black chalk, the small nude in red chalk; inscribed in ink in a sixteenth-century hand: *di Jacopo da puntormmo.* Fig. 196.

Bibliography: Berenson 1903, no. 2032; Clapp 1914, 134–135; Berenson 1938, no. 2032.

Clapp dated this drawing 1520–1523 and thought the black chalk studies might be first ideas for the figure above the St. Veronica. They certainly resemble this figure in pose and in proportions, but they are also similar to the St. Veronica herself, and may have been preliminary studies for any one of the figures to the left of the composition. Pontormo's new canon of proportions in the Certosa frescoes is most evident in these nudes. These brittle, elongated forms with their small heads are not angular in themselves like the Poggio a Caiano figures, but are aphysical, weightless props for the complicated and angular folds of drapery that will be piled on them in the fresco. The softened line and sparse modelling of these two nudes is that of the other studies for the fresco, but in black rather than red chalk. Clapp thought the small reclining nude was connected with Poggio a Caiano, but it is an idea for Bronzino's Certosa *St. Lawrence*, a motive that Pontormo also sketched on the recto of this sheet.

203 · Rome, GNS F.N. 2943 *verso*: Study for the *Way to Golgotha*. Nude seen to the knees and almost from behind turned to the right with the right arm extended; to the left, faint sketch (for a figure with a child?). (*Recto*: Study for a *Madonna and Child with St. John*, cat. 14.) 341 x 257, red chalk on pink prepared paper. Fig. 197.

Bibliography: Grassi 1946, 42, fig. 11; Grassi 1947, 122; Berenson 1961, no. 2368A–1.

Grassi connected this drawing with the Pitti *Martyrdom* of 1529–1530. However, the nude is easily recognizable by its slender proportions and unassertive draughtsmanship as a drawing of the Certosa period. It is very close in type and in style to the St. Veronica studies (cat. 200–201) and to cat. 202, and must also have been a preliminary study for one of the figures to the left of the composition.

204 · Venice, Accademia di Belle Arti. *Verso*: Study for the *Way to Golgotha*. Upper half of a partially draped figure seen from behind who leans to the left. (*Recto*: Putto study, cat. 257.) 204 x 187, black chalk; edges partly covered by old mount. Fig. 195.

Bibliography: Bassi 1945, 82–85, illustrated; Bassi 1959, 50, no. 22, illustrated.

This slight study was published by Bassi as a drawing for the woman with her back turned on the right of the Poggio a Caiano lunette. However, the action of that figure is actually quite different and her head is not turned away. Bassi later (1959) suggested that the drawing might be connected with the Certosa, but did not specify a particular figure. This sketch, fragmentary as it is, is recognizable as a drawing of the Certosa period. It is identical in style with its recto, a study that has close stylistic associations with works of ca. 1524–1525. This study is for the woman in the right lower corner of the *Way to Golgotha*, a figure that is identical in pose, even to the bare back and upper arm with the drapery below, to the woman sketched here. Cf. Empoli's copy (fig. 189) for this figure, which is damaged in the fresco.

205 · Florence, Uffizi 6687F *recto*: Study for the *Way to Golgotha*. Page from a sketchbook: Bust of a nude with his right arm across his chest, looking to the left. (*Verso*: Faint indication of lower part of a nude with legs apart, not catalogued.) 152 x 93, red chalk on pink prepared paper. Fig. 194.

Bibliography: Berenson 1903, no. 2172; Clapp 1914, 234; Berenson 1938, no. 2172.

Both Berenson and Clapp dated this drawing at the time of S. Felicita, Clapp connecting it with the figure who supports Christ's shoulders in the *Deposition*. The action of this figure is somewhat similar, but the head and expression are different and the draughtsmanship is not as refined and ornamental as in the drawings for the *Deposition*. A very similar facial type does appear in cat. 269 and 274 for the *Deposition*, but in cat. 274 the line is tighter, finer, and more intricately handled, while in cat. 269 there is more emphasis on surface luminosity. This head, with its full lips, wide nostrils, and prominent ears is found in such Certosa drawings as cat. 207 and 211 for the *Nailing to the Cross*. However, the motive (in reverse) and expression of the face are so close to both the Christ and the man carrying the cross above to the right in the *Way to Golgotha*, that this study is most logically placed in relation to that fresco.

STUDIES FOR A NAILING TO THE CROSS

206 · Florence, Uffizi 6671F: Compositional study for a *Nailing to the Cross*. Within an arched picture space with a doorway indicated to the right, Christ being nailed to the cross surrounded by a crowd of figures; in the foreground, four half-length figures. 173 x 165, black chalk heightened with white, squared in red chalk; some outlines incised for transfer; sheet cut in lunette shape. Fig. 198.

Bibliography: Ferri 1890, 119; Berenson 1903, no. 1997; *MPA* 1910, 36; Clapp 1911, 12; Clapp 1914, 222–223; Clapp 1916, 40, 43, fig. 85; Giglioli 1926, 784, illustrated; Berenson 1938, 313, no. 2159A; Becherucci 1943, 9, pl. 15; Becherucci 1944, 17, fig. 32; Marcucci 1955, 251; *MP* 1956 (Marcucci), no. 109, fig. 142; Gamba 1956, 11, fig. 16; Berenson 1961, no. 2159A, fig. 928.

Clapp first recognized this important drawing as a study for an unexecuted

Nailing to the Cross planned for the Certosa. However, it has not been noted that the composition was intended for the space adjoining the *Way to Golgotha*. Not only does the narrative connection tie the two scenes together, but the two frescoes would have been virtually mirror images of one another. The indications of the door to the right show that Pontormo intended to reverse this composition, since the door is actually on the left side of the space. With the composition reversed the diagonal of Christ on the cross would repeat the diagonal of Christ carrying the cross, both originating in the corner between the two frescoes; the figure at Christ's feet would repeat the pose of the man carrying the end of the cross; and the elongated, bent figures that close the composition to the right would perform the same function as the figures to the left of the *Way to Golgotha*. These two compositions are so closely linked stylistically that they must have been planned at approximately the same time, even though the *Nailing to the Cross* was never executed. In both compositions the arched space is completely filled by a complex panorama of jagged rhythms, and in both cut-off figures rise up into the foreground. Furthermore, a peculiarity unique to these two compositions is the unusual number of faces that are turned, sometimes with an effect of dislocation, to stare out of the picture in insistent communication with the spectator.

When the date of this project has been considered at all it has generally been assumed that it should be placed at the end of Pontormo's work at the Certosa. Clapp and Marcucci dated it as late as 1525 as related to the *Supper at Emmaus* and as marking the transition from the style of the Certosa to that of S. Felicita. They found that here the influence of Dürer had been replaced by a greater equilibrium and sense of spaciousness that anticipated Pontormo's mature style. However, in view of the affinities with the *Way to Golgotha* and the close dependence of the composition on Dürer's woodcut of the *Nailing to the Cross* (*Small Passion*, 1509–1511, Bar. 39), this project would more logically be placed 1523–1524, before the simplified schemes of the *Pietà* and the *Supper at Emmaus*.

207 · Florence, Uffizi 6665F: Study for the *Nailing to the Cross* (cat. 206). The nude figure of Christ lies across to the left, the arms outstretched and legs bent; below left, the head restudied; in reverse direction, the bust restudied with the right arm raised. 236 x 380, black chalk heightened with white, the head studies in red chalk; left corner of the sheet has been cut out and reattached. Fig. 199.

Bibliography: Berenson 1903, no. 2155; *MPA* 1910, 36; Clapp 1914, 216–217; Clapp 1916, 43, fig. 86; Berenson 1938, no. 2155; Becherucci 1943, 9, pl. 16; Becherucci 1944, 17; *MP* 1956 (Marcucci), no. 110, fig. 144; Berenson 1961, no. 2155, fig. 927.

This study was first connected by Berenson with cat. 206, which Clapp then recognized as an unexecuted project for the Certosa. As in the case of the compositional study, Clapp and Marcucci have associated this drawing in style with S. Felicita, Clapp dating it as late as 1525–1526. This drawing is more finished than most of the Certosa studies and thus more complex in its linear elaboration and vibrant surface effects. It is the only Certosa study conspicuously heightened in white, suggesting Pontormo's revival of interest in luminous surfaces in the S. Felicita drawings. Furthermore, in its transparent beauty and delicacy the reprise of the head of Christ below is a striking anticipation of the drawing for the head of the S. Felicita Christ (cat. 276) and other heads for the *Deposition*, such as cat. 275. However, on close comparison, the line in this drawing is coarser and less finespun than in the S. Felicita studies and a closer parallel would be the head of the monk in cat. 216 for the *Supper at Emmaus*. In the study for the whole figure of Christ, the contours of the body and the *pentimenti* of the arms suggest multiple nervous vibrations and tensions between movement and restraint that are much less marked in the drawings for the S. Felicita Christ (cat. 267 and 276). The extremely long and narrow proportions of the figure are also quite unlike the more curved and graceful proportions of the S. Felicita figures, and the broken rhythms of the figure recall more closely those of the reclining nude on a sheet for the *Way to Golgotha* (cat. 198). Pontormo later used this figure in reverse for one of the crucified martyrs in the Pitti *Martyrdom* of 1529–1530.

208 · Florence, Uffizi 6657F: Study for the *Nailing to the Cross* (cat. 206). Nude turned to the right with his head turned away, left arm extended, right hand holding a hammer; to the left above, head and shoulder restudied. 326 x 206, red chalk; some outlines incised for transfer. Fig. 200.

Bibliography: Berenson 1903, no. 2148; *MPA* 1910, 32; Clapp 1911, 13; Clapp 1914, 210; Clapp 1916, 43; Berenson 1938, no. 2148; *MP* 1956 (Marcucci), no. 112, fig. 145; Marcucci 1956, 15, fig. 18.

Berenson originally called this figure a soldier for a *Judgment of Solomon*, but Clapp has seen that it is a study for the figure to the extreme left of the *Nailing to the Cross*. Clapp dated it 1522–1525, while Marcucci placed it 1525. This drawing is a preliminary action study from the model executed in a rhythmic, uncomplicated, almost Raphaelesque manner that is quite different from the style of the finished study for the same figure (cat. 209).

209 · Florence, Uffizi 447F *verso*: Study for the *Nailing to the Cross* (cat. 206). Standing partially draped figure turned to the right with the left hand raised, the right hand holding a hammer; above to the right, the shoulder restudied. (*Recto*: Studies for the Certosa, cat. 210.) 307 x 190, red chalk. Fig. 201.

Bibliography: Giglioli 1926, 784, illustrated; Berenson 1938, 313, no. 1972A; Toesca 1943, 12, fig. 15; Grassi 1946, 42, fig. 15; Marcucci 1955, 251; *MP* 1956 (Marcucci), no. 111, fig. 143b; Gamba 1956, 11, fig. 18; Marcucci 1956, 15, fig. 17; Berenson 1961, no. 1972A, fig. 924.

This drawing was identified by Giglioli as a final study for the figure to the far left of the composition. The changes from the original action study are characteristic of Pontormo's evolution of an idea toward its definitive form. In contrast to the expansive and flexible action of the nude in cat. 208, this figure has been tightened and contracted within itself. The normative proportions of cat. 208 have been elongated; the head is now small and delicately shaped, the hands have become expressively large, and the sense of ponderation in the figure is all but eliminated. The line has become the instrument of a nervous complicating activity like that in cat. 207, 210, and 211, all for the same composition.

210 · Florence, Uffizi 447F *recto*: Studies for the *Nailing to the Cross* (cat. 206). Draped figure seen to the knees with the left arm across the body; to the left, the upper part of the figure restudied with the right arm pouring from a pitcher; below, the legs lightly indicated. (*Verso*: Study for the Certosa, cat. 209.) 307 x 190, red chalk. Fig. 202.

Bibliography: Ferri 1890, 116; Berenson 1903, no. 2006; *MPA* 1910, 36; Clapp 1914, 95–96; Clapp 1916, 43, fig. 89; Giglioli 1926, 783–784; Berenson 1938, 313, no. 1972A; Marcucci 1953, 122, fig. 10; Marcucci 1955, 251; *MP* 1956 (Marcucci), no. 111, fig. 143a; Gamba 1956, 11, fig. 17; Marcucci

1956, 15, fig. 16; Berenson 1961, no. 1972A, fig. 926.

This drawing was identified by Clapp as a study for the figure just above the head of Christ. He dated it 1525, considering the influence of Dürer no longer operative and the drapery similar to that in S. Felicita studies, cat. 270, 274, and 277. Marcucci also dated it 1525, finding it Sartesque in the delicacy of the chiaroscuro. These figures do not seem any less Dürereresque than the figure on the verso or than equivalent figures in the *Way to Golgotha* and the *Christ Before Pilate*. Nor does the drapery resemble that in the S. Felicita drawings closely enough to date this project as late as 1525. The forms are not the broad oval ones of S. Felicita, but are still fragmented into smaller, irregular units; and the drapery has more substance than the immaterial draperies of S. Felicita, winding itself into tight knots of folds. Aside from cat. 196 for the *Agony in the Garden*, there are no drapery studies for the Certosa frescoes for comparison, but the handling of drapery in this drawing is very similar to that of the St. Veronica in the *Way to Golgotha* fresco.

211 · Florence, Uffizi 6652F *recto*: Study for the *Nailing to the Cross* (cat. 206). Partially draped man seen to the knees standing with his arms raised and hands to his head, looking up wildly to the right. (*Verso*: Nude study, cat. 240.) 306 x 190, red chalk squared. Fig. 203.

Bibliography: Berenson 1903, no. 2144; Clapp 1911, 13; Clapp 1914, 207–208, pl. 4; Clapp 1916, 43; Berenson 1938, no. 2144.

Clapp connected this study with the figure holding his hands to his head to the upper right of the composition, dating it 1525 as close in style to the S. Felicita drawings. Yet, in comparison with cat. 271, a study for a comparable *Deposition* figure, this drawing seems distinctly earlier in style. The shapes are still too eccentric and unrelated by an insistent linear organization, the line is too broken, and the expression too agitated to stand direct comparison with the *Deposition* studies. Typically of the *Nailing to the Cross* drawings, the body seems to be moving in many directions at once; organically as well as in its linear style it is a fragmented image. A similar full-featured facial type was later used in the *Deposition* (cat. 274), but it is also found earlier in Certosa drawings such as cat. 205 and 207.

STUDY FOR A DEPOSITION

212 · Florence, Uffizi 6622F: Compositional study for a *Deposition*. Within an arched picture space with a doorway indicated to the left, Christ is being carried by two figures; to the right, another figure; to the left, five figures. 126 x 100, red chalk. Fig. 204.

Bibliography: Berenson 1903, no. 2119; *MPA* 1910, 35; Clapp 1911, 12; Clapp 1914, 191–192; Clapp 1916, 43, fig. 83; Berenson 1938, 315, no. 2119, fig. 971; *MF* 1952, 63; *MP* 1956 (Marcucci), no. 108, fig. 158a.

Clapp and Marcucci both dated this study 1522–1525 as for an unexecuted Certosa fresco. Because of its close connections with the last fresco in the series, the *Pietà*, it can probably be placed ca. 1524. This small sketch is a discarded idea for the space in the far right corner of the cloister where the *Pietà* was actually painted. As in the *Pietà*, the double level compositions of the earlier Certosa compositions, with their crowds of agitated figures and multiplication of small rhythms across the surface, have been reduced to a simplified group of less than a dozen figures connected by a slow rhythm. Also as in the *Pietà*, the spatial ambiguities of the earlier compositions with their floating half-figures, have been notably reduced.

Berenson thought this composition was

inspired by Andrea del Sarto's Pitti *Pietà* of ca. 1524, but Clapp rightly pointed out that it was derived from Dürer's *Descent from the Cross* (*Small Passion*, 1509–1511, Bar. 42) and that the woman who holds her hand to her face in the background was taken from the *Crucifixion* of the same series (Bar. 40). The unusual motive of the Christ over the shoulders of a man with his back turned comes directly from Dürer's *Descent from the Cross*, but Pontormo has typically deprived the motive of any functional basis, making out of it a more abstract pattern. The draughtsmanship, according to Clapp, approaches the "simplicitè naïve" of a woodcut. In this drawing, as in cat. 196, there is certainly a sense of the strong visual impression that Dürer's *Small Passion* woodcuts must have made on Pontormo. While Pontormo is in no sense copying Dürer, the flat, simple patterns of the forms and the bold, strong outlines can only have been suggested by the graphic mode of the woodcut.

STUDIES FOR THE PIETÀ

213 · Florence, Uffizi 6702F *verso*: Studies for the *Pietà*. The figure of Christ supported by a figure leaning down from above; to the right, draped seated figure; over these studies on a larger scale, nude moving forward, his left arm pointing ahead, his right arm behind him. (*Recto*: Putto study, cat. 248.) 288 x 188, black chalk, the nude in red chalk. Fig. 206.

Bibliography: Berenson 1903, no. 2185; Clapp 1911, 11; Gamba 1912, 2; Clapp 1914, 246–247; Clapp 1916, 38, 42; Berenson 1938, no. 2185; *MDM* 1954 (Marcucci), no. 51; *EMI* 1954, no. 71; *MP* 1956 (Marcucci), no. 115, fig. 153b.

Clapp first connected the black chalk sketches on this sheet with the Certosa *Pietà*, dating them 1522–1524. Gamba dated the drawing as early as 1522, but Marcucci has placed it at the end of the Certosa period, toward 1525. The study for the seated figure is identical to the woman at the right, except for the hands. The study for the Christ and the man bending over him is adapted from Dürer's *Lamentation* (*Small Passion*, 1509–1511, Bar. 43). As in cat. 212 for a *Deposition*, Pontormo did not copy Dürer's figures directly but completely changed their principle of organization so that the group becomes emphatically Pontormesque. In Pontormo's sketch Dürer's compact group is readjusted so that the effect is one of greater verticality. The man forms a high arc above the Christ, while Christ's body has been elongated and his legs dislocated to increase the angular, vertical effect. The result is curiously like the motive of Christ and the man above him in Rosso's Volterra *Deposition* of 1521. However, the two figures in the fresco suggest neither Dürer nor Rosso. The figure of the man bending over is retained, but the Christ is changed so effectively into a horizontal arabesque placed parallel to the picture plane, that without benefit of the drawing it would not be evident that Dürer had been Pontormo's starting point.

As Clapp first noted, this sheet of sketches for the *Pietà* also contains a recollection of the *Haman* of the Sistine Ceiling. Pontormo was repeatedly fascinated by the *Haman* motive (cf. cat. 184 of ca. 1520) but he seems never to have used it in a painting. Clapp suggested that it might have been drawn here in connection with the *Resurrection* or with the *Crucifixion* that Vasari says (V/M, VI, 269) Pontormo planned but never executed at the Certosa. While this figure does not resemble the Christ of Pontormo's *Resurrection*, it may have been a very preliminary idea for the *Crucifixion*. This subject was planned for the space next to the *Pietà*, and thus its preparatory studies would logically appear on the same sheet with studies for the *Pietà*.

214 · Marseilles, Musée de Longchamp: Study for the *Pietà*. Standing nude leaning over looking to the left with his arms extended down and hands together; to the right below, upper part of the nude lightly restudied. 270 x 180, black chalk. Fig. 207.

Collection: Unidentified stamp recto; Ecole des Beaux-Arts, Marseilles (until 1870).

Bibliography: *Marseilles Exhib.* 1861, no. 1430; Auquier 1908, 366; Berenson 1938, 313, no. 2256A.

This drawing has been attributed to Michelangelo, but in Auquier's list and at present it goes under the name of Sebastiano del Piombo. Berenson attributed the drawing to Pontormo as a study for the figure who bends down to the left of the Virgin in the *Pietà*. This drawing may have been reworked in some of the contours (notably those of the right arm), but in the smaller sketch at the right the hand of Pontormo is unmistakable. In this drawing, as well as in cat. 212, we begin to find parallels with the studies for the *Supper at Emmaus*, finished in 1525; with the drawing for the Uffizi *Madonna Enthroned* of ca. 1525; and with the earlier studies for the S. Felicita cupola. Cf. cat. 217, 222, and 263 for the long-limbed, curved proportions of the figure, the flatness and regularity of the modelling, and the lack of tension and strong accents in the line. This "relaxed style" of ca. 1525 is a prelude to the newly cohesive formulation of Pontormo's drawing style in 1526–1528.

1525. SUPPER AT EMMAUS. Florence, Uffizi 8740. I. Canvas, 230 x 173 cm. Dated *1525* on the *cartella* in the foreground. Fig. 208.

Bibliography: Goldschmidt 1911, 8, 44; Clapp 1916, 41, 114–115, fig. 82; Gamba 1921, 9; Venturi 1932, 141–144, fig. 83; Berenson 1936, 401; Weihrauch 1937/38, 25–29, fig. 1; Becherucci 1944, 17, figs. 35–37; Nicco Fasola 1946, 46–47, fig. 17; Nicco Fasola 1947, 48–49, figs. 26–29; *Amsterdam Exhib.* 1955, no. 92, fig. 2; *MP* 1956 (Berti), no. 50, fig. 42; Nicco Fasola 1956, 5–14, fig. 2; Marcucci 1956, 15–16, fig. 19.

The *Supper at Emmaus* is dated 1525 and there is also a record in the accounts of the Certosa of payment to Pontormo on June 4, 1525 "per tanti colori e la cornice per fare lo cenaculo de la despensa." (See Clapp 1916, app. II, doc. 15.) Vasari describes this picture along with two others that Pontormo painted for the Certosini after he had finished the frescoes in the cloister and returned to Florence.[29] It was also noted by Borghini 1584, 483, as at the Certosa. Milanesi (V/M, VI, 270n1), saw the picture after it had come to the Accademia and misread the date as 1528, a mistake that was repeated by Goldschmidt and Gamba.

[29] V/M, VI, 269–270: ". . . spese in questi lavori [the Passion Series] parecchi anni: e poichè fu finita la peste, ed egli tornatosene a Firenze, non lasciò per questo di frequentare assai quel luogo, ed andare e venire continuamente dalla Certosa alla città; e così seguitando, sodisfece in molte cose a que' padri . . . Per la Foresteria de' medesimi padri fece in un gran quadro di tela colorita a olio, senza punto affaticare o sforzare la natura, Cristo a tavola con Cleofas e Luca, grandi quanto il naturale . . ." The other two works mentioned by Vasari are lost. Pontormo painted a lay brother, age one hundred and twenty, in fresco over a door leading to the chapel. For the prior's chamber he painted a *Nativity* in which Joseph held a lighted lantern. Since Vasari (*ibid.*) notes that this motive was derived from German prints, we can guess that Dürer's *Nativity* from the *Small Passion* (Bar. 20), in which precisely this motive appears, might have been Pontormo's source.

Besides making copies of the Passion Series, Empoli copied the *Supper at Emmaus* on the same small scale (126 x 115 cm), probably adding the triangular *occhio divino* to the original.[30] The copy differs from Pontormo's picture only in the addition of a grey stone doorway that frames the composition. Nicco Fasola believed that such a doorway was part of Pontormo's original conception, suggesting that it was either part of the painting or painted on the wall around it. It is quite possible that Pontormo's *Supper at Emmaus* originally had a *trompe l'oeil* frame, but not a painted one. It is more likely that the picture was framed by a normal wooden frame resembling a doorway, the *cornice* for which Pontormo was paid on June 4, 1525. Framed in this way, the painting must have hung very low on the wall so that an illusion was created of figures seen through a doorway seated in another space on a level with those in the room. The picture is almost exactly the height of the doorways in the monastery and the view of figures and table from above certainly suggests that it hung below eye level. As to the shape of the original frame, it is probable that only the inner mouldings in Empoli's copy reflect Pontormo's frame and that he added the flanking pilasters to make the picture exactly the same size as the copies of the Passion Series. Furthermore, Empoli extended Pontormo's composition at the top above the *occhio divino*, making the doorway arched. It is probable that this arch is Empoli's invention and that Pontormo's frame resembled a post and lintel doorway. If the mouldings of the doorway in the copy are compared with those of the doors in the monastery, it is evident that with a horizontal rather than an arched top Pontormo's frame would have been similar to the actual doors in the building — and thus to those in the very room where the picture hung.

[30] Nicco Fasola suggested that the *occhio divino* was added by Empoli to Pontormo's painting in accordance with the precepts of the Counter Reformation, this form of representing the Trinity having come into use only in the later part of the century.

There is further evidence that the original setting of the *Supper at Emmaus* was an illusionistic one. In the Dürer woodcut of the same subject from which Pontormo derived his composition (*Small Passion*, 1509–1511, Bar. 48) there is an arched doorway with a ledge in the foreground behind which the scene takes place. Since Pontormo adapted other illusionistic devices from the woodcut, such as the *cartella* with the date (the only instance of this device in his painting), it is logical to suppose that Dürer was also the source for the illusionistic framing of the scene.

STUDIES FOR THE SUPPER AT EMMAUS

215 · London, British Museum 1936–10–10–10 *verso*: Study for the monks on the left, *Supper at Emmaus.* Three-quarter length figures of two monks, one behind the other. (*Recto*: Nude study, cat. 253.) 284 x 202, red chalk. Fig. 210.

Bibliography: Berenson 1938, no. 2250B; Popham 1939, 29; Gamba 1956, 11, fig. 20; Berenson 1961, no. 2255A, fig. 932.

This drawing was identified by Berenson as a study for the *Supper at Emmaus.* This sheet and cat. 216 are studies for the monk portraits that Vasari praised so highly.[31] These two studies are evidence

[31] V/M, VI, 270: ". . . fra coloro che servano a quella mensa, ritratto alcuni conversi di que' frati, i quali ho conosciuto io, in modo che non possono essere nè più vive nè più pronti di quel che sono." In a similar naturalistic style was probably the portrait of a lay brother that Vasari says (*ibid.*, 269) was ". . . tanto bene e pulitamente fatta con vivacità e prontezza, ch'ella merita che per lei sola si scusi il Pontormo della stranezza e nuova ghiribizzosa maniera che gli pose adosso quella solitudine, e lo star lontano dal commerzio degli uomini."

of a naturalistic tendency in Pontormo's drawings between the completion of the Certosa cloister and the beginning of the Capponi Chapel, a naturalism that was one aspect of a general relaxation and simplification of style that had already begun in the last phase of the Certosa (cat. 212–214) and was to continue through the S. Felicita cupola studies. As in the other drawings of this group, Pontormo's draughtsmanship here is unassuming, the line without involvement, and the modelling quietly understated rather than asserting the plasticity of the forms.

In contrast to the relation of Pontormo's preparatory drawings to his paintings — both before in the Certosa frescoes, and after in the *Deposition* — the direct contact with reality evident in these monk studies is retained in the painting. This specific realism, the *tenebroso* light, and the extraordinary rendering of the still-life in the painting have suggested to some authors the term "proto-Caravaggesque" and other seventeenth-century analogies.[32] Such comparisons are suggestive, but Pontormo's naturalism remains different in kind from that of a Baroque artist. The singular juxtaposition of the two heads in the drawing; and, in the painting, the apparitional context and warped space in which these naturalistic portraits occur, effectively removes them from the reality of physical presence that is the essence of a seventeenth-century conception.

216 · Florence, Uffizi 6656F *verso*: Study for the monk on the right, *Supper at Emmaus*. Three-quarter length figure of a monk with arms at his sides. (*Recto*: Study for the *Supper at Emmaus*, cat. 217.) 293 x 210, red chalk. Fig. 209.

Bibliography: *MPA* 1910, 22; Clapp 1911, 12; Clapp 1914, 209–210; Clapp 1916, 42, fig. 84; Tinti 1925, fig. 11; Weihrauch 1937/38, 26; Berenson 1938, 313, no. 2147; *MDF* 1939, 25; *MC* 1940, 51; Becherucci 1943, 9, pl. 19; *MDM* 1954 (Marcucci), no. 50; *EMI* 1954, no. 70.

This drawing was recognized by Clapp as a study for the *Supper at Emmaus*. Like cat. 215 it is a study from nature for one of the monks in the painting. While it is typical of his "relaxed style" of ca. 1525, in this drawing for the figure on the right Pontormo achieves a measure of monumentality through directness of approach and unmannered, understated draughtsmanship.

217 · Florence, Uffizi 6656F *recto*: Study for the man on the left, *Supper at Emmaus*. Seated nude seen from behind with his right leg pulled up, his left hand on his knee. (*Verso*: Study for the *Supper at Emmaus*, cat. 216.) 293 x 210, red chalk. Fig. 211.

Bibliography: Berenson 1903, no. 2147; Clapp 1914, 209; Berenson 1938, 313, no. 2147; *MDM* 1954 (Marcucci), no. 50; *EMI* 1954, no. 70.

This nude study was recognized by Clapp as the first idea for the figure in the left foreground. As is also evident in cat. 218, this man was at first intended to look up toward the Christ in the center of the picture. However, in the final study (cat. 219) and in the painting, his absorbtion in his pouring contrasts with the other figure's awareness of Christ. This is the only nude study for the painting, but it is close in style to other nude, or seminude, studies of ca. 1524–1525, such as cat. 214 for the Certosa *Pietà*, cat. 222 for the Uffizi *Ma-*

[32] See Becherucci 1944, 17, and Smyth 1949, 185, who mention an anticipation of Caravaggio. See also R. Longhi, "Un San Tomaso del Velasquez e le congiunture italo-spagnole tra il '5 e il' 600," *Vita Artistica 2* (1927), 7, and Nicco Fasola 1947, 48, who are reminded of Ribalta, Zurbaran, and Velasquez. Marcucci, *MDM* 1954, 34, noted that cat. 216 for the painting was an anticipation of Velasquez, while the painting itself she found more Düreresque.

donna Enthroned, or cat. 260 for the S. Felicita cupola. In all these studies we find larger and fuller forms that are less elongated than those of the Certosa figures, and the relaxed line with flattening diagonal shading that is typical of Pontormo's drawings of this date.

218 · Munich, Staatliche Graphische Sammlung 10142 *verso*: Studies for the man on the left, *Supper at Emmaus*. Bust of a man in profile right with his right arm raised; below, the motive restudied twice. (*Recto*: Study for the *Supper at Emmaus*, cat. 220.) 267 x 153, black chalk. Fig. 212.

Bibliography: Weihrauch 1937/38, 26–28, fig. 4; *MDM* 1954 (Marcucci), 34; Cox 1956, 17; *MP* 1956 (Marcucci), no. 113, fig. 147a; Berenson 1961, no. 2256B–1.

This drawing is one of a group of four studies on two sheets that were attributed to Pontormo as for the *Supper at Emmaus* by Weihrauch, who dated them 1524. However, since the picture is dated 1525, there is little cause to predate its final studies into the previous year. Weihrauch thought that only the sketch at the top was for the man who pours and that the others were for the figure on the right in reverse. However, the pouring action is also specified in the lower sketches, which take up the motive from cat. 217, where the man also looks up.

While Berenson accepted these drawings as Pontormo, Marcucci has called them Jacopo da Empoli copies after lost Pontormo studies for the picture, drawings that are "quasi . . . una contraffazione." The attribution of these sheets to an imitator suggests that the range and mentality of the copyist has not been fully considered. While Empoli could execute a finished study such as cat. 219 without betraying his hand, he would immediately reveal a lack of spontaneity in copying a sheet of sketches such as this one, where the motive is developed in a series of overlapping studies from the bottom of the sheet to the top. In judging the authenticity of these studies we must also consider the style of Pontormo's other drawings of this date; drawings that, if similar to these, must be rejected with them. The phase between the Certosa Passion Series and the S. Felicita *Deposition* was a momentary *détente* in Pontormo's development, a period when naturalism of concept and lack of linear tension and excitement were primary characteristics of his drawings. Besides the other studies for the *Supper at Emmaus*, cat. 222, 252, 255, 261, and 262 are similar studies of draped figures from this period, although stylistic parallels can also be found in many other drawings. It is not surprising that certain late sixteenth-century artists of the Mannerist *détente* found in this relaxed style an affinity with their own stylistic intentions and imitated the drawings of precisely this period. Many of these imitations, deceptively and superficially similar to Pontormo's drawings, have been wrongly attributed to him.[33] However, it would be unwise to carry the correction of these misattributions so far as to ascribe original drawings to the imitators.

219 · Munich, Staatliche Graphische Sammlung 14043 *recto*: Study for the man on the left, *Supper at Emmaus*. Draped figure seated on a stool in profile right pouring from a pitcher into a glass. (*Verso*: Study for the *Supper at Emmaus*, cat. 221.) 268 x 157, black chalk. Fig. 213.

Collection: Mannheim: Graphische Sammlung, stamp recto (L. 2723), stamp verso (L. 2673).

Bibliography: Weihrauch 1937/38, 26–28, fig. 2; *MDM* 1954 (Marcucci), 34; Cox 1956, 17, fig. 18; *MP* 1956 (Marcucci), no. 114, fig. 146a; Gamba 1956, 12, fig. 22; Berenson 1961, no. 2256B–3, fig. 930.

[33] See cat. A37, A63, A71, A163, A165, A217.

See the discussion of cat. 218 for the critical opinions on this drawing. This drawing was also mentioned by Gamba as a study for the *Supper at Emmaus.* This study is the most finished of the group of four drawings for the painting, following cat. 217–218 as a final study for the man on the left. There are certain differences between the figure in the drawing and that in the painting. The draperies are changed in some details, such as the drapery that falls over the man's right shoulder and down his back in the drawing, and they are in general less complex in arrangement. In the drawing the feet are crossed, the left behind the right, but they are not crossed in the painting. Furthermore — and this is true also of cat. 220 — the figure in the drawing is seen from a normal point of view slightly from below, while in the painting it is accommodated to the warped convex perspective of the picture in such a way that we look down on the upper part of the figure and his legs slide away at a sharper angle into the picture.

220 · Munich, Staatliche Graphische Sammlung 10142 *recto*: Study for the man on the right, *Supper at Emmaus.* Draped figure seated on a stool in profile left, above, the head restudied. (*Verso*: Study for the *Supper at Emmaus*, cat. 218.) 267 x 153, black chalk. Fig. 214.

Collection: Mannheim; Graphische Sammlung, stamp recto (L. 2723), stamp verso (L. 2673).

Bibliography: Weihrauch 1937/38, 26–28, fig. 5; *MDM* 1954 (Marcucci), 43; Cox 1956, 17; *MP* 1956 (Marcucci), no. 113, fig. 146b; Gamba 1956, 12, fig. 23; Berenson 1961, no. 2256B–1.

See the discussion of cat. 218 for the critical opinions on this drawing. This study was also mentioned by Gamba as for the *Supper at Emmaus.* It is the pendant drawing to cat. 219 and, like it, is a model study from a normative point of view for a figure whose position is subtly shifted in the painting. The modelling of the legs in curved parallel lines recalls certain Certosa studies that were imitative of Dürer's woodcut technique, such as cat. 196 and 212. The drapery, with its broad, flat folds and occasional Düreresque involvement (cf. the bunched folds over the stool) is very close to that of the St. Jerome study of ca. 1525 for the Uffizi *Madonna Enthroned* (cat. 222).

221 · Munich, Staatliche Graphische Sammlung 14043 *verso*: Study for Christ, *Supper at Emmaus.* Seated draped Christ seen to the knees blessing the bread. (*Recto*: Study for the *Supper at Emmaus*, cat. 219.) 268 x 157, black chalk. Fig. 215.

Bibliography: Weihrauch 1937/38, 26–28, fig. 3; *MDM* 1954 (Marcucci), 34; Cox 1956, 17; *MP* 1956 (Marcucci), no. 114, fig. 147b; Berenson 1961, no. 2256B–3, fig. 931.

See the discussion of cat. 218 for the critical opinions on this drawing. This study, which shows the figure before the introduction of the table, is the closest of the group to the earlier Certosa drawings, contrasted in its slender proportions with the more solidly naturalistic forms in the other studies for the picture. The involved folds of the drapery and the delicate features of the face recall Certosa drawings such as cat. 210 for the *Nailing to the Cross.* However, in the painting, the contrast between Christ and the other figures is not so emphatic: the gentle curve of the body is straightened to a more monumental vertical, the head is less tilted, the features enlarged, and the hand not as expressively large in relation to the rest of the figure.

PART III: 1522–1525

Ca. 1525. MADONNA AND CHILD ENTHRONED WITH ST. FRANCIS, ST. JEROME, AND TWO PUTTI. Florence, Uffizi 1538. III. (Executed, and partly designed by Bronzino.) Panel, 72 x 60 cm. Fig. 217.

Bibliography: Berenson 1896, 126; Gamba 1904, 18; Goldschmidt 1911, 46; Clapp 1914, 271; Clapp 1916, 20, 139; Gamba 1921, fig. 20; Venturi 1932, 126, fig. 67; Stscherbatscheva 1934/36, 181, fig. 198; Berenson 1936, 401; Smyth 1955, 91; *MP* 1956 (Berti), no. 41, fig. 33; Sanminiatelli 1956, 242; Seilern 1959, 35–36, fig. 16.

According to Berti, this picture belonged to the heirs of Cardinal Carlo de' Medici as a Pontormo, but was later also attributed to Rosso. Berenson restored it to Pontormo without suggesting a date, while Clapp dated it 1517–1518 as associated with the Visdomini altar. Gamba, Stscherbatscheva, and Sanminiatelli dated it 1520–1521. On the other hand, Berti has suggested that Bronzino executed it about 1520–1525 on the basis of Pontormo's design, and Smyth considered the picture to be possibly designed by Bronzino as well.

The connection with Pontormo rests primarily on a preparatory study (cat. 222), undoubtedly his, that establishes at least Pontormo's invention of the St. Jerome about 1525, the date indicated by the style of the drawing. Several studies by Pontormo from this period are suggestive of the central figures (cf. cat. 244–246, 248, and 257 for the putti, cat. 249 for the Madonna and Child), but none are close enough to the picture to be definitely associable with it. There is a general compositional analogy to the *Supper at Emmaus* of 1525, and we suggest that Pontormo may have indeed a similar duality in this picture: apparitional unreality coexisting with pervasive naturalism. However, in the picture as it was painted, the visionary quality of the *Supper at Emmaus* is lost (the group appears frozen rather than transfixed) and the naturalism is intensified. The rigid figures of the saints — especially the St. Francis, who is likely to be Bronzino's own invention — are contrasted with the doll-like Madonna and with fragile putti, whose wings and draperies are quite un-Pontormesque. This static group is placed in a curiously archaic architectural setting of a type that had never appeared in Pontormo's paintings. Furthermore, the composition is derivative in a way that would have been rather unusual for Pontormo. As can be seen from the framing figures around the central space, the unusually restive putti, and the profile saints who converse across the picture, the composition goes back to Rosso's S. M. Nuova *Madonna and Saints* (Uffizi) of 1518.

The intervention of Bronzino certainly seems likely not only for the execution but for an indeterminate part of the design as well. Not only are there parallels to be found in Bronzino's Washington *Holy Family* of ca. 1527–1528, but both the archaicisms and the color scheme are typical of Pontormo's pupil in the period before 1530. However, in resolving the problems presented by this picture, note should be taken of the little *Madonna and Child with St. John* in the Corsini Gallery,[34] a picture that is also derivative from Pontormo of the early to midtwenties and is

[34] Panel, 52 x 40 cm. This picture has generally been given to Pontormo. See *Corsini Cat.*, no. 185; Clapp 1916, 129–130; Venturi 1932, 156, fig. 90. It has been dated contemporary with S. Felicita except by Sanminiatelli 1956, 242, who dated it before the Certosa frescoes. This picture is derivative from Rosso as well as from Pontormo (cf. the Madonna and the kneeling woman to the left in Rosso's *Marriage of the Virgin* of 1523.)

in some aspects extraordinarily close in style to the Uffizi *Madonna Enthroned*, yet presents a number of difficulties as a Bronzino.

STUDY FOR THE
MADONNA ENTHRONED

222 · London, Count Seilern Collection 92 *verso*: Study for St. Jerome, *Madonna Enthroned*. Partially draped man standing in profile right with his hands to his chest. (*Recto*: Figure study, cat. 254.) 404 x 280, red chalk. Fig. 216.

Bibliography: Popham 1935, 83, pl. 38; Berenson 1938, no. 1957A; *MP* 1956 (Berti), 27; Seilern 1959, no. 92, pl. 50.

Popham associated this study with the St. Jerome, dating it 1517–1518. Berenson dated it in the Certosa period as already Düreresque, while Seilern has placed it more broadly, 1521–1525. In style this drawing is extremely close to the studies for the *Supper at Emmaus* and aids in locating the Uffizi *Madonna Enthroned* at about the same time. The broad, flat folds of drapery and the unassertive quality of the line appear in cat. 220; the type, and perhaps even the model, is identical to that of the monk in the foreground of cat. 215; and the modelling of the nude parts of the figure recalls cat. 217. The St. Jerome in the painting, a figure that was probably executed by Bronzino after this drawing, is identical to Pontormo's saint, except that in the drawing he looks up as if at the Madonna, while in the painting, his head juts forward as he stares across at the St. Francis.

Ca. 1525. PORTRAIT OF ALESSANDRO DE' MEDICI. Lucca, Pinacoteca 75. I. Panel, 85 x 61 cm. Fig. 218.

Bibliography: Trapesnikoff 1909, 77; Clapp 1916, 57, 84, 159–160, 258, fig. 115; Voss 1920, 176; Gamba 1921, 11, fig. 43; Tinti 1925, fig. 1; Venturi 1932, 175, fig. 104; *Paris Exhib.* 1935, no. 383; Berenson 1936, 402; Steinbart 1939, 12, illustrated; *MC* 1940, 40; Toesca 1943, 23, fig. 50; Becherucci 1944, 18, fig. 46; Nicco Fasola 1947, fig. 39; Alazard 1948, 150–151, fig. 43; *MF* 1952, no. 9, fig. 9; *Brussels Exhib.* 1954, no. 58; *Amsterdam Exhib.* 1955, no. 94; *MP* 1956 (Berti), no. 62, fig. 54; Baldini 1956, 11, fig. 13.

This picture, which came from the Medici Villa of Poggio Imperiale, is identifiable with the *Portrait of Alessandro de' Medici* that Vasari says Pontormo painted. According to Vasari, Alessandro (b. 1512) and his brother Ippolito (b. 1511) were painted by Pontormo while they were in the custody of Silvio Passerini.[35] Since the boys were sent to Florence in 1524 and exiled in 1527, Pontormo's portraits must have dated from those years. The *Portrait of Ippolito* has disappeared, but Pontormo's study for it survives (cat. 223).

In spite of adequate comparative material that includes Pontormo's own *Portrait of Alessandro de' Medici* of less than a decade later,[36] there has been consider-

[35] V/M, VI, 273: " . . . essendo stati mandati in Firenze da papa Clemente settimo, sotto la custodia del legato Silvio Passerini cardinale di Cortona, Alessandro ed Ipolito de' Medici, ambi giovinetti; il magnifico Ottaviano, al quale il papa gli aveva molto raccomandati, gli fece ritrarre amendue dal Puntormo, il quale lo servì benissimo e gli fece molto somigliare, come che non molto si partisse da quella sua maniera appressa dalla tedesca."

[36] Philadelphia, Johnson Collection (see note 12 on p. 293). Cf. also the *Portrait of Alessandro de' Medici* by Vasari (Uffizi, ca. 1534) and numerous other likenesses of the Duke (*MM* 1939, 46, 48, 132, 135, 136).

able disagreement on the identity of the sitter and on the date of the picture. In a study of Medici portraits, Trapesnikoff thought it was a posthumous portrait of Giuliano di Piero de' Medici (1435–1478), but this idea was already rejected by Clapp. Clapp did not suggest another identification, but dated the portrait ca. 1529–1530. A more widely held theory has been that the person represented is Giuliano di Pier Francesco Il Giovane. Aside from the question of resemblance, this identification would place the portrait at a very uncomfortable date stylistically. Since Giuliano was born 1520/21, the portrait could not have been painted until at least 1535. Gamba suggested that the picture might be one of the portraits Vasari mentions, although he dated it 1530. The correct identification and date has been reasserted by Becherucci, tentatively by Berti and Baldini, but is still not generally accepted.

STUDY FOR A PORTRAIT OF IPPOLITO DE' MEDICI CA. 1525

223 · Florence, Uffizi 452F *recto*: Compositional study for a *Portrait of Ippolito de' Medici* (a pendant to the *Portrait of Alessandro de' Medici*), ca. 1525. Three-quarter length standing draped boy wearing a hat, his left hand holding a glove(?), his right hand on his hip; below the right arm the head of a dog is faintly indicated. (*Verso*: Study for Poggio a Caiano, cat. 141.) 332 x 211, black chalk heightened with white squared on bluish prepared paper. Fig. 219.

Bibliography: Ferri 1890, 116; Berenson 1903, no. 1975; *MPA* 1910, 22; Clapp 1914, 98; Clapp 1916, 26, 84, fig. 38; Berenson 1938, 318, no. 1975, fig. 980; Becherucci 1944, 18.

Clapp thought this drawing dated 1518–1520 and associated the drapery style with Poggio a Caiano. Berenson mentioned the stylistic connection with the *Portrait of Alessandro de' Medici*, while Becherucci has suggested that it was a study for Pontormo's lost pendant to the *Alessandro*, dating 1526–1527. As noted by Vasari, the sitter for that picture was Ippolito de' Medici accompanied by his dog.[37] Although Ippolito's more regular features are not as easily recognizable as Alessandro's, there is no objection to this identification on the basis of likeness.[38] The apparent age and the dress of the two youths are almost identical, as is the three-quarter length frontal pose. In his final elaboration of the drawing in preparation for its transfer Pontormo eliminated a strip across the bottom so that the proportions of the squared area are exactly those of the *Portrait of Alessandro*.

The technique of softened black chalk heightened with white is that of most of Pontormo's squared compositional studies of the period 1522–1528 (cf. cat. 192, 206, 224, 261, 272, and 289), but this drawing is the only portrait study in this style. It is especially close to the study for God the Father of the S. Felicita cupola (cat. 261), a drawing that must have been contemporary with it.

Berenson remarked that the youth of this portrait was of a type that appealed to Puligo, mentioning specifically a *Portrait of a Prelate* (ex-Plymouth Collection) and a *Portrait of a Youth* (Seville Museum). Even closer in composition and in costume would be Puligo's *Portrait of Carnesecchi* (Pitti), painted in 1527. However, these comparisons would apply equally well to

[37] V/M, VI, 273: "In quel d'Ipolito ritrasse insieme un cane molto favorito di quel signore, chiamato Rodon; e lo fece così proprio e naturale, che pare vivissimo." Pontormo's lost portrait may have influenced Bronzino's *Guidobaldo da Urbino* (Pitti, ca. 1531), in which the dog and his owner are arranged in a similar composition, but with the dog on the right instead of on the left as in Pontormo's drawing.

[38] Cf. Titian's *Portrait of Ippolito* (Pitti, 1532).

the *Portrait of Alessandro*, which is identical to this drawing in type, costume, and composition. Because of its softer forms and *sfumato*, the drawing naturally looks more Puligesque; while in the painting, the similarities are much less striking.

STUDIES FOR THE ISRAELITES DRINKING THE WATER IN THE WILDERNESS
CA. 1522–1525

224 · Florence, Uffizi 6675F: Compositional study for an *Israelites Drinking the Water in the Wilderness*, ca. 1522–1525. Moses stands conversing with Aaron and pointing to the left; to the left, a boy riding a horse forward; in the center and background, many figures, one of which leans over with cupped hands while another lies face down drinking the water. 285 x 283, black chalk heightened with white squared; outlines incised for transfer; the reverse of the Aaron and the boy on the horse blackened for transfer; inscribed verso in ink in a seventeenth-century hand: *di Jacopo Po. .no.* Fig. 220.

Bibliography: Berenson 1903, no. 2160; *MPA* 1910, 37; Clapp 1914, 225; Berenson 1938, 315, no. 2160, fig. 965; Becherucci 1944, 15.

Berenson connected this composition with the Pitti *Martyrdom* of 1529–1530 and associated the boy on horseback with the standard-bearer in the middle of the picture. The association with the *Martyrdom* is unconvincing not only on the basis of the earlier style of this drawing and its preparatory studies, but because the rider in the *Martyrdom* is seen only to the shoulders and carries a banner high in his right hand, while the other figures in this drawing do not appear in the painting at all. Since he incorporated this scene into the *Martyrdom*, the subject of this drawing was not problematic for Berenson, but for Becherucci it was "una composizione imprecisata," and for Clapp, who dated it 1523–1526, the subject remained a mystery.[39]

The purpose of this drawing is still unknown, but it certainly represents the *Israelites Drinking the Water in the Wilderness*. While *Moses Striking the Rock* was not an uncommon subject at this time (cf. Beccafumi in the Siena Cathedral *pavimento*; Bronzino in the Cappella Eleanora), the subsequent moment was rarely represented separately. However, the scene in this drawing accords perfectly with the subject: the hooded figure of Moses stands with Aaron to the right, while the rest of the composition is taken up with numerous figures drinking or waiting to drink, with a figure on horseback (a motive that often occurs in *Moses Striking the Rock* scenes), and with various subordinate figures that are not clearly delineated in this compositional drawing. In the preparatory studies (cat. 225–233) some of these motives are clarified, providing further evidence for our identification of the subject. Primary among these are six studies on four large sheets in the Uffizi (cat. 225–231) that are in black chalk on the same paper and in the same style, but which have never been related as a group to cat. 224. Cat. 226, 228, and 232 are studies for the supine drinking figure in the center of the compositional study, while cat. 225 and 227 are studies for the horse and rider, but also contain studies for the children who are invariably present in representations of *Moses Striking the Rock*, and thus would occur in the subsequent scene as well.

Both in draughtsmanship and in composition this drawing may be dated in the

[39] However, Clapp did suggest that it might have been a study for a lost *St. George* mentioned by Bocchi (actually Cinelli). In discussing the pictures in San Clemente, Cinelli 1677, 7, wrote: ". . . vi è anche un quadro entrovi un S. Giorgio di Jacopo da Pontormo." Clapp later (1916, 256) noted that Cinelli had mistaken a *St. Augustine* by Pontormo for a *St. George*.

period 1522–1525. Black chalk compositional drawings of these years, such as cat. 206 for the Certosa *Nailing to the Cross* or cat. 223 for the *Portrait of Ippolito de' Medici*, provide a basis for direct comparison in style, while the similarity to certain of the Certosa compositions is striking. The tightly packed picture space, the *repoussoir* figure of Aaron to the right, the round-eyed stares of the figures, and the general agitation of the composition suggest the *Nailing to the Cross* or the *Way to Golgotha*, while the figures on the right side of the drawing recall the elongated soldiers and the broadly gesturing man above Christ in the *Christ Before Pilate*. The drawing could, perhaps, be dated more closely at the time of these frescoes (1523–1524), yet it is impossible to tell at this early, somewhat nebulous stage in the development of the composition whether in its final form it would have approximated the radical spatial and psychological inventions of the Certosa frescoes. For this reason we have dated it more generously, as it might have been done just after or, more likely, just before the frescoes in the Certosa cloister.

225 · Florence, Uffizi 6516F *recto*: Study for the *Israelites Drinking the Water in the Wilderness* (cat. 224). Draped figure of a child seen from behind. (*Verso*: Study for the *Israelites Drinking the Water in the Wilderness*, cat. 226.) 402 x 265, black chalk heightened with white; W: Acorn (B. 7435).

Bibliography: Berenson 1903, no. 2021; Clapp 1914, 125–126; Berenson 1938, no. 2021; *MP* 1956 (Marcucci), no. 129, fig. 160a.

Clapp dated this study 1519–1522 and Berenson also thought it was early, but neither connected it with cat. 224. Marcucci suggested that the drawing dated ca. 1530, associating it with the man in the foreground of the Pitti *Martyrdom*. However, there is little connection between this child and the serpentine forms of the Michelangelesque figure in the *Martyrdom*. Rather, this study is a more finished version of the children sketched on cat. 227, a drawing that we know was intended for cat. 224 because the horse and rider of cat. 224 have been traced onto the same sheet. As only a few of the figures in the crowd can be distinguished in the compositional study, it is not possible to determine exactly where this child would have appeared. However, since this figure and those on cat. 227 point to the right, they were perhaps intended to be placed at the left of the horse and rider in a part of the composition cut off in cat. 224.

226 · Florence, Uffizi 6516F *verso*: Studies for the *Israelites Drinking the Water in the Wilderness* (cat. 224). Nude lying face down toward the right supporting himself on his hands; below, the figure restudied twice on a smaller scale. (*Recto*: Study for the *Israelites Drinking the Water in the Wilderness*, cat. 225.) 265 x 402, black chalk; inscribed: [Franco Ros]*i 266*. Fig. 221.

Bibliography: Berenson, 1903, no. 2021; Clapp 1914, 126; Clapp 1916, fig. 47; Berenson 1938, no. 2021; Becherucci 1943, 7, pl. 4; Becherucci 1944, 15; *MF* 1952, 62; *MP* 1956 (Marcucci), no. 129, pl. 160b.

Clapp dated this drawing 1523–1526 and saw that these nudes were studies for the figure in the center foreground of cat. 224, the figure that Berenson accurately described as "drinking from a stream," although he did not connect the motive with the actual subject of the composition. This figure, which is also studied on cat. 228 and 232, is an important clue to the subject of cat. 224 and may be compared with the very similar drinking figure in Bronzino's *Moses Striking the Rock* of ca. 1542 (Cappella Eleanora). Marcucci connected this study with cat. 224, but, following Berenson, she associated cat. 224 with the Pitti *Martyrdom* and thus dated the preparatory studies toward 1530.

227 · Florence, Uffizi 6518F: Studies for the *Israelites Drinking the Water in the Wilderness* (cat. 224). Boy riding a horse forward; to the right, draped child seen from behind; above sideways on the sheet, draped child seen from behind. 390 x 280, black chalk; inscribed verso: [Fran^co^ Ros]*i 240;* inscribed verso in ink in a sixteenth-century (?) hand: *Di Jacopo.* Fig. 223.

Bibliography: Berenson 1903, no. 2023; Clapp 1914, 127; Berenson 1938, no. 2023; *MDM* 1954 (Marcucci), 33.

This sheet has not been associated with cat. 224. Berenson originally related it to the Pitti *Martyrdom*, but later (1938) concurred with Clapp in connecting the three studies with figures in the Pitti *Adoration of the Magi* of ca. 1522. Clapp found the stumpy proportions of the draped figures close to those in the *Adoration*, and the horse and rider identical to the group in the middle ground of the picture, dating the sheet 1518–1522. Marcucci also thought the drawing was for the *Adoration*. Aside from the fact that neither the horse and rider nor the children are to be found in the *Adoration*, there is a conclusive connection with cat. 224 that has not been noted: the horse and rider have been transferred by tracing from cat. 224 and only some of the traced lines have been redrawn. The two sketches of children are for the same figure that is drawn on cat. 225, a child with its back turned that may have served as a *repoussoir* figure to the far left of the composition.

228 · Florence, Uffizi 6558F *recto*: Studies for the *Israelites Drinking the Water in the Wilderness* (cat. 224). Nude lying on his left side, his face to the ground and legs bent back; sideways on the sheet at either end, a draped head. (*Verso*: Studies for the *Israelites Drinking the Water in the Wilderness*, cat. 229.) 280 x 420, black chalk. Fig. 222.

Bibliography: Berenson 1903, no. 2059; *MPA* 1910, 33; Clapp 1914, 153–154; Clapp 1916, 42; Berenson 1938, no. 2059; *MDF* 1939, 30; *MC* 1940, 45.

Berenson connected these studies with the Pitti *Adoration;* the head for the Madonna, the nude for the kneeling king. The other head he took for a cast of drapery. Clapp connected the nude with the figure in the center of cat. 224 and dated the sheet 1521–1526. Like cat. 226 and 232, this nude is a study for the drinking figure, only here his legs are drawn back and he lies on his side. The heads are related to the draped head of Moses, but were probably studies for other hooded figures in the crowd. As early as 1517 (cf. cat. 27) Pontormo had already tended to accentuate the angular possibilities of drapery, but here there is a complicated and involved activity of folds that is quite independent of the forms underneath. These heads resemble the draped heads of the Certosa figures, for which no studies have survived. The head to the left recalls any number of heads in the *Way to Golgotha* and the Germanic type of high round headdress with the veil is consistently worn by the women in the frescoes. The head to the right is similar to that of Pilate's wife in the *Christ Before Pilate*. This head particularly is so cubistic in construction as to recall the contemporary radical experiments of Rosso in this direction, such as the head of the woman to the far left in the Volterra *Deposition* of 1521.

229 · Florence, Uffizi 6558F *verso*: Studies for the *Israelites Drinking the Water in the Wilderness* (cat. 224). Horse seen to the knees moving forward and turned slightly to the right; four studies of horse's legs. (*Recto*: Studies for the *Israelites Drinking the Water in the Wil-*

derness, cat. 228.) 280 x 420, black chalk; inscribed in ink: *P°*.

Bibliography: Berenson 1903, no. 2059; Clapp 1914, 154; Berenson 1938, no. 2059. (Photo G.)

Berenson and Marcucci connected these studies for a horse with the Pitti *Adoration* of ca. 1522. Clapp dated the sheet 1522–1524, noting the connection with cat. 230, which he related to the *Adoration*. While there are similar horses in the middle distance of the *Adoration*, a work contemporary with this project in date, the connection with cat. 224 and with the detail studies for the horse and rider (cat. 230–231, 233) is more explicit. Since the horse is facing left rather than right in cat. 224, this was probably one of Pontormo's preliminary sketches for the motive.

230 · Florence, Uffizi 6722F *recto*: Studies for the *Israelites Drinking the Water in the Wilderness* (cat. 224). Boy riding a horse forward slightly to the left; to the right, the front left side of the horse restudied. (*Verso*: Study for the *Israelites Drinking the Water in the Wilderness*, cat. 231.) 403 x 270, black chalk; inscribed in ink in an eighteenth-century hand: *Anda del Sarto*. Fig. 226.

Bibliography: Ferri 1890, 119; Berenson 1903, no. 2205; *MPA* 1910, 38; Gamba 1912, no. 6, pl. 6; Clapp 1914, 256; Clapp 1916, 24, fig. 34; *Paris Exhib.* 1935, no. 653; Berenson 1938, 315, no. 2205, fig. 964; *MDF* 1939, 30; *MC* 1940, 47; Becherucci 1944, 15; *MDM* 1954 (Marcucci), no. 49; *EMI* 1954, no. 68; Sinibaldi 1960, no. 49, fig. 49.

Gamba thought this sheet was a study for a lost picture of 1518–1519; Berenson connected it with the standard-bearer in the Pitti *Martyrdom* of 1529–1530; while Clapp, Becherucci, Marcucci, and Sinibaldi agreed in associating it with the figure riding in from the right in the background of the Pitti *Adoration*. Clapp dated it 1518–1522, Marcucci 1523. The vigorous draughtsmanship of this study does not preclude an association with the *Adoration* of ca. 1522, but there is little connection in motive with that picture. While the horse is similar in pose, the rider is not a boy but a heavily draped man who leans forward and to the left almost dwarfing his mount. In any case, the connection with the horse and rider in cat. 224 is explicit. Except that the horse's head is turned slightly more to the right, the pose of the horse and rider is identical to that in cat. 224 and 227.

231 · Florence, Uffizi 6722F *verso*: Study for the *Israelites Drinking the Water in the Wilderness* (cat. 224). Boy dressed in a full-sleeved blouse riding a horse forward slightly to the left. (*Recto*: Study for the *Israelites Drinking the Water in the Wilderness*, cat. 230.) 403 x 270, black chalk. Fig. 224.

Bibliography: Ferri 1890, 119; Berenson 1903, no. 2205; Clapp 1914, 257; Berenson 1938, no. 2205; *MDM* 1954 (Marcucci), no. 49; *EMI* 1954, no. 68; Sinibaldi 1960, no. 49.

See the discussion of the recto (cat. 230) for the critical opinions on this drawing. In this somewhat less excited, almost Sartesque, version of the motive on the recto, the boy is seen dressed in the then currently fashionable puffed-sleeved blouse that is also worn by some of the figures in the contemporary Pitti *Adoration* and in cat. 172 of ca. 1521.

232 · London, British Museum 1946–7–13–380: Study for the *Israelites Drinking the Water in the Wilderness* (cat. 224). Nude lying face down with his legs slightly apart and his hands under his chest. 123 x 342, black chalk heightened with white squared; inscribed in red: *N°*

24; inscribed on the mount: *Battista Naldini Pitt. Fior^{no}.* Fig. 225.

Collection: Martelli (?) no. 24; Ottley (sold Sotheby, June 14, 1814, lot 874); Lawrence; Woodburn (sold Christie's June 4–16, 1860, lot 878, no. 6); Phillipps; Fenwick.

Bibliography: Popham 1935, 69.

This squared study for the drinking figure in cat. 224 has been briefly noted by Popham, who retained Ottley's attribution to Naldini, as has the museum. However, this drawing is decidedly too authoritative and coherent, too close to Pontormo in its morphological details, to be considered as a product of his pupil's hand. The linear spontaneity, the *pentimenti*, and luminous surface of this drawing are quite removed from the scrubby quality of the contours, the scratchy angularity of the strokes, and the flat modelling of the average Naldini drawing. The black chalk and white high lights are manipulated in a manner similar to some of the later studies for the Poggio a Caiano putti, as well as to certain Certosa drawings, such as cat. 207 for the *Nailing to the Cross*. This is probably the last study for the drinking figure, following cat. 226 and 228. As in the compositional study, cat. 224, the figure is seen more from above with the legs apart and the elbow closer to the body.

233 · Naples, Galleria Nazionale Capodimonte 0283: Study for the *Israelites Drinking the Water in the Wilderness* (cat. 224). Horse seen from the front turned slightly to the left; above, two clenched hands. 284 x 215, red chalk; the hands in black chalk; inscribed in ink: *Jacomo da Pontormo.*

Bibliography: Berenson 1938, no. 2256F; Becherucci 1944, 15. (Photo Sop. Naples)

This drawing was first published as Pontormo by Berenson, who dated it in the Certosa period. Becherucci connected it with the horses in the background of the Pitti *Adoration* of ca. 1522. However, this horse is more likely to be still another study for the *Israelites Drinking the Water in the Wilderness.* Except that the head is more frontal, it is identical in pose to the horse in the compositional study, cat. 224.

MISCELLANEOUS DRAWINGS CA. 1522–1525

234 · Edinburgh, National Gallery D. 1612 *recto*: Ca. 1523–1525. Nude youth leaning over to the left grasping a nude child who stands at his knees with his back turned. (*Verso*: Nude and child, cat. 235.) 384 x 239, black chalk; upper left corner of the sheet repaired. Fig. 228.

Collection: Laing, given to the Royal Scottish Academy in 1789, stamp recto (L. 2188); given to the National Gallery in 1910, stamp recto.

Bibliography: Berenson 1938, no. 1959B (as no. 2330 and as red chalk); Andrews 1958, 439, fig. 37.

Berenson thought this drawing might have been a discarded idea for the S. Felicita *Deposition.* According to Andrews, it could be connected with the Certosa *Way to Golgotha* as well as with S. Felicita, works which he considered as executed at the same time. There are close analogies with Pontormo's drawings of 1523–1525. The greyish-black chalk, lighter than is usual in Pontormo's drawings, occurs in only two other studies, cat. 254 and 257, both of ca. 1525. The figure type, with the broad, curving shapes, the long arms, the full-featured face, appears in drawings for the Certosa (cat. 205, 208, 211), for the *Supper at Emmaus* (cat. 217), and for the S. Felicita cupola (cat. 260, 268). Yet, the motive and subject of this drawing link it especially with the Certosa *Way to Gol-*

gotha and *Nailing to the Cross* (cat. 206). The man who bends over while looking out at the spectator is repeated several times in the *Way to Golgotha*, most conspicuously in the man carrying the end of the cross, a figure very similar to this one. Among the Certosa frescoes a person with a child could only occur in the *Way to Golgotha*. Indeed, there is such a group in the lower right corner of the fresco, a group for which this study could conceivably have been a discarded idea. This drawing might also have been connected with the *Israelites Drinking the Water in the Wilderness* project of about the same date, a subject in which children generally appear. However, the motive does not occur in the compositional study (cat. 224).

235 · Edinburgh, National Gallery D. 1612 *verso*: Ca. 1523–1525. Nude standing turned to the right with his left foot on a stone and his arms around the shoulders of a child who stands just behind his left leg facing forward. (*Recto*: Nude and child, cat. 234.) 384 x 239, black chalk. Fig. 227.

Bibliography: *Leicester Exhib.* 1952, no. 45; Andrews 1958, 439, fig. 36.

There is one aspect of this drawing that makes its date in Pontormo's *oeuvre* somewhat problematic: it appears to have been considerably reworked by a later hand, most notably in the face of the child, in some of the contours, and in the shading of the background. Thus, while it may date from the midtwenties with the recto as Andrews suggests, there is a suggestion of a somewhat earlier moment in Pontormo's draughtsmanship. Figures such as this one, modelled in the same manner with the deep shadowing of the eyes and mouth, appear in Pontormo's drawings of ca. 1520, such as cat. 124 for Poggio a Caiano. In any case, this was probably a first version of the nude with child motive (taken from a sculptural source?) that was then refined and worked out as a more coherent design on the recto, a sequence which would remain the same whatever the difference in date between the two sides of the sheet.

236 · Florence, Uffizi 449F *recto*: Ca. 1523–1524. Figure seen to the waist with arms folded, dressed in a shirt and an elaborate headdress. (*Verso*: Study for the *Portrait of Two Men*, cat. 193.) 247 x 148, red chalk. Fig. 234.

Bibliography: Ferri 1890, 116; Berenson 1903, no. 1974, pl. 175; *MPA* 1910, 21; Clapp 1914, 96–97; Clapp 1916, 49, 84, fig. 101; Tinti 1925, fig. 3; Giglioli 1926, 778; Stscherbatscheva 1934/36, 182; Dussler 1938, no. 36, fig. 36; Berenson 1938, 318, no. 1974, fig. 981; Becherucci 1943, 9, pl. 18; Becherucci 1944, 17, fig. 47; Alazard 1948, 149; *MF* 1952, 63; *MDM* 1954 (Marcucci), no. 48; *EMI* 1954, no. 67.

This drawing is generally dated 1522–1525, except by Clapp and Stscherbatscheva, who placed it 1527 as closely associated with S. Felicita, and Dussler, who dated it ca. 1530. This drawing does not represent a girl, nor is it a portrait as is often supposed. It is essentially a drapery study for the elaborate headdress of a Madonna from the period 1522–1525, such as those in cat. 192 and the Hermitage *Holy Family*, the Uffizi *Madonna Enthroned*, or the two Pontormesque Madonnas in the Corsini Gallery (nos. 185 and 141). This exact headdress does not appear in any of these works, but the delicate features that are pulled close together, the waved center-parted hair, the prominent ears, and the general lines of the Düreresque headdress are duplicated very closely in Corsini no. 185, a picture that must have been derived from a Pontormo invention such as this one. In draughtsmanship, precise analogies may be found in red chalk drawings for the

Certosa *Nailing to the Cross* such as cat. 209 and 210, where the same slender, elongated type with its small featured face and intricately involved handling of drapery appears.

237 · Florence, Uffizi 6513F *verso*: Ca. 1522–1525. Lower part of a draped seated figure turned to the left; below, study for a *Madonna and Child* on a smaller scale and fragments of two heads and a pair of eyes. (*Recto*: Study for S. Felicita, cat. 263.) 222 x 363, red chalk, smaller sketches in red and black chalk.

Bibliography: Berenson 1903, no. 2018; Clapp 1914, 122–123; Berenson 1938, no. 2018. (Photo G.)

Neither Berenson nor Clapp commented on this drawing. It occupies the same somewhat equivocal position in Pontormo's *oeuvre* of the midtwenties as cat. 241 and 250, which are identical in style. A certain hesitation in the line and stiffness in form give the impression that this drawing is a copy; however, Pontormo himself may have been the copyist in this case. In certain Certosa drawings Pontormo employed a type of regular shading that seemed to be imitative of Dürer's woodcut technique (cf. cat. 196, 199, 212, 214). This same kind of modelling appears here; furthermore, the sharp demarcation of the edges of the forms against the white of the paper is suggestive of a woodcut. The way the drapery breaks at the ground is also Düreresque (cf. the *Adoration of the Magi*, 1511, Bar. 3) and recalls the drapery of another Düreresque drawing of a seated figure from these same years (cat. 252). Judging from the small sketch below, these sketches must have been made in preparation for a *Madonna and Child*.

238 · Florence, Uffizi 6539F *recto*: Ca. 1522–1523. Upper part of a seated nude looking over his right shoulder; below, drapery study. (*Verso*: Study for Castello, cat. 339.) 280 x 184, red chalk; W: Small eagle; inscribed: *Franco Rosi 190.*

Bibliography: Berenson 1903, no. 2042; Clapp 1914, 139–140; Clapp 1916, 42; Berenson 1938, no. 2042. (Photo G.)

Clapp dated this drawing 1525, comparing the drapery in style with cat. 273 for S. Felicita. The drapery is even closer to that of cat. 210 and 236 of the Certosa period, while the nude certainly dates no later than 1522–1523.

239 · Florence, Uffizi 6632F *verso*: Ca. 1523–1525. Boy dressed in short trousers asleep on a wall; below, head and arms restudied. (*Recto*: Study for S. Felicita, cat. 262.) 284 x 395, red chalk, sketch below in black chalk. Fig. 233.

Bibliography: Berenson 1903, no. 2125; Clapp 1914, 196; Berenson 1938, no. 2125.

Berenson and Clapp connected this study with Poggio a Caiano, but there is no relation in motive or style with any of the lunette figures. Furthermore, like cat. 254 and 255 from these same years, this drawing is clearly not for a specific pictorial motive but is an informal study from the model, probably one of the *garzoni* in the studio. The figure type, with the elongated body, long arms, and enlarged hands, is that of the Certosa (cf. cat. 209–210) and the S. Felicita cupola drawings (cf. cat. 263).

The black chalk sketch below has escaped notice, but is interesting as an example of Pontormo's reference back to his early drawings in his later years. Here he has transformed the angular, broken forms of the original model study into an intricate pattern of curved shapes. This rhythmic reinterpretation of the motive of the sleeping figure appears first in a sleeping Christ Child of the thirties (cat. 333) and then in the sleeping figure of Adam in the San Lorenzo *Christ in Glory with the Creation of Eve* (cat. 359–363).

240 · Florence, Uffizi 6652F *verso*: Ca. 1523–1525. Nude standing with his left arm at his side, his right arm raised holding a sling. (*Recto*: Study for the Certosa, cat. 211.) 306 x 190, red chalk. Fig. 229.

Bibliography: Berenson 1903, no. 2144; Clapp 1911, 23; Clapp 1914, 207; Berenson 1938, no. 2144.

Clapp connected this drawing with Michelangelo's lost bronze *David* of 1502, with the study for it in the Louvre, or with the wax model in the Casa Buonarroti that he considered preparatory to it.[40] However, Pontormo's figure is not similar in pose to any of these works. Berenson considered the drawing to be after Michelangelo's "bozzetto for the David of c. 1517." Berenson may have meant the terracotta *bozzetto* in the Casa Buonarroti (no. 413).[41] This terracotta, or perhaps the bronze original that included the right arm, was the source of Pontormo's drawing. The proportions of the body, the movement of the legs, head, and left arm correspond exactly in the sculpture and in Pontormo's figure. Thus, it is possible that Pontormo's drawing may also record the original position of the raised right arm in Michelangelo's figure. In any case, since his figure is holding what appears to be a sling, Pontormo may have been thinking in terms of the *David* subject when he made this drawing.

Pontormo's attempt to transform Michelangelo's sculptured figure into his own graphic idiom has resulted in the exaggerated curving contours and the unusually brilliant surface of this nude, a figure that is an extraordinary anticipation of El Greco's luminous spiraling forms. While this figure is unique in Pontormo's *oeuvre* because of these qualities, Clapp's date of 1517 seems decidedly too early for it, and there is no objection to placing it at the same date as its recto, a study for a figure in the *Nailing to the Cross* of ca. 1523–1524. While this nude is not a study for that Certosa project (cat. 206), there is a certain affinity in the proportions and movement of the figure with the half-length soldiers in the foreground of the composition.

[40] See C. Tolnay, *Michelangelo* I (Princeton, 1943), 205–209, 232–233, figs. 93, 288. Pontormo could not have known the bronze *David*, since it was sent to France in 1508; the Louvre drawing (Berenson 1938, no. 1585) provides no basis for this drawing; and the wax model (Casa Buonarroti no. 422) is unconnected with the *David*.

[41] See Tolnay, *Michelangelo* I, 231–232, figs. 286–287. According to Tolnay, this terracotta is a copy after a lost Michelangelo model of 1505–1506, of which other copies exist. Cf. Tolany, figs. 289–292.

241 · Florence, Uffizi 6667F *recto*: Ca. 1525. Bust of a boy in a cap looking over his left shoulder; to the right on a smaller scale, the bust restudied; below, torso faintly indicated. (*Verso*: Nude and drapery studies, cat. A124.) 296 x 273, red chalk, the torso in black chalk. Fig. 230.

Bibliography: Ferri 1890, 118; *MPA* 1910, 23; Clapp 1914, 218; Clapp 1916, 49, 84, fig. 102; Berenson 1938, 318, no. 2156A, fig. 982; Steinbart 1939, 3, illustrated; *MDF* 1939, 26; *MC* 1940, 49; King 1940, 82.

Clapp has rightly suggested that this drawing was for a lost portrait of 1525–1530, while King noted the similarity between this boy and the young Cosimo in the Baltimore *Portrait of Maria Salviati and Cosimo de' Medici* of 1526–1527. The close resemblance between these two heads is partly due to the way in which Pontormo adjusted his sitter's faces to a preconceived portrait image in the middle twenties: in the *Alessandro* and *Ippolito* portraits (cat. 223), the *Halberdier*, the self-portrait for the *Deposition* (cat. 277), and especially in the *Boy with the Lute*,[42]

[42] Ex-Guicciardini Collection, Florence (panel, 73 x 57 cm). Gamba 1921, 11, fig. 29, dated this

we find the tendency that is so evident in this drawing to reform the features into a pattern of very rounded plastic shapes pulled close together into the middle of the face.

While this drawing has always been attributed to Pontormo, it has recently been ascribed to Bronzino by the museum. The graphic mode of this study is generally Pontormesque, but there is a certain hardening of the forms and an overprecision of the line that might suggest Bronzino in a closely imitative moment in the late twenties, such as that of the Pontormesque *Portrait of a Boy* in Milan.[43] Thus, the possibility of Bronzino's authorship is not to be excluded. In resolving the problem of this drawing, two other red chalk studies of the midtwenties that are identical in style to this drawing should be considered (cat. 237 and 250).

242 · Florence, Uffizi 6668F *recto*: Ca. 1522–1525. Page from a sketchbook: Bust of a bearded man in a cap turned in profile left. (*Verso*: Portrait study, cat. 243.) 196 x 125, red chalk on pink prepared paper. Fig. 231.

Bibliography: Berenson 1903, no. 2157; *MPA* 1910, 22; Clapp 1914, 218–219; Berenson 1938, no. 2157; *MP* 1956 (Marcucci), no. 137, fig. 164a; Berti 1956, 9–10, fig. 7.

Clapp dated this study and the verso 1518–1522, while Marcucci and Berti placed both in the period of San Lorenzo, 1545–1550. The early date is more convincing than the later for this sheet because of close parallels in style with drawings for the Certosa frescoes in red chalk on the same pink prepared sketchbook paper (cat. 196, 197, 200, 201, 205). Pontormo used this combination later as well, but in this sheet the line is simplified and soft, quite without the tightness and ornamental precision of his linear mode in the late drawings.

The sitter for this profile portrait study is unknown. Clapp suggested that the sitter was the same as in the Uffizi *Portrait of a Man*,[44] while Berti considered it to be a self-portrait. The resemblance to the Uffizi man (a portrait in three-quarter view) is not striking, nor is there any firm basis for calling this drawing a self-portrait.[45]

243 · Florence, Uffizi 6668F *verso*: Ca. 1522–1525. Page from a sketchbook: Bust of a man in a cap turned in profile left.

picture 1535, but it has been more generally associated with the *Portrait of a Halberdier* and dated in the late twenties. See Becherucci 1944, 19, fig. 48; Berti, *MP* 1956, no. 63, fig. 55. As pointed out by Berti, the forms in this portrait are more abstracted than those of the *Halberdier* and are quite suggestive of Bronzino at this same date. The possibility of Bronzino's authorship of this picture is not to be excluded, especially in view of its connections with the problematic drawing (cat. 241) and with Bronzino's Milan portrait (see note 43).

[43] Museo del Castello Sforzesco. This portrait was attributed to Pontormo by B. Berenson, *The Florentine Painters of the Renaissance* (New York, 1909), 176, an attribution that has generally been accepted. See Clapp 1916, 160–161 (dated 1521–1522); Gamba 1921, 11, fig. 46 (dated ca. 1535); and Berti, *MP* 1956, no. 78, fig. 71 (dated ca. 1535). However, Becherucci 1949, fig. 5; R. Longhi, "Un Ritratto del Pontormo," *Paragone* 35 (1952), 41; and Emiliani 1960, pl. 16, have rightly returned to the traditional attribution to Bronzino, dating the picture in the early thirties.

[44] Florence, Uffizi 2220 (panel, 65 x 50 cm). Clapp 1916, 141, accepted this portrait as a Pontormo dating 1530–1532. However, Longhi's attribution to Foschi is more convincing. See R. Longhi, "Arrivo a Pier Francesco Toschi," *Paragone* 43 (1953), 54 (as Uffizi 1183). Berti, *MP* 1956, no. 80, fig. 73, dated it before 1535 as a Pontormo, but with reservations as to its authenticity.

[45] For a list of the portraits of Pontormo see note 16 on p. 112. There are no profile portraits of Pontormo for direct comparison.

(*Recto*: Portrait study, cat. 242.) 196 x 125, red chalk on pink prepared paper; inscribed: *Fran^co Rosi 185*. Fig. 232.

Bibliography: Berenson 1903, no. 2157; Clapp 1914, 219; Berenson 1938, no. 2157; *MP* 1956 (Marcucci), no. 137, fig. 164b; Berti 1956, 9–10, fig. 6.

See the discussion of the recto for the critical opinions and the dating of this drawing. The sitter for this portrait study is also unknown. Marcucci quoted Sinibaldi as believing that this person was the same one as represented in cat. 331 (by Sinibaldi considered a portrait of Pontormo by Bronzino, here called a self-portrait). Berti considered this drawing to be a self-portrait like the recto of this sheet. While these two profile studies are identical in style, they certainly do not represent the same person (as is evident from the differently shaped noses) and thus cannot both be self-portraits. In both there are suggestive resemblances to the self-portraits of this period (cf. this head with the portrait in the Pitti *Adoration* of ca. 1522; cf. the recto with cat. 253), but since there are no profile portraits of Pontormo for comparison, it would be hazardous to identify either as such.

244 · Florence, Uffizi 6669F *recto*: Ca. 1524–1525. Seated putto turned to the right and leaning backward; to the left, putto dressed in a shirt seated turned to the left; to the right, legs of a putto, the left restudied below. (*Verso*: Putto studies, cat. 245.) 279 x 403, red chalk; W: Eagle. Fig. 237.

Bibliography: Ferri 1890, 118; Berenson 1903, no. 2158; *MPA* 1910, 33; Clapp 1911, 6; Clapp 1914, 219–220; Clapp 1916, 32, fig. 67; Popham 1931, no. 228, pl. 192; Berenson 1938, no. 2158; *MDF* 1939, 30; *MC* 1940, 44; Gamba 1956, 8, fig. 4.

Berenson originally thought these putti studies and those on the verso were for the boy on the steps in the SS. Annunziata *Visitation* of 1514–1516, while Clapp connected them with the Visdomini altar. Clapp later (1914) dated the sheet 1518–1519 as for the Poggio a Caiano putti and Berenson agreed. Gamba has suggested that these were all sketches for the putti in a *Madonna della Carità*, the lower section of which he attributed to Pontormo.[46] These putti studies and those on the verso do not have any connection in motive or style with those of Poggio a Caiano, but belong in the midtwenties. Compared with the studies for the putti of the lunette (cat. 152–160), the forms in these drawings are flatter, the line more regular and less vibrating, and the modelling more precise. It is possible that these studies from the model may have been related to Pontormo's preparation for the poses of the two putti in the Uffizi *Madonna Enthroned* of ca. 1525, but the connection is one of coincidence in date and general style rather than of specific motive.

245 · Florence, Uffizi 6669F *verso*: Ca. 1524–1525. Seated putto turned to the right with the right leg drawn up; to the right, the chest restudied and the legs restudied three times. (*Recto*: Putto studies, cat. 244.) 279 x 403, red chalk.

Bibliography: Ferri 1890, 118; Berenson 1903, no. 2158; Clapp 1911, 6; Clapp 1914, 220–221; Clapp 1916, 32, fig. 68; Popham 1931, no. 230; Berenson 1938, no. 2158.

[46] Museo dell'Ospedale degli Innocenti, Florence. See Gamba 1921, 6, fig. 7, who dated it ca. 1517. This picture is a pastiche of motives from Pontormo and Andrea del Sarto: The putto to the far left is from the Visdomini altar, the one next to it from Andrea's Scalzo *Caritas*, the one in the left foreground from the Dublin *Pietà*, the Virgin from Andrea's Scalzo *Salome*, and the putto nearest her on the right from Andrea's *Assumption*, Pitti 191. Berti, *MP* 1956, no. 30, fig. 20, suggested the authorship of Jacopino del Conte, Carlo Portelli, or Jacone.

See the discussion of the recto for the critical opinions and dating of this drawing. Unlike the recto, this side of the sheet contains studies for a single putto, with parts of the figure repeated to the right. The pose recalls that of the putto on the left of the Uffizi *Madonna Enthroned*, although not with enough precision to be considered definitely as a study for it. Cf. cat. 246, 248, and 257 for other studies that may have been associated with these putti.

246 · Florence, Uffizi 6678F *recto*: Ca. 1524–1525. Putto seated on a step with his left arm raised. (*Verso*: Study for the Capponi *Madonna*, cat. 258.) 282 x 198, red chalk; lower right corner of the sheet replaced. Fig. 235.

Bibliography: Berenson 1903, no. 2163; *MPA* 1910, 32; Clapp 1914, 228–229; Berenson 1938, no. 2163.

Berenson noted the connection in pose between this putto and the one on the left of the Uffizi *Madonna Enthroned* of ca. 1525, considering it to be for another similar altar. Clapp dated it 1517–1518 as possibly for the St. John the Baptist of the Visdomini altar, but also noted the similarity to the putto in the Uffizi picture, which he dated at the same time as the Visdomini altar. Of the group of studies that recall the putti in the Uffizi picture without being definitely studies for them (cat. 244–245, 248, 257), this one is the closest to the putti in the painting. The slender, rather elongated proportions of the torso and legs, the position of the head and facial expression are close to the putto on the left, while the bent leg is identical to that of the putto on the right.

247 · Florence, Uffizi 6682F *verso*: Ca. 1523–1525. Page from a sketchbook: Lower torso and thigh of a seated nude in profile right. (*Recto*: Study for the Certosa, cat. 196.) 199 x 158, red chalk on pink prepared paper.

Bibliography: Giglioli 1926, 781; Berenson 1938, no. 2167; *MP* 1956 (Marcucci), no. 107, fig. 141b.

Giglioli thought this drawing was for the Christ of the S. Felicita *Deposition*, but Marcucci dated it at the same time as the recto. There seems no reason to dissociate this very fragmentary sketch from the date of the recto.

248 · Florence, Uffizi 6702F *recto*: Ca. 1524–1525. Putto seated with his left leg pulled up, his left hand to his head. (*Verso*: Studies for the Certosa, cat. 213.) 288 x 188, red chalk; W: Small eagle.

Bibliography: Berenson 1903, no. 2185; *MPA* 1910, 32; Gamba 1912, no. 12, pl. 12; Clapp 1914, 246; Berenson 1938, no. 2185; *MDM* 1954 (Marcucci), no. 51; *EMI* 1954, no. 71; *MP* 1956 (Marcucci), no. 115, fig. 153a.

Gamba dated this putto study 1522 on the basis of the Certosa study on the verso, which actually must have dated in 1524. Clapp, however, found the style of the putto different and dated it 1517–1520. Marcucci dated it rightly toward 1525 as close to cat. 217 for the *Supper at Emmaus* of that year. This drawing may be associated with cat. 244–246, and 257, drawings of putti that recall those of the Uffizi *Madonna Enthroned* of ca. 1525. The contours in this drawing are a little less flexible than those of the others in the group, but the putto type and the parallel strokes of the modelling that flatten the forms associate it with them.

249 · Florence, Uffizi 6728F *recto*: Ca. 1524–1525. Study for a *Madonna and Child*. Seated draped woman holding a child on her lap to the right; the child restudied held higher to the left. (*Verso*: Leg and head, cat. 250.) 327 x 276, black chalk heightened with white; W: Fruit (cf. B. 7392). Fig. 238.

Bibliography: Berenson 1903, no. 2211; Clapp 1914, 261–262; Berenson 1938, no. 2211; *MP* 1956 (Marcucci), no. 125, fig. 155b.

Berenson dated this drawing early as perhaps for a *Charity*. Clapp placed it no later than 1520, comparing it with Andrea del Sarto's *Madonna di Porta a Pinti*, which he dated 1520, and with the *Madonna and Child with St. John* (Florence, Corsini Gallery no. 185), which he accepted as Pontormo. Marcucci has dated the drawing much later, ca. 1528, as a study for the Louvre *Madonna and Saints*. She compared it in draughtsmanship with cat. 290 for the *Birthplate* and with cat. 225. The style of this vigorous study is quite different from the brittle, fragmented style of cat. 290 of ca. 1529, but there are close parallels among the drawings of ca. 1522–1525, such as the black chalk studies for the *Israelites Drinking the Water in the Wilderness* (cat. 224–233). The drapery is similar to that in cat. 225, mentioned by Marcucci; the flexible line and slender round-headed figure type are found conspicuously in cat. 230.

There are so many links with works of the early to midtwenties that this drawing must be dated at that time. The composition is distantly dependent on the Pinti *Madonna*, which was also reflected in Pontormo's Hermitage *Holy Family*. It also suggests the Madonna and Child of the Corsini picture, itself an adaption of Andrea's idea. However, it seems closer still in motive to the Uffizi *Madonna Enthroned* of ca. 1525. The resemblance to Andrea's composition and its derivatives is based in part on the presence of two children in this drawing. However, these are actually alternate ideas for the position of the Christ Child, the right one similar in pose to the Child (reversed) in the Corsini *Madonna*, the left one close to the Child in the Uffizi *Madonna Enthroned*. The doll-like proportions of the Madonna, her very round head, the frontal pose, and the arrangement of the draperies also recall the Madonna of both pictures. Thus, this drawing is a link with two problematic pictures of the same period, both of which evidently derive from Pontormo, but neither of which is from his hand.

250 · Florence, Uffizi 6728F *verso*: Ca. 1524–1525. Right leg from the knee down; in reverse direction, head of a child. (*Recto*: Madonna and Child, cat. 249.) 276 x 327, red chalk; inscribed: *Franco Rosi 269*.

Bibliography: Clapp 1911, 8; Clapp 1914, 262; Clapp 1916, 32; Berenson 1938, no. 2211; *MP* 1956 (Marcucci), no. 125.

Clapp dated this sheet ca. 1520 and connected it with figures in the Poggio a Caiano fresco; the leg with Pomona, the head with the putto to the right above the window. Marcucci considered it to be a copy after a Pontormo drawing of the Poggio a Caiano period by the same hand as cat. 241. The child's head is virtually identical to the head on the right in cat. 241, a problematic drawing that has been given by some authors to Bronzino. In these two drawings and in cat. 237, which may be grouped with them, there is an insistence on the volume of the forms, a slightly mechanical touch in the modelling, and a hardening of the line that might suggest Bronzino, but certainly not conclusively.

251 · Florence, Uffizi 6729F *verso*: Ca. 1522. Draped head of an old woman looking up to the right; to the left, the head restudied without the drapery. (*Recto*: Study for the Hermitage *Holy Family*, cat. 192.) 189 x 255, red chalk, the head to the left in black chalk. Fig. 239.

Bibliography: Ferri 1890, 120; Berenson

1903, no. 2003; Clapp 1914, 263; Berenson 1938, no. 2211A; Smyth 1949, 199, fig. 15; *MDM* 1954 (Marcucci), no. 47 & p. 57; *EMI* 1954, no. 66; Emiliani 1960, 61.

Clapp thought this drawing was for a *Pietà* of 1516–1519, while Smyth dated it in the midtwenties and recognized that Bronzino used it as a model for the head of his St. Elizabeth in the Washington *Holy Family*. While the painting and Bronzino's own drawing for the bust of the figure (cat. A75) may be placed ca. 1527–1528, the style of this drawing — the vibrant contours and luminous surface of the head to the right — suggests a date earlier in the twenties. There are parallels to this plastic, energetic manner in the red chalk Poggio a Caiano drawings, but the closest analogies are found in the red chalk compositional studies of ca. 1522 (cat. 194–195), where there is the same brilliant chiaroscuro and richly individualized characterization of the heads. Furthermore, the head of St. Anne in the Pitti *Adoration of the Magi* of ca. 1522 is the exact painted counterpart of this head.

The authorship of the black chalk head to the left has not been questioned. However, it was probably drawn by Bronzino in preparation for the St. Elizabeth. The two heads are placed in an odd relation to one another if they are both by Pontormo. There is no example in Pontormo's drawings of a reprise of exactly the same motive in a different medium on the same scale and at the same angle on the sheet; whereas this is just what we would expect if Bronzino were copying his master's drawing. Furthermore, since he copied the head again on cat. A75, also in black chalk, we know that this sheet was in his hands. These imprecise, unmodulated lines bear little resemblance to Pontormo's cohesive setting down of the idea, but they are strikingly similar to the graphic mode of cat. A75; while certain aspects of the head, such as the nose, the placement of the eye, and the handling of the jawbone, show the copyist's only approximate comprehension of its structure.

252 · London, British Museum 1933-8-3-13 *recto*: Ca. 1524–1525. Draped figure of a woman seated turned to the left with hands clasped in her lap and looking out at the spectator. (*Verso*: Study for S. Felicita, cat. 276.) 287 x 201, red chalk. Fig. 242.

Collection: Reynolds, stamp recto (L. 2364); Hone, stamp recto (L. 2793); acquired by the museum August 2, 1933 (Sotheby, lot 59).

Bibliography: Popham 1933, 66, fig. 21; Berenson 1938, no. 2252C; Berenson 1961, no. 2252C, fig. 934.

Popham placed this study at the time of S. Felicita on the basis of the date of the verso, but compared it rightly with cat. 236, a Düreresque drapery study of the Certosa period. Berenson noted that it dated earlier than the verso, at the time of the Certosa frescoes. It certainly should be placed contemporary with the last phase of Pontormo's work at the Certosa. The simple, broad areas of the forms, the relaxed line, and the careful parallel shading are characteristic of most of the drawings for the *Pietà* and the *Supper at Emmaus* (cat. 212–221). Like these studies it is specifically Düreresque in character. As in cat. 212 and 214, the simplified modelling recalls the linear mode of a woodcut. The drapery folds indicate that Pontormo must have studied figures such as the Madonna in Dürer's *Adoration of the Magi* (1503, Bar. 87). The head is thrust forward to the point of dislocation and the facial expression must, like that in cat. 196 and 214, reflect a Northern prototype. This figure does not appear in the Certosa frescoes, but might have been a discarded idea for a mourning figure in the *Pietà*, the unexecuted *Deposition* (cf. cat. 212), or the unexecuted *Crucifixion*.

253 · London, British Museum 1936–10–10–10 *recto*: Ca. 1525. Nude seen almost to the knees turned to the right with the left arm extended, the right arm pointing out toward the spectator. (*Verso*: Study for the *Supper at Emmaus*, cat. 215.) 284 x 202, red chalk; W: Fleur-de-lis; inscribed in ink: *Pontormo/ nº. 2.* Fig. 241.

Collection: Oppenheimer (sold Christie's July 13, 1936, cat. no. 149); Koenigs (no. 1149).

Bibliography: Popham 1931, no. 232, pl. 196; Berenson 1938, no. 2250B; Popham 1939, 29; Gamba 1956, 11, fig. 19.

As Popham has suggested, this vigorous study is contemporary with the *Supper at Emmaus*. The simple, unelaborated linear structure and the broad diagonal shading bring it close to such studies for the *Supper at Emmaus* as its verso and cat. 216. This unusual drawing was evidently not done in connection with a pictorial motive, but is a self-portrait of the artist pointing at himself in the mirror. Of Pontormo's many self-portraits, it is closest as a likeness to the one in the Pitti *Adoration of the Magi* of ca. 1522 and to cat. 306 of toward 1530.[47]

254 · London, Count Seilern Collection 92 *recto*: Ca. 1525. Youth in contemporary costume seated with his right arm resting on a block, the left supporting his chin. (*Verso*: Study for the *Madonna Enthroned*, cat. 222.) 404 x 280, black chalk. Fig. 243.

Collection: Lawrence; Woodburn (sold Christie's, June 4, 1860, lot 21, no. 10); Phillipps; Fenwick.

Bibliography: *VS* 1931, XII, no. 8, pl. 8; Popham 1935, 83; Berenson 1938, no. 1957A; Seilern 1959, no. 92, pl. 49.

[47] For a list of Pontormo's self-portraits see note 16 on p. 112.

This study of a boy in artisan's clothes has been considered by Popham and Berenson in connection with the drawings for Poggio a Caiano. However, there is little relation between the relaxed line and naturalistic basis of this drawing and the tense linear angularity and expressive distortions of the studies for the lunette. The normative proportions of the figure, the broad strokes of the modelling and the uncomplicated style of the drapery find parallels in numerous drawings of ca. 1525, such as the verso of this sheet, the *Supper at Emmaus* studies (cat. 215–221), and figure studies such as cat. 252 and 255.

255 · Rotterdam, Museum Boymans-Van Beuningen I117 *recto*: Ca. 1525. Two seated boys in contemporary dress, the one to the right holding a book across his leg. (*Verso*: Head, cat. 256.) 277 x 379, red chalk. Fig. 240.

Collection: Richardson Sr., stamp recto (L. 2183); Spencer; Wauters, stamp recto (L. 911); Koenigs; Van Beuningen, given to the museum in 1941.

Bibliography: Juynboll 1938, 19, illustrated; *Amsterdam Exhib.* 1955, no. 235; Berenson 1961, no. 2368A–2.

No date has been suggested for this drawing, but it may be placed about 1525, as in the same general style as the *Supper at Emmaus* studies (cat. 215–221) and the study for the Uffizi *Madonna Enthroned* (cat. 222). However, like cat. 254, this drawing was done quite independently of any pictorial purpose and is thus without the directed intensity of feeling connected with the preparation for a picture. Both this study and cat. 254 are informal studies of a type that became more common later in the century. In fact, it was precisely this kind of drawing that was a favored starting point in Pontormo's work for a number of draughtsmen of the late sixteenth century who turned to Pontormo's style of the midtwenties in their reaction against the refined surfaces and ornamental linear style of the *Maniera*. Pontormo's studies of this type in the midtwenties (cf. also cat. 239 and 254) are rather different in style from their earlier counterparts. There is a relaxation of the incisive, angular characterization of form and of expression that were typical of analogous drawings from ca. 1521 (cat. 172 and 186).

256 · Rotterdam, Museum Boymans-Van Beuningen I117 *verso*: Ca. 1525. Head of a man in a hat looking up almost in profile left. (*Recto*: Two boys, cat. 255.) 277 x 379, black chalk.

Bibliography: Berenson 1961, no. 2368A–2. (Photo Museum)

This study is on a smaller scale than the recto, occupying only a small part of the large sheet. As a Pontormo attribution, it is somewhat puzzling. It has a linear bravura and a lack of substance that brings to mind later sixteenth-century drawings by draughtsmen who were influenced by Pontormo's work of the midtwenties, such as Boscoli, Poccetti, and Jacopo da Empoli. However, there are several heads that are very close to this one in the crowd along the right side of cat. 194 of ca. 1522, and a similar head with the same Düreresque hat appears in the *Supper at Emmaus* in the right foreground. Thus, the sketch may be tentatively placed about 1525 at the time of the recto.

257 · Venice, Accademia di Belle Arti. *Recto*: Ca. 1524–1525. Seated boy seen to the knees with the left leg drawn up, the left arm extended (holding a staff?) and the right arm across his leg; underneath, scrawl of a figure. (*Verso*: Study for the Certosa, cat. 204.) 204 x 187, black chalk; sketch underneath in red chalk; W: Object in a circle (fragmentary); inscribed in ink: *Jacopo*. Fig. 236.

Bibliography: Bassi 1945, 82–85, illustrated; Bassi 1959, 51, no. 21, illustrated; Berenson 1961, no. 2368B–1.

Bassi attributed this study to Pontormo and associated it with the putto to the left above the window in the Poggio a Caiano fresco, a connection that was accepted by Berenson. Later (1959) Bassi also mentioned a connection with the St. John the Baptist of the Visdomini altar. While this sketch may have been intended for a St. John, there is little resemblance to Pontormo's drawings of 1517–1518 for the Visdomini altar. Nor is there any connection in motive or style with the Poggio a Caiano putti, for which we have a well-defined series of studies (cat. 152–160). The unusual, almost grey tonality of the black chalk is similar to that of two drawings of the midtwenties (cat. 234 and 254), while the relaxed handling of the line is much closer to the simplified manner of the *Supper at Emmaus* studies than to the complex vibrations and sharp accents of the Poggio a Caiano drawings. The flattened forms and relatively normative proportions of this figure contrast with the swelling limbs and tiny joints of the Poggio a Caiano putti, bringing this putto closer in type to those in the Uffizi *Madonna Enthroned* of ca. 1525. This drawing may be grouped with several others of similar putti in the same style that are related to the Uffizi picture but not closely enough to be considered definitely as studies for it (cat. 244–246, 248).

PART IV · 1525–1530

Catalogue entries 258–306

PART IV · 1525–1530

Ca. 1525–1526. MADONNA AND CHILD. Florence, Conte Ferrante Capponi Collection. I. Panel, 88 x 80 cm; paint surface of the tondo, 77 cm diameter. Fig. 244.

Bibliography: *MP* 1956 (Berti), no. 59, fig. 46; Gamba 1956, 12; Sanminiatelli 1956, 242.

According to Vasari, Pontormo painted a *Madonna and Child* and a portrait of one of Lodovico's daughters as the Magdalen for Lodovico Capponi at the same time as he was decorating the Capponi Chapel.[1] These works were also noted by Borghini 1584, 483. Both were listed as lost pictures by Clapp 1916, 257. While the portrait has not been found,[2] the *Madonna and Child* is still in the possession of the Capponi family in the chapel of the Palazzo Capponi. Until 1956, when it was identified by Gamba, it was in an unrecognizable state, having been completely repainted and transformed from a tondo on a square panel into an oval in order to fit into an oval frame over the altar of the chapel. This altar is eighteenth-century in style and the picture was presumably adjusted to fit it when it was constructed.

While the tondo as it exists today is extremely damaged and still repainted in part, there is little doubt that it is the picture that Pontormo painted for Capponi's bedroom while he was working at S. Felicita. The style of the tondo suggests the earlier part of the S. Felicita period. In contrast to the Uffizi *Madonna and Child with St. John*, an analogous subject of almost identical size whose complex curvilinear style surely postdates most of the work in the chapel, the Capponi picture is closer in style to the less involved tondo compositions of the S. Felicita *Evangelists*. Further evidence in favor of a dating in the early part of the S. Felicita period — not later than 1526 — is the sketch for the Child, which is stylistically more compatible with Pontormo's drawings of ca. 1525 than with the later studies for the *Deposition* and *Annunciation*.

[1] V/M, VI, 272: "Al medesimo Lodovico fece un quadro di Nostra Donna per la sua camera, della medesima maniera; e nella testa d'una Santa Maria Maddalena ritrasse una figliuola di esso Lodovico, che era bellissima giovane."

[2] An attempt has been made to identify it with a *Magdalen* in the Palazzo Capponi to which an inscription identifying it as Pontormo's portrait has been added. See F. Massai, "Notizie del Ritratto di Francesca di Lodovico Capponi dipinto da Jacopo da Pontormo," (Florence, 1924). The picture actually derives from the St. Julia in Andrea del Sarto's Berlin *Madonna and Saints*.

STUDY FOR THE MADONNA AND CHILD

258 · Florence, Uffizi 6678F *verso*: Study for the *Madonna and Child*. Putto seated in profile right with his right arm raised and looking over his shoulder; to the left, part of a left arm. (*Recto*: Putto study, cat. 246.) 282 x 198, red chalk; the arm in black chalk. Fig. 245.

Bibliography: Berenson 1903, no. 2163; Clapp 1914, 229; Stscherbatscheva 1934/36, 183, fig. 199; Berenson 1938, no. 2163.

This drawing has not been previously connected with the Capponi *Madonna and Child*. Of those who wrote before the identification of the picture in 1956, Berenson thought the drawing was probably for a young St. John the Baptist in an altar similar to the Uffizi *Madonna Enthroned.* He also noted the similarity in pose to a putto in Andrea del Sarto's drawing for the Wallace Collection *Madonna and Angels* (British Museum 1896–8–10–1; Berenson 1938, no. 131). Clapp dated the drawing 1517, connecting it in pose with the putto to the right on the steps in the Uffizi picture. Clapp also mentioned the analogy in pose with the Christ Child in cat. 192 for the Hermitage *Holy Family*, while Stscherbatscheva considered the drawing to be a study for the Christ in the Hermitage picture. The *Holy Family* dates ca. 1522 and the study for it is closely related in style to the Poggio a Caiano drawings. This drawing is not only unrelated in style to cat. 192, but the child here is posed rather differently from the Christ in that drawing, whose legs are more bent, who sits more erectly, who is in fullface, and who holds a bird in both hands. On the other hand, the connection with the Uffizi picture does suggest the correct date for this drawing. There are parallels in type between the putti in the picture and the child in this drawing. Furthermore, the recto of this drawing, another study of a putto in identical style, is quite possibly connected with the Uffizi picture. However, contrary to Clapp's opinion, this child can hardly have been a study for one of the putti seated on the steps. It is evident both from the pose and from the blank space left near his buttocks that this child was intended to be held rather than to sit independently. Indeed, his pose and his type correspond exactly with those of the child in the Capponi picture, as do details such as the angle of the head, the features and expression of the face, the relation of the torso to the bent right leg, and the position of the arm. Thus, considering the similarity in motive together with the date indicated by the style of this drawing, it may be identified as the only surviving study for the Capponi *Madonna and Child.*

1525–1528. DECORATION OF THE CAPPONI CHAPEL: *God the Father with the Four Patriarchs; Four Evangelists; Deposition*; and *Annunciation.* Florence, S. Felicita.

Bibliography: Clapp 1916, 122; see also the individual works below.

According to Vasari, Lodovico Capponi bought the Barbadori chapel in S. Felicita[3] and commissioned Pontormo to decorate it.[4] Vasari implies a date of 1525 for the beginning of the work. Just before his account of Pontormo's work at S. Felicita, he mentions (V/M, VI, 269–270) a group of works that Pontormo painted when he returned from the Certosa; among them the *Supper at Emmaus*, which is dated 1525. A date of 1525 is also indicated for the commission by documentary evidence that Capponi acquired the chapel May 22, 1525, and, according to Balocchi, began to have it redecorated immediately.[5] Vasari states that Pontormo

[3] The first chapel on the right side of the church was built by Brunelleschi in the early 1420's for the Barbadori family. See Balocchi 1828, 34; Paatz 1952/55, II, 64–65.

[4] V/M, VI, 270–271: "Non molto dopo, essendo tornato da Roma Lodovico di Gino Capponi, il quale aveva compero in Santa Felicita la cappella che già i Barbadori feciono fare a Filippo di ser Brunellesco all'entrare in chiesa a man ritta si risolvè di far dipignere tutta la volta, e poi farvi una tavola con ricco ornamento. Onde avendo ciò conferito con messer Niccolò Vespucci cavaliere di Rodi, il quale era suo amicissimo; il cavaliere, come quelli che era amico anco di Jacopo, e da vantaggio conosceva la virtù e valore di quel valent'uomo, fece e disse tanto, che Lodovico allogò quell'opera al Puntormo."

[5] See Balocchi 1828, 34: "Finalmente nell' anno 1525 da Bernardo da Gherardo di Antonio Paganelli per contratto di vendita passò in Lodovico

kept the chapel closed for three years.[6] Thus, the work was probably not completed until into the year 1528. Pontormo painted the now destroyed *God the Father with the Four Patriarchs* in fresco in the vault, the tondi of *Four Evangelists* in the pendentives, both with Bronzino's assistance; the altarpiece of the *Deposition*; and the fresco of the *Annunciation* on the wall to the right of the altar.

di Gino di Lodovico Capponi, quale si diede subito a restaurla, e quasi tutta la rifece di nuovo, adornandola riccamente nella maniera come ora si vede, per essere stata lasciata intatta nella restaurazione della chiesa." Clapp 1916, app. II, doc. 17, cites a document that records the payment of two hundred *scudi* by Lodovico Capponi for the chapel. The exact date of the sale is found in the archive of the Palazzo Capponi, filza 33, no. 2. According to Balocchi 1828, 37, the chapel was consecrated July 1, 1525.

[6] V/M, VI, 271: "E così fatta una turata, che tenne chiusa quella cappella tre anni, mise mano all'opera."

1525. GOD THE FATHER WITH THE FOUR PATRIARCHS. Fresco in the vault, S. Felicita (destroyed).

Bibliography: Clapp 1916, 46, 257; Paatz 1952/55, II, 72; Cox 1956, 17–18; Gamba 1956, 12; *MP* 1956 (Berti), 34.

Because of its location in the vault we would expect to find that this fresco was the first part of the chapel to be executed. A date of 1525 is certainly indicated; indeed, Vasari implies this date when he states (V/M, VI, 271) that Capponi "si risolvè di far dipignere tutta la volta, e poi farvi una tavola con ricco ornamento." Vasari continues (*ibid.*,): "Nel cielo della volta fece un Dio Padre, che ha intorno quattro patriarchi molto belli." Apparently Bronzino had some part in the execution of this work as Vasari notes elsewhere in his life of Bronzino (*ibid.*, VII, 594): "nella volta colorì alcune figure." The vault fresco was also mentioned by Borghini 1584, 483, and Richa 1754/62, IX, 311–312. The vault of the Capponi chapel was destroyed in 1736 in the rebuilding of the western end of the church and the present shallow dome was substituted for the original.[7] Pontormo's drawings (cat. 259–266) verify the descriptions of the destroyed work and give us a clear impression of a scheme in which God the Father was seated in the center of the vault with the four Patriarchs sitting below and looking up at him. Bronzino's fresco of ca. 1540 in the vault of the Cappella Eleanora, Palazzo Vecchio, is surely a reflection of Pontormo's general arrange-

[7] Balocchi 1828, 10, 25, 35. Milanesi (V/M, VI, 271n1) gives the date of the destruction of the vault as 1766. Remnants of the original dome found by Niccoli indicate that it was hemispheric. See R. Niccoli, "Su alcuni recenti saggi eseguiti alla brunelleschiana Cappella Barbadori in Santa Felicita," *Atti del 1° Congresso di Storia della Architettura*, (Florence, 1936), 146. Niccoli suggested that both the dome and the present pendentives were not part of Brunelleschi's structure but were built during Capponi's alterations of 1525. However, H. Saalman, "Further Notes on the Cappella Barbadori in S. Felicita," "*Burl.* 100 (1958), 270–274, found the hemispheric dome with pendentives consistent with Brunelleschi's intentions. He cited an *Annunciation* attributed to Paolo Schiavo (Collegiata, Castiglione d'Olona) that he believed records a lost Uccello fresco of ca. 1430 that reflected the Capponi chapel in its original state. Since Vasari mentions (V/M, II, 206) Four Evangelists in the pendentives of the chapel of the Uccello fresco that do not appear in the copy, it is likely that Pontormo's tondi of the Evangelists were replacements for older representations that already existed in the chapel.

ment. Cat. A217 is a copy after one of the Patriarchs or after a drawing for the figure.

STUDIES FOR GOD THE FATHER WITH THE FOUR PATRIARCHS

259 · Florence, Uffizi 6686F *verso*: Study for *God the Father with the Four Patriarchs.* Fragment of a sketch of a bearded man seated turned to the right looking up to the left and extending his right arm out toward the spectator. (*Recto*: Study for the same figure, cat. 260.) 257 x 245, black chalk; sheet cut irregularly.

Bibliography: Cox 1956, 17; *MP* 1956 (Berti), 34; Berenson 1961, no. 2171. (Photo Sop.)

With the aid of the recto and of cat. 261, this slight sketch may be identified as Pontormo's first idea for the God Father. Even though the drawing has been considerably cut down, one can see the torso of the seated figure, the beard, and the beginning of the extended right arm.

260 · Florence, Uffizi 6686F *recto*: Study for *God the Father with the Four Patriarchs.* Nude seated turned to the right with his right arm extended toward the spectator. (*Verso*: Study for the same figure, cat. 259.) 257 x 245, black chalk; some of the outlines incised for transfer; sheet cut irregularly close to the figure. Fig. 247.

Bibliography: Berenson 1903, no. 2171; Clapp 1914, 233–234; Berenson 1938, no. 2171; Smyth 1955, 71; Cox 1956, 17, fig. 19; *MP* 1956 (Berti), 34.

Berenson thought this drawing was a study for a figure in the unexecuted *Nailing to the Cross* for the Certosa (cat. 206). Clapp doubted its authenticity, although he related it in style to cat. 265 and 266, which are here associated with the Patriarchs, and dated it 1525–1535. Smyth also questioned the attribution to Pontormo and suggested that this drawing was a discarded Bronzino idea for one of the Evangelist tondi. The connection of both sides of the sheet with cat. 261 leaves no doubt as to the Pontormo attribution and the association with the cupola fresco. The rather indifferent quality of the drawing is due in part to the silhouetting of the figure and to the incising of some of the contours, but there is little cause to remove it from Pontormo's *oeuvre*. In this study from a young nude the definitive pose of the God Father is established, although the more vigorous gesture of the arm seen in cat. 261 is still to be worked out. In style this study is a typical example of the relaxed, rather flat draughtsmanship and the characteristic figure type that we have seen in other drawings of 1525, such as the *Supper at Emmaus* study, cat. 217.

261 · Florence, Uffizi 8966S: Study for *God the Father with the Four Patriarchs.* Draped old man with a beard seated with his legs and torso turned to the right, the right arm extended out to the left and the head turned up to the left. 273 x 342, black chalk heightened with white, squared in red chalk; laid down; written in Pontormo's hand to the right above: *Finiscila e non la . . .* Fig. 246.

Collection: Santarelli, given to the Uffizi in 1866, stamp recto (L. 907).

Bibliography: Santarelli 1870, 606; Cox 1956, 17–18, fig. 1; *MP* 1956 (Berti), 34; Berenson 1961, 2248D.

In Santarelli's catalogue this drawing was attributed to Niccolò dell'Abate and described as a "figure sendente, forse rappresentante il Tempo." This squared drawing may be identified as Pontormo's final study for the God Father. As such it is a most important drawing in his *oeuvre*, not only because it documents a destroyed work, but because it provides a term of comparison for other drawings that heretofore could only be tentatively associated with the vault fresco. In this study the final conception of the draped, bearded figure has taken shape. The broad, spread-out design of the figure in cat. 260 has been contracted and condensed so that the legs are pulled closer to the body and the contrapposto of the torso and arm is more striking. However, the expressive gesture of the arm is still in a fluid, evolutionary stage. In style this drawing is closer to the drawings of 1525 than to the studies for the *Deposition* and *Annunciation*. The ornamental beauty and luminosity of surface, the elongated proportions of the forms, and the complex linear refinement of these studies are not yet in evidence. The solid form of the God Father does not have the weightlessness of the *Deposition* figures, nor does his forceful gesture have the will-less quality of the gestures in the altarpiece. In draughtsmanship, especially in the handling of the draperies, there are close parallels in this drawing to the *Supper at Emmaus* studies and to a portrait drawing of about 1525 such as cat. 223.

262 · Florence, Uffizi 6632F *recto*: Study for *God the Father with the Four Patriarchs*. Boy in contemporary costume seated leaning on his right arm, while his left arm is raised and he looks up to the right; in reverse direction, the same figure in a more frontal position lightly indicated. (*Verso*: Boy asleep, cat. 239.) 395 x 284, red chalk over faint black chalk, the reverse sketch in black chalk. Fig. 249.

Bibliography: Berenson 1903, no. 2125; *MPA* 1910, 30; Gamba 1912, no. 11, pl. 11; Clapp 1914, 195–196; Clapp 1916, 32; *Paris Exhib.* 1935, no. 651; Berenson 1938, 311, no. 2125; *MDF* 1939, 28; *MC* 1940, 48; Berenson 1961, no. 2125, fig. 913.

Both Berenson and Clapp connected this drawing with Poggio a Caiano, Clapp relating the figure to the boy on the wall to the left and the sketch in reverse to the Pomona. Gamba considered the drawing to be possibly for the second unexecuted lunette. There is not a single Poggio a Caiano drawing that is like this study in style, although the motive of a seated figure reaching up might suggest the boy on the wall to the left. Furthermore, there are none of the distortions that Pontormo's angular shorthand of the Poggio a Caiano studies creates, nor is there a trace of the agitated psychological state of most of the figures in the lunette drawings. Rather, the content of the drawing is unaggressive, the line relaxed and without insistent accent. While the drawing is essentially a model study similar in type to cat. 254 of the same date, the motive suggests that it was done with one of the seated Patriarchs of the vault in mind.

263 · Florence, Uffizi 6513F *recto*: Study for *God the Father with the Four Patriarchs*. Seated nude with the left leg drawn up, gesturing with both arms and looking up in profile left; to the left, the head and arms restudied. (*Verso*: Drapery study, cat. 237.) 363 x 222, red chalk; W: Fruit (cf. B. 7392). Fig. 250.

Bibliography: Ferri 1890, 117; Jacobsen 1898, 282; Berenson 1903, no. 2018; *MPA* 1910, 27; Clapp 1914, 122; Berenson 1938, no. 2018; *MDF* 1939, 31; *MC* 1940, 45.

There has been general agreement in connecting this study with Poggio a Caiano, Clapp relating it to the boy with the basket to the left of the window. However, both the motive and the style suggest more strongly that it is a study for one of the Patriarchs who gestures and looks up toward the God Father. The draughtsmanship is closer to drawings of the midtwenties such as cat. 246 than to the earlier lunette drawings. The proportions of the figure are very close to those of cat. 260 and 265 for the S. Felicita vault, both of which have the flattened, curving limbs and very large hands that are evident in this nude.

264 · Florence, Uffizi 6519F *recto*: Study for *God the Father with the Four Patriarchs.* Bust of a nude with the right arm held up. (*Verso*: Drapery study, cat. 296.) 142 x 215, red chalk. Fig. 248.

Bibliography: Berenson 1903, no. 2024; Clapp 1914, 127–128; Berenson 1938, no. 2024; *MP* 1956 (Marcucci), no. 121, fig. 144b.

Berenson related this drawing to Poggio a Caiano, while Clapp thought it was for the Virgin of the *Deposition* and dated it 1525–1526. As Marcucci has also concluded, this nude is for one of the Patriarchs of the vault. The model seems to be the same one as was used for cat. 260 for the God Father. In draughtsmanship the study is identical to a drawing that is without doubt for a Patriarch (cat. 265), even to details of expression, the blowing hair, and the raised, enlarged hand.

265 · Florence, Uffizi 6613F *recto*: Study for *God the Father with the Four Patriarchs.* Draped seated man with the left arm raised, his head turned up to the left. (*Verso*: Studies for S. Felicita, cat. 270.) 307 x 270, red chalk. Fig. 251.

Bibliography: Berenson 1903, no. 2112; *MPA* 1910, 25; Gamba 1912, no. 10, pl. 10; Clapp 1914, 185–186; Clapp 1916, 49; Berenson 1938, 311, no. 2112; Cox 1956, 17, fig. 17; *MP* 1956 (Marcucci), no. 119, fig. 149a; Emiliani 1960, pl. 5; Berenson 1961, no. 2112, fig. 945.

Berenson thought this figure was a study for the Vertumnus of the Poggio a Caiano fresco, while Gamba dated it later, and Clapp suggested that it might be for a S. Felicita Patriarch, dating it ca. 1527. In accordance with our earlier dating of the vault, the drawing should be placed in 1525. This study and cat. 266 are the most completed of the Patriarch drawings, showing the figures in a *sotto-in-su* perspective, foreshortened as they would have been on the curved surface of the vault.

266 · Florence, Uffizi 6590F: Study for *God the Father with the Four Patriarchs.* Nude seated with legs apart, his left hand resting on a book (?). 279 x 213, black chalk heightened with white, squared in red chalk; inscribed in ink: *Jacopo.* Fig. 252.

Bibliography: Ferri 1890, 118; Jacobsen 1898, 282; Berenson 1903, no. 2089; *MPA* 1910, 26; Clapp 1914, 171; Clapp 1916, 49; Berenson 1938, 311, no. 2089; Gamba 1956, 12, fig. 24; Berenson 1961, no. 2089, fig. 944.

This study was associated with the Poggio a Caiano lunette by Jacobsen, Berenson, and Clapp, but Clapp later (1916) suggested a connection with the S. Felicita Patriarchs, followed by Gamba, who specifically named Adam. There seems no reason to identify this figure as Adam, but the drawing is certainly a model study from the nude for the pose of one of the Patriarchs. The physical type and the handling of the black chalk are very close to cat. 260 for the God Father; the figure is seen from below at the same angle as cat. 265; and it is squared for enlargement in the same scale as the finished study for the God Father (cat. 261).

PART IV: 1525–1530

Ca. 1525–1526. FOUR EVANGELISTS: *St. John* (Pontormo), *St. Luke* (Bronzino), *St. Mark* (Bronzino), and *St. Matthew* (Pontormo and Bronzino?). Tondi in the pendentives, S. Felicita. II. Panels, 76 cm diameter.

Bibliography: Goldschmidt 1911, 45, 53 (John?); Schulze 1911, 5, ix (Luke); Clapp 1916, 122–123 (Mark); Voss 1920, 170 (John); McComb 1928, 5, 52 (Luke); Berenson 1936, 401; Becherucci 1944, 43 (Mark); Nicco Fasola 1947, 46–47, figs. 21–23; Procacci 1947, 50–52 (Mark); Becherucci 1949, 2, fig. 1 (Mark); Smyth 1949, 188–192, figs. 4–5, 8–9 (Mark and Luke); Paatz 1952/55, II, 67; Cox 1956, 17 (Mark and Matthew?); *MP* 1956 (Berti), nos. 55–58, figs. 48–51 (Mark); Sanminiatelli 1956, 242 (Mark); Emiliani 1960, pl. 4–6 (Mark and Luke).

In his account of Pontormo's work at S. Felicita Vasari continues directly after mentioning the vault fresco (V/M, VI, 271): ". . . e nei quattro tondi degli angoli fece i quattro Evangelisti, cioè tre ne fece di sua mano, ed uno il Bronzino tutto da sè." However, in his life of Bronzino (*ibid.*, VII, 594), Vasari says "fece . . . in due tondi a olio due Evangelisti . . ." Borghini 1584, 483; Richa 1754/62, IX, 311–312; and Balocchi 1828, 41, all followed Vasari's first version, giving Bronzino only one tondo. However, in the modern literature there have been attempts to attribute another tondo to Bronzino. (See the bibliography above for the tondo or tondi given to Bronzino.)

There has been general agreement on the attribution of the *St. John* panel to Pontormo, although no drawings by Pontormo for it or for any of the tondi have survived. Since Clapp there has been a fairly general agreement that the tondo surely by Bronzino is the *St. Mark*. However, cat. A9, believed by Smyth to be a Pontormo drawing used by Bronzino for the *St. Mark*, is more likely to be Bronzino's own study for the *St. Mark*, confirming the ascription of this tondo to him. Cat. A125, also considered by Smyth to be Pontormo's drawing used by Bronzino for the *St. Mark*, is more probably Bronzino's study for the *St. Matthew*. The *St. Luke* has been attributed variously to both Pontormo and Bronzino. This tondo has been identified — we now believe correctly — as Bronzino's second tondo by Schulze, McComb (who called it *St. John* in error), Smyth, and Emiliani. In addition to the *St. Mark* and the *St. Luke*, it is possible, in spite of Vasari's restriction of Bronzino to two tondi, that Bronzino had a part in still a third tondo — the *St. Matthew*. On the basis of evidence from the restorer (quoted by Procacci) that there was an earlier version of the design on the panel, Smyth suggested that Bronzino began the tondo and perhaps did the angel-head but it was completely reworked by Pontormo. Further evidence for Bronzino's participation in the design of this tondo is his preparatory study for it (cat. A125), usually called Pontormo's drawing for the *St. Mark*. The style of this drawing is more characteristic of Bronzino, while the youthful, curly-haired, half-nude figure can only be that of the *St. Matthew*, even though the pose was changed before the final solution. Therefore, there is considerable evidence for Bronzino's role in the design of the *St. Matthew* tondo, even though in its present damaged condition, it is impossible to draw firm conclusions as to the hand or hands involved in its execution. Cat. A214 is a copy after this tondo.

Ca. 1526–1527. DEPOSITION. Altarpiece, S. Felicita. I. Panel, 313 x 192 cm. Fig. 253.

Bibliography: Goldschmidt 1911, 8, 45, pl. 4; Clapp 1916, 45–46, 120–122, fig. 92; Voss 1920, 168–169; Gamba 1921, 9, fig. 33; Wild 1932, 182–185, figs. 114–115; Venturi 1932, 158–161, figs. 91–93; *Paris Exhib.* 1935, no. 381; Berenson 1936, 401; Steinbart 1939, 8, illustrated; *MC* 1940, 41, fig. 22; Toesca 1943, 14–16, figs. 24–27; Becherucci 1944, 18–19, figs. 40–43; Nicco Fasola 1947, 44–46, figs. 18–19; Smyth 1949, 205; Paatz 1952/55, II, 67; *MP* 1956 (Berti), no. 54, fig. 47; Berti 1956, 12, fig. 10; Marcucci 1956, 16–18, fig. 20.

Vasari describes this altarpiece in detail after the vault fresco and the tondi and remarks on how different it is from them in style (V/M, VI, 271–272). The altar is also mentioned by Borghini 1584, 488; Cinelli 1677, 117; Richa 1754/62, IX, 311; and Balocchi 1828, 41. In the modern literature there has been general agreement in dating the *Deposition* 1525/26–1528, the years indicated by the documentary evidence and Vasari's statements. Only Gamba has placed it 1524–1526. Because of the precedence of the vault fresco, it seems likely that the altarpiece was not started until 1526; and, since the *Annunciation* was probably executed last, the altarpiece may not have occupied Pontormo beyond the year 1527.

STUDIES FOR THE DEPOSITION

267 · Florence, Uffizi 6619F: Study for the Christ, *Deposition.* Seated partly draped man seen to the knees turned to the right; to the right above, the neck restudied. 353 x 280, red chalk; W: Crossed arrows in a circle with a star (B. 6305). Fig. 255.

Bibliography: Berenson 1903, no. 2117; Gamba 1912, no. 15, pl. 15; Clapp 1914, 190; Clapp 1916, 48, fig. 99; Berenson 1938, 316, no. 2117, fig. 972; Toesca 1943, 15, fig. 23; *MP* 1956 (Marcucci), no. 122, fig. 145b.

As was first observed by Berenson, this is a study for the Christ of the *Deposition.* It is quite different from Pontormo's final concept of the figure and should be placed rather early in the evolution of the idea. Cat. 276 is a later sheet of detail studies for the Christ, probably done after the compositional drawing, cat. 272. Pontormo had drawn the motive of a half-seated dead Christ before, about 1519, when he designed a lunette *Pietà* (cat. 103) that apparently was never executed. Here, in this most elaborately finished of the S. Felicita studies, Pontormo experimented again with the motive on a naturalistic, almost academic basis. There is no indication that the figure will ultimately become a weightless arabesque; it is intentionally stabilized and lacks completely the impression of expanding forms that was so evident in the fluctuating contours and expressively enlarged limbs of the vault drawings. Here, too, setting this drawing apart from the other *Deposition* studies, there is a sculptural smoothness of surface that is strikingly like that of the painting but quite unrelated to the mode of the other drawings for it.

The prominent motive of the bent right wrist and turned hand may have been derived from Michelangelo, who used it frequently to suggest the related states of death or sleep (cf. the *Madonna of the Stairs*, the Sistine Ceiling *Creation of Eve*, the *Lorenzo de' Medici* of the Medici Tombs). However, in this drawing Pontormo may have been the first to use it in the context of a *Pietà.*

268 · Florence, Uffizi 6576F *recto*: Study for the St. John, *Deposition.* Nude youth standing looking down to the left. (*Verso*: Nude study, cat. A 87.) 390 x 215, black chalk heightened with white; lower left corner replaced; inscribed in ink: cxxx. Fig. 257.

Bibliography: Berenson 1903, no. 2076; *MPA* 1919, 24; Clapp 1914, 163–164; Clapp 1916, 49, fig. 100; Berenson 1938, 316, no. 2076, fig. 976; *MDF* 1939, 30; *MC* 1940, 46; Becherucci 1943, 9, pl. 20; *MF* 1952, 63.

As has been noted by Clapp, this nude is a study for the figure to the upper right of the *Deposition*. However, only the upper part of this figure was actually used in the subsequent drapery study (cat. 273) and in the painting. This study for the St. John is one of the earliest drawings that has survived for the altar and is similar in effect to a preliminary red chalk study for the Virgin, cat. 269. Here, the proportions of the figure and the bold modelling are still close to the style of the vault studies, especially cat. 264 and 265. However, in contrast to the vault drawings there is here an increased intensity of feeling that takes the form of a rarefied emotionalism, a new fluency and tension in the slowly attenuated line, a concern with ornamental beauty of surface (seen also in cat. 267), and a shift toward a more refined physical type.

269 · Florence, Uffizi 6666F *recto*: Study for the Virgin, *Deposition*. Bust of a nude staring forward. (*Verso*: Drapery study, cat. 303.) 165 x 146, red chalk. Fig. 256.

Bibliography: Berenson 1903, no. 2156; Clapp 1914, 217; Clapp 1916, 48, fig. 93; Berenson 1938, no. 2156; Becherucci 1943, 9, pl. 21; *MF* 1952, 64.

Clapp has rightly suggested that this is a study for the Virgin. It is close in style to cat. 268 for the St. John and is at once more refined in line and more brilliant in its modelling than the studies for the vault figures, such as an analogous Patriarch study, cat. 264. The use of a male model for a female figure had been a common practice in Pontormo's drawings, but with studies like this one a genuine ambiguity of sex appears, anticipating a conspicuous feature of Pontormo's later drawings.

270 · Florence, Uffizi 6613F *verso*: Studies for the man to the far left, *Deposition*. Lower torso and legs of a nude walking to the right; above, a bit of drapery; in reverse direction, the whole figure sketched twice. (*Recto*: Study for S. Felicita, cat. 265.) 307 x 270, red chalk. Fig. 260.

Bibliography: Berenson 1903, no. 2112; Clapp 1911, 13; Clapp 1914, 186; Clapp 1916, 48, fig. 98; Berenson 1938, no. 2112; *MP* 1956 (Marcucci), no. 119, fig. 149b.

Clapp has seen that these studies are all for the figure who supports Christ's shoulders, but Berenson placed the drawing earlier as unconnected with S. Felicita. While Clapp dated this drawing about 1526, Marcucci dated it as early as 1525 because of its stylistic similarity to the vault study on the recto, although she placed the painting 1527–1528. 1526 would seem a reasonable date for the first ideas for the altar and even for the beginning of its execution. Even after these detailed studies Pontormo still seemed to be more undecided about this figure than any other in the composition. In the compositional study the other figures are drawn with considerable assurance, but repeated *pentimenti* almost blot out the forms and precise action of this figure. One subsequent study for the drapery of the figure has survived (cat. 273).

271 · Florence, Uffizi 6536F: Study for the woman to the left of the Virgin, *Deposition*. Page from a sketchbook: Partially draped figure seen to the knees looking up to the right with arms held out.

222 x 161, red chalk squared on pink prepared paper. Fig. 258.

Bibliography: Berenson 1903, no. 2039; *MPA* 1910, 27; Clapp 1914, 138; Voss 1928, 11, illustrated, 48; Berenson 1938, no. 2039; *MDF* 1939, 29; *MC* 1940, 49; *MDM* 1954 (Marcucci), no. 55; *EMI* 1954, no. 76.

Berenson thought this drawing was a study for Poggio a Caiano. While Clapp and Voss dated it 1528, Marcucci 1525–1526, it has not been associated with the *Deposition.* The head of this figure was used for the woman just to the left of the Virgin in the center of the picture. Cat. 274 is a later sheet of studies for the head alone, probably subsequent to the compositional study, cat. 272. Even though he used only the head in the painting, Pontormo conceived it in relation to the expressive action of the torso, the arms, and the clenched hands. The procedure is similar to his development of the half-length St. John, a figure whose psychic state was suggested in the drawing through the motion of the entire body (cat. 268).

272 · Oxford, Christ Church Library F68: Compositional study for the *Deposition.* Within an arched picture space the Dead Christ carried by two figures, one crouching in the foreground, the other standing to the left; above, the Virgin supported by a woman seen from behind; to the left, two women's heads; above on the left, a woman leans down; above on the right, St. John leans down; at the top, a woman; at the right edge, a head; and in the background on the left, bust of a figure and a ladder faintly indicated. 445 x 276, black chalk heightened with white with a little bistre wash, squared in red chalk; the top two figures gone over in pen; sheet cut to an arched shape and laid down. Fig. 254.

Collection: J. Richardson Sr., stamp recto (L. 2184); Guise, given to Christ Church in 1765.

Bibliography: Jeudwine 1959, 114–115, fig. 2; *Christ Church Exhib.* 1960, no. 60, pl. 43.

This important drawing was discovered in the reserves of the Christ Church Library as a Baroccio by Philip Pouncey, who brought it to the author's attention in 1955. As a compositional study in black chalk heightened with white it is closely related in style to Pontormo's other compositional drawings of the late twenties, such as cat. 223 for the *Portrait of Ippolito de' Medici*, cat. 261 for the S. Felicita *God the Father with the Four Patriarchs*, and cat. 289 for the Carmignano *Visitation.* The compositional study has been placed at this point in our sequence of *Deposition* studies because it is clearly subsequent to cat. 267–271, but may have been made before cat. 273–277, which show refinements in detail that are closer to the painting than to this drawing. In any case, at the moment of this study Pontormo had established the general scheme of the composition and had worked out many of its parts in detail, but the exact final proportions of the composition and the spatial relations within it were still evolving. The changes that were made after this drawing were all toward one end — that of taking the action out of a definite time and space context and turning all the forms inward, connecting them by and through a slow whirlpool of curves into which there is a prescribed entrance but from which there is no exit. For this reason the elements that suggested depth and overlapping forms were altered in the painting: the small figure in the left distance was removed, the woman at the top was enlarged so that she comes forward, the head of the woman by the Virgin's arm was raised so that it is tangent to but not behind the arm, a concrete object that suggests a supporting ground such as the ladder was taken out, and the self-portrait head on the right was brought out of the background into an ambiguous spatial relation to the rest of the figures. In order to remove these forms even further from our reality, Pontormo shifted the whole structure of the lower part of the composition so that the composition becomes a precariously inverted pyramid. To this end, the legs of the figure holding Christ's body and the woman with her back turned are pulled back so that only the single foot and the wisp of drapery remain to support the entire composition.

273 · Florence, Uffizi 6730F *recto*: Studies for the St. John and the man to the far left, *Deposition*. Lower part of a draped figure seen to the knees walking to the right; above, draped torso without the head. (*Verso*: Scrawl in black chalk, not catalogued.) 334 x 125, red chalk. Fig. 261.

Bibliography: Berenson 1903, no. 2212; Clapp 1911, 13; Clapp 1914, 263–264; Clapp 1916, 48–49, fig. 97; Berenson 1938, no. 2212.

As Clapp noted, the upper study is for the St. John, who was first studied on cat. 268, and the legs below are for the figure who holds the shoulders of Christ, first studied on cat. 270. It is likely that these rather careful studies were executed after the Oxford compositional drawing (cat. 272). The draperies of these two figures had not been worked out to this extent in the compositional study, but are identical in every detail to the draperies in the painting.

274 · Florence, Uffizi 6627F *recto*: Studies for the woman to the left of the Virgin, *Deposition*. Page from a sketchbook: Draped heads of two women. (*Verso*: Nude studies, cat. 301.) 202 x 140, red chalk on pink prepared paper. Fig. 259.

Bibliography: Berenson 1903, no. 2122; *MPA* 1910, 24; Clapp 1914, 193; Clapp 1916, 48, fig. 94; Berenson 1938, 316, no. 2122, fig. 973; *MDF* 1939, 29; *MC* 1940, 50; Becherucci 1943, 9, pl. 22; Becherucci 1944, 19.

As has been observed by Berenson, these are studies for the head of the woman in the center of the *Deposition*. Like cat. 275 and 277, also head studies, they were probably executed after the compositional drawing. The upper head is a more immediate study of the delicately anguished expression of the face, while the lower head is more crystallized in form and closer to the head in the painting in details such as the slightly sharper angle from below and in the form of the headdress. In both studies the line is more precise and ornamental than the freer, less involved line of the preliminary idea for the head that also included a suggestion of the figure in action (cat. 271).

275 · Florence, Uffizi 6577F: Study for the man in the center foreground, *Deposition*. Page from a sketchbook: Head of a man turned to the right. 216 x 153, red chalk on pink prepared paper; W: Heart (cf. B. 4196). Fig. 262.

Bibliography: Ferri 1890, 118; Jacobsen 1898, 279; Berenson 1903, no. 2077; *MPA* 1910, 24; Clapp 1914, 164; Clapp 1916, 48, fig. 95; Berenson 1938, 316, no. 2077, fig. 974.

Jacobsen first connected this drawing with the youth who supports the body of Christ. Like cat. 274 and 277 this drawing is a final study for the head of a figure in the *Deposition*; however, in this case we lack any of the earlier studies for the action of the figure. The notion of equating the compositional pivot of the painting with our means of entrance into the picture had not been developed up to the point of the compositional study. In cat.

272 this figure looks down to the right, avoiding rather than insisting on any contact with the spectator. However, in this final study the head is identical in form and feeling to the painted version. His expression is precisely the bewildered half-frown of the face in the painting, who looks upon us as intruders yet compels us to participate in his experience.

276 · London, British Museum 1933–8–3–13 *verso*: Studies for the Christ, *Deposition*. Bust of a nude with a hand supporting the head to the right; sideways on the sheet, a three-quarter length seated nude in profile right with the head looking forward; to the left, part of the torso; to the right, outline sketch of part of the torso. (*Recto*: Seated woman, cat. 252.) 287 x 201, red chalk. Fig. 264.

Bibliography: Popham 1933, 66; Berenson 1938, no. 2252C; Popham 1939, 29; Berenson 1961, no. 2252C, fig. 940

This sheet of studies for the Dead Christ was first published by Popham. With the exception of the first model study (cat. 267), it is the only surviving drawing for the Christ and is among the most refined and subtle of Pontormo's S. Felicita drawings. Like cat. 274, 275, and 277, which are also drawn in this ultrasensitive manner, it was probably executed after the compositional drawing. Details of Christ's head and the supporting hand that were somewhat blurred in the compositional drawing are here clarified. This group of drawings are final studies — not finished in the sense of an academic definition of every line — but complete as a definition of the form and feeling of each figure as it is to be in the painting. Therefore, although the Christ is beardless in the drawing, there was no further step to be taken in the evolution of Pontormo's idea of the figure.

277 · Florence, Uffizi 6587F: Study for the self-portrait, *Deposition*. Page from a sketchbook: Bust of a man in a hat looking over his right shoulder at the spectator. 155 x 107, red chalk on pink prepared paper. Fig. 263.

Bibliography: Berenson 1903, no. 1995; *MPA* 1910, 24; Clapp 1914, 169; Berenson 1938, 316, no. 2086A.

Berenson recognized this head as a study for the man to the far right of the *Deposition*, but it has not been noted that the drawing is a self-portrait. The figure in the painting, who is in contemporary dress and clearly has no connection with the action other than that of observer, must be either the artist or the donor. If the face is compared with the known likenesses of Pontormo, it is clear that it too is a self-portrait, and that the likeness is quite consonant with Pontormo's age in about 1528.[8] As in the self-portrait that appears in the Pitti *Adoration of the Magi* of ca. 1522, Pontormo has taken liberties with his features in order to accommodate the head into the curvilinear organization of the picture. This image of himself is no more a literal transcription of reality than is the scene of the *Deposition* itself. If it is compared with another more objective self-portrait drawing of the same approximate date (cat. 306), it can be seen that here the tilt of the head makes the face seem rounder and that each feature is fuller and more curved in shape in accord with the cursive patterns of the picture. The ornamental delicacy of the line and the rarefied emotional state conveyed link this drawing with cat. 274–276.

[8] For a discussion of the portraits of Pontormo see note 16 on p. 112. Berti 1956, 12, fig. 10 noted that the head in the painting is a self-portrait, but did not mention this drawing for it.

Ca. 1527–1528. ANNUNCIATION. S. Felicita. I. Fresco, each side 250 x 110 cm. Figs. 265, 267.

Bibliography: Clapp 1916, 122; Nicco Fasola 1947, 46–47, figs. 24–25; Paatz 1952/55, 67; *MP* Supplement 1956 (Berti).

Vasari mentioned this part of the decoration of the Capponi Chapel last (V/M, VI, 272). The style of this fresco does indeed suggest that it was the final phase of Pontormo's work at S. Felicita, dating ca. 1527–1528. These monumental figures are closely related to works that certainly postdate the Capponi Chapel, such as the Uffizi *Madonna and Child with St. John* and the Carmignano *Visitation.* Especially in the *Visitation,* we see the same precarious stance of the figures, the identical reformation of each figure into a sequence of long oval shapes. In both the *Annunciation* and *Visitation,* in contrast to the *Deposition,* the effect is one of transfixed motion rather than constantly turning movement. In all aspects, including the important evidence of the two preparatory studies (cat. 278–279), the *Annunciation* represents a stage in Pontormo's development just subsequent to rather than contemporary with the *Deposition.*

STUDIES FOR THE ANNUNCIATION

278 · Florence, Uffizi 448F: Study for the Virgin, *Annunciation.* Heavily draped woman standing turned toward the right with her left hand resting on a ledge, her head turned back to the left; in the lower right corner, a small drapery study. 393 x 217, red chalk squared. Fig. 268.

Bibliography: Ferri 1890, 116; Jacobsen 1898, 279; Berenson 1903, no. 1973; *MPA* 1910, 23; Gamba 1912, no. 16, pl. 16; Clapp 1914, 96; Clapp 1916, 47, fig. 88; Voss 1920, 170, fig. 50; Voss 1928, 45, pl. 5; Popham 1931, no. 231, pl. 195; Berenson 1938, no. 1973; *MDF* 1939, 25; *MC* 1940, 44; Toesca 1943, 14, fig. 22; Becherucci 1944, 19, fig. 44; *MDM* 1954 (Marcucci), no. 53, fig. 11; *EMI* 1954, no. 73, fig. 13; Procacci 1958, 29, fig. 14; Berenson 1961, no. 1973, fig. 946.

Jacobsen first connected this drawing with the Virgin Annunciate. This extremely finished study for the figure gives support to the idea that the *Annunciation* was the last part of the chapel to be executed. The ornamentalism of line and complex elaboration of surface that is characteristic of many S. Felicita drawings is extended here as far as seems possible within such a refined manner of drawing. In this respect the drawing is closely related in style to the final study for the Hannover *St. Jerome* of ca. 1527–1528 (cat. 287), especially in its meticulous detail and in the exceptionally brilliant quality of the red chalk surface.

279 · Florence, Uffizi 6653F: Study for the Angel, *Annunciation.* Heavily draped figure moving in profile to the right. 391 x 215, black chalk over faint red chalk heightened with white, squared in red chalk; brown-yellow wash added by a later hand; W: Eagle. Fig. 266.

Bibliography: Ferri 1890, 118; Berenson 1903, no. 2145; *MPA* 1910, 23; Gamba 1912, 3; Clapp 1914, 208; Clapp 1916, 47, fig. 87; Voss 1920, 170, fig. 50; Voss 1928, 45, pl. 5; Berenson 1938, no. 2145; *MDF* 1939, 25; *MC* 1940, 44; Becherucci 1943, 9, pl. 23; Becherucci 1944, 19, fig. 44; *MDM* 1954 (Marcucci), no. 52; *EMI* 1954, no. 72.

Berenson first connected this drawing with the Angel. It is a final study for the figure, a pendant to cat. 278 except that it is executed in black rather than red chalk. Critical attention has been mainly focussed on the effects of luminosity in this drawing, Becherucci mentioning a prelude to Bernini. It is true that Pontormo was much concerned with light in the fresco and carried this interest to the point of setting up an ambiguous relation between the natural light from the window between the figures and the unreal luminosity of the angel. However, it would seem that in the drawing — and this is more apparent in the original than in the reproduction — the luminosity was suggested only by black chalk heightened with white. The wash appears to be a later addition. It is of a color never used by Pontormo, whose infrequent bistre washes are of a delicate greyish tonality, and it is applied with little consideration for the forms of the drawing, perhaps in an attempt to imitate the painting. For example, the arm and the drapery billowing behind it are rendered almost incoherent by the addition of the wash. The more dramatic light and shade effects produced by the use of wash appealed to the later sixteenth-century Florentine draughtsman, one of whom must have added the wash to this drawing and also reworked some of the outlines. Originally, this study was of a type familiar in Pontormo's drawings of the late twenties. It is a large study of a single figure in black chalk heightened with white similar to cat. 268 for the St. John of the *Deposition*, and to cat. 300 and 305, nude studies of ca. 1528.

Ca. 1527–1528. MADONNA AND CHILD WITH ST. JOHN. Florence, Uffizi 4347. III. Panel, 86 x 73 cm. Fig. 269.

Bibliography: Gamba 1907, 20–22, illustrated; Goldschmidt 1911, 46; Clapp 1916, 53, 145–146; Gamba 1921, 10, fig. 32; Venturi 1932, 154, fig. 88; Berenson 1936, 401; Toesca 1943, 16, fig. 30; Becherucci 1944, 20, fig. 54; Nicco Fasola 1947, 51, fig. 32; *MP* 1956 (Berti), no. 60, fig. 52.

According to the museum, this painting was already in the Tribuna of the Uffizi in 1589. It was discovered in 1907 in the Uffizi storerooms and first published by Gamba, who dated it 1530. Becherucci dated it 1529–1531 as associated with the Michelangelesque moment of the Pitti *Martyrdom*, while Berti placed it 1528–1530. However, it has generally been dated slightly earlier; by Clapp 1526–1528, by Gamba 1525–1528. Certainly a date of 1527–1528 seems most logical because of the close stylistic affinity with the work at S. Felicita. The Christ Child and the St. John are similar to their older counterparts in the *Deposition*, and the Madonna is closely related to the woman to the upper right in the *Deposition* and to the Angel of the *Annunciation*. The interweaving of curving rhythms, the composition that turns in on itself with mounting complexity, the refined agony of the expressions, the dreamlike gesture of the Christ, and the spaceless *ambiente* in which the complex of forms is suspended all suggest the style of S. Felicita.

Clapp and Berti have indicated that there is some dependence on Michelangelo's Doni tondo in this picture. The heroic Madonna type, the St. John, and the elaborate foreshortening are certainly symptomatic of Pontormo's revaluation of Michelangelo's early as well as his current works in the period toward 1530. However, possible recollections of other High Renaissance artists are also significant and suggest that at this time Pontormo restudied certain aspects of the classical style. Raphael's later Madonna paintings of the type of the *Madonna della Tenda* are a starting point within his style for this kind of Mannerist extension, while Leonardo's *Madonna with St. Anne* certainly provides an authority for the complex interweaving of forms in this picture. Since Pontormo's *St. Jerome* of this same date also depends to some extent on Leonardesque models, this period may have been a time when Pontormo investigated Leonardo's works especially with renewed interest.

STUDIES FOR THE MADONNA AND CHILD WITH ST. JOHN

280 · Florence, Uffizi 6697F *recto*: Studies for the Madonna, *Madonna and Child with St. John*, and other studies. (a) Partly draped man seen from behind turned to the left with his left arm extended; (b) underneath, bust of a woman leaning to the right; below, the draped upper arm restudied; (c) to the lower right on a smaller scale partly underneath, a standing figure holding a child and a figure in profile left; (d) in reverse direction in the upper right corner, a scene with ships and figures lying on a deck; (e) in the lower left corner, an undecipherable sketch. (*Verso*: Studies for the *Birthplate*, cat. 290.) 407 x 278, red chalk, sketches (a) and (e) in black chalk. Fig. 270.

Bibliography: Berenson 1903, no. 2181; Clapp 1914, 242–243; Fraenckel 1933, 170–172; Fraenckel 1935, 214, pl. 18; Berenson 1938, no. 2181; Grassi 1946, 42, fig. 14; *MP* 1956 (Marcucci), no. 128, fig. 118a.

Since the studies for the drapery and arm of the Madonna (b) are the only ones on this sheet that correspond to a painting, the drawing has been placed here in connection with the Uffizi picture. Clapp dated (b) 1518 as for a lost *Holy Family* that he thought was also drawn on the verso (actually a study for the Uffizi *Birthplate*). Marcucci thought sketch (b) was for the woman above to the left in the *Deposition*, a figure that is very close to this Madonna in pose. The nude study (a) has also been dated variously. Fraenckel placed it 1516 as a study for the figure to the far right of Andrea del Sarto's Scalzo *Baptism*. Clapp dated it 1518 as derived from the Scalzo figure. Marcucci and Grassi dated it 1524–1525 in the Certosa period. Any connection with the Andrea fresco is quite unconvincing, in addition to the fact that stylistically this nude cannot date before 1525 and is probably of the same date as sketch (b). Cat. 291 and 294 of the late twenties are nudes of the same general type and are drawn in the same manner as this figure. Sketch (c) was considered by Fraenckel to be connected with sketch (a) in that she believed it was for the group of figures in the woods in the background of the Scalzo *Baptism*. However, Clapp noted rightly that sketch (a) is for the figure to the right of sketch (c). This sketch seems to be an idea for a *Presentation in the Temple*. Sketches (d) and (e) are somewhat difficult to place, (d) perhaps depicting a naval battle. Clapp and Marcucci would date sketch (d) 1524 as after a German print, but there seems little cause to remove it in date from the rest of the sheet.

281 · Florence, Uffizi 6649F *recto*: Study for the Madonna, *Madonna and Child with St. John*. Seated nude boy turned to the right with his right hand to his chest; below on a larger scale, the right leg restudied. (*Verso*: Study for the *Madonna and Child with St. John*, cat. 282.) 250 x 167, red chalk; W: Crown. Fig. 271.

Bibliography: Berenson 1903, no. 2141; Clapp 1914, 205; Giglioli 1920, 36, illustrated; Berenson 1938, no. 2141; *MDF* 1939, 29; *MC* 1940, 48.

Clapp dated this study 1527–1532, but it was first connected with the painting by Giglioli, who dated it 1530. Here the figure of the Madonna, which was first sketched in part on cat. 280, is studied for the details of the pose from a nude boy model. This sheet is closely linked with three others of the S. Felicita period: cat. 286 and 287 for the *St. Jerome* and cat. 288 for the *Halberdier*. All are on the same small sheets of paper with the crown watermark and all are in the same delicate red chalk style. This ultrarefined manner is found also in several of the latest studies for the *Deposition*, notably cat. 274–277. This whole group of studies represents for us the momentary crystallization of Pontormo's mature style and marks the apogee of disembodied refinement in his draughtsmanship.

282 · Florence, Uffizi 6649F *verso*: Study for the Christ, *Madonna and Child with St. John*. Nude boy seated on the legs of another figure, indicated only by the right leg; below, the knees of the boy restudied. (*Recto*: Study for the *Madonna and Child with St. John*, cat. 281.) 250 x 167, red chalk. Fig. 272.

Bibliography: Berenson 1903, no. 2141; Clapp 1914, 205; Giglioli 1920, 36, illustrated; Berenson 1938, no. 2141.

Clapp unaccountably dated this side of the sheet ca. 1520, while placing the recto 1527–1532. Giglioli first connected these sketches with the Christ Child in the picture, dating them 1530. The drawing is after the same boy model that Pontormo had used for the Madonna's pose on the recto. The Child is drawn seated on the lap of the Madonna in the same pose as the figure in the picture except that his legs are crossed and the head is not shown.

Ca. 1527–1528. ST. JEROME IN THE WILDERNESS. Hannover, Landesgalerie. III. Panel, 105 x 80 cm (unfinished). Fig. 273.

Bibliography: Schuchhardt 1904, 120, no. 44; *MF* 1952, no. 10, fig. 10; Bertini 1952, 147, illustrated; Molajoli 1952, 369, fig. 1; *Hannover Cat.* 1954, no. 279; Oertel 1955, 111–120, figs. 1, 4, 7–8; Gamba 1956, 12.

According to the museum, this painting came to first the Kestner Museum, then the Städtische Gallerie from the collection of August Kestner (no. 134), where it was evidently attributed to Leonardo, although Schuchhardt lists it simply as Italian school. In 1951 it was found by Oertel in the storerooms of the museum and was shown for the first time as Pontormo at the Naples exhibition in 1952. While the catalogue of the museum allowed a broad dating of 1525–1530, Oertel proposed a date of 1525, emphasizing affinities with Pontormo's pre-S. Felicita style.[9] However, the painting undoubtedly belongs to the same stylistic moment as the S. Felicita *Annunciation* and the Uffizi *Madonna and Child with St. John*. The pose of the upper body and head is exactly that of the Uffizi Madonna in reverse (although it should be noted that Pontormo had earlier used a similar motive in the Certosa *Way to Golgotha* of ca. 1523). The way the figure is composed of serpentine curves, balanced on a point of drapery, and totally unrelated to any axis except its own is reminis-

[9] Oertel considered that strong, unconnected colors such as the red in this picture did not occur in Pontormo's work after the Certosa period. He also found a harshness of expression and nervous disquiet that he thought incompatible with the idealized *Deposition*. Furthermore, Oertel believed that Bronzino's *St. Benedict* (Badia) of ca. 1525–1526 was dependent on the *St. Jerome* and thus Pontormo's picture must date earlier. However, there is precedent for Bronzino's *St. Benedict* in Pontormo's drawings of the Certosa period (cf. cat. 198). Oertel also suggested a connection with the Christ in Dürer's *Agony in the Garden* woodcut (Bar. 6), but the relation between the two does not extend beyond a similarity in the position of the legs.

cent especially of the Angel of the *Annunciation*. Figures of this type did not occur in Pontormo's work before S. Felicita. The drapery behind the saint, which should locate it in space but does not, the singular tangential insertion of the lion's head to the side (cf. the self-portrait in the *Deposition*), and the curved space that allows the crucifix to appear in front of a figure already occupying the front plane of the picture are further links with Pontormo's style of the late twenties.

STUDIES FOR ST. JEROME
IN THE WILDERNESS

283 · Florence, Uffizi 6561F *recto*: Study for *St. Jerome*. Nude kneeling turned to the left looking out at the spectator. (*Verso*: Study for the same figure, cat. 284.) 225 x 164, red chalk. Fig. 274.

Bibliography: Berenson 1903, no. 2062; Clapp 1914, 155; Clapp 1916, 57, 61, fig. 121; Berenson 1938, no. 2062; *MP* 1956 (Marcucci), no. 132, fig. 161a.

Clapp dated this drawing ca. 1520 and Berenson thought it was for a St. John the Baptist looking into a fountain. Although it is remotely derived from Pontormo's earlier St. John the Baptist studies, such as cat. 163, the drawing is probably associated with the *St. Jerome*, as Marcucci has also seen. Here, although the legs are disposed almost as they are in the painting, the final pose of the torso has not yet been determined. This is a preliminary study for the general position of the figure, an experiment in the contrapposto of the torso and legs in which the left shoulder is pulled forward so that the figure twists violently and flexibly toward the spectator. In the draughtsmanship and movement of the figure we find a foretaste of Pontormo's boneless, pliable nudes of after 1530.

284 · Florence, Uffizi 6561F *verso*: Study for *St. Jerome*. Bust of a nude leaning forward to the left; above, part of a torso. (*Recto*: Study for the same figure, cat. 283.) 225 x 164, red chalk, torso in black chalk.

Bibliography: Berenson 1903, no. 2062; Clapp 1914, 155–156; Berenson 1938, no. 2062; *MP* 1956 (Marcucci), no. 132, fig. 161b.

Clapp dated this drawing ca. 1545 in spite of the fact that it is another study for the figure on the recto and is not notably different in style. Marcucci associated the sketch with the *St. Jerome*. Here the torso is very lightly sketched with the right shoulder forward as it will be in the following studies and in the painting.

285 · Florence, Uffizi 6638F *recto*: Study for *St. Jerome*. Half-length nude leaning forward to the left, his left hand raised to his chest. (*Verso*: Two nudes, cat. 302.) 265 x 196, black chalk. Fig. 275.

Bibliography: Berenson 1903, no. 2130; Clapp 1914, 198; Berenson 1938, no. 2130; *MP* 1956 (Marcucci), 102.

Both Berenson and Clapp thought this figure was reclining, Clapp connecting it with the soldier to the right of the Certosa *Resurrection*. As Marcucci has also seen, it is certainly the study following cat. 284 in the preparatory work for the *St. Jerome*. Here, with the emphasis on the flattened and exaggerated arc of the shoulders, Pontormo began to refine the pose and proportions of the figure away from nature in accord with his concept of the abstract design of the picture.

286 · Florence, Uffizi 6664F: Study for *St. Jerome*. Nude kneeling turned to the left with his left hand holding a stone to his chest, his right arm across his legs. 190 x 130, red chalk; sheet cut out around the figure; W: Crown. Fig. 276.

Bibliography: Berenson 1903, no. 2154; Clapp 1914, 216; Berenson 1938, no. 2154;

Oertel 1955, 116–117, fig. 5; *MP* 1956 (Marcucci), 102.

Berenson and Clapp connected this drawing with cat. 287, the final study for the *St. Jerome*. According to Oertel, who first associated it with the Hannover picture, this was Pontormo's first study after the model because of its spontaneity and its naturalness of proportions. While the drawing is certainly less elaborated than cat. 287, it is in no sense a first model study because considerable ornamental reformation of the limbs and idealization of the features has already occurred. This drawing belongs in style with a group of drawings of ca. 1527–1528 that are all in the same delicate red chalk manner: cat. 287, the final study for the figure, cat. 288 for the *Halberdier*, cat. 281–282, for the *Madonna and Child with St. John*; as well as cat. 274–277 for the *Deposition.*

287 · Florence, Uffizi 441F *recto*: Study for *St. Jerome*. Partly draped nude kneeling turned to the left with his left hand holding a stone to his chest, his right arm across his legs; under and behind the figure, draperies; to the left, the cardinal's hat; to the right, head of the lion. (*Verso*: Nude study, cat. 295.) 266 x 199, red chalk over faint black chalk, squared in red chalk; W: Crown. Fig. 277.

Bibliography: Ferri 1890, 116; Berenson 1903, no. 1968; *MPA* 1910, 37; Gamba 1912, no. 17, pl. 17; Clapp 1914, 91–92; Clapp 1916, 53–54, fig. 109; Meinhof 1931, 123, fig. 14; Berenson 1938, no. 1968; *MDF* 1939, 29; *MC* 1940, 48; Becherucci 1943, 10, pl. 24; Becherucci 1944, 19; *MF* 1952, 9; *Hannover Cat.* 1954, 122; Oertel 1955, 116–117, fig. 6; *MP* 1956 (Marcucci), no. 133, fig. 167a.

Berenson originally dated this important finished drawing 1520 or later, but Clapp placed it at the time of S. Felicita, a date that was generally accepted until the discovery of the Hannover picture. In his publication of the painting Oertel dated the drawing 1525. In support of his early dating he compared it with cat. 207 for the unexecuted *Nailing to the Cross* for the Certosa, finding the model the same in both drawings. While there is a general similarity in type between the Christ and the St. Jerome, Pontormo's frequent repetition of types cautions against the use of this argument in dating the *St. Jerome*. In any event, since the drawing, like the painting, is intimately associated with Pontormo's S. Felicita style, Oertel's early dating cannot be accepted. It is closely linked in draughtsmanship to cat. 274–277 for the *Deposition*, cat. 281–282 for the Uffizi *Madonna and Child with St. John*, and cat. 288 for the *Halberdier*. However, as a finished red chalk compositional study, it is also especially close to the final study for the S. Felicita Virgin Annunciate (cat. 278). In both drawings we find the same meticulous red chalk finish and preoccupation with a complex luminosity, the same intricate involvement of the draperies, as well as a line so calculated and refined as to be almost without independent energy. Marcucci has also accepted this traditional dating, placing the drawing toward 1530 and associating it with cat. 284–286 (but not cat. 283) as for the Hannover picture. However, she also includes cat. 170, an earlier *St. Jerome* project of ca. 1521, as part of the series.

The changes between this final study and the painting are subtle, but they are significant in determining the final steps in Pontormo's elaboration of the design. In the otherwise carefully finished drawing there is a single *pentimento* indicating that Pontormo intended to lower the original line of the head. In the painting, where the *pentimenti* are easily visible through the thin application of the paint, the reason for this change becomes clear. The major *pentimento* in the painting is the shift of the head down and forward to the left so that the angle between the head and the left shoulder is less abrupt and so that the head projects more boldly forward from the plane of the shoulders. To make even more dramatic the projection of the small head from the massive shoulders, their outlines have been extended slightly. Both *pentimenti* together constitute the final refinement of Pontormo's design, a last adjustment of the exaggerated arc of the shoulders that had been Pontormo's central preoccupation in the preparatory studies. The third *pentimento* in the painting also shows a change from the drawing. The right knee has been moved from its original position in toward the other knee and slightly down. This change creates at once a stronger contrast to the forceful projection of the left knee and, together with the other knee, a smaller pivot on which the top-heavy figure turns.

Berenson has rightly noted the connection between this composition and Leonardo's Vatican *St. Jerome*, a similarity that was surely the reason for the former attribution of the Hannover picture to Leonardo. However, even more indicative of Pontormo's renewed interest in Leonardo at this time is the close relation in the design of this figure to Leonardo's lost *Leda* (see Berenson 1938, nos. 1013A and 1020A, fig. 546), a composition that Pontormo has transformed into his own Mannerist idiom. Pontormo's earlier assimilation of Leonardo's style at the time of the Visdomini altar involved only the borrowing of certain effects of chiaroscuro and eccentricities of facial expression, but in compositions of his maturity such as the *St. Jerome* he saw the possibilities for Mannerist inversion and elaboration in Leonardo's compositions.

Ca. 1527–1528. PORTRAIT OF A HALBERDIER. New York, Chauncey Stillman Collection. II. Panel, 92 x 72 cm. Fig. 278.

Bibliography: Voss 1920, 174–175, fig. 53; Gamba 1921, 11, fig. 31; Mather 1922, 66–69, illustrated; Clapp 1923, 65–66, fig. 46; Giglioli 1926, 790–791; Venturi 1931, pl. 345; Venturi 1932, 172–174, fig. 102; Berenson 1936, 402; Steinbart 1939, 12; *N. Y. Exhib.* 1939, no. 287, fig. 28; Toesca 1943, 23, fig. 51; Becherucci 1944, 19, fig. 49; Alazard 1948, 150; *Indianapolis Exhib.* 1954, no. 11, fig. 11; *MP* 1956 (Berti), no. 64, fig. 56; Baldini 1956, 12; Marcucci 1956, 18–19, fig. 23; Keutner 1959, 149–150, 152, figs. 9, 11.

This portrait first appears in the Riccardi Collection, Florence, listed as Pontormo in an inventory of 1612.[10] It later belonged to Cardinal Fesch with an attribution to Bronzino. When this collection was dispersed in 1844, the picture was bought by Leroy d'Etiolles, who sold it in 1861 to Princess Mathilde Bonaparte. In the 1904 sale of Princess Mathilde's collection, it was bought by James Stillman as a Bronzino.[11]

[10] See Keutner 1959, 149–150, 152. The picture is described as "un ritratto della stessa grandezza [1 and ¼ *braccia*] si crede di mano di Jac.° dell' Ecc.mo Duca Cosimo quand' era giovanetto, con calze rosse, e berretta rossa, ed una picca in mano con arme a'canto, e giubbone bianco, e collana al' collo . . ." The size given is 15 cm smaller than the height of the *Halberdier*, but there is no doubt that it is the picture described. However, the identification of the subject as Duke Cosimo is probably an error (see p. 270).

[11] See L. H. George, *Catalogue des Tableaux Composant la Galerie de Feu S.E. le Cardinal Fesch* (Rome, 1844), no. 682; F. Masson, *Catalogue de la Collection de S.A.I. Madame la Princess Mathilde* (Paris, 1905), no. 53. At some point after it passed from the Riccardi Collection, the identification of the sitter as Duke Cosimo was dropped and the original attribution to Pontormo changed to Bronzino.

There has been a history of confusion in the literature concerning this painting. The primary difficulty has been the mistaken assumption that it is the *Portrait of Francesco Guardi* that Vasari (V/M, VI, 275) says Pontormo painted during the seige of Florence (1529–1530). Voss first attributed the picture to Pontormo as the Guardi portrait, an identification that was accepted by Gamba, Toesca, and Becherucci, among others. Even those, such as Clapp and Berti, who did not accept the Guardi identification have placed the picture about 1530, Marcucci dating it as late as 1530–1535. Mather also dated the portrait 1529–1530, but he satisfactorily disproved the identification of the sitter as Francesco Guardi. According to Vasari, the *Pygmalion and Galatea* (Florence, Palazzo Vecchio) was the cover for the *Francesco Guardi.* Since that picture measures 79 x 62 cm, it is clearly too small to cover the *Halberdier*. Still further error has resulted from the association with the *Halberdier* of a drawing that probably was for the lost *Francesco Guardi* (cat. 292) and with two drawings that are merely copies after the *Halberdier* (cat. A248 and A265).

More recently there has been an attempt by Keutner — based on the identification in the Riccardi inventory — to identify this picture as the *Portrait of Cosimo de' Medici* that Vasari says (V/M, VI, 282) Pontormo painted at the beginning of the work at Villa Castello. In order to be identifiable with that lost picture the portrait must not only resemble Cosimo at about age eighteen, but it must be consonant in style with Pontormo's other portraits in the thirties. First, and of primary importance, it is difficult to see in this youth any resemblance to Cosimo. (Cf. Pontormo's drawing of him in profile of ca. 1537, cat. 334; or the familiar likenesses of him by Bronzino, such as the half-length portrait in armor in the Uffizi.) Furthermore, this portrait is inseparable in style from the S. Felicita phase of Pontormo's development, years in which Cosimo was a child of seven to nine years. The elongated oval shapes of this figure are fitted together into a rhythmic sequence of curves that is infused with an overrefined elegance is perhaps even more decisive than in the Capponi Chapel itself. The figure has an extreme elongation and a formal rigidity that is similar to that of the figures in the Carmignano *Visitation.* The cold, rectangular surfaces of the stone architecture that in both pictures serves as a background for the figures, contributes to this effect. The *Halberdier*, and its preparatory study as well (cat. 288), would seem to fit perfectly into Pontormo's chronology at exactly the moment of the *Visitation.* It is quite unlikely that this portrait could have been painted, instead, in the middle thirties, close to the heavy and somber Philadelphia *Portrait of Alessandro de' Medici* of 1534–1535.

While at this moment we can make no definitive identification of the subject of the portrait, the cap brooch worn by the Halberdier[12] suggests a line of inquiry that may aid in dating the picture and identifying the sitter. Becherucci has suggested that the *Hercules and Anteus* design on the brooch was connected with Michelangelo's projects of 1525–1528 for a statuary group of the same subject.[13]

[12] For a discussion of Italian early sixteenth-century cap brooches, see J. Evans, *History of Jewellry*: 1100–1870 (London, 1953), 88–92, figs. 42, 43, 45b, 48. The one worn by the halberdier is close to the gold *repoussé* medallion in fig. 45b, but less elaborate. Benvenuto Cellini, *La Vita Scritta da lui medesimo*, ed. F. Tassi (Florence, 1829), I, 138, affirms the popularity of these ornaments: "Si usava in questo tempo alcune medagliette d'oro, che ogni signore e gentiluomo gli piaceva fare scolpire in esse un suo capriccio o impressa; e le portavano nella beretta. Di queste opere io ne fece assai, ed erano molto difficili a fare."

[13] Since Pontormo's portrait — and presumably

While this connection cannot be absolutely proved, the coincidence in date is certainly suggestive. Furthermore, the scene on the brooch may also be an indication of the sitter's name. Ercole, as the personification of *Fortitude*, would have been an appropriate ornament for any soldier's cap, yet there may have been a more personal meaning in the choice of subject. If the sitter's name was Ercole, he might possibly be identifiable with a Conte Ercole Rangone, who is mentioned in the accounts of the seige of Florence (1529–1530).[14] The soldier may actually have owned such a hat medal, or Pontormo may have invented it, possibly basing himself on Michelangelo's design, solely for the purpose of his portrait.

---

the brooch — date from the years ca. 1527–1528, it is possible that the design of the brooch is derived from his invention. Michelangelo's drawing in Oxford, Ashmolean Museum, cat. no. 317, shows a group that is identical (reversed) in every detail to the figures on the brooch. We know from Cellini (*ibid.*, 195–197), that it was common practice for the medallist to borrow designs from other artists and that Michelangelo supplied drawings for such medallions. Cellini himself made a medal for Federigo Ginori in 1528 showing *Atlas Holding up the World*, for which he asserts a Michelangelo design was considered and rejected.

[14] This identification was suggested (verbally) by S. J. Freedberg. See B. Varchi, *Storia Fiorentina*, ed. L. Arbib (Florence, 1838/41), I, 495; II, 210, 225 (references to the year 1529); S. Ammirato, *Istorie Fiorentine* (Florence, 1849), pt. II, 6, 140; C. Roth, *The Last Florentine Republic* (London, 1925), 230, 236.

STUDY FOR THE HALBERDIER

288 · Florence, Uffizi 6701F *recto*: Study for the *Halberdier*. Three-quarter length standing youth dressed in military costume and holding a lance in his right hand. (*Verso*: Nude study, cat. 304.) 209 x 169, red chalk; W: Crown. Fig. 279.

Bibliography: Ferri 1890, 119; Berenson 1903, no. 2184; *MPA* 1910, 22; Clapp 1914, 245; Clapp 1923, 65, fig. 48 (as Uffizi 463F); Giglioli 1926, 790–791; Venturi 1932, 174, fig. 103; Berenson 1938, 318, no. 2184, fig. 986; *MDF* 1939, 29; *MC* 1940, 49; Berenson 1954, pl. 50.

Clapp originally dated this drawing 1531 as for a lost portrait, but he later was the first to associate it with the *Halberdier*, dating both toward 1530. This study corresponds with the painting except that the figure has been turned from a frontal to a three-quarter view in the painting. This change brings the lance into play as a diagonal deviation from the axis of the figure, pushes the hilt of the sword forward out of the picture, and focusses attention on the wide sweep of the luxurious sleeve. Against the slight turn of the figure, the full-face is more effective than it is in the drawing, where it is not so dramatically accented by the composition. The style of this drawing, even without its association with the portrait, indicates a date of ca. 1527–1528. It belongs with a group of red chalk studies on the same paper that are all executed in the ultrarefined red chalk manner of the S. Felicita period (cat. 281–282, 286–287; see also cat. 274–277 for the *Deposition*).

Ca. 1528. VISITATION. Carmignano, Pieve. I. Panel, 202 x 156 cm. Fig. 280.

Bibliography: Gamba 1904, 13–18, fig. 1; Goldschmidt 1911, 10, 43, pl. 3; Clapp 1916, 55, 106–107, fig. 111; Gamba 1921, 10, fig. 34; Venturi 1932, 170–172, fig. 101; Berenson 1936, 401; Steinbart 1939, 8; *MC* 1940, 42, fig. 21; Toesca 1943, 16, fig. 31; Becherucci 1944, 19, fig. 45; Nicco Fasola 1947, 50–51, fig. 33; *MP* 1956 (Berti), no. 61, fig. 53.

The *Visitation* is mentioned by Cinelli

1677, 286, as in the villa of the Pinadori in Carmignano. Therefore, it is likely that it was painted for the Pinadori family and came only later to the church in Carmignano. The picture has generally been dated ca. 1528–1530, except by Goldschmidt, who placed it 1536, and the 1940 exhibition, where it is unaccountably dated 1525. The style of this painting is that of S. Felicita; more precisely, of the moment just subsequent to the *Deposition*. Like the *Annunciation*, there is a faintly perceptible shift toward a more crystalline conception in which the figures seem literally transfixed. This effect is heightened by the rectilinear forms of the architecture that give the scene a specific setting and tend to arrest slightly the continuous slow movement that was the essence of the *Deposition*. The figures themselves are more elegant and attenuated, and, if possible, still more transluscent than those in the Capponi Chapel.

Clapp noted that this group was derived from Dürer's *Four Naked Women* (1497, Bar. 75). There is certainly an exploitation of that composition in Pontormo's *Visitation*, although the *Visitation* from Dürer's *Life of the Virgin* (Bar. 84) is equally important as a source.

STUDY FOR THE VISITATION

289 · Florence, Uffizi 461F: Compositional study for the Carmignano *Visitation*. The Virgin and St. Elizabeth stand facing each other in profile; behind them, two attendant women facing forward; in the background, a street with buildings with a doorway and steps to the right. 327 x 240, black chalk heightened with white, squared in red chalk; W: Eagle. Fig. 281.

Bibliography: Ferri 1890, 116; Berenson 1903, no. 1980; Gamba 1904, 13, fig. 2; *MPA* 1910, 34; Clapp 1914, 104–105; Clapp 1916, 55, fig. 112; Panofsky 1927, 47, fig. 6; Berenson 1938, no. 1980; *MDF* 1939, 25; *MC* 1940, 44, fig. 104; Toesca 1943, 16, fig. 32; *MF* 1952, 63; *MDM* 1954 (Marcucci), no. 54; *EMI* 1954, no. 75; Berenson 1961, no. 1980, fig. 948.

This drawing was recognized as a compositional study for the *Visitation* by Gamba, who dated it toward 1530. Clapp placed it 1528–1530. The style of this drawing is further reason for placing the *Visitation* as early as 1528. The Virgin, in type, is identical to the Virgin Annunciate in cat. 278 for the S. Felicita *Annunciation*. As in the compositional study for the *Deposition* (cat. 272), also in black chalk heightened with white, the foreground figures are modelled in great detail as they will be in the painting. However, also as in cat. 272, the other figures are more summarily indicated, occasionally with differences from the final composition. The attendant to the left is quite different from the figure in the painting. In the drawing she leans away from the other figures to the left covering the perspective view along the street that makes a setting for the group in the painting. With the slight change in the position of this figure in the painting, the four women become a more compact and self-contained group that floats in front of the severe architectural background. Finally, as we find so often in Pontormo's drawings, the facial expressions of the two attendant figures betray an agitation and disquiet that is masked over in the final painted version.

Clapp and Marcucci have identified this drawing as the "modello . . . in piccolo" for the *Visitation* that Cinelli 1677, 286, mentions as belonging to Andrea Pitti. However, the differences between this drawing and the painting are such that it seems unlikely that this was actually the final *modello* for the painting. Perhaps another drawing, like the painting in all details, belonged to Pitti but has not survived.

Ca. 1529. BIRTHPLATE: *The Naming of St. John the Baptist.* Florence, Uffizi 1532. III. Wood, 54 cm diameter. Fig. 282.

Bibliography: Goldschmidt 1911, 46; Schubring 1915, 407; Clapp 1916, 57, 140–141, fig. 114; Gamba 1921, fig. 30; Venturi 1932, 164, fig. 96; Berenson 1936, 401; Toesca 1943, fig. 29; Becherucci 1944, 18; Nicco Fasola 1946, 46, fig. 16; Nicco Fasola 1947, 50, fig. 30; *Amsterdam Exhib.* 1955, no. 93, fig. 1 and back cover; *MP* 1956 (Berti), no. 53, fig. 43; Baldini 1956, 11, fig. 12.

It is generally agreed that the arms on the reverse of Pontormo's *Birthplate* are those of the Della Casa and Tornaquinci families. According to Becherucci, the plate was commissioned for the birth in 1526 of Aldighieri della Casa, first son of Girolamo della Casa and Lisabetta di Giovanni Tornaquinci, who were married in 1521. Gamba, Berti, and Baldini agreed with this dating, while Toesca and Clapp dated the *Birthplate* 1529–1530.

In spite of the birth of a child to this family in 1526, the dating of this work before S. Felicita, or even during the beginning of the S. Felicita period, is not entirely convincing. There remains the possibility that it was ordered for the birth, or expected birth, of a later child. The style of this panel reflects the break away from Pontormo's S. Felicita style that occurs on a more monumental scale in the Louvre altar,[15] the tondo at the bottom of the altar providing a direct comparison for Pontormo's handling of small-scale figures ca. 1529. In the altar and in the *Birthplate* we find the same relaxed rhythms, the same listless movement of brittle figures, the same luminosity that makes the forms seem even less substantial. Both pictures are conceived as heraldic compositions with framing profiles at the sides. The St. Elizabeth and the St. Anne, the St. Benedict and the St. Zachary, the St. Philip and the profile figure to the right of the *Birthplate* are identical types. In the Louvre picture Pontormo recalled the classical compositional formula developed by Fra Bartolommeo in his altarpieces; here, he adapts into his own rhythmic style an almost contemporary composition by his former master, Andrea del Sarto. Andrea's Scalzo *Naming of the Baptist* of 1526 is clearly the source of Pontormo's composition and provides a *terminus post quem* for the *Birthplate.*

STUDY FOR THE BIRTHPLATE

290 · Florence, Uffizi 6697F *verso*: Study for the woman with the child and the wo-

[15] *Madonna and Child with St. Anne, St. Peter, St. Sebastian, St. Benedict, and St. Philip* (Paris, Louvre 1240; panel, 228 x 176 cm). According to Vasari, who mentions this altar after the Capponi Chapel (V/M, VI, 272–273), the picture was commissioned by the Signoria for the nuns of S. Anna a Verzaia. The scene in the tondo depicts a yearly commemoration, which took the form of a procession of the Signoria to the convent, of a rebellion that occured on St. Anne's day (July 26) in 1343. Berenson 1896, 127, and Goldschmidt 1911, 47, interpreted this to mean that the picture was painted for the 200th anniversary of the rebellion, and dated it 1543. Gamba 1912, 3, dated it 1534; Becherucci 1944, 18, dated it 1527; and Clapp 1916, 51–53, 167–169, fig. 104, dated it 1528. Since the picture was executed after the Capponi Chapel and the convent for which it was painted was destroyed September 21, 1529 (see Moreni 1791/95, IV, 25), it is likely that it was commissioned for the St. Anne's day celebration of 1529 and delivered to the convent shortly before the nuns were forced to vacate, taking their possessions with them. They occupied several buildings before the church of S. Anna sul Prato, where the altar was seen by Cinelli, 1677, 211; and, among others, Richa 1754/62, IV, 222. There are no surviving studies for this important work. Cat. A43 and A167 are copies after a lost compositional study for the altar.

man to the left, *Naming of St. John the Baptist*. Seated draped woman leaning over a child held to the right; behind, vague indications of other figures; below right, bust in profile right of a woman with drapery over her head; sideways on the sheet, two profiles of men. (*Recto*: Studies for the *Madonna and Child with St. John*, cat. 280.) 407 x 278, black chalk, the bust and the scribbles to the left in red chalk; inscribed: *Fran^co Rosi 268*. Fig. 283.

Bibliography: Berenson 1903, no. 2181; Clapp 1914, 243; Berenson 1938, no. 2181; *MP* 1956 (Marcucci), no. 128, fig. 159b.

Berenson, Clapp, and Marcucci have called this sheet a study for a *Holy Family*, Clapp dating it ca. 1518, Marcucci 1528–1530. While the crouched woman and child do suggest the *Holy Family* subject, the group is extremely close to the woman and child in the center of the *Birthplate*, even though the position of the child is shifted somewhat in the painting. A further link with the *Birthplate*, noted also by Marcucci, is the draped profile bust at the lower right, a figure that occurs to the left of the composition. The profiles of the old man that are drawn sideways on the sheet are, as has been remarked, Leonardesque, and are a further indication of Pontormo's renewed interest in Leonardo at this time. In style, this drawing is indicative of the complex changes from Pontormo's extremely refined draughtsmanship of the S. Felicita period in the years immediately following his work in the Capponi Chapel. The nervous searching for forms and the agitated, nondescriptive hooked strokes suggest a new tendency in Pontormo's development. However, in its angular freedom of handling and eccentricity of form, this study is an isolated phenomenon in this period. It is possible that it represents a significant aspect of Pontormo's draughtsmanship at this time, although no other studies of this genre have survived.

Marcucci considered this drawing most interesting as a document of Pontormo's interest in Michelangelo about 1528. She found the woman and child group closely dependent on the Medici *Madonna*. While there was certainly some connection with Michelangelo's sculpture, Marcucci's other comparisons with Michelangelo are not convincing. She compared this drawing with Louvre 4112 (see Berenson 1938, no. 1599, fig. 627), Louvre 110, and British Museum cat. 31. The first is not by Michelangelo, the second is a much earlier Michelangelo drawing and not conspicuously connected, and the last is a study for the Child of the Medici *Madonna* in a somewhat similar pose to the child in the *Birthplate*, but not to the one in this drawing.

1529–1530. PYGMALION AND GALATEA. Florence, Palazzo Vecchio. II. Panel, 81 x 60 cm (with Bronzino). Fig. 284.

Bibliography: Morelli 1892, 130; Goldschmidt 1911, 31, 55; Clapp 1916, 56, 182–183; Tinti 1920, 6; Voss 1920, 207; Gamba 1921, 11, fig. 42; McComb 1928, 78–79; Berenson 1936, 402; Becherucci 1944, 43; Smyth 1949, 204; Becherucci 1949, 2, fig. 2; Smyth 1955, 103–107; Emiliani 1960, 62, pl. 7–9.

Vasari attributes this painting to Bronzino as the cover of Pontormo's *Portrait of Francesco Guardi*.[16] Vasari does not

[16] V/M, VI, 275: "Ritrasse similmente, nel tempo dell'assedio di Fiorenza, Francesco Guardi in abito di soldato, che fu opera bellissima: e nel coperchio poi di questo quadro dipinse Bronzino, Pigmalione che fa orazione a Venere, perchè la sua statua, ricevendo lo spirito, s'avviva e divenga . . . di carne e d'ossa." Pontormo's portrait has been lost or destroyed. Unsuccessful attempts

repeat this attribution in his life of Bronzino, and the picture is not mentioned in the other early accounts. It was formerly in the Barberini Collection (no. 83), where it was attributed to Peruzzi, according to Morelli. Morelli gave it to Pontormo, an attribution that was accepted by Berenson and Gamba, while Clapp and McComb considered it a collaboration in which Pontormo was responsible for the figures. On the other hand, Goldschmidt, Tinti, Voss, Becherucci, Smyth, and Emiliani all accepted Vasari's statement that Bronzino executed the picture. However, it is not impossible that Vasari, misinterpreting his friend Bronzino's account, gave to him the entire execution of a picture for which he was only partially responsible. While the landscape and background accessories are admittedly Bronzinesque (cf. the landscape in the Hermitage *Apollo and Marsyas* of ca. 1531), the figures are quite consonant with Pontormo's style in 1530 and the color recalls specifically his Pitti *Martyrdom* of this same year. Details such as the singular distortion of Galatea's left hand are uniquely Pontormesque (cf. the pointing hand of St. Benedict in the Louvre altar). The tightly wound drapery of both figures is like the involved draperies of the King and the foreground figure in the Pitti *Martyrdom*. The precise indication of muscular patterns and the play of light on the flesh finds its parallel only in Pontormo's Michelangelesque nudes in the *Martyrdom* and never in Bronzino at this early date. However, in contrast to the spaceless and timeless world of Pontormo's pictures of 1526–1528, there is here and in the *Martyrdom* a reassertion of stability in the precise definition of locale. Accessories are multiplied as if in an attempt to give the image a concrete reality that its structure denies. The participation of Bronzino in the execution of the background would only serve to intensify this effect of discordance between the compositional and spatial illogic of the picture and the exact description of its parts.

The subject, which corresponds exactly with Vasari's description, is taken from Ovid, *Metamorphoses* X, 246–298. The figure of Galatea is derived from the same Venus Pudique type that appeared much earlier in Pontormo's drawing (cat. 15) of a *Venus and Cupid* and in the statue in the *Joseph in Egypt*. Here, while quoting the pose of the Venus in a statuary context, Pontormo has subtly altered it so that the figure is not harmoniously balanced like the Venus in cat. 15, but turns her head to stare out of the picture in a most unclassical manner. The altar in the background is a Mannerist fantasy on an antique relief of *Venus and Mars*.[17]

STUDY FOR PYGMALION AND GALATEA

291 · Florence, Uffizi 6742F *verso*: Study for Pygmalion, *Pygmalion and Galatea*. Nude standing in profile left leaning forward with his left leg bent back, his hands clasped in front of him; sideways on the sheet over the nude, a lunette with a circular window incised with a compass; under the window, two figures reclining with their backs turned; to the right, a crouched figure looking out at the spectator, the head leaning on the left hand; to the far left, a seated figure with legs crossed leaning forward looking out at

have been made to identify the *Halberdier* with this portrait, but it is larger than its supposed cover. Cat. 292–293 are probably Pontormo's studies for the *Francesco Guardi*.

[17] This part of the composition was almost certainly by Bronzino, who has indulged at this early date his penchant for incorporating sculptural motives (antique or otherwise) into his paintings. These herm figures are part of an imaginary composition, but such groups occurred in antique altars. See S. Reinach, *Répertoire de la Statuaire Grecque et Romaine* (Paris, 1930), I, 367, no. 6. A similar altar appears in Parmigianino's *Portrait of a Priest* of 1523 (Wrotham Park).

the spectator. (*Recto*: Nude study, cat. 305.) 400 x 265, black chalk, the lunette and small figures in red chalk. Fig. 285.

Bibliography: Berenson 1903, no. 2224; Clapp 1914, 271–272; Clapp 1916, 20, 30; Berenson 1938, no. 2224; *MP* 1956 (Marcucci), no. 117, fig. 148b.

Clapp and Berenson believed that this figure was connected with the St. Francis of the Visdomini altar of 1518. However, Marcucci rightly noted that the pose of the nude occurs repeatedly in Pontormo's work and that its style is far from that of the other Visdomini studies, such as the certain drawing for the St. Francis (cat. 48). While the pose of the nude recalls that of the St. Francis, it is clearly a study for the Pygmalion, to which it corresponds in motive (even though the nude does not actually kneel in the drawing), in type and proportions, and in the strong plastic accents of the draughtsmanship. It is closely related in style to a nude study for the Pitti *Martyrdom* of exactly the same date (cat. 294).

Clapp and Berenson thought that the lunette sketch was for the Poggio a Caiano lunette, while Marcucci found it indecipherable. However, the figures in this sketch are quite distinct (at least in the original drawing where the red chalk contrasts with the black chalk of the nude) and some connection with Poggio a Caiano is undeniable. It is possible that this sketch is a recollection of the *Vertumnus and Pomona* lunette, perhaps drawn at the time Pontormo was commissioned to paint the second lunette in 1532. The nervous and brittle drawing of these small figures is much like that of the *Birthplate* drawing (cat. 290) of ca. 1529.

STUDIES FOR THE PORTRAIT OF FRANCESCO GUARDI(?)

292 · Florence, Uffizi 463F *recto*: Study for the *Portrait of Francesco Guardi* (?). Three-quarter length standing man dressed in a soldier's costume, his left hand on the hilt of his sword, his right hand on his hip. (*Verso*: Studies for the same figure, cat. 293.) 253 x 204, black chalk; W: Fruit (cf. B. 7392). Fig. 286.

Bibliography: Ferri 1890, 117; Berenson 1903, no. 1982; *MPA* 1910, 21; Gamba 1912, no. 20, pl. 20; Clapp 1914, 106; Clapp 1916, 57, 85, fig. 120; Mather 1922, 69; Giglioli 1926, 790–791; Berenson 1938, 318, no. 1982, fig. 987; *MDF* 1939, 26; *MC* 1940, 51; Becherucci 1944, 21; Alazard 1948, 150.

Berenson and Clapp have called this drawing a study for the lost portrait of Francesco Guardi in soldier's costume that, according to Vasari (V/M, VI, 275), Pontormo painted during the seige of Florence (1529–1530). However, Mather believed it was for the *Halberdier*, Becherucci dated it ca. 1535 as close to Pontormo's self-portrait (cat. 331), and Gamba dated it 1530–1535. The costume of the sitter and the date indicated by the style of the drawing agree so exactly with Vasari's description that this drawing seems most likely to have been for the *Francesco Guardi*.[18] It is an excellent example of one kind of change in Pontormo's draughtsmanship toward 1530. In comparison with an analogous subject, the *Halberdier* study (cat. 288), there is a relaxation of the insistent rhythmic organization of the earlier

[18] It should be noted that in refuting the identification of Pontormo's *Halberdier* as Francesco Guardi, Keutner 1959, 148n33, cited a document that refers to a Francesco Guardi who was born on December 6, 1466, and would thus have been too old to fight as a soldier in the seige of Florence. Since there is no question of identifying the *Halberdier* with Pontormo's lost picture, this document has no bearing on that painting. Nor does it seem sufficient objection to admitting Vasari's statement (V/M, VI, 275) as evidence that there was a soldier bearing this name in 1529–1530 whom Pontormo painted. Furthermore, a Francesco di ser Battista Guardi is mentioned as a member of the new Signoria of 1529. See Varchi, *Storia Fiorentina*, I, 524.

drawing that leaves the parts somewhat separated, their individual identity becoming more important than their relation to the composition as a whole. The extremely delicate, refined line and transparent surface of the *Halberdier* drawing has given way to a harder, more isolating line and to a greater sense of substantial form. This type of drawing begins to resemble the portrait drawings of the thirties, such as cat. 324, 331, and 335.

293 · Florence, Uffizi 463F *verso*: Studies for the *Portrait of Francesco Guardi* (?). Three-quarter length standing man studied twice. (*Recto*: Study for the same figure, cat. 292). 253 x 204, black chalk squared. Fig. 287.

Bibliography: Ferri 1890, 117; Clapp 1914, 106.

These two preliminary studies for the pose of the soldier on the recto show the way in which Pontormo has first drawn the figure from the nude and then, in the other sketch, begun to visualize it in costume, but always with a vacancy of expression in the face that forecasts the depersonalization of his later portraits. This drawing shows a facet of Pontormo's style of the late twenties that is also seen in cat. 283 and 295. In these three drawings the line is limp and sinuous, quite without the tension and subtle complications of Pontormo's line in the S. Felicita drawings.

1529–1530. LEGEND OF THE TEN THOUSAND MARTYRS. Florence, Pitti 182. I. Panel, 65 x 73 cm.[19] Fig. 288.

Bibliography: Goldschmidt 1911, 8–9, 46, pl. 5; Clapp 1916, 53–54, 131–132, fig. 106; Gamba 1921, 10, fig. 41; Venturi 1932, 167–168, fig. 99; Berenson 1936, 401, Toesca 1943, 17; Becherucci 1944, 20, fig. 52; *MP* 1956 (Berti), no. 65, figs. 57–58.

This picture is discussed in some detail by Vasari, who says it was commissioned by the Hospital of the Innocents and was still there at the time of his writing.[20] Vasari's narrative clearly implies the date of the seige of Florence (1529–1530) for this picture. However, there have been minor variations in the interpretation of this passage, Clapp dating the picture 1528–1529, Berti 1530–1531. Stylistically the *Martyrdom* finds a logical niche in Pontormo's development between the Louvre altar, the *Pygmalion and Galatea*, and the Boldrone tabernacle on one hand, and the drawings for the second project at Poggio a Caiano (cat. 307–311) on the other. This was a moment of intensive Michelangelo research. There are reminiscences of the *Cascina* cartoon via the

[19] A copy after the *Martyrdom* (New Haven, Yale University; panel, 69 x 73 cm) shows that the original has been cut at the sides. See O. Sirén, *Catalogue of the Jarves Collection*, Yale University (New Haven, 1916), 200.

[20] V/M, VI, 274–275: In un quadro d'un braccio e mezzo fece alle donne dello spedale degl'Innocenti, in uno numero infinito di figure piccole, l'istoria degli undici mila Martiri, stati da Diocleziano condennati alla morte, e tutti fatti crucifiggere in un bosco: dentro al quale finse Jacopo una battaglia di cavalli e d'ignudi molto bella; ed alcuni putti bellissimi, che volando in aria avventano saette sopra i crucifissori. Similmente intorno all'imperadore che gli condanna sono alcuni ignudi, che vanno alla morte, bellissimi. Il qual quadro, che è in tutte le parti da lodare, è oggi tenuto in gran pregio da don Vincenzio Borghini, spedalingo di quel luogo e già amicissimo di Jacopo." Borghini 1584, 484, repeats Vasari's statement on the location of the picture, but Bottari (ed. Borghini, Florence, 1730, 395), notes that it was no longer at the hospital. However, Richa 1754/62, VIII, 130, lists it as still there. It was in the Pitti by 1828. See F. Inghirami, *La Galleria dei quadri di Palazzo Pitti* (Florence, 1834), no. 182.

earlier *Martyrs* drawing (cat. 195), on which part of this composition is based. These recollections are overlaid with fresh impressions of the Medici Tombs. A stylistic split is thus created within the picture by the up-to-date Michelangelisms that appear in the foreground (actually a platform that has been inserted between the spectator and the battle and martyrdom scenes) and the reminiscences of an earlier Michelangelo in the fighting figures. On this platform are the King, in pose a pastiche of the *Lorenzo de' Medici* and *Giuliano de' Medici* figures, and a man with his back turned whose sinuous contrapposto is dependent on the multidirectional movements of the tomb *Allegories*. The scene of the crucified martyrs at the upper right is also a new invention that did not appear in the earlier drawing; and, like the foreground group, is dependent on Perino del Vaga's earlier cartoon (see cat. 195). The figures in this part of the picture are delicate and brittle like those of the *Birthplate* and reveal a degree of elongation that is not found in the nudes of the battle scene, but only in Pontormo's style of the late twenties. Furthermore, the crucified figure to the right center refers specifically to the Christ in the Boldrone tabernacle of ca. 1528–1529.[21]

STUDY FOR THE LEGEND OF THE TEN THOUSAND MARTYRS

294 · Florence, Uffizi 6588F: Study for the man in the foreground, *Martyrdom*. Nude in profile right looking away and pointing into the distance with his right arm; to the right, a shoulder; below, bust of a man; to the left, neck and part of the head of a man looking down to the left. 375 x 260, black chalk; W: Greek cross in a circle (B. 5540); inscribed verso in ink: *Pontormo*. Fig. 290.

Bibliography: Berenson 1903, no. 2087; *MPA* 1910, 28; Clapp 1914, 169–170; Berenson 1938, 316, no. 2087, fig. 975; Grassi 1946, 42, fig. 12.

Berenson connected each of these studies with a figure in the S. Felicita *Deposition*, while Clapp dated the sheet 1530–1533, noting its generally Michelangelesque character. Grassi has rightly associated the figure with the man in the foreground of the *Martyrdom*. Although the precise movement of this nude is rather different from that of the man in the painting, the rhythm of his action, his heavily muscled, elongated proportions, and even his blowing hair are sufficiently close to the painted figure to justify the connection. This drawing is further evidence of Pontormo's study of the Medici Tombs. The slow, swelling movement and the torsion of the nude are reminiscent of the *Aurora*, while the head at the left is drawn after the *Notte*. The study of a head at the lower right may have been an idea for the King's head in the *Martyrdom* painting.

MISCELLANEOUS DRAWINGS CA. 1526–1530

295 · Florence, Uffizi 441F *verso*: Ca. 1528–1529. Nude lying face down look-

[21] *Crucifixion with St. John and the Virgin, St. Julian and St. Augustine* (Florence, Forte di Belvedere, formerly Boldrone; detached fresco, center, 307 x 175 cm, sides each 275 x 127 cm). Vasari (V/M, VI, 272) mentions this work directly after the Capponi Chapel, which was finished in 1528. However, his comment on its Düreresque qualities has persuaded most authors to date it before the Capponi Chapel. Becherucci 1944, 17–18, figs. 38–39, dated it 1525; Berti, *MP* 1956, nos. 42–44, figs. 34–36, before 1525; Sanminiatelli 1956, 242, as early as 1520–1521. However, Clapp 1916, 44–45, 103–104, placed it 1526–1527; and Gamba 1921, 10, figs. 37–39, has seen that it is very close in style to the Louvre altar and must date 1528–1530. Like the Louvre altar, this work reveals the return to a more traditional scheme of composition and a general simplification of style that is one facet of Pontormo's development after S. Felicita.

ing out at the spectator. (*Recto*: Study for *St. Jerome*, cat. 287.) 199 x 266, red chalk. Fig. 289.

Bibliography: Ferri 1890, 116; Berenson 1903, no. 1968; Gamba 1912, 3; Clapp 1914, 92; Clapp 1916, 54, fig. 110; Berenson 1938, no. 1968; *MP* 1956 (Marcucci), no. 133, fig. 152b.

Gamba dated this study in the late twenties, Clapp ca. 1528, Marcucci just after S. Felicita. This nude study certainly belongs about 1528–1529 on the basis of its similarity in style to cat. 283 for the *St. Jerome* and cat. 293 for the lost *Portrait of Francesco Guardi.*

296 · Florence, Uffizi 6519F *verso*: Ca. 1526–1528. Fragment of drapery. (*Recto*: Study for S. Felicita, cat. 264.) 142 x 215, red chalk.

Bibliography: Clapp 1911, 8; Clapp 1914, 128; Clapp 1916, 32; Berenson 1938, no. 2024; *MP* 1956 (Marcucci), no. 121, fig. 150b.

Clapp thought this drapery study was for the Pomona in the Poggio a Caiano lunette, while Marcucci dated it 1525 as associated with S. Felicita. This slight study surely belongs in date with its recto. The luminous red chalk draughtsmanship is typical of the S. Felicita drawings and this is probably one of the many drapery studies that Pontormo must have made at that time.

297 · Florence, Uffizi 6537F: Ca. 1529. Cast of drapery over an extended right arm. 235 x 113, red chalk. Fig. 294.

Bibliography: Berenson 1903, no. 2040; Clapp 1914, 138–139; Berenson 1938, no. 2040.

Clapp dated this study 1516–1520, while Berenson connected it specifically with the figure on the extreme left of the *Joseph in Egypt* of 1518–1519. The drawing is difficult to place, but its connection with the pre-1520 period is not convincing. It is more careful and calculated than any red chalk study of those years and for this reason belongs in the twenties, probably toward the end of the decade. Although the exact motive is not to be found in the fresco, the elaborate piling up of the stiff, heavy folds with deep shadows between them, as well as the shape and gesture of the hand suggests the style of the Boldrone tabernacle of ca. 1528–1529; in particular, the figure of St. Julian.

298 · Florence, Uffizi 6604F *recto*: Ca. 1529–1530. Nude seated turned to the left but pointing forward to the right. (*Verso*: Nude study, cat. 299.) 412 x 256, black chalk heightened with white; W: Eagle. Fig. 291.

Bibliography: Berenson 1903, no. 2103; *MPA* 1910, 28; Clapp 1914, 180–181; Berenson 1938, 310, no. 2103, fig. 946.

Berenson originally considered this drawing to be for Poggio a Caiano and Clapp also dated it 1520, noting the similarity in pose to cat. 143 for the lunette. Berenson later (1938) rightly concluded that the drawing was more mannered than the Poggio a Caiano drawings and suggested that it might have been for the later, unexecuted lunette. While it cannot be connected with the second lunette without further evidence, this nude is a characteristic study of the post-S. Felicita years. In its extremely refined curvilinear organization and detailed modelling it is close in style to cat. 294 for the Pitti *Martyrdom* of 1529–1530. Conceivably, it might have been a part of Pontormo's preparation for the figure of the King in the *Martyrdom*, a figure whose pose and pointing gesture are not far removed from those of this nude.

299 · Florence, Uffizi 6604F *verso*: Ca. 1529–1530. Nude seen from behind looking over his right shoulder. (*Recto*: Nude study, cat. 298.) 412 x 256, black chalk heightened with white.

Bibliography: Berenson 1903, no. 2103; Clapp 1914, 181; Berenson 1938, no. 2103. (Photo G.)

Neither Berenson nor Clapp suggested a date for this drawing. This nude study is identical in style to its recto and to cat. 294 for the Pitti *Martyrdom* of 1529–1530. Like its recto, it was probably connected with that picture, although the exact motive is not to be found in the painting.

300 · Florence, Uffizi 6610F: Ca. 1526–1528. Nude stepping down from a rock and bending over in profile to the right. 340 x 257, black chalk heightened with white; left lower corner replaced.
Fig. 293.

Bibliography: Berenson 1903, no. 2109; *MPA* 1910, 33; Clapp 1914, 184; Berenson 1938, no. 2109; Schlegel 1961, 32, fig. 2.

Clapp dated this study ca. 1520, grouping it with cat. 298 and 305, both of the late twenties. There is no connection with Pontormo's vigorous early style in this drawing, with its slowly pulled-out contours, extremely refined modelling, and graceful curvilinear organization of the forms. While cat. 298 may be slightly later, this drawing and cat. 305 are closely related, even to the use of the same model, to the drawing for the St. John of the S. Felicita *Deposition* (cat. 268). It is tempting to connect this study with the preparation for one of the figures who leans down from above in the *Deposition*, although there is no trace of the motive in the painting.

301 · Florence, Uffizi 6627F *verso*: Ca. 1526–1528. Page from a sketchbook: Sketch of a left shoulder. (*Recto*: Study for S. Felicita, cat. 274.) 202 x 140, black chalk on pink prepared paper.

Bibliography: Clapp 1914, 192. (Photo G.)

This very minor sketch is datable with its recto, but it is too slight to be associated with any pictorial motive.

302 · Florence, Uffizi 6638F *verso*: Ca. 1526–1530. Nude standing facing forward and holding the head of a figure crouched in front of him that is seen only to the shoulders. (*Recto*: Study for *St. Jerome*, cat. 285.) 265 x 196, red chalk; inscribed: [Franco] *Rosi 180*.

Bibliography: Berenson 1903, no. 2130; Clapp 1914, 198; Berenson 1938, no. 2130; *MP* 1956 (Marcucci), 103. (Photo G.)

Marcucci suggested that this drawing might be connected with the *Nudes Playing Calcio* (cat. 307) of 1532–1534, while Clapp dated it ca. 1535 as possibly for a *Sacrifice of Isaac*. Clapp's designation of the subject is surely correct, but the drawing most likely dates with its recto. Although it is only a light outline sketch, it is close in its loose, rhythmic style to cat. 283–284 for *St. Jerome*, and to cat. 293, for the *Portrait of Francesco Guardi*.

303 · Florence, Uffizi 6666F *verso*: Ca. 1526–1528. Draped torso of a man turned to the left with his left hand on his hip. (*Recto*: Study for S. Felicita, cat. 269.) 165 x 146, red chalk; inscribed in black chalk across the figure: *14*.

Bibliography: Berenson 1903, no. 2156; Clapp 1914, 217; Berenson 1938, no. 2156. (Photo G.)

Neither Clapp nor Berenson dated this study. The drapery folds are similar to those in the studies for the *Deposition* and the brilliant handling of the red chalk is the same as that of the recto, a study for the *Deposition*. This drawing is clearly a study for a portrait contemporary with

S. Felicita. It is conceivable that it may be a study for the drapery of the left arm of the *Halberdier* of 1527–1528, but the relation is not close enough to associate it definitely with the painting.

304 · Florence, Uffizi 6701F *verso*: Ca. 1528–1530. Three-quarter length nude seen almost from behind with his head turned away and leaning on his left arm. (*Recto*: Study for the *Halberdier*, cat. 288.) 209 x 169, red chalk.

Bibliography: Berenson 1903, no. 2184; Clapp 1914, 245–246; Berenson 1938, no. 2184. (Photo G.)

Clapp dated this drawing 1530–1535, comparing it in pose to cat. 170, for a *St. Jerome* of ca. 1521. The pose is similar to that of the *St. Jerome*, but it is difficult to associate this drawing in style with the Poggio a Caiano period. The elongated proportions, sinuous flexibility of the torso, and the patterning of the muscles suggest the period towards 1530. Some of the nudes in the Pitti *Martyrdom* of 1529–1530 (cf. especially the group in the lower left corner of the picture) are very close to this figure both in motive and in the dry, exaggerated handling of the modelling. However, this exact figure does not appear in the painting.

305 · Florence, Uffizi 6742F *recto*: Ca. 1526–1528. Nude seated on a rock turned to the left with his hands to the right. (*Verso*: Study for *Pygmalion and Galatea*, cat. 291.) 400 x 265, black chalk heightened with white. Fig. 292.

Bibliography: Berenson 1903, no. 2224; *MPA* 1910, 33; Clapp 1911, 20; Clapp 1914, 271; Berenson 1938, no. 2224; *MP* 1956 (Marcucci), no. 117, fig. 148a; Marcucci 1956, 17, fig. 21.

Berenson thought this drawing was a study for the Evangelist of the Visdomini altar, Clapp dated it ca. 1520 as derived from the Ignudo to the left of the Delphic Sibyl of the Sistine Ceiling, while Marcucci rightly connected it in style with cat. 268 for the S. Felicita *Deposition*, dating it 1525. This drawing is one of a group of three black chalk studies after the same model, one of which is cat. 268, the other cat. 300. The type, with the long arms and curved legs, expressive face and flying hair, is the same in all three drawings and the forms are organized according to an ornamental principle that was operative only at this period in Pontormo's drawings. In the study for the angel of the S. Felicita *Annunciation* (cat. 279, a drawing that was like this one in style before the addition of the wash) there is the same reformation of the figure into long oval shapes, the same absence of a weight-support relation between these shapes, and the same tapering of the composition to a point. It is even possible, in view of the similarities, that this drawing was a discarded early model study for the Virgin Annunciate in the same fresco.

306 · Florence, Horne Foundation 5542: Ca. 1528–1530. Study for a self-portrait. Bust of a man with a small beard wearing a hat. 121 x 83, red chalk on pink prepared paper; laid down. Fig. 295.

Collection: Horne, stamp recto (L. 1266C).

Comparison with the known self-portraits by Pontormo [22] can only lead to the conclusion that this unpublished drawing is also a likeness of Pontormo. The pose is the characteristic pose of the self-portrait, with the artist looking directly at

[22] See note 16 on p. 112 for a listing of the portraits of Pontormo. See especially the picture from the Contini-Bonacossi Collection (panel, 52 x 37 cm), a damaged self-portrait that is similar to this drawing in likeness and in pose and may have been done a few years after it. Berti 1956, 12, fig. 11, suggested that Naldini painted this picture after 1550 based on an earlier likeness of Pontormo.

the spectator (himself) over his right shoulder. If this likeness is compared with the *Deposition* self-portrait and its drawing (cat. 277), it is evident that the features and the approximate age of the sitter are the same. However, these two studies of the same face are quite different in character and purpose. The Horne drawing is the most straight-forward of Pontormo's likenesses of himself, while the likeness in cat. 277 is used only as a starting point and the features are completely reformed in order to accommodate them to the unique cursive style of the *Deposition.* In style this drawing is close in its delicate red chalk draughtsmanship to the S. Felicita head studies (cat. 274–275, 277), but it is distinctly more crystalline in form, the contours are slightly harder and less flexible, and the chiaroscuro not quite as subtle. For these reasons this drawing might be placed very close to 1530.

PART V · 1530–1545

Catalogue entries 307–346

PART V · 1530–1545

STUDIES FOR NUDES PLAYING CALCIO 1532–1534

307 · Florence, Uffizi 13861F: Compositional study for a *Nudes Playing Calcio*, Poggio a Caiano, 1532–1534. To the right, a group of three players; behind them to the left, two embracing players; behind further to the left, a player kicking the ball; behind him further to the left, four players jumping for the ball; to the far left, a player runs forward; in the left foreground, two players leaning over with heads touching (helping up a fallen player?). 394 x 695, black chalk on heavy brown paper; laid down; sheet rubbed and torn. Fig. 296.

Collection: Lodovico Capponi (?).

Bibliography: Clapp 1911, 15; Clapp 1914, 283–284; Clapp 1916, 58–62; Berenson 1938, no. 2240C; Becherucci 1944, 21; *MP* 1956 (Marcucci), 103.

Clapp recognized this drawing as a study for one of the three frescoes that Pontormo planned for Poggio a Caiano but never executed. According to Vasari, after the seige of Florence Clement VII directed Ottaviano de' Medici to have the *Salone* of Poggio a Caiano completed. Franciabigio and Andrea del Sarto, who had worked with Pontormo on the original frescoes, were dead, and the whole commission was given to Pontormo.[1] In his life of Franciabigio Vasari says that the commission was given to Pontormo by Duke Alessandro in 1532.[2] Pontormo made the cartoons but had not yet executed any of the frescoes when the project was abandoned after the death of Clement VII (September 25, 1534).[3] Confirmation for the dating of the project is found in the dependence of a study for one of the *calcio* players (cat. 308) on Michelangelo's *Tityus* drawing, executed for Cavalieri late in 1532.[4] In spite of the ample evidence in favor of 1532–1534 as the years in which Pontormo made the Poggio a Caiano cartoons, the *Nudes Playing Calcio* has been dated 1531–1533 by Clapp, 1530–1532 by Marcucci.

Vasari is quite explicit on the subjects of the projected frescoes (V/M, VI, 276): ". . . in uno de' quali cartoni, che sono oggi per la maggior parte in casa di Lodovico Capponi, è un Ercole che fa scoppiare Anteo; in un altro, una Venere e Adone; ad in una carta, una storia d'ignudi che giuocano al calcio." The last subject mentioned is identifiable with this drawing. There is no easy explanation for this unusual choice of subject, which has no evident relation to either the Roman historical themes of the earlier frescoes at Poggio a Caiano or to the mythological subjects of the other cartoons that Vasari

---

[1] V/M, VI, 275–276. The seige ended August 12, 1530 and Andrea died in September 1530.

[2] V/M, V, 196: "Ma questa opera [Poggio a Caiano] per la morte di Leone rimase imperfetta, e poi fu di commissione del duca Alessandro de' Medici, l'anno 1532, ricominciata da Jacopo da Puntormo; il quale la mandò tanto per la lunga, che il duca si morì, ed il lavoro resto a dietro."

[3] V/M, VI, 276. Vasari blames Pontormo's lack of progress on the fact that his pupil Bronzino was not there to help him. Actually, since Bronzino stayed no more than a year and a half in Pesaro, he had most likely returned by 1532. Information from C. H. Smyth, "Bronzino and the Dossi at Pesaro" (unpublished paper, 1956).

[4] Windsor 12771. Cavalieri thanks Michelangelo for the drawing in a letter of January 1, 1533. See C. Tolnay, *Michelangelo* III (Princeton, 1948), 111, fig. 155.

names. The game of *calcio* was at that time a popular sport and a logical, if somewhat startling, vehicle for a virtuoso display of Michelangelesque nudes. However, we have no clue to any special reference that this subject might have had.[5] There is only a somewhat tenuous connection with the *Anointing of the Athlete* (cat. 124) that was planned for one of the end walls of the *Salone* in 1520, but never executed. It is, however, certain that this drawing was intended for one of these spaces — rectangular areas below the lunettes that are similar in proportion to this drawing. The remaining fields in the *Salone* are more nearly square in shape and would have been suitable for the projected *Venus and Adonis* or the *Hercules and Anteus*.

308 · Florence, Uffizi 6505F: Study for the *Nudes Playing Calcio* (cat. 307). Nude sprawled on the ground on his right side; behind him, a nude seen from behind from the waist down who pulls at the left arm of the fallen figure. 263 x 403, black chalk; inscribed in ink in a seventeenth-century hand: *Jacopo da Pontormo.* Fig. 299.

Bibliography: Berenson 1903, no. 2013; Clapp 1914, 116–117; Berenson 1938, no. 2013.

Berenson associated this drawing with San Lorenzo, while Clapp noted the connection with the *Nudes Playing Calcio.* These figures cannot be clearly made out in the damaged compositional study, but this fallen player being pulled up by another player was intended for the foreground center of the composition, where one can see vestiges of just such a group.

The derivation of the fallen player from Michelangelo's *Tityus* drawing of 1532, first noted by Berenson, aids in placing this study and, by association, the project, after that date. It might also be noted that the pose of both the *Tityus* and Pontormo's player is that of the Venus (reversed) in the *Venus and Cupid*, which Michelangelo designed and Pontormo painted in 1532–1533. In this drawing not only are the pose and canon of proportions taken from Michelangelo, but for the first time in Pontormo's drawings, the technique is a wholesale exploitation of Michelangelo's black chalk manner. The smooth, meticulously detailed modelling of the muscles and the extreme plasticity of the forms are imitative of Michelangelo. However, in Pontormo's hands the contour line still dominates the interior modelling; it flattens and violently deforms the figure in a way that is foreign to the more normative three-dimensionality of Michelangelo's forms.

309 · Florence, Uffizi 6616F *recto*: Study for the *Nudes Playing Calcio* (cat. 307). Nude boy running forward with his arms held out; below, a laughing head and an arm; on a smaller scale, two entangled nudes. (*Verso*: Study for the *Nudes Playing Calcio*, cat. 310.) 288 x 197, red chalk; fig leaf added to the boy in pencil by a later hand. Fig. 297.

Bibliography: Berenson 1903, no. 2115; Clapp 1911, 15; Clapp 1914, 188; Clapp 1916, 62; Berenson 1938, no. 2115.

As Clapp has noted, this drawing is a study for the figure who runs forward on the far left of the *Nudes Playing Calcio.* Both Berenson and Clapp called the small sketch of two entangled figures a rape. However, since one figure seems to be

[5] The famous *calcio* game played during the seige in the Piazza S. Croce on February 15, 1530 was a notable recent event, but this would hardly have been a suitable occasion to commemorate in a Medici villa. See F. D. Guerrazzi, *L'Assedio di Firenze* (Paris, 1836), ch. 27. Both Clement VII and Alessandro de' Medici played *calcio* themselves; but, again, this does not seem to hold any particular significance in reference to Pontormo's projected fresco. See C. Gandi, *Il Calcio Fiorentino* (Florence, 1936), with bibliography.

attempting to lift the other off the ground, it is not impossible that this is an idea for the *Hercules and Anteus*, which we know from Vasari (V/M, VI, 276) was also planned for the *Salone*, but for which no drawings have survived.

310 · Florence, Uffizi 6616F *verso*: Study for the *Nudes Playing Calcio* (cat. 307). Nude boy in profile left with his left arm held out and looking over his shoulder. (*Recto*: Study for the *Nudes Playing Calcio*, cat. 309.) 288 x 197, red chalk; inscribed in ink in a sixteenth-century (?) hand: *Jacopo*. Fig. 298.

Bibliography: Berenson 1903, no. 2115; Clapp 1914, 188–189; Berenson 1938, no. 2115.

Clapp has rightly identified this drawing as a slight sketch for the figure on the right of the pair of embracing nudes in the right background of the *Nudes Playing Calcio*.

311 · Florence, Uffizi 6738F: Study for the *Nudes Playing Calcio* (cat. 307). Two three-quarter length nudes bending over toward each other with their arms extended down and their heads touching and turned away. 112 x 255, red chalk. Fig. 300.

Bibliography: Berenson 1903, no. 2220; Clapp 1911, 15; Clapp 1914, 267; Clapp 1916, 62; Berenson 1938, no. 2220; *MP* 1956 (Marcucci), no. 134, fig. 163a.

Clapp recognized this drawing as a study for the two almost invisible figures in the left foreground of the *Nudes Playing Calcio*. In these nudes we see Pontormo's new figure type, which first appeared about 1530 in the foreground figures of the Pitti *Martyrdom* and in the Galatea of the *Pygmalion and Galatea*. The extremely slender body with long arms and a very small head is so pliable as to seem almost boneless, and its parts are freely manipulated to form arabesques in which overlapping planes are carefully avoided. The draughtsmanship of this drawing is a translation into red chalk of the Michelangelesque black chalk manner of cat. 308, also for the *Nudes Playing Calcio*.

1535–1536. DECORATION OF THE CAREGGI LOGGIA: *Fortune*, *Justice*, *Peace*, *Prudence*, *Fame*, *and Love* (in the pendentives); *Flying Putti with Animals* (in the vault). Environs of Florence, Villa Careggi. Oil on plaster (destroyed).

Bibliography: Clapp 1916, 65–66, 262.

Vasari describes Pontormo's work at Careggi in detail.[6] As part of the restoration of the old Medici villa, Duke Alessandro commissioned Pontormo to decorate the loggias on either side of the cortile.[7] The first loggia was completed

[6] V/M, VI, 281: "Avendo dunque Jacopo chiamato il Bronzino, gli fece fare in cinque piedi della volta una figura per ciascuno; che furono la Fortuna, la Justizia, la Vittoria, la Pace e la Fama; e nell'altro piede (che in tutto son sei) fece Jacopo di sua mano un Amore. Dopo, fatto il disegno d'alcuni putti, che andavano nell'ovato della volta, con diversi animali in mano, che scortano al disotto in su, gli fece tutti, da uno in fuori, colorire dal Bronzino, che si portò molto bene: e perchè, mentre Jacopo ed il Bronzino facevano queste figure, fecero gli ornamenti intorno Jacone, Pierfrancesco di Jacopo, ed altri. . . ."

[7] V/M, VI, 280–281. The *cortile* with its two open loggias still exists, apparently unaltered architecturally, as part of the hospital at Careggi. The loggia that Pontormo decorated on the left has six pendentives (two on each side and one at each end), exactly the number described by Vasari. See G. Carocci, *La Villa Medicea di Careggi, Memorie e Ricordi* (Florence, 1888) pl. facing p. 48.

December 13, 1536, just before the assassination of the Duke, and the second loggia was never executed.[8] We do not know the proposed subjects of the second loggia, but the first was part of a decorative program designed to glorify Alessandro; in this instance through a number of allegorical figures selected to personify various aspects of his rule of Florence. Vasari was unsure of the exact identity of all these figures, since he substituted *Prudence* for *Victory* when he mentioned the project in his life of Bronzino (V/M, VII, 596). However, since a drawing for a figure probably identifiable as *Prudence* survives (cat. 314), it is likely that Vasari's second version of the subject is correct. The only other allegory that can be provisionally identified from Pontormo's drawings is the *Justice* (cat. 316). The vault with the putti and animals seems to have been purely decorative in character. For it only a small compositional design (cat. 319) and two putti studies (cat. 312 and 320) have survived. Since the Duke wanted the loggias completed as quickly as possible, Pontormo needed assistance in order to finish the large project. He obtained the aid of Bronzino for the execution of all the *Allegories* except the *Love*. Jacone, Pierfrancesco di Jacopo (Foschi) and others helped with the grotesques and other ornamental decoration (see V/M, VI, 281, 452; VII, 596). This decoration consisted partly of garland borders around the pendentives, as can be seen in the little sketch for a pendentive (cat. 312), and also included the Medici arms, designed by Pontormo (cat. 313).

[8] V/M, VI, 281: ". . . restò in poco tempo tutta finita quell'opera con molta sodisfazione del signor duca, il quale voleva far dipignere l'altra loggia, ma non fu a tempo; perciocchè essendosi fornito questo lavoro a dì 13 di dicembre 1536, alli sei di gennaio sequente fu quel signor illustrissimo ucciso dal suo parente Lorenzino: e così questa ed altre opere rimasono senza la loro perfezione."

Since Vasari notes (V/M, VI, 282) that damage from humidity had already occurred, these decorations had evidently begun to deteriorate shortly after their execution. The fact that they are not mentioned at all by Borghini may indicate that by the later sixteenth century they were too severely damaged to merit his attention.[9] Like the Castello frescoes, which have also disappeared, they were probably executed "a olio sulla calcina secca," a technique that had none of the permanency of fresco. In the modern literature on Pontormo there has been no attempt to discuss this destroyed work by way of the surviving drawings, with the exception of Clapp, who associated one drawing (cat. 319) with the project.

STUDIES FOR THE CAREGGI LOGGIA

312 · Florence, Uffizi 6644F *recto*: Studies for the Careggi loggia. Two pages from a sketchbook: On the left page, a putto seen from below with his arms raised, holding the end of a garland (?); behind him, torso of a putto seen from behind. On the right page, a winged figure in a pendentive edged with a garland decoration; the figure is half seated with the legs turned to the right, the head to the left, the arms bent, slightly extended and raised; above, buttocks lightly indicated. (*Verso* of the right page: slight sketch of part of a nude; *verso* of the left page: an arm, not catalogued.) 212 x 280, black chalk on pink prepared paper, the putto drawn over in red chalk; inscribed: *Franco Rosi 176*. Fig. 302.

Bibliography: Berenson 1903, no. 2136; Clapp 1914, 201; Berenson 1938, no. 2136.

Berenson dated both of these pages before 1525, while Clapp associated them with the Castello loggia, dating them 1536–1543. However, the sketch of a fig-

[9] There is no later commentary on the destroyed frescoes. Moreni 1791/95, I, 58–59, simply repeats Vasari's description.

ure to the right clearly indicates that this drawing was for Careggi. The allegorical figures of Castello were in lunettes, while Vasari says specifically (V/M, VI, 281) that those at Careggi were in pendentives. This small sketch gives us a valuable clue to the appearance of the Careggi decorations, indicating a scheme of allegorical figures in garland-framed pendentives that is reminiscent of the Loggia di Psiche in the Palazzo Farnesina. With the aid of this study we are able to identify cat. 314 and 316 securely with the Careggi project because of their similarity in pose to this figure and because of the suitability of their compositions to the shape of the pendentive indicated here. However, while cat. 314 and 316 can be at least provisionally identified as to subject, this sketch is too small to tell more than that the figure is winged, as any of the allegories might have been.

The putto sketched on the other side of the sheet must have been for the vault because of the strongly foreshortened view from below. He would not have belonged to the group of flying putti with animals in the center, but might have been placed at the lower part of the vault, perhaps holding the end of a garland like those around the pendentives.

313 · Florence, Uffizi 416 orn.: Study for the Careggi loggia. Compositional sketch for a tondo with two winged putti supporting the arms of Duke Alessandro de' Medici; the putto on the left sits astride a wall with only his right leg visible; the putto on the right is faintly indicated. 219 x 150, red chalk on pink prepared paper; W: Cornet (cf. B. 7697); inscribed in ink: *Jacopo da puntorno.*

Fig. 303.

Bibliography: Ferri 1890, 120.

This important drawing has gone unnoticed in the recent literature. It may be identified as a study for the arms of Alessandro de' Medici for the Careggi loggia. While not mentioned specifically by Vasari, these arms would surely have been part of the decoration, perhaps over one of the two doorways. Since Vasari says (V/M, VI, 281) that Pontormo did not execute any of the ornamental decoration of the loggia, it is probable that one of the assistants actually painted these arms. In style, this drawing is identical to cat. 312 and 320, studies for the putti of the vault. The soft handling of the red chalk as well as the small sheet of pink prepared paper indicate that this study and cat. 312 may have been part of the same sketchbook.

314 · Hamburg, Kunsthalle 21173 *recto*: Study for the Careggi loggia. Partly draped seated woman with her left leg drawn up, her left hand holding a mirror (?) against her knee; her right arm is extended and her head is turned to the right; above to the right, the chin, neck, and shoulders lightly sketched; below to the right, the left side of the torso lightly sketched; below left, the figure drawn on a smaller scale with the legs turned to the left. (*Verso*: Study for a *Madonna and Child*, cat. 333.) 353 x 262, black chalk heightened with white; narrow black border added by a later hand.

Fig. 305.

Collection: Harzen; Kunsthalle, stamp verso (L. 1328).

Bibliography: *Hamburg Exhib.* 1920, no. 119; Pauli 1927, no. 19, pl. 19; Fischel 1930/31, 480; Berenson 1938, 319, no. 2252A, fig. 993; *Brussels Exhib.* 1954, no. 116; *Amsterdam Exhib.* 1955, no. 236; Gamba 1956, 13, fig. 28; *Hamburg Exhib.* 1957, no. 89.

This drawing was associated with Careggi by Pauli. It is the most finished and certainly the most important surviving study for the loggia. This allegorical figure is varied only slightly in pose from the figure in the pendentive design (cat. 312). Her right arm is extended and she holds what appears to be a large mirror against her left knee. Since the mirror is frequently an attribute of *Prudence*, this figure may tentatively be identified as the *Prudence* that Vasari lists among the Careggi *Allegories* (V/M, VII, 596).[10] Gamba calls her a *Truth*, which is not among the subjects that Vasari mentions. The small sketch below is a preliminary study for the figure in a more twisted contrapposto with her legs to the left and the right arm pulled across the body. This arrangement was superceded by the ornamental, planar display of curved shapes that we find in the larger study.

The kind of developed *Maniera* design and figure type that Pontormo evolved in this allegory as early as 1536 did not occur more widely in Florence until the next decade, when nudes like this one frequently appear, conspicuously in the works of Bronzino. (Cf. the Venus of the London *Allegory* or the nude in the *Primavera* tapestry in the Palazzo Vecchio, which is like this figure both in composition and type.) Since Bronzino was the executant of all but one of the Careggi *Allegories*, it is logical to suppose that he was to some degree influenced by them. This type of figure continues to appear later, still within the Bronzino tradition, in works such as Allori's finished black chalk drawing for a *Fortune* (Uffizi 609E), which is closely related to this figure in type and in pose, even to the raised arms.

315 · Florence, Uffizi 6759F *recto*: Study for the Careggi loggia. Seated nude woman seen to the knees with her left leg drawn up and her arms extended; above, the figure restudied on a smaller scale. (*Verso*: Faint sketch of a nude, not catalogued.) 257 x 172, black chalk; holes and tears especially along the left and lower edges of the sheet; W: Anchor in a circle. Fig. 304.

Bibliography: Berenson 1903, no. 2239; Clapp 1914, 280–281; Berenson 1938, no. 2239.

Clapp compared this sheet in motive with cat. 312 and with cat. A172, a copy related to the Careggi drawings, but he dated it 1545–1550. While Pontormo used this pose for the Eve in the San Lorenzo *Labor of Adam and Eve* (cat. 370), the style of this study is closer to that of the thirties and it is evident from the pose of the figure that it is a preliminary study for cat. 314.

316 · Florence, Uffizi 6584F *recto*: Study for the Careggi loggia. Seated nude woman seen to the knees turned to the right with her right leg drawn up, her right arm resting on a large book, and looking over her right shoulder. (*Verso*: Faint sketch in black chalk, not catalogued.) 269 x 295, black chalk. Fig. 306.

Bibliography: Berenson 1903, no. 2084; Clapp 1911, 15; Clapp 1914, 168; Clapp 1916, 68, fig. 132; Berenson 1938, 319, no. 2084; Wallis 1939, 180, fig. 3; Toesca 1943, 18, illustrated; Becherucci 1944, 21, fig. 53.

Clapp and Becherucci considered this drawing to be for one of the allegorical figures at Castello, while Berenson thought it was "perhaps for a sibyl." This nude is a study for one of the *Allegories* in the pendentives at Careggi, and is composed on the same ornamental principles as the figure in cat. 314. If this figure is imagined full-length, it is evident that she would fit ideally into the pendentive space. The

[10] The *Prudence* in the Casa Vasari, Arezzo, is very like Pontormo's in the design of the seated half-draped figure holding the mirror. See L. Berti, *La Casa del Vasari in Arezzo e il suo Museo* (Florence, 1955), no. 32, fig. 4b, who attributes it to Doceno.

book that she holds suggests that this figure may be identifiable with the *Justice* that Vasari mentions as among the *Allegories.*

The influence of Michelangelo is evident in this drawing, both in the draughtsmanship and in the type and pose of the nude. The tight and granular black chalk manner betrays the influence of Michelangelo's technique of the Cavalieri drawings, just as did cat. 308 for the *Nudes Playing Calcio.* The pose of the figure is close to that of the *Giorno* from the Medici Tombs, except for the legs, and the physical type is influenced by the tomb *Allegories* as well as by the lost *Leda* of 1529–1530, and the *Venus and Cupid* of 1532–1533. Michelangelo's heavy and monumental female type does not seem to have influenced Pontormo decisively until toward the midthirties. Indeed, it was only with his study of Michelangelo's nudes that drawings of nude females begin to appear in Pontormo's work. The only surviving drawing of a female nude before the Careggi studies of the midthirties is an early and slight sketch after a Venus statue (cat. 91), and the only female nude in a painting is the Galatea — also a Venus statue — in the *Pygmalion and Galatea* of 1529–1530. These figures are cast in a quite different, more personal mold, with the slender, almost masculine proportions that still appear in the *Three Graces* (cat. 321) of ca. 1535–1536. However, in the midthirties and later the monumental female type of Michelangelo appears frequently (cf. cat. 314, 325, 329, 333), until it is finally transformed in the San Lorenzo drawings.

317 · Florence, Uffizi 6583F: Study for the Careggi loggia. Seated three-quarter length nude seen from behind leaning on the right arm with the left arm raised straight up; to the right, the figure restudied showing the raised right leg; below, the torso restudied with another torso facing to the left. 204 x 265, red chalk; W: Crown. Fig. 307.

Bibliography: Berenson 1903, no. 2083; Clapp 1914, 167; Berenson 1938, no. 2083.

These studies are connected with cat. 316, which is not for Castello, as Clapp supposed. The genesis of the figure is clearly indicated: the sketch to the lower left is after Michelangelo's *Giorno* from the Medici Tombs; the nude is then sketched with the back completely turned and the arm raised; finally, the figure is drawn to the right as it is in cat. 316 with the bent right arm faintly indicated. A torso like the one to the left is sketched in black chalk on a red chalk drawing of 1517–1518 (cat. 66). It is possible that Pontormo might have had this figure in mind when he reused the earlier sheet. In any case, both drawings are of the same date and refer to the same Michelangelo source.

318 · Florence, Uffizi 6605F: Study for the Careggi loggia. Three-quarter length seated nude seen from behind leaning to the left; to the left, part of a torso. 227 x 288, black chalk; W: Ladder in a shield with star (cf. B. 5927).

Bibliography: Berenson 1903, no. 2104; Clapp 1914, 181; Berenson 1938, no. 2104. (Photo G.)

Berenson and Clapp dated this study late but did not connect it with Careggi. The drawing is a model study for the motive in the center of cat. 317, which in turn is preparatory to cat. 316.

319 · Florence, Uffizi 458F *recto*: Study for the Careggi loggia. Two flying putti with birds in their hands; below on a smaller scale, a putto with a bird flying in the other direction; to the left, an oval containing six flying putti. (*Verso*: Bird, cat. A41.) 173 x 255, black chalk, the oval with putti in ink. Fig. 301.

Bibliography: Berenson 1903, no. 2009; Clapp 1911, 15; Clapp 1914, 101–102; Clapp 1916, 66; McComb 1928, 35; Berenson 1938, no. 1977A; Emiliani 1960, 87.

Clapp identified this sheet as preparatory to the vault of the Careggi loggia that is described by Vasari (V/M, VI, 281): "Dopo, fatto il disegno d'alcuni putti, che andavano nell'ovato della volta, con diversi animali in mano, che scortano al disotto in su. . . ." As it is evidently a study for the putti that Vasari saw, this drawing is a keystone of our knowledge of Pontormo's work at Careggi. It gives us a term of comparison for cat. 313 and 320, which otherwise could not be related to the loggia frescoes. Furthermore, like the foliate borders of the pendentives, these putti flying with animals and birds recall the *amoretti* of Raphael's Loggia di Psiche, suggesting the possible influence of that scheme on Pontormo. Clapp has noted Bronzino's imitation of these putti in his *Nativity* of 1565 (S. Stefano, Pisa).

320 · Florence, Uffizi 6637F: Study for the Careggi loggia. Lower part of a flying putto; below, part of a torso seen from behind. 270 x 195, red chalk; cut irregularly on three sides.

Bibliography: Berenson 1903, no. 2129; Clapp 1914, 198; Berenson 1938, no. 2129. (Photo G.)

Clapp dated this sheet 1532–1535 and thought that the torso was a study for the central figure in the *Three Graces* (cat. 321). While this sketch is very faint, it does resemble the second study of the torso on cat. 322, a study for the *Three Graces* that is contemporary in date with Careggi. The more important sketch on this sheet is a study for the lower half of one of the flying putti of the Careggi vault. The extremely soft and unaccentuated red chalk style with very little elaboration of the interior modelling is like that of cat. 315, a preliminary study for one of the Careggi *Allegories.*

STUDIES FOR A THREE GRACES
CA. 1535–1536

321 · Florence, Uffizi 6748F: Compositional study for a *Three Graces*, ca. 1535–1536. Nude woman with her back turned extending her arms to clasp the hands of two nude women who stand on either side of her facing forward and holding a light drapery above and behind them. 295 x 212, red chalk; outlines incised for transfer; W: Large Greek cross in a circle (B. 5540); inscribed in ink in an eighteenth-century (?) hand: *Jacopo da Pontormo.* Fig. 310.

Bibliography: Ferri 1890, 120; Berenson 1903, no. 2229; Clapp 1911, 14–15; Gamba 1912, no. 21, pl. 21; Clapp 1914, 275–276; Clapp 1916, 61, fig. 122; Berenson 1938, no. 2229; *MDF* 1939, 26; *MC* 1940, 48; Toesca 1943, 18, fig. 35; Becherucci 1943, 10, pl. 26; Becherucci 1944, 21; *MF* 1952, 64; *MDM* 1954 (Marcucci), no. 57; *EMI* 1954, no. 78; Marcucci 1956, 19, fig. 24.

This drawing has always been dated in the thirties, but with considerable variation. Clapp dated it 1532–1535 and Gamba 1530–1535, while Toesca thought it was for the Careggi loggia, and Becherucci thought it was for Castello. According to Vasari's descriptions, none of Pontormo's decorative programs of the thirties included this subject; nor, in fact, would the shape of this composition have been appropriate for either the pendentives of Careggi or the lunettes of Castello. Rather than being connected with the loggias, it was more likely a project for some other decoration that was never executed. These long, flexible, defeminized bodies with their unstable movements and weightless gestures are similar to such Careggi nude studies as cat. 314. However, they are executed in a more refined and personal mode than many of the extremely Michelangelesque female nudes of the mid-thirties, such as cat. 316 and 329.

As Clapp has pointed out, the composition of intertwined floating women recalls Pontormo's earlier Carmigano *Visitation.* Clapp also noted the clear reference to Marcantonio's *Three Graces* (Bar. 340), which in turn is based on the antique group in Siena. A small painting of a *Three Graces* by Naldini in Budapest is freely derived from Pontormo's drawing or from the lost painting for which it was preparatory.[11]

322 · Florence, Uffizi 6747F: Study for the *Three Graces* (cat. 321). Standing nude seen from behind to the knees looking down to the right. 267 x 164, red chalk. Fig. 308.

Bibliography: Berenson 1903, no. 2228; Gamba 1912, 3; Clapp 1914, 275; Berenson 1938, no. 2228; *MDF* 1939, 26; *MDM* 1954 (Marcucci), no. 58; *EMI* 1954, no. 79.

Although this figure is not in exactly the same pose and the model is a man, it is certainly a study for the central figure in the *Three Graces*, as Gamba and Clapp have noted. Marcucci, however, believed it unlikely that Pontormo would use an elderly man as a model for this figure and did not connect this drawing with the *Three Graces.* She dated it 1532–1536 as related in style to the *Nudes Playing Calcio.*

323 · Florence, Uffizi 6620F: Study for the *Three Graces* (cat. 321). Nude woman seen from behind with her arms held out and leaning slightly to the left; to the right, part of the torso restudied. 292 x 207, red chalk. Fig. 309.

Bibliography: Berenson 1903, no. 2118; Clapp 1914, 190; Berenson 1938, no. 2118; Schlegel 1961, 32, fig. 13.

As Clapp has noted, this drawing is a study for the central figure in the *Three Graces.* With cat. 322, the other study for the figure, it is similar in style to some of the model studies for the Careggi *Allegories*, such as cat. 317. In these drawings the slender, pliable forms are modelled in a meticulously detailed red chalk technique that does not have quite the same curvilinear and ornamental emphasis as the final study for the *Three Graces* or the more finished Careggi studies.

MISCELLANEOUS DRAWINGS CA. 1530–1536

324 · Florence, Uffizi 443F *recto*: Ca. 1530–1535. Portrait study of a boy. Three-quarter length seated boy turned to the left wearing a cloak and hat, and holding a horn in his right hand. (*Verso*: Study for the *Portrait of Giovanni della Casa*, cat. 345.) 272 x 196, red chalk; W: Pascal lamb (B. 50). Fig. 324.

Bibliography: Berenson 1903, no. 1970; *MPA* 1910, 21; Clapp 1914, 93; Clapp 1916, 86; Tinti 1925, fig. 12; Berenson 1938, 318, no. 1970, fig. 983; *MDF* 1939, 26; *MC* 1940, 50; Parigi 1951, no. 930.

Clapp dated this finished portrait study ca. 1540, but it is more likely to date not later than 1535. There is a close stylistic affinity with Pontormo's *Portrait of Alessandro de' Medici* of 1534–1535,[12] and with

[11] Panel, 20 x 14 cm. See *Catalogue Szépművészeti Múzeum* (Budapest, 1954), 383. This picture was formerly attributed to Vasari. (See *Die Gemälde Galerie des Museums für Bildende Künste in Budapest* (Budapest, 1916), no. 207 fig. 207).

[12] Philadelphia, Johnson Collection (panel, 97 x 79 cm). This portrait is discussed in detail by Vasari (V/M, VI, 278) and documented by a letter that places its execution at the time when Alessandro was in mourning for his father, Clement VII, who died September 25, 1534. See

his *Portrait of a Boy* of about the same date,[13] which might almost be after the same model as this drawing. The strict pyramidal organization of the figure, the quiet silhouette, the broad, flat areas of drapery, and the antiornamental quality of the tightly disciplined line are common to all these portraits. The closest parallels among the other drawings of this period are the more naturalistically handled red chalk nudes such as cat. 317 or 323, rather than those in which ornamentalism of line and shape is emphasized.

325 · Florence, Uffizi 6534F *recto*: Ca. 1535–1536. Study for a *Madonna and Child* (?). Nude woman reclining to the left on a piece of drapery, holding a book in her right hand and holding a child to her breast with her left arm. (*Verso*: Nude studies, cat. 326.) 280 x 405, black chalk. Fig. 311.

Bibliography: Berenson 1903, no. 2037; *MPA* 1910, 37; Clapp 1911, 14; Clapp 1914, 136–137; Clapp 1916, 63; Berenson 1938, 319, no. 2037, fig. 991; Cecchi 1956, fig. 6.

This drawing is closely connected with the *Venus and Cupid* that Pontormo painted from Michelangelo's cartoon about 1533.[14] Berenson called it a "happier variant of the Michelangelo composition" and Clapp dated it 1533–1534 as after the painting. In still another variant of the Michelangelo invention, which may date just before this drawing, Pontormo had drawn a Venus that greatly exaggerated the pose and proportions of Michelangelo's figure (cat. 329). Here he has apparently transformed the Venus and Cupid of his model into a Madonna and Child by changing the position of Venus' right arm so that she holds a book and by turning the cupid into a nursing child. This drawing is close in style to Careggi studies such as cat. 314 and 316, where we find the same monumental type with swelling curved limbs, high breasts, and small head. This type, as well as the soft handling of black chalk, is found in another *Madonna and Child* drawing of these same years (cat. 333). Both these drawings are connected with a still later *Madonna and Child* painting (known only in copies), which is a reworking of elements of this composition in less bizarre terms (see p. 317, n. 8).

326 · Florence, Uffizi 6534F *verso*: Ca. 1535–1536. Three small scale nude studies of a torso, a profile, and a back. (*Recto*: Study of a *Madonna and Child*?, cat. 325.) 280 x 405, black chalk. (Photo G.)

These little nudes in the corner of a large sheet are minor sketches from the same date as the recto and were probably done in connection with, or at least contemporary with, Pontormo's work at Careggi. The profile bust is of a similar type as the profile of the allegorical figure (cat.

Clapp 1916, 64–65, 170–173, app. II, doc. 22, fig. 124. Cat. A1, a copy after a lost preparatory study for this portrait, shows that Pontormo's original drawing must have had a close affinity in style with cat. 324.

[13] Florence, Contini-Bonacossi Collection (tile, 66 x 51 cm). Toesca 1943, fig. 49, accepted this portrait as Pontormo, but it has been attributed to Foschi by Berti, *MP* 1956, no. 87, fig. 81. The fact that this picture is painted on tile together with its damaged condition makes a final judgment as to its authenticity difficult.

[14] See Tolnay, *Michelangelo* III (Princeton, 1948), 108–109. Michelangelo made the cartoon ca. 1532–1533 for Bartolommeo Bettini, who had Pontormo paint it. See V/M, VI, 277, 291–295 (note by Milanesi on the Accademia version); Benedetto Varchi, *Due Lezzioni* (Florence, 1549), 104. The cartoon is lost, but a copy exists in Naples. There are numerous copies of the painting, of which only the Florence, Accademia (no. 1284) version has been widely accepted as the original. See also Clapp 1916, 62–64, 142–145, fig. 123; and Berti, *MP* 1956, no. 70, fig. 65.

314). The torso, which is drawn after the nude in Michelangelo's so-called *Dream of Human Life* (see Berenson 1938, no. 1748B, fig. 693), is still another instance of Pontormo's study of Michelangelo in the early and middle thirties.

327 · Florence, Uffizi 6570F *recto*: Ca. 1530–1534. Study for a *Venus* (?). Partially draped woman standing leaning against a rock with the left foot placed forward on a rock and the right arm raised; to the right, the right foot restudied; underneath, lower part of a nude seen from behind. (*Verso*: Nude studies, cat. 328.) 402 x 274, black and red chalk heightened with white, the nude in red chalk, squared in red chalk; some outlines incised for transfer; W: Eagle.
Fig. 313.

Bibliography: Berenson 1903, no. 2070; *MPA* 1910, 29; Gamba 1912, no. 19, pl. 19; Clapp 1914, 159–160; Clapp 1916, 48, 258; Berenson 1938, no. 2070.

Berenson thought this drawing was intended for an allegorical figure contemporary with the Louvre altarpiece, which he dated 1543. Clapp believed that the figure might have been a first idea for the Virgin in the S. Felicita *Annunciation* or, following Gamba's suggestion, a study for the *Pomona* that Vasari says (V/M, VI, 274) Pontormo painted for Filippo del Migliore. While this figure could very well be a Pomona, Vasari implies a date for the *Pomona* near to S. Felicita that would seem a few years early for the style of this drawing. This sheet must date at least 1530, possibly toward the midthirties. The torso to the left is, as Clapp has noted, related to the nude studies on the verso, studies that evidently date shortly after 1530 at the time of the *Nudes Playing Calcio* for Poggio a Caiano. The monumental type of the half-draped woman, with her elongated torso, small head, small high breasts, and heavy thighs, as well as the ornamentalizing curves of her pose, recalls Pontormo's Careggi *Allegories* of 1535–1536 (cat. 314 and 316). Yet, the conception of the figure is less rigidly elegant here, the forms more flexibly arranged in overlapping planes, the line freer, and the modelling less tight than in most of Pontormo's drawings from the midthirties. It is possible that this study is slightly earlier than Careggi and that it was connected with the projected Poggio a Caiano frescoes of 1532–1534. One of the cartoons mentioned by Vasari (V/M, VI, 276) was a *Venus and Adonis*, a subject for which this drawing could possibly have been a study.

Also very suggestive of a dating in the early thirties — and possibly of the *Venus* subject as well — is the relation between this figure and the Madonna of Bronzino's Panciatichi *Holy Family*, painted after his return from Pesaro in 1532 in exactly the period in which we have placed Pontormo's drawing on the basis of its style. Clearly there was some contact between these works. (Cf. also the reflection of Bronzino's picture in Allori's drawing, Munich 2249, for a signed and dated *Holy Family*, Easton Neston, Lord Hesketh Coll.) In Bronzino's and Pontormo's works the physical type is close, though Bronzino's Madonna has a more classicized face. The lines of the drapery and the pose with the right hip thrown out are very similar, even though the position of the head and right arm in Bronzino's figure has been adjusted in order to focus the action of the Madonna toward the Child at the right. Given the similarities between these two figures and the well-known dependence of the Bronzino on antique sculpture, it is possible that Pontormo's figure also derives — directly or indirectly through Bronzino — from an antique Venus.[15] If this is the case, this drawing

[15] While no specific sculpture may be named, there are several half-draped Venus types who stand in a hip-shot pose with one leg forward

would be evidence of Pontormo's momentary turn to classical sculpture in the early thirties, a direction which he, unlike Bronzino, did not pursue further. And, if we are correct in associating this drawing with the motive of an antique Venus, then the connection between this drawing and the Poggio a Caiano *Venus and Adonis* might become a stronger possibility.

We know from Vasari that the *Venus and Adonis* of Poggio a Caiano never progressed beyond the cartoon stage, and this figure does not appear elsewhere in Pontormo's surviving works. However, it is interesting to note that Pontormo's invention in this drawing must have been known, for there exists at least one instance of a close adaption of it by another artist into quite a different context. With the exception of the exact arrangement of the legs, this Venus appears as the Eve in a Pontormesque painting of *Adam and Eve*.[16]

---

like the figure in Pontormo's and Bronzino's works. Cf. S. Reinach, *Répertoire de la Statuaire Greque et Romaine* (Paris, 1897), I, 341, nos. 4, 7. See B. Schweitzer, "Zum antikenstudium des Angelo Bronzinos," *Mitt. des Deutschen Arch. Inst.* 33 (1918), 17ff, on Bronzino's picture and the antique, especially the influence of a Praxitelean Venus on the Madonna. As Smyth 1949, 206, has pointed out, there is the possibility that Bronzino's exposure to the Raphaelism of Raffaellino del Colle in Pesaro may also have had some formative influence on the Panciatichi *Holy Family*, an influence that could have underscored Bronzino's interest in the antique.

[16] New York Art Market (panel, 74 x 58 cm). This unpublished picture is attributed to Pontormo, but it is derivative from at least two periods of his activity and probably dates after 1550. The Eve is based on this drawing of shortly after 1530, and the Adam is of the type found in the drawings for the *Nudes Playing Calcio* of the same date (cf. cat. 307–311). However, the God Father with putti derives from compositions of the San Lorenzo period such as the *Moses Receiving the Tables of the Law* (cat. 354–355).

328 · Florence, Uffizi 6570F *verso*: Ca. 1530–1534. Standing nude seen from behind; to the left, the neck and right shoulder restudied twice and a knee; to the right, the neck and right shoulder restudied three times and a knee. (*Recto*: Figure study, cat. 327.) 402 x 274, red chalk. Fig. 314.

Bibliography: Berenson 1903, no. 2070; Clapp 1914, 160; Clapp 1916, 48; Berenson 1938, no. 2070; Gamba 1956, 12, fig. 21 (as in Dresden); Berenson 1961, no. 1958A (as in Dresden).

Clapp dated this drawing 1525–1527 as for the Angel of the S. Felicita *Annunciation*, while Gamba dated it 1525. The connection with the Angel, based on the similarity in motive of the bust to the upper right, is very tenuous. Furthermore, the tight linear descriptiveness and the Michelangelesque treatment of the muscles in this study definitely places it after 1530. There is a close analogy with the heavily muscled nudes of the Pitti *Martyrdom* of 1529–1530. Although the exact figures do not appear in the painting, this sheet of studies might have been connected with that picture. There is also the possibility of some relation to the unexecuted Poggio a Caiano frescoes of 1532–1534 (cf. the *Nudes Playing Calcio* studies, cat. 308 and 311).

329 · Florence, Uffizi 6586F: Ca. 1532–1534. Nude woman reclining on a mass of drapery with legs apart, her head turned to the left and her left hand resting on a sphere. 167 x 153, black chalk. Fig. 315.

Bibliography: Berenson 1903, no. 2086; *MPA* 1910, 37; Clapp 1911, 14; Gamba 1912, no. 23a, pl. 23a; Clapp 1914, 168–169; Clapp 1916, 63, 68, fig. 133; Berenson 1938, 319, no. 2086, fig. 994; *MDF* 1939, 5; *MC* 1940, 46; Cecchi 1956, fig. 5.

This nude is derived from Michelangelo's works of ca. 1532–1533. The motive is taken from the *Venus and Cupid* as well as from the *Tityus* (reversed), and the drawing is related to the Cavalieri drawings in technique. Berenson also noted the connection with another drawing attributed to Michelangelo of the same period in which a female nude is posed against drapery.[17] Clapp dated this drawing ca. 1538 as for Careggi or Castello. However, it does not seem to have been designed for either a pendentive or a lunette space, and its close relation to the Michelangelo works of 1532–1533 makes a date nearer to them more probable. The extremely exaggerated proportions of the figure and the Michelangelesque black chalk draughtsmanship suggest that Pontormo did this drawing while the impact of the Michelangelo invention was still fresh, not several years later at a time when he had assimilated and disciplined his impressions of Michelangelo into his own more linear and ornamental style. The only other drawing that has this quality of immediate dependence on a Michelangelo model is cat. 308 for the *Nudes Playing Calcio of* 1532–1534, which is also derived from the *Tityus*.

330 · Florence, Uffizi 6606F: Ca. 1532–1534. Nude seen from behind almost to the knees with the left arm wound around his head. 276 x 212, black chalk.

Bibliography: Berenson 1903, no. 2105; Gamba 1912, no. 24, pl. 24; Clapp 1914, 181; Berenson 1938, no. 2105.

Gamba thought this drawing was for the *Nudes Playing Calcio*, while Clapp dated it ca. 1542. The exact figure cannot be located in the *Calcio* drawing (cat. 307), but this Michelangelesque study is undoubtedly connected with it and is perhaps a discarded idea for one of the players.

331 · Florence, Uffizi 6698F: Ca. 1533–1534. Study for a self-portrait. Seated man seen to the knees dressed in an artisan's costume and hat, his left arm resting on a table holding a piece of paper, his right hand on his leg, and his head turned slightly to the right; to the right, the left hand restudied holding a piece of paper. 388 x 258, black chalk, squared on the verso in black chalk; formerly on a mount with an old inscription: *Portrait de lui-même* (according to Clapp). Fig. 325.

Bibliography: Ferri 1890, 119; Berenson 1903, no. 2002; *MPA* 1910, 22; Gamba 1912, no. 18, pl. 18; Clapp 1914, 243–244; Clapp 1916, 85; McComb 1928, 8; Popham 1931, no. 233, pl. 197; Berenson 1938, 217, no. 2181A; *MDF* 1939, 26; *MC* 1940, 51; Toesca 1943, 23, fig. 46; Becherucci 1943, 10, pl. 25; Becherucci 1944, 20–21, fig. 50; *Paris Exhib.* 1950, no. 425; Tietze 1953, 365; *MDM* 1954 (Marcucci), no. 56, fig. 12; *EMI* 1954, no. 77, fig. 14; Berti 1956, 8–9, fig. 5; Del Massa 1959, pl. 27; Berenson 1961, no. 2181A, fig. 971.

Ferri identified this drawing as a self-portrait on the basis of the old inscription on the mount. Berti, citing Longhi and Sinibaldi in agreement, accepted the identification but not the authorship, dating the drawing ca. 1535–1540 as a portrait of Pontormo by Bronzino. It is now listed as Bronzino in the museum. Other authors have accepted the drawing as a Pontormo but not as a self-portrait, Gamba dating it in the midtwenties, Clapp and Popham 1525–1530, Becherucci 1534–1535 (mentioning the self-portrait possibility), and Marcucci ca. 1535. Clapp objected to the identification as a self-portrait on the basis of a comparison with Bronzino's like-

[17] Albertina no. S.R. 169 (Berenson 1938, no. 1606). The pose of the figure is not the same, but the proportions of the nude, the way it is set off against the drapery, and the meticulous black chalk draughtsmanship recall Pontormo's drawing. Both this drawing and Pontormo's may reflect a lost Michelangelo original of the period of the Cavalieri drawings.

ness of Pontormo in his *Christ in Limbo* of 1552. However, there is ample evidence that this is a self-portrait by Pontormo when he was about forty, dating ca. 1534–1535. If we compare the face with the known likenesses of Pontormo,[18] especially the woodcut in Vasari, the portraits in the Uffizi, and even the head in the *Christ in Limbo*, there is little doubt that this is the same face at an earlier date. The long nose, the high forehead, the unusual cut of the eye, the prominent ears, and the sparse beard are the same in all the portraits, regardless of date. Furthermore, the artisan's clothing, the rather self-conscious posture and critical expression of the face, the difficulty with the hands and with the proportioning of the body, all seem characteristic of the self-portrait. The tight precision in the handling of the black chalk and the nervous rigidity of the form are characteristic of Pontormo's draughtsmanship in the midthirties (cf. cat. 314), but not of Bronzino's, which was not yet as intricate and controlled (cf. cat. A16). The style of this drawing, together with the dependence of certain Bronzino portraits on it, indicates a date of not after 1535 for this self-portrait. Similarities to Bronzino's portraits of the thirties have already been pointed out by Clapp and McComb. Furthermore, it is quite possible that this drawing may have been the first example of new tendencies in Florentine Mannerist portraiture that were later to crystallize into a formula that was the common property of both Pontormo and Bronzino, although it became more closely identified with the latter. The earliest of Bronzino's portraits of this group, the *Youth with the Lute* (ca. 1534, Uffizi) and the drawing for it (formerly attributed to Pontormo, cat. A16) are dependent on Pontormo's invention in the self-portrait drawing, while the later *Ugolino Martelli* (Berlin, ca. 1535–1538) and the *Bartolommeo Panciatichi* (Uffizi, ca. 1540) are Bronzino's extensions upon the same invention.[19] Since Bronzino was working with Pontormo from about 1535 to 1543 at Careggi and Castello and must have been in close contact with his former master, there is no reason to doubt Pontormo's formative influence on Bronzino's portrait style; even though, as has often been remarked, there was at the same time a reciprocal influence of Bronzino's maturing style on that of Pontormo.

332 · Florence, Uffizi 6760F *verso*: Ca. 1535–1536. Profile bust of a youth facing left. (*Recto*: Study for Castello, cat. 341.) 241 x 184, black chalk.

Bibliography: Giglioli 1926, 780; Berenson 1938, no. 2240. (Photo G.)

This slight study was first noted by Giglioli, but he did not suggest a date. It is connected in style and in the type of the head with Pontormo's Careggi and Castello drawings, but cannot be specifically related to either project. A somewhat similar bust appears on cat. 326.

333 · Hamburg, Kunsthalle 21173 *verso*: Ca. 1535–1536. Study for a *Madonna and Child*. Half-length seated woman holding a sleeping child across her lap; to the left sideways on the sheet, bust of a nude with the left arm but lacking the head. (*Recto*: Study for Careggi, cat. 314.) 262 x 353, black chalk. Fig. 312.

Bibliography: Pauli 1927, no. 19; Berenson 1938, 319, 365, no. 2252A, fig. 992.

This rapid, unelaborated study, which Berenson justly called a "monumental Madonna . . . magnificently Michelangelesque," is one of Pontormo's two surviving drawings of the subject from the period

[18] For a discussion of the portraits of Pontormo see note 16 on p. 112.

[19] See Smyth 1949, 195, for the dating of these portraits, which he notes may also be connected with Michelangelo's recently (1533) completed *Giuliano de Medici*.

after 1530. This drawing and cat. 325, the other *Madonna and Child* study, are similar in their Michelangelesque style to the drawings for the Careggi *Allegories*, one of which is drawn on the recto of this sheet. One of these drawings (more likely this one) might have been a study for a lost *Madonna and Child* mentioned by Vasari that must have dated from the mid-thirties.[20] Both these drawings are also related to a later *Madonna and Child* of ca. 1545–1550 that is known only through copies (see p. 317, n. 8). In the later composition the seated Madonna's pose and type, her full, curving shapes and encircling arm are close to this drawing, while the motive of the book in her right hand and the pose of the child are related to cat. 325.

Michelangelo's *Venus and Cupid* was the source for cat. 325, and this drawing may also reflect a Michelangelo composition of the early or middle thirties. Berenson thought this drawing might be related to an earlier variant of a *Madonna and Child* drawing in the British Museum, which he dated ca. 1535 (Berenson 1938, no. 1508, fig. 707). The British Museum drawing may reflect a Michelangelo original, but closer to Pontormo's drawing is another Michelangelesque *Madonna and Child* drawing in the Kenneth Clark Collection (Berenson 1938, no. 1694, fig. 797). Berenson pointed out that the head in the Clark drawing is after a Michelangelo head of the early thirties (Windsor no. 434). However, there certainly must have been a Michelangelo invention behind the rest of the composition as well; a drawing that Pontormo may also have known. The Madonna in the Pontormo drawing is similar to that in the Clark drawing in pose and in her monumental proportions, and the motive of the Child is the same in reverse. The Child in both these drawings (and presumably in the Michelangelo source) refers back to a motive that was quite common in Florentine and Roman classicizing circles in the earlier part of the century.[21] This motive probably derives from an antique prototype, but here it has been completely transformed by the rhythmic monumentality of Pontormo's Michelangelesque composition.

[20] V/M, VI, 279–280. This picture, which later belonged to Alessandro, son of Ottaviano de'Medici, was given by Pontormo to Rossino, the mason who worked on his house. Vasari implies (*ibid.*, 279) that Pontormo finished his house about 1535, and Clapp 1916, app. II, doc. 23, cites evidence that it was built before 1536.

STUDIES FOR PORTRAITS OF COSIMO DE' MEDICI AND OF MARIA SALVIATI CA. 1537

334 · Florence, Uffizi 6528F *verso*: Study for a *Portrait of Cosimo de' Medici*, ca. 1537. Head of a young man with curly hair in profile left; below right, the eye restudied. (*Recto*: Study for San Lorenzo, cat. 377.) 421 x 215, black chalk; inscribed: *Franco Rosi 186*. Fig. 326.

Bibliography: Gamba 1910, 125–127, illustrated; *MPA* 1910, 21; Gamba 1912, no. 25, pl. 25; Clapp 1914, 133–134; Clapp 1916, 68; Berenson 1938, 319, no. 2031, fig. 985; *MC* 1940, 128; Toesca 1943, 18 (as no. 2031).

This drawing was published by Gamba as connected with a *Portrait of Cosimo de' Medici* in the Museo Mediceo, which he also attributed to Pontormo.[22] However,

[21] See for example, a Fra Bartolommeo drawing of ca. 1500 (Uffizi 482E *verso*); a Raphael drawing of ca. 1510–1512 (British Museum, Fischel 305); and the *Madonna and Child* tondo (London, Philip Pouncey Collection) of ca. 1513–1515 by Sebastiano del Piombo. While the Christ Child in all these examples, especially the last, is close to Pontormo's, in none of them is the Child asleep as in Pontormo's drawing.

[22] This picture (panel, 47 x 37 cm) has generally been identified as the *Portrait of Cosimo de' Medici* that Vasari says Pontormo painted at

this painting is surely a copy after this drawing or after the lost portrait for which it was preparatory. Gamba believed that Pontormo used this likeness for a portrait of Cosimo in frecso — "un medaglione" at Villa Castello. We know from both Vasari and Borghini that Pontormo did a portrait of Cosimo and one of his mother, Maria Salviati, at the beginning of the work at Castello (probably late 1537), but neither Vasari nor Borghini say these portraits were in fresco.[23] The implication is rather that they were conventional portraits on panel or canvas. Since these portraits have not survived, we cannot be certain whether this sketch was for the Castello portrait of Cosimo or for still another portrait. However, it does represent Cosimo as a young man of eighteen in 1537, the year in which he came to power. As Gamba has pointed out, profile likenesses of Cosimo on medals of the next year show him with the beard that he wore consistently after that date.[24]

In style there are parallels with Pontormo's Careggi and Castello drawings that also indicate ca. 1537 as the most probable date for the drawing. The hard, unevenly accentuated contours are the same as those which describe the ornamental forms in cat. 314 for Careggi. The modelling of the face, the drawing of the ear, the mop of curly hair, and other details are identical to such a drawing for a Castello loggia putto as cat. 336.

Castello (see n. 23). See Gamba 1910, illus. pp. 125–127; Clapp 1916, 68, 146–147; *MM* 1939, 144; Becherucci 1944, 21; Berti, *MP* 1956, no. 81, fig. 74. Keutner 1959, 144, 148, has rightly rejected the attribution to Pontormo. He attributes the picture to Vasari's shop; a logical association, since this profile likeness of the young Cosimo appears several times in Vasari's Palazzo Vecchio frescoes.

[23] See V/M, VI, 282: ". . . il che [the loggia frescoes] potea fare commodamente, avendo per ciò otto scudi il mese da Sua Eccellenza; la quale ritrasse, così giovinetta come era, nel principio di quel lavoro, e parimente la signora donna Maria sua madre." See Borghini 1584, 484: ". . . il qual lavoro [the loggia frescoes] il tempo, e l'aria consumano à poco à poco, e vi ritrasse di naturale il Duca Cosimo in quella età giovane, e Madonna Maria sua Madre." It is possible that Gamba's idea that the portraits were in fresco is based on an editorial note appended to Borghini's passage. See Bottari (ed. Borghini, 1730, 306n1): "Ora sono consumatissime, e solo vi è rimaso il contorno." This remark does not necessarily refer to the portraits, but was simply placed at the end of a long sentence that refers to both the loggia frescoes and the portraits. In any event, since so little remained, it is unlikely that Bottari would have been able to determine whether there were portraits in the loggia or not.

335 · Florence, Uffizi 6680F: Study for a *Portrait of Maria Salviati*, ca. 1537. Bust of a woman wearing a high-necked dress and a widow's veil. 202 x 123, black chalk; inscribed in ink in an eighteenth-century (?) hand: *Jacopo da Pon.*

Fig. 327.

Bibliography: Ferri 1890, 119; Berenson 1903, no. 2165; *MPA* 1910, 21; Clapp 1914, 230; Clapp 1916, 86; Berenson 1938, 317, no. 2165, fig. 979; Steinbart 1939, 12; King 1940, 81, fig. 8; *MDM* 1954 (Marcucci), no. 59; *EMI* 1954, no. 80; *MP* 1956 (Berti), 53.

Before the discovery of the Uffizi *Portrait of Maria Salviati*, Berenson dated this drawing in the "later middle period" and Clapp placed it ca. 1540. Since the Uffizi picture came to light and was identified by Lányi as the one that Vasari says (V/M, VI, 282) Pontormo did at the beginning of his work at Castello, this drawing has generally been associated with it. King, however, has connected this drawing with the much earlier double portrait of Maria and Cosimo painted in 1526–1527 after

[24] Cf. A. Heiss, *Les Médailleurs de la Renaissance* (Paris, 1892), Florence, II, pl. 1, fig. 10, for the medal by Domenico di Polo.

the death of her husband, Giovanni delle Bande Nere.[25] While Pontormo's various representations of Maria Salviati pose problems as yet unresolved, it seems likely that this drawing refers neither to the earlier Baltimore double portrait nor to the Uffizi portrait (which must date at least 1543 and is therefore not the one mentioned by Vasari as painted at Castello), but to the still unidentified or lost Castello portrait. While the likeness in this drawing is strikingly similar to that of the Baltimore portrait, the draughtsmanship is quite unlike Pontormo's portrait drawings of the late twenties, as for example, the study for the *Halberdier* (cat. 288) or the self-portrait (cat. 277). The line is drier and more meticulous, the forms more rigid and less curvilinear than those of any drawing of the S. Felicita period. The drawing is extremely unlikely to date between 1527 and 1537 because Maria and Cosimo lived in retirement at Trebbia in the Mugello during this period before Cosimo came to power. The immediate difficulty in connecting the drawing with the Uffizi portrait of ca. 1543–1545 is that this drawing represents a younger woman than Maria appears to be in the Uffizi picture and, especially, in the drawing that is unquestionably for it (cat. 346). Furthermore, the style of this drawing is very different from the soft red chalk style of cat. 346. It is closer to the style of the Careggi drawings of 1535–1536 or to that of the black chalk self-portrait drawing of ca. 1533–1534 (cat. 331). The precise modelling of the face, the clarity with which the features are delineated, and the rigidity of a figure with a disproportionately large head and exaggerated sloping shoulders are close links with the self-portrait drawing.

[25] Baltimore, Walters Art Gallery 37.596 (panel 87 x 71 cm). This picture is the earliest of Pontormo's representations of Maria Salviati, the others being cat. 335 of ca. 1537, cat. 346 of ca. 1543, and the Uffizi painting, probably done after her death. This portrait is listed in the Riccardi Collection inventory of 1612 (see Keutner 1959, 151), where it is described as "un quadro di bra.a uno e mezzo della Sig.[ra] D. Maria Medici con una puttina [sic]." In its overpainted state it was rejected by Clapp 1916, 194, but was identified after cleaning by King 1940, 75–84, figs. 1–3. The identity of the subject is confirmed by Vasari's medallion portrait of Maria (Palazzo Vecchio), which is based on this representation. The date is easily established as late 1526 or early 1527. Maria wears the widow's veil and holds a medallion that must have represented her husband, who died November 30, 1526. Maria and Cosimo went into exile in the spring of 1527. The child can be none other than Cosimo (b. 1519), who is represented here at about the age of seven. Furthermore, the hieratic placement of the mother and child, the interweaving of the hands, and the prominent position of the medallion are clearly references to Cosimo's succession and destiny as a Medici ruler. The date 1526–1527 has not been accepted by Berti, *MP* 1956, 53, who identified the picture as the lost Castello portrait mentioned by Vasari and interpreted it as a retrospective likeness of Cosimo and his mother at his coming to power in 1537. Neither the date nor the identification of the child has been accepted by Keutner 1959, 144–147, fig. 8. He based himself on the apparently mistaken reference to a "puttina" in the Riccardi inventory and identified the portrait as Pontormo's lost Castello portrait of Maria accompanied by one of her young female relatives.

Late 1537/38–1543. DECORATION OF THE CASTELLO LOGGIA: *Philosophy, Astrology, Geometry, Music, Arithmetic, and Ceres* (in lunettes; stories connected with these figures in medallions); *Flying Putti, Saturn with the Sign of Capricorn, Mars with the Sign of Leo, and Mercury with the Sign of Gemini* (in the vault). Environs of Florence, Villa Castello. Oil on plaster (destroyed).

Bibliography: Clapp 1916, 66–67, 262–263.

According to Vasari, after the battle of Montemurlo (August 2, 1537) Cosimo initiated a large-scale redecoration of the gardens and the villa of Castello.[26] Allegedly to please his mother, Maria Salviati, he commissioned Pontormo to paint "la prima loggia che si truova entrando nel palazzo di Castello a man manca." [27] Vasari states (V/M, VI, 282) that Pontormo kept the scaffolding up for five years until Maria ordered the work uncovered. Since Maria died December 12, 1543, the frescoes were probably not started until sometime in 1538, although the preparatory work may have begun late in 1537. Also late in that year, according to Vasari "nel principio di quel lavoro" (*ibid.*), Pontormo painted portraits of the new Duke Cosimo and of Maria Salviati (see cat. 334–335). The first work in the loggia was the ornamental decoration, which Bronzino and the others who had worked with Pontormo at Careggi executed after his drawings (*ibid.*, 282; VII, 596). Then Pontormo shut himself up in the loggia and painted without assistance the figures in the vault, the *Allegories*, and their medallions.[28]

Since the frescoes of the loggia had already begun to deteriorate in Vasari's time because they were executed in oil on dry plaster (see V/M, VI, 283), there is no satisfactory notice of the details of Pontormo's work after the sixteenth century. According to Borghini 1584, 484: "Dipinse a Castello la prima loggia, che si trova entrando nel palagio a man manca, faccendovi alcune historie degli Dei antiche, e arti liberali, lavorate a olio sula calcina secca, il qual lavora il tempo, e l'aria consumano a poco a poco." Subsequent writers were no longer able even to comment on the subjects of the frescoes.[29]

Clapp associated several drawings (cat. 336–337, 343) with the loggia, but there has been no attempt in modern literature to deal with the loggia and its program as a whole. A detailed reconstruction of the

[26] V/M, VI, 282. See the life of Tribolo (*ibid.*, 71–85) for a full description of Cosimo's plans for the gardens. For the villa itself see Moreni 1791/95, I, 101–110; G. Anguillesi, *Notizie Storiche dei Palazzi e Ville appartenti alla I. e R. Corona di Toscana* (Pisa, 1815), 214–221; *Mostra del Giardino italiano*, Palazzo Vecchio (Florence, 1931), fig. 6.

[27] Today the loggia is closed in, but it appears otherwise unaltered. There are three lunettes on the rear wall, two on the left wall, and one on the right wall. Since the space on the right wall nearest to the rear wall is taken up by an archway leading to a staircase, the number of lunettes agrees with the number of *Allegories* named by Vasari (see n. 28).

[28] V/M, VI, 283; "Vi fece dunque nel mezzo della volta un Saturno col segno del Capricorno, e Marte ermafrodito nel segno del Leone e della Vergine, ed alcuni putti in aria che volano come quei di Careggi. Vi fece poi, in certe femminone grandi e quasi tutte ignude, la Filosofia, l'Astrologia, la Geometria, la Musica, l'Arismetica, ed una Cerere, ed alcune medaglie di storiette fatte con varie tinte di colori ed appropriate alle figure."

[29] Bottari (ed. Borghini, 1730, 396n1) remarks that only the outlines of the decoration described by Borghini remain. Moreni 1791/95, I, 103, could only repeat Vasari's description and clearly could tell nothing for himself: "Se ne deplora di queste [the frescoes] la perdita totale." Finally, Milanesi (V/M, VI, 283n1) noted that they were completely lost and the wall whitewashed.

loggia decoration is not possible with the present evidence, but the sixteenth-century descriptions may be clarified and, on the basis of the surviving preparatory studies (cat. 336–344), a few additional suggestions may be made. The allegorical figures that Vasari names are the *quadrivium* of the Liberal Arts (*Astrology*, *Geometry*, *Music*, *Arithmetic*) with the related discipline of *Philosophy*. Borghini refers to these figures as "arti liberali" but does not name them individually. From Vasari (V/M, VI, 83–84) we know that Cosimo's elaborate plans for the Castello garden sculpture were to be executed according to a program devised by Benedetto Varchi that included *Seasons*, *Virtues*, *Law*, *Peace*, *Sciences*, *Languages*, and the *Arts*, all conceived as allegorical references to the Medici dynasty and to Duke Cosimo himself. In such a scheme Pontormo's *Allegories of the Liberal Arts* would have found a natural place. According to Vasari, these figures were, together with a *Ceres*, "feminone grandi e quasi tutte ignude." The Castello loggia has six lunettes — exactly the number of figures mentioned by Vasari — and the *Allegories* must have been painted in these spaces rather than in pendentives as in the Careggi loggia. Furthermore, cat. 343 and 344 are studies of reclining nudes that are identical in style to the drawings for the vault and that are ideally designed for such lunette spaces. The most logical place for the *medaglione* that accompanied these figures would have been in the pendentives between the lunettes. In this case there would have been six scenes with a medallion corresponding to each figure. However, no drawings survive for these scenes and we have no further evidence on their subjects or location.

The figures of the vault are described by Vasari as "Saturn with the Sign of Capricorn, Mars hermaphrodite in the Sign of Leo and the Virgin," by Borghini as "ancient Gods." It may be suggested with some certainty that this vault decoration was intended as a pictorial rendering of Cosimo's horoscope, a scheme that would have been something of a novelty in Florence, but not without precedent in Rome.[30] Cosimo was born June 11, 1519.[31] In his horoscope Saturn was in the Sign of Capricorn 22°. The ascendant was at 27°

[30] The signs of the zodiac and the planets had occurred both in church and in secular decoration but their configuration as the horoscope of an individual was unusual. The combination of the planets, the signs of the zodiac, and the liberal arts that is seen in Pontormo's Castello loggia appeared in Florence within the late medieval encyclopedic tradition in, for example, the Spanish chapel of S.M. Novella. The Sala della Ragione in Padua, the Palazzo Schifanoia in Ferrara, and the Tempio Malatestiano in Rimini are representative Quattrocento examples, later manifestations of the same tradition in which the signs of the zodiac occur in conjunction with apostles, planetary gods, labors of the months, etc. Examples of a different point of view in which the sky is shown in a cupola as it would have appeared at a given moment of time appear in Quattrocento Florence in the Old Sacristy, San Lorenzo, and in the Pazzi Chapel; later, in Rome, in Raphael's Chigi Chapel, S.M. del Popolo, of 1515–1516. In these examples the signs of the zodiac were still projected within a religious context; however, in Rome in the early sixteenth century, this device was used for the glorification of an individual and the "picture of the sky" at the moment of his birth made the basis for secular ceiling decorations. The earliest example is Peruzzi's horoscope of Agostino Chigi (1510–1511, Palazzo Farnesina). See F. Saxl, *La Fede Astrologica di Agostino Chigi* (Rome, 1934). This was followed in 1521 by that of Leo X on the ceiling of the Sala dei Pontefici in the Vatican (see Freedberg 1961, I, 566–567). There are several examples of elaborate astrological programs in the later sixteenth century, such as Zuccari's at Caprarola and Zucchi's in the Galleria Ruccellai of the Palazzo Ruspoli, Rome. See F. Saxl, *Antiker Götter in der Spätrenaissance* (Berlin, 1927).

[31] I am indebted to Mr. Eric Schroeder, who interpreted Cosimo's horoscope as quoted, with positions recalculated roughly, from Gauricus and Junctinus.

and, as ruler of the Sign of Capricorn, Saturn was "Lord of the Ascendant." This position was most significant for Cosimo, who would have regarded Saturn as his best planet with respect to "dignity," We have considerable evidence that Cosimo did, indeed, place great emphasis on the Sign of Capricorn, since the goat appears frequently as a decorative motive in works that he commissioned, at least one of which dates as early as 1538.[32] Furthermore, in another decorative cycle contemporary in date with Castello, Cosimo's horoscope based on the Sign of Capricorn played a significant part. Among the decorations, probably temporary, for his marriage to Eleanora in 1539 Cosimo had had painted "le stelle che entrano nel segno del Capricorno, nella camera dedicata all' Honore . . ." [33] Thus, it is probable that *Saturn with the Sign of Capricorn* occupied a prominent or even central place on the Castello vault. For this group we have been able to identify two preparatory studies (cat. 336 and 340), the first showing the figure of Saturn astride the goat, the second showing the nude Saturn alone.

[32] The medal with a portrait of Cosimo cited above in note 24 has Capricorn with eight stars on the reverse. Cf. Heiss, pl. 1, 8. The goat frequently appears as a device in conjunction with Cosimo's arms in such diverse works as the frescoes in the Sala degli Elementi, Palazzo Vecchio; a drawing for a frontispiece (Uffizi 394 orn.); the borders of the tapestries of the *Story of Joseph* for the Sala de' Dugento. Cosimo had adapted Capricorn as his device, not because it was the sign of his birth, but because of its key position in his horoscope and because it was the sign of Emperor Charles V, who had given Cosimo his title, and of Emperor Augustus, who had defeated Marcantonio and Cleopatra on the same day of the year (August 2) that Cosimo had won the decisive battle at Montemurlo. See Paolo Giovio, *Dialogo dell' Imprese Militari et Amorose di Monsignor Giovio Vescovo di Nocera: Con un Ragionamento di Messer Lodovico Domenichi, nel medesimo soggetto* (Florence, 1556), 32–33.

[33] *Ibid.*, 33.

It is characteristic of Pontormo's canon of design at Castello that Saturn and the goat are not depicted separately but are interwoven as a single compositional unit. In comparison with earlier representations of Saturn and the goat, this seems to have been an entirely novel concept.[34]

The next part in Vasari's description, "Marte ermafradito nel segno del Leone e della Virgine," is more problematic, since Vasari has evidently identified these figures incorrectly. In Cosimo's horoscope Mars was in the Sign of Leo 22°. Cat. 341 can easily be identified as Pontormo's study for *Mars with the Sign of Leo.* The nude Mars lies over the lion, the two figures forming the same kind of intertwined group as the *Saturn with the Sign of Capricorn.* However, Mars is not an hermaphrodite and is not depicted as such in the drawing. It may be suggested that the hermaphrodite that Vasari saw was actually Mercury, who is often shown as an hermaphrodite and who figures prominently closely conjunct to Venus in this horoscope. Mercury and Venus were in the Sign of Cancer, the sign of Cosimo's birth, and thus would naturally have been included in Pontormo's representation. Since the Sign of Cancer and the Sign of Virgo are both adjacent to the Sign of Leo, Vasari must have mistaken Pontormo's Venus (actually in the Sign of Cancer) for Virgo, a sign that plays no important part in this horoscope at all. Among Pontormo's drawings for Castello there is one that probably represents

[34] *Cf.* Perugino in the Udienza del Cambio, where the goat is placed in the right wheel of Saturn's chariot; Agostino di Duccio in the Tempio Malatestiano, where the goat and Saturn are in separate panels; or Perino del Vaga in the Sala dei Pontefici, where the goat occupies its own square field to the left of Saturn. In the most important example after Pontormo's loggia, Zucchi's representation in the Galleria Ruccellai, the goat is placed between Saturn's legs as in Pontormo's drawing. See Saxl, *Antiker Götter*, pl. 2.

Mercury with the Sign of Gemini. The nude figure in cat. 342 strongly suggests an hermaphrodite, he wears a helmet, and the object he holds may have been intended as the caduceus. Intertwined with the reclining figure are two putti who would represent the Sign of Gemini, since Mercury rules that sign and the twins usually accompany representations of Mercury in an astrological context.

The last part of Vasari's description of the vault is a reference to "alcuni putti in aria che volano come quei di Careggi." Like those at Careggi (cf. cat. 319–320), these putti may have been represented flying around the edges of the vault, leaving the center free for the representation of the horoscope. Several studies for these figures have survived (cat. 336–339). Cat. A151 (fig. 322) is a copy after some of these putti and after the lunette *Allegories* of the loggia.

STUDIES FOR THE CASTELLO LOGGIA

336 · Florence, Uffizi 6510F: Studies for the Castello loggia. Bust of a flying putto with his arms extended; to the right on a smaller scale, the entire figure flying to the right; above sideways on the sheet, nude with a beard seated astride a goat. 257 x 178, black chalk; upper left corner of the sheet replaced. Fig. 316.

Bibliography: Berenson 1903, no. 2017; Clapp 1914, 120–121; Clapp 1916, 68; Berenson 1938, no. 2017.

Berenson originally associated this sheet with San Lorenzo, but later agreed with Clapp in connecting it with the Castello loggia. These putti, along with those on cat. 337–339, are studies for the flying putti of the vault. They are similar in general type and action to the Careggi putti, but the line is softer and details such as the exaggerated roundness of the face, the mop of hair, and the very large ears, are peculiar to Pontormo's Castello drawings (cf. cat. 343–344). As Clapp has noted, the old man astride the goat (which he called a monster) is a study for the Saturn mentioned by Vasari (V/M, VI, 283): "Vi fece dunque nel mezzo della volta un Saturno col segno del Capricorno." Cat. 340 is a study for the figure alone.

337 · Florence, Uffizi 6592F *recto*: Studies for the Castello loggia. Nude boy flying with arms outstretched studied twice; in reverse direction, faint study of the same figure. (*Verso*: Scrawl in black chalk, not catalogued.) 233 x 173, black chalk; lower corners replaced. Fig. 317.

Bibliography: Berenson 1903, no. 2091; Clapp 1914, 172; Berenson 1938, no. 2091.

Berenson thought these flying figures were for San Lorenzo, but Clapp saw that they were studies for the putto sketched on cat. 336 and thus intended for the vault of the Castello loggia.

338 · Florence, Uffizi 6734F: Studies for the Castello loggia. Three-quarter length nude boy flying upward with arms raised; to the right, two details of the figure restudied. 208 x 280, red chalk; three corners replaced; laid down.

Bibliography: Berenson 1903, no. 2216; Clapp 1914, 265; Berenson 1938, no. 2216. (Photo G.)

Clapp dated this drawing 1545–1550 but did not connect it with any painting. It is for the putti of the Castello vault, who are also studied on cat. 336–337 and 339.

339 · Florence, Uffizi 6539F *verso*: Study for the Castello loggia. Three-quarter length nude boy with his arms raised above his head; above, the left arm restudied. (*Recto*: Nude and drapery, cat. 238.) 280 x 184, black chalk.

Bibliography: Clapp 1914, 140; Berenson 1938, no. 2042. (Photo G.)

This sketch was dated 1545–1555 by Clapp as connected with San Lorenzo and with a drawing on page four of Pontormo's diary (cf. fig. 379). Although it is a very slight, unelaborated sketch, it is actually more closely associated with the studies for the flying putti of the Castello vault, especially cat. 337.

340 · Cambridge (Mass.), Fogg Art Museum 1932.144: Study for the Castello loggia. Nude seen to the knees seated in profile right and leaning back on his hands looking over his right shoulder. 292 x 194, red chalk; W: Pascal lamb (B. 50). Fig. 318.

Collection: Loeser, given to the museum in 1932.

Bibliography: Clapp 1914, 85; Berenson 1938, no. 1955B; Mongan and Sachs 1940, I, 83, II, fig. 82.

Clapp rejected this drawing from Pontormo's *oeuvre* and Berenson thought it was a poor study from the San Lorenzo period. However, Mongan and Sachs accepted it as Pontormo, comparing it with cat. 316, a nude study for the Careggi loggia that is close in pose to this figure, and with cat. A126, probably a copy after a lost study for San Lorenzo. The connection with cat. 336, a small sketch for the *Saturn with the Sign of Capricorn* for the Castello vault, has not been noted. This drawing is a study for the figure that most likely occupied the central position in the vault (see V/M, VI, 283). Even without cat. 336 to identify the motive, this drawing is recognizable as a study for Castello. The figure is composed in an arabesque with the head turned to look out at the spectator, a motive that runs through the loggia studies (cf. cat. 343–344 and cat. A151, a copy after some of the figures). In this study and in others for the loggia there is a refinement in the rubbed red chalk modelling, a softening of hard contours, and less insistence on the minute description of the forms that had characterized many of the drawings of the earlier thirties.

341 · Florence, Uffizi 6760F *recto*: Study for the Castello loggia. Nude reclining to the left against a lion with his legs crossed and his left arm over his head. (*Verso*: Profile study, cat. 332.) 184 x 241, black chalk, the lion in red chalk; W: Anchor in a circle. Fig. 319.

Bibliography: Berenson 1903, no. 2240; Clapp 1914, 281; Clapp 1916, fig. 153; Berenson 1938, no. 2240.

Clapp connected this drawing with San Lorenzo and with a sketch on page four of Pontormo's diary (cf. fig. 381). We know from a copy after the San Lorenzo *Resurrection of the Dead* (cat. A216) that there was a similar figure in the fresco, but this drawing is an earlier version of the motive. It is identifiable as the *Mars with the Sign of Leo* that Vasari describes (V/M, VI, 283) as having been with the *Saturn* in the middle of the vault. The lion under his body to the left is unmistakable and the languid, reclining pose inspired after the Medici Tomb figures of *Crespusculo* and *Notte* is still another variant of cat. 340, 342–344, studies for the Castello loggia. Such a figure with a lion would have had no place in the San Lorenzo fresco cycle, although the pose of the figure without the lion was certainly used again, as were numerous motives from Pontormo's repertory of the thirties and forties.

342 · Florence, Uffizi 17405F: Study for the Castello loggia. Nude reclining to the right on an inclined surface resting on his left arm and looking up to the right; behind him, two putti. 153 x 172, black chalk; paper discolored by old glue on the verso; W: Mermaid in a circle with a star (cf. B. 13899). Fig. 320.

This unpublished drawing may be identified as a study of *Mercury with the Sign of Gemini* for the Castello vault. In his account of the Castello vault Vasari describes an hermaphrodite figure, but mistakenly identifies it as Mars. However, Mars is not usually represented as an hermaphrodite and cat. 341 is unmistakably Pontormo's drawing for the *Mars with the Sign of Leo*. The hermaphrodite seen by Vasari was probably Mercury, who is also prominent in Cosimo's horoscope. He is shown here with Gemini, the sign of his "Night House" and his usual attribute in an astrological context. The position of the nude, especially the legs, is strongly reminiscent of the classic hermaphrodite pose in antique sculpture, and there seems little doubt, in spite of the lack of very pronounced female characteristics, that Pontormo intended this figure as an hermaphrodite.[35] The *sotto-in-su* perspective from which the figure is seen also makes it likely that it was intended for the vault. In style this drawing is especially close to cat. 344 for one of the lunette *Allegories*, but the elongated, boneless, small-headed type also anticipates the figure type of Pontormo's San Lorenzo drawings, begun only a few years later.

343 · Florence, Uffizi 6630F: Study for the Castello loggia. Reclining nude leaning on the left elbow looking out at the spectator from behind the raised right arm. 212 x 289, red chalk; repair top center of the sheet; W: Star in a circle (B. 6086). Fig. 323.

Bibliography: Berenson 1903, no. 2123; *MPA* 1910, 37; Gamba 1912, no. 22, pl. 22; Clapp 1914, 194; Clapp 1916, 68; Berenson 1938, no. 2123; *MP* 1956 (Marcucci), no. 135, fig. 163b; Marcucci 1956, 20, fig. 25; Sinibaldi (*Uffizi Exhib.*) 1960, no. 94.

Berenson dated this study late, while Gamba apparently placed it in the thirties. Marcucci, followed by Sinibaldi, suggested that it was intended for the Adonis of the *Venus and Adonis* projected for Poggio a Caiano and dated it 1530–1532. However, this drawing differs sharply in style from the studies of the early and even middle thirties. The date of the Poggio a Caiano project (1532–1534) was exactly the period when Pontormo's draughtsmanship was hard and Michelangelesque, the contours firm and the muscles insistently emphasized (cf. cat. 308), while this nude approaches the San Lorenzo drawings in its softness and refinement of surface. The delicate handling of the red chalk also brings it close to the two portrait drawings of the early forties, cat. 345 and 346. Clapp rightly thought this study was for Castello, but identified it with the Mars Hermaphrodite mentioned by Vasari. However, cat. 337 is explicitly a study for the *Mars with the Sign of Leo*, while this drawing and cat. 344 must have been studies for the allegorical figures in the lunettes. Cat. A151 (fig. 322), a copy after some of the figures from the Castello loggia, contains a sketch after a figure very close to this one in reverse.

344 · Florence, Uffizi 6683F: Study for the Castello loggia. Reclining nude leaning on the right arm with the left arm behind the head and looking out at the spectator. 199 x 318, black chalk. Fig. 321.

Bibliography: Berenson 1903, no. 2168; Clapp 1914, 231; Berenson 1938, no. 2168; Becherucci 1943, 10, pl. 27; Becherucci 1944, 21; Marcucci 1956, 22, fig. 26.

Clapp dated this study 1545–1550, while Becherucci and Marcucci connected it with the Castello *Allegories*. The reclining pose of the figure would have been suitable for one of the lunettes of the loggia and

[35] The sexual ambiguity of Pontormo's nudes in the late period becomes increasingly evident. Even the females of the Castello loggia (cat. 343 and 344) and the *Three Graces* (cat. 321) are more masculine than feminine.

the pose is exactly that of the other lunette figure study turned around (cat. 343). On a sheet of studies after the Castello loggia (cat. A151), this nude appears almost as in this drawing, except for the position of the left arm.

Ca. 1540–1544. PORTRAIT OF GIOVANNI DELLA CASA. Washington, National Gallery, Kress Collection 1902. III. Panel, 98 x 70 cm. Fig. 330.

Bibliography: Lafenestre 1909, 12, illustrated; Bode 1914, 6; Dussler 1942, 148–149; Suida 1946, 143–144, fig. 8; Suida 1956, no. 55, illustrated; *MP* 1956 (Berti), no. 84, fig. 77.

After passing as Sebastiano del Piombo from its first publication in 1909, this important portrait was attributed to Pontormo by Suida and dated 1541–1544. There is little difficulty in confirming the traditional identification of the portrait as Monsignor Giovanni della Casa and in dating it within a few years after 1540 when Della Casa was in Florence and had become a monsignor.[36] The chronological relation of Pontormo's portrait to those by Salviati and Titian confirms this identification and dating. The earliest is the portrait by Salviati showing Della Casa as a younger man not yet in clerical dress.[37] Salviati's portrait must date before 1540, by which time Della Casa had been made a monsignor, and probably was painted in 1537 or 1538, the year in which he commissioned Salviati's *Visitation* in S. Giovanni Decollato (V/M, VI, 579). Pontormo's portrait may be dated at the earliest in 1540, the year Della Casa is documented as a monsignor in Florence, and at the latest in 1544, the year he became Archbishop of Benevento. In Pontormo's portrait Della Casa's dress is that of a monsignor, he appears somewhat older than the man in Salviati's portrait, and he has grown a longer, fuller beard. Pontormo shows Della Casa holding a book, a reference to his activity as a man of letters, while his increasingly important role in the Church is underscored by the ecclesiastical setting. Titian's portrait is the only one that is documented and it serves to confirm the identity of the sitter in the other two portraits. It was begun March 1545 and not yet finished January 15, 1546.[38] While this lost work is known

[36] Della Casa was born in 1503 and in 1529 he was in Rome pursuing both literary and clerical careers. See *Enciclopedia italiana* 12 (1931), 545. He visited Florence briefly in 1531 and in the winter of 1533–1534, returning to Rome in the spring of 1534 and remaining there until 1540. See also U. Scoti-Bertinelli, ed., *Il Galateo* (Turin, 1921), 2–4. From 1537 he was in the service of Paul III, being named Apostolic Clerk on March 12, 1537 (*Enc. ital.*, 545). The exact date on which he became a monsignor is not clear. According to Scoti-Bertinelli, he took orders before 1538, but he had not yet assumed the title of monsignor by July 8, 1537, when he signed himself "Ser. Giovanni della Casa." (See *Opere di Monsig. Giovanni della Casa*, Florence, 1707, "Lettere," 91.) In 1540 he was sent to Florence as Apostolic Commissioner for tax collection. While there he was admitted to the Florentine Academy at its founding, February 11, 1540. Cardinal Alessandro Farnese wrote to him in Florence late in 1540 addressing him as Monsignor (*Opere*, "Introduction," 39). It is not known how long Monsignor della Casa stayed in Florence, but he had definitely returned to Rome by April 2, 1544, when he was made Archbishop of Benevento (*Opere*, 41). In August of the same year he was made papal nuncio to Venice and remained in that post until the death of Paul III in 1549.

[37] Vienna, Kunsthistorisches Museum no. 2681 (panel, 63 x 49 cm; inscribed on the back "Ritratto di M. della Casa"). See L. Baldass, "Uber ein Porträt von Francesco Salviati," *Belvedere* 10 (1931), 11–12, fig. 9. The portrait was attributed to Salviati and dated ca. 1540 by Wilde.

[38] See *Lettere da Giovanni della Casa a Carlo*

only through the copy in the Uffizi inscribed "Joannes Casa," in this picture Della Casa appears costumed and bearded much as in Pontormo's portrait.[39]

Pontormo's *Della Casa* is close to his *Maria Salviati* of ca. 1543–1545 in the format, the pose of the figure, the elongated pyramid of the slope-shouldered, small-headed figure, in the elliptical shapes into which the arms and hands are pulled, and in the sharp light that falls on the abstracted forms. However, it is more immediately communicative of the sitter's personality, and considering the special circumstances under which the *Maria Salviati* may have been painted, the *Della Casa* is probably more characteristic of Pontormo's portrait style in this period. Berti has suggested an analogy with the *Portrait of a Man with a Book* attributed to Pontormo by Longhi, a picture that is close in pose to this one but somewhat less precise and rhythmic in style.[40] The relation of the figure to the background in the portrait of Della Casa recalls Pontormo's use of the partly open door behind the figure in his *Portrait of Alessandro de' Medici* of 1534–1535. However, in the later portrait this device is employed with a more dramatic effect of spatial illogic, much as in the extension of space to the upper right of the slightly later *Madonna and Child* (known only in copies, see p. 317, n. 8). Pontormo's use of architecture in this portrait contrasts with Bronzino's portrait architecture of the same period, such as in the *Ugolino Martelli* and the *Bartolommeo Panciatichi*. In Bronzino's portraits the units of the architecture tend to lock the figure rigidly into place; in the Della Casa the figure is not imprisoned by the church in which he is standing, but seems to float in front of it — a characteristic late Pontormo image.

Gualteruzzi da Fano, ed. L. M. Rezzi (Imola, 1824), 16; and *Opere*, "Lettere," 51. The first letter from Della Casa mentions the portrait as commissioned and the second notes it as not yet finished.

[39] See Suida, 1946, 134–144. An engraving after the lost Titian appears as the frontispiece in the *Opere di Giovanni della Casa* (Venice, 1728).

[40] See R. Longhi, "Un Ritratto del Pontormo," *Paragone* 35 (1952), 40–41, illustrated, who published this portrait as in a private collection, Florence, dating it ca. 1534. The analogy to Pontormo's portrait of Della Casa, as well as to Bronzino's *Portrait of a Man* (Metropolitan Museum) perhaps indicates a date closer to 1540 for this portrait, although it is difficult to judge either its authenticity or its date from Longhi's reproduction.

STUDY FOR THE PORTRAIT OF GIOVANNI DELLA CASA

345 · Florence, Uffizi 443F *verso*: Study for the *Portrait of Giovanni della Casa*. Three-quarter length standing bearded man wearing a clerical robe and cape with a biretta on his head; his left hand held to his breast; his right hand studied twice: once holding a book, once holding his biretta out to the left; to the right above, the lower part of the head studied in profile. (*Recto*: Portrait of a boy, cat. 324.) 272 x 196, red chalk. Fig. 331.

Bibliography: Berenson 1903, no. 1970; Clapp 1914, 93–94; Clapp 1916, 86; Berenson 1938, no. 1970.

Clapp thought this drawing was a study of ca. 1540 for the lost *Portrait of Bishop Ardinghelli* that is mentioned by Vasari (V/M, VI, 273–274). It has not been noted that these studies are for the *Portrait of Giovanni della Casa*. The sitter is unquestionably the same and the costume and pose identical. In this drawing Pontormo has experimented with the position of the Monsignor's right arm and hand, once holding the book and once holding his biretta, which he wears alternatively on his head. In the painting Pontormo used the less conventional idea of having the Monsignor hold his hat rather than wear it, and placed the book in his left hand instead. The style of these studies is close to that of the studies for the *Portrait of Maria Salviati* (cat. 346), where Pontormo has also concentrated on the head and not worked out the rest of the figure in the same detail. Both are executed in an ultra-refined and sensitive red chalk manner that is softer and less sharply linear and descriptive than the black chalk portrait drawings of the thirties, such as cat. 331 and 335.

Ca. 1543–1545. PORTRAIT OF MARIA SALVIATI. Florence, Uffizi 3565. III. Panel, 87 x 71 cm. Fig. 328.

Bibliography: Berenson 1932, 467; Lányi 1932/34, 88–102, figs. 1–2; Berenson 1936, 401; *MM* 1939, 130–131; King 1940, 81–82, fig. 6; Becherucci 1944, 21, fig. 51; Nicco Fasola 1947, 58, fig. 44; *MDM* 1954 (Marcucci), 38–39; *Amsterdam Exhib.* 1955, no. 95; *MP* 1956 (Berti), no. 82, fig. 75; Gamba 1956, 15–16, fig. 31; Keutner 1959, 144–146, fig. 6.

According to the museum, this picture was acquired in Siena in 1911 as a Sienese painting. It was first given to Pontormo by Berenson and was identified by Lányi as the portrait of Maria Salviati that Vasari says (V/M, VI, 282) Pontormo painted at the beginning of his work at Castello. King accepted the identification of the picture, but doubted that it could have been the Castello portrait of ca. 1537 because of Maria's apparently advanced age. He placed it with its preparatory study (cat. 346), which emphasizes her age even more, toward the time of her death in 1543. Berti tended to place the picture even later, suggesting that it might be an idealized representation done after her death. Thus, with some differences in dating between ca. 1537 and ca. 1543, this picture has generally been accepted as Pontormo's *Portrait of Maria Salviati.* Only Gamba and Keutner have disagreed, maintaining that it does not represent Maria at all and that it is probably not even by Pontormo, Gamba supposing that it was done by a Sienese artist after Pontormo's preparatory study (cat. 346).

In spite of these objections, the identification of this woman as Maria Salviati cannot be seriously doubted. The face is the same as in Pontormo's double portrait of Maria with Cosimo (Baltimore), painted about seventeen years earlier, and in Vasari's medallion in the Palazzo Vecchio, which is based on the Baltimore representation. However, as King and Berti have noted, this portrait is not the one that Pontormo painted about 1537 at Castello. The painting and its preparatory study both show a woman older than Maria probably appeared in 1537 at the age of thirty-eight and well before the three-year illness that ended in her death. Furthermore, there is another representation of Maria that does show her as a younger woman, a drawing that might well have been done for the lost Castello portrait (cat. 335). Cat. 346, the study for this picture, shows Maria more aged than in cat. 335, and was probably made as late as 1543. As has been pointed out, Maria does appear somewhat younger — or at least smoother — in the painting than in the drawing. Lányi has indicated that repaint may be partially responsible for these differences. However, as Berti has suggested, it is certainly possible that this is an idealized post mortem representation of Maria, possibly painted for Cosimo shortly after her death.

STUDY FOR THE PORTRAIT OF MARIA SALVIATI

346 · Florence, Uffizi 6503F *recto*: Studies for the *Portrait of Maria Salviati.*

Woman seen from the neck to below the waist dressed in a high-necked, full-sleeved dress with her left arm across her waist; below, head of a woman wearing a headdress and veil. (*Verso*: Head, the outlines of which show through on the recto, cat. A56.) 265 x 188, red chalk; W: Angel (cf. B. 613). Fig. 329.

Bibliography: Berenson 1903, no. 2011; Clapp 1914, 115; Lányi 1932/34, 93–94, fig. 3; Berenson 1938, 319, no. 2011; King 1940, 81–82, fig. 7; *MP* 1956 (Berti), 52–53; Gamba 1956, 15, fig. 32; Berenson 1961, no. 2011, fig. 960.

Clapp dated this drawing ca. 1545 without knowledge of the portrait for which it is a study. When Lányi published the Uffizi picture, he dated both drawing and painting about 1537. However, King and Berti tended to place the drawing toward the end of Maria's life, ca. 1543. Only Berenson has not accepted the association of the two works. He dated the Uffizi picture 1537 but believed that Maria could not have looked as old as she does in the drawing in that year, and implied that the drawing dated some years later.

While differences between the drawing and the painting certainly exist, there is little doubt that these are studies for the Uffizi picture. The upper study is for the costume exactly as it appears in the painting, and the head study certainly shows the same features. The differences from the painting are not a matter of shape, but of a general abstraction of forms and smoothing over of details, such as the lines under the eyes. The face is the same one that Pontormo had painted in the Baltimore portrait of 1526–1527 and that he had drawn in cat. 335 of ca. 1537. The difference between this likeness and the earlier ones lies mainly in a lessened fullness in the face, due to her more advanced age and probably augmented by her illness.

The style of the drawing bears out this dating. Its soft red chalk *sfumato*, a subtle and understated modelling that veils rather than insisting on the plasticity of the forms, is that of the study for the *Portrait of Giovanni della Casa* of the early forties (cat. 345) and of one of the Castello drawings (cat. 343). As in the Della Casa portrait study, the only other portrait drawing surviving from this late period, there is a sense of intimacy and communication of the personality of the sitter that was not as evident in the portrait drawings of the thirties, such as Pontormo's own earlier study of Maria herself (cat. 335).

PART VI · 1545–1556

Catalogue entries 347–383

PART VI · 1545–1556

Ca. 1545–1549. CARTOONS FOR TAPESTRIES: *Benjamin at the Court of the Pharaoh; The Lamentation of Jacob* (destroyed; tapestries in Rome, Palazzo Quirinale). II. 565 x 278 cm; 550 x 270 cm. Fig. 332.

Bibliography: Geisenheimer 1909, 137–147, illustrated; Goldschmidt 1911, 48; Clapp 1916, 70–72, 183–187, fig. 134; Voss 1920, 172; McComb 1928, 21–25, 165–168; Berenson 1936, 402; *MF* 1952, no. 17; Longhi 1953, 15; *MP* 1956 (Berti), nos. 75 and 77, figs. 68 and 70; Emiliani 1960, 73–76.

Vasari mentions a series of tapestries of the *Story of Joseph* that were made by the Flemish weavers Rost and Karcher from cartoons by Pontormo, Bronzino, and Salviati for the Sala de' Dugento.[1] According to Vasari, Pontormo did the cartoons for a *Lamentation of Jacob* and a *Joseph and Potiphar's Wife*.[2] In an inventory of July 1549 Pontormo is listed as the author of the *Joseph and Potiphar's Wife* and of a tapestry called "la coppa di Josef." [3] The *Lamentation of Jacob* mentioned by Vasari is readily identifiable as the tapestry now in the Palazzo Quirinale, but the others are more problematic. The *Joseph and Potiphar's Wife* in the Quirinale is certainly attributable to Bronzino rather than Pontormo. Its rigid and static composition is quite unlike the suave, rhythmic style of Pontormo's designs, but it is close in style to Bronzino's other tapestries. Therefore, either another tapestry actually by Pontormo has been misnamed or there was once a Pontormo tapestry of *Joseph and Potiphar's Wife* that has not survived. It is possible that Pontormo's tapestry of this subject was made but that it was not acceptable to the Duke and Bronzino designed one to replace it, the change not being noted since the commission was originally given to Pontormo. Such an explanation is credible in view of Vasari's statement that neither the Duke nor the weavers liked Pontormo's cartoons and that he ceased to participate in the project.[4] The "Coppa di Josef" attributed to Pontormo in the inventory is not identifiable unless it is, as Clapp has suggested, a misnaming for the *Benjamin at the Court of the Pharaoh* now in the Palazzo Quirinale. This tapestry is clearly a Pontormo invention and there are three preparatory studies for it (cat. 347–349).

There are various critical opinions on

[1] V/M, VI, 283: "Avendo poi condotto il signor duca in Fiorenza maestro Giovanni Rosso e maestro Niccolò Fiamminghi, maestri eccellenti di panni d'arazzo, perchè quell'arte si esercitasse ed imparasse dai Fiorentini, ordinò che si facessero panni d'oro e di seta per la sala del consiglio de'Dugento, con spesa di sessanta mila scudi, e che Jacopo e Bronzino facessero nei cartoni le storie di Joseffo." See also V/M, VII, 28–29 in connection with Salviati's cartoon, and *ibid.*, 599, where Vasari says that Pontormo did two of the cartoons for the series, Salviati one, and Bronzino fourteen.

[2] V/M, VI, 283–284: "Ma avendone fatte Jacopo due, in uno de'quali è quando a Jacob è annunziata la morte di Joseffo, e mostratogli i panni saguinosi, e nell'altro il fuggire di Joseffo, lasciando la veste dalla moglie di Putifaro . . ."

[3] See C. Conti, *Ricerche storiche sull'Arte degli Arazzi in Firenze* (Florence, 1875), 48–49; and Geisenheimer 1909, 142–143.

[4] See V/M, VI, 284: ". . . non piacquero nè al duca nè a que'maestri che gli avevano a mettere in opera, parendo loro cosa strana e da non dover riuscire ne' panni tessuti ed in opera; e così Jacopo non seguitò di fare più cartoni altrimenti."

the authorship and dating of the three tapestries in question. Goldschmidt and McComb gave only the *Lamentation* and the *Joseph and Potiphar's Wife* to Pontormo, while Clapp added the *Benjamin* to the group. Berenson and Berti accepted all three of them as Pontormo, but Longhi and Emiliani have given all of the tapestries to Bronzino, believing that Vasari's comment on the poor reception of the cartoons meant that no tapestries were made from Pontormo's cartoons at all. The tapestries have been dated variously between 1545 and 1553. Berenson dated them before 1546, Clapp dated the *Lamentation* and the *Joseph and Potiphar's Wife* 1545–1546 and the *Benjamin* 1546–1553 (although he identified it as mentioned in the 1549 inventory). Berti dated the *Benjamin* before 1549 and the *Lamentation* 1546–1553. The inconsistencies in the inventories as to the titles of the tapestries make it difficult to date them precisely. We know from a letter of September 1545 that Cosimo planned to initiate the production of tapestries in Florence, and from a letter of December 1545 that Bronzino had already made a cartoon.[5] According to an inventory of November 1553, the series of twenty tapestries was finished.[6] However, there is good reason to suppose that Pontormo did not continue to work as late as 1553. According to Vasari (V/M, VI, 284), he was dismissed from the project at some time before the series was finished. Furthermore, two tapestries from his cartoons are mentioned in the inventory of 1549. Therefore, 1549 is a likely terminal date for his cartoons, which may have been executed even earlier.

Since Pontormo probably began work at San Lorenzo in 1546, his tapestry designs are an integral part of the formulation of his late style, preceding by a short time his compositional studies for the frescoes of the upper range of the choir.

[5] See Geisenheimer 1909, 137–138.

[6] See Geisenheimer 1909, 138–139.

The tapestry cartoons are preliminary essays in decorative terms (which would have been compatible with the formalized idiom of Bronzino and Salviati) for the highly subjective and anti-decorative expressionism of the San Lorenzo frescoes. The compositions of the tapestries and the compositional drawings for the upper-range frescoes are remarkably similar. In the tapestries, as in cat. 350, 354, 364, and 370 (see these entries for more detailed comparisons), a new compositional image has emerged that is reminiscent of Pontormo's rhythmic style of the late twenties; only now all narrative values have been subordinated to the demands of decorative organization. The loosely sprawling figures of the thirties are hung along the central axis like a garland, little distinction being made between the interweaving of the fruits of the real garland around the tapestry border and the handling of the figures within the narrow picture field. As in the San Lorenzo compositions these figures are connected by a slow and complex rhythm that is generated at the bottom of the composition, most characteristically in a pointed foot. If these singular compositions are compared with those of Bronzino, it is evident that they are, as Vasari reports, incompatible with the predominant style of the series, and some credence must be given to his story of their poor reception by Duke Cosimo and the weavers.

STUDIES FOR BENJAMIN AT THE COURT OF THE PHARAOH

347 · Florence, Uffizi 6593F *recto*: Study for *Benjamin at the Court of the Pharaoh.* Page from a sketchbook: Three-quarter length nude seen from behind bending to the left; below, head looking down. (*Verso*: Nude study, cat. A91.) 225 x 165, black chalk on pink prepared paper. Fig. 333.

Bibliography: Berenson 1903, no. 2092;

Clapp 1914, 172–173; Clapp 1916, 71, fig. 135; Berenson 1938, no. 2092.

Clapp rightly identified the figure as a study for the nude at the right behind the Pharaoh, reversed in the tapestry. This nude and the other nude studies for the tapestry (cat. 348–349) are of the same tightly muscled type that appears in the figure studies for the upper-range San Lorenzo frescoes, such as cat. 356, 358, and 371. However, here the line and the modelling are a little less delicately handled, and it is possible that the drawing was somewhat reworked by the artist who drew the nude on the verso. The head below is similar to faces in the tapestry, especially that of the Pharaoh, but also recalls heads in two works of this period for which no drawings have survived. The exact facial type with the ample, slightly drooping features and the heavy-lidded eyes appears in the *Isaac Blessing Jacob*,[7] and even more precisely in an important *Madonna and Child* that is known only from copies.[8]

[7] Uffizi, Gabinetto Disegni e Stampe 91466 (canvas, 121 x 214 cm). This work, also known as *Lot and his Daughters*, may be identical with Pontormo's *chiaroscuro* of that subject recorded in the 1612 inventory of the Riccardi Collection (see Keutner 1959, 153). O. Giglioli, "Un chiaroscuro inedito del Pontormo nella Galleria degli Uffizi," *Boll. d'A.* 28 (1934/35), 341–343, fig. 1, considered it a part of a decorative series dating ca. 1539. Berti, *MP* 1956, no. 74, fig. 67, connected it in style with the tapestries and dated it ca. 1545. This *chiaroscuro*, which certainly must have been part of a decorative frieze, is associable in composition and in the figure types with the drawings for the upper-range San Lorenzo frescoes as well as with the tapestries and may date as late as 1550. The Isaac may be compared with the God Father in cat. 354 and 359, with the Abraham in cat. 366, as well as with the Jacob in the *Lamentation* tapestry. The other figures, with their long flexible arms and their full features, are related to such San Lorenzo drawings as cat. 358 and 370.

[8] The Madonna and Child are seated in the foreground, with St. Joseph, Christ, St. Elizabeth, and St. John the Baptist in the right background. The composition is attributed to Pontormo on the basis of the inscription on the Madonna's book in several of the versions, such as the one in Munich. An inscription on the verso of cat. 107, a seventeenth-century drawing after the composition, indicates that a version of the painting belonged at that time to Cardinal Carlo de' Medici. However, this picture was not necessarily Pontormo's original, since most of the copies now known already existed by the later seventeenth century. This composition was Pontormo's most copied invention, there being at least twelve versions of it. Of these, only the Munich and the Ferroni-Frascione (now New York Art Market) versions have been seriously considered as the original. For discussion of the various copies see Clapp 1916, 194, 195, 201, 211, 212, 217, 223; M. Pittaluga, "Per un quadro smarrito del Pontormo," *L'Arte* n.s. 4 (1933), 354–366, figs. 1–2 (Poggio Imperiale version); and Berti, *MP* 1956, nos. 67–68, figs. 60–61 (Munich and Frascione versions). Berti dated the composition ca. 1529–1530, Pittaluga dated it 1540–1543, and Clapp placed it 1540–1550. It is unlikely to be identifiable, as Pittaluga has suggested, with the picture mentioned by Vasari (V/M, VI, 280) that Pontormo gave to Rossino the mason for finishing his house, since that picture must have dated 1536 or earlier (see p. 299, note 20). The composition surely dated ca. 1545–1550 and it might be the "quadro di Nostra Donna" that Vasari placed directly after the tapestry cartoons (V/M, VI, 284), but we have no more precise description of that picture. In any case, it is closely related in style to the tapestries and their drawings. The serpentine arrangement of the figures in the high, narrow background scene reflects the compositions of the tapestries, the St. Joseph is identical in movement to the figure at the top of the *Benjamin*, while the type of the Madonna occurs in the tapestries and in cat. 347. Cf. cat. 325 and 333, *Madonna and Child* drawings of the midthirties that are prototypes for this group.

348 · Florence, Uffizi 6572F: Study for *Benjamin at the Court of the Pharoah*. Page from a sketchbook: Half-length nude seen from behind turned to the right with his left arm bent up to his neck and looking over his shoulder. 218 x 156, black chalk on pink prepared paper. Fig. 334.

Bibliography: Berenson 1903, no. 2072; Clapp 1914, 162; Berenson 1938, no. 2072.

Clapp dated this drawing 1535–1540. It may be identified as a preliminary study for the Benjamin. The figure is reversed in the tapestry, the bent left arm becoming the right arm, and the curve of the torso is slightly shifted, but Pontormo certainly had this figure in mind when he drew this pliable and ornamentalized sequence of muscles.

349 · Florence, Uffizi 6643F *recto*: Study for *Benjamin at the Court of the Pharaoh.* Page from a sketchbook: Right leg and foot seen from the side, bent at the kne in reverse direction, right leg and part o a torso. (*Verso*: Study for the Certos cat. 197.) 218 x 153, black chalk on pin prepared paper; W: Greek Cross in circle (B. 5543). Fig. 33

Bibliography: Berenson 1903, no. 213 Clapp 1914, 200; Berenson 1938, no. 213

Clapp has dated this drawing 1535–154 The swelling forms and the exaggerate musculature are similar to cat. 348 an certainly indicate a date in the forties. Th bent leg may be connected with the tapes try cartoons as a study for the Benjamin leg in reverse.

Ca. 1546–1550/51. DECORATION OF THE SAN LORENZO CHOIR: *The Sacrific of Cain and the Death of Abel*; *The Benediction of the Seed of Noah and the Buildin of the Ark*; *Moses Receiving the Tables of the Law*; *The Expulsion*; *Christ in Glor with the Creation of Eve*; *The Original Sin*; *The Four Evangelists*; *The Sacrifice o Isaac*; *The Labor of Adam and Eve.* Florence, San Lorenzo. Frescoes in the upper rang of the choir (destroyed).

Ca. 1552–1556. *The Deluge with Noah Speaking with God*; *The Ascension of Soul with the Martyrdom of St. Lawrence*; *The Resurrection of the Dead.* Frescoes in th lower range of the choir (finished by Bronzino; destroyed).

Expulsion	*Christ in Glory*	*Original Sin*
Moses		*Four Evangelists*
Noah		*Sacrifice of Isaac*
Cain and Abel		*Labor of Adam and Eve*
Skeletons	*Ascension of Souls Martyrdom of St. Lawrence*	*Skeletons*
Deluge with Noah		*Resurrection of the Dead*

Bibliography: Clapp 1916, 74–79, 263–264 Tolnay 1950, 38–52; Cecchi 1956, 136–166

According to Vasari, the Medici ha planned to decorate the choir of Sa Lorenzo for some years and finally gav the coveted commission to Pontormo.[9]

[9] V/M, VI, 284: "E perchè Sua Eccellenza seguitando le vestigia de'suoi maggiori, ha sempr cercato di abbellire ed adornare la sua città essendole ciò venuto in considerazione, si risolv di fare dipignere tutta la cappella maggiore de magnifico tempio di San Lorenzo, fatta già da gran Cosimo vecchio de'Medici. Perchè daton il carico a Jacopo Puntormo . . ." According to Vasari (*ibid.*, 147), Clement VII commissioned Bandinelli to decorate the choir in about 1525. Bandinelli was to paint the *Martyrdom of Sts. Cosmos and Damian* on one side of the choir and the *Martyrdom of St. Lawrence* on the other,

The exact date of this commission is not known. It was certainly before 1548, the year in which Salviati wrote to Vasari from Rome that his plan for the choir had been rejected and the commission given to Pontormo.[10] However, by 1548 Pontormo had surely been working for two or possibly three years. Vasari reports that Pontormo kept the choir closed for eleven years.[11] Since Pontormo died on January 1, 1557,[12] this would place the commission as early as 1545. However, Lapini says that Pontormo worked on the choir for only ten years, which would indicate 1546 as the date of the commission.[13] Considering Salviati's concern with the affair as late as 1548, the most likely year for the commission — and certainly for the beginning of the work — would seem to be 1546.

We know of no documents concerning Pontormo's work in the choir that refer to these earlier years. There is a reference to payments to an assistant of Pontormo's for the period March 1, 1554, to February 28, 1557 (see Clapp 1916, app. II, doc. 27), and there are documents referring to Pontormo's purchase of colors "per dipigniere il coro di San L^zo^" that go back as early as June 5, 1549.[14] This is also the year in which the first critical notice of the choir occurs. Writing from Venice about works of art to be seen in Florence, Doni advises his readers to see the pictures by Pontormo in the choir, "se per sorte saranno finite." [15] Doni's comments would imply that, while the work was still unfinished, enough had been done on which to base his recommendation.

Pontormo's diary (see pp. 347–356) gives us first-hand documentation for the later years of his work on the choir, 1554–1556. While he mentions by name only the *St. Lawrence*, his marginal sketches make it clear that he was working on the lower range of the choir, as we would expect at this late date. Since Pontormo worked in the normal way from the top of the choir to the bottom, the upper-range frescoes must have been finished in about 1550 or 1551, if we allow about half of the total period for their execution. The three large walls of the lower range would thus have been begun about 1552. The frescoes on

---

but they were not executed. Marcantonio's engraving after the *St. Lawrence* (Bar. 104) shows that Bandinelli's designs were for the large, almost square fresco fields of the lower lateral walls of the choir, the spaces that were later filled by Pontormo's *Deluge* and *Resurrection of the Dead*. Later, ca. 1545–1546, Salviati submitted a design of unspecified subject for the choir. See note 10.

[10] See V/M, VII, 30. Salviati wrote that he had done "un disegno per la capella maggiore di San Lorenzo, che di ordine del signor duca s'aveva a dipignere." He goes on to say that since his drawing was not shown to the duke, the commission was given to Pontormo instead, and he departed for Rome. While we have no further evidence to this effect, there is certainly the possibility that some sort of competition was involved in which Salviati was an unsuccessful participant.

[11] V/M, VI, 285: "Avendo egli adunque con muri, assiti e tende turata quella cappella, e datosi tutto alla solitudine, la tenne per ispazio d'undici anni in modo serrata, che da lui in fuori mai non vi entrò anima vivente, nè amici, nè nessuno."

[12] See Clapp 1916, app. II, doc. 28, 29. Pontormo was buried in the courtyard of SS. Annunziata on January 2, 1557 [new style].

[13] See *Diario fiorentino di Agostino Lapini dal 252 al 1596*, ed. G. O. Corazzini (Florence, 1900), 112. See note 17 for a quotation of this passage.

[14] I am indebted to Mr. Edward Sanchez for bringing these documents to my attention. A.S.F., Fabbriche Medicee no. 1 rosso (Libro Debitorie Creditori B. del Duca Cosimo attenente a Muraglie del suo Palazzo ed altri luogi, 1549–1552).

[15] See Anton Francesco Doni, *Disegno* (Venice, 1549), 48: ". . . fatevi aprire la ricchezza dei broccati et veduto i pergami di bronzo andate a cena, ma se per sorte saranno finite le pitture del choro del Pontorno, vi raccomando a Dio che sarà mezza notte tanto havrete che fare insieme con la tavola del Rosso."

these walls — the *Deluge*, the *Resurrection of the Dead*, and the *St. Lawrence* — were left unfinished when Pontormo died and were all completed by Bronzino.[16] The choir was finally unveiled July 23, 1558.[17]

Besides the authors already mentioned, Pontormo's frescoes were noted by Borghini 1584, 195, 484–485, described by Bocchi 1591, 253–254, noted by Del Migliore 1684, 166, and Cinelli 1677, 515–516. The frescoes were destroyed in 1742 when the sinking of the foundation arches of the crossing necessitated the rebuilding of the lateral walls of the choir.[18] Richa 1754/62, V, 29, writing soon after the destruction, remarks: ". . . non ci dispiaccia di vedere tolte via in occasione di dover fare alcuni archi, ed altri rifarcimenti, le pitture, che tutta adornavano la Tribuna."

Clapp and Tolnay have attempted to reconstruct the original placement of Pontormo's destroyed frescoes. Clapp's order for the upper range was based on the drawings and on the descriptions of Vasari and Bocchi. Clapp placed them from left to right around the choir: *The Creation of Adam*, *The Temptation*, *The Expulsion from Paradise*, *Moses Receiving the Law and the Sacrifice of Isaac*, *Christ in Glory as Judge*, *The Four Evangelists*, *The Tilling of the Soil*, *The Sacrifice of Cain and the Death of Abel*, *The Benediction of the Seed of Noah and the Building of the Ark*. However, we know there was no separate representation of the *Creation of Adam* in the choir, nor were the *Moses* and the *Isaac* combined in a single scene. Furthermore, this reconstruction is rendered obsolete by Tolnay's discovery of a print that shows the choir as it was decorated for a funeral service for King Philip II of Spain on November 12, 1598 (fig. 336).[19] As can be seen in the print the frescoes of the end wall are the *Christ in Glory with the Creation of Eve* in the center, the *Original Sin* to the right, and the *Expulsion* to the left. Tolnay placed the remaining subjects mentioned by Vasari and Bocchi (or occuring in Pontormo's drawings) on the side walls as follows: *Cain and Abel* on the left wall nearest the arch, the *Four Evangelists* in the center field, and the *Labor of Adam and Eve* in the far field. He placed the *Sacrifice of Abraham* in the far field of the right wall,

[16] See V/M, VII, 602: "Avendo alla sua morte lasciata Jacopo Puntormo imperfetta la capella di San Lorenzo, ed avendo ordinato il signor duca che Bronzino la finisse, egli vi finì dalla parte del Diluvio molti ignudi che mancavano a basso, a diede perfezione a quella parte; e dall'altra, dove a piè della Resurrezione de'morti mancavano, nello spazio d'un braccio in circa per altezza nel largo di tutta la facciata, molte figure, le fece tutte bellissime a della maniera che si veggiono; ed a basso, fra le finestre, in un spazio che vi restava non dipinto, finì un San Lorenzo ignudo sopra una grata, con certi putti intorno . . . il ritratto del qual Puntormo fece di sua mano il Bronzino in un canto della detta capella a man ritta del San Lorenzo."

[17] See Lapini, *Diario*, 121–122: Et a dì 23 detto luglio [1558], in sabato, si scopersono le pitture della cappella e coro dell'altar maggiore di S. Lorenzo, cioe il Diluvio e la Resurrezione dei morti, dipinti per mano di maestro Jacopo da Puntormo, la quale a chi piacque a chi no. Peno anni x a condurla; et anco poi morse avanti la finissi, e gli dette il suo fine maestro Agnolo detto Bronzino . . ."

[18] See D. Moreni, *Continuazione delle Memorie istoriche dell'Ambrosiana Imperiale Basilica di San Lorenzo* (Florence, 1817), 112, 115–121. P. Conti, *La Basilica di S. Lorenzo di Firenze e la Familia Ginori* (Florence, 1939), 144–146, gave the date of the restoration and destruction of the frescoes as 1738. Milanesi (V/M, VI, 287n1) noted that the walls were whitewashed in 1738, but did not mention the actual destruction. It is possible that the whitewashing occured in 1738, but there is little doubt that the frescoes were destroyed in 1742. Moreni (p. 115), is specific on this point: "In tal congiuntura colla demolizione delle due pareti laterali del Coro si perderono . . . le pitture che l'adornavano . . ."

[19] See Tolnay 1950, 39, fig. 37; and D. Moreni, *Pompe Funebri celebrate nell'Imperial e Reale Basilica di San Lorenzo* (Florence, 1827), 167–169.

the *Moses* in the center field, and the *Noah* nearest the arch. However, Tolnay's reconstruction, like Clapp's, must be revised on the basis of more recently discovered evidence.

Since the choir was rebuilt in the eighteenth century when the frescoes were destroyed, the funeral print is a useful guide to the appearance of the choir in the late sixteenth century as well as to the placement of the frescoes. The upper rear wall, now covered by an organ loft, had two high arched windows, placed so that the space between them was about half again as large as the spaces between the windows and the corners of the choir. These windows were similar in design to those in the clearstory of the nave and transepts of the church. The upper end walls of the transepts (which are the same width as the choir) with their two windows give a good idea of the original appearance of the upper end wall of the choir. The subjects of the frescoes on the end wall in the funeral print may be identified on the basis of Vasari's and Bocchi's descriptions.[20] In the center is the *Christ in Glory with the Creation of Eve*, to the left the *Original Sin*, and to the right the *Expulsion*. In addition, the funeral print shows that pairs of embracing putti were used as decorative motives under each of the windows. Since the print shows the choir in reverse, the *Original Sin* was actually on the right and the *Expulsion* on the left. Compositional drawings have survived for the *Christ in Glory* (cat. 359) and the *Expulsion* (cat. 357), but not for the *Original Sin*. These drawings, as well as the other compositional studies for the choir, are squared for enlargement in *braccia*.[21] The drawing for the *Expulsion*, intended for the narrower side field, is squared approximately four by ten *braccia*, while the drawing for the *Christ in Glory* in the center is squared approximately five and one half *braccia*, and another study for this subject (cat. 360) is inscribed "b° 5 ½." If the measurements indicated by Pontormo's drawings are added together, estimating about three *braccia* each for the windows on the basis of their size in relation to the fresco fields, the total is nineteen and one half *braccia*, which closely coincides with the actual width of the choir.[22]

In the funeral print the perspective is too abrupt to show how the scenes were

[20] V/M, VI, 285: ". . . fece nella parte di sopra in più istorie la creazione di Adamo ed Eva, il loro mangiare del pomo vietato, e l'essere scacciati di Paradiso." *Ibid.*, 286: "A sommo del mezzo della facciata sopra le finestre fece nel mezzo in alto Cristo nella sua maestà, il quale circondato da molti Angeli tutti nudi fa resuscitare que'morti per guidicare. Ma io no ho mai potuto intendere la dottrina di questa storia, se ben so che Jacopo aveva ingegno da sè, e praticava con persone dotte e letterate; cioè quello volesse significare in quella parte dove è Cristo in alto che risuscita i morti, e sotto i piedi ha Dio Padre che crea Adamo ed Eva." (It will be noted that in this passage Vasari mentions the *Christ in Glory with the Creation of Eve* in the context of the story of Adam and Eve, and then a second time in the context of the *Last Judgment*.) Bocchi 1591, 254: "Si vede in alto Adamo, ed Eva di mano del Puntormo, ed il mangiare del Pome vietato di colorito bellissimo, e poscia quando sono cacciati del Paradiso . . ."

[21] Cat. 350, 354, 357, 360, 364, 366, and 370 are squared for enlargement, the points for the squaring are marked and numbered on cat. 359. Each square is equal to a *braccio*, except in cat. 357, 360, and 366, where two squares equal one *braccio*. Pontormo's *braccio* was about 60 cm (see note 14 on p. 7).

[22] The width of the end wall is 11.55 meters or 19 1/5 *braccia*. There is no evidence that the dimensions of the choir were altered in the restorations of 1742; indeed, the width of the choir, being determined by the width of the crossing arch, must have remained constant. That the dimensions of the choir were not changed to any appreciable extent is indicated by Buontalenti's plan for the Cappella dei Principi (Uffizi 4489A), dated October 1592 and inscribed "coro b[a] 20."

arranged on the side walls. However, we can see that there are two windows on each wall, similar in size and shape to those on the end wall, dividing the wall into three fields. The upper side walls appear very similar to this arrangement today; however, since these walls were rebuilt, it is impossible to determine with certainty the original placing of the windows or the exact size of the fresco fields. Tolnay thought that the corner fields were narrower, but there is no evidence for this in the print and this idea is contradicted by the drawings, none of which is squared for a field of less than four *braccia* in width. While one might imagine that the center fields of the side walls were larger, like that of the end wall, this was not the case. Cat. 366, clearly intended for one of the central fields, is squared four *braccia* in width. Thus, Pontormo's drawings indicate that the side walls consisted of three equal fields four *braccia* wide, separated by two windows like those of the end wall. Since there was no wider central field, the side walls would measure only eighteen *braccia* in width.[23]

For the placement of the scenes on the side walls we must rely on the descriptions of Vasari and Bocchi and on the compositional studies for the frescoes, which survive for all the scenes on the lateral walls except the *Noah*. There are indications of location on three of the compositional studies. On the drawing for the *Cain and Abel* (cat. 350) the arched window to the right and the inscription to the left, "parte diverso larco," indicate that this fresco was on the left wall next to the arch of the crossing. The other drawings that give a clue to the placement of the subject are the studies for the *Sacrifice of Isaac*. Cat. 367 shows a window drawn to the right, but cat. 366, the final study, shows windows to both sides, indicating that this composition belonged in one of the central fields. To determine whether this fresco was painted in the central field of the right or the left wall and to determine how the remaining four scenes were arranged, we must turn to the contemporary accounts of the choir. The quite independent descriptions of Vasari and Bocchi, different in wording and in the scenes mentioned, contain a number of clues as to the disposition of the frescoes. As we have seen, both Vasari and Bocchi note the end wall first, describing its three scenes accurately. Vasari then mentions the *Labor of Adam and Eve* (cat. 370), the *Cain and Abel* (cat. 350), and the *Noah*.[24] Since we already know that the *Cain and Abel* was on the left wall next to the arch, if Vasari is progressing around the choir from one fresco to another, the *Labor of Adam and Eve* would precede it across the choir on the right side next to the arch. If this was the case, the *Noah* must have occupied the space in the center of the left wall after the *Cain and Abel*. Bocchi's description of the side wall frescoes,[25] like Vasari's, begins with the *Labor of Adam and Eve*,

[23] The side walls measure 11.2 meters or 18 3/5 *braccia*, while Pontormo's drawings indicate only 10.8 meters or 18 *braccia*. Thus, the side walls are actually narrower than the end wall, but not by as much as Pontormo's drawings suggest. It should be noted that Vasari states that the size of the frescoes of the lower side walls was "braccia quindici per ogni verso" (V/M, VI, 286), a sight estimate that is several meters short of the width of the walls.

[24] V/M, VI, 285–286: ". . . fece nella parte di sopra in più . . . il zappare la terra, il sacrifizio d'Abel, la morte di Caino [sic] la benedizione del seme di Noè, e quando egli disegna la pianta e misure dell'Arca."

[25] Bocchi 1591, 254: Si vede in alto Adamo, ed Eva . . . e quando col sudore del volto zappando deono procacciarsi la vita. Bellissima è la figura di Abraam, quando sacrifica il figliuolo; e l'attitudine d'Isaac molto è lodata; dove gli artefici, quando commendano il disegno di queste due figure, non si possono saziare. Si mostra la fierezza di Cain, quando uccide il fratello, di bellissimo artifizio; ed Abel, che da tanto furore

which we have tentatively placed next to the arch on the right wall. Bocchi then identifies the subject of the next, or central, field of the right wall as the *Sacrifice of Isaac*. As we have noted, the compositional drawing for this fresco (cat. 366) indicates that it was planned for a field between two windows. Bocchi then describes the *Cain and Abel* on the other side of the choir, but does not mention the *Noah* or the subjects of either of the two corner fields adjacent to the end wall. Thus, if we combine the accounts of Vasari and Bocchi with the evidence of the drawings themselves, a picture of the placement of the four subjects of the end and central fields of the side walls emerges. This arrangement is also suggested by another description of the choir, apparently independent of Vasari's and Bocchi's, that is quoted by Cirri: "Dispinse nella parete superiore a destra diverse Storie di Adamo ed Eve ed il Sacrifizio d'Abramo. A sinistra la morte di Caino e la Storia di Noè." [26]

If we are correct in our interpretation of the evidence cited to this point, only the two corner fields of the side walls remain unfilled. While Bocchi mentions no further subjects for the upper range of the choir, Vasari identifies the subject of one of these corner fields. After his description of the upper-range frescoes, ending with the *Noah*, he discusses the entire lower range of the choir, beginning with the *Deluge* under the *Noah* and coming back to the *Christ in Glory* via the *Resurrection of the Dead* and the *Ascension of Souls*. Vasari then notes, almost as a postscript, that "in uno de'canti" there was a *Four Evangelists*, a scene that interrupted the "ordine di storia" of the choir.[27] Since this was the only fresco that did not represent an Old Testament subject, Vasari could not connect it by narrative (the only level on which he understood the program) with the other scenes. However, Vasari does say that it was in a corner field, although there is nothing in his text to indicate which corner. If, as we may suppose, the *Four Evangelists* occupied one of the corner fields, the other corner field across from it must have been filled by the *Moses Receiving the Tables of the Law* (cat. 354). This subject is not mentioned in any of the accounts of the choir, but it is a logical pendant to the *Four Evangelists*, and three drawings for it have survived.

Turning to the lower range of the choir, we find that in the funeral print this part of the choir is covered by hangings that completely obscure the frescoes. However, an early seventeenth-century painting of the *Funeral of Michelangelo in San Lorenzo* shows the choir in the background (fig. 337).[28] Unfortunately, Pon-

---

si vuol fuggire, esser non puote più singulare, ne più raro."

[26] A. Cirri, "Le Chiese di Firenze e Dintorni: Sepoltuario," V, 2368 (MS, Florence, Biblioteca Nazionale). I am grateful to Mr. Edward Sanchez for indicating to me this previously uncited description of the frescoes, which it may be useful to quote in full: "42. Coro. Fu tutto adornato di affreschi di Jacopo Pontormo che vi rappresento diverse storie del Vecchio e del Nuovo Testamento . . . Dipinse nella parete superiore a destra diverse Storie di Adamo ed Eva e il Sacrifizio d'Abramo. A sinistra la Morte di Caino e la Storia di Noè. Nelle facciate inferiore: Il Diluvio universale e Noè che parla con Dio e il Giudizio finale. Di fronte all'altare figurò diversi nudi che salgono l'uno sulle spalle dell' altro per dare la scalata al Paradiso. Nel centro sopra alle finestre: Christo in Gloria che ordina la Resurrezione dei Morti sotto l'Eterno Padre che crea Adamo ed Eva e negli angoli i quattro Evangelisti."

[27] V/M, VI, 286: "Oltre ciò, in uno de' canti dove sono i quattro Evangelisti nudi con libri in mano, non mi pare, anzi in niun luogo, osservato nè ordine di storia, nè misura, nè tempo . . ."

[28] This ceiling painting by Agostino Ciampelli is part of a series in the Casa Buonarroti that depicts the life of Michelangelo. See Voss 1920, II, 390, fig. 152.

tormo's frescoes have been deleted — a not unexpected omission in view of the seventeenth-century opinion of them — but this picture is a useful guide to the architecture of the choir before the eighteenth-century alterations. The painting shows the large approximately square fields of the side walls with pilasters in the corners supporting the entablature that separates the lower from the upper range of the choir. These fields are unbroken by the moulding that now cuts across the rebuilt walls. Vasari is precise in his description of these lateral walls. He mentions the *Deluge with Noah Speaking with God* on one side and the *Resurrection of the Dead* on the other side.[29] Bocchi adds that the *Resurrection of the Dead* ("Giudizio Universale") was on the right and the *Deluge with Noah* on the left.[30] Clapp and Tolany placed these subjects according to Bocchi's indications. No compositional drawings have survived for the frescoes of the side walls, but cat. 377–379 may be associated with the *Resurrection of the Dead* and cat. 373–375 with the *Deluge*. In addition, cat. A88 (fig. 365), A208 (fig. 366), A216 (fig. 371), and A237–240 (figs. 367–370) are copies after the *Resurrection of the Dead*.

The end wall of the lower range has presented more problems than the side walls. According to Clapp, there was a window in the center with the *Ascent into Heaven* and the *Descent of the Damned* on either side of it. However, no *Descent of the Damned* is mentioned in the descriptions of the choir. As Tolnay has concluded on the basis of Vasari's detailed account of the end wall,[31] there was an *Ascension of Souls* between two windows, and to either side of these windows there were two skeletons carrying flaming torches. It is clear from Ciampelli's painting as well as from Vasari's description that there were two windows in the end wall of the choir. This wall, at present covered by an organ loft supported by two columns, was identical to the side walls except for two rectangular windows placed just below the entablature on a line with the two windows of the upper range. These windows were similar in size and shape to those still in the chapels lateral to the choir. Thus, while the lower side walls presented large, uninterrupted picture spaces, the upper part of the lower end wall was divided into three fields approximately the same size as those of the upper range. The two columns of nudes ascending into paradise that Vasari describes were in the space between the windows. A preparatory study for one of these columns (cat. 376) is squared about three *braccia* in

[29] V/M, VI, 286: "In una poi delle facciate di sotto, ciascuna delle quali è braccia quindici per ogni verso, fece la inondazione del Diluvio, nella quale sono una massa di corpi morti ed affogati, e Noè che parla con Dio. Nell'altra faccia è dipinta la Resurrezione universale de' morti, che ha da essere nell'ultimo e novissimo giorno, con tanta e varia confusione . . ."

[30] Bocchi 1591, 253–254: "Nella parte destra adunque è dipinto il Giudizio universale. Si mostrano in varie, e bizzarre attitudini da basso molti, che risuscitano . . . Ha figurati in aria molti Angeli di colorito dolce, e morbido, e con movenza di persona molto fiera, e bizzarra . . . Di costa poi si vede il Diluvio. E grande la moltitudine dei corpi morti, che sono dipinti: Ma si veggono in cima del monte alcuni campati dall' acque, effigiati con molta industria; ed in compagnia di Noè con bellissime attitudini, e con gran disegno assai fanno sede . . . Gli Angeli, che sono per l'aria, sono effigiati con artifizio sopra ogni stima raro."

[31] V/M, VI, 286: "Dirimpetto all'altare, fra le finestre, cioè nella faccia del mezzo, da ogni banda è una fila d'ignudi, che presi per mano e aggrappatisi su per le gambe e busti l'uno dell' altro si fanno scala per salire in paradiso, uscendo di terra; dove sono molti morti che gli accompagnano, e fanno fine da ogni banda due morti vestiti, eccetto le gambe e le braccia, con le quali tengono due torce accese." Cirri also noted this fresco. See note 26.

width, approximately half of the size of the space between the windows. This scene probably occupied, in addition, a portion of the large space remaining below the windows, and on either side of the windows were the "due morti vestiti" that Vasari describes.

Neither Tolnay nor Clapp have mentioned the *Martyrdom of St. Lawrence* as part of the fresco cycle in San Lorenzo. In his account of Bronzino's work in finishing the choir, Vasari says (V/M, VII, 602) that Bronzino completed the lower part of the *Deluge*, the *Resurrection of the Dead*, and "a basso, fra le finestre, in uno spazio che vi restava non dipinto, finì un San Lorenzo ignudo sopra una grata, con certi putti intorno . . ." Bocchi also mentions the *St. Lawrence* as by Bronzino in his description of the choir.[32] It is evident from both these accounts that the *Martyrdom of St. Lawrence* occupied the central part of the end wall below the *Ascension of Souls*. However, since Vasari and Bocchi implied that Bronzino was responsible for this fresco and no Pontormo drawings have survived for it, no mention has been made of the *St. Lawrence* in connection with Pontormo. Nevertheless, it was planned as part of the cycle and it was designed and at least partially executed by Pontormo himself. Bocchi knew of a drawing by Pontormo in which was depicted "il Giudizio universale, e da basso il martiro di S. Lorenzo." [33] This drawing must have been a compositional study for the entire central portion of the lower end wall with the *Ascension of Souls* above and the *Martyrdom of St. Lawrence* below. According to Bocchi it was three quarters of a *braccio* (40 cm) in size and in black chalk, exactly the size and medium of the compositional studies for the choir that have survived (cf. cat. 350, 354, 359, etc.). Thus, we know that Pontormo at least made a drawing for the lower end wall. Furthermore, no note has been made of the fact that Pontormo records in his diary the design and partial execution of the *Martyrdom of St. Lawrence* from August to October of 1556 (see p. 356). In his diary he mentions preparing the cartoon for the St. Lawrence and painting in fresco putti with the crown of martyrdom and a chalice. Since the three months following before his death were months in winter when Pontormo would have worked little if at all, the *Martyrdom of St. Lawrence* was probably his final painting, left unfinished to be completed by Bronzino with the other frescoes in the lower range of the choir.[34]

[32] Bocchi 1591, 254: "Molte figure, che sono da basso in ciascuna di queste due storie [the *Deluge* and the *Resurrection of the Dead*] sono di mano di Agnolo Bronzino, e di vero lodate da tutti, e con ragione. E il S. Lorenzo ignudo sopra la graticola con alcuni puttini, sono altresì di sua mano; appresso ci ha il ritratto del Puntormo fatto di estrema vivezza."

[33] Bocchi 1591, 183–184: This drawing, which belonged to Baccio Valori, is described as a "tavoletta, di tre quarti di braccio, dove in un foglio bianco di mano di Jacopo da Puntormo è stato effigiato di matita nera il Giudizio universale, e da basso il martiro di S. Lorenzo . . . Il S. Lorenzo posato sopra la graticola di grazioso aspetto è bellissimo: e quattro Angeletti nella freschezza delle carni, e toccati con gentil maniera non possono essere più leggiadri, nè più belli." Bocchi continues to say that he preferred the drawing to the fresco of the St. Lawrence in the choir. Borghini 1584, 485, also mentions this drawing: "Di quest'opera [the San Lorenzo choir] ha un piccolo disegno molto ben fatto quì M. Baccio con un'ornamento à uso di spera, il coperchio del quale è stato dipinto da Battista Naldini . . ."

[34] In completing this fresco Bronzino undoubtedly added the portrait of Pontormo that is mentioned by Vasari (V/M, VII, 602) and Bocchi 1591, 254, as part of the scene, Vasari specifying that it was on St. Lawrence's right. Bronzino later (1565–1569) painted his own, much larger and more complex representation of the *Martyrdom of St. Lawrence* on the left

Clapp did not attempt to interpret the program of the San Lorenzo choir, but Tolnay explained his arrangement of the scenes as a cycle of the history of man, beginning with the *Creation* in the central field of the end wall and ending in the same field with the *Christ in Glory*: the triumph of Grace over Sin.[35] While Tolnay suggested valid interrelations among the subjects represented in the choir, his reconstruction of the program is not without inconsistencies and it does not link the upper- and lower-range frescoes convincingly. Tolnay's arrangement is a narrative one that begins with the three scenes of *Adam and Eve* on the end wall and then, starting with the field next to the arch on the left wall, progresses around the choir to the right in historical order, skipping over the symbolic compositions of the *Four Evangelists* and the *Moses*. Tolnay placed these as pendants in the central fields of the left and right walls, pointing out that the right side of the choir was traditional for Old Testament scenes, the left side for New Testament scenes. The resulting order of the frescoes was, Tolnay indicated, contrary to Renaissance practice, where cycles generally began at the entrance and progressed toward the altar. The order was rather a reversion to medieval concepts, where the cycle often began over the altar and then moved around the choir. However, especially if the *Moses* and the *Four Evangelists* are considered as symbolic compositions that interrupt the historical order, there remain only four scenes with which to make such a narrative sequence, and no two of these (according to Tolnay's reconstruction) are contiguous. If we consider the presence in the cycle of the two nonnarrative subjects, together with Pontormo's unusual choice of the central field of the end wall for the symbolic uniting of the beginning and the end, it is evident that (no matter how the other scenes are placed) there can be no convincing narrative succession of the frescoes. On the contrary, Pontormo's scheme is a symbolic one in which the sequence of events in time and their separation in space plays no significant part. This point of view is manifest in the end wall, where the *Christ in Glory with the Creation of Eve* is flanked by the two initial episodes from the History of Man: the *Original Sin* and the *Expulsion*. The left wall, with its scenes of *Cain and Abel* and *Noah* above, the *Deluge* below, depicts the evil of man and its punishment. The right wall, with its

---

nave wall of the church, one of a pair of scenes commissioned by Cosimo de' Medici, the second of which was never executed. This fresco, like the descriptions of Pontormo's fresco in the choir, shows St. Lawrence on the grate with putti holding a crown and a chalice above, and a portrait of Pontormo to the saint's right. To what extent Bronzino's fresco repeated other elements of Pontormo's earlier representation of the subject in the same church is impossible to determine.

[35] See Tolnay 1950, 49: "C'est l'histoire de la création de l'homme, sa chute, la décadence de sa race (Caïn, Noé), son annihilation (Déluge), et ensuite la Résurrection et l'envol des âmes vers les cieux grâce au Sacrifice du Rédempteur qui a vaincu le péché et la mort de l'humanité. Ce n'est donc pas un Jugement Dernier traditionnel (la Chute des damnés n'y figure pas) mais plutôt un triomphe de la grâce sur le péché, prédit par les Évangélistes, et l'Ancienne Loi, et c'est sans doute pourquoi Pontormo a si curieusement réuni sur un même champ la *Création d'Eve*, début du péché et la fin de ce drame, le *Triomphe du Rédempteur*, juste au-dessus. C'est donc une allégorie religieuse du drame éternel de l'âme humaine dont la chute est représentée par des cercles horizontaux et dont l'ascension et la rédemption finale sont figurées par les courants verticaux culminant dans le Christ en Gloire, qui dépasse les cercles fatals." According to Tolnay, the iconography of the San Lorenzo frescoes was influenced by the Counter Reformation teachings of the Spaniard Valdés, who was in Italy from 1531 to 1541 and whose doctrines of justification by faith alone commanded a large following.

scenes of the *Labor of Adam and Eve* and the *Sacrifice of Isaac* above, the *Resurrection of the Dead* below, represents the sacrifice of man and the promise of redemption. From the right wall we are led back up to the *Christ in Glory* by the *Ascension of Souls*. The *Martyrdom of St. Lawrence* below makes a suitable epilogue, linking the patron saint of the church with the theme of sacrifice and redemption.

In the light of this interpretation a problem remaining in the reconstruction of the upper range may be resolved. We suggested that the *Four Evangelists* and the *Moses Receiving the Tables of the Law* were pendants in the corner fields, but it was not possible to determine from the drawings or the descriptions of the choir which fresco belonged on which side. As we have noted, Tolnay placed these pendants in the center fields instead, citing the left side as traditional for New Testament subjects and the right side for Old Testament scenes. However, since the *Four Evangelists* is an isolated New Testament subject among eight Old Testament scenes, it does not seem imperative to impose the right vs. left tradition in this case. In fact, if we consider the location of the other scenes, there is every indication that the subjects were placed in just the opposite way: the *Moses Receiving the Tables of the Law* symbolizes the Old Law and belongs on the left wall with the *Cain and Abel*, the *Noah*, and the *Deluge*; while the *Four Evangelists* symbolizes the New Law and belongs on the right wall with the *Labor of Adam and Eve*, the *Sacrifice of Isaac*, and the *Resurrection of the Dead*. Placed as they are in the corners, nearer to the *Christ in Glory* than the other scenes, these two symbolic compositions proclaim the respective themes of the two sides of the choir, referring both the sin of the left wall and the sacrifice of the right to the Christ in Glory of the *Last Judgment*.

STUDIES FOR THE SACRIFICE OF CAIN AND THE DEATH OF ABEL

350 · Florence, Uffizi 6739F *recto*: Compositional study for the *Sacrifice of Cain and the Death of Abel*, San Lorenzo. Cain slaying Abel, who cringes below him on a rock; above, Cain and Abel kneeling on either side of a circular altar on which a flaming sacrifice is placed; to the right, indication of the left half of a high arched window. (*Verso*: Study for San Lorenzo, cat. 372.) 405 x 218, black chalk squared in black and red chalk; written in Pontormo's hand to the left: *parte diverso larco*; to the right below: *9 emezo*; to the left the squares are numbered 1–7 and to the right 1–4. Fig. 338.

Bibliography: Ferri 1890, 120; Berenson 1903, no. 2221; *MPA* 1910, 38; Voss 1913, 310, fig. 14; Clapp 1914, 267–268; Clapp 1916, 72, 76, fig. 141; Voss 1920, 174, fig. 51; Berenson 1938, 321, no. 2221, fig. 996; *MDF* 1939, 26; *MC* 1940, 47; Tolnay 1950, 39, fig. 45; Cecchi 1956, fig. 11.

Berenson recognized this drawing as for the San Lorenzo *Cain and Abel*. Clapp placed it in the center of the right wall; however, as Tolnay has seen, it belongs in the left field of the left wall. The inscription "parte diverso larco" and the lines of the window to the right indicate that this composition was designed for the space next to the arch of the crossing. This study is squared for enlargement to the dimensions of approximately four by ten *braccia*, as are the other compositional studies for the upper-range frescoes. As is indicated by the line drawn from Abel's foot, the lowest point in the composition, and the notation "9 emezo," Pontormo intended the actual figural composition to be nine and one half *braccia* in height.

This drawing is the final compositional study for the *Cain and Abel*, which is the pendant to the *Labor of Adam and Eve* (cat. 370), next to the arch on the other side of the choir. It follows the preliminary sketch for the composition (cat. 351) in which Cain has his back turned and Abel leans to the right. This arrangement was discarded in favor of one in which both figures are frontal. Their violent movements, which implied a turning in space, are now pressed flat into a surface pattern of interlocking curves. This composition closely recalls Pontormo's tapestry designs of ca. 1545–1549, especially the *Lamentation of Jacob*. Not only are these two figures related in the same way as the Jacob and the figure above him, but the high narrow format and the rising composition with its large, rhythmically interrelated figures below and the group of smaller figures above are the same as in the tapestry. The Abel is similar in pose to the Jacob, while the Cain is reminiscent of the nude boy to the left in the *Benjamin* tapestry. The figure of Abel appears again in the San Lorenzo drawings with slight variations in the analogous figure of Isaac (cat. 366). Clapp dated this composition 1550–1555. However, considering how close in style this study is to the tapestries and considering that by 1550 some of the work in the upper range of the choir was completed, this study should be placed ca. 1546–1550/51.

351 · Florence, Uffizi 168S *verso*: Studies for *Cain and Abel* (cat. 350), *Moses Receiving the Tables of the Law* (cat. 354), and the *Labor of Adam and Eve* (cat. 370), San Lorenzo. Enclosed in a rectangular frame, Cain killing Abel and the sacrifice of Cain; to the right, a figure turned to the right shoveling studied twice; above, kneeling figure with arms held up studied twice. (*Recto*: Study for San Lorenzo, cat. 365.) 257 x 80, black chalk. Fig. 340.

Bibliography: Santarelli 1870, 18, no. 2.

This sheet was listed as Michelangelo in Santarelli's catalogue, but it was attributed to Pontormo as for San Lorenzo by Smyth (verbally). The most completed sketch on this sheet of studies is the drawing for the *Cain and Abel*, a preliminary idea in which the Cain stands with his back turned in front of Abel, who leans back to the left. Cat. 353 is a detail study for the Abel in this pose. The other studies on this sheet are preliminary ideas for the *Labor of Adam and Eve* (cat. 370), the pendant to the *Cain and Abel* on the right side of the choir, and for the *Moses* (cat. 354), at the other end of the left wall. The figure of Adam with his spade is studied twice as he appears in cat. 370, while the kneeling Moses is studied in two alternate directions. This sheet, the sketch for the *Four Evangelists* on the recto, cat. 355 for the *Moses*, and cat. 367 for the *Sacrifice of Isaac* are the only surviving preliminary sketches for the compositions of the upper range frescoes. The pliable little figures of these sketches, as well as the slackness of the line, recall drawings such as cat. 336 for the Castello loggia of ca. 1537–1543. Since this sheet is reminiscent of earlier studies and contains ideas for several of the frescoes, it may be dated early in the San Lorenzo period, certainly well before 1550.

352 · Florence, Uffizi 6746F: Study for *Cain and Abel* (cat. 350). Three-quarter length nude looking down to the right with his left arm raised. 232 x 137, black chalk; W: Shield with five crescents.

Bibliography: Berenson 1903, no. 2227; Clapp 1914, 274–275; Clapp 1916, 76, fig. 142; Berenson 1938, no. 2227.

Clapp recognized this nude study as for the torso, raised right arm, and head of Cain, just as he appears in the compositional drawing. However, he dated it 1550–1555, by which time Pontormo would certainly have executed many of the frescoes in the upper range of the choir. This muscled torso recalls the studies for the tapestries, such as cat. 347–348, but it is handled with a less insistently ornamental accentuation of the muscle patterns.

353 · Florence, Uffizi 15665F: Study for *Cain and Abel* (cat. 350). Seated nude leaning to the left with his arms over his head, the left leg bent under him; to the left below, a torso. 266 x 207, black chalk; paper discolored by old glue on the verso; W: Fleur-de-lis in a circle (B.7106).

Bibliography: Berenson 1903, no. 2244; Clapp 1914, 285–286; Berenson 1938, no. 2244. (Photo G.)

Berenson thought this drawing was probably for San Lorenzo and Clapp connected it with the Abel in cat. 350 reversed, dating it 1550–1555. Actually, the pose is close to the Abel in Pontormo's first idea for the composition (cat. 351) and the drawing must date closer to 1550 than 1555. Clapp connected the faint torso below with cat. A172, which he also thought was for San Lorenzo. However, the torso is connected with the figure of Cain as he is sketched on cat. 351.

STUDIES FOR THE MOSES RECEIVING THE TABLES OF THE LAW

354 · Florence, Uffizi 6749F *recto*: Compositional study for *Moses Receiving the Tables of the Law*, San Lorenzo. Moses kneels with his back turned and his arms raised holding the Tables of the Law; above, God the Father with two angels. (*Verso*: Outlines of the right half of a high arched window to the left, not catalogued.) 385 x 148, black chalk squared; W: Ladder in a shield with a star (cf. B. 5927); written in Pontormo's hand in ink below: *10*/[br]*accia dua dita.*

Fig. 339.

Bibliography: Berenson 1903, no. 2230; *MPA* 1910, 38; Clapp 1914, 276; Clapp 1916, 76, fig. 139; Berenson 1938, 321, no. 2230; Tolnay 1950, 40, fig. 48; *MP* 1956 (Marcucci), no. 139, fig. 167b.

Berenson (1903) identified this study and cat. 355 as *Noah Conversing with the Lord*, a subject that Vasari (V/M, VI, 286) describes as part of the *Deluge*. However, Clapp identified the two compositional studies correctly as for the *Moses Receiving the Tables of the Law*. While this subject is not mentioned by either Vasari or Bocchi, this drawing and cat. 355 were clearly intended for one of the narrow fresco fields of the upper part of the choir, and one of the nine fields is unaccounted for in their listing of the subjects. Clapp thought of this composition as a pendant to the *Four Evangelists* (cat. 364) and placed it to the left of the rear wall. Tolnay also interpreted these subjects as pendants, with the *Moses* on the right and the *Evangelists* on the left of the choir in the central spaces between the windows. However, Clapp's placement is ruled out by the funeral print, which shows other scenes on the end wall, and Tolnay's by the drawing for the *Sacrifice of Isaac* (cat. 366), which is designed for a field between two windows. Furthermore, Vasari implies (V/M, VI, 286) that the pendant to the *Moses* — the *Four Evangelists* — was in a corner. Therefore, it is most logical to place this fresco in the corner on the left side wall as a pendant to the *Evangelists* in the corner on the right side. Like the *Four Evangelists*, this composition is squared to proportions of approximately four by ten *braccia*, and the vertical dimension is verified by Pontormo's notation "10 [br]accia dua dita" below.

Clapp dated this drawing 1545–1556 and he dated cat. 355, 1550–1555. Considering that the upper range of frescoes must have been finished by about 1550 or 1551, Clapp tended to date this composition too late. On the other hand, Marcucci has considered this to be one of the earliest drawings for San Lorenzo. She dated it 1545–1546 and thought that here Pontormo was strongly influenced by Michelangelo's *Last Judgment*, which he could have seen on his alleged trip to Rome in 1539 or possibly on another later trip (see n. 37). Like the other compositions for the upper-range frescoes, this design has a strong aura of *Romanità*, although not a specific relation to the *Last Judgment*. Also, like the other upper-range compositions, the calculated ornamental arrangement of these figures is closely related to Pontormo's tapestry designs of ca. 1545–1549. The kneeling Moses is a reworking of the Benjamin (reversed in the tapestry) in the *Benjamin at the Court of the Pharaoh*.

355 · Florence, Uffizi 6508F *recto*: Study for *Moses Receiving the Tables of the Law* (cat. 354). Within a rectangular picture field squared for enlargement, Moses kneels with his back turned and his arms raised holding the Tables of the Law; above, God the Father with two angels; outside this scheme, four studies for the shoulders of the God Father. (*Verso*: Study for San Lorenzo, cat. 380.) 270 x 140, black chalk. Fig. 341.

Bibliography: Berenson 1903, no. 2016; Clapp 1914, 119; Berenson 1938, 321, no. 2016; Tolnay 1950, 40, fig. 47.

See cat. 354. This drawing is a first compositional study for the Moses, differing from the final version in the position of the angels accompanying God the Father, and showing in the *pentimenti* Pontormo's indecision as to the exact pose of the Moses. Like cat. 365 for the *Four Evangelists* and cat. 367 for the *Isaac*, this drawing is a preliminary sketch for the composition of the fresco, executed on a much smaller scale than the final drawings. However, unlike the other sketches, the format of the fresco field is marked out and squared well within the limits of the sheet. The composition is squared for enlargement approximately four by ten *braccia*, the same as in cat. 354 and in the other studies for the frescoes of the upper range of the choir, except for the *Christ in Glory*. Clapp noted the similarity of the shoulder studies outside the compositional scheme to cat. 336 for the Castello loggia, a comparison that points up the close link in style between the first drawings for San Lorenzo and Pontormo's studies for the decorations of the late thirties and early forties.

356 · Florence, Uffizi 6582F: Study for *Moses Receiving the Tables of the Law* (cat. 354). Three-quarter length nude seen from behind with his arms held up, looking up to the right. 266 x 171, black chalk. Fig. 352.

Bibliography: Berenson 1903, no. 2082; Clapp 1914, 167; Berenson 1938, no. 2082.

Clapp dated this drawing after 1545, noting that there was a rapport in pose with the Moses in cat. 354. This nude is a study for the figure of Moses that is related to the earliest ideas for the figure, two sketches on cat. 351. In one of these two ideas for the Moses the figure is drawn with his legs turned to the left as they are in this study. Thus, it is probable that this drawing preceded both the compositional studies for the fresco. As Berenson has remarked, this study is Michelangelesque. Indeed, the pose of the figure turned away holding the large book and the emphasis given to the muscled back suggests a distant echo of the Libyan Sibyl, whose forceful contrapposto is here reduced to a purely surface pattern.

STUDIES FOR THE EXPULSION

357 · Dresden, Kupferstichkabinett C65: Compositional study for the *Expulsion*, San Lorenzo. Nude figures of Adam and Eve walk to the left, the Adam bent over with his face hidden, the Eve looking up with her hands to her head; above them,

the angel flying to the right. 385 x 140, black chalk squared, the angel also squared in red chalk; outlines of Eve's breast and shoulder reworked by a later hand; laid down; written in Pontormo's hand to the left: [di]*segnato/a dare 1°/ . . a . . .* [fare?] / *aq°* [questo] *per 4 . . .* [a?] *dare 1° b°* [braccio] *etc. fa . .* [fare?]
Fig. 342.

Bibliography: Voss 1913, 309, fig. 13; Berenson 1938, 321, no. 1959A, fig. 998; Tolnay 1950, 39–40, fig. 40.

Formerly attributed to Bronzino and to Allori, this drawing was first published by Voss as for the San Lorenzo *Expulsion*. Tolnay placed it to the left of the rear wall of the choir on the basis of the funeral print, which shows the *Expulsion* to the left of the *Christ in Glory* with the design in reverse. Tolnay thought that Pontormo might have used his cartoons for all the frescoes in reverse, in this case because the Adam and Eve move contrary to the usual left to right direction seen in other *Expulsion* scenes, such as those of Masaccio and Michelangelo. However, if Pontormo reversed his cartoon, would not the subsequent reversing of the design in the print make the figures move from right to left again? Since the figures move to the right in the print, we can only assume that they moved to the left in the fresco as they do in this drawing. (Cf. Pontormo's own earlier *Expulsion* of ca. 1519–1520 in which the figures move from right to left as they do here.)

This composition is squared for enlargement in the usual proportions for the upper-range frescoes: four by ten *braccia*. However, here as in cat. 360 and 366 a system of squaring is used in which two squares (rather than one) are equal to one *braccio*. The drawing has been cut slightly at the sides and the inscription to the lower left is not completely legible. However, the "per 4" probably refers to the width of the composition.

358 · Florence, Uffizi 6715F: Study for the *Expulsion* (cat. 357). Nude woman seen to the knees walking to the left with her hands raised to her head and looking up to the right. 290 x 210, black chalk; the right leg reworked by another hand.
Fig. 346.

Bibliography: Berenson 1903, no. 2198; Clapp 1914, 253; Clapp 1916, 76, fig. 137; Berenson 1938, 320, no. 2198, fig. 997; *MDF* 1939, 27; Tolnay 1950, 39, fig. 42; *MDM* 1954 (Marcucci), no. 60; *EMI* 1954, no. 81; Cecchi 1956, fig. 10; Marcucci 1956, 23, fig. 28.

Berenson thought this was a study for the Eve of an *Expulsion*, probably for San Lorenzo. Clapp also identified it as for the San Lorenzo *Expulsion*, which he placed on the left wall in the field nearest the rear wall. Clapp recorded an inscription on the mount: "Bronzino per la cacciata del Paradiso terr. Dresda." Thinking this referred to a painting, he did not connect it with the compositional study in Dresden (cat. 357), which was then attributed to Bronzino. Tolnay has pointed out that this is a study for the Eve just as she appears in cat. 357 and (reversed) in the funeral print.

This nude study is very close in style to cat. 371 for the Adam in the *Labor of Adam and Eve*. Although Clapp dated it 1546–1556, it probably dates ca. 1546–1550/51. The precisely finished, ornamentalizing style of this study is related to the drawings for the tapestries (cat. 347–348), and the calculated and flattening manipulation of the forms parallel to the picture plane recalls such figures as the Benjamin in the *Benjamin at the Court of the Pharaoh* and the two figures above Jacob in the *Lamentation*.

STUDIES FOR THE CHRIST IN GLORY WITH THE CREATION OF EVE

359 · Florence, Uffizi 6609F: Compositional study for the *Christ in Glory with the Creation of Eve*, San Lorenzo. Christ seated with his hands raised in benediction surrounded by a circle of fourteen nudes, some of which are only heads; below, to the right, God the Father; further below, the sleeping Adam lying across to the left with the upper part of Eve behind him facing to the right. 326 x 180, black chalk; written in Pontormo's hand at the lower left: *b*° [braccio]; numbered along the left edge 1–9 with a mark in the center of the lower edge. Fig. 345.

Bibliography: Berenson 1903, no. 2108; *MPA* 1910, 38; Goldschmidt 1911, 12, pl. 4; Clapp 1914, 182–183; Clapp 1916, 75–76, fig. 138; Berenson 1938, 321, no. 2108; Steinbart 1939, 10; Wallis 1939, 280, fig. 5; *MDF* 1939, 27; Becherucci 1943, 11, pl. 28; Becherucci 1944, 22, fig. 55; Tolnay 1950, 39, 49, fig. 39; *MDM* 1954 (Marcucci), no. 62; *EMI* 1954, no. 83; Cecchi 1956, fig. 9.

Berenson thought that this drawing was for San Lorenzo, while Clapp specified that it was for the *Christ in Glory with the Creation of Eve* mentioned by Vasari (V/M, VI, 286) as in the middle of the upper rear wall of the choir. This exact composition is seen (reversed) between the windows of the rear wall in the funeral print. The central field was larger than those to the sides of the windows or those of the side walls. Accordingly, this drawing is measured for enlargement to five and one half by ten *braccia* rather than the four by ten *braccia* of the other compositional drawings. Tolnay thought that Pontormo might have used this drawing in reverse for the fresco because in the drawing God the Father takes Eve's hand with his left hand and Christ's left hand is higher than his right hand. However, the composition as it appears in this drawing is reversed in the print and thus must have been transferred to the wall just as it is here.

Since it is placed in the wide field high in the center of the wall opposite the altar, the *Christ in Glory with the Creation of Eve* is the climax of the San Lorenzo fresco cycle. It is also related in a complex way to the subjects of the rest of the cycle and holds the key to its meaning. The *Christ in Glory* is the Christ of the *Last Judgment* and must be seen in relation to the *Ascension of Souls*, which was directly below it, and to the *Resurrection of the Dead*, which was below on the right wall. Vasari described the Christ as "Cristo in alto che risuscita i morti" (V/M, VI, 286). Christ and three of the four angels who carry the symbols around him look down to the right toward the fresco of the *Resurrection of the Dead*, and it is Christ's hand on the right that is raised higher as if in the act of raising the dead. Furthermore, as Tolnay has pointed out, this Christ is at once the Christ of the *Last Judgment* and the Christ of the Passion. The angels carry the instruments of the Passion: the angel to the right holds the crown of thorns in his left hand over the head of Christ and holds the nails in his right hand. This drawing is cut at the top, but cat. 360 shows that the angel in the right corner held the sponge and the angel on the left held the lance. The two angels below hold large books that must refer to the Old Law and the New Law, represented on the side walls by the *Moses Receiving the Tables of the Law* on the left and the *Four Evangelists* on the right. While Vasari interpreted the *Christ in Glory* as the Christ of the *Last Judgment* in relation to the *Ascension of Souls* and the *Resurrection of the Dead*, he was puzzled by the inclusion of the *Creation of Eve* in the same scene.[36] However, as

[36] V/M, VI, 286. Compare note 20. Bocchi 1591, 254, referred to this composition simply as "Adamo ed Eva," not connecting the *Christ in Glory* with the scenes of the lower range. The scene is rightly described by Cirri's source, however, except that the angels in the corners are wrongly called the four Evangelists. See note 26.

Tolnay has pointed out, the first and last events of the San Lorenzo cycle are united in this symbolic central composition.

The composition of the *Christ in Glory with the Creation of Eve* is more elaborate than the others in the upper range of the choir because of the larger field that it occupies and because of this complex double subject. The composition is dominated by the same serpentine curves that determine the narrower compositions of the other fields. Only here, in this more ample space, there is also a rotary movement around the Christ that springs from the crossed figures of Adam and Eve and weaves endlessly through the complex maze of the angels. While this kind of composition may be seen as a reminiscence of Pontormo's earlier S. Felicita *Deposition*, there is also a certain analogy with Michelangelo's *Last Judgment* in the way the Judging Christ is the pivot around which the other figures dependently revolve. However, the exact scheme of the design and the pose of the Christ seems to depend more precisely on a Michelangelo invention of the midforties: the *Pietà* for Vittoria Colonna, a link that underscores an interpretation of this Christ as the Christ of the Passion as well as of the Last Judgment. Pontormo may have known these later works of Michelangelo from copies, but it is more likely that he saw them on a final trip to Rome in the forties before he began work on the San Lorenzo choir.[37]

According to Vasari (V/M, VI, 286–287), Pontormo's contemporaries did not understand or appreciate the frescoes of the San Lorenzo choir. However, ornamentalizing versions of this particular composition do appear in the years after Pontormo's death, especially in the works of Bronzino. The Uffizi *Allegory of Fortune* is directly related to it, as are even the schemes of large altarpieces such as the SS. Annunziata *Resurrection*. However, the *Trinity* of 1571 (Cappella di San Luca, SS. Annunziata) is the most direct adaptation of this composition.[38] Bronzino's *Trinity* is ultimately related also to Michelangelo's *Pietà*, but apparently only by way

---

[37] This trip is not to be confused with Pontormo's alleged trip of 1539, which Clapp (1916, 69, app. II, doc. 24) has shown is based on Milanesi's mistaken interpretation of a letter written by Annibal Caro that referred to a painter called Pastermo in Rome in that year. (See V/M, VI, 273n5.) However, Clapp believed that Pontormo was in Rome between 1535 and 1543, citing as "definite and conclusive proof" the drawings after Roman monuments attributed to Pontormo from the Baldinucci collection in the Louvre (cat. A261–A318). Since these drawings are not by Pontormo, they do not constitute proof of a trip to Rome. However, such a trip — possibly between the completion of the Castello loggia in 1543 and the beginning of the tapestry cartoons ca. 1545 — is certainly a strong possibility. The aura of *Romanità* in Pontormo's works of ca. 1545–1550 (the tapestry cartoons, the lost *Madonna and Child*, the *Isaac Blessing Jacob*, San Lorenzo designs such as the *Christ in Glory*) cannot be accounted for by his presumed knowledge of copies of Michelangelo's later works or by his exposure to the semi-Romanized style of Bronzino and Salviati. Rather, these works suggest that Pontormo had been re-exposed to a direct stimulus of Michelangelo's art. Furthermore, what fragmentary evidence that has survived of the composition of the *Resurrection of the Dead* (cat. 377–379, A216) indicates that Pontormo must have seen Michelangelo's *Last Judgment* before he painted his own fresco in San Lorenzo. See Marcucci, *MP* 1956, 108, who apparently accepted the 1539 trip, but allowed that Pontormo might also have gone to Rome later.

[38] Note the pose of the Christ, the angels supporting him, and the angels who hold the instruments of the Passion above. In fact, this work is so Pontormesque in design that Cinelli 1677, 464, attributes the invention to Pontormo and its execution to Bronzino. While the composition is certainly Bronzino's, it is sufficiently reminiscent of Pontormo's *Christ in Glory* to justify Cinelli's statement. Clapp 1916, 200, did not find this work related to either Pontormo or Bronzino.

of Pontormo's previous translation of it in the San Lorenzo *Christ in Glory*.

360 · Leningrad, Hermitage 291A: Study for the *Christ in Glory with the Creation of Eve* (cat. 359). Christ seated with his hands raised in benediction surrounded by a circle of twenty nudes, some of which are only heads; below to the right, God the Father; further below, the sleeping Adam lying across to the left with the figure of Eve lying across to the right in front of him. 330 x 170, black chalk squared; written in Pontormo's hand to the left: *b° 5 e ½*. Fig. 347.

Collection: Yaremitch; Dobroklonsky.

Bibliography: Dobroklonsky 1940, no. 291A; Dobroklonsky 1941, 39–40, fig. 2.

This drawing was once attributed to Cavaliere d'Arpino, but it was given to Bronzino by Lippart, and subsequently to Pontormo as a study for the *Christ in Glory with the Creation of Eve*. Dobroklonsky considered this study to be the final drawing for the fresco, subsequent to cat. 359. However, in the print that shows this fresco in the choir, the figures are arranged exactly as in cat. 359. Therefore, this study must be an earlier version of the composition. It differs from cat. 359 in the pose of the angel on the upper left; in the Eve, who lies in front of Adam; and in details of Adam's pose. This version also includes a bit of the top of the composition that has been cut off in cat. 359, showing that the angel in the right corner held the sponge and the angel to the left held the lance, thus accounting for the two instruments of the Passion that are missing in cat. 359. The measurements on cat. 359 indicate that the composition was intended to be enlarged to about five and one half by ten *braccia*. This size is confirmed by the squaring of this drawing (in Pontormo's alternate system of two squares to a *braccio* also used in cat. 357 and 366) and by the inscription "b° [braccio] 5 e ½," which must refer to the intended width of the composition.

361 · Florence, Uffizi 465F *verso*: Study for the *Christ in Glory with the Creation of Eve* (cat. 359). On the lower part of the sheet a nude lying to the left with his head resting on his right arm while the left arm falls down across his chest; to the left, the figure restudied in a more upright position and seen only to the shoulders. (*Recto*: Study for a *Creation of Eve*, cat. 104.) 423 x 315, black chalk. Fig. 343.

Bibliography: Berenson 1938, no. 1983.

Berenson dated this sketch in the San Lorenzo period. This drawing for the figure of the sleeping Adam indicates that the source of that figure was Pontormo's own earlier *Creation of Eve* composition of ca. 1520 (cat. 104). In that drawing Adam is reclining in the foreground of the composition in an almost identical pose to the Adam in the studies for the San Lorenzo fresco. Since the *Creation of Eve* is on the recto of this sheet, it is clear that Pontormo simply returned to his earlier drawing and restudied the motive on the verso, transforming the relatively vigorous and naturalistic nude of the Poggio a Caiano period into the limp, attenuated forms and calculated contours of his later style.

362 · Florence, Uffizi 6615F *verso*: Studies for the *Christ in Glory with the Creation of Eve* (cat. 359). Torso reclining to the left; above, a torso; to the left, a bent right arm, shoulders, and a left arm. (*Recto*: Study for San Lorenzo, cat. 371.) 212 x 289, black chalk.

Bibliography: Berenson 1903, no. 2114; Clapp 1914, 188; Berenson 1938, no. 2114. (Photo Sop.)

Clapp dated these studies 1550–1555, connecting the left arm and shoulders (reversed) with the Christ in cat. A97, but calling this sketch a study for the Adam in the *Labor of Adam and Eve* (cat. 370). All the studies on this sheet are related to the reclining Adam in the *Christ in Glory* and probably date not after 1550. The torso is studied in the same pose as in the other studies for the figure, but here the left arm is drawn as it was in cat. 361, extended down rather than under Adam's head. In cat. 363 and in the compositional study Pontormo returned to the original motive of the crossed arms that he had drawn in his Adam of 1520.

363 · Florence, Uffizi 6733F: Study for the *Christ in Glory with the Creation of Eve* (cat. 359). Nude reclining to the left seen to the knees, his head resting on his crossed arms. 216 x 290, black chalk; W: Pascal lamb in a circle (B. 50). Fig. 344.

Bibliography: Berenson 1903, no. 2215; Clapp 1914, 265; Berenson 1938, no. 2215.

As Clapp has noted, this is a study for the reclining Adam. It is a final study for the figure, subsequent to cat. 361 and 362. As a drawing for a figure in the upper range of the choir, it probably dates ca. 1550 or even earlier, not 1550–1554 as Clapp thought.

STUDIES FOR THE FOUR EVANGELISTS

364 · Florence, Uffizi 6750F: Compositional study for the *Four Evangelists*, San Lorenzo. Four floating intertwined nudes holding large books; below them, an angel blowing a trumpet; at the bottom of the sheet, detailed study of the shoulder of the second Evangelist from the top. 413 x 177, black chalk squared; W: Ladder in a shield with a star (cf. B. 5927). Fig. 350.

Bibliography: Berenson 1903, no. 2231; *MPA* 1910, 38; Clapp 1914, 277; Clapp 1916, 76, fig. 140; Berenson 1938, no. 2231; *MDF* 1939, 27; *MC* 1940, 47; Becherucci 1944, 22; Tolnay 1950, 40, fig. 46; Parigi 1951, no. 932; Cecchi 1956, fig. 14.

Berenson recognized this drawing as for San Lorenzo, but connected it with the *Last Judgment*, calling the figures Prophets or Apostles. Cecchi also identified it with the *Last Judgment*, the fresco on the right in the lower part of the choir. However, the format and proportions of this composition (squared four by ten *braccia*) clearly indicate that it was intended for one of the fields of the upper range. Clapp identified the subject as the *Four Evangelists*, placing it on the right side of the rear wall as a pendant to the *Moses Receiving the Tables of the Law* on the left side. Tolnay also considered this composition as a pendant to the *Moses*, but placed the two frescoes in the center fields of the side walls, seeing them as the pendant Old and New Testament subjects with the *Moses* on the right and the *Four Evangelists* on the left side of the choir. These two frescoes were certainly pendants, but the relations with the other subjects of the side walls indicate that the *Four Evangelists* was on the right, the *Moses* on the left. Furthermore, Vasari (V/M, VI, 286) gives a specific indication as to the location of the Four Evangelists as "in uno de'canti." This fresco is a pendant to the *Moses* in composition as well as in subject. In both there is a complex interweaving of forms that unwinds from a narrow base (in each case a leg), the forms swelling out in the center and then diminishing again toward the top of the composition. Like the *Cain and Abel*, these compositions are closely related to Pontormo's tapestry designs and should be dated not later than about 1550. Clapp dated this drawing more broadly, 1546–1556, but the upper range of the choir was certainly completed not along after 1550. In the bearded St. John the Evangelist of this drawing there is a reminiscence in both type and pose of Pontormo's earlier St. John tondo for S. Felicita.

365 · Florence, Uffizi 168S *recto*: Study for the *Four Evangelists* (cat. 364). Four floating intertwined nudes holding large books; below them, a putto blowing a trumpet; at the bottom of the sheet on a smaller scale, the foremost nude and the putto restudied. (*Verso*: Studies for San Lorenzo, cat. 351.) 257 x 80, black chalk. Fig. 348.

Collection: Santarelli, given to the Uffizi in 1866, stamp recto (L. 907).

Bibliography: Santarelli 1870, 18, no. 2.

This drawing was listed as Michelangelo in Santarelli's catalogue, but was attributed to Pontormo as for San Lorenzo by Smyth (verbally). This sketch is a first idea for the *Four Evangelists* in which the basic serpentine disposition of the four nudes and the putto is established. However, the shape of the composition is still rather amorphous in this sketch, while in cat. 364 the arrangement of the figures is tightened and the silhouette of the group is more sharply defined. This change is partly accomplished by the attenuation of the uppermost Evangelist and of the angel with the trumpet so that the elongated oval shape of the composition emerges more clearly, and by turning the two lower Evangelists into ornamentalizing profiles that are very like those of the two figures above Jacob in the *Lamentation* tapestry.

STUDIES FOR THE SACRIFICE OF ISAAC

366 · Bergamo, Accademia Carrara 2357: Compositional study for the *Sacrifice of Isaac*, San Lorenzo. On a sacrificial altar Abraham half kneels over the seated Isaac, whom he pushes to the right with his left hand; Abraham looks up to the left at the angel, who is flying to the left and wrests the knife from Abraham's right hand; to the left, the outline of half of a high arched window; to the right, the outline of half of a high arched window; below, a line indicating the bottom of the picture field. 230 x 165, black chalk squared in red chalk; laid down; written in ink in Pontormo's hand below: *b IX e tre quarti*; inscribed in ink: *di Jacopo Pontormo*. Fig. 351.

Bibliography: Collobi and Ragghianti 1962, 51, fig. 112.

This finished drawing for the *Sacrifice of Isaac* makes it evident that this fresco was in one of the central fields of the side walls, not in the far field of the right wall where Tolnay had placed it on the basis of the preliminary compositional study, cat. 367. As we have noted, its position in the center of the right wall can be deduced from the contemporary descriptions of the choir. Of all the compositional studies for the upper range, this drawing is the most specific in the indication of the exact proportions of the fresco fields and their relation to the windows. Like the other squared drawings, this one is squared for enlargement to approximately four by ten *braccia* (as in cat. 357 and 360, two squares are equal to a *braccio*). The notation below "b[raccia] IX e tre quarti" refers, like the notation "9 emezo" on the *Cain and Abel* (cat. 350) and the notation "10[br]accia dua dita" on the *Moses* (cat. 354), to the actual vertical dimension of the figures in the composition. This drawing also shows — and this is confirmed by the funeral print — that Pontormo's frescoes almost completely filled the available space in the upper range of the choir.

The composition of the *Sacrifice of Isaac* is a vertical arrangement of interlocking forms of the type first found in Pontormo in the *Lamentation of Jacob* tapestry and then in several other drawings of the San Lorenzo series. The two figures of Abraham and Isaac are only slightly varied from the Cain and Abel group (cat. 350), but such a complex interlacing of rising forms is found only in the *Four Evangelists* (cat. 364) and, apparently, in the *Original Sin*. Judging from the funeral print, the design of the three figures with the lower, seated Adam linked to the angel above by the attenuated, serpentine Eve, was very close to the composition of this drawing. The types and motives in this drawing also occur in the studies for the other upper-range frescoes: the Isaac appears again as Abel (cat. 350); the contorted angel is a slightly varied mirror image of the angel in the *Expulsion* (cat. 357); while the Abraham is the same bearded type that Pontormo used for the St. John the Evangelist (cat. 364) and the God Father (cat. 354 and 359).

367 · Florence, Uffizi 6568F: Study for the *Sacrifice of Isaac* (cat. 366). The half-kneeling Abraham turns and looks up at the angel who floats above with his arms raised; below, the Abraham and Isaac studied on a smaller scale; to the right in ink, the outline of the left half of a high arched window; to the left, above and below, the edges of the picture field indicated in chalk and ink. 249 x 114, black chalk; written in Pontormo's hand in ink below: *b 3 e sete otavi.* Fig. 349.

Bibliography: Berenson 1903, no. 2068; Clapp 1914, 158; Berenson 1938, no. 2068; Tolnay 1950, 39, fig. 44.

Berenson thought that this composition was probably for San Lorenzo, while Clapp identified it with the *Fall of the Damned*, a subject that he placed to the right on the lower rear wall of the choir, dating it 1550–1555. However, the *Fall of the Damned* is not mentioned in the descriptions of the San Lorenzo frescoes, and the high arched window in this drawing indicates without doubt that it was for the upper range of the choir and thus datable ca. 1550 or earlier. Tolnay recognized the subject of this drawing as the *Sacrifice of Isaac* that is mentioned by Bocchi 1591, 254. Since the window appears to the right of the composition, Tolnay placed this fresco in the only logical field: on the right wall in the far field. However, the finished drawing for the fresco shows a window to either side of the composition, indicating that it must have been in the center field instead. Although this preliminary sketch is not squared, the proportions of the fresco field and the window are the same as in the more elaborated drawings. We know from the final study that the composition was to be four *braccia* wide; therefore, the notation "b[raccia] 3 e sete otavi" below must refer to the actual width of the figures themselves.

Among the preliminary studies for the compositions of the upper-range frescoes (cat. 351, 355, and 364), this drawing is the least elaborated, the most fluid and rhythmic in its draughtsmanship. Like cat. 351 for the *Cain and Abel*, the composition sketched here is quite different from the final solution. The first idea for the Abraham and Isaac figures is sketched on a small scale below, where the Abraham kneels with his left knee on the Isaac. Above, the relation between the Abraham and the angel is worked out with the Isaac suggested but not actually drawn in under Abraham's knee. In this grouping there are reminiscences of Michelangelo that do not appear in the final composition. The Abraham and Isaac are very like the *Victory*, while the sudden spiraling upward of the angel recalls Michelangelo's drawings for a *Resurrection* ca. 1526–1532.[39] The dynamic relation between the angel and the Abraham is not at all like that of the final composition. Here the figure of the angel continues the vertical accent of the Abraham in a way that does not occur in any of

[39] See Michelangelo's studies for a projected *Resurrection* for the Medici Chapel (British Museum 1860-6-16-133, Windsor cat. 219; Louvre 691 bis.).

the upper-range compositions; he is suspended between ascent and descent, between turning away and turning toward the Abraham. In the final drawing there is an acute sense of the physical struggle between the two figures; here they are not connected physically but only by way of the emphatic serpentine rhythm that dominates the composition. This study is the only instance in the drawings for the upper-range frescoes in which there is an indication of the extremes to which Pontormo would carry the idea of suspended, unoriented, rising and falling forms in the studies for the *Deluge* and the *Resurrection of the Dead*.

368 · Florence, Uffizi 6585F: Study for the *Sacrifice of Isaac* (cat. 366). Three-quarter length nude leaning to the right with his head on his left shoulder and his arms behind his back; to the right, two smaller indecipherable sketches. 280 x 194, black chalk; inscribed verso in ink: . . . *da Puntormo*. Fig. 355.

Bibliography: Berenson 1903, no. 2085; Clapp 1914, 168; Berenson 1938, no. 2085.

Berenson thought this nude was a late study for a *Dead Christ* or a *Christ at the Column* and connected it with cat. A80 and A83. Clapp dated the drawing 1540–1550 as for a *Christ at the Column*. This drawing is a study for the figure of Isaac in exactly the same pose as in the compositional study, with the torso fully elaborated, but the head and the beginning of the legs only faintly indicated. The style of this black chalk study is specifically that of other detail studies for figures in the upper range frescoes, especially cat. 352, 353, 356, and 363.

369 · Florence, Uffizi 15662F: Study for the *Sacrifice of Isaac* (cat. 366). Angel flying to the left with the left arm raised and the legs crossed. 175 x 225, black chalk; laid down. Fig. 354.

Bibliography: Berenson 1903, no. 2243; Clapp 1914, 285; Berenson 1938, no. 2243.

This drawing was dated "rather early" by Berenson and dated 1535–1545 by Clapp, who saw it as a figure flying vertically rather than horizontally. This faint, rather damaged drawing is a study for the angel in the *Sacrifice of Isaac* in which the pose has been determined but its details not yet worked out. Here the action of the arms is different from those in the final study, with the left arm raised rhetorically and the right arm placed on the sword. Pontormo's indecision about the exact position of the right leg is also evident: the figure was first drawn lightly with the right leg bent down and forward, but when the modelling was added to the figure, the position of the right leg was changed so that it was parallel to and behind the left leg. In the final compositional study this second position of the legs is retained, while the figure is placed in a more diagonal position with the head higher to accommodate the more aggressive restraining action of the angel's arms. This angel is similar to the angel in the *Expulsion* (cat. 357) in type and pose, and it is the sort of flying angel that became a stock motive in the later Bronzino (cf. the *Martyrdom of St. Lawrence*, San Lorenzo).

STUDIES FOR THE LABOR OF ADAM AND EVE

370 · Florence, Uffizi 6535F: Compositional study for the *Labor of Adam and Eve*, San Lorenzo. Enclosed in a rectangular frame, Adam facing right digging with his spade; above, Eve seated turned to the left holding a spindle and distaff; behind her to the left, a torso; to the right, a head; outside this scene to the right, right half of a nude man seen to the knees; above on a smaller scale, lower half of a floating figure. 203 x 158, black chalk squared in black and red chalk. Fig. 356.

Bibliography: Berenson 1903, no. 2038; Clapp 1914, 137–138; Clapp 1916, 76, fig. 143; Berenson 1938, 320, no. 2038; Tolnay 1950, 39, fig. 43.

Clapp identified this compositional study and nude study with the *Labor of Adam and Eve*, dating it 1550–1555. Since the upper range of the choir was surely finished well before 1555, Clapp's date must be considered too late for this drawing. Clapp placed this composition on the right wall in the far field, while Tolnay placed it on the left wall in the far field because of its narrative association with the Adam and Eve scenes of the rear wall. However, as we have noted, the location of this subject on the right wall next to the arch may be deduced from the descriptions of the choir and indications on certain of the other drawings. Like the other compositional studies for the upper-range frescoes, except for the *Christ in Glory*, this study is squared for enlargement to approximately four by ten *braccia*.

The composition of the *Labor of Adam and Eve* recalls Pontormo's tapestry designs of ca. 1545–1549. The pose of the half-seated Eve and the balancing of the two opposed curves of the figures are like the relation of the two protagonists in the *Benjamin at the Court of the Pharaoh*. The Eve recalls the third figure in the *Lamentation of Jacob* tapestry, and she appears in a similar pose in the *Original Sin* (cf. the funeral print), but her type and her pose go back ultimately to the kind of monumental female that Pontormo had invented in the Careggi *Allegories* of a decade earlier (cat. 314 and 316). As Clapp has noted, the fragmentary nude to the right and partly under the compositional study may have been a preliminary idea from a male model for the pose of the Eve in reverse.

371 · Florence, Uffizi 6615F *recto*: Study for the *Labor of Adam and Eve* (cat. 370). Nude seen to the knees turned to the right digging with a spade; to the right, his left hand restudied. (*Verso*: Studies for San Lorenzo, cat. 362.) 289 x 212, black chalk; W: Star in a circle with a cross (B. 6088). Fig. 353.

Bibliography: Berenson 1903, no. 2114; Clapp 1914, 187–188; Berenson 1938, no. 2114; Tolnay 1950, 39, fig. 41.

Clapp identified this study as for the Adam digging with his spade, but dated it 1550–1555, certainly too late for a drawing for the upper-range frescoes. This study is a careful elaboration of the figure as it is drawn in the compositional study. It is similar in style to analogous drawings for other figures in the upper range, such as the study for the Eve of the *Expulsion*, cat. 358.

372 · Florence, Uffizi 6739F *verso*: Study for the *Labor of Adam and Eve* (cat. 370). Bust of a nude in profile right with the right arm raised; above, part of the legs and feet of a figure. (*Recto*: Study for San Lorenzo, cat. 350.) 405 x 218, black chalk. (Photo Sop.)

These very faint unpublished sketches are on the verso of the finished study for the *Cain and Abel*. They are ideas for its pendant across the choir, the *Labor of Adam and Eve*, in which we see the legs and feet of Eve and the head and shoulders of Adam.

STUDIES FOR THE DELUGE

373 · Florence, Uffizi 6752F *recto*: Study for the *Deluge*, San Lorenzo. Mass of ten intertwined nude figures. (*Verso*: Faint sketch of a nude, not catalogued.) 156 x 244, black chalk; W: Fleur-de-lis (B. 6895); inscribed in ink in an eighteenth-century hand on a paper used to repair a damage: *Jac° da Pontormo.*

Fig. 357.

Bibliography: Berenson 1903, no. 2233;

Clapp 1914, 278; Clapp 1916, 76, fig. 145; Tinti 1925, fig. 5; Berenson 1938, no. 2233; Nicco Fasola 1947, 55, fig. 35; Tolnay 1950, 49; *MP* 1956 (Marcucci), no. 140, fig. 167a; Cecchi 1956, fig. 12; Marcucci 1956, 22, fig. 27.

Berenson thought this drawing and cat. 374–375 were for the *Deluge* or the *Last Judgment* of San Lorenzo, while Clapp identified the group as for the *Deluge*, dating them 1550–1555. Tolnay, Marcucci, and Cecchi have also affirmed the connection with the *Deluge*. As the only surviving drawings for the *Deluge* fresco on the left side of the choir, these three studies may be identified as drawings for the "massa di corpi morti ed affogati" described by Vasari (V/M, VI, 286) as part of the *Deluge*.

374 · Florence, Uffizi 6753F: Study for the *Deluge*, San Lorenzo. Group of five nudes wound around one another; to the right, a sprawled nude. 135 x 306, black chalk; inscribed in ink in an eighteenth-century hand: *Jacopo da Pontormo.* Fig. 358.

Bibliography: Berenson 1903, no. 2234; Clapp 1914, 278–279; Clapp 1916, 76, fig. 144; Berenson 1938, no. 2234; Grassi 1946, 44, fig. 17; Tolnay 1950, 49, fig. 50; Cecchi 1956, fig. 13; Berenson 1961, no. 2234, fig. 979.

See cat. 373. These five figures (but not the sprawled nude to the right) are careful detail studies for the group in the center of cat. 375. These two studies are the most precisely datable of the San Lorenzo drawings, since sketches corresponding to these nudes occur in Pontormo's diary between May 14 and June 7, 1555 (cf. figs. 378–379). Therefore, these studies for the *Deluge* must have been executed toward the end of Pontormo's work in the choir.

375 · Florence, Uffizi 6754F *recto*: Study for the *Deluge*, San Lorenzo. Mass of about fourteen intertwined nudes. (*Verso*: Study for a *Venus and Cupid*, cat. 383.) 266 x 402, black chalk; some outlines incised for transfer; right lower corner of the sheet replaced. Fig. 359.

Bibliography: Berenson 1903, no. 2235; Clapp 1914, 279, pl. 8; Tinti 1925, fig. 6; Berenson 1938, no. 2235; Becherucci 1943, 11, pl. 29; Becherucci 1944, 23, fig. 56; Tolnay 1950, 49, fig. 51.

See cat. 373. This drawing is the most elaborate of the surviving studies for the lower-range frescoes. In this study and in cat. 373–374 there has been a sharp break from the style of the studies for the upper range of the choir, and even from the drawings for the *Resurrection of the Dead* (cat. 377–379) and the *Ascension of Souls* (cat. 376). In this shifting complex of swollen and distorted forms there is a radical departure from the still ornamental figures of the earlier San Lorenzo drawings. These nudes are no longer individualities in any sense. The earlier nudes were still anatomically intact, but these will-less figures have been distended, twisted, and manipulated so that their proportions no longer approximate those of the human form and they no longer represent actual physical beings. Back views now predominate and contact with the spectator through the power of facial expression (such a conspicuous feature of Pontormo's earlier drawings) is sharply reduced. It comes somewhat as a surprise within this context to find Pontormo still making oblique reference to Michelangelo. The figure upside down on the left (seen more clearly in cat. 374) is derived from the *Fall of Phaeton* drawings, while the figure to the right with his arm twisted behind him is an often-used Michelangelo image (cf. the nude above the *Jesse* spandrel in the Sistine Ceiling).

STUDY FOR THE ASCENSION OF SOULS

376 · Venice, Gallerie 550: Compositional study for the *Ascension of Souls*, San

Lorenzo. Four intertwined nudes: two figures with their arms raised supported by two crouched figures. 288 x 190, black chalk squared in red chalk; inscribed in ink: *Jacopo.* Fig. 360.

Collection: Accademia delle Belle Arti, Venice, stamp recto (L. 188).

Bibliography: Clapp 1914, 348–349; Clapp 1916, 76, fig. 147; Berenson 1938, no. 2368B; Tolnay 1950, 49.

This drawing was formerly attributed to Tintoretto, but it was given to Pontormo by Clapp, who associated it with the *Ascension of Souls* and dated it 1550–1556. This drawing agrees exactly with Vasari's description of the figures on either side of the space between the windows as "una fila d'ignudi, che presi per mano e aggrappatisi su per le gambe e busti l'uno dell'altro si fanno scala per salire in paradiso . . ." (V/M, VI, 286). Since the space between the windows was about five and one half *braccia* in width and this drawing is squared for enlargement to slightly under three *braccia*, it is clear that this study is for a part of one of the two columns of nudes that Vasari describes. In Pontormo's diary there is a sketch dating March 11, 1555 (see fig. 373) that corresponds very closely to these figures and may also have been done in connection with the *Ascension of Souls.*

STUDIES FOR THE RESURRECTION OF THE DEAD

377 · Florence, Uffizi 6528F *recto*: Studies for the *Resurrection of the Dead*, San Lorenzo. On the lower part of the sheet a mass of sprawling intertwined nudes; above, part of a nude back, a small kneeling nude; to the left sideways on the sheet, heads and raised arms of two figures facing each other fighting (?). (*Verso*: Portrait study of Cosimo de' Medici, cat. 334.) 421 x 215, red chalk over a little black chalk; sketches above in black chalk; W: Hand. Fig. 363.

Bibliography: Gamba 1910, 126; Gamba 1912, 4; Clapp 1914, 132–133; Clapp 1916, 76–77, fig. 146; Berenson 1938, 320, no. 2031, fig. 995; Becherucci 1943, 11, pl. 30; Becherucci 1944, 23, fig. 57; Nicco Fasola 1947, 55, fig. 36; Tolnay 1950, 49.

Berenson, Gamba, and Clapp thought the mass of nudes on this sheet were for the *Deluge*, Clapp associating them with sketches on page thirteen of Pontormo's diary (cf. fig. 393), while Tolnay connected this study with the *Resurrection of the Dead*. It is somewhat difficult to make a definitive distinction between the drawings for the various lower-range frescoes because of Pontormo's frequent repetition of motives and of groups of sprawling, entangled nudes. However, these figures are alive while those in the studies for the *Deluge* are not, and they rise up energetically, looking upward with raised arms in a way that suggests the *Resurrection of the Dead*. This drawing is also quite different in style from those for the *Deluge* (cat. 373–375). It is a preliminary sketch in red chalk (the only San Lorenzo drawing in red chalk), while the *Deluge* studies are carefully finished black chalk drawings; it is executed in a fluid, energetic manner that recalls the first sketches for the upper range, such as cat. 351; and the nudes themselves are not as anormative and distended in form as those in the *Deluge* studies. The other sketches on this sheet also link this drawing with the upper-range studies. The two fighting figures might have been an idea for the *Cain and Abel*, sketched on cat. 351, while the small nude to the right is, as Clapp has noted, identical in pose to the Abel in cat. 350. The torso is close in style to the nudes of the upper range and even to those of the tapestry studies. These connections all suggest that this drawing is an early study for the *Resurrection of the Dead*, possibly dating from shortly after 1550, not toward 1555, as Clapp dated it.

378 · Florence, Uffizi 17411F *recto*: Studies for the *Resurrection of the Dead*, San Lorenzo. Four intertwined nudes; below, a reclining nude, a half-length nude seen from behind, a bone. (*Verso*: Studies for San Lorenzo, cat. 379.) 243 x 184, black chalk. Fig. 361.

Bibliography: Berenson 1903, no. 2247; Gamba 1912, no. 23b, pl. 23b; Clapp 1914, 287; Berenson 1938, no. 2247; *MDF* 1939, 5; *MC* 1940, 46; Grassi 1946, 44, fig. 18; Tolnay 1950, 49.

This sheet has been variously connected with both the *Deluge* and the *Resurrection of the Dead*. Gamba and Clapp thought it might be for either fresco, Clapp dating it 1550–1555; while Berenson connected it with the *Deluge* and Tolnay with the *Resurrection of the Dead*. As in the case of cat. 377, this drawing could have been for either fresco, but it was more likely for the *Resurrection*. This knot of writhing, muscular figures is quite different in character from the inert, dead forms of the *Deluge* drawings (cat. 373–375). These nudes are of the same type that appear in the drawing for the *Ascension of Souls* (cat. 376), and their action suggests that this is a more finished study for a group like that in the center of cat. 377. Groups of figures similar to this one appear in cat. A216, a copy after the *Resurrection of the Dead*, while in another copy (cat. A238) there is a nude that is extremely close to the central figure in this group. The torso and nude below must also have been connected with the *Resurrection of the Dead*, although Clapp thought the torso was a study for the foremost nude in the *Four Evangelists* (cat. 364). There is some connection in pose, but Pontormo's constant repetition of motives is such that the association with the earlier drawing is unlikely. As Clapp has noted, the reclining nude is inspired by the Medici Tomb *Allegories* (cf. the *Giorno*).

379 · Florence, Uffizi 17411F *verso*: Studies for the *Resurrection of the Dead*, San Lorenzo. Bust of a nude holding a hat in his left hand, a staff in the right hand and looking upward; to the left, a bone traced from the recto. (*Recto*: Studies for San Lorenzo, cat. 378.) 184 x 243, black chalk. Fig. 362.

Bibliography: Berenson 1903, no. 2247; Clapp 1914, 288; Berenson 1938, no. 2247.

This drawing has not been related to the San Lorenzo frescoes. It is a study for the *Resurrection of the Dead*, a connection that is confirmed by the occurrence of an identical figure in the center of cat. A216, a copy after a part of the fresco. This type of nude, with his Michelangelesque bulging muscles, appears also on the recto of this sheet and in cat. 376 for the *Ascension of Souls*.

MISCELLANEOUS DRAWINGS
CA. 1545–1556

380 · Florence, Uffizi 6508F *verso*: Ca. 1545–1550. Torso of a nude seen from behind; to the left in reverse direction, a small nude with arms raised flying upward. (*Recto*: Study for San Lorenzo, cat. 355.) 140 x 270, black chalk; written in Pontormo's hand across the sheet to the left: *o segno / basta 3 e ½/ e 8 lu*[n]*go/ alt*º *4 e ½ e 7/ alt*º *10 e 4/* [s]*e no*[n] *4 e 6/ 85 fog* [l]*i imperiale/ nel cartone gra*[n]*de.*

Bibliography: Berenson 1903, no. 2016; Clapp 1914, 120; Berenson 1938, no. 2016. (Photo G.)

Clapp connected this torso with cat. A94. The emphatic muscular patterning and curved shapes of this torso recall the tapestry drawings (cat. 347–348) and the detail studies for figures in the upper-range San Lorenzo frescoes, such as the shoulders on the recto of this sheet or cat. 356, both for the *Moses*. However, this figure cannot be definitely associated with any one of the compositions. The partially legible inscription is of considerable interest because it is Pontormo's figuring in *braccia* for the proportions of the frescoes of the upper range, the first figure in each set referring to the width (all but one of the frescoes were about four *braccia* wide), and the second to the height of a composition or a part of it (the frescoes were a maximum of about ten *braccia* in height). The last part of the inscription apparently refers to the number of sheets of *imperiale* paper that went to make up a large cartoon, possibly the cartoon for two of the upper-range frescoes.[40]

381 · Florence, Uffizi 6560F: Ca. 1545–1556. Nude reclining on his left side with his arms wound around his head. 210 x 277, black chalk; inscribed verso in ink: *Puntormo.* Fig. 364.

Bibliography: Berenson 1903, no. 2061; Clapp 1914, 155; Clapp 1916, fig. 148; Berenson 1938, no. 2061; *MDF* 1939, 27; Tolnay 1950, 49.

Clapp associated this drawing with the San Lorenzo *Deluge*. He noted the connection in pose with the central figure in cat. 378 and cat. A82, both of which he considered for the *Deluge*. However, cat. 378 is probably for the *Resurrection of the Dead* and cat. A82 is a copy after a Pontormo drawing similar to this one. Clapp also connected this study with a sketch on page four of Pontormo's diary, a figure that was drawn June 20–22, 1555 (cf. fig. 380). While this nude is closely related in pose to the diary sketch and to cat. 378, Pontormo's constant repetition of motives cautions against connecting it definitely with either the *Resurrection of the Dead* or the *Deluge*. Furthermore, the sinuous, ornamental contours and the calculated curvilinear relations of the forms in this figure are suggestive of detail studies for figures in the upper-range frescoes such as cat. 358 and cat. 371. However, there is no figure in the upper-range compositions, except possibly the Adam of the *Original Sin* in a preliminary version, that would have been posed in this way.

382 · Florence, Uffizi 6654F: Ca. 1550–1556. Three-quarter length seated nude turned to the right hiding his face with his right arm. 144 x 89, black chalk.

Bibliography: Berenson 1903, no. 2146; Clapp 1914, 208; Berenson 1938, no. 2146. (Photo G.)

Berenson and Clapp both called this nude a late drawing, Clapp comparing it with cat. A126. This nude is close in style to drawings for the lower-range San Lorenzo frescoes such as cat. 378, and the action of the figure suggests either the *Deluge* or the *Resurrection of the Dead*, but this figure cannot be precisely connected with any of the studies for the frescoes.

383 · Florence, Uffizi 6754F *verso*: Ca. 1550–1556. Study for a *Venus and Cupid*. Reclining nude Venus with Cupid astride her hip kissing her; below, fragment of a reclining figure. (*Recto*: Study for San Lorenzo, cat. 375.) 266 x 402, black chalk. (Photo Sop.)

This unpublished study is the only surviving drawing of the San Lorenzo period that is definitely not connected with the frescoes in the choir. In this very faint sketch, Pontormo has reconsidered the theme and motive of the Michelangelo *Venus and Cupid* of 1533–1534. However, in comparison with cat. 325 and 329, Pon-

[40] *Imperiale* paper was 740 x 500 in size. See Meder 1919, 174; and C. M. Briquet, *Les Filigranes* (Leipzig, 1923), I, 3–4.

tormo's earlier variants on the Michelangelo invention, he has here transformed the *Maniera* group into the fluid, expressive style of his San Lorenzo drawings. The pose of the Venus also refers to Pontormo's nudes for the lunettes of Villa Castello (cf. cat. 344 for the legs), as does the pose of cat. 381 of this same period. Cat. A120 may be a copy after a more finished version of this composition.

PONTORMO'S DIARY AND THE SAN LORENZO CHOIR

PONTORMO'S DIARY AND THE SAN LORENZO CHOIR

The original manuscript of Pontormo's diary [1] was identified by Colosanti,[2] but it was not until Clapp's transcription (1916, app. III) that it was published in full. Clapp retained Pontormo's spelling and abbreviations in his text, appending a synopsis of the contents of the diary as well as a topical analysis and a reconstruction of the sequence of the entries. Before his publication of the full text Clapp had connected some of the marginal sketches in the diary with drawings attributed to Pontormo as studies for the San Lorenzo choir.[3] After Clapp's work there were no notable studies of the diary until Cecchi's edition at the time of the *Mostra del Pontormo* in 1956.[4] In Cecchi's transcription spelling and abbreviations are modernized, resulting in a readable edition that should be consulted for the many interesting aspects of the diary that are not considered here. Cecchi appended an essay on the diary in general as well as quotations from various authors on the destroyed San Lorenzo frescoes. However, he did not concern himself with the text and the marginal sketches as sources of information about Pontormo's work, considerations that must be of primary interest here.

In this section the parts of the diary that are directly concerned with Pontormo's frescoes at San Lorenzo (apparently the only project on which he was engaged at the time) have been excerpted in chronological order so that an

[1] "Diario di Jacopo da Pontorno [sic] fatto nel tempo che dipingeva il Coro di San Lorenzo," Florence, Biblioteca Nazionale, Miscellanea magliabecchiana cl. VII, no. 1490. Sixteen sheets (twenty-three pages), 218 x 150; written in ink with forty-three marginal sketches 1 to 3 cm in size on pp. 1–8, 10–14, and 21. The first recorded owner of the diary was Carlo di Tommaso Strozzi, who acquired it in 1625. It was bought from the Strozzi family by Leopoldo de' Medici in 1786 (see Clapp 1916, 295n1).

[2] See A. Colosanti, "Il Diario di Jacopo Carucci da Pontormo," *Bollettino della Società Filologica Romana* 2 (1902), 35–59. Previous to this publication a seventeenth-century copy of pp. 1–6 and 20–23 of the diary (Biblioteca Nazionale, Palatino 621 E, 5, 6, 32) was published by G. Gaye, *Carteggio inedito d'artisti dei secoli XIV, XV, XVI* (Florence, 1840), III, 166–169. See also C. von Fabriczy, "Das Tagebuch Jacopos da Pontormo," *Rep. KW* 26 (1904), 95–96; and F. Maggini, "Un Diario del Pontormo," *Giornale Storico della Letteratura italiana* 63 (1914), 301–305.

[3] Of the 11 drawings that Clapp associated with the diary, cat. A88, A114, A159, A171, and A208 are copies after Pontormo drawings for San Lorenzo, while A151 is after his Castello frescoes. Cat. 339 and 341 are studies for the Castello loggia. Cat. 374 is a study for the San Lorenzo *Deluge*, cat. 377 for the *Resurrection of the Dead*, and cat. 381 is for San Lorenzo but not definitely associable with any one of the frescoes.

[4] See E. Cecchi, ed., *Jacopo da Pontormo: Diario* (Florence, 1956). See also an earlier article: E. Cecchi " 'Diario' del Pontormo," *Parallelo* I (1943), 29–30.

account of Pontormo's artistic activity emerges from the much longer text of the entire diary. The translation of these passages into English follows as closely as possible Pontormo's often abbreviated and irregular syntax, the ellipsis being used to indicate material omitted and brackets to enclose explanatory insertions or queries. The marginal sketches that Pontormo drew in conjunction with much of the text have been connected, where possible, with his drawings for the frescoes of the lower range of the choir and with copies after the *Resurrection of the Dead*.

Pontormo's diary contains a record of his work at San Lorenzo during the two years before his death (January 1, 1557), with two entries going back to 1554. From it emerges a picture of a painstakingly slow and virtually solitary process — as much physical labor as intellectual activity — that makes understandable why a decade was required to paint the choir. While Vasari's statement (V/M, VI, 285): ". . . da lui in fuori mai non vi entrò anima vivente, nè amici, nè nessuno," is surely an exaggeration, Pontormo records no assistance in the actual work, including plastering the wall in preparation for the color and the transferring of the cartoons as well as the painting itself. We know that Pontormo had other assistants (see Clapp 1916, app. II, doc. 27), but we do not know the nature of their work or whether Pontormo had any assistance in the actual painting of the frescoes. In any case, in the diary he mentions only Marco Moro, who assisted him on June 9, 1554, in repairing holes in the walls and in walling up the choir, and Battista Naldini, who helped him in fetching and carrying supplies from July 20 to 22, 1555.

As can be seen immediately from the excerpted sections of the diary, Pontormo's account of his work at San Lorenzo is fragmentary, abbreviated, and often inexplicit, especially considering that we cannot turn to the frescoes themselves for corroboration and correlation of his remarks. Aside from the two entries in 1554, Pontormo reports working between January and November of 1555 and from February to October of 1556. At this time Pontormo must long since have finished the frescoes of the upper range, which, being at the top of the choir, would normally have been painted first. Thus, as Pontormo's remarks in the text of the diary and the marginal sketches confirm, his account of work in the years 1554–1556 can only have been concerned with the *Deluge*, on the left lower wall; the *Resurrection of the Dead*, on the right lower wall; the *Ascension of Souls* and the *Martyrdom of St. Lawrence*, both on the rear lower wall. However, it is impossible to deduce too rigid a chronology for Pontormo's work on these frescoes. The first problem is that Pontormo worked on all three walls of the choir during this two-year period.

The contemporary reports that Pontormo left all the frescoes unfinished along the bottom when he died are corroborated in the diary by sketches for and indirect references to all the subjects of the lower-range frescoes. Thus, it appears that Pontormo worked almost simultaneously from the top down on the three walls, finishing the *Ascension of Souls*, which occupied only the upper part of the lower rear wall, but not the *Martyrdom of St. Lawrence* below it, nor the *Deluge* and the *Resurrection of the Dead*. Not only did Pontormo move back and forth, working on one fresco for a period and then switching to another, but there is another obstacle to determining the sequence of his work. It is often impossible to be sure which sketch refers to which fresco because Pontormo habitually repeated motives that carried certain meanings for him. Judging from the drawings (cat. 373–379) and from the copies after the *Resurrection of the Dead*, there was more than the usual repetition of motives in these later years. Therefore, caution must be used in associating the diary sketches.

Keeping these various problems in mind, we may suggest the following sequence for the work that Pontormo records in the diary: the two entries from 1554 tell us nothing about the fresco on which Pontormo was working, while the only sketch (fig. 372) is an example of the motive repetition mentioned above. The figure recalls one in cat. A216 after the *Resurrection of the Dead*. However, especially considering the similarities in motive that we know existed between figures in the *Resurrection*, *Ascension of Souls*, and the *Deluge*, it is difficult to associate this sketch definitely with the *Resurrection of the Dead*. However, from January to March 1555, it is reasonably clear that Pontormo was painting the *Ascension of Souls*, as sketches (fig. 373) can be associated with cat. 376 for that fresco. Since the *Ascension of Souls* was on the upper part of the lower rear wall, since it was not among the frescoes left unfinished at Pontormo's death, and since he later records work on the fresco directly below it, it is probable that he completed it at this time. From April to June 1555 Pontormo was almost certainly working on the *Deluge*. Marginal sketches (figs. 378–379) refer explicitly to two nudes that appear together in studies for the fresco (cat. 374–375). On June 25th Pontormo notes that scaffolding was taken down, indicating that a large portion of this fresco must have been completed. Since no further entries or sketches refer to the *Deluge*, it is possible that Pontormo did not return to work on it again. From this point on Pontormo worked almost continuously on the *Resurrection of the Dead*. Marginal sketches (figs. 381, 383, 384, 387) from July to November 1555 may be associated with cat. A88, A208, A216, and A238, copies after the fresco. There is a break in Pontormo's work (or of his record of it) during the winter months of December 1555 and January 1556, but in February and March he was working steadily, probably still on the *Resurrection of the Dead.* We can be certain of this in April, when Pontormo writes that he was painting the wall of the choir opposite the Old Sacristy. Sketches (fig. 393) from May and June refer again to figures in cat. A216 and on June 13 Pontormo notes that part of a fresco — evidently the *Resurrection of the Dead* — was finished. During July Pontormo continued to work on the *Resurrection of the Dead*, but late in the month it is certain that he turned to the *Martyrdom of St. Lawrence.* While there are no marginal sketches in this part of the diary, Pontormo is unusually explicit. He mentions preparing the cartoon of the *St. Lawrence* for transfer in August, and in September and early October he painted the putti with the symbols of martyrdom. Pontormo records work on this fresco until October 6. Although the diary continues for another two weeks, this is the last entry that concerns his painting.

EXCERPTS FROM PONTORMO'S DIARY

1554

Wed. March 21 [5]
[p. 21] . . . I did the figure above the bald head.[6]

Sat. June 9
[p. 22] . . . Marco Moro began to wall up the choir of San Lorenzo and to fill holes in the walls.

1555

Wed.–Thurs. Jan. 30–31, Fri. Feb. 1, Tues. Feb. 5, Sat. Feb. 16
[p. 1] On the 30th of January 1555 I began the loins of the figure who laments for the child. On the 31st I did the little bit of drapery around her . . . On the first of February I did some drapery below and on the 5th I finished her, and on the 16th I did the legs of the child below her . . .

Thurs. Feb. 28
. . . during the day I did the head of the figure who is above the one that goes like this.[7]

Mon. March 4
. . . I did the torso that is below the head mentioned above . . .

Mon.–Wed. March 11–13
. . . Monday I did the arm of the figure at the top who rises up and I left it up to here as this sketch shows.[8] Tuesday and Wednesday I did the old man and his arm that goes like this.[9]

[5] It should be noted that Pontormo does not, as one might expect, follow the Florentine calender in dating the entries in his diary. Had he done so, entries dated January, February, and March of 1556 would refer to a period after his death.

[6] Page 21, sketch A (fig. 372). Cf. a figure in cat. A216 after the *Resurrection of the Dead.*

[7] Page 1, sketch A (fig. 373). There is a similar sketch on p. 14, sketch A. The motive of two figures, one carrying the other, could have occurred in any of the frescoes. However, considering Pontormo's remark of Jan. 30th that he painted a figure lamenting for a child, it is possible that this sketch refers to the *Deluge.*

[8] Page 1, sketch B (fig. 373). Figures like this one occurred in the *Ascension of Souls* (cf. cat. 376).

[9] Page 1, sketch C (fig. 373). While a figure like this one appears to the upper left of cat. A216 after the *Resurrection of the Dead*, this sketch was more likely to have been done in

Fri. March 15, Mon.–Wed. March 18–20
On March 15th I began the arm that holds the strap . . .[10] Wednesday on the 20th I finished the arm [I had done] Friday and Monday; before that, I did the bust and on Tuesday I did the head that belongs to the arm of which I am speaking.

Fri.–Sat. March 22–23
Friday I did the other arm that goes across; and Saturday [I did] a little bit of blue background . . .[11]

Tues.–Wed. March 26–27
Tuesday I did the head of the child who is bending over . . . Wednesday I did the rest of the child . . .

Fri. March 29
[p. 2] . . . I did the hand and half of the arm of the large figure, the knee with a piece of the leg where he puts his hand . . .[12]

Wed. April 3
. . . I did the leg from the knee down with great difficulty with the darkness, and wind, and plastering.

Fri. April 5
. . . I began . . . the back that is under it [the leg] . . .

Tues. April 9
. . . I did the leg that has its thigh under the back mentioned above . . .[13]

Sat. April 13
. . . I worked on the large rock and the Duke [Cosimo] came to mass at San Lorenzo.

Thurs.–Sat. April 18–20
Thursday I worked on the two arms.[14] . . . Friday I did the head with the large rock below it . . . Saturday I did [a] large branch and [a] rock and the hand . . .

Sat. April 27
[p. 3] . . . during the day I finished the leg by itself that goes like this.[15]

Tues. May 7, Thurs. May 9
Tuesday . . . I began the arm of the figure that goes like this[16] . . . and Thursday I finished it . . .

Tues.–Wed. May 14–15
. . . Tuesday I began to do the torso that is upside down like this[17] . . . Wednesday I did a plastering that was so difficult that I don't think it went well . . .[18]

Thurs.–Sat. May 16–18, Mon.–Wed. May 20–22, Fri. May 24
Thursday I did an arm. Friday [I did] the other arm. Saturday [I did] the thigh of the figure that goes like this . . .[19] Monday I began the arm of the above-

connection with the *Ascension of Souls* like sketch B on this page.

[10] Page 1, sketch D (fig. 373). Compared with sketch B on the same page, also depicting figures rising up, this sketch is suggestive of the *Ascension of Souls*.

[11] None of the descriptions of Pontormo's frescoes mention specific colors, Vasari noting only that Pontormo's color scheme was "fatta a suo modo" (V/M, VI, 287). Since Pontormo elsewhere (see note 53) mentions the blue background of the *Resurrection of the Dead*, we may safely assume that this was the background color of the choir.

[12] Page 2, sketch A (fig. 374).

[13] Page 2, sketch B (fig. 375).

[14] Page 2, sketch C (fig. 376).

[15] Page 3, sketch A (fig. 377).

[16] Page 3, sketch B (fig. 378).

[17] Page 3, sketch C (fig. 378). A nude posed like this is conspicuous in cat. 374 and 375 for the *Deluge*.

[18] The text continues "che sono tucte le poppe come si vede la comettitura," meaning that the surface of the plastering was rough and one could see where the section Pontormo had just prepared joined the others.

[19] Page 3, sketch D (fig. 378). This figure appears in the center of cat. 374 and 375 for the *Deluge* to the right of the figure in sketch C on this page. The conjunction of these two motives makes it virtually certain that these sketches were done in connection with work on the *Deluge* fresco.

mentioned figure that goes like this . . .[20] Tuesday [I did] the other arm. Wednesday the 22nd [I did] the torso . . . Friday [I did] the thigh . . . and I finished the figure.

Wed.–Sat. May 29–June 1
[p. 4] Wednesday I did the head that is under the figure like this.[21] Thursday [I did] the thigh. Friday [I did] the back. Saturday I finished the figure . . .

Wed.–Fri. June 5–7
Wednesday . . . I did the shoulders of the figure that goes like this.[22] Thursday I did the arm. . . . Friday I finished it . . .

Wed.–Sat. June 19–22
Wednesday I did the head of the dead man with a beard that is above this figure.[23] Thursday I did the head and arm of the figure who goes like this.[24] Friday I did the torso. Saturday [I did] the legs and I finished it . . .

Tues.–Thurs. June 25–27
Tuesday the scaffolding was taken down, Wednesday the holes [in the wall] were filled; Thursday I did that which goes as far as the . . .[25]

Thurs.–Sat. July 4–6, Tues. July 9, Thurs. July 11
Thursday on the 4th of July I began the figure that goes like this [26] [p. 5] . . . Friday, Saturday I did as far as the legs . . . Tuesday I did a thigh . . . Thursday I did the other leg . . .

Sat. July 13
. . . during the day I worked on that long [27] . . . close to the scaffolding.

Tues. July 16, Thurs. July 18
On Tuesday the 16th I began this figure . . .[28] Thursday . . . I finished the figure.

Sat. July 20
Battista [Naldini] came for all the ground colors and brushes and oil.

Mon.–Tues. July 22–23
On Monday the 22nd . . . during the day I pricked the cartoon that Battista brought. Tuesday I did a piece of drapery.

Fri. July 26
[p. 6] . . . I did the head that looks over there, that is, the one on the sheet that I brought, which goes like this.[29]

Tues.–Sat. July 30–Aug. 3
Tuesday the 30th I began the figure. Wednesday [I did] up to the legs. On Thursday the first of August I did the leg . . . Friday I did the arm that it leans on [30] . . . Saturday [I did] the head of the figure below it that goes like this.[31]

[20] A line is drawn up to sketch D.

[21] Page 4, sketch A (fig. 379). This torso appears in cat. 374 and 375 for the *Deluge*.

[22] Page 4, sketch B (fig. 380). This torso may be connected with the torso directly to the right of the one to which sketch A refers in cat. 374 and 375 for the *Deluge*. Clapp related this sketch to cat. 339 for the Castello loggia.

[23] Page 4, sketch C (fig. 381).

[24] Page 4, sketch D (fig. 381). Cat. 381 for the *Deluge* or the *Resurrection of the Dead* is similar in pose to this figure.

[25] A word beginning "co" is incomplete at the edge of the page. Pontormo probably wrote "cornice" or "coro."

[26] Page 4, sketch E (fig. 381). This figure occurs in cat. A208 and A216, both copies after the *Resurrection of the Dead*. Clapp associated it with cat. 341 for the Castello loggia, an earlier version of the same motive.

[27] The word Pontormo wrote is "docc[i]one." Since this word means drainpipe, its meaning is not clear in this context. See note 55.

[28] Page 5, sketch A (fig. 382).

[29] Page 6, sketch A (fig. 383). This figure appears in copies after the *Resurrection of the Dead*, cat. A208 and A216.

[30] Page 6, sketch B (fig. 383). This sketch is for the left arm of the figure in sketch A on this page.

[31] Page 6, sketch C (fig. 383). In cat. A216 after the *Resurrection of the Dead* this figure appears below the figure drawn in sketches A and B on this page.

Wed.–Thurs. Aug. 7–8
Wednesday [I did] the head that the figure puts his hand on. Thursday I did the head with the laurel.

Tues.–Wed. Aug. 13–14, Fri.–Sat. Aug. 16–17
Tuesday . . . I began the head of the figure that goes like this.[32] Wednesday [I did] the arm . . . Friday [I did] the body. Saturday [I did] the thighs.

Mon.–Wed. Aug. 19–21
Monday, Tuesday I began the loins under the head.[33] Wednesday I finished it.

Mon.–Sat. Sept. 2–7
On Monday the 2nd, I began to work above a cornice.[34] Tuesday I did the head of this figure[35] . . . [p. 7] Wednesday [I did] as far as the hips . . . Thursday [I did] the thighs and the hips. Friday [I did] the arm. Saturday [I did] the head of the dead man that is beside it.

Mon.–Sat. Sept. 8–14, Mon. Sept. 16
Monday . . . I didn't work and until Saturday I stayed home to draw . . . Monday I drew.

Tues.–Thurs. Sept. 17–19
Tuesday I began the figure below the head.[36] Wednesday [I did] the body under the breasts. Thursday [I did] all of the leg.

[32] Page 6, sketch D (fig. 384).

[33] Page 6, sketch E (fig. 384). These two nudes are similar to several in cat. A216 after the *Resurrection of the Dead.* Clapp connected this sketch with cat. A159, a copy after a figure in the *Resurrection of the Dead* that also appears to the right in cat. A216.

[34] ". . . comincai a fare sopra una cornice . . ." Pontormo's reference to a cornice is not clear in the context, since the sketches on this page indicate that he was working on the *Resurrection of the Dead* on the right lower wall of the choir. The only cornice in the choir is part of the entablature that divides the upper and lower ranges of the choir. See note 40.

[35] Page 6, sketch F (fig. 384).

[36] Page 7, sketch A (fig. 385).

Mon.–Wed. Oct. 7–9, Sat. Oct. 12
Monday . . . I did the head that is below the figure sketched above. Tuesday I did the other hand that is beside it and Wednesday [I did] the rest.[37] Saturday I did the body again.

Mon.–Sat. Oct. 14–19
Monday [I did] the helmet. Tuesday [I did] the head like this.[38] Wednesday [I did] the bust . . . Thursday [I did] the arm . . . Friday [I did] the body. . . . Saturday [I did] the arm and his buttocks.

Mon.–Sat. Oct. 21–26
Monday, Tuesday, Wednesday, Thursday, Friday I worked under the above-mentioned figure[39] drawing as far as the large cornice.[40] Saturday I prepared the cartoon that goes beside it.

Sun.–Mon. Oct. 27–28
These two days I stayed at home to draw . . .

Sat. Nov. 9, Tues. Nov. 12
[p. 8] On the 9th I did the head below the figure that goes like this.[41] On the 12th I did the head again, which is something to remember.

Sat. Nov. 16
. . . the cartoon came and I brought the other one and put it in place to begin to work.

Tues. Nov. 19
. . . I worked on the two heads of the dead men that are below her buttocks.[42]

[37] Page 7, sketch B (fig. 386).

[38] Page 7, sketch C (fig. 386).

[39] Pontormo refers to p. 7, sketch C.

[40] ". . . insino al cornicione." Pontormo probably refers here to the cornice that divides the lower from the upper range of the choir.

[41] Page 8, sketch A (fig. 387). These two figures are similar to two nudes in the center of cat. A216 after the *Resurrection of the Dead.* Clapp connected this sketch with cat. A151, a copy after the Castello loggia frescoes.

[42] Page 8, sketch B (fig. 387). A figure like this one appears in cat. A238, and in cat. A216

Wed. Nov. 27
. . . I began under the figures that are like this.[43]

1556

Thurs. Feb. 6
[p. 10] On the 6th I began to work.

Sat. Feb. 8
. . . in the evening I finished the figure that is drawn [above].[44]

Thurs. Feb. 20
[p. 11] . . . I did the torso of the figure that goes like this.[45]

Thurs.–Sat. Feb. 27–29
On Thursday the 20th [sic] I did the head that screams . . . and up to the 29th I finished everything below that head as far as the ground.[46]

Tues.–Wed. March 3–4, Fri.–Sat. March 6–7, Mon. March 9, Wed.–Sat. March 11–14
On the 3rd of March I did the head of the figure drawn here.[47] On the 4th of March I did a bit of torso as far as the breasts . . . On the 6th I did all of the torso. On the 7th I finished the legs . . . Monday the 9th I did a head under them . . . Wednesday [I did] a head under them. Thursday I took out the tacks that were nailed up there. Friday [I did] a head under them . . . Saturday I did the plastering by myself for a head.[48]

Wed. March 18
. . . I did the plastering of stone under the windows.[49]

Thurs.–Sat. March 26–28, Mon. March 30, Wed. April 1, Fri. April 3, Thurs. April 9
[p. 12] On the 26th I began the arm of the child who is below him.[50] Friday . . . I did the torso from the arm down. Saturday I did a thigh . . . Monday I did the head of the child[51] . . . Wednesday I did the other thigh with all the leg and the foot . . . Friday . . . I did the child's torso.[52] . . . Thursday I did the legs . . .

Fri.–Sat. April 10–11
Friday [I did] a blue background[53] . . . Saturday I did the stone near the figure who is to go there below the windows opposite the Old Sacristy.[54]

Mon.–Sat. April 13–18, Mon. April 20
Monday I worked on these . . . [?] under the windows.[55] . . . Tuesday, Wednesday the scaffolding was put up in order to work. [p. 13] Thursday . . . I began the figure below the head that goes like this.[56] Friday [I did] the torso. Saturday

---

after the *Resurrection of the Dead*. Clapp connected it with cat. A88.

[43] Page 8, sketch C (fig. 387).

[44] Page 10, sketch A (fig. 388).

[45] Page 11, sketch A (fig 389).

[46] Page 11, sketch B (fig. 389).

[47] Page 11, sketch C (fig. 389).

[48] Pontormo refers to heads in sketch C.

[49] "Intonico di macigno." The windows are those in the upper range of the choir above where Pontormo was working. Pontormo also mentions these windows in his entries of April 11 and 13 of the same year, making it clear that he was working on the right side of the choir. See notes 54–55.

[50] Page 12, sketch A (fig. 390).

[51] A line is drawn to sketch A.

[52] A line is drawn to sketch A.

[53] Pontormo also mentions the blue background of his frescoes in connection with the *Ascension of Souls*. See note 11.

[54] Since the Old Sacristy of San Lorenzo is to the left of the choir, the windows opposite it would be those in the upper part of the right wall of the choir, above the *Resurrection of the Dead*.

[55] The windows are those of the right wall of the upper range of the choir above where Pontormo was working, but it is not clear what the "docioni" were (see note 27).

[56] Page 13, sketches A and B (fig. 393). A line is drawn to sketch A, while sketch B is the nude on which Pontormo was working. Clapp connected these and other sketches on p. 13 with cat. 377, which he considered to be for the *Deluge* but which is more likely to have been a study for the *Resurrection of the Dead*.

the 18th of April [I did] the legs . . . Monday [I worked] under them as far as the top of the choir stalls.

Mon.–Sat. May 4–9
Monday I began the figure that goes like this.[57] Tuesday I did the head. Wednesday [I did] the torso . . . Thursday [I did] the legs. Friday and Saturday [I worked] under them.

Tues.–Wed. May 12–13, Fri.–Sat. May 15–16
Tuesday I began the arm of the figure that goes like this[58] . . . Wednesday [I did] the other arm and the leg . . . Friday and Saturday I finished the figure.

Thurs.–Sat. May 28–30
Thursday the 28th I began the figure under the head that goes like this[59] and Friday I finished it. Saturday I did the book.

Mon. June 1
. . . I did the little negro.

Tues. June 9, Fri.–Sat. June 12–13
On the 9th I began the figure that goes like this[60] . . . Friday, Saturday I did the little bit of the arm and finished it so that all the figures of one episode are finished.

Fri.–Sat. June 19–20
[p. 14] Friday the 19th I began the figure that goes like this.[61] Saturday I did the arms.

Thurs.–Sat. June 25–27
Thursday I did those two heads that are drawn above[62] . . . Friday all those holes in the first episode above the choir stalls were plastered.[63] Saturday I did the two arms.

Mon.–Tues. June 29–30
Monday I did the undergrounding.[64] Tuesday [I did] the other undergrounding.

Sat. July 4
. . . I drew.

Tues.–Thurs. July 14–16, Sat. July 18, Mon. July 20, Wed. July 22
Tuesday the 14th I began the torso of this large figure. Wednesday [I did] this little bit of the arm.[65] Thursday two holes were plastered up. Saturday [I did] the back that is here under him . . . [p. 15] Monday the 20th I did the bit of arm and a piece of the leg that goes with the back mentioned above . . . Wednesday the 22nd I did the head and a little part of the shoulder . . .

Thurs.–Sat. July 23–25, Mon. July 27, Wed. July 29
Thursday I worked in the corner of the finished episode above the choir stalls. Friday I did the leg of the large full length figure . . . Saturday the 25th I did the large thigh . . . Monday . . . I did the torso that is below [the thigh]. Wednesday I did the shin that goes with the large thigh.

Wed. July 29–Wed. Aug. 26, Thurs. Aug. 27

[57] Page 13, sketch C (fig. 393). A similar nude appears in the lower center of cat. A216 after the *Resurrection of the Dead.*

[58] Page 13, sketch D (fig. 393). There is a nude similar to this one in cat. A216 after the *Resurrection of the Dead* to the right of the nude related to sketch C.

[59] Page 13, sketch E (fig. 393). As Pontormo notes, the nude holds a book.

[60] Page 13, sketch F (fig. 393). This sketch is similar in motive to p. 8, sketch B (see note 42) and both were probably drawn in connection with the *Resurrection of the Dead.*

[61] Page 14, sketch A (fig. 391). This sketch is very similar to p. 1, sketch A. Clapp associated it with cat. A171, a copy after San Lorenzo.

[62] Pontormo refers to sketch A.

[63] Pontormo refers back to the part of the fresco of the *Resurrection of the Dead* that he had completed on June 13th.

[64] "Terretta," the chiaroscuro underpainting of the fresco.

[65] Page 14, sketch B (fig. 392). Clapp connected this sketch with cat. A114, a copy after a San Lorenzo drawing.

Concerning the work from the day mentioned above, that is, the 29th of July until the 26th of August, I have done the figure . . . [?] [66] with the little bit of background and I ordered the St. Lawrence [67] . . . On the 27th I brought the cartoon of St. Lawrence and pricked it in order to work on it.

[66] The text continues "non[?] vestita di testa", a phrase whose meaning is unclear in this context.

[67] The *Martyrdom of St. Lawrence*, the only fresco that Pontormo mentions by name in the diary, occupied him from July 29 until October 6, 1556, after which Pontormo no longer recorded his work in the San Lorenzo choir.

Sat. Sept.12, Mon. Sept. 14, Wed. Sept. 16, Fri.–Sat. Sept. 18–19, Wed. Sept. 23, Mon.–Tues. Oct. 5–6

[p. 16] Saturday I did the head of the putto who holds the crown . . . Monday [I did] the crown. Wednesday . . . I did the arm . . . Friday I did the torso . . . Saturday [I did] the legs . . . Wednesday I began the putto with the chalice . . . Monday I did the head of the putto with the hair . . . Tuesday . . . I did the torso of the putto who holds the chalice.

LIST OF ATTRIBUTED DRAWINGS

Catalogue entries A1-A378

LIST OF ATTRIBUTED DRAWINGS

A1. Amsterdam, Rijksmuseum 59:02: Portrait study of Alessandro de' Medici. 238 x 190, red chalk; inscribed in a sixteenth-century (?) hand: *Lo Ill*^{mo} *et Ecc.*^{mo} *Sig.*^{n} *Duca Alex.*^{o} *Medici di mano di Jac.*^{o} *da Puntormo.* Collection: Hone, stamp recto (L. 2793); Rogers, stamp recto (L. 624); A. G. B. Russell, stamp recto (L. 2770a), sold Sotheby, June 9, 1955 (as Bronzino).

Bibliography: *MM* 1939, 134, fig. 55; *Drawings and Watercolors of Five Centuries*, Slatkin Galleries, New York, 1959; Berenson 1961, no. 2256I, fig. 969.

According to the inscription, this drawing is a Pontormo study of Alessandro de' Medici. Although it is related in style to Pontormo's portrait drawings of the mid-thirties (cf. cat. 324), the handling of the red chalk is timid and the articulation of the figure incoherent. It is probably a contemporary copy after a Pontormo drawing for the Philadelphia *Alessandro de' Medici* of 1534–1535. The drawing certainly represents Alessandro, the costume is close to that in Pontormo's portrait, and he is shown drawing on a tablet as he is in the painting. Vasari says (V/M, VI, 278) that Pontormo made a preparatory study for the picture, a *quadretto* that was in the *guardaroba* of Duke Cosimo. This drawing, similar to the painting in all elements except the pose, might easily reflect Pontormo's preparatory study. On the mat of this drawing is pasted a line engraving signed by an English nineteenth-century engraver, F. C. Lewis, and inscribed "Jac pixit." This engraving is identical in all details to the drawing, but the form of the inscription would normally imply that it was after a painting. It is therefore possible that Pontormo's *quadretto*, the probable source of both this drawing and the engraving, survived into the nineteenth century.

A2. Berlin-Dahlem, Kupferstichkabinett 401: Seated nude boy holding drapery. 233 x 160, red and black chalk. Collection: Pacetti, stamp recto (L. 2057).

This unpublished drawing is attributed to Pontormo by the museum. However, it is Cecco Bravo's study for the youth with drapery to the right of his fresco in the Sala delle Porcellane, Palazzo Pitti.

A3. ——— 465 *recto*: Nude study. (*Verso*: Study for Poggio a Caiano, cat. 159.) 405 x 215, pen and bistre.

Bibliography: Goldschmidt 1915, 84–85, fig. 32; Voss 1920, 178, fig. 55; Berenson 1938, no. 1954A.

First published and dated 1520 by Goldschmidt, this Michelangelesque pen study was also accepted as Pontormo's by Voss and Berenson. Although it is the reverse of an authentic study, it is difficult to accept this ill-proportioned figure and crudely hatched technique as Pontormo's. In Pontormo's few pen studies pen was used for accents (cf. cat. 40), or to define the structure of a figure under a wash (cf. cat. 131), but never as an instrument for modelling form. Like similar pen studies wrongly given to Pontormo (cf. cat. A35, A42, A46, A48, A131), this drawing is probably by Naldini.

A4. ——— 4626 *verso*: Seated nude. (*Recto*: Nude study, cat. 171.) 402 x 265, black chalk.

Bibliography: Berenson 1938, no. 1754A.

The recto of this sheet is a Pontormo study of ca. 1520 that has been gone over by a later artist, who apparently added this figure on the verso. Berenson is probably correct in attributing this brittle and structureless imitation of Pontormo's drawing style of the Poggio a Caiano period to Naldini.

A5. ——— 5153: Nude and head studies. 410 x 283, red and black chalk; inscribed: *Tiziano*. Collection: Beckerath.

Bibliography: Clapp 1914, 79; Berenson 1938, no. 1754D; *Wiesbaden Exhib.* 1946, 24.

Clapp thought this drawing and cat. A6 were modern forgeries, but Berenson gave them rightly to Naldini, noting the similarity in the head and that of a woman in the foreground of Naldini's *Presentation in the Temple* of 1572–1573 (S. M. Novella). The nude may be a study for the figure to the left of the priest in the painting of the same subject in S. Pier Maggiore. The angular, scrubby contours and unfinished hands and feet of this nude are characteristic of Naldini's draughtsmanship (cf. Uffizi 17808F for the identical style).

A6. ——— 5716: Nude studies. 417 x 287, red chalk with touches of black; inscribed: *Tiziano*. Collection: Beckerath.

Bibliography: Clapp 1914, 80; Berenson 1938, no. 1754E.

See cat. A5. These may be Naldini's studies for the standing and seated figures to the left of the S. Pier Maggiore *Presentation*. Cf. Uffizi 7518F.

A7. ——— 7715 *recto*: Copy after Pontormo's Certosa *Resurrection*. (*Verso*: Architectural motive.) 214 x 195, pen and bistre. Collection: Pacetti, stamp recto (L. 2057).

Bibliography: Goldschmidt 1915, 88–89, fig. 35; Voss 1920, 168; Friedlaender 1925, 66, fig. 7.

Goldschmidt published this drawing as Pontormo's study for the fresco, but it was recognized as a Boscoli copy by Voss and Friedlaender and is now given to Boscoli in the museum. Boscoli has made the proportions of the composition slightly higher and narrower than those of the fresco, but otherwise this is a faithful copy. For other copies after the same fresco cf. cat. A252 and A326.

A8. Berlin, ex-Beckerath Collection (present location unknown): Nude study. 365 x 235, red and black chalk.

Bibliography: Berenson 1903, no. 1954; Clapp 1914, 79; Berenson 1938, no. 1954.

This drawing has never been reproduced and was no longer in the Beckerath collection when Berenson included it in his second edition.

A9. Besançon, Musée D.1511: Draped man seen to the waist. 195 x 145, red chalk. Collection: Gasc, stamp recto (L. 1131); C. Gasc, stamp recto (L. 542).

Bibliography: Berenson 1938, no. 1954C (as no. 1411); Smyth 1949, 190, fig. 6; Cox 1956, 17; *MP* 1956 (Berti), 34; Emiliani 1960, pl. 5.

Berenson identified this drawing as a Pontormo study for one of the S. Felicita tondi and Smyth associated it with the *St. Mark*, which he attributed to Bronzino. Since the *St. Mark* is one of the tondi that is securely attributable to Bronzino, it would follow that a study for it that is identical except for a slight shift in the angle of the figure might also be by Bronzino. There is a considerable difference in style between this drawing and an analogous Pontormo study for one of the Patriarchs (cat. 264), a drawing that is at once more expressive and more exaggerated. The facial expressions are similar, but this face is an artificial mask, frozen into place. Pontormo's luminous surfaces are deadened and the line is less vibrant in a way that is quite typical of Bronzino in the late twenties (cf. cat. A66 and A75).

A10. Bremen, Kunsthalle 1475: Full-length portrait study of a man. Chalk; inscribed: *A B il suo ritratto . . . di mano proprio . . . Baccio Bandinelli.*

Bibliography: Berenson 1938, no. 2370A.

This drawing was given by Berenson to school of Pontormo. It has no connection with Pontormo's style and is much closer to Bandinelli, as the inscription suggests. Cf. Uffizi 538F *verso* and 6933F, school of Bandinelli drawings that are probably by the same hand as this study, and Windsor, cat. 72, fig. 23, which is not by the same hand but is similar in type and pose.

A11. Brunswick (Maine), Bowdoin College, Walker Art Museum 204: Draped figure of a woman. 285 x 133, red chalk.

Bibliography: F. J. Mather, "Drawings by Old Masters at Bowdoin College," *Art in America* 1 (1913), 246–247, fig. 13; *Bowdoin Museum of Fine Arts, Walker Art Building: Descriptive Catalogue* 1930, 63.

This late sixteenth-century drawing is given to Andrea del Sarto by the museum and to Pontormo by Mather. However, it has no connection with the drawings of either artist.

A12. Cambridge (Eng.), Fitzwilliam Museum: Reclining nude. 215 x 330, red chalk. Collection: Clough.

Bibliography: Berenson 1938, no. 1754F.

This study is attributed to Pontormo by the museum but given to Naldini by Berenson. This drawing has no connection with the style of Pontormo, and although certainly late sixteenth-century Florentine, it is equally unrelated to Naldini.

A13. Cambridge (Mass.), Fogg Art Museum 1932. 143 *recto*: Seated draped figure holding a scroll. (*Verso*: Head and arm.) 286 x 206, red chalk; verso black chalk with pen and bistre. Collection: Loeser, given to the museum in 1932.

Bibliography: Berenson 1938, no. 1754G; Mongan and Sachs 1940, I, 77–78.

This drawing was formerly attributed to Pontormo, but Berenson and Mongan and Sachs now give it rightly to Naldini. The sibyl on the recto recalls Pontormo's *St. Cecilia* drawing of ca. 1519 (cat. 93), while the head on the verso is derivative from his drawings of the Certosa period, such as cat. 236.

A14. ——— 1932.212 *recto*: Kneeling draped youth. (*Verso*: Various studies.) 405 x 230, black chalk; verso in pen and bistre; W: Shield with a unicorn head (cf. B. 1884 and Mongan and Sachs W. 9). Collection: Loeser, given to the museum in 1932.

Bibliography: Mongan and Sachs 1940, I, 84.

This drawing was given by Mongan and Sachs to the school of Pontormo, but it is surely by Jacopo da Empoli. Cf. Uffizi 1823S, 3462F, 3463F, and 9335F. The watermark on this sheet is the same as that on cat. A71, also attributed here to Empoli.

A15. Chantilly, Musée Condé 103: Portrait study of a seated girl. 195 x 160, red chalk; inscribed: *André del Sarte.*

Bibliography: G. Morelli, "Handzeichnungen italienischer Meister . . ." *Kunstchronik* 4 (1892/93), 488; Berenson 1903, no. 1956; Clapp 1914, 80–81; O. Giglioli, "Note su Franciabigio e Jacopo del Conte," *Riv. d'A.* 18 (1936), 191–194, fig. 1; Berenson 1938, no. 1956.

This portrait drawing has been attributed to Puligo by Morelli, Franciabigio by Giglioli, Andrea del Sarto by the museum, and Pontormo by Clapp and Berenson. Clapp dated it 1518–1521, Berenson 1525-1530. There are certainly no parallels in style between this drawing and Pontormo's portrait studies (cf. cat. 85, 223, 288, 335, etc.), nor does it seem to date as early as Clapp and Berenson have placed it. While the draughtsmanship is influenced by Andrea del Sarto and the soft roundness of the forms recalls Puligo (cf. the *Woman with Spindles*, Uffizi), the portrait seems closer in style to those of Bronzino around 1540 (cf. *Lucrezia Panciatichi* or the *Girl with a Missal* in the Uffizi). However, the draughtsmanship is unconnected with Bronzino and the drawing must have been done by a follower of Andrea del Sarto.

A16. Chatsworth, Duke of Devonshire Collection. Portrait study of a seated man. 260 x 180, black chalk squared. Collection: Flinck, inscribed recto (L. 959), sold 1756; Duke of Devonshire, stamp recto (L. 718).

Bibliography: S. Strong, *Reproductions of Drawings by Old Masters in the Collection of the Duke of Devonshire at Chatsworth* (London, 1902), 7, pl. 16; Berenson 1903, no. 1957; Clapp 1914, 81; A. G. B. Russell, "Collection of the Duke of Devonshire," *VS*, ser. II (1925), VI, no. 9, pl. 9; Popham 1931, no. 234, fig. 198; Berenson 1938, 318, no. 1957, fig. 984; Becherucci 1944, 44; J. Gere, "Some Drawings at the Chatsworth Exhibition," *Burl.* 91 (1949), 169–170, fig. 29; Smyth 1949, 195; Smyth 1955, 60–61; Emiliani 1960, pl. 18.

Clapp accepted this portrait drawing as a Pontormo of the same type as cat. 331 and dated it 1534. Berenson also gave it to Pontormo but thought that Bronzino used it for his *Youth with the Lute* (Uffizi). Russell, Popham, Becherucci, Gere, and Smyth attributed the drawing rightly to Bronzino himself, associating it with the Uffizi portrait. However, Smyth thought the drawing might have been done as early as 1530 and used only later for the portrait. This portrait study, which appears to be strongly influenced by Pontormo's self-portrait drawing (cat. 331), is surely a study for the Uffizi painting, and both probably date ca. 1534.

A17. ——— Nude study. 275 x 192, red chalk. Collection: Flinck.

Bibliography: Clapp 1914, 81–82.

Morelli attributed this drawing and cat. A18 and A19 to Pontormo, but Clapp has rightly rejected them.

A18. ——— Head of a woman. 322 x 270, black chalk on green paper.

Bibliography: Clapp 1914, 82.

See cat. A17.

A19. ——— Seated draped figure of a woman. 262 x 198, pen and bistre wash.

Bibliography: Clapp 1914, 82.

See cat. A17.

A20. Dijon, Musée des Beaux-Arts 819: Head of a man and a hand. 195 x 115, red chalk. Collection: Reynolds, stamp recto (L. 2364); His de la Salle, stamp recto (L. 1333).

Bibliography: Berenson 1903, no. 1958; Clapp 1914, 82–83; Berenson 1938, no. 55H, fig. 858.

Berenson (1903) gave this drawing to Pontormo, but later identified it as Andrea del Sarto's study for the St. Zachary in the Scalzo *Visitation* of 1524. Clapp wrongly considered it a copy after the fresco, suggesting Lappoli or Naldini.

A21. Dresden, Kupferstichkabinett: *Holy Family with St. John the Baptist and St. Francis*. 350 x 220, red chalk on pink prepared paper.

Bibliography: Clapp 1914, 84.

Clapp rejected this drawing as Pontormo. In 1961 it was not possible to locate it in the Dresden Kupferstichkabinett.

A22. Edinburgh, National Gallery 2230: Two studies of a standing putto mounted together. 236 x 207, red chalk; inscribed: *Coreggio*. Collection: W. F. Watson, given to the museum in 1886.

Bibliography: *Catalogue of the National Gallery of Scotland* (Edinburgh, 1936), 347; Andrews 1958, 436–437, fig. 34; Berenson 1961, no. 1959B-1.

These putti, evidently inspired by those of the Sistine Ceiling, were attributed to Pontormo by Andrews, who connected them with a presumed trip to Rome about 1520. Berenson considered them to be perhaps for Poggio a Caiano. These putti have little in common with the putto studies for Poggio a Caiano (cat. 152–160) and are certainly drawings of the very late sixteenth century. Their soft chiaroscuro and pliant line is close to the graphic style of Lodovico Carracci, although the occurrence of similar figures in almost identical poses in Annibale's frescoes in the Palazzo Mangani, Bologna, suggest that they may be Annibale studies done under the influence of Lodovico. These two drawings, wrongly mounted so that the putti face one another, were designed as caryatid or console figures flanking a central pier. Cf. Lodovico's study for a monument (Louvre 7724), in which a similar pair of figures appear. Cf. also examples in Annibale's Farnese Ceiling.

A23. Florence, Biblioteca Marucelliana B.175: Nude studies of women. 125 x 165, red chalk.

Bibliography: P. Ferri, "I Disegni e le Stampe della R. Biblioteca Marucelliana di Firenze," *Boll. d'A.* 5 (1911), 293, fig. 4; Clapp 1914, 85–86; E. Tietze-Conrat, "Ein Plastisches Modell des Pontormo," *ZBK* 63 (1929/30), 165–168, illustrated; Schlegel 1961, 37n42.

This drawing was attributed to Pontormo by Ferri as for San Lorenzo, rejected by Clapp, and associated with Pontormo again by Tietze-Conrat. Tietze-Conrat connected the central figure of this drawing with a terracotta (Bloch Collection, Vienna), which she attributed to Pontormo, and with a bronze copy after it from the school of Giambologna (Pierpont Morgan Collection). The figure in the drawing is related in pose to these sculptures and may be based on them, but neither sculptures nor drawing is in any way connected with Pontormo. The drawing is very close in style to Jacopo da Empoli (cf. cat. A71 and A258) and may tentatively be attributed to him.

A24. Florence, Uffizi 122F: Head of a boy. 104 x 96, red chalk; laid down.

Bibliography: Berenson 1903, no. 1960; Clapp 1914, 86; Berenson 1938, no. 1960.

This drawing was accepted by Berenson but rejected rightly by Clapp as totally unrelated to Pontormo's drawings.

A25. ——— 272F: Study of a putto. 225 x 150, red chalk; inscribed in red chalk: *Andrea.*

Bibliography: Ferri 1890, 134; Jacobsen 1898, 277; Berenson 1903, no. 1961; F. Knapp, *Andrea del Sarto* (Leipzig, 1907), 133; *MPA* 1910, 9; Clapp 1914, 86–87; Berenson 1938, no. 1961; Marcucci 1955, 250, fig. 18.

This putto was given to Andrea del Sarto by Ferri, Jacobsen, and Knapp (as for the Dresden altar), to Pontormo by Berenson and Marcucci, and to an Andrea assistant of ca. 1515–1518 by Clapp. Although this study recalls both Andrea's and Pontormo's drawings of ca. 1513–1515 (cf. cat. 15), it is not by either artist. The extremely soft quality of the surface, the lack of an underlying structure to the forms, and the somewhat mechanical modelling suggest Puligo, who was Andrea's assistant at the time of the Dresden altar and in the years following.

A26. ——— 295F *recto*: Seated draped woman. (*Verso*: Nudes with putti and a decorative design.) 293 x 208, red chalk, verso pen and bistre with design in red chalk.

This unpublished sheet is ascribed to Pontormo in the museum, but the studies on the verso (for a *Massacre of the Innocents*?) are very close to Bandinelli (cf. Uffizi 546F, 1526E) and the sheet probably comes from his circle.

A27. ——— 301F *recto*: Study for a portrait bust. (*Verso*: Same.) 130 x 125, red chalk.

Bibliography: Berenson 1903, no. 68; *MPA* 1910, 10; F. Di Pietro, *I Disegni di Andrea del Sarto negli Uffizi* (Siena, 1911), 30, figs. 23–24; Clapp 1914, 87–88; Fraenckel 1935, 170–171; Berenson 1938, no. 110J.

This drawing was formerly attributed to Pontormo, but Berenson gave it rightly to Andrea del Sarto as a study for the *Portrait of a Sculptor* (National Gallery, London) of ca. 1517–1518, and it is now catalogued as Andrea by the museum.

A28. ——— 325F: *St. John the Baptist.* 406 x 170, black chalk; laid down.

Bibliography: Berenson 1903, 287, no. 76; Knapp 1907, 133; *MPA* 1910, 8; Di Pietro 1910, 102; Fraenckel 1935, 189; Berenson 1938, no. 117A, fig. 876; Marcucci 1955, 250–252, fig. 17; J. Shearman, "A Lost Altar-piece by Andrea del Sarto 'The Madonna of S. Ambrogio,'" *Burl.* 103 (1961), 226, fig. 46.

This study was ascribed to the early Andrea del Sarto by Berenson, who considered it as a possible study for Andrea's lost altar of 1511–1513 for S. M. delle Neve. Di Pietro also gave it to Andrea, but Fraenckel ascribed it to an assistant. The connection with the lost Andrea altar has recently been reaffirmed by Shearman on the basis of Empoli's copy of the picture, in which a figure similar to this one appears. Shearman dated the altar and this drawing 1514–1515. Only Marcucci has given this drawing to Pontormo, connecting it with cat. 15 of ca. 1515 and cat. A25, which we have ascribed to Puligo. This drawing certainly derives more closely from the style of Andrea than from that of Pontormo and it is undoubtedly related to the saint in the S. Ambrogio altar. However, the top-heavy proportions of the figure, the exaggerated curving of the arms and legs, and the somewhat mechanical modelling suggest that it may not be by Andrea but by his assistant Puligo. There is another version of this drawing (black chalk, 420 x 160) in Christ Church Library, Oxford, where it is listed as Tuscan school.

A29. ——— 414E: Portrait study of a woman. 390 x 266, red chalk; laid down.

Bibliography: Ferri 1881, 25; Berenson 1903, no. 1964, pl. 173; *MPA* 1910, 23; Clapp 1914, 89; Clapp 1916, 86; Berenson 1938, 312, no. 1964, fig. 978; Toesca 1943, 23, fig. 37.

This portrait drawing has been ascribed to numerous hands, including Leonardo, Franciabigio, and Sodoma. Berenson, Clapp, and Toesca gave it to Pontormo, Clapp dating it 1530 and Berenson not before 1525. The impersonality and distance of the Mannerist portrait of toward 1530 is not evident in this drawing, which is more closely linked in style with the late Quattrocento, in particular with the tradition of Leonardo. The museum now gives it to Bacchiacca, an attribution that is more tenable than that to Pontormo, but not entirely satisfactory.

A31. ——— 415 orn.: Tondo with putti and Medici arms. 199 x 202, black chalk, the left side redrawn in ink; on two sheets and laid down.

Bibliography: Ferri 1890, 120.

This drawing has no connection in style with Pontormo's study for Medici arms (cf. cat. 313) and, in any case, cannot date before 1569 because the arms are those of Cosimo I, Grand Duke of Tuscany.

A31. ——— 417 orn.: Arms of Pope Leo X with two figures. 186 x 218, pen and bistre; sheet cut to an oval and laid down.

Bibliography: Ferri 1890, 120; Berenson 1903, no. 1965, pl. 169; *MPA* 1910, 26; Clapp 1911, 4–5; Clapp 1914, 89–90; Clapp 1916, 11; Berenson 1938, no. 2248A; Berenson 1961, no. 2248A–2.

Berenson associated this drawing with the visit of Leo X to Florence in 1515, while Clapp thought it might be connected with the lost arms of Leo X that Vasari says (V/M, VI, 250) Pontormo painted in 1513. This drawing was certainly done in connection with the festivities of ca. 1513–1515 for the Medici Pope, but it has no relation in style with Pontormo's early drawings.

A32. ——— 418 orn.: Medici arms with allegorical figures of Faith and Strength (?). 159 x 186, pen and bistre on brownish paper; cut to an oval and laid down.

Bibliography: Ferri 1890, 120; Berenson 1903, no. 1966; *MPA* 1910, 26; Clapp 1911, 4; Clapp 1914, 90; Clapp 1916, 11; Berenson 1938, no. 2248B.

Gamba (*MPA*) connected this drawing and cat. A31 with Pontormo's decorations for the Cappella del Papa in 1515. However, as Clapp has pointed out, these are not the arms of Leo X because the papal keys are not included. Clapp identified the figures as St. John the Baptist and another saint and dated the drawing 1512–1514. Berenson called the figure to the left St. Philip. Since these half-draped figures are women and carry a large cross and a column, it is possible that they were intended to symbolize Faith and Strength. In any case, this pen drawing is unrelated to Pontormo's style and is probably by the same unidentified hand as cat. A31.

A33. ——— 442F: Nude studied three times. 416 x 269, red chalk; W: Eagle in a circle with a crown (B. 207).

Bibliography: Ferri 1890, 116; Berenson 1903, no. 1969; *MPA* 1910, 30; Clapp 1914, 92–93; Goldschmidt 1915, 85; Clapp 1916, 23, fig. 44; Berenson 1938, no. 1969.

Berenson dated this drawing early, Clapp placed it 1516–1520, and Goldschmidt associated it with cat. A3, which he dated 1520. While it has been uncontested as an original, this drawing appears to be a good copy, probably by Naldini, after Pontormo's study (cat. 25) of ca. 1517 for *Joseph* (III). The line lacks the sharpness and sureness of Pontormo's drawings of this period (cf. the right leg of the figure to the left), while the modelling is unusually even and without Pontormo's wide range of chiaroscuro. This study would even seem to betray knowledge of Pontormo's later drawings, in which he employed a similar soft, granular kind of modelling. It might also be remarked that the watermark on this sheet is not noted by Briquet as appearing before 1573.

A34. ——— 444F *recto*: Venus and putti. (*Verso*: Arm.) 101 x 141, black chalk.

Bibliography: Berenson 1903, no. 2005; Clapp 1911, 14; Clapp 1914, 94; Clapp 1916, 63; Berenson 1938, no. 1970A.

Clapp and Berenson both accepted this

study and its variant cat. A36, Clapp dating both 1534–1535 as variants of the Michelangelo-Pontormo *Venus and Cupid* of 1533–1534. The motive is not very close and the pictorial pen and bistre technique certainly places these studies in the last quarter of the century.

A35. ——— 445F: Flying putto. 157 x 63, pen and bistre; sheet cut close to the figure; W: Fruit (B. 7388).

Bibliography: Berenson 1903, no. 1971; Clapp 1914, 94; Berenson 1938, no. 1971.

This study is for the angel to the right of God the Father in cat. A45, here attributed to Naldini.

A36. ——— 446F: *Venus and Cupid*. 97 x 142, pen and bistre wash over black chalk; laid down.

Bibliography: Berenson 1903, no. 1972; Clapp 1911, 14; Clapp 1914, 94–95; Clapp 1916, 63; Berenson 1938, no. 1972.

See cat. A34.

A37. ——— 450F *recto*: Standing youth holding a staff. (*Verso*: Nude study for the same.) 345 x 158, black chalk; W: Hammer and anvil (cf. B. 5963).

Bibliography: Ferri 1890, 116; Berenson 1903, no. 2007; *MPA* 1910, 34; Clapp 1914, 97; Giglioli 1926, 784; Berenson 1938, no. 1974A; L. Marcucci, "Appunti per Mirabello Cavalori disegnatore," *Riv. d'A.* 28 (1953), 94, figs. 17–18.

Clapp, who knew only the recto, doubted the authenticity of this sheet, considering it perhaps by the same hand as cat. 15. Giglioli published the verso as a study for the *Halberdier*. The extremely Pontormesque verso may be derived from a Pontormo drawing such as cat. 253 of ca. 1525, but the recto is an elaboration of the motive in a graphic manner that leaves no doubt as to its late sixteenth-century origins. Marcucci has convincingly attributed the sheet to Cavalori and it is now listed as Cavalori in the museum.

A38. ——— 453F *recto*: Heads of children. (*Verso*: Head of a child and hands.) 190 x 258, red and black chalk; inscribed: *del Pontormo*.

Bibliography: Clapp 1914, 98.

This drawing was correctly rejected by Clapp as unrelated to Pontormo's style.

A39. ——— 456F: *Death of St. Peter Martyr*. 313 x 400, yellow wash and white gouache over black chalk; inscribed: *Jacopo da Pontormo*.

Bibliography: Ferri 1890, 116; Clapp 1914, 101.

This compositional study, which must be a fragment of a larger drawing, was rejected by Clapp and dated after 1575. It has no connection with Pontormo and is now listed by the museum as anonymous late sixteenth-century Florentine.

A40. ——— 457F: *Pietà*. 370 x 489, red chalk.

Bibliography: Clapp 1914, 101; A. Forlani, *Mostra di Disegni di Andrea Boscoli*, Gabinetto Disegni e Stampe degli Uffizi, Florence, 1959, no. 13, fig. 4.

This drawing was formerly attributed to Pontormo, but was given by Clapp, the museum, and Forlani to Boscoli. Forlani considered it probably for a *Resurrection of Lazarus* rather than a *Pietà*.

A41. ——— 458F *verso*: Study of a bird. (*Recto*: Study for Careggi, cat. 319.) 173 x 255, bistre wash over black chalk.

This study on the verso of a Pontormo drawing has not been noted in the literature because the drawing was formerly laid down. It has no counterpart in Pontormo's drawings and may have been done by one of the assistants who did the decorative work of the Careggi loggia. Smyth (verbally) thought it might be by Bronzino.

A42. ——— 459F *recto*: *St. John the Baptist in the Wilderness.* (*Verso*: Study for a Virgin at the foot of the Cross.) 324 x 222, pen and bistre; W: Crown with a star (B. 4835); inscribed: *dal Ponto.*

Bibliography: Ferri 1890, 116; Berenson 1903, no. 1978; *MPA* 1910, 37; Gamba 1912, no. 14, pl. 14 (recto); Clapp 1914, 102–103; Berenson 1938, no. 1978.

Gamba and Clapp accepted this drawing as Pontormo, dating it respectively 1520–1530 and 1524. Clapp connected the verso with the Madonna of Pontormo's Boldrone tabernacle of ca. 1529, while Berenson considered it to be close to Fra Bartolommeo. This drawing is similar in style to cat. A48 and A131 and all three pen studies are attributable to Naldini.

A43. ——— 460F: Copy after Pontormo's compositional drawing for the Louvre *Madonna and Saints.* 245 x 184, pen and bistre wash over black chalk, squared; inscribed verso in a late sixteenth-century (?) hand: *Jacopo da pontormo.*

Bibliography: V/M, 1878/85, VI, 273n2; Ferri 1890, 116; Berenson 1903, no. 1979, pl. 171; Clapp 1911, 16; Clapp 1914, 103–104; Clapp 1916, 52, fig. 105; Berenson 1938, 314, no. 1979, fig. 962; Toesca 1943, 17, fig. 33; *MF* 1952, 64; Berenson 1954, pl. 49; *MP* 1956 (Marcucci), 95.

This drawing has been considered as Pontormo's study for the Louvre altarpiece by all except Marcucci, who has also concluded that it is a copy. The difference in a few details from the painting — the tondo with the procession of the *Signoria* is absent, as are St. Peter's keys and the halos on all the figures, while St. Sebastian does not have an arrow in his neck but holds the martyr's palm — together with the existence of another copy in which these same differences occur (cat. A167) suggest that this drawing is a copy after a lost preparatory study by Pontormo for the Louvre altarpiece. The hand of the copyist is not precisely identifiable, but the drawing belongs to a group of late sixteenth-century Florentine copies in pen and bistre after Pontormo, some of which are close to Boscoli (cf. cat. A7, A167, A199, A265, A326, A336).

A44. ——— 462F: Group of sprawling nudes. 158 x 283, black chalk and bistre wash, squared.

Bibliography: Ferri 1890, 117; Jacobsen 1898, 280; Berenson 1903, no. 1981; Clapp 1914, 105–106; Berenson 1938, no. 1981; Tolnay 1950, 49; *Mostra del Demoniaco nell'Arte*, Florence, 1952, no. 69; Smyth 1955, pp. 56–57.

Jacobsen, Berenson, Clapp, and Tolnay considered this drawing to be a Pontormo study for the San Lorenzo *Resurrection of the Dead.* Clapp suggested that it might be one of Bronzino's studies for the completion of the fresco and compared it in style with Uffizi 570F, a Bronzino study for one of the *Story of Joseph* tapestries of the late forties. The drawing is certainly not Pontormo's, as is evident if it is compared with the authentic studies for the lower-range frescoes (cf. cat. 373–379), nor is the attribution to Bronzino entirely convincing. However, this study may come from Bronzino's circle and may even record a lost original study for the lower portion of the *Resurrection* fresco.

A45. ——— 464F: *Madonna and Child.* 430 x 318, red chalk.

Bibliography: Clapp 1914, 106–107; A. Forlani, *Mostra di Disegni di Andrea Boscoli*, Gabinetto Disegni e Stampe degli Uffizi, Florence, 1959, no. 12, fig. 1.

This drawing was formerly catalogued as Pontormo, but it was given rightly to Boscoli by Clapp, Forlani, and the museum.

A46. ——— 526E *recto*: *God the Father Commanding Noah to Build the Ark.* (*Verso*: Flying putto and architectural sketch.) 305 x 253, pen and bistre; verso in red chalk with the sketch in pen.

Bibliography: Ferri 1890, 115; Berenson 1903, no. 1984; Clapp 1914, 108; Berenson 1938, no. 1959C.

Formerly attributed to Raphael, this drawing was given to Pontormo by Ferri as a copy after the loggia composition. It was accepted as Pontormo by Berenson and Clapp, the latter dating it 1520–1540. The verso of this sheet is more Pontormesque than the recto, deriving from his red chalk manner of ca. 1520, but both drawings are certainly by Naldini. The tiny architectural sketch recalls the design of the end walls of the Poggio a Caiano *Salone*.

A47. ——— 625E *recto*: Studies of hands. (*Verso*: Head and hand studies.) 169 x 207, red chalk; pen study by a different hand on a sheet added at the top of the verso.

Bibliography: *MPA* 1910, 27; Clapp 1914, 108–109.

This sheet was rightly rejected by Clapp as unconnected with Pontormo. As is suggested by a former attribution to Andrea del Sarto it derives much more specifically from Sarto's red chalk manner than from Pontormo's. It is now classified rightly by the museum as Santi di Tito.

A48. ——— 671E *recto*: Studies of putti. (*Verso*: Same.) 398 x 278, pen and bistre.

Bibliography: Ferri 1881, 40; Ferri 1890, 115; Berenson 1903, no. 1986; *MPA* 1910, 34; Clapp 1914, 109–110; Berenson 1938, no. 1959E.

Berenson and Clapp dated this sheet ca. 1515, Berenson associating it with the Cappella del Papa decorations. Like cat. A42 and A131, this sheet is probably by Naldini. Cf. the putti in the foreground of the *Allegoria dei Sogni* of 1570–1572 (Palazzo Vecchio).

A49. ——— 1210E: Dead Christ. 154 x 224, red chalk; laid down.

Bibliography: Ferri 1881, 64; Berenson 1903, no. 2398; Clapp 1914, 112; Kusenberg 1931, 152; Berenson 1938, no. 2398; Barocchi 1950, 218.

This study carried a traditional attribution to Pontormo that was rightly rejected by Clapp. It has since been given to Rosso by Berenson, but not by Kusenberg, to Bacchiacca by Barocchi, and by the museum to Polidoro da Caravaggio.

A50. ——— 1485 orn.: Putto and a dolphin. 135 x 196, red chalk; laid down.

Bibliography: Berenson 1903, no. 1990; Clapp 1914, 112–113; Berenson 1938, no. 1990; Marcucci 1955, 250.

Clapp rightly rejected the attribution of this drawing to Pontormo, but Marcucci has reasserted the Pontormo attribution, associating it in style with cat. 15 and with cat. A25, which we have given to Puligo. This study after a sculpture is not connected with either artist and surely dates from the later sixteenth century.

A51. ——— 1564E *recto*: Designs for arabesques. (*Verso*: Drapery studies.) 282 x 195, red chalk; verso with black chalk; inscribed verso: [Fran^co] *Rosi 184*.

Bibliography: Ferri 1881, 79; Ferri 1890, 115; Berenson 1903, no. 1991; *MPA* 1910, 26; Clapp 1914, 113; Berenson 1938, no. 1991; Thiem 1961, 5–6, fig. 7.

These sketches were accepted by Berenson and Clapp, who dated them 1514–1518, and by Gamba (*MPA*), who connected them with Pontormo's work at S.M. Novella in 1515. These frothy inventions are certainly not from Pontormo's hand and are surely by an ornament specialist. The drawing has recently been attributed convincingly to Andrea di Cosimo Feltrini by C. and G. Thiem.

A52. ——— 6424F: Drapery study. 208 x 147, red chalk on pink prepared paper; W: Crown.

Bibliography: Berenson 1903, no. 121; F. Knapp, *Andrea del Sarto* (Leipzig, 1907), 134; Clapp 1914, 113; Berenson 1938, no. 121.

Formerly attributed to Pontormo, this drapery study was given to Andrea del Sarto by Berenson and Knapp, and is now attributed to Andrea by the museum. According to S. J. Freedberg (cited by Berenson 1961), it is a study for the apostle at the extreme right of Andrea's *Last Supper* at San Salvi.

A53. ——— 6436F: Nude study. 213 x 138, black chalk on pink prepared paper; W: Cornet (cf. B. 7697).

Bibliography: Clapp 1914, 113–114.

This study was rightly rejected from Pontormo's *oeuvre* by Clapp and is now given by the museum to Alessandro di Barbiere.

A54. ——— 6437F *recto*: Drapery study. (*Verso*: Fragment of drapery.) 265 x 246, red chalk; W: Acorn (B. 7435).

Bibliography: Clapp 1911, 8; Clapp 1914, 114; Clapp 1916, 31; Berenson 1938, no. 1991A.

Clapp and Berenson both considered these studies to be for the Pomona of the Poggio a Caiano lunette, Clapp comparing the study on the recto with cat. 144. Cat. 144 contains a sketch for a seated figure in a similar pose, but it is not a study for the Pomona, not is the resemblance between this drapery study and the motive of the Pomona more than a superficial one. The angular and nervous handling of the red chalk in this drawing is closely based on Pontormo's Poggio a Caiano draughtsmanship, but exhibits none of his spare economy of line or solid articulation of forms. The museum currently gives this sheet to Clemente Bandinelli, but it is difficult to substantiate this attribution.

A55. ——— 6438F: *Madonna and Child with St. John*. 180 x 146, red and black chalk squared on pink prepared paper.

Bibliography: Berenson 1903, no. 2010; Clapp 1914, 114–115; Berenson 1938, no. 1991B; Smyth 1955, 71–72.

Formerly attributed to Andrea del Sarto, this study was given to Pontormo by Berenson, who connected it with the Louvre altar and with the Pontormesque *Madonna and Child with St. John* in the Corsini Gallery (no. 141). The composition is not similar to that of the Corsini picture and resembles the Louvre altar only in the position of the Christ Child. Clapp, who retained the Pontormo attribution, was reminded of the composition of Bronzino's *Holy Family* in Vienna, while Smyth attributed the drawing to Bronzino, dating it in the midtwenties. The composition is certainly Bronzinesque, but the closest analogy is with his later works, notably the *Madonna with St. John and St. Elizabeth* (London, National Gallery) of the midforties. Although the attribution to Bronzino himself is not secure, this study could well come from his circle.

A56. ——— 6503F *verso*: Head of a laughing child. (*Recto*: Study for the *Portrait of Maria Salviati*, cat. 346.) 265 x 188, black chalk.

Bibliography: Clapp 1914, 115; Berenson 1938, no. 2011.

This head is on the verso of an authentic study but it is probably not by Pontormo. While Clapp also doubted the authenticity of this slight sketch, Berenson called it a copy by Pontormo after a Quattrocento head.

A57. ——— 6506F *verso*: Standing nude. (*Recto*: Study for the S. Michele altar, cat. 101.) 393 x 260, red chalk.

Bibliography: Berenson 1903, no. 2014; Clapp 1914, 118; Berenson 1938, no. 2014.

This academic study inspired by Michelangelo's *David* is on the reverse of an authentic drawing of ca. 1519, but it is not by Pontormo's hand. Berenson and Clapp accepted it, Clapp dating it not later than 1519.

A58. ——— 6507F *recto*: Two nudes. (*Verso*: Nude studies.) 407 x 260, black chalk; verso with pen; lower left corner replaced.

Bibliography: Berenson 1903, no. 2015; *MPA* 1910, 29; Clapp 1914, 118–119; Berenson 1938, no. 2015.

Berenson accepted this sheet as a Pontormo close to Andrea, while Clapp thought it might be by Naldini. This drawing has none of the characteristics of Naldini's style and is more likely by an artist close to Andrea and Pontormo toward 1520. Comparisions with Puligo, such as the group of figures standing to the left of the Borghese *Story of Joseph* of ca. 1520, suggest that this drawing may be from his hand. Cf. also drawings given here to Puligo (cat. A25 and A28).

A59. ——— 6509F: Study after a statue of Venus. 230 x 166, black chalk on pink prepared paper.

Bibliography: Berenson 1903, no. 2016A; Clapp 1914, 120; Berenson 1938, no. 2016A.

This weak Bartolommesque drawing has no connection with Pontormo's style, but it has been accepted by Berenson and Clapp, the latter dating it 1520–1535.

A60. ——— 6517F: Putto study. 343 x 243, black chalk with yellow wash on brown paper; pricked for transfer; cut irregularly and laid down.

Bibliography: Berenson 1903, no. 2022; Clapp 1914, 126–127; Berenson 1938, no. 2022.

This drawing was doubted by Clapp, but called an early Pontormo by Berenson. It is Beccafumi's cartoon for the putto in the center middle distance of the *Prophets of Baal*, Siena Cathedral *pavimento*.

A61. ——— 6521F *recto*: Skeleton studies. (*Verso*: Same.) 339 x 210, black chalk; inscribed verso: *di Jacopo*.

Bibliography: Berenson 1903, no. 2026; Clapp 1914, 129; Berenson 1938, no. 2026; *MP* 1956 (Marcucci), no. 136, fig. 165 (as no. 652).

Clapp compared this drawing with cat. 355 for San Lorenzo and Marcucci dated it ca. 1545. The delicate handling of black chalk in these anatomical sketches is suggestive of Pontormo's late drawing style, but there is nothing in this sheet that conclusively points to his hand.

A62. ——— 6522F: Anatomical studies. 290 x 201, red chalk; written in red chalk in the same hand: *schemezzo;* inscribed verso: *di Jacopo* and [Fran]co *Rosi 267*.

Bibliography: Berenson 1903, no. 2027; *MPA* 1910, 36; Clapp 1914, 129–130; Berenson 1938, no. 2027.

Clapp dated this study 1530–1540. Of the anatomical studies in the Uffizi attributed to Pontormo (cat. A61, A65, A132, and A139–141) this red chalk drawing is the closest in draughtsmanship to his authentic drawings, recalling his brilliant manipulation of red chalk in the early twenties. However, lacking further more definite connections with his drawings, this study must remain in the attributed category.

A63. ——— 6523F *recto*: Heavily draped man. (*Verso*: Draped arm.) 290 x 202, red chalk.

Bibliography: *MPA* 1910, 31; Clapp 1914, 130.

Clapp dated this sheet 1517–1520. However, it is a late sixteenth-century imitation of Pontormo's style of ca. 1525, recalling his studies for the monks in the *Supper at Emmaus* (cat. 215–216). This drawing is now attributed to Naldini by the museum, but it has little connection with his style. It is much closer to cat. A37, attributed to Cavalori, and may also be given to him.

A64. ——— 6524F *recto*: Nude boy walking. (*Verso*: Nude kneeling.) 403 x 247, red chalk.

Bibliography: Berenson 1903, II, 124; Clapp 1914, 130–131; Berenson 1938, II, 246.

Berenson and Clapp have rightly given this sheet to Naldini, as a copy after a lost Andrea del Sarto study for the servant to the right of the Scalzo *Dance of Salome*. Berenson noted an almost identical Naldini drawing, Uffizi 311F.

A65. ——— 6526F *recto*: Anatomical studies. (*Verso*: Same.) 227 x 181, red and black chalk; recto squared; W: letter R; inscribed verso: *Van* . . .

Bibliography: Berenson 1903, no. 2029; Clapp 1914, 132; Berenson 1938, no. 2029.

Clapp dated these skeleton studies 1525–1530 but they have little relation to Pontormo's style.

A66. ——— 6527F: Study of legs. 245 x 163, red chalk; inscribed verso: *Di Jacopo.*

Bibliography: Berenson 1903, no. 2030; Clapp 1914, 132; Berenson 1938, no. 2030; Smyth 1955, 54.

Both Clapp and Berenson accepted this drawing as Pontormo's study for the legs of Christ in the S. Felicita *Deposition.* However, as Smyth has seen, it is Bronzino's study for the S. Trinita *Pietà* of ca. 1528. As such it is a valuable term of comparison for Bronzino's drawing style of before 1530 while he was still with Pontormo.

A67. ——— 6532F: *Christ at the Column.* 229 x 141, black chalk; cut close to the figure.

Bibliography: Berenson 1903, no. 2035; Clapp 1914, 136; McComb 1928, 149; Berenson 1938, no. 2035.

Berenson accepted this drawing as a late Pontormo, but Clapp and McComb attributed it to Bronzino, dating it ca. 1549, and it is now listed by the museum as Bronzino. The condition of the drawing makes judgment as to its quality difficult, but an attribution to the circle of Bronzino is more convincing than that to Bronzino himself.

A68. ——— 6538F *recto*: Seated nude. (*Verso*: Nude and bone.) 284 x 193, red chalk.

Bibliography: Berenson 1903, no. 2041; Clapp 1914, 139; Berenson 1938, no. 2041.

Berenson dated this drawing late and Clapp dated it 1540–1545, although he gave another version of the recto (cat. A152) to Bronzino. This study belongs to the circle of Bronzino and is probably by the same follower as cat. A78, A89, A93, and A96.

A69. ——— 6540F *recto*: Half-length seated nude. (*Verso*: Lower part of a nude.) 267 x 179, black chalk on rough blue paper.

Bibliography: Berenson 1903, no. 2043; Clapp 1914, 140–141; Berenson 1938, 316, no. 2043.

Clapp dated this sheet 1520, while Berenson connected the recto with the Christ of the S. Felicita *Deposition*, the verso with the figure in the foreground of the same picture. The sheet is a characteristic black chalk study by Naldini. As suggested by Michael Rinehart (verbally), the recto is a study for the seated nude to the left in Naldini's *Allegoria dei Sogni* of 1570–1572 (Palazzo Vecchio).

A70. ——— 6544F: Reclining nude. 234 x 409, red chalk; W: Eagle with a crown (B. 95).

Bibliography: Berenson 1903, no. 2047; *MPA* 1910, 26; Clapp 1914, 144; Clapp 1916, 30, fig. 59; Berenson 1938, 302, 312, no. 2047, fig. 955.

This drawing and cat. A77, which is related in motive and by the same hand, were considered to be studies for the reclining woman on the far right of the Poggio a Caiano lunette by Berenson and Clapp. However, these academic nude studies are quite different in style from Pontormo's drawings for the women in the lunette (cf. cat. 144–149) and must date from the very end of the sixteenth century. The watermark on this sheet was not found by Briquet prior to 1565–1568.

A71. ——— 6546F: Bust of a woman. 233 x 177, red chalk; W: Shield with a unicorn head (B. 1884).

Bibliography: Berenson 1903, no. 2049; *MPA* 1910, 35; Clapp 1914, 145, pl. 5; Clapp 1916, 50; Tinti 1925, fig. 7; Berenson 1938, no. 2049; Becherucci 1943, 9, pl. 17; Becherucci 1944, 17; *MP* 1956 (1 ed., Marcucci), no. 108, fig. 117a; Berenson 1961, no. 2049, fig. 936; A Forlani, *Mostra di Disegni di Jacopo da Empoli*, Gabinetto Disegni e Stampe degli Uffizi, Florence, 1962, no. 61, fig. 32.

This study has been generally accepted as Pontormo, Clapp dating it 1530 as possibly for the Magdalen painted for Capponi, Marcucci and Becherucci placing it in the Certosa period, and Tinti connecting it with the San Lorenzo *Last Judgment*. However, while accepting this drawing without question as a Pontormo, Clapp compared it with a *Magdalen* by Lorenzo Lippi (cat. A165), Marcucci mentioned a *Magdalen* by Jacopo da Empoli (Uffizi 9278F), and Berenson thought the figure was "worthy of the seicento." While this drawing shows a strong awareness of Pontormo's style of about 1525, it is certainly from the late sixteenth century and has been convincingly attributed to Jacopo da Empoli by the museum and by Forlani. The watermark on this sheet was not found by Briquet before 1576.

A72. ——— 6547F: Head of a woman. 88 x 70, black chalk; cut close around the head.

Bibliography: Berenson 1903, no. 2050; Clapp 1911, 9; Clapp 1914, 146; Clapp 1916, 32, fig. 64; Berenson 1938, no. 2050.

Clapp and Berenson thought this drawing was a study for Pomona's head in the Poggio a Caiano lunette. However, in the fresco figure, the face is rounder, the chin shorter, and the hairline curves up instead of down. There may once have been a fragment of a Pontormo study here, but the drawing has been silhouetted, rubbed, and possibly reworked, so that its authenticity is difficult to determine.

A73. ——— 6549F: Two kneeling nudes and a leg. 264 x 200, red chalk.

Bibliography: Berenson 1903, no. 2052; Clapp 1914, 147; Goldschmidt 1914, 88; Berenson 1938, no. 2052.

Berenson thought the nudes were possibly for a *Pietà* and Clapp connected the leg with the putto on the wall below the window to the right of the Poggio a Caiano lunette. This drawing is a study by Bandinelli for a composition of *Adam and Eve with God the Father and Angels* that is preserved in a pen drawing in the Ecole des Beaux-Arts. See O. Kurz, "Giorgio Vasari's Libro de' Disegni," *OMD* 12, no. 47; 39, pl. 35. This composition may have been connected with a project of this subject for the choir of the Duomo in 1547.

A74. ——— 6550F *recto*: Standing nude. (*Verso*: Architectural sketch.) 281 x 192, red chalk; verso in black chalk.

Bibliography: Clapp 1914, 148.

This drawing was rejected by Clapp, but is still catalogued as Pontormo. It is a copy after a drawing attributed to Michelangelo at Windsor (see Berenson 1938, no. 1607, fig. 637).

A75. ——— 6552F *recto*: Bust of an old woman. (*Verso*: Bust of a woman in profile.) 348 x 254, black chalk retouched in ink by a later hand; verso heightened with white; W: Large acorn (cf. B. 7435).

Bibliography: Berenson 1903, no. 2054; Clapp 1914, 148–149; Berenson 1938, no. 2054; Smyth 1949, 196–198, figs. 10–11; *MDM* 1954 (Marcucci), no. 95; *EMI* 1954, no. 117; Smyth 1955, 59–60; Berenson 1961, no. 2054.

Clapp and Berenson accepted this sheet as a Pontormo dating 1525–1530, but Berenson later (1961) doubted the authenticity of the verso. Smyth first correctly gave the sheet to Bronzino, an attribution that has been accepted by Marcucci and the museum. The bust on the recto is a study for Bronzino's Washington *Holy Family* of ca. 1527–1528, a motive that is derived from an earlier drawing by Pontormo, a sheet on which Bronzino also drew a version of the St. Elizabeth's head (cat. 251). Smyth noted that the verso is based on a relief attributed to Desiderio da Settignano in the Victoria and Albert Museum (see C. Tolnay, *Michelangelo* I, Princeton, 1943, 129–131, fig. 137). There are several versions of this relief as well as a number of sixteenth-century drawings after it. See Tolnay, figs. 138–141 (drawings by Fra Bartolommeo, attributed to Lorenzo di Credi, after Bandinelli, and Bandinelli); in addition to a drawing after this composition by Maso da San Friano (Oxford, Christ Church Library E28). Bronzino's drawing differs from the others in that it shows only the half-length Madonna, but otherwise it is closely based on the relief. It is a preparatory study for a *Madonna and Child* (Florence, Art Market; panel, 73 x 61 cm) brought to the author's attention by Philip Pouncey. This picture is attributed to Pontormo, but is actually a Bronzino of ca. 1528–1530, probably just subsequent to the Washington *Holy Family* for which the recto of this sheet is a study. The figure in the painting is identical to Bronzino's drawing not only in the pose but in details such as the folds of the veil and the soft, reflected lights on the figure.

A76. ——— 6553F: *Crucifixion.* 375 x 263, black chalk; inscribed: *Jacopo*; inscribed verso: *Batista Venetians.*

Bibliography: Berenson 1903, no. 2055; Clapp 1914, 149; Berenson 1938, no. 2055.

Clapp accepted this drawing with some reservations and dated it 1535–1545. Berenson considered it a copy after the Michelangelo at Windsor (Berenson 1938, no. 1621, fig. 724), probably by Battista Franco, but he nonetheless listed the drawing under Pontormo. This study is a pastiche based on late Michelangelo *Crucifixion* drawings and has no connection with Pontormo.

A77. ——— 6555F: Reclining nude. 246 x 394, red chalk.

Bibliography: Berenson 1903, no. 2056; Clapp 1914, 150–151; Clapp 1916, 31, fig. 60; Berenson 1938, 302, 312, no. 2056.

See cat. A70.

A78. ——— 6562F: Nude woman seen from behind. 399 x 151, black chalk.

Bibliography: Berenson 1903, no. 2063; Clapp 1914, 156; McComb 1928, 149; Berenson 1938, 63, no. 601A.

This drawing was listed as Pontormo by Berenson, who later agreed with Clapp's attribution to Bronzino. McComb doubted the Bronzino attribution but rightly accepted it as from his circle. This study is very close to Bronzino, and is by the same hand as cat. A68, A89, A93, and A96.

A79. ——— 6563F: Kneeling nude. 356 x 264, black chalk; W: Eagle.

Bibliography: Berenson 1903, no. 2064; Clapp 1914, 156; Fraenckel 1933, 177n22; Berenson 1938, no. 2064.

Clapp dated this drawing 1530 as close to cat. 268, while Berenson thought it was for the same *Pietà* as cat. 67. However, as Fraenckel has pointed out, this is actually a copy after a Pontormo drawing of ca. 1517–1518 (cat. 83), probably for a figure in an *Adoration*. While the motive derives from this early Pontormo nude study, the elongated proportions of the figure and the reflections of Pontormo's rhythmic style of the late twenties (cf. cat. 298, 300, 305) indicate that this drawing dates from at least 1530 if not still later in the century. It is certainly by the same hand as cat. A117, A150, and A157, which we have attributed to Cavalori on the basis of stylistic resemblance to figures in his paintings. For this figure, cf. especially the priest in the *Sacrifice of Lavinia* from the *Studiolo*, or the kneeling apostles in the Badia *Pentecost*. There are also close parallels, notably in the hands and facial type, with the so-called *Conversation* (London, National Gallery 3941), attributed to Pontormo but surely by Cavalori.

A80. ——— 6565F: Nude being supported. 390 x 247, black chalk; inscribed: *Jacopo da Pon . . .*

Bibliography: Berenson 1903, no. 2066; Clapp 1914, 157; Berenson 1938, no. 2066.

Berenson called this drawing late and Clapp dated it 1545–1550 as for a *Deposition*. This drawing is a study for the figure to the right in cat. A97 and both are by a draughtsman strongly influenced by the late Pontormo. The museum now ascribes these studies to Bronzino.

A81. ——— 6566F: Nude boy. 410 x 268, red chalk squared in black chalk; W: Eagle in a circle (cf. B. 203).

Bibliography: Clapp 1914, 157.

Clapp rightly gave this study to Naldini, noting that the motive suggests *Salome with the Head of St. John the Baptist*, and it is now catalogued as Naldini in the museum. This Sartesque drawing is very close to cat. A5, A6, and A64, also attributed here to Naldini.

A82. ——— 6567F: Reclining nude seen to the knees. 187 x 238, black chalk.

Bibliography: Berenson 1903, no. 2067; Clapp 1914, 157–158; Berenson 1938, no. 2067.

Berenson dated this study late and Clapp thought it was a study for the same figure as Pontormo's cat. 381 for San Lorenzo. There is an analogy in motive with cat. 381, but the draughtsmanship in this drawing is less secure and the modelling labored. It is most likely to be a copy after a similar Pontormo study for San Lorenzo.

A83. ——— 6569F: Nude seen to the knees. 220 x 165, black chalk; inscribed: [J]*acopo da Pontormo.*

Bibliography: Berenson 1903, no. 2069; Clapp 1914, 158–159; Berenson 1938, no. 2069.

Clapp dated this drawing ca. 1543, connecting it with cat. A80 and A97. While not by the same hand as cat. A80 and A97, this drawing is also related to Pontormo's late style and may be a copy after a study for San Lorenzo.

A84. ——— 6573F: Draped woman. 192 x 155, black chalk on blue paper.

Bibliography: Berenson 1903, no. 2073, pl. 176; *MPA* 1910, 22; Clapp 1911, 16; Clapp 1914, 162; Clapp 1916, 84; Berenson 1938, 318, no. 2073, fig. 989.

Berenson dated this study late and Clapp placed it a little before 1530. It is diffcult to understand how this drawing became associated with Pontormo. The blurred, imprecise handling of the chalk and the lack of articulation in the forms are not only quite foreign to Pontormo's style, but the drawing is probably not even Florentine.

A85. ——— 6574F: Nude in profile seen to the knees. 215 x 154, red chalk on pink prepared paper; W: Cornet (cf. B. 7697).

Bibliography: Berenson 1903, no. 2074; Clapp 1914, 162–163; Berenson 1938, no. 2074; Marcucci 1953, 121, fig. 9.

Clapp dated this drawing 1530–1540 and Berenson placed it in Pontormo's middle period. As Clapp has pointed out, this nude may be related to cat. A94; however, neither drawing is closely connected with Pontormo. Marcucci has attributed this study to Macchietti and it is now listed as Macchietti by the museum. Although this drawing probably dates from the later part of the century, it is difficult to see any specific relation to Macchietti's drawings.

A86. ——— 6575F *recto*: Nude leaning over to the right. (*Verso*: Leg and arm.) 390 x 260, red chalk; leg on the verso in black chalk.

Bibliography: Berenson 1903, no. 2075; *MPA* 1910, 25; Clapp 1914, 163; Berenson 1938, no. 2075.

Berenson connected this drawing with Poggio a Caiano and Clapp dated it 1519–1520. While this nude study is derived in style from Pontormo's drawings of ca. 1520, the muddled profile, weak articulation of limbs and hands, suggest the hand of a pupil, probably Naldini.

A87. ——— 6576F *verso*: Three-quarter length nude with back turned. (*Recto*: Study for S. Felicita, cat. 268.) 390 x 215, black chalk.

Bibliography: Berenson 1903, no. 2076; Clapp 1914, 164; Berenson 1938, no. 2076.

This nude on the verso of a Pontormo drawing was dated 1535–1545 by Clapp. The excessively elongated figure type with the small head derives from Pontormo's figures in the *Story of Joseph* tapestries, but it never appears in Pontormo's drawings in such extreme form. The draughtsmanship is also closely based on Pontormo's drawings of this period (cat. 347–349), but is more academically insistent on the articulation of the surface and less fluid in line than in any of Pontormo's studies.

A88. ——— 6580F: Nude torso seen from behind. 200 x 190, black chalk; W: Pascal lamb (B. 50). Fig. 365.

Bibliography: Berenson 1903, no. 2080; Clapp 1914, 165–166; Berenson 1938, no. 2080.

Berenson called this drawing late, while Clapp connected it with San Lorenzo, comparing it in motive with a figure in cat. 374 and 375 and with a sketch on page eight of Pontormo's diary. The weak structure of the forms and the mechanical modelling of this drawing indicate that it is a copy, probably after a Pontormo study for a figure in the *Resurrection of the Dead*. Cf. a figure that appears in the upper right of a copy after the fresco (cat. A216). Cf. cat. A159 for another copy of the same figure with the head included.

A89. ——— 6589F: Three-quarter length nude with back turned. 276 x 167, black chalk; W: Animal in a double circle.

Bibliography: Berenson 1903, no. 2088; Clapp 1914, 170–171; McComb 1928, 149; Berenson 1938, no. 2088; *MDM* 1954 (Marcucci), no. 96; *EMI* 1954, no. 118.

Berenson placed this drawing in Pontormo's middle period, but Clapp gave it to Bronzino, dating it 1545–1555. Marcucci accepted Clapp's attribution and McComb considered it to be possibly Bronzino. It is now attributed to Bronzino by the museum. While this study is close in style to Bronzino, an attribution to his circle — the same hand as cat. A68, A78, A93 and A96 — is preferable.

A90. ——— 6591F: Nude torso seen from behind. 190 x 148, black chalk on pink prepared paper.

Bibliography: Berenson 1903, no. 2090; Clapp 1914, 171–172; Berenson 1938, no. 2090.

Berenson called this drawing late and Clapp dated it after 1545. It is a weak imitation of the style of Pontormo's tapestry drawings (cat. 347–349).

A91. ——— 6593F *verso*: Nude torso. (*Recto*: Tapestry study, cat. 347.) 225 x 165, black chalk on pink prepared paper.

Bibliography: Berenson 1903, no. 2092; Clapp 1914, 173; Berenson 1938, no. 2092.

Clapp connected this drawing with a figure in the left background of cat. 307 for the *Nudes Playing Calcio*, but there is no figure in that drawing similar in pose to this nude. This study is the reverse of a Pontormo drawing for a tapestry of the late forties and also dates from that period. There was probably a Pontormo sketch on this side of the sheet, but as is evident — notably in the modelling of the left arm — it has been reworked by another hand.

A92. ——— 6598F: Seated nude. 407 x 275, red chalk; left upper corner replaced; W: Eagle in a circle (cf. B. 203).

Bibliography: Berenson 1903, no. 2097; *MPA* 1910, 32; Clapp 1914, 176; Berenson 1938, no. 2097.

Berenson considered this drawing to be a study for Poggio a Caiano, while Clapp dated it 1519–1521, noting analogies with the Ignudi of the Sistine Ceiling. The motive of this figure is derived from the Ignudo to the left above the Prophet Isaiah in reverse. It is very close in style to Pontormo's red chalk drawings of ca. 1520 and must be by a contemporary working directly under his influence.

A93. ——— 6600F: Standing nude in profile right. 438 x 196, red chalk.

Bibliography: Berenson 1903, no. 2099; Clapp 1914, 177; Berenson 1938, no. 2099; *MDF* 1939, 5.

This study was dated "latish" by Berenson, in the early thirties by Clapp. While the style of this drawing as well as the figure type derives ultimately from Pontormo's nude studies of the thirties, the figure is more elongated and mannered, the draughtsmanship more academic than in any of the authentic studies. This drawing, together with a group of studies probably by the same hand (cat. A68, A78, A89, and A96), belongs to the circle of Bronzino. In this group, notably in this drawing, there is a suggestion of the red chalk manner of Macchietti (cf. the studies for the *Bagni di Pozzuoli* in the Louvre and Uffizi 6415F, 12138F, 17585F). However, these drawings are more precisely ornamental in style and closer to Bronzino than the Macchietti studies.

A94. ——— 6602F: Compositional study of nudes around a fire burning books. 290 x 313, black chalk and yellow wash; W: Crossed arrows with a star (B. 6305); inscribed: *Jacopo da Pontormo.*

Bibliography: Berenson 1903, no. 2101; Clapp 1914, 179, pl. 7; Berenson 1938, no. 2101, fig. 990.

Berenson dated this compositional drawing ca. 1535, Clapp ca. 1540. The scene in the background of this enigmatic subject recalls Pontormo's *Isaac Blessing Jacob* (Uffizi) of ca. 1545–1550, but the foreground composition, the exaggerated muscular figure types, and the pictorial wash technique have no counterpart among his drawings.

A95. ——— 6603F *recto*: Nude woman seated on steps. (*Verso*: Nude.) 401 x 250, red chalk.

Bibliography: Berenson 1903, no. 2102; *MPA* 1910, 28; Clapp 1911, 7; Clapp 1914, 180; Clapp 1916, 16, fig. 6; Fraenckel 1933, 178; Berenson 1938, no. 2102, fig. 936; Toesca 1943, 9, fig. 2; *MP* 1956 (Marcucci), 63.

Berenson, Clapp, Toesca, and Marcucci thought this drawing was a study for the woman on the steps in Pontormo's SS. Annunziata *Visitation.* However, as Fraenckel has seen, it is certainly a copy after a lost preparatory study for the figure. Weak contours, schematic facial features, and the formless feet suggest the hand of Naldini, an attribution that is confirmed by the nude study on the verso, which is close in style to a series of Naldini copies after Pontormo in the Louvre (cf. especially cat. A322). Cf. cat. A377 for another copy after the lost study for the SS. Annunziata figure.

A96. ——— 6607F: Nude standing in profile to the left. 415 x 258, black chalk.

Bibliography: Berenson 1903, no. 2106; Clapp 1914, 182; Berenson 1938, no. 2106.

Berenson called this study a late Pontormo, but Clapp considered it a Bronzino of about 1560 and it is now catalogued as Bronzino by the museum. This nude is more likely to be from the hand of a Bronzino follower, probably the same hand as cat. A68, A78, A89, and A93.

A97. ——— 6608F: Two nudes, one supporting the other. 410 x 259, black chalk.

Bibliography: Berenson 1903, no. 2107; Clapp 1914, 182; Berenson 1938, no. 2107.

This study, probably for figures in a *Last Judgment*, was dated 1545–1550 by Clapp, but is now given to Bronzino by the museum. This drawing is certainly influenced by the late Pontormo but the hand of Bronzino is not evident. Cat. A80 is a more finished study for the figure to the right.

A98. ——— 6611F *recto*: Dead Christ. (*Verso*: Nude studies.) 266 x 255, black chalk.

Bibliography: Berenson 1903, no. 2110; Clapp 1914, 184–185; Berenson 1938, no. 2110, fig. 969 (recto).

Berenson and Clapp accepted this drawing as Pontormo, Clapp dating it 1533–

1545, but it is now ascribed to Bronzino by the museum. The attribution to Bronzino is not convincing, but this study is evidently by the same imitator of the late Pontormo as cat. A80, A97, and possibly A120.

A99. ——— 6614F *recto*: Head of a youth. (*Verso*: Dead Christ.) 343 x 245, red chalk; verso in black chalk on grey prepared paper; W: Acorn (B. 7435).

Bibliography: Berenson 1903, no. 2113; Clapp 1914, 187; Berenson 1938, 313, no. 2113.

Clapp dated this sheet 1521–1523 and considered the verso to be a study for the Certosa *Pietà* derived from Dürer's woodcut from the *Small Passion*. Berenson also connected the verso with the preparation for the Certosa fresco. If it is compared with Pontormo's sketch for this motive (cat. 213), it is evident that the thin and lifeless contours of this study are not Pontormo's. However, the style of this drawing is suggestive of Sogliani, an attribution that is confirmed by the head on the recto. Cf. British Museum 1862–2–32, and Munich 12867 (listed as Italian sixteenth century) for typical head studies by Sogliani of this type.

A100. ——— 6617F: Composition of many draped figures. 260 x 666, black chalk on brownish paper; squared; laid down.

Bibliography: Ferri 1890, 118; Berenson 1903, no. 2556; Clapp 1914, 189; Berenson 1938, no. 2556.

This study was formerly attributed to Pontormo but has been given rightly to Sogliani by Berenson, Clapp, and the museum.

A101. ——— 6618F *recto*: Nude seen from behind and two legs. (*Verso*: Drapery studies.) 362 x 216, red chalk.

Bibliography: Berenson 1903, no. 2116; Clapp 1914, 189–190; Clapp 1916, 33; Berenson 1938, no. 2116.

Clapp dated this sheet 1518–1520 and Berenson also considered it early. The stiff drapery studies of the verso have no connection at all with Pontormo and the style of the somewhat academic nude is only superficially related to his drawings of ca. 1517–1518.

A102. ——— 6621F: Nude seen from behind. 410 x 133, red chalk; inscribed verso: *Jacopo da Pon*[tor]*mo*.

Bibliography: Clapp 1914, 191; McComb 1928, 150; Berenson 1938, no. 601B.

This study was formerly attributed to Pontormo but has been given to Bronzino by Berenson, Clapp (dated ca. 1560), and the museum. McComb's doubts as to the Bronzino attribution were justified as this drawing is certainly a copy after Bronzino. Cat. A188 is another copy of the same figure.

A103. ——— 6623F: Nude study. 157 x 193, black chalk; W: Circle.

Bibliography: Berenson 1903, no. 2120; Clapp 1914, 192; Berenson 1938, no. 2120.

Clapp dated this drawing 1550–1556 and Berenson called it late. It is a copy or imitation of Pontormo's San Lorenzo drawing style of the same type as cat. A82 and A83.

A104. ——— 6624F: Nude seen from behind. 400 x 136, red chalk; inscribed verso: *Jacopo da Pontor*[mo].

Bibliography: Clapp 1914, 192; Berenson 1938, no. 2458H.

Clapp rejected this drawing as Pontormo, noting that it was derived from Michelangelo's *David* seen from behind. Berenson gave it to school of Rosso as a copy of the *David*. Actually, it is not after the *David* but after the same lost Michelangelo sculpture of ca. 1505–1506 as cat. 240 by Pontormo and several school of Michelangelo drawings (see L. Dussler, *Die Zeichnungen des Michelangelo*, Berlin, 1959, cat. 369, fig. 183).

A105. ——— 6626F *recto*: *Rape of the Sabines*. (*Verso*: Heads and architectural motive.) 126 x 176, pen and bistre over black chalk; verso pen and bistre with red ink.

Bibliography: Clapp 1914, 193.

The traditional attribution of this drawing to Pontormo has been rightly rejected by Clapp as it is quite unrelated to Pontormo's style.

A106. ——— 6628F: Copy of the central part of Pontormo's S. Ruffillo altar. 399 x 283, black chalk partly redrawn in ink; W: Eagle with a star.

Bibliography: Clapp 1914, 193–194.

Clapp recognized this drawing as a copy after the S. Ruffillo altar. It probably dates from the seventeenth century.

A107. ——— 6629F: Copy after Pontormo's lost *Madonna and Child*. 308 x 242, black chalk; inscribed verso in a seventeenth-century hand: *Di Jacopo da Pontormo il quadro è in mano del Illmo Cardinale Carlo de' Medici nel casino di San Marco*; inscribed recto: *Pontormo*; *Jacopo*; *Po*[ntormo].

Bibliography: Clapp 1914, 194.

Clapp recognized this drawing as a copy after a Pontormo composition that is preserved in many versions (see p. 317, n. 8). While Clapp dated it in the eighteenth century, the inscription, which states that the painting belonged to Carlo de' Medici (d. 1666), would seem to place this copy in the seventeenth century.

A108. ——— 6631F: Nude boy. 185 x 188, red chalk with touches of black; W: Star in a circle (B. 6086); laid down.

Bibliography: Berenson 1903, no. 2124; Clapp 1914, 195; Berenson 1938, no. 2124.

Clapp thought this drawing was a study for the *Nudes Playing Calcio* and Berenson dated it late. The type of the boy and his flying action recall Pontormo's studies for the Castello loggia putti (cat. 336–339). In addition, the paper is the same as a sheet used by Pontormo in a study for one of the *Allegories* of the loggia (cat. 343, with the same watermark). While the weak articulation of the figure and the hesitant line do not suggest Pontormo's hand, it is likely that this sketch was executed by one of his assistants at Castello, probably Bronzino (cf. cat. A121).

A109. ——— 6633F: Study for the Christ in a *Noli Me Tangere* and other studies. 383 x 282, red and black chalk; laid down.

Bibliography: Clapp 1914, 196.

This drawing was rejected by Clapp as a Pontormo and is now given convincingly by the museum to Clemente Bandinelli.

A110. ——— 6634F: Nude torso and legs. 186 x 164, black chalk; torn irregularly and laid down.

Bibliography: Berenson 1903, no. 2126; Clapp 1914, 196–197; Clapp 1916, 33; Berenson 1938, no. 2126.

Berenson placed this drawing late, but Clapp dated it 1518–1521 as a study for the boy on the wall in the Poggio a Caiano lunette. This slight sketch is very close in style to Pontormo's studies for the vault of the Careggi loggia (cat. 312–313) and it may be by his hand, although it is more likely to be by an assistant.

A111. ——— 6635F: Two nude studies mounted together. 373 x 158, black chalk on pink prepared paper; upper study retouched in ink; inscribed in red chalk: *andrea.*

Bibliography: Berenson 1903, no. 2127; Clapp 1914, 197; Berenson 1938, no. 2127.

Berenson dated these studies early and Clapp dated them 1516–1522. The soft, pictorial treatment of the nude in these slight sketches is unrelated to Pontormo's drawing style.

A112. ——— 6636F *recto*: Studies of shoulders. (*Verso*: Shoulder.) 182 x 150, black chalk on pink prepared paper.

Bibliography: Berenson 1903, no 2128; Clapp 1914, 197–198; Berenson 1938, no. 2128.

Clapp rightly doubted the authenticity of these slight sketches, but connected them with cat. 374 and 375 for San Lorenzo. This sheet seems to derive more specifically from Pontormo's slightly earlier drawings for the tapestries (cat. 347–349).

A113. ——— 6639F: Upper part of a sleeping child and a hand. 265 x 190, black chalk; W: Angel (cf. B. 613); inscribed verso in a seventeenth-century (?) hand: *Jacopo da Pontormo.*

Bibliography: Berenson 1903, no. 2131; Clapp 1914, 199; McComb 1928, 150; Berenson 1938, no. 601C, fig. 999; Smyth 1949, 195; Smyth 1955, 38–39; Emiliani 1960, pl. 61.

This drawing was given to Pontormo by Berenson (1903), but was recognized by Clapp as Bronzino's study for the Christ in the Panciatichi *Holy Family* of the early thirties. This association has been generally accepted and the drawing is now listed as Bronzino in the museum.

A114. ——— 6640F *recto*: Nude. (*Verso*: Nude.) 214 x 154, red and black chalk on pink prepared paper; inscribed: *Fran*[co] *Rosi 165.*

Bibliography: Berenson 1903, no. 2132; Clapp 1914, 199–200; Berenson 1938, no. 2132; Tolnay 1950, 49.

Clapp, Berenson, and Tolnay connected the recto of this sheet with the San Lorenzo *Deluge*, Clapp noting a sketch for a figure in a similar pose on page fourteen of Pontormo's diary. Clapp dated the verso 1532–1535. The verso is totally unPontormesque in draughtsmanship, while the recto derives in style from Pontormo's drawings of the thirties and forties.

A115. ——— 6641F: Reclining nude. 160 x 261, black chalk; W: Mermaid in a circle (cf. B. 13893).

Bibliography: Berenson 1903, no. 2133; Clapp 1914, 200; Berenson 1938, no. 2133.

Clapp and Berenson dated this study late, but it is surely a contemporary imitation of Pontormo's late drawing style.

A116. ——— 6642F: Bust of a woman. 213 x 154, black chalk on pink prepared paper.

Bibliography: Berenson 1903, no. 2134; Clapp 1914, 200; Berenson 1938, no. 2134.

Berenson considered this study to be possibly for the Virgin in the S. Felicita *Deposition*, but its style is unrelated to Pontormo's and suggests a late sixteenth-century draughtsman close to Jacopo da Empoli.

A117. ——— 6647F *recto*: Head of a woman. (*Verso*: Bust of a man.) 205 x 265, pen and bistre on grey prepared paper; verso in black chalk; inscribed: *Fran*[co] *Rosi 25*[?]*6.*

Bibliography: Berenson 1903, no. 2139;

Clapp 1911, 13; Clapp 1914, 203; Clapp 1916, 44, 49, fig. 91 (recto); Berenson 1938, no. 2139; Smyth 1949, 207; Berenson 1954, pl. 47 (recto); Cecchi 1956, fig. 16 (recto).

Berenson associated the head on the recto with the Virgin in the S. Felicita *Deposition*, while Clapp and Cecchi thought it was a study for the *S. Quentin* (Borgo S. Sepolcro), Clapp dating it 1522–1525. Berenson connected the verso with the S. Felicita *Evangelists*, Clapp dated it 1521–1525, Smyth ca. 1520. It is difficult to perceive any connection with Pontormo's drawings of the twenties in these sketches. The sheet is by the same hand as cat. A37, A63, A79, and A157, here attributed to Cavalori, while the bust on the verso is close to Uffizi 472F, given by Marcucci (*Riv. d'A.* 28, 1953, 88, fig. 12) to Cavalori. Both sides of this sheet may possibly be connected with Cavalori's *Pentecost* (Badia), the recto with the head of the Virgin, the verso with one of the apostles to the right.

A118. ——— 6648F *recto*: Seated draped torso. (*Verso*: Sketches of interiors.) 250 x 172, black chalk; verso in pen and bistre.

Bibliography: Berenson 1903, no. 2140; Clapp 1911, 11; Clapp 1914, 204–205; Clapp 1916, 39, 42; Berenson 1938, 313–314, no. 2140, fig. 961 (recto).

Berenson and Clapp thought this drawing was Pontormo's imitation of Dürer's manner and that it dated in the Certosa period. While the mode of this study is Düreresque, it is not as close to Pontormo's studies of the Certosa period as it is to Bacchiacca's studies after Dürer, notably Uffizi 14564F. This drawing is now attributed to Bacchiacca by the museum.

A119. ——— 6650F: Reclining nude and a head. 211 x 264, black chalk and ink; inscribed verso: [Franco] *Rosi 241.*

Bibliography: Berenson 1903, no. 2142; Clapp 1914, 205–206; Berenson 1938, no. 2142; Tolnay 1950, 49.

Clapp dated this drawing after 1548 and connected it with a figure to the right in cat. 375 for the San Lorenzo *Deluge*. There is a general resemblance in motive to the figure in Pontormo's drawing but none at all in style. This drawing is more closely derived in draughtsmanship from the late Bronzino and is by an artist of his circle, possibly Allori.

A120. ——— 6655F: *Venus and Cupid.* 133 x 202, black chalk; laid down.

Bibliography: Clapp 1914, 208.

This drawing was not accepted as Pontormo by Clapp and it is now listed as Bronzino by the museum. Clapp considered it to be based on the Michelangelo-Pontormo *Venus and Cupid*, but there are several differences in pose. However, it is identical in motive with a Pontormo sketch of the fifties for a *Venus and Cupid* (cat. 383) and it may be a copy of a more finished version of the composition. It is possibly by the same hand as cat. A80, A97, and A98.

A121. ——— 6658F *recto*: Two kneeling nudes. (*Verso*: Reclining nude and a putto.) 180 x 254, red chalk; W: Star in a circle (cf. B. 6086); inscribed verso in a sixteenth-century (?) hand: *bronzino.*

Bibliography: Berenson 1903, no. 2149; Clapp 1914, 210–211; Berenson 1938, no. 2149; Smyth 1955, 52–53.

Berenson accepted this drawing as Pontormo on the basis of the recto, while on the same evidence Clapp gave it to Lappoli or Pichi, dating it 1525–1540. Smyth has attributed the sheet to Bronzino of the early twenties. While the figures of the recto cannot be associated with a painting, the nude on the verso may be connected with Bronzino's *St. Lawrence*, painted at the Certosa in 1523–1524. Cf. two Pontormo sketches on Certosa studies (cat. 198 and 202), which might have been his suggestions to Bronzino for the pose of the figure.

A122. ——— 6659F *recto*: Seated nude torso. (*Verso*: Seated nude.) 219 x 150, red chalk on pink prepared paper; verso in black chalk; W: Heart (cf. B. 4196); inscribed in an eighteenth-century hand: *Puntormo*; inscribed in a later hand: . . . *ia copia*.

Bibliography: Berenson 1903, no. 2150; Clapp 1914, 211; Berenson 1938, no. 2150.

Clapp dated the recto of this sheet ca. 1535, the verso ca. 1540. In motive these studies are derived from figures on the Sistine Ceiling (the recto from the Ignudo to the left above Isaiah, reversed, the verso from the Jonah) and in draughtsmanship they are based on the style of the late Pontormo.

A123. ——— 6663F *recto*: Standing woman holding a child with another child beside her. (*Verso*: Copy after a figure from the *Battle of the Cascina*.) 404 x 268, red and black chalk on brown paper; W: Fruit (B. 7392); inscribed: *Franco Rosi 237*.

Bibliography: Clapp 1914, 216; Berenson 1938, no. 2556A.

These studies have been rightly attributed to Sogliani by Clapp and Berenson. The recto is close in style to many black chalk studies by Sogliani in the Uffizi (cf. 16989F–17049F).

A124. ——— 6667F *verso*: Nude and drapery studies. (*Recto*: Portrait study, cat. 241.) 296 x 273, black chalk.

Bibliography: Clapp 1914, 218; Berenson 1938, no. 2156A.

Clapp discussed only the drapery study, considering it an idea for the woman to the far right in the Poggio a Caiano lunette that was gone over about 1545. Although it is the verso of a Pontormo study of the twenties, this drawing consists of two copies from originals of widely separated dates. The drapery is copied after that of the Poggio a Caiano woman, while the nude must reflect a drawing of ca. 1545–1549, the period of the *Story of Joseph* tapestry cartoons (cf. cat. 347–349).

A125. ——— 6674F: Nude youth seen to the waist with drapery around his shoulders. 207 x 165, black chalk on grey paper; cut to an arch at the top.

Bibliography: Ferri 1890, 119; Berenson 1903, no. 2000; *MPA* 1910, 24; Clapp 1914, 224–225; Berenson 1938, no. 2159D; Smyth 1949, 190, fig. 7; Emiliani 1960, pl. 5.

Ferri, Berenson, and Clapp considered this drawing to be for one of the S. Felicita *Evangelists* but did not specify which one. Smyth and Emiliani thought it was Pontormo's study for the *St. Mark*, which they attributed to Bronzino. This drawing is certainly connected with the tondi, but it is probably by Bronzino rather than Pontormo and it is preparatory to the *St. Matthew* rather than the *St. Mark*. The style of the drawing contrasts sharply with the delicate and lucid manner of Pontormo's S. Felicita studies, while the heavy contours, awkward articulation of arms and shoulders, and frozen quality of the facial expression are close to Bronzino's drawings of this period (cf. cat. A75). A similar position (reversed) was used for the *St. Mark*, but it is evident that this drawing was preparatory to the *St. Matthew*, the only one of the Evangelists who is depicted as a youthful nude with a drapery behind his shoulders, curly-headed, with round eyes, a short nose, and a small full mouth. This drawing, in which the tondo format is not yet indicated, must have been made early in the preparation for the *St. Matthew*, since a slightly different pose was subsequently worked out for the figure. However, the general aspect of the figure as noted above remained the same in the painting.

A126. ——— 6679F: Seated nude. 280 x 172, black chalk; W: Latin cross (B. 5641).

Bibliography: Berenson 1903, no. 2164; Clapp 1914, 229–230; Clapp 1916, 77, fig. 149; Berenson 1938, no. 2164; Cecchi 1956, fig. 8.

Berenson called this drawing late and Clapp dated it 1545–1555. This study is a copy of poor quality, probably after a study for the San Lorenzo *Resurrection of the Dead*. Cf. the figure in the lower center of cat. A216.

A127. ——— 6681F: Head of a woman. 151 x 115, red chalk; inscribed in a seventeenth-century (?) hand: *Jacopo da Pont.*

Bibliography: Berenson 1903, no. 2166; Clapp 1914, 230; Berenson 1938, 314, no. 2166.

Berenson suggested that this drawing was a Pontormo study for the Louvre altar, while Clapp thought it was by Bronzino and related to cat. 192. It is a copy after the Madonna's head in Bronzino's *Holy Family* (Washington, National Gallery) of ca. 1527–1528.

A128. ——— 6684F *recto*: Nude studies. (*Verso*: Nude studies.) 254 x 196, black chalk; W: Angel (cf. B. 613).

Bibliography: Berenson 1903, no. 2169; Clapp 1914, 231–232; Berenson 1938, no. 2169; *MDF* 1939, 27; Tolnay 1950, 49; Cecchi 1956, fig. 7 (verso).

Clapp thought that the recto was a sheet of studies for the San Lorenzo *Last Judgment* and the verso was datable 1535–1540. Berenson, Tolnay, and Cecchi also connected the sheet with San Lorenzo. With the exception of the reclining nude on the verso, which is an exaggerated imitation of Pontormo's Michelangelesque drawings of the midthirties (cf. cat. 329), these sketches are inspired by studies for the San Lorenzo *Resurrection of the Dead* or perhaps by figures in the fresco itself.

A129. ——— 6695F *recto*: Bust of a nude boy. (*Verso*: Peacock.) 190 x 270, black chalk; verso red chalk squared.

Bibliography: Berenson 1903, no. 2179; Clapp 1914, 241; Berenson 1938, no. 2179; Smyth 1955, 62.

Clapp dated the boy 1525 and the peacock 1535, but Smyth has rightly given the sheet to Bronzino and it is now listed as Bronzino in the museum. The figure on the recto is close to cat. A121, while it is executed in the same soft black chalk technique as cat. A75 of ca. 1525–1526. The peacock seems later in style and may possibly be a study for the peacock in Bronzino's cat. A260 of 1565, a compositional drawing squared in the same scale as this study.

A130. ——— 6696F: Masked figure. 169 x 143, black chalk.

Bibliography: Berenson 1903, no. 2180; Clapp 1914, 241–242; Berenson 1938, no. 2180.

Clapp dated this study 1535–1545 but it has no specific connection with Pontormo's style and may date toward the end of the sixteenth century.

A131. ——— 6699F *recto*: Flying putti. (*Verso*: Same.) 399 x 285, pen and bistre.

Bibliography: Ferri 1890, 119; Berenson 1903, no. 2182; *MPA* 1910, 34; Clapp 1914, 244–245; Berenson 1938, no. 2182.

Gamba (*MPA*) connected this sheet and cat. A48 with the Cappella del Papa decorations, while Clapp doubted the authenticity of this drawing, but accepted cat. A48 as Pontormo. Both sheets may be given to Naldini.

A132. ——— 6700F: Skeleton. 421 x 281, black chalk; W: Crossbow in a circle with fleur-de-lis above (B. 761).

Bibliography: Berenson 1903, no. 2183; Clapp 1914, 245; Berenson 1938, no. 2183.

Clapp dated this drawing and the other skeleton studies from the same series (cf. cat. A139–A141) 1535–1550 and Berenson called them late. While none of the anatomical studies in the Uffizi attributed to Pontormo is securely by his hand, this group is especially distant from his drawing style. The dry, literal execution and the academicism of these studies is very suggestive of Allori's black chalk drawings and this group of skeleton studies may be attributed to him.

A133. ——— 6703F: Standing nude. 405 x 242, red chalk.

Bibliography: Berenson 1903, no. 2186; Clapp 1914, 248; Berenson 1938, no. 2186.

Clapp dated this nude ca. 1530 and Berenson placed it in Pontormo's early middle period as perhaps for a *St. John the Baptist*. The accentuated brilliance of the modelling is close to the red chalk style of Boscoli, to whom this drawing may be ascribed. It is now catalogued as Boscoli by the museum.

A134. ——— 6704F: Nude seen from behind. 423 x 156, black chalk on yellow prepared paper.

Bibliography: Berenson 1903, no. 2187; Clapp 1914, 248–249; McComb 1928, 150; Berenson 1938, no. 601D; Smyth 1949, 195; *MDM* 1954 (Marcucci), no. 97; Smyth 1955, 11–12; Berenson 1961, no. 601D, fig. 981.

This drawing was given to Pontormo by Berenson, but it was recognized by Clapp as Bronzino's study for a figure in the *Crossing of the Red Sea* in the Cappella Eleanora, Palazzo Vecchio. Clapp dated it 1545–1546, Marcucci placed it 1550–1551, but it should be dated a decade earlier — 1540–1541.

A135. ——— 6705F *recto*: Child asleep. (*Verso*: Arm.) 164 x 202, red chalk; sheet cut irregularly.

Bibliography: Berenson 1903, no. 2188; Clapp 1914, 249; Berenson 1938, no. 2188.

Clapp dated this study toward 1518, but it is too *retardataire* in draughtsmanship to be attributed to Pontormo at the time of the Visdomini altar. It might have been executed by a less advanced contemporary such as Bugiardini, with whose children there are analogies in type.

A136. ——— 6706F *recto*: Putto seen from below. (*Verso*: Fragment of a nude.) 149 x 155, red chalk; sheet cut irregularly; W: Fleur-de-lis in a circle (B. 7106).

Bibliography: Berenson 1903, no. 2189; Clapp 1911, 5n; Clapp 1914, 249; Clapp 1916, 10; Berenson 1938, no. 2189.

Clapp dated this drawing 1514–1515, suggesting that it might have been for one of the putti in Pontormo's *Faith and Charity* of 1514. None of the putti in the damaged fresco correspond to this one in pose and, in any case, this later sixteenth-century sketch is unrelated in style to Pontormo's early Sartesque drawings.

A137. ——— 6707F: Reclining nude seen from behind. 217 x 181, black chalk on blue paper.

Bibliography: Berenson 1903, no. 2190; Clapp 1914, 249–250; Berenson 1938, no. 2190.

This slight, later sixteenth-century sketch has no connection with Pontormo's drawings of any period and is executed on a rough blue paper of a type that never occurs in Pontormo's surviving drawings.

A138. ——— 6708F: Nude boy falling backwards. 200 x 252, black chalk on blue paper; lower left corner replaced.

Bibliography: Berenson 1903, no. 2191; Clapp 1914, 250; Berenson 1938, no. 2191.

Clapp doubted the authenticity of this drawing, but dated it 1535–1550. Berenson dated it in the S. Felicita period. It is a Federigo Zuccaro study for a figure in the cupola of the Duomo, Florence. Cf. Uffizi 11066F for the complete compositional study including this figure.

A139. ——— 6709F: Skeleton. 423 x 288, black chalk; W: Crossbow in a circle with a fleur-de-lis above (B. 761); inscribed verso: *Di Jacopo.*

Bibliography: Berenson 1903, no. 2192; Clapp 1914, 250; Berenson 1938, no. 2192; Nicco Fasola 1947, 40, fig. 20.

See cat. A132.

A140. ——— 6710F: Skeleton. 405 x 280, black chalk; W: Crossbow in a circle with a fleur-de-lis above (B. 761).

Bibliography: Berenson 1903, no. 2193; Clapp 1914, 251; Berenson 1938, no. 2193.

See cat. A132.

A141. ——— 6711F: Skeleton. 423 x 293, black chalk; W: Crossbow in a circle with a fleur-de-lis above (B. 761).

Bibliography: Berenson 1903, no. 2194; Clapp 1914, 251; Berenson 1938, no. 2194.

See cat. A132.

A142. ——— 6712F *recto*: Flayed limbs. (*Verso*: Same.) 284 x 202, red and black chalk; W: Crown; inscribed verso: *Fran*[co] *Rosi 227.*

Bibliography: Berenson 1903, no. 2195; Clapp 1914, 251–252; Berenson 1938, no. 2195.

Clapp dated these studies and cat. A143 (by the same hand) ca. 1540. The draughtsmanship has nothing in common with that of Pontormo and these drawings are similar to studies of this same type in the Louvre, where they are attributed to Allori.

A143. ——— 6713F *recto*: Flayed limbs. (*Verso*: Same.) 287 x 203, red chalk; W: Fragment of a ladder in a shield (B. 5928); inscribed verso: *Fran*[co] *Rosi 228.*

Bibliography: Berenson 1903, no. 2196; Clapp 1914, 252; Berenson 1938, no. 2196.

See cat. A142.

A144. ——— 6714F *recto*: Reclining nude. (*Verso*: Flayed torso.) 215 x 305, black chalk.

Bibliography: Berenson 1903, no. 2197; Clapp 1914, 252–253; Berenson 1938, no. 2197; Tolnay 1950, 49.

Clapp attributed this drawing to Bronzino as a study for his portion of the San Lorenzo *Deluge*, but Berenson and Tolnay retained the Pontormo attribution. This study is certainly a copy after a drawing for San Lorenzo, possibly by Allori.

A145. ——— 6716F: Five flayed figures. 281 x 430, black and red chalk; inscribed verso: *Pontormo.*

Bibliography: Berenson 1903, no. 2199; Clapp 1914, 253–254; Berenson 1938, no. 2199.

Clapp dated these flayed torsos 1540–1550, but this gross and exaggerated handling of muscular forms is quite foreign to Pontormo's style.

A146. ——— 6717F: Head of a man. 109 x 69, black chalk.

Bibliography: Berenson 1903, no. 2200; Clapp 1914, 254; Berenson 1938, no. 2200.

Clapp thought this study was from the period of S. Felicita. This head closely resembles many of the heads in the *Story of Joseph* tapestry series by Pontormo, Bronzino, and Salviati, but cannot be specifically identified. It is most likely by the hand of an assistant, probably from the shop of Bronzino.

A147. ——— 6718F: Skeletonlike head. 346 x 229, black chalk.

Bibliography: Berenson 1903, no. 2201; Clapp 1914, 254; Clapp 1916, 57, fig. 117; Berenson 1938, no. 2201; *MP* 1956 (Marcucci), no. 126, fig. 158b; Cecchi 1956, fig. 15.

Clapp dated this study 1520–1530 and Marcucci placed it 1528–1530, noting that it might have been a study for Pontormo's lost *Raising of Lazarus* of ca. 1529–1530 (see V/M, VI, 274). Marcucci also mentioned a connection in motive with cat. 251, Pontormo's study of the head of an old woman that Bronzino used in his Washington *Holy Family* of ca. 1527–1528. A comparison with Bronzino's own study for the St. Elizabeth (cat. A75) suggests that this head is another Bronzino drawing of the same period. The soft and rather dry line, the sudden darker accent of the eye, its large flat shape, and the accentuated neck muscles are characteristic of both drawings.

A148. ——— 6720F: Standing nude seen from behind. 388 x 158, black chalk with bistre wash.

Bibliography: Berenson 1903, no. 2203; Clapp 1914, 255; Berenson 1938, no. 2203.

Berenson thought this nude was possibly for the uppermost figure in the S. Felicita *Deposition* and Clapp dated it 1535. This drawing must be a copy, probably related to the *Story of Joseph* tapestries by Pontormo and Bronzino (cf. cat. 347).

A149. ——— 6721F: Nude walking. 393 x 141, red chalk; sheet cut irregularly and laid down; inscribed: [Ja]*c*° *da Pont*°.

Bibliography: Berenson 1903, no. 2204; Clapp 1914, 255–256; Berenson 1938, no. 2204.

Berenson called this drawing early and Clapp dated it ca. 1517. This Sartesque study may be by Puligo, with whom we have also connected cat. A58, which is close in many details to this drawing.

A150. ——— 6723F *recto*: Standing nude boy. (*Verso*: Seated draped woman.) 404 x 249, black chalk on tan paper; triangular repair center of sheet; W: Eagle.

Bibliography: Berenson 1903, no. 2206; Clapp 1914, 257; Clapp 1916, 56, fig. 113 (recto); Giglioli 1926, 779; Berenson 1938, no. 2206; *MP* 1956 (Marcucci), 96.

Clapp dated the recto 1529–1530 as a study for a lost *Raising of Lazarus* by Pontormo mentioned by Vasari. Giglioli thought it might be for a *Sacrifice of Isaac* and Berenson dated it fairly early. Although the style of the recto derives closely from Pontormo's drawings of the late twenties (cf. cat. 268, 300), the lack of fluidity in the line and the lumpy forms are not characteristic of his nude studies of this period, while the blurred and tentative handling of the chalk in the study on the verso is never found in Pontormo's drawings. This sheet has recently been ascribed to Bronzino by the museum, but it is closer to a group of studies that we have given to Cavalori (cf. cat. A37, A63, A79, A117, A157) and may also be by his hand.

A151. ——— 6724F: Nude studies. 230 x 330, black chalk; inscribed verso in a late sixteenth-century (?) hand: *Pontormo.* Fig. 322.

Bibliography: Berenson 1903, no. 2207; Clapp 1914, 257–258; Berenson 1938, no. 2207.

Berenson called these nudes late and Clapp dated them in the San Lorenzo period. These studies are probably contemporary copies after figures from Pontormo's Castello loggia. The flying figures on a large scale are after the putti of the vault (cf. cat. 336–339), the reclining nude at the upper right is after the figure studied by Pontormo on cat. 344, the nude below is after one of the other allegorical females, the sketch at the upper left is after a figure very like the one on cat. 343, and the figure sketched at the lower right is reminiscent of the pose of the Saturn (cf. cat. 340).

A152. ——— 6725F: Seated nude. 248 x 205, red chalk; W: Undecipherable.

Bibliography: Berenson 1903, no. 2208; Clapp 1914, 259; Berenson 1938, no. 2208.

Clapp called this drawing a Bronzino of 1540–1545, although he accepted the other version of the drawing (cat. A68) as a Pontormo. This study is now catalogued as Bronzino by the museum, but it is a copy after cat. A68 from the school of Bronzino.

A153. ——— 6731F *recto*: Lower part of a draped figure seated on a wall. (*Verso*: Nude seen from behind.) 400 x 271, black chalk; W: Fruit (cf. B. 7392); inscribed verso: *di Jacopo* and [Fran]^{co} *Rosi 239.*

Bibliography: Berenson 1903, no. 2213; Clapp 1911, 8; Clapp 1914, 264; Clapp 1916, 32, fig. 61 (recto); Berenson 1938, 312, no. 2213, fig. 959 (recto).

The recto of this sheet was considered by Berenson and Clapp to be a preparatory study for the drapery of the Pomona in the Poggio a Caiano lunette. This rather dry and academic study contrasts in style with Pontormo's drawing for the Pomona (cat. 149) and the final studies for the other women (cat. 145 and 148). Furthermore, the uncertainty in the modelling and the timidity of the line suggest that it is not by Pontormo but a copy after a lost drawing for the Pomona. The verso is certainly not by Pontormo, although it was accepted as a late drawing by Clapp. The Michelangelesque draughtsmanship and the elongated proportions of the figure suggest that this side of the sheet was inspired by Pontormo's drawings of the forties, such as those for the tapestries (cat. 347–349).

A154. ——— 6732F: Drapery study. 249 x 177, red chalk on pink prepared paper.

Bibliography: Berenson 1903, no. 2214; Clapp 1914, 264–265; Berenson 1938, no. 2214.

Berenson dated this study of drapery on a kneeling figure early and Clapp placed it 1515–1522, although he questioned its authenticity. There is no example of this type of conservative quattrocentesque drapery study in Pontormo's early work. This drawing is identifiable as Ridolfo Ghirlandaio's study for the kneeling St. Catherine in the *Marriage of St. Catherine* (La Quiete, Florence).

A155. ——— 6736F: Nude woman. 227 x 168, black chalk.

Bibliography: Berenson 1903, no. 2218; Clapp 1914, 266; Berenson 1938, no. 2218.

The authenticity of this slight sketch was rightly doubted by Clapp.

A156. ——— 6737F *recto*: Nude torso. (*Verso*: Same.) 155 x 195, black and red chalk on pink prepared paper.

Bibliography: Berenson 1903, no. 2219; Clapp 1914, 266–267; Berenson 1938, no. 2219.

Clapp dated this sheet 1530–1550. It is close in style to Pontormo's studies for the Careggi loggia (cf. cat. 312) and may be by one of his assistants on that project.

A157. ——— 6740F *recto*: Seated nude. (*Verso*: Studies for a *St. John the Baptist in the Wilderness*, cat. 166.) 410 x 286, red chalk.

Bibliography: Ferri 1890, 120; Berenson 1903, no. 2222; *MPA* 1910, 30; Gamba 1912, no. 7, pl. 7; Clapp 1914, 268–269; Berenson 1938, no. 2222.

This drawing has generally been accepted as a study for a *St. John the Baptist in the Wilderness* of ca. 1520–1521, part of a series of studies of this subject by Pontormo (cat. 161–166). It is closely related to cat. 161, but careful examination suggests that it is a copy after a lost variant of that drawing. Note especially the caricature of Pontormo's intense facial expression, the unsure articulation of the right hand, the inconsistent modelling and flat outline of the left leg. Certain characteristics of the draughtsmanship are very close to cat. A37, A79 (also a copy of a Pontormo), and A117, all given here to Cavalori, and this study may also be attributed tentatively to him.

A158. ——— 6743F: Seated nude. 264 x 390, red chalk.

Bibliography: Berenson 1903, no. 2225; *MPA* 1910, 28; Clapp 1914, 272–273; Berenson 1938, no. 2225.

Clapp and Berenson considered this drawing to be a study for the Vertumnus of Poggio a Caiano, but it is a mannered exaggeration of Pontormo's drawing style of ca. 1520. Note the self-consciously curved and attenuated figure, the small feet and head, the patterning of the muscles. This study is now rightly attributed to Naldini in the museum.

A159. ——— 6745F *recto*: Nude torso seen from behind. (*Verso*: Writing.) 201 x 167, black chalk; W: Fleur-de-lis (B. 6895).

Bibliography: Berenson 1903, no. 2226; Clapp 1914, 274; Berenson 1938, no. 2226.

Berenson and Clapp accepted this variant of cat. A88, but both drawings are copies after a lost Pontormo study for the San Lorenzo *Resurrection of the Dead*.

A160. ——— 6751F: Five putti in clouds. 344 x 260, black chalk with touches of red chalk, squared.

Bibliography: Berenson 1903, no. 2232; Clapp 1914, 277–278; Berenson 1938, no. 2232.

Clapp dated this Correggesque study 1518–1522. It has no connection in style with Pontormo and is certainly not Florentine. It may be by one of the Campi, possibly Bernardino.

A161. ——— 6755F *recto*: Sprawling nude boy. (*Verso*: Architectural studies.) 280 x 330, red chalk. Collection: Leopoldo de' Medici, stamp recto (L. 2712).

Bibliography: Clapp 1914, 279; Berenson 1938, no. 2430A; Barocchi 1950, 145, 201–202, fig. 171 (recto).

This study was rejected by Clapp, given to Rosso by Berenson and Barocchi, the latter dating it before 1523. The drawing is certainly closely derived from Rosso in style and is now catalogued as follower of Rosso by the museum.

A162. ——— 6756F: Standing putto. 289 x 203, red chalk; laid down; inscribed:

Di Jacopo da Pontormo. Collection: Leopoldo de' Medici, stamp recto (L. 2712).

Bibliography: Berenson 1903, no. 2236; *MPA* 1910, 32; Clapp 1914, 279–280; Berenson 1938, no. 2236.

Clapp dated this putto study ca. 1518, while Berenson called it early. It is probably a Naldini inspired by a Pontormo original of that date such as cat. 34. Cf. Uffizi 7469F, a red chalk study by Naldini in this same manner, and, in this catalogue, cat. A86 and A158.

A163. ——— 6757F *recto*: Heavily draped figure. (*Verso*: Bust.) 206 x 83, red chalk; verso in black chalk and pen; inscribed verso: *Jacopo*. Collection: Leopoldo de' Medici, stamp recto (L. 2712).

Bibliography: Berenson 1903, no. 2237; Clapp 1914, 280; Berenson 1938, no. 2370B.

Clapp rejected this drawing and cat. A164, while Berenson at first accepted them and later assigned them to the school of Pontormo. These elongated figures and flattened masses of drapery certainly derive from the very late sixteenth century, although the hand is difficult to identify. Cat. A163 may be by the same hand as Uffizi 6440F, attributed unconvincingly by Marcucci (*Riv. d'A.* 28, 1953, 94, fig. 19) to Cavalori.

A164. ——— 6758F *recto*: Draped figure. (*Verso*: Bust of a woman.) 203 x 90, red chalk; verso in black chalk; inscribed verso: *Jacopo*. Collection: Leopoldo de' Medici, stamp recto (L. 2172).

Bibliography: Berenson 1903, no. 2238; Clapp 1914, 280; Berenson 1938, no. 2370C.

See cat. A163.

A165. ——— 7322F: Woman seen to the waist. 190 x 165, red chalk.

Bibliography: Tinti 1925, fig. 8; Berenson 1938, no. 2240A.

Berenson placed this drawing in Pontormo's middle period, but rightly remarked on its "seicento feeling." It is at present given convincingly to Lorenzo Lippi by the museum. Cf. Uffizi 2277S.

A166. ——— 13849F: Standing nude. 265 x 108, red chalk.

Bibliography: Berenson 1903, no. 2431; Clapp 1914, 283; Kusenberg 1931, 153; Berenson 1938, no. 2431; Barocchi 1950, 218, fig. 199.

Formerly attributed to Pontormo, this drawing was given to Rosso by Berenson, but was not accepted as such by Clapp, Kusenberg, or later by Berenson himself. This nude is too conventional and academic for either Pontormo or Rosso and Barocchi's attribution to Bacchiacca is more satisfactory. The drawing is now listed as Bacchiacca in the museum.

A167. ——— 13850F: Copy after Pontormo's lost compositional study for the Louvre *Madonna and Saints*. 275 x 204, pen and bistre over black chalk. Collection: Leopoldo de' Medici, stamp recto (L. 2712).

Bibliography: V/M, 1878/85, VI, 273n2; Clapp 1914, 104, 284.

This drawing was considered by Milanesi and Clapp to be a late sixteenth-century copy after cat. A43, which they thought to be Pontormo's compositional study for the Louvre altar. However, both cat. A43 and this much weaker drawing are copies after a lost Pontormo drawing.

A168. ——— 14415F *recto*: Standing boy in a full-sleeved blouse. (*Verso*: Nude boy.) 401 x 233, red chalk; inscribed verso: *Andrea del Sarto* and *Scuola di* . . .

Bibliography: Berenson 1903, II, 125; Berenson 1938, II, 247.

This sheet is still given to Pontormo although Berenson has rightly attributed it to Naldini. Berenson (no. 1674, fig. 853) noted another version of this drawing also by Naldini in Munich and considered both to be copies after a lost Andrea del Sarto study for the executioner in the Scalzo *Capture of the Baptist.* In these studies the figure moves in an opposite direction from the soldier in Andrea's study (Uffizi 659E) and thus they are more likely to be free variants of Andrea's drawing than copies after a similar study. This sheet is especially close in draughtsmanship to cat. A86 and A95, also given here to Naldini.

A169. ——— 14433F *recto*: Nude torso. (*Verso*: Faint landscape sketch.) 281 x 118, red chalk.

Bibliography: Berenson 1903, no. 2241; Clapp 1914, 284–285; Berenson 1938, no. 2241.

This study was dated about 1530 by Berenson and Clapp. There is no counterpart in Pontormo's drawings for this academic drawing after a statue.

A170. ——— 15661F *recto*: *Pietà.* (*Verso*: Tracing of figure on recto.) 228 x 169, black chalk; paper discolored by glue on verso.

Bibliography: Berenson 1903, no. 2242; Clapp 1914, 285; Berenson 1938, no. 2242.

This study for a Michelangelesque *Pietà* was dated late by Berenson, after 1545 by Clapp. In draughtsmanship it is imitative of Pontormo's San Lorenzo drawings.

A171. ——— 15666F: Three nude torsos. 197 x 247, black chalk; paper discolored by glue on verso.

Bibliography: Berenson 1930, no. 2245; Clapp 1914, 286; Berenson 1938, no. 2245.

Berenson and Clapp connected these studies with San Lorenzo, Clapp relating the figure on the left with a sketch on page fourteen of Pontormo's diary. The pose is somewhat related but this sheet is by an imitator of Pontormo's San Lorenzo drawing style.

A172. ——— 17410F: Torso of a seated nude woman. 257 x 196, black chalk.

Bibliography: Berenson 1903, no. 2246; Clapp 1914, 286; Berenson 1938, no. 2246; Tolnay 1950, 49.

Berenson, Clapp, and Tolnay considered this drawing to be a study for the San Lorenzo *Resurrection of the Dead.* However, it is closely related to Pontormo's drawing for one of the Careggi *Allegories* (cat. 314), and is probably a copy after a lost preliminary study for that figure. While close to Pontormo's Careggi nude studies (cf. cat. 315–318), the tight, mechanical quality of the modelling and the finishing of only certain parts of the figure suggest the hand of a copyist.

A173. ——— 17769F: Portrait study of a woman seen to the waist wearing a turban. 228 x 173, red chalk; W: Animal in a circle.

Bibliography: Berenson 1903, no. 2248; *MPA* 1910, 23; Clapp 1914, 288; Clapp 1916, 86; Berenson 1938, 317, no. 2248, fig. 977; Toesca 1943, 23, fig. 47; Becherucci 1943, 8, pl. 13; Becherucci 1944, 19; Alazard 1948, 155, fig. 44; *MF* 1952, 63; Marcucci 1953, 122n8; *MP* 1956 (Berti), 54.

This portrait drawing has been generally accepted as Pontormo, Clapp dating it 1530–1540, Becherucci and Berti toward 1540. However, if this study is compared with cat. 345 and 346, portrait studies of precisely this period, its unPontormesque qualities — an over-insistent fussiness in the definition of the features, a thin wavering line, and strong overtones of academicism — are immediately evident. While it is based in pose on a portrait formula developed by Bronzino (cf. the Frankfurt *Portrait of a Lady* or the *Lucrezia Panciatichi*) and Pontormo (cf. *Maria Salviati*), the resemblance is a generic one only and the draughtsmanship suggests a hand of the next generation. Marcucci has ascribed the drawing convincingly to Macchietti and it is now listed as Macchietti by the museum.

A174. ——— 17812F: Cupid. 368 x 199, red chalk.

Bibliography: Clapp 1914, 288.

This drawing was rightly rejected by Clapp and is now called anonymous Italian sixteenth-century by the museum.

A175. ——— 17819F: *St. Lawrence.* 214 x 360, red chalk; W: Acorn (B. 7435).

Bibliography: Berenson 1903, no. 2439; Clapp 1914, 288–289; K. Kusenberg, "Agnolo Bronzino," *OMD* 4 (1929), 37–38, pl. 42; Berenson 1938, no. 604A; Smyth 1949, 186; Emiliani 1960, pl. 61.

The erroneous attribution of this study for a *Martyrdom of St. Lawrence* to Pontormo was rejected by Berenson, who gave it to Rosso, an attribution with which Clapp agreed. Kusenberg identified it as Bronzino's study for his lunette of *St. Lawrence* at the Certosa. Berenson (1938) also gave the drawing to Bronzino and it is now listed as Bronzino by the museum. However, as Smyth has pointed out, Bronzino's *St. Lawrence* has quite a different composition and this drawing is unrelated to his early drawing style.

A176. ——— 17872F: Flying angel. Red chalk.

Bibliography: Clapp 1914, 289.

A drawing attributed to Baroccio that bears this inventory number in the Uffizi is not the flying angel that Clapp discussed and rejected as Pontormo.

A177. ——— 692S: *St. John the Baptist.* 236 x 227, red chalk.

This drawing and the following numbers (cat. A178–A198) from the Santarelli collection all bear the stamp of Emilio Santarelli (L. 907) and all are laid down. They are listed as Pontormo in the Santarelli catalogue, 1870, 61–62. This particular study is surely seventeenth-century. An attribution to Vanni is written on the mount.

A178. ——— 693S: *Holy Family.* 194 x 160, black chalk with bistre wash, squared.

This drawing is a pastiche of Andrea del Sarto motives by Jacopo da Empoli. Cf. Uffizi 9394F.

A179. ——— 694S: *Madonna and Child* 246 x 139, black chalk.

This Sartesque *Madonna and Child* is probably attributable to Maso da San Friano. For the same black chalk style cf. Uffizi 14426F.

A180. ——— 695S: *Madonna and Child.* 146 x 117, red chalk.

An attribution to Sguazzella is written on the mount of this study.

A181. ———696S: Bust of a female saint. 185 x 147, red chalk.

Santi di Tito is suggested on the mount as the author of this drawing.

A182. ——— 697S: Nude study. 321 x 213, red chalk.

An attribution to Vanni is written on the mount of this drawing.

A183. ——— 698S: Group of figures. 297 x 209, pen and bistre.

This drawing is a copy after the left side of the *Reconciliation of Pope Alessandro II and Federico Barbarossa* (Sala Regia, Vatican, Rome) by Giuseppe Porta, Il Salviati.

A184. ——— 699S: Angel. 129 x 103, red chalk.

This drawing is unrelated to Pontormo and may be late sixteenth-century Roman.

A185. ——— 700S: Sketches for a wall and ceiling decoration. 206 x 160, red chalk.

These studies for a decorative project with sketches of signs of the zodiac to the right may be by a mid- or late-sixteenth-century Florentine, but are not by Pontormo's hand.

A186. ——— 701S: Putto study. 98 x 101, red chalk.

This slight sketch of a reclining putto probably dates from the seventeenth century.

A187. ——— 702S: *St. John the Baptist.* 77 x 72, red chalk; sheet cut irregularly.

This drawing is a study for a kneeling infant Baptist to the left of a *Madonna and Child* group and is very close both in motive and draughtsmanship to Franciabigio. Cf. Uffizi 638S.

A188. ——— 703S: Nude woman seen from behind. 424 x 134, black chalk.

This drawing is another version of cat. A102, a copy after Bronzino.

A189. ——— 704S: Putto head. 321 x 226, black chalk.

In type and in draughtsmanship this putto head belongs to the circle of the late Bronzino.

A190. ——— 705S: *Madonna and Child.* 230 x 174, black chalk on yellow paper.

This drawing is possibly by Maso da San Friano.

A191. ——— 706S: *Madonna and Child with St. Anthony and a Bishop.* 280 x 211, black chalk.

This compositional study for an altarpiece is possibly by Foschi. Cf. the drawings published by M. Pouncey, "Five Drawings by Pier Francesco di Jacopo di Domenico Toschi," *Burl.* 99 (1957), 159, especially Oxford, Christ Church add. 8.

A192. ——— 707S: *Annunciation.* 154 x 307, red chalk.

Bibliography: Berenson 1903, no. 905; Berenson 1938, no. 905.

This drawing is quite unconnected with Pontormo. It is given to Ridolfo Ghirlandaio by the museum, to school of Ridolfo Ghirlandaio by Berenson.

A193. ——— 708S: *Visitation.* 299 x 224, pen and bistre over black chalk.

This drawing is a copy, by Battista Franco as suggested on the mount, of the central figures and the figure to the right behind them in Pontormo's SS. Annunziata *Visitation.*

A194. ——— 709S: *Madonna and Child.* 287 x 238, red chalk.

Attributions to Sguazzella and Siciolante, neither verifiable, are written on the mount of this drawing.

A195. ——— 710S. *Pietà.* 190 x 120, pen and bistre.

This compositional study for a *Pietà* is close in style to Naldini.

A196. ——— 711S: Lower part of a seated draped figure. 321 x 228, red chalk.

This drawing is rightly identified by a notation on the mount as an eighteenth-century copy after Baroccio.

A197. ——— 712S: *Madonna and Child with St. John.* 329 x 243, red chalk.

This compositional study of poor quality is unconnected with Pontormo.

A198. ——— 713S: Studies of heads. 159 x 130, red chalk.

This is a sheet of copies, probably after Andrea del Sarto.

A199. Florence, ex-Davanzati Collection (present location unknown): Copy after Pontormo's Uffizi *Birthplate.* 410 x 320, pen and bistre heightened with white on grey paper.

Bibliography: Clapp 1916, 130; *Art Treasures and Antiquities from the Famous Davanzati Palace*, American Art Galleries, New York, November 21–29, 1916, no. 996, illustrated.

As Clapp has noted, this copy probably dates from the very late sixteenth century.

A200. Florence, ex-Gabburri Collection (present location unknown): Copy after Pontormo's Visdomini altar. Ink and watercolor.

Bibliography: G. Campori, *Raccolta di Cataloghi ed inventarii inediti* (Modena, 1870), 524; Clapp 1916, 127.

In the description of the Gabburri Collection published by Campori, this drawing is described as follows: "No. 13. Altro compagno con quantità di figure di penna e acquarelli rappresentante la Virgine che siede in alto col Bambino Gesù, S. Giovambattista piccolo, S. Francesco e altri Santi. Opera singolarissima del celebre Jacopo da Pontormo: ed e lo stesso che si vede in una tavola da altare nella chiesa di S. Michele Bisdomini in Firenze." The work described was evidently a watercolor copy after the Visdomini altar. According to Clapp, the Gabburri Collection was sold to Kent in 1742 and later sold in London.

A201. Florence, ex-Lamponi Collection (present location unknown) *recto*: Bust of an old woman. (*Verso*: Head of a child.) 220 x 140, red chalk.

Bibliography: *Catalogue de la Collection Lamponi*, Florence, November 10–19, 1902, no. 356, pl. 20; Clapp 1916, 141.

The recto of this drawing is a copy after the figure to the extreme left of the Uffizi *Birthplate.*

A202. Frankfurt a/M., Städelsches Kunstinstitut 599: Study after a relief. 144 x 321, pen and bistre.

Bibliography: Clapp 1914, 289.

Clapp has rightly noted that this copy after an antique sarcophagus has no connection with Pontormo.

A203. Haarlem, ex-Koenigs Collection 292: Portrait of a man seated in a chair. 385 x 265, black chalk; inscribed: *Bronzino* and *N* [?]*: 016*. Collection: Wauters, stamp recto (L. 912); D'Hendecourt, sold Sotheby May 8–10, 1929, lot 242, fig. 100.

Bibliography: F. Lees, *The Art of the Great Masters as exemplified by drawings in the collection of Emile Wauters* (London, 1913), 87, fig. 100; V. R. Altena 1934, no. 619; Berenson 1938, no. 2250A.

Lees considered this drawing to be a portrait by Pontormo of Ottaviano de' Medici or his son Alessandro, while Berenson called it a portrait of a Florentine lawyer. Since it was destroyed in World War II (according to the Boymans-Van Beuningen Museum), we have not seen this drawing. However, the pictorial treatment and soft line as well as the general blandness of the conception do not accord with Pontormo's style. The drawing probably comes from a later sixteenth-century Florentine hand, perhaps an artist close to Cavalori. Cf. the very similar figures in Cavalori's *Conversation* (London, National Gallery 3941).

A204. Hamburg, Kunsthalle 21147: Study of a saint. 405 x 240, black chalk.

Bibliography: Berenson 1903, no. 2251; Clapp 1914, 290; Berenson 1938, no. 2251.

Berenson attributed this drawing to Pontormo, but Clapp rightly rejected it and it is now given to Cigoli by the museum.

A205. Kansas City (Mo.), William Rockhill Nelson Gallery of Art 44–58: Portrait study of a woman. 346 x 234, black chalk. Collection: Barnard; Dimsdale; Bale; Heseltine, sold Amsterdam, 1913, cat. no. 1, illustrated; Oppenheimer, sold Christie's July 13, 1936, cat. no. 174 (as Andrea del Sarto).

Bibliography: Berenson 1938, no. 140A; *Loan Exhibition of Old Master Drawings from Midwestern Museums*, Detroit Institute of Arts, 1950, no. 43, pl. 43; *Baltimore Exhib.* 1961, no. 61; Berenson 1961, no. 129C.

Berenson listed this portrait drawing as Andrea del Sarto, but it has been exhibited as a copy by Pontormo after Andrea. It is certainly a copy after a Sarto drawing (Paris, Lugt Collection J5572), but its timid and mechanical draughtsmanship has no connection whatever with Pontormo.

A206. London, British Museum 1854–6–28–11: Seated man. 361 x 248, black chalk heightened with white on blue paper.

Bibliography: Clapp 1914, 290–291.

The erroneous attribution of this drawing to Pontormo was already rejected by Clapp and it is now listed as Daniele da Volterra by the museum.

A207. ——— 1870–8–13–891 *recto*: Seated man. (*Verso*: Same.) 315 x 186, red chalk. Collection: Richardson, inscribed recto (L. 2184); Spencer, stamp recto (L. 1532); Parsons.

Bibliography: G. Morelli, "Handzeichnungen italienischer Meister . . . ," *Kunstchronik* 3 (1891/92), 525; Clapp 1914, 292–293; A. E. Popham, *Correggio's Drawings* (London, 1957), 169, fig. 50; A. O. Quintavalle, *Michelangelo Anselmi* (Parma, 1960), 119, fig. 70.

This drawing was formerly called Pontormo, but was rejected by Morelli and Clapp and is now rightly attributed to Anselmi.

A208. ——— 1910–10–13–4: Reclining nude and parts of four other nudes. 257 x 205, black chalk. Collection: Reynolds, stamp recto (L. 2364); Champernowne, inscribed recto (L. 153). Fig. 366.

Bibliography: Clapp 1914, 293–294.

Clapp dated this drawing 1550–1556 as a study for San Lorenzo, noting the connection in pose between the central figure and a sketch on page four of Pontormo's diary. Both the nude with his arm raised and the figure with his back turned who looks out over his shoulder occur in various San Lorenzo drawings (cf. cat. 373–375, 377–378) and in the copy after part of the *Resurrection of the Dead* (cat. A216). In cat. A216 the first figure appears just below the center to the right and the second at the right edge below. This drawing is not far from Pontormo's San Lorenzo studies in style, but the dryness and hesitancy of the line, together with the way the figures are arbitrarily cut off, suggest that it is not a preparatory study but a copy after a group from the *Resurrection of the Dead*.

A209. ——— 1946–7–13–627 *recto*: Study of a saint. (*Verso*: Hooded figure.) 330 x 155, red chalk heightened with white. Collection: Woodburn; Phillipps-Fenwick.

Bibliography: Popham 1935, 84, no. 3.

This drawing was wrongly attributed to Pontormo by Popham. It is now classified by the museum as after Taddeo Zuccaro.

A210. ——— 1946–7–13–1374 *recto*: Head of a man. (*Verso*: Studies after the Scalzo frescoes.) 255 x 182, red chalk. Collection: Woodburn; Phillipps-Fenwick.

Bibliography: Popham 1935, 84, no. 2.

According to Popham the head on the recto is Pontormo's study for the Evangelist in the Visdomini altar. It is now classified as after Andrea del Sarto.

A211. ——— 1946–7–13–1375 *recto*: Nude studies. (*Verso*: Studies of a flying figure.) 103 x 273, pen and brown ink. Collection: Lawrence; Woodburn; Phillipps-Fenwick.

Bibliography: Popham 1935, 84, no. 4.

According to Popham this drawing was for the San Lorenzo *Deluge*. It is now listed by the museum as anonymous Italian.

A212. ——— P.p. 1–57 *recto*: Nude studies. (*Verso*: Figure with putti.) 200 x 273, red chalk; verso in black chalk. Collection: Payne-Knight, stamp verso (L. 1577).

Bibliography: Berenson 1903, no. 2253; Clapp 1914, 294; Berenson 1938, no. 2253; Popham 1939, 29.

Popham found this drawing to be an example of Pontormo's "later mannerism." Berenson considered the recto of this sheet to be a study for the San Lorenzo *Deluge*, but there is little connection between these decorative nudes and those in Pontormo's *Deluge* studies (cat. 373–375). Rather, they derive in type from studies for the Careggi and Castello loggias of the thirties and may have been done by one of Pontormo's assistants at that time.

A213. ——— P.p. 2–101: *Madonna and Child with St. John.* 225 x 190, red chalk.

Bibliography: Wickhoff 1899, 214; Berenson 1903, no. 2254; Clapp 1914, 294–295; Berenson 1938, no. 2254.

This study was rightly rejected by Clapp. It is a characteristic drawing by Sogliani, preparatory to a picture similar to his *Madonna and Child with St. John* in the Uffizi.

A214. ——— P.p. 2–102: Half-length nude youth in a tondo. 242 x 222, red chalk; laid down.

Bibliography: Wickhoff 1899, 214; Berenson 1903, no. 2253A; Clapp 1914, 295; Clapp 1916, 49; Berenson 1938, no. 2253A; Smyth 1949, 189; Cox 1956, 17; *MP* 1956 (Berti), 34; Emiliani 1960, pl. 5; Berenson 1961, no. 2253A, fig. 942.

Clapp considered this drawing to be Pontormo's study for the *St. Matthew*, S. Felicita, an association that has been generally accepted. However, the imprecise definition of the face, the prettified features, the hard contours of the torso and arms, and the confused shading of the background are unparalleled in Pontormo's S. Felicita drawings. This drawing is, therefore, a copy after the tondo probably dating from the late sixteenth century. It will be noted that when this copy was made the tondo was mounted turned to the left so that the elbow did not mark the lower center of the composition and the lower arm was more nearly horizontal.

A215. ——— Sloane 5226: *Naming of St. John the Baptist.* 163 x 200, red chalk.

Bibliography: Clapp 1914, 295; Berenson 1938, no. 1763A; Berenson 1961, no. 1763A, fig. 785.

Clapp and Berenson both rejected this drawing as Pontormo, Berenson giving it to Naldini. However, it is correctly listed in the museum as Andrea del Sarto and is a preparatory study for the Scalzo fresco of this subject.

A216. London, Victoria and Albert Museum D.2154–1885: Copy after Pontormo's *Resurrection of the Dead*, San Lorenzo. 341 x 240, black chalk and bistre wash. Fig. 371.

This unpublished drawing is listed as Pontormo by the museum, but it is a copy of the late sixteenth or seventeenth century after a portion of his destroyed *Resurrection of the Dead*. The composition, with the rising floating nudes and the angels with trumpets above, is unmistakable. There are also several exact coincidences in motive between figures in this drawing and Pontormo's drawings for the fresco (cat. 378–379) or in other copies after the fresco (cat. A88, A208, A238, and A240).

A217. London, Victor Bloch Collection: Partially draped seated figure. 185 x 151, black chalk with touches of red chalk; W: Fleur-de-lis in a circle (B. 2109).

Bibliography. Cox 1956, 18, fig. 16.

This drawing is attributed to Pontormo but is a copy after one of the Patriarchs from the destroyed cupola of the Capponi Chapel. The *sotto-in-su* placement of the figure, its pose and proportions, and even the quality of the silhouette are singularly close to Pontormo's studies for the Patriarchs (cat. 264–266). This copy may be attributed to Jacopo da Empoli, by whom there are numerous similar chalk drawings (cf. Uffizi 9344F, 3453F etc.).

A218. London, ex-A. G. B. Russell Collection (present location unknown): Two studies of a horse.

Bibliography: "Drawings in the Collection of G. B. Russell," *Connoisseur* 66 (1923), 5, fig. 3; Berenson 1938, II, 301.

Berenson attributed this study to Pontormo as close in style to cat. 233, but it has no relation to his drawings and is probably North Italian.

A219. Milan, ex-Morelli Collection (present location unknown): *Tobias and the Angel*. Red chalk.

Bibliography: G. Frizzoni, *Collezione di Quaranta Disegni scelti dalla raccolta del Senatore Giovanni Morelli* (Milan, 1886), pl. 9; Clapp 1914, 295–296.

Clapp has rightly rejected the attribution of this very late sixteenth-century drawing to Pontormo.

A220. Munich, Staatliche Graphische Sammlung 10440: Nude studies. 75 x 136, black chalk; inscribed: *Pontormo*.

This unpublished study is attributed to Pontormo in the museum. It is an imitation of Pontormo's late style in the drawings for Careggi and Castello, perhaps by the same hand as cat. A151.

A221. ——— 11123 *recto*: Kneeling youth. (*Verso*: Hands.) 225 x 154, red chalk.

Bibliography: Berenson 1938, no. 2256B (as no. 11125). J. Shearman, "Andrea del Sarto's Two Paintings of the Assumption," *Burl.* 101 (1959), 133n44; Berenson 1961, no. 141C–1.

Berenson thought this drawing was datable ca. 1530 and that the kneeling figure on the recto was a possible study for the Pygmalion in Pontormo's *Pygmalion and Galatea*. Shearman has identified the recto as a study for the St. Margaret and the verso as a study for the St. James in Andrea del Sarto's *Assunta* (Pitti 225). Berenson later (1961) listed the sheet as Andrea, but also suggested the possibility that its author is Naldini. While evidently related to the *Assunta* figures, these drawings may well be copies after lost Andrea studies for the altar.

A222. ——— 12899 *recto*: Head of a child. (*Verso*: Studies for a *Madonna and Child.*) 268 x 203, red chalk heightened with white.

Bibliography: Weihrauch 1937/38, 29–30, fig. 6 (recto); Berenson 1961, no. 2256B–4 (as no. 14855).

Weihrauch connected the head of a child with the Christ in the *Madonna and Child with St. John* (Florence, Corsini Gallery 185), which he accepted as a Pontormo of ca. 1528. There is no more than a general similarity of type between the two heads, while the sketches on the verso place the sheet without doubt in the seventeenth century.

A223. ——— 14855: Nude bending to the right. 436 x 373, black chalk heightened with white on grey paper; W: Monogram of Christ (B. 94).

Bibliography: Weihrauch 1937/38, 30, fig. 7; Berenson 1961, no. 2256B–2 (as no. 12899).

Weihrauch gave this study to Pontormo and dated it 1521–1526. However, the museum attributes it to Annibale Carracci, to whose circle it certainly belongs.

A224. ——— 34948: Seated draped man. 245 x 160, black chalk on blue paper; W: Anchor in a circle (cf. B. 454–72).

Bibliography: Berenson 1938, no. 2256C.

This study and cat. 225 by the same hand were given to Pontormo by Berenson, who dated them in Pontormo's "Düreresque phase." However, this tight, carefully hatched manner of drawing has no connection with Pontormo's style, even when he was influenced by Dürer.

A225. ——— 34949: Drapery study. 140 x 125, black chalk on blue paper.

Bibliography: Berenson 1938, no. 2256D.

See cat. A224.

A226. ——— 42448: Draped arms and profile of a man. 270 x 195, red chalk; inscribed in the same hand: *Jacopo da Pontormo*; W: Fragment of a star. Collection: R. von Hoerschelmann, given to the museum in 1947.

This unpublished drawing is attributed to Pontormo by the museum. Since it is inscribed by the artist with Pontormo's name, it is undoubtedly a copy after motives from a Pontormo painting, probably of ca. 1518–1519 (cf. the profile with one to the far left of the *Joseph in Egypt*).

A227. Munich, ex-Private Collection (present location unknown): Copy after Pontormo's Carmignano *Visitation.* 225 x 165.

Bibliography: *Handzeichnungen*, A. Weinmüller, Munich, 1938, cat. 17, no. 573, pl. 23.

This drawing is a copy after Pontormo's *Visitation.*

A228. Naples, Galleria Nazionale Capodimonte 265 *recto*: Three studies of a kneeling woman. (*Verso*: Study for same.) Red chalk, 265 x 205; incribed: *Jacopo da Pontormo.*

Bibliography: C. Ricci, "Un Disegno di Andrea del Sarto," *Riv. d'A.* 3 (1905), 142–143, illustrated; Clapp 1914, 296; Fraenckel 1935, 180, pl. 28; Berenson 1938, no. 141D, fig. 917; Berenson 1961, no. 141D, figs. 863–864.

This sheet was formerly attributed to Pontormo. As was noted by Ricci, these are studies by Andrea del Sarto for the kneeling St. Catherine in the *Virgin in Glory* (Pitti 123).

A229. New York, Metropolitan Museum of Art: Compositional study of a *Madonna and Child with St. John the Baptist, St. Elizabeth, St. Francis, and a female martyr Saint.* 270 x 275, red chalk. Collection: Earl of Pembroke.

Bibliography: S. Strong, *Reproductions of Drawings by the Old Masters at Wilton House* (London, 1900), pt. 3, no. 26; Berenson 1903, no. 2370; Clapp 1914, 352; Berenson 1938, no. 2256G; *Italian Drawings 1330–1780*, Smith College Museum, 1942, no. 41; "Some Italian Drawings in the Metropolitan Museum," *Connoisseur* 110 (1942), 151, no. 7; Gamba 1956, 10, fig. 11; *Baltimore Exhib.* 1961, no. 64.

Strong attributed this drawing to Pontormo and it was accepted by Berenson, who dated it first ca. 1530 and then ca. 1520. Gamba placed it before Poggio a Caiano, reproducing the Louvre copy as the original. Clapp, however, noted that the St. John was the only figure close to Pontormo and thought it might be by a draughtsman such as Lappoli with corrections by Pontormo. This drawing is a pastiche based on motives from Pontormo's works between ca. 1515 and 1522. The saint to the left reflects Pontormo's drawings of ca. 1515–1516 (cf. cat. 14–15), and the St. Francis is related in conception if not in the exact pose to the St. Francis in the Visdomini altar. The arrangement of the Madonna, Child, and St. John is based on that of the Visdomini, but the precise motive of the Madonna and Child does not appear in Pontormo's work until the Pitti *Adoration* and cat. 194 of ca. 1522. The St. Elizabeth has no counterpart in Pontormo's work, while the way in which this figure and the saint on the left are disposed as firm vertical accents to the sides of the composition is quite uncharacteristic of Pontormo. We have not been able to verify Clapp's attribution to Lappoli, but the author of this drawing must have been someone like Lappoli who was close to Pontormo in these years. There is a copy of this drawing (Louvre Bible 1991) by Francesco Vanni, and another copy also attributed to Vanni (Uffizi 4725S) that shows only the Madonna, Children, and St. Elizabeth.

A230. New York, Pierpont Morgan Library IV 20: Four draped women, one with a child. 245 x 110, black chalk with pen and bistre heightened with white.

Bibliography: *J. Pierpont Morgan Collection of Drawings by the Old Masters formed by C. Fairfax Murray* (London, 1912), IV, pl. 20; Clapp 1914, 296–297; Berenson 1938, no. 2448D; Barocchi 1950, 226, fig. 224.

This study for a group of figures for a *Moses Striking the Rock* was wrongly attributed to Pontormo. Clapp rejected it and Berenson gave it to the early Rosso. Barocchi rightly doubted the Rosso attribution, suggesting that the drawing was Emilian, perhaps Girolamo da Carpi.

A231. ——— IV 21: Two drawings of arms mounted together. 75 x 135; 75 x 165, red chalk.

Bibliography: *Fairfax Murray Cat.* 1912, pl. 21; Berenson 1938, no. 2448E.

This drawing was attributed to Pontormo but was given to Rosso by Berenson. In these slight sketches there is no convincing connection with the drawings of either artist.

A232. New York, Robert Lehman Collection G. 242: Portrait study of a woman. 175 x 133, silverpoint and red chalk on grep prepared paper. Collection: Fairfax

Murray; A. G. B. Russell, stamp recto (L. 2770a), sold Sotheby May 22, 1928, lot 68 ill.; Oppenheimer, sold Christie's July 13, 1936, cat. no. 150, pl. 37.

Bibliography: Berenson 1938, no. 2370D; *Collection Lehman de New York*, Musée de l'Orangerie, Paris, 1957, no. 120; *The Lehman Collection*, Cincinnati Art Museum, 1959, no. 217, pl. 217.

This portrait drawing has been ascribed to Lorenzo di Credi, but Parker gave it to Pontormo in the catalogue of the Oppenheimer sale and Berenson listed it as school of Pontormo. Pontormo's early drawings are quite unconnected in style and in media with the late Quattrocento tradition from which this study derives. However, neither does it come from such a *retardataire* hand as Lorenzo di Credi. Eugene Carroll has made a plausible attribution to Rosso, dating the drawing ca. 1515 (verbal communication).

A233. ——— Seated nude turned to the left holding a pan pipes; below, the figure restudied with drapery on a smaller scale. 372 x 205, black chalk. Collection: Reynolds, stamp recto (L. 2364); Lawrence, stamp recto (L. 2445); Reitlinger, stamp verso (L. 2274a).

Bibliography: H. M. Calmann, *Old Master Drawings*, London, 1958, no. 9; Seiferheld, *Master Drawings*, New York, 1961, no. 2, pl. 2; Berenson 1961, no. 2255B.

This drawing has been ascribed to Pontormo, although without any suggestions as to date or other drawings with which it might be associable in style. There is a superficial connection with Pontormo's nudes of the late thirties (cf. cat. 316, 343), but the chiaroscuro is softer than Pontormo's and lacks his usual precise definition of forms, while the line is flat and without rhythmic accent (note especially the legs). The figure type — a standard academic derivation from Michelangelo's nudes — reveals the influence not so much of Pontormo but of the later Bronzino, to whose tradition this drawing of toward 1600 probably belongs.

A234. New York, Janos Scholz Collection: Bust of a nude youth. 157 x 127, red chalk. Collection: Piancastelli; Brandegee.

Bibliography: *Indianapolis Exhib.* 1954, no. 10, fig. 10; *Drawings of the Italian Renaissance from the Scholz Collection*, Indiana University etc., 1958, no. 38, fig. 38; Berenson 1961, no. 2256J.

This drawing has been called an autograph replica of cat. 269, Pontormo's study for the Virgin in the S. Felicita *Deposition*, to which it is virtually identical. However, there is no example in Pontormo's *oeuvre* of this sort of repetition, and this drawing must be a sixteenth-century copy after Pontormo's study.

A235. New York, Art Market (now William Hayes Ackland Memorial Art Center, Chapel Hill, N.C.): *Pietà*. 162 x 330, red chalk; inscribed: *Andrea nº 152*.

Bibliography: *Baltimore Exhib.* 1961, no. 63, fig. 63.

This drawing is a later sixteenth-century copy after Pontormo's compositional study for a *Pietà* of ca. 1520 (cat. 103).

A236. Oxford, Christ Church Library B. 29: *Pietà*. 342 x 320, black chalk; inscribed: *Alessandro Allorio*. Collection: J. Richardson.

Bibliography: Berenson 1903, no. 2257; C. F. Bell, *Drawings by the Old Masters in the Library of Christ Church Oxford* (Oxford, 1914), 76, fig. 91; Clapp 1914, 297 (as no. 224); Berenson 1938, no. 2257; *Christ Church Exhib.* 1960, no. 1, fig. 49.

Berenson, Bell, and Clapp considered this drawing to be a study for the S. Felicita *Deposition*. However, the composition is not similar to that of Pontormo's picture and the author of the drawing is Allori, as the inscription suggests. Cf. Allori's painting of a *Dead Christ with Angels* (Budapest. Szépmúvészeti Múzeum no. 166). An attribution to Allori has also been made by Philip Pouncey (quoted in the Christ Church Exhibition catalogue).

A237. ——— B. 30 *recto*: Reclining nude woman seen to the knees, bust of a woman, and a head of a bearded man. (*Verso*: Architectural studies.) 260 x 200, black chalk; W: Eagle in a circle with a crown above; fragment, the other half on cat. A238 (B. 207). Fig. 367.

Bibliography: Berenson 1903, no. 2258; Bell 1914, 76; Clapp 1914, 298 (as no. 318); Berenson 1938, 321n, no. 2258.

Clapp recorded an inscription on the former mount of this drawing: *Pontormo San Lorenzo di Firenze*. This drawing and cat. A238–A240 are still attributed to Pontormo, although Berenson, Bell, and Clapp have considered them to be copies after San Lorenzo. Berenson suggested that the copyist might be Bronzino or Allori and Clapp thought the hand was the same as cat. A259, which he gave to Allori. An attribution to Allori or his circle is convincing for this group of copies. A date in the last quarter of the century is also indicated by the watermark, which Briquet does not record before 1578. These drawings are almost certainly copies after the *Resurrection of the Dead*, part of the composition of which is recorded in cat. A216. The figures in this drawing are not found in cat. A216, but the reclining nude appears reversed at the center right of the drawing.

A238. ——— B. 31 *recto*: Two reclining nude women, one seen from behind. (*Verso*: Landscape.) 190 x 267, black chalk; W: Other half of a cat. A237; inscribed: *Jacopo da Pontormo*. Fig. 368.

Bibliography: Berenson 1903, no. 2259; Bell 1914, 76; Clapp 1914, 298–299 (as no. 319); Berenson 1938, 321n, no. 2259.

See cat. A237. Clapp recorded an inscription on the former mount of this drawing, which was also found on cat. A239 and A240: *di Jacopo da Pontormo studio per il quadro di San Lorenzo di Firenze*. The nude at the left appears twice in the copy of the *Resurrection of the Dead* (cat. A216) and the nude to the right occurs just above the center of the same copy.

A239. ——— B. 32 *recto*: Nude seen to the waist and a bust of a bearded man. (*Verso*: Horse head.) 276 x 195, black chalk; W: Eagle in a circle with a crown above (B. 207). Fig. 369.

Bibliography: Berenson 1903, no. 2260; Bell 1914, 76; Clapp 1914, 299 (as no. 320); Berenson 1938, 321n, no. 2260.

See cat. A237.

A240. ——— B. 33: Nude woman seen to the knees leaning to the right; to the left, indication of the arm of another figure who supports her. 280 x 210, black chalk. Fig. 370.

Bibliography: Berenson 1903, no. 2261; Bell 1914, 76; Clapp 1914, 299–300 (as no. 645); Berenson 1938, 321n, no. 2261.

See cat. 237. A similar figure is found to the right of the center of cat. A216, the copy after the *Resurrection of the Dead.*

A241. Paris, Bibliothèque Nationale B. 3a rés., p. 13: Seated nude boy with legs apart. 260 x 201, black and red chalk. Collection: Bibliothèque Sainte Geneviève, stamp recto (L. 2352).

Bibliography: Berenson 1903, no. 2335; Clapp 1914, 300; Berenson 1938, no. 2335.

Berenson's attribution of this drawing to Pontormo was rejected by Clapp. This drawing is Francesco Salviati's study for the Adam in the *Temptation* (Rome, Galleria Colonna no. 84) of ca. 1553.

A242. ——— B. 3a rés., p. 14: Seated nude seen from behind. 255 x 145, black chalk; inscribed: *Jacopo.*

Bibliography: Berenson 1903, no. 2336; Clapp 1914, 300; Berenson 1938, no. 2336.

Berenson accepted this study as Pontormo, but Clapp gave it to Allori. While not conspicuously close to Allori's style, this sketch certainly belongs to the circle of Bronzino and is perhaps by the same hand as cat. A68, A78, A89, A93, and A96.

A243. Paris, Ecole des Beaux-Arts 34163 *recto*: Portrait study of a woman. (*Verso*: Studies for the same.) 272 x 207, red chalk; written in the hand of the artist: *Biago . . . turch*[ino]. . . *naz*[o] *agu* [to]; and on the verso: *biago . . . turch* [ino]. Collection: Armand; Valton.

Bibliography: O. Fischel, "Eine Bildnisstudie von Andrea del Sarto," *Belvedere* I (1922), 32–33, fig. 12; Lavallée 1935, 30; Fraenckel 1935, 184; Berenson 1938, 289, no. 159A; *Paris Exhib.* 1958, no. 48.

Fischel, Fraenckel, and Berenson considered this drawing to be Andrea del Sarto's study for the *Portrait of Maria del Berrettaio* in the Uffizi, Fraenckel dating it ca. 1528. In spite of this clearly correct attribution, Lavallée gave this drawing to Pontormo as a copy after the painting, which he dated 1511–1513, and he mistook the handwriting for Pontormo's. This drawing is not comprehensible as a copy, and the image has the directness, solid roundness, and rich chiaroscuro that are specifically characteristic of Andrea's draughtsmanship. In the 1958 exhibition this drawing was restored to Andrea.

A244. ——— 34901 *recto*: Nude study. (*Verso*: Nude study.) 390 x 274, red chalk. Collection: Armand; Valton.

Bibliography: Lavallée 1935, 31; Berenson 1938, no. 998B.

This sheet was formerly attributed to Fra Bartolommeo, but was given by Lavallée to Pontormo, with whose style it has no connection. Berenson gave it to Granacci, dating it 1520–1530.

A245. ——— *recto*: Nude woman and two small nudes. (*Verso*: Kneeling figure.) 256 x 137, black chalk heightened with white, the small figures in pen, the verso in black chalk. Collection: Flury-Hérard, stamp recto (L. 1015); J. Masson, stamp recto (L. 1494A).

Bibliography: Lavallée 1935, 30; *Paris Exhib.* 1958, no. 36.

Lavallée suggested that this sheet was a Pontormo of ca. 1520, but in the 1958 exhibition it is listed as Naldini. The verso of this drawing is an early stage of Baroccio's preparation for the Virgin in the Prado *Notte* of ca. 1595. The figure is a rapid study of the pose, with only a slight suggestion of drapery. For later studies of the same figure cf. Uffizi 11550F, 11634F, 11636F. For the style of the recto cf. Uffizi 11339F and 11343F; and for the pen studies cf. Uffizi 1396F.

A246. ——— *recto*: Seated nude. (*Verso*: Standing nude.) 427 x 183, red chalk. Collection: Desperet, stamp recto (L. 721); Gigoux, stamp recto (L. 1164).

Bibliography: Lavallée 1935, 31; Berenson 1938, no. 605D, fig. 1003 (verso).

This drawing was formerly given to Michelangelo, but was attributed to Bronzino by Berenson, to Pontormo by Lavallée. Both sides of this academic sheet must be copies and there is no connection with either Pontormo or Bronzino. The nude on the recto is a free variant of the Ignudo to the right above the Cumaean Sibyl. The figure on the verso appears, slightly changed, in cat. A357.

A247. ——— Nude woman reclining. 388 x 268, red chalk. Collection: Mariette; Cornu.

Bibliography: Lavallée 1935, 32.

The old Mariette attribution of this sheet to Palma Giovane was seconded by Popham (note on mount), but it was wrongly given to Pontormo School by Lavallée.

A248. Paris, Institut Néerlandais (Lugt Collection) 3457: Copy after Pontormo's *Portrait of a Halberdier.* 220 x 167, black chalk squared; inscribed: *Zuccaro.*

Bibliography: V. R. Altena 1934, no. 618.

This drawing is given to Pontormo as a study for the *Halberdier*, but it is certainly a later sixteenth-century copy after the painting or after a completed study for it.

A249. ——— 4025 *recto*: Study for a fainting Virgin with three figures. (*Verso*: Hands.) 177 x 185, black chalk; inscribed: *Raffaelle.* Collection: Bateson, stamp recto (L. 2604A).

This drawing is attributed to Pontormo in the Lugt Collection, but it is Battista Franco's sudy for the group in the right background of his *Christ Falling under the Cross* (Bergamo) of 1552.

A250. ——— 4026: Bust of a dressed figure, right shoulder restudied. 275 x 413, black chalk on pink prepared paper. Collection: A. G. B. Russell, stamp recto (L. 2770a).

Bibliography: V. R. Altena 1934, no. 617.

These studies have been given to Pontormo, but they are much closer to Pocetti (cf. Uffizi 1564S).

A251. ——— 5906: Copy of Michelangelo's *Giuliano de' Medici.* 242 x 143, black chalk.

This copy is attributed to Pontormo in the Lugt Collection, but it is executed in a decorative manner that is quite unrelated to his style.

A252. Paris, Louvre, Cabinet des Dessins R.F. 497: Copy after Pontormo's Certosa *Resurrection.* 235 x 208, pen and bistre wash. Collection: Mariette, stamp recto (L. 1852); His de la Salle, stamp recto (L. 1333).

Bibliography: Clapp 1914, 332–333.

Clapp recognized this drawing as a copy after the Certosa fresco. It may be by Boscoli, to whom is ascribed another copy after the same work (cat. A7). Cf. also cat. A326.

A253. ——— 946: *Birth of the Virgin.* 420 x 570, red chalk; inscribed: *Pontormo.*

Bibliography: Clapp 1914, 302.

An old inscription gave this drawing to Pontormo, but as Clapp has seen, it has no relation to his style.

A254. ——— 947: Five dead nudes. 123 x 190, red chalk.

Bibliography: Berenson 1903, no. 2265; Clapp 1914, 302; Berenson 1938, no. 2265; Tolnay 1950, 49.

This drawing has been connected with the San Lorenzo *Deluge* by Clapp and Berenson, but called a youthful work by Tolnay. The subject of this study is reminiscent of the *Deluge*, but its style has no connection with Pontormo's drawings for that fresco (cat. 373–375).

A255. ——— 948: Kneeling man and woman holding a small nude figure. 270 x 235, black chalk.

Bibliography: Clapp 1914, 302–303; L. Marcucci, "Appunti per Mirabello Cavalori disegnatore," *Riv. d'A.* 28 (1953), 96, fig. 20.

The attribution of this drawing to Pontormo was rejected by Clapp, who rightly placed it after 1570. Marcucci has given it to Cavalori, dating the sheet 1570–1572. While this attribution is not convincing, this drawing is certainly by a Florentine draughtsman from the late sixteenth century.

A256. ——— 949: Five draped figures. 280 x 180, red chalk.

Bibliography: M. Reiset, *Notice des Dessins, Cartons, etc. . . . au Musée National du Louvre* (Paris, 1866), 60; Berenson 1903, no. 2450, pl. 179; Clapp 1914, 301–302 (as no. 517); Kusenberg 1931, 145, pl. 68; Berenson 1938, 323, no. 2450, fig. 1004 (as no. 189); Barocchi 1950, 200, fig. 172; Bacou 1955, no. 72.

This drawing was given by Reiset to Pontormo, but by Berenson to Rosso, an attribution that has been accepted by Clapp, Kusenberg, Barocchi, and Bacou, all of whom dated it before 1523.

A257. ——— 950: Composition with figures in front of a façade. 250 x 370, black chalk with bistre.

Bibliography: Clapp 1914, 303.

As Clapp has noted, this later sixteenth-century drawing has no connection with Pontormo.

A258. ——— 951: Nude boy squatting in profile left. 135 x 90, red chalk.

Bibliography: Berenson 1903, no. 2266; Clapp 1914, 303; Berenson 1938, no. 2266; C. Tolnay, *Michelangelo* III (Princeton, 1948), 153, fig. 273; Smyth 1955, 61.

Clapp rejected this drawing as Pontormo, but Berenson accepted it, and Tolnay believed that it was a Pontormo copy after a statuette in Leningrad attributed to Michelangelo as executed in 1524 for the tomb of Lorenzo de' Medici. Smyth has given the drawing to Bronzino, dating it ca. 1524. While the drawing may be derived in motive from the Leningrad sculpture, the puffy, structureless forms and the soft line place it in the later sixteenth century. It may probably be attributed to Jacopo da Empoli. Cf. cat. A23 and A71.

A259. ——— 952: *Isaac Blessing Jacob.* 208 x 360, black chalk. Collection: Baldinucci I, 161.

Bibliography: Clapp 1914, 303–304; O. Giglioli, "Un Chiaroscuro inedito del Pontormo nella Galleria degli Uffizi," *Boll. d'A.* 28 (1934/35), 341–343, fig. 2; Berenson 1938, 321, no. 2266A.

Clapp called this drawing a copy after a late Pontormo painting, although he did not know the *chiaroscuro* in the Uffizi. Giglioli considered it a copy after the Uffizi painting (see p. 317, n. 7). As Clapp suggested, the hand is probably Allori. This drawing and the following cat. A260–A319, as well as cat. A327–A333, are from the Baldinucci Collection. Most of them are sketchbook studies after Roman antiquities and other decorative studies that are quite unrelated to Pontormo's style and require no separate listings. Berenson 1938, nos. 2266A–2333, accepted most of these drawings as Pontormo (nos. 952, 954, 958–965, 969–1011, 1020–1025), while Clapp 1914, 304–331, accepted all but nos. 966, 967, and 1012 as authentic. In attributing these studies to Pontormo Clapp relied heavily on the identification of the handwriting that appears on them as Pontormo's. He dated the drawings 1535–1543, years during which he postulated a Roman trip for Pontormo. For detailed descriptions of these drawings see Clapp 1914, 304–331. For those drawings of the Baldinucci group that are of sufficient interest to merit individual discussion, see the entries below (cat. A260, A265, A327, A328, A329, A330, A332, and A333).

A260. ——— 953: *Venus and Cupid with the Three Graces.* 400 x 310, black chalk with bistre wash, squared. Collection: Baldinucci I, 162.

Bibliography: Voss 1913, 308–309, fig. 12; Clapp 1914, 304; Voss 1920, fig. 71; McComb 1928, 152–153; Berenson 1938, no. 605E; Smyth 1955, 57–58; Emiliani 1960, 89.

This drawing was identified by Voss as a study by Bronzino for the Ponte alla Carraia decorations for the marriage of Francesco de' Medici and Joanna of Austria in 1565. Clapp and Berenson considered it a copy after Bronzino, but McComb and Smyth rightly accepted it as a Bronzino. As noted by Philip Pouncey, a pendant to this drawing for the same series is found in Oxford, Christ Church Library (no. add. 1).

A261–A264. ——— See cat. A259.

A265. ——— 958 *recto*: Seated putto and a copy after Pontormo's *Portrait of a Halberdier.* (*Verso*: Architectural studies.) 224 x 158, pen and bistre wash over black chalk. Collection: Baldinucci I, 169.

Bibliography: Berenson 1903, no. 2268; Clapp 1914, 307; Clapp 1923, 65–66, fig. 47; Berenson 1938, no. 2268.

Clapp dated this sheet 1530, considering the putto for the second, unexecuted lunette at Poggio a Caiano. Berenson thought the putto was probably for the *Vertumnus and Pomona.* Clapp noted the connection of the other sketch with cat. 288 and thought it was a study for the same lost portrait. This sketch is a late sixteenth-century copy of the *Portrait of a Halberdier,* for which cat. 288 is the preparatory study. The putto is a copy after a lost Pontormo study for the putto seated on the wall to the left in the Poggio a Caiano lunette.

A266–A319. ——— See cat. A259.

A320. ——— 1013: *Madonna and Saints.* 353 x 335, pen and bistre wash heightened with white.

Bibliography: Clapp 1914, 325–326.

The attribution of this compositional study to Pontormo was quite rightly rejected by Clapp. His suggestion that it is by Pontormo's pupil Lappoli is not convincing, since the drawing is most certainly Roman, probably close to Perino del Vaga.

A321. ——— 1014: Lower part of a Trinity. 85 x 70, black chalk with bistre wash. Collection: Jabach, inscribed verso (L. 2959).

Bibliography: Clapp 1914, 326.

Clapp has rightly rejected the attribution of this drawing to Pontormo.

A322. ——— 1015: Nude standing profile right. 395 x 202, red chalk; inscribed: *Jacopo da Pontormo.*

Bibliography: Berenson 1903, no. 2327 (as no. 1018); Clapp 1914, 326; Berenson 1938, no. 2327 (as no. 1018); Bacou 1955, no. 69.

Clapp and Bacou dated this study 1519–1521. However, like cat. A324, this drawing is imitative of Pontormo's style of that period and is probably by Naldini.

A323. ——— 1016: Two ewers. 190 x 227, pen with bistre wash.

Bibliography: Clapp 1914, 326–327.

Clapp accepted this drawing as by Pontormo, but it is quite unconnected with his style.

A324. ——— 1017: Seated nude boy turned to the right, his torso restudied to the right. 400 x 285, red chalk heightened with white; inscribed: *J° Pmo*. Collection: Royal Collection, initials of A. Coypel recto (L. 478).

Bibliography: Berenson 1903, no. 2326; Clapp 1914, 327; Berenson 1938, no. 2326; Grassi 1947, 123, pl. 25; Bacou 1955, no. 70; W. R. Valentiner, "An Early Work by Francesco da San Gallo," *Scritti di Storia dell'arte in Onore di Lionello Venturi*, 1956, I, 364, fig. 4.

Clapp and Bacou dated this study 1519–1521, Grassi placed it 1520–1530, and Valentiner cited it as an instance of Pontormo's unbalanced Mannerist poses. This drawing certainly derives from Pontormo's drawings of the period around 1520 and, like cat. A322, is attributable to Naldini.

A325. ——— 1018: *Massacre of the Martyrs*. 540 x 455, black chalk with bistre wash. Collection: Jabach, inscribed verso of mount (L. 2959); Pricolt, inscribed verso of mount (L. 2953).

Bibliography: Berenson 1903, no. 2750; Clapp 1914, 327; Berenson 1938, no. 2750.

This drawing was rightly rejected by Clapp and was listed by Berenson as Sogliani.

A326. ——— 1019: Study for a *Resurrection*. 425 x 345, pen and bistre wash. Collection: Jabach, inscribed verso of mount (L. 2959); Pricolt, inscribed verso of mount (L. 2953).

Bibliography: Clapp 1914, 327–328.

Clapp recognized this drawing as a late sixteenth-century variant on the composition of Pontormo's Certosa *Resurrection*.

A327. ——— 1020: Seated nude boy with left leg drawn up. 425 x 282, red chalk. Collection: Baldinucci I, 163.

Bibliography: Berenson 1903, no. 2328; Clapp 1914, 328; Berenson 1938, no. 2328.

Clapp connected this drawing and cat. A328–A330 with Poggio a Caiano, dating them 1519–1521. This study is one of a series of four copies after Pontormo from the Baldinucci Collection, two of them (cat. A328 and A330) derived from known originals. This nude may be related to a lost Pontormo study for the Vertumnus of the Poggio a Caiano lunette (cf. cat. 135). Cat. 146, also for Poggio a Caiano, is an exact prototype for the draughtsmanship and physical type of the nude in this drawing. The author of this group of copies is probably Naldini.

A328. ——— 1021: Nude turned with arms lifted over his head. 420 x 275, black and red chalk heightened with white; W: Mountains. Collection: Baldinucci I, 164.

Bibliography: Berenson 1903, no. 2329; Clapp 1914, 328; Berenson 1938, no. 2329.

See cat. A327. This drawing is a copy, probably by Naldini, after a Pontormo study of ca. 1521 (cat. 189).

A329. ——— 1022: Two seated nudes. 295 x 420, red chalk. Collection: Baldinucci I, 165.

Bibliography: Berenson 1903, no. 2330; Clapp 1914, 329; Berenson 1938, no. 2330.

See cat. A327.

A330. ——— 1023: Three nudes. 415 x 285, red chalk; W: Mountains. Collection: Baldinucci I, 166.

Bibliography: Berenson 1903, no. 2331; Clapp 1914, 329; Berenson 1938, no. 2331.

See cat. A327. This drawing is a copy,

probably by Naldini, after a Pontormo study of ca. 1521 (cat. 188).

A331. ——— See cat. A259.

A332. ——— 1025: Old man and nude woman led by a blindfold cupid. 260 x 142, black chalk on grey prepared paper. Collection: Baldinucci I, 168.

Bibliography: Berenson 1903, no. 2333; Clapp 1914, 330–331; Berenson 1938, no. 2333.

Berenson dated this drawing late and Clapp placed it ca. 1545. This drawing is unconnected with Pontormo's late works, but the types closely correspond to those found in drawings and paintings of ca. 1519–1522. As Clapp has pointed out, the old man may be compared with the God Father in cat. 104 and with the *St. Anthony* (Uffizi). The woman is comparable in type to the Eve in cat. 104 and to the woman in the right lower corner of cat. 131 for Poggio a Caiano. The excited putto is very similar to the Christ Child in cat. 194 of ca. 1522. The mechanical regularity of the draughtsmanship and incompleted portions of the figures such as the man's left arm might suggest that this drawing is a copy after a lost Pontormo of ca. 1520. However, the friezelike arrangement of the figures is not at all Pontormesque and the drawing is more likely to be a pastiche by a close follower, similar in type to cat. A229 and perhaps by the same hand.

A333. ——— 1026: Group of entangled dead nudes, some in water. 260 x 742, black chalk. Collection: Baldinucci II, 3.

Bibliography: Clapp 1914, 331; V. Mariani, "Due Disegni del Bronzino al Louvre," *L'Arte* 29 (1926), 58–60, fig. 1; McComb 1928, 153; Berenson 1938, 321, no. 605A; Smyth 1949, 195; Smyth 1955, 78–79.

Clapp, Mariani, McComb, and Berenson believed this drawing was Bronzino's study for the part of Pontormo's San Lorenzo *Deluge* that he finished, Clapp allowing the possibility that it might be a copy by Bronzino after Pontormo. Smyth has, probably rightly, removed this drawing another step from Pontormo, considering it to be a copy after a Bronzino study or after Bronzino's part of the fresco, which we know from Vasari (V/M, VII, 602) was a strip one *braccio* in height at the bottom of the fresco. Cf. Louvre 1027 for a related study by the same hand.

A334. ——— 1029: *Venus and Cupid*. 280 x 410, black chalk.

Bibliography: Clapp 1914, 331.

This drawing was recognized by Clapp as a copy after the Michelangelo-Pontormo *Venus and Cupid* and is now catalogued as a copy by the museum.

A335. ——— 1674: *St. John the Evangelist*. 350 x 325, red chalk. Collection: J. Barnard, inscribed verso (L. 1420); J. Richardson Sr., stamp recto (L. 2183).

Bibliography: Berenson 1903, no. 2377; C. Gamba, "A Proposito di alcuni disegni del Louvre," *Ras. d'A.* 9 (1909), 37, fig. 1; Clapp 1914, 301 (as no. 461); Berenson 1938, no. 2377, fig. 929.

Formerly attributed to Andrea del Sarto, this study was given to Pontormo by Gamba, who considered it a study for the SS. Annunziata *Visitation*. Clapp rejected the attribution to Pontormo and Berenson has rightly ascribed it to Puligo. See Berenson 1938, no. 2370, fig. 928, for an analogous Puligo study of about the same date.

A336. ——— 1725: Copy after Pontormo's *Joseph in Egypt*. 210 x 280, pen and bistre wash.

Bibliography: Clapp 1914, 331.

As Clapp has noted, this drawing is a

copy after Pontormo's *Joseph in Egypt*, probably of the late sixteenth century.

A337. ——— 11094 *recto*: Decorative motives. (*Verso*: Same.) 300 x 260, pen and bistre.

Bibliography: Clapp 1914, 331–332.

This drawing is listed by the museum as sixteenth-century Italian school, but attributed wrongly to Pontormo by Clapp.

A338. Paris, ex-Rodrigues Collection (present location unknown): Head of a youth in a high cap. 235 x 170, black and red chalk.

Bibliography: Sale of the Rodrigues Collection, Drouot, Paris, November 28–29, 1928, no. 208, pl. 15; Berenson 1938, no. 2336C.

This drawing was given to school of Andrea del Sarto in the Rodrigues sale and to Pontormo by Berenson, but it is unrelated to either artist.

A339. Paris, ex-Private Collection (present location unknown): Seated nude. 250 x 110, red chalk with bistre wash. Collection: A. P. E. Gasc, stamp recto (L. 1131).

Bibliography: Sale of the Collection of Mme. X, Drouot, Paris, May 23, 1928, no. 42, pl. 5; Berenson 1938, no. 2336D.

Berenson attributed this drawing to Pontormo as for Poggio a Caiano, but it has no connection at all with his drawings and probably dates from the seventeenth century.

A340. Princeton (N.J.) Art Museum: *Raising of Lazarus*. 307 x 203, black chalk with pen and bistre wash heightened with white, squared. Collection: F. J. Mather.

Bibliography: F. J. Mather, "A Drawing for Pontormo's Lost Raising of Lazarus," *Art in America* (1927), 132–136, illustrated.

This compositional study was thought by Mather to be a preparatory drawing for Pontormo's lost *Raising of Lazarus* mentioned by Vasari (V/M, VI, 274). It certainly dates from later in the sixteenth century, is Roman rather than Florentine, and may be by Taddeo Zuccaro (cf. Uffizi 11218F).

A341. ——— 44.264: Bust of a boy in a cap. 345 x 210, red chalk. Collection: F. J. Mather, stamp recto (L. 1853A).

Bibliography: Berenson 1938, no. 2369B; Berenson 1961, no. 2336D-1.

Berenson gave this drawing to Pontormo, but it is a copy after the head of the youth to the left in Gozzoli's *Adoration of the Magi*.

A342. ——— 44.265: *Mars and Venus*. 366 x 272, pen and bistre on brown paper. Collection: F. J. Mather, stamp recto (L. 1853A).

Bibliography: A. Neumeyer, *Exhibition of Old Master Drawings*, Mills College Art Gallery, 1937, no. 49.

This drawing was exhibited as "manner of Pontormo," but it is unrelated to his drawings.

A343. Rome, GNS F.C. 116: Three putto heads. 165 x 268, red chalk. Collection: Corsini; R. Accademia dei Lincei, stamp verso (L. 1683).

Bibliography: Berenson 1903, no. 2337; Clapp 1914, 334; Berenson 1938, no. 2337.

Clapp dated this drawing 1517–1520, while Berenson accepted it in 1903 but rightly rejected it in 1938. It is unconnected with Pontormo in style and may date from the seventeenth century.

A344. ——— F.C. 131: Scene of a *Martyrdom.* 167 x 123, red chalk with bistre wash; laid down. Collection: Corsini; R. Accademia dei Lincei.

This unpublished sheet is ascribed to Pontormo in the museum but it is a later sixteenth-century drawing.

A345. ——— F.C. 134 *recto*: Saint with a book and a cross. (*Verso*: Draped head and a figure.) 200 x 138, red chalk; figure on verso in black chalk. Collection: Corsini; R. Accademia dei Lincei, stamp verso (L. 2187).

This unpublished drawing is attributed to Pontormo by the museum, but it is probably Roman seventeenth-century.

A346. ——— F.C. 136: *Massacre of the Innocents.* 243 x 179, red chalk. Collection: Corsini; R. Accademia dei Lincei.

Bibliography: Clapp 1914, 347.

This drawing was rejected as Pontormo by Clapp. It is a study by Pocetti for the fresco of 1610 in the Ospedale degli Innocenti, Florence.

A347. ——— F.C. 141: Seated nude boy. 265 x 263, black chalk on tan paper; laid down. Collection: Corsini; R. Accademia dei Lincei.

This unpublished drawing is given by the museum to Pontormo or Pocetti, but it is not related in style to either artist. It is probably north Italian from the second half of the sixteenth century.

A348. ——— F.C. 142 *recto*: Seated nude and other sketches. (*Verso*: Nude studies, and a sketch for a *Holy Family*.) 408 x 290, red chalk; other sketches in black chalk; verso in red chalk with hand in black chalk; inscribed: *copia*. Collection: Corsini; R. Accademia dei Lincei, stamp recto (L. 1683).

Bibliography: Berenson 1903, no. 2368; Clapp 1914, 345–346; Berenson 1938, no. 2368; Schlegel 1961, 38n61.

Clapp dated this drawing 1517–1520 on the basis of the nude studies and *Holy Family* sketch, but did not know the recto. The seated nude on the recto is a copy after a lost Pontormo drawing of ca. 1520–1521, of which there exists another copy in Lille, Musée des Beaux-Arts no. 410 (incorrectly ascribed to Salviati).

A349. ——— F.C. 143 *recto*: Three studies of a nude woman. (*Verso*: Saint with a book, a profile and a head.) 262 x 198, black chalk over faint red chalk. Collection: Corsini; R. Accademia dei Lincei, stamp recto (L. 2187).

Bibliography: Berenson 1903, no. 2353; Clapp 1914, 345; Berenson 1938, no. 2366C.

Clapp dated this drawing ca. 1530 on the basis of the recto. Both draughtsmanship and figure types indicate a date later in the sixteenth century for this drawing.

A350. ——— F.C. 144 *recto*: Nude with a stick and a seated putto. (*Verso*: Nude.) 401 x 256, red chalk; putto in black chalk and ink. Collection: Corsini; R. Accademia dei Lincei, stamp recto and verso (L. 2187).

This unpublished sheet is ascribed to Pontormo by the museum. All three studies on this sheet are Pontormesque, yet in none of them is the attribution entirely satisfactory. The seated putto is the closest to Pontormo (cf. cat. 33 and 40 for the Visdomini altar), while the nude with the stick is an exaggerated imitation of his Sartesque drawings of ca. 1516 (cf. cat. 12 and 21). The more carefully academic nude on the verso is more distantly related to Pontormo, but there are analogies with studies such as cat. 8 of ca. 1514. This sheet must be by a contemporary imitator of Pontormo's pre-1520 drawings, but the hand is difficult to identify.

A351. ——— F.C. 145: Nude study. 399 x 265, red chalk; laid down. Collection: Corsini; R. Accademia dei Lincei.

This unpublished drawing is attributed to Pontormo in the museum, but it is a very late sixteenth-century study, probably after a sculpture. Berti (note on mount) has suggested school of Jacopo da Empoli.

A352. Rome, Private Collection: Nude seated in profile left. 290 x 100, red chalk. Collection: Vallardi, stamp recto (L. 1223); Locarno.

Bibliography: Grassi 1946, 41, fig. 7.

Grassi dated this drawing at the time of Poggio a Caiano, comparing it in style with cat. 137. While it shows a certain influence of Pontormo's drawings of this period, it is closer in style to drawings of the school of Bandinelli (cf. Uffizi 6541F and 14006F).

A353. Rotterdam, Museum Boymans-Van Beuningen I391 *recto*: *Madonna and Child.* (*Verso*: Head and hand.) 290 x 215, red chalk on grey prepared paper. Collection: Vallardi, stamp recto and verso (L. 1223); Böhler; Koenigs, stamp verso.

Bibliography: Berenson 1938, no. 2442B; Barocchi 1950, 227; Berenson 1961, no. 2458D–2.

This sheet is ascribed to Pontormo by the museum, given to Rosso by Berenson, but not accepted as such by Barocchi. This drawing is not by either Pontormo or Rosso, but both recto and verso show analogies with the drawings of Foschi, a younger contemporary influenced by both of them. Cf. the drawings published by M. Pouncey, "Five Drawings by Pier Francesco di Jacopo di Domenico Toschi," *Burl.* 99 (1957), 159, especially Oxford, Ashmolean Museum cat. 495.

A354. San Francisco, Art Market: Copy of Pontormo's *St. Cecilia*; below, drapery study. 260 x 203, black chalk; drapery study in red chalk. Fig. 95 (detail).

This unpublished drawing is considered to be Pontormo's study for the *St. Cecilia* lunette. However, it is a copy after the destroyed lunette or after Pontormo's *modello* for it. As such, it is of considerable documentary interest. It shows the figure with the "rose in mano" that Vasari mentioned (V/M, VI, 257), but which are only faintly indicated in Pontormo's compositional drawing for the lunette (cat. 93). This copy shows that the saint in the final composition was not half-draped as in cat. 94, but fully clothed as in another preliminary sketch (cat. 96). The copy also suggests that the putti indicated in cat. 93 were not present in the final version of the composition. This drawing certainly dates from the very late sixteenth century and is very close in style to Boscoli.

A355. Stockholm, National Museum 57: Two seated girls. 328 x 250, black chalk.

Bibliography: O. Sirén, *Dessins et tableaux de la Renaissance italienne dans les collections de Suède* (Stockholm, 1902), 46; Clapp 1914, 347; O. Sirén, *Italienska Handteckningar fran 1400– och 1500–Talen i Nationalmuseum* (Stockholm, 1917), 31.

This drawing was attributed to Pontormo by Sirén, but it was rejected by Clapp and subsequently restored to Allori by Sirén.

A356. ——— 58: Standing monk. 210 x 152, black chalk heightened with white on pink prepared paper.

Bibliography: Sirén 1902, 46; Clapp 1914, 347.

This drawing, once ascribed to Botticelli, was attributed to Pontormo by Sirén. However, as Clapp has seen, it is unconnected with his style.

A357. ——— 123: Two studies of a nude winged figure. 270 x 175, red chalk.

Bibliography: Sirén 1917, 28; Berenson 1938, no. 2370E.

Sirén gave this drawing to the school of Andrea del Sarto, while Berenson called it school of Pontormo and considered it to be close to Pontormo of ca. 1540. This late sixteenth-century drawing has no possible connection with the tradition of Andrea and Pontormo.

A358. Turin, Biblioteca Reale 15606 *recto*: Portrait study of a woman. (*Verso*: Three figures.) 254 x 213, black chalk; W: Fruit. Collection: Richardson, stamp recto (L. 2184).

Bibliography: Clapp 1914, 348; A. Bertini, "Disegni inediti del Pontormo e della Cerchia del Rosso nella Biblioteca Reale di Torino," *Boll. d'A.* 37 (1952), 312, fig. 5; A. Bertini, *I disegni italiani della Biblioteca Reale di Torino* (Rome, 1958), no. 379; Berenson 1961, no. 2458D–3.

This study was formerly attributed to Andrea del Sarto and to Pontormo, but it was rightly given to Sogliani by Clapp. Among the numerous drawings by Sogliani in the Uffizi that are close in style to this one cf. 14542F and 17015F. Bertini has given this drawing to the early Rosso. However, while it shows the influence of Rosso's types (cf. the woman with the book in the *Marriage of the Virgin* or the St. Catherine in the Dei altar), it is typical of Sogliani in draughtsmanship.

A359. ——— 15661 *recto*: Two embracing reclining nudes and a putto. (*Verso*: Standing nude woman.) 250 x 365, black chalk heightened with white on yellowish prepared paper; verso in red chalk heightened with white; W: Latin Cross (cf. B. 5641).

Bibliography: Bertini 1952, 310–311, figs. 1–2; *MP* 1956 (Berti), 17; Bertini 1958, no. 352; Berenson 1961, no. 2368A–3 (as no. 1565).

Bertini connected the recto with cat. 131 and 132 for Poggio a Caiano, relating the figures to those in the lower left corner of Pontormo's compositional studies. He dated the verso ca. 1520 as similar in draughtsmanship to cat. 103. Berti connected the figure on the verso with the statues in Pontormo's *Joseph in Egypt*. This sheet undoubtedly dates from ca. 1515–1520, but the analogies with Pontormo's works are not convincing. The planar arrangement of the figures on the recto as well as the secular subject indicate that it might have been a design for a frieze, a decoration of the sort executed by Andrea del Sarto (cf. the *chiaroscuri* in the Uffizi). The verso is also closer to Andrea than Pontormo and was probably a preparatory study for an allegorical figure in a similar decorative project. While the attribution may be made only tentatively, both sides of the sheet are suggestive of the drawing style of Sogliani.

A360. ——— 16007: Tritons and female nudes. 100 x 185, pen and bistre.

Bibliography: Clapp 1914, 348; Berenson 1938, no. 2460A; Bertini 1958, no. 383; Berenson 1961, no. 2460C.

This study (after an antique relief?) was formerly attributed to Pontormo, but given to the school of Rosso by Berenson and Bertini. As Clapp has pointed out, it is closer to the school of Raphael.

A361. ——— 16182 *recto*: Two standing nudes. (*Verso*: Legs of a figure seated on an ornamental throne.) 230 x 120, red chalk, verso squared; W: Shield with crossed keys and a fleur-de-lis with a star above.

Bibliography: A. Bertini, *Prima Mostra dei Disegni italiani della Biblioteca Reale*, Turin, 1950, 21, no. 56; Bertini 1952, 311–

312, figs. 3–4; *MP* 1956 (Berti), 40; Bertini 1958, no. 353.

This drawing was formerly attributed to Parmigianino, but was given to Pontormo by Bertini, who dated it ca. 1530 and associated the recto with the Pitti *Martyrdom*. These extremely attenuated and ornamentalizing figures are more characteristic of the later sixteenth century in Florence, in particular of the Studiolo painters. The pair of nudes on the recto is so close to those in the foreground of Maso da San Friano's *Diamond Mine* of ca. 1570 (Palazzo Vecchio) that an attribution of this drawing to him is quite plausible. The watermark on this sheet is not cited by Briquet prior to 1584–1585.

A362. Venice, Accademia di Belle Arti *recto*: Copy after the Christ from Pontormo's Certosa *Way to Golgotha*. (*Verso*: Lower part of a putto.) 370 x 261, red chalk; cut irregularly.

Bibliography: Bassi 1959, no. 23, fig. 23.

This (seventeenth-century?) copy is with the Pontormo drawings in the Accademia, but it was not recognized as such by Bassi, who called it a Tuscan drawing of ca. 1521.

A363. ——— *Brazen Serpent*. 270 x 190, black chalk.

Bibliography: Clapp 1914, 349.

This drawing and the following were rejected by Clapp. We have not been able to locate them in the collections of the Accademia.

A364. ——— Head of a man in a turban. 255 x 152, red chalk.

Bibliography: Clapp 1914, 349.

See cat. 363.

A365. Vienna, Albertina 86: *Birth of the Virgin*. 159 x 125, black chalk; laid down.

Bibliography: F. Wickhoff, "Die italienischen Handzeichnungen der Albertina: II. Die römische Schule," *Jahrbuch der Kunsthistorischen Sammlungen* 13 (1892), 16; Clapp 1914, 349; A. Stix and L. Fröhlich-Bum, *Beschreibender Katalog der Handzeichnungen in der Graphischen Sammlung Albertina*: III. Die Zeichnungen der Toskanischen, umbrischen und römischen Schulen (Vienna, 1932), no. 156.

This drawing was attributed to Pontormo by Wickhoff, but was listed as possibly Fra Bartolommeo by Stix and Fröhlich-Bum. It is perhaps by a late follower of Andrea del Sarto.

A366. ——— 138: Copy after Andrea del Sarto's Scalzo *Salome*. 274 x 421, red chalk.

Bibliography: Wickhoff 1892, 20; Clapp 1914, 350.

Wickhoff thought this copy after Andrea's fresco was by Pontormo, but it has no connection with his style.

A367. ——— 164: Portrait study of a woman. 390 x 244, black chalk with touches of red chalk in face and hands.

Bibliography: *Pantheon* 10 (1932), 301; Stix and Fröhlich-Bum 1932, no. 220; Berenson 1938, no. 2368C.

This drawing has been given to Pontormo, but is a copy of the later sixteenth century after a portrait of ca. 1510–1515 of the type of Bugiardini's *La Monaca* (Pitti).

A368. ——— 255: Seated nude. 343 x 243, red chalk; laid down.

Bibliography: Stix and Fröhlich-Bum, 1932, no. 221.

This drawing was attributed to the school of Pontormo, but it derives more closely from the style of Rosso. Michael

Hurst (note on mount) has suggested Bandinelli.

A369. ——— 261 *recto*: Head of a man, an ear, and a compositional sketch. (*Verso*: Compositional studies.) 274 x 202, red chalk, compositional studies in pen and bistre.

Bibliography: Stix and Fröhlich-Bum 1932, no. 219; Berenson 1938, no. 1766B; Berenson 1961, no. 1766G.

This drawing is wrongly attributed to Pontormo by Stix and Fröhlich-Bum. Berenson gave it to Naldini, but it is by Pocetti. The sketch to the right on the verso is a study for the *Sposalizio* in S. Pier Maggiore, while the head and the ear on the recto correspond to figures in the *Martyrdom of St. James Minor* in the same church.

A370. ——— 374: Copy after Pontormo's SS. Annunziata *Visitation*. 272 x 205, pen and bistre heightened with white. Collection: Vasari; Crozat; Mariette; Fries.

Bibliography: Wickhoff 1892, 37; Clapp 1914, 350.

Wickhoff and Clapp have noted that this sheet, traditionally attributed to Pontormo, is actually a copy after his *Visitation*.

A371. ——— 375: *Holy Women at the Foot of the Cross*. 101 x 60, pen and bistre wash.

Bibliography: Wickhoff 1892, 37; Clapp 1914, 350.

As Clapp has noted, this drawing and cat. A372–A373 were attributed wrongly to Pontormo. They are now listed by the museum as late sixteenth-century Florentine.

A372. ——— 376: *Christ in the House of Mary and Martha*. 102 x 86, pen and bistre wash.

Bibliography: Wickhoff 1892, 37; Clapp 1914, 351.

See cat. A371.

A373. ——— 377: *Christ in the House of Mary and Martha*. 101 x 85, pen and bistre wash.

Bibliography: Wickhoff 1892, 37; Clapp 1914, 350.

See cat. A371.

A374. ——— 378: Copy after Michelangelo's *Lorenzo de' Medici*; other sketches sideways on the sheet. 288 x 181, black chalk with touches of red chalk heightened with white on brown paper; laid down. Collection: Mariette, stamp recto (L. 1852); Fries, stamp recto (L. 2903).

Bibliography: Wickhoff 1892, 37; Berenson 1903, no. 2369; Clapp 1914, 351; Stix and Fröhlich-Bum 1932, no. 217; Berenson 1938, no. 2369.

Clapp rightly rejected this copy as unconnected with Pontormo. It may be by Federigo Zuccaro, to whom is attributed another stylistically identical study after the same statue (Earl of Rosebery Collection).

A375. ——— 444: *Triumph of Bacchus*. 262 x 405, pen and bistre over black chalk.

Bibliography: Wickhoff 1892, 41; H. Tietze, "Annibale Carraccis Gallerie im Palazzo Farnese," *JPK* 26 (1906), 115; Clapp 1914, 351; F. Antal, "Observations on Girolamo da Carpi," *AB* 30 (1948), 88n42; E. Wind, "A Note on Bacchus and Ariadne," *Burl.* 92 (1950), 85n2.

Wickhoff listed this drawing under Perino del Vaga, but inexplicably considered it closer to Pontormo. Clapp rejected this association and the drawing has been rightly discussed in the other literature as Raphael shop.

A376. ——— 24532 *recto*: Standing draped man and smaller figures. (*Verso*: Seated boy playing a violin.) 367 x 246, black chalk heightened with white, smaller figures and squaring of verso in red chalk.

Bibliography: Stix and Fröhlich-Bum 1932, no. 218.

This sheet is attributed to Pontormo, but it is surely by Cigoli. Cf. Uffizi 8918F (*Mostra del Cigoli*, San Miniato, 1959, no. 51, fig. 44).

A377. Vienna, ex-Geiger Collection (present location unknown): Nude woman seated on steps. 267 x 192, black chalk. Collection: Grahl; Geiger, sold Sotheby December 1920, no. 244.

Bibliography: L. Planiczig and H. Voss, *Drawings of Old Masters from the Collection of Dr. Benno Geiger* (Vienna, n.d.), no. 13, pl. 13; Berenson 1938, II, 287.

This drawing has been considered to be Pontormo's study for the woman on the steps in the SS. Annunziata *Visitation*, but it is a copy after a lost study for the figure. Cat. A95 is another copy after the same drawing.

A378. Vienna, ex-Klinkosch Collection (now Cleveland, Museum of Art 51.492): Half-length draped figure. 394 x 170, red chalk. Collection: Klinkosch, sold Vienna, April 15, 1889, no. 825, illustrated; von Lanna; Delacre, sold Berne, Gutekunst and Klipstein, June 21–22, 1949, no. 419, illustrated.

Bibliography: Berenson 1938, no. 2369A; Berenson 1961, no. 1957B and no. 2369A.

This drawing was attributed to Andrea in the Klinkosch and Delacre sales, but given to Pontormo by Berenson. It was acquired by the Cleveland Museum in 1951 as Andrea and listed by Berenson (1961) under Andrea with an attribution to Pontormo, but without reference to the earlier listing, which still stands in the 1961 edition. This study is unrelated to either Pontormo or Andrea, but is by Allori. Cf. Uffizi 10282F.

BIBLIOGRAPHY

CONCORDANCE: DRAWINGS OF THE FLORENTINE PAINTERS

REGISTER OF PLACES FOR DRAWINGS IN THE CATALOGUE RAISONNÉ

INDEX

BIBLIOGRAPHY

This chronologically arranged bibliography includes all items referred to in abbreviated form in the bibliographies for each entry (both drawing and painting) in the Catalogue Raisonné. It does not include items that occur only in the notes or in the List of Attributed Drawings. Full references for these items will be found in their first citation in the text.

1568 Vasari, G., *Le Vite de' più eccellenti pittori, scultori ed architettori*, 2 ed., Florence. *See also* Vasari 1878.

1584 Borghini, R., *Il Riposo di Raffaello Borghini*, Florence. *See also* Bottari 1730.

1591 Bocchi, F., *Le Bellezze della città di Fiorenza*, Florence. *See also* Cinelli 1677.

1677 Cinelli, G., ed., F. Bocchi, *Le Bellezze della città di Firenze*, Florence.

1684 Del Migliore, F., *Firenze città nobilissima*, Florence.

1730 Bottari, G., ed., R. Borghini, *Il Riposo di Raffaello Borghini*, Florence.

1754 Richa, G., *Notizie istoriche delle chiese Fiorentine*, 10 vols., Florence, 1754–1762.

1791 Moreni, D., *Notizie istoriche dei contorni di Firenze*, 6 vols., Florence, 1791–1795.

1828 Balocchi, G., *Illustrazione dell' I. e R. Chiesa Parrochiale di S. Felicita*, Florence.

1854 Waagen, G., *Treasures of Art in Great Britain*, vol. III, London.

1861 *Exposition des Beaux-Arts, concours régional de 1861*, Marseilles.

1867 *Catalogue Descriptive and Historical of the Works of Art in the National Gallery of Ireland*, Dublin.

1870 Santarelli, E., *Catalogo della raccolta di disegni autografi antichi e moderni, donata dal Prof. Emilio Santarelli alla R. Galleria di Firenze*, Florence.

1877 Gonse, L., "Musée de Lille: Le Musée Wicar," *Gazette des Beaux-Arts* n.s. 16, 555.

1878 Vasari, G., *Le Vite de' più eccellenti pittori, scultori ed architettori scritte da Giorgio Vasari pittore aretino*, G. Milanesi, ed., 9 vols., Florence, 1878–1885. *See also* Vasari 1568.

1881 De Tauzia, B., *Notice des Dessins de la Collection His de la Salle exposés au Louvre*, Paris.

Ferri, P., *Catalogo dei Disegni Esposti al Pubblico . . . nella R. Galleria degli Uffizi*, Florence.

1884 Jan, J., *Catalogue du Musée de la Ville de Rennes*, Rennes.

1889 Pluchart, H., *Notice des Dessins, Cartons, Pastels, Miniatures, et Grisailles exposés*, Lille.

1890 Ferri, P., *Catalogo riassuntivo della raccolta di disegni antichi e moderni posseduta dalla R. Galleria degli Uffizi di Firenze*, vol. I, Rome.

1892 Morelli, G., *Italian Painters: The Borghese and Doria-Pamfili Galleries in Rome*, trans. J. Ffoulkes, London.

BIBLIOGRAPHY

1896 Berenson, B., *The Florentine Painters of the Renaissance*, New York and London.

Woermann, K., *Handzeichnungen alter Meister im Königlichen Kupferstichkabinett zu Dresden*, vol. VI, Munich, 1896–1898.

1897 Schönbrunner, J., and J. Meder, *Handzeichnungen alter Meister aus der Albertina und anderen Sammlungen*, vol. IV, Vienna.

1898 Jacobsen, E., "Die Handzeichnungen der 'Uffizien' in ihren Beziehungen zu Gemälden, Sculpturen und Gebäuden in Florenz," *Repertorium für Kunstwissenschaft* 21, 263–283.

1899 Wickhoff, F., "Uber einige italienische Zeichnungen im British Museum," *Jahrbuch der preussischen Kunstsammlungen* 20, 202–215.

1903 Berenson, B., *The Drawings of the Florentine Painters*, 2 vols., London. *See also* Berenson 1938 and 1961.

1904 Gamba, C., "Un quadro del Pontormo a Carmignano," *Rivista d'Arte* 1, 13–18.

Schuchhardt, C., *Führer durch das Kestner Museum*, Hannover.

1905 Giglioli, O., "Il San Giovanni Evangelista e il San Michele dipinti dal Pontormo per la Chiesa di San Michele a Pontormo presso Empoli," *Rivista d'Arte* 3, 146–151.

The Vasari Society for the Reproduction of Drawings by Old Masters, Oxford, series 1, pt. 1, 1905–1906.

1907 Gamba, C., "Quadri nuovamenti esposti agli Uffizi," *Bollettino d'Arte* 1, no. 7, 20–22.

Rusconi, A., "I disegni di antichi maestri nella Galleria Corsini," *Emporium* 25, 262–275.

1908 Auquier, P., *Catalogue des Peintures, Sculptures, Pastels et Dessins, Ville de Marseille*, Musée des Beaux-Arts, Marseilles.

1909 Geisenheimer, H., "Gli arazzi nella Sala dei Dugento a Firenze," *Bollettino d'Arte* 3, 137–147.

Lafenestre, G., "Une Exposition de Tableaux Italiens," *La Revue de L'Art* 25, 5–22.

Trapesnikoff, T., *Die Porträtdarstellungen der Mediceer des XV Jahrhunderts*, Strasbourg.

1910 Gamba, C., "Un Ritratto di Cosimo I del Pontormo," *Rivista d'Arte* 7, 125–127.

Exhibition catalogue: *Mostra dei Disegni di Andrea del Sarto e del Pontormo*, Gabinetto Disegni e Stampe degli Uffizi, Florence.

1911 Clapp, F. M., *On Certain Drawings of Pontormo*, Florence.

Goldschmidt, F., *Pontormo, Rosso und Bronzino*, Leipzig.

Schulze, H., *Die Werke Angelo Bronzinos*, Strassburg.

1912 Di Pietro, F., "Due disegni di Jacopo da Pontormo finora attribuiti al Correggio," *Vita d'Arte* 10, 77–89.

Gamba, C., "Disegni di Jacopo Carucci detto il Pontormo," *I Disegni della R. Galleria degli Uffizi*, series I, fasc. 1, Florence.

1913 Voss, H., "Uber einige Gemälde und Zeichnungen von Meistern aus dem Kreise Michelangelos," *Jahrbuch der preussischen Kunstsammlungen* 34, 297–320.

1914 Bode, W., "Ein Paar Neuaufgefundene Gemälde des Sebastiano del Piombo," *Jahrbuch der preussischen Kunstsammlungen* 35, 5–8.

Clapp, F. M., *Les Dessins de Pontormo*, Paris.

Crowe, J. A., and G. B. Cavalcaselle, *A New History of Painting in Italy*, vol. XVI, New York.

1915 Goldschmidt, F., "Zeichnungen von Jacopo Carucci da Pontormo," *Amtliche Berichte aus den Königlichen Kunstsammlungen* 36, 84–93.

Schubring, P., *Cassoni: Truhen und Truhenbilder der italienischen Frührenaissance*, Leipzig.

1916 Clapp, F. M., *Jacopo Carucci da Pontormo, His Life and Work*, New Haven.

1919 Meder, J., *Die Handzeichnungen: Ihre Technik und Entwicklung*, Vienna.

1920 Giglioli, O., "Di un Disegno del Pontormo non identificato," *Bollettino d'Arte* 14, 36.

Tinti, M., *Bronzino*, Florence.

Voss, H., *Die Malerei der Spätrenaissance in Rom und Florenz*, vol. I, Berlin.

Exhibition catalogue: *Ausstellung von Zeichnungen alter Meister aus der Sammlung der Kunsthalle zu Hamburg*, Hamburg.

1921 Gamba, C., *Il Pontormo*, Florence.

1922 Mather, F., "The Halberdier by Pontormo," *Art in America* 10, 66–69.

1923 Clapp, F. M., "A Letter to Pontormo," *Art Studies* 1, 65–66.

1925 Friedlaender, W., "Die Entstehung des antiklassischen Stiles in der italienischen Malerei um 1520," *Repertorium für Kunstwissenschaft* 46, 49–86; trans. as "The Anti-Classical Style," in *Mannerism and Anti-Mannerism in Italian Painting*, New York, 1959.

Sinibaldi, G., "Una Predella del Pontormo attribuita ad Andrea del Sarto nella Galleria di Dublino," *L'Arte* 28, 153–158.

Tinti, M., "Un Romantico del Cinquecento," *Belvedere* 7, 113–119.

1926 Giglioli, O., "Disegni sconosciuti di Filippino Lippi e del Pontormo," *Dedalo* 7, pt. 3, 777–791.

1927 Panofsky, E., "Ein Bildentwurf des Jacopino del Conte," *Belvedere* 11, 43–50.

Pauli, G., *Zeichnungen alter Meister in der Kunsthalle zu Hamburg: Italiener*, Frankfurt am Main.

Schrey, R., "Frankfurt, Städelsches Kunstinstitut," *Stift und Feder*, Frankfurt am Main.

1928 McComb, A., *Agnolo Bronzino: His Life and Works*, Cambridge, Mass.

Voss, H., *Zeichnungen der italienischen Spätrenaissance*, Munich.

1929 Byam Shaw, J., "Andrea del Sarto," *Old Master Drawings* IV, 1929/30, 23–25.

1930 Fischel, O., "Dreizehnte Veröffentlichung der Prestel-Gesellschaft: Zeichnungen italienischer Meister in der Kunsthalle zu Hamburg," *Kunst und Künstler* 29, 480.

Hoffmann, E., *Italian Drawings*, Budapest Department of Prints and Drawings, Budapest.

1931 Bodmer, O., "Die Fresken in der Papstkapelle im Chiostro Grande von S. Maria Novella," *Mitteilungen des Kunsthistorischen Institutes in Florenz* 3, 355.

Delacre, M., "Sur deux dessins de Pontormo," *Bulletin des Musées de France* 3, 139–140.

Kusenberg, K., *Le Rosso*, Paris.

Meinhof, W., "Leonardos Hieronymus," *Repertorium für Kunstwissenschaft* 52, pt. 3, 14–124.

Popham, A. E., *Italian Drawings Exhibited at the Royal Academy, Burlington House, London, 1930*, Oxford.

Venturi, L., *Pitture italiane in America*, Milan.

The Vasari Society for the Reproduction of Drawings by Old Masters, Oxford, series II, pt. 12.

1932 Berenson, B., *Italian Pictures of the Renaissance*, Oxford; Milan 1936.

Lányi, J., "Pontormos Bildnis der Maria Salviati de' Medici," *Mitteilungen des Kunsthistorischen Institutes in Florenz* 4, 1932/34, 88–102.

Venturi, A., *Storia dell'arte italiana*, vol. IX, pt. 5, Milan.

Wild, D., "Ein Selbstbildnis Pontormos," *Josef Strzygowski-Festschrift*, Klagenfurt, 182–185.

1933 Fraenckel, I., "Jugendwerke Pontormos," in "Festschrift für Walter Friedlaender," 145–179; unpub. ms. in the Kunsthistorisches Institut, Florence.

Popham, A. E., "'Sheet of Studies by Jacopo Pontormo," *British Museum Quarterly* 8, 65–66.

Exhibition catalogue: *Mostra del Tesoro di Firenze Sacra*, Convento di San Marco, Florence.

1934 Stscherbatscheva, M., "Ein neu aufgefundenes Bild Pontormos," *Belvedere* 12, 1934/36, 179–184.

Van Regteren Altena, J.Q., *Italiaansche Kunst in Nederlandsch Bezit*, Stedelijk Museum, Amsterdam.

1935 Fraenckel, I., *Andrea del Sarto*, Strasbourg.

Lavallée, P., *Art Italien des XVme et XVIme Siècles*, Ecole Nationale Supérieure des Beaux-Arts, Paris.

Popham, A. E., *Catalogue of Drawings in the collection formed by Sir Thomas Phillipps, Bart., F.R.S., now in the possession of his grandson, T. Fitzroy Phillipps Fenwick of Thirlestaine House, Cheltenham*, London.

Exhibition catalogue: *Exposition de l'Art Italien de Cimabue à Tiepolo*, Petit Palais, Paris.

1936 Berenson, B., *Pitture italiane del Rinascimento*, Milan.

1937 Weihrauch, H., "Einige unbekannte italienische Handzeichnungen in der Graphischen Sammlung zu München," *Münchner Jahrbuch der bildenden Kunst* n.f. 12, 1937/38, XXV–XXXII.

1938 Berenson, B., *The Drawings of the Florentine Painters*, 2 ed., 3 vols., Chicago. *See also* Berenson 1903 and 1961.

Dussler, L., *Italienische Meisterzeichnungen*, Frankfurt am Main.

1939 Popham, A. E., *A Handbook to the Drawings and Water-colours in the Department of Prints and Drawings*, British Museum, London.

Steinbart, K., "Der Gotiker Jacopo Carucci aus Pontormo," *Pantheon* 23, 3–12.

Wallis, A. A., "A Pictorial Principle of Mannerism," *Art Bulletin* 21, 280–283.

Exhibition Catalogue: *Mostra di Disegni Fiorentini del Cinquecento*, Gabinetto Disegni e Stampe degli Uffizi, Florence.

Exhibition Catalogue: *Mostra Medicea*, Palazzo Medici, Florence.

Exhibition Catalogue: *Masterpieces*

of Art: Catalogue of European Paintings and Sculpture from 1300–1500, New York World's Fair, New York.

1940 Dobroklonsky, M., *Catalogue of the Italian Drawings of the 15th and 16th Centuries, Collection of the Hermitage*, Leningrad; title trans. from the Russian.

King, E., "An Addition to Medici Iconography," *Walters Journal* 3, 75–84.

Mongan, A., and P. Sachs, *Drawings in the Fogg Museum of Art*, 3 vols., Cambridge, Mass.; 2 ed., 1946.

Exhibition Catalogue: *Mostra del Cinquecento Toscano*, Palazzo Strozzi, Florence.

1941 Dobroklonsky, M., "Un dessin de Pontormo à L'Hermitage," *Travaux du départment de l'art Européen, Musée de l'Ermitage* I, 29–40.

1942 Dussler, L., *Sebastiano del Piombo*, Basel.

1943 Becherucci, L., *Disegni del Pontormo*, Bergamo.

Toesca, E., *Il Pontormo*, Rome.

Tolnay, C., *History and Technique of Old Master Drawings: A Handbook*, New York.

1944 Becherucci, L., *Manieristi toscani*, Bergamo; 2 ed., 1949.

1945 Bassi, E., "Due Disegni inediti del Pontormo," *Emporium* 101, 82–85.

1946 Grassi, L., "Appunti sul Pontormo e i suoi Disegni," *Emporium* 103, 29–46.

Nicco Fasola, G., "Pontormo e Dürer," *Arti figurative* 2, 37–48.

Suida, W., "Titian's Portraits, Originals and Reconstructions," *Gazette des Beaux-Arts*, ser. 6, 29, 139–152.

Exhibition Catalogue: *Old Master Drawings*, Central Collecting Point, Landesmuseum, Wiesbaden.

1947 Grassi, L., *Storia del disegno*, Rome.

Nicco Fasola, G., *Pontormo o del Cinquecento*, Florence.

Procacci, U., *Mostra di opere d'arte trasportate a Firenze durante la guerra e di opere d'arte restaurate*, Florence.

1948 Alazard, J., *The Florentine Portrait*, trans. B. Whelpton, London and Brussels.

1949 Becherucci, L., *Bronzino*, Florence; 2 ed., 1952.

Smyth, C. H., "The Earliest Works of Bronzino," *Art Bulletin* 31, 184–210.

1950 Barocchi, P., *Il Rosso Fiorentino*, Rome.

Tolnay, C., "Les fresques de Pontormo dans le choeur de San Lorenzo à Florence," *Critica d'Arte* 33, 38–52.

Exhibition catalogue: *Trésors des Bibliothèques d'Italie IV–XVI Siècles*, Bibliothèque National, Paris.

1951 Marcucci, L., *Mostra di disegni d'arte decorativa*, Gabinetto Disegni e Stampe degli Uffizi, Florence.

Parigi, L., *I disegni musicali del Gabinetto degli Uffizi e delle minore collezione pubbliche a Firenze*, Gabinetto disegni e stampe degli Uffizi, Florence.

1952 Bertini, A., "Fontainebleau e la Maniera Italiana," *Emporium* 116, 147–164.

Molajoli, B., "La Mostra 'Fontainebleau e la Maniera italiana,'" *Bollettino d'Arte* 37, 368–369.

Paatz, W. and E., *Die Kirchen von Florenz*, 6 vols., Frankfurt am Main, 1952–1955.

Exhibition catalogue: *Old Master Drawings*, Leicester Museum and Art Gallery.

Exhibition catalogue: *Fontainebleau e la Maniera italiana*, Palazzo dell' Arte, Naples.

1953 Marcucci, L., "Girolamo Macchietti disegnatore," *Mitteilungen des Kunsthistorischen Institutes in Florenz* 7, 121–132.

Longhi, R., "Fontainebleau e la Maniera italiana," *Paragone* 43, 15.

Scharf, A., "The Exhibition of Old Master Drawings at the Royal Academy," *Burlington Magazine* 95, 351–356.

Tietze, H., "A Self-Portrait by Pontormo," *Gazette des Beaux-Arts*, ser. 6, 41, 365–366.

Wischnitzer, R., "Jacopo Pontormo's Joseph Scenes," *Gazette des Beaux-Arts*, ser. 6, 41, 145–166.

Exhibition Catalogue: *Drawings by Old Masters*, Royal Academy, London.

1954 Berenson, B., *Disegni di Maestri Fiorentini del Rinascimento in Firenze*, Florence.

Katalog der Gemälde alter Meister in der Niedersächsischen Landesgalerie Hannover, Hannover.

Exhibition catalogue: *Het Eerste Manierisme in Italië*, 1500–1540, Rijksmuseum, Amsterdam. Pontormo: L. Bianchi and L. Marcucci.

Exhibition catalogue: *L'Europe Humaniste*, Palais des Beaux-Arts, Brussels.

Exhibition catalogue: *Mostra di Disegni dei Primi Manieristi italiani*, Gabinetto Disegni e Stampe degli Uffizi, Florence. Pontormo: L. Marcucci.

Exhibition catalogue: *Pontormo to Greco: The Age of Mannerism*, John Herron Art Museum, Indianapolis.

1955 Bacou, R., "Choix de Dessins de Maîtres Florentins et Siennois," Louvre, Cabinet des Dessins, Paris.

Baldini, U., *Mostra di opere d'arte restaurate*, Ottava Esposizione, Gabinetto dei Restauri, Florence.

Marcucci, L., "An Early Drawing by Pontormo," *Burlington Magazine* 97, 250–252.

Oertel, R., "Pontormos büssender Hieronymus," *Mitteilungen des Kunsthistorischen Institutes in Florenz* 7, 111–120.

Sanminiatelli, D., "Mostra di Disegni dei Primi Manieristi italiani," *Burlington Magazine* 97, 96.

Smyth, C. H., "Bronzino Studies"; unpub. diss., Princeton University.

Exhibition catalogue: *Le Triomphe du Maniérisme Européen: de Michelange au Greco*, Rijksmuseum, Amsterdam.

1956 Baldini, U., *Itinerario del Museo della Collegiata*, Empoli.

Baldini, U., *Quaderni Pontormeschi* no. 1, "Catalogo," Empoli.

Berti, L., *Quaderni Pontormeschi* no. 5, "Sembianze del Pontormo," Empoli.

Cecchi, E., ed., *Jacopo da Pontormo: Diario*, Florence.

Cox, J., "Pontormo's Drawings for the Destroyed Vault of the Capponi Chapel," *Burlington Magazine* 98, 17–18.

Gamba, C., *Contributo alla Conoscenza del Pontormo*, Florence.

Marcucci, L., *Quaderni Pontormeschi* no. 3, "La 'Maniera' del Pontormo," Empoli.

Nicco Fasola, G., *Quaderni Pon-*

tormeschi no. 4, "Alcune Revisioni sul Pontormo," Empoli.

Sanminiatelli, D., "The Pontormo Exhibition in Florence," *Burlington Magazine* 98, 241–243.

Suida, W., *Paintings and Sculpture from the Kress Collection*, National Gallery of Art, Washington.

Vayer, L., *Meisterzeichnungen aus der Sammlung des Museums der Bildenden Künste in Budapest*, Budapest.

Catalogue of Pictures of the Italian Schools, National Gallery of Ireland, Dublin.

Exhibition catalogue: *Die Schönsten Zeichnungen des Museums*, Szépmüvészeti Múzeum, Budapest.

Exhibition catalogue: *Mostra del Pontormo e del Primo Manierismo Fiorentino*, Palazzo Strozzi, Florence. Paintings: L. Berti; drawings: L. Marcucci; paintings by other artists: U. Baldini.

1957 Bacou, R., "Ils Existent. Le saviez-vous?", *L'Oeil* no. 28, 22–29.

Lavin, I., "Observations on 'Medievalism' in Early Sixteenth Century Style," *Gazette des Beaux-Arts*, ser. 6, 50, 113–118.

Exhibition catalogue: *Italienische Zeichnungen 1500–1800*, Hamburger Kunsthalle, Hamburg.

Exhibition catalogue: *Treasures from the Pierpont Morgan Library, Fiftieth Anniversary Exhibition*, New York.

1958 Andrews, K., "Three Pontormo Drawings in the National Gallery of Scotland," *Burlington Magazine* 100, 436–437.

Baldini, U., and L. Berti, *II Mostra di Affreschi Staccati*, Forte di Belvedere, Florence.

Degenhart, B., P. Halm, and W. Wegner, *Hundert Meisterzeichnungen aus der Staatlichen Graphischen Sammlung München*, Munich.

Procacci, U., *La Tecnica degli antichi affreschi e il loro distacco e restauro*, Florence.

Musée de l'Ermitage, Départment de l'Art Occidental, Catalogue de Peintures, Moscow.

Exhibition Catalogue: *La Renaissance italienne et ses prolongements européens*, Ecole Nationale Supérieure des Beaux-Arts, Paris.

1959 Bassi, E., "Disegni dell'Accademia di Belle Arti," *Atti e Memorie dell' Accademia di Belle Arti di Venezia*, 50–53.

Del Massa, A., *Maestri italiani del Disegno*, Rome.

Friedlaender, W., "The Anti-Classical Style," in *Mannerism and Anti-Mannerism in Italian Painting*, New York. *See also* Friedlaender 1925.

Jeudwine, W. R., "Old Master Drawings — XII," *Apollo* 69, 114–116.

Keutner, H., "Zu einigen Bildnissen des frühen Florentiner Manierismus," *Mitteilungen des Kunsthistorischen Institutes in Florenz* 8, 139–154.

Seilern, A., *Italian Paintings and Drawings at 56 Princes Gate, London SW 7*, 2 vols., London.

Exhibition catalogue: *Great Master Drawings of Seven Centuries: A Benefit Exhibition of Columbia University*, M. Knoedler and Company, New York.

1960 Emiliani, A., *Il Bronzino*, Busto Arsizio.

Sinibaldi, G., *Italian Drawings: Masterpieces of Five Centuries*,

Exhibition organized by the Gabinetto Disegni, Galleria degli Uffizi, Florence, and circulated by the Smithsonian Institution, 1960–1961.

Sinibaldi, G., *Mostra di Disegni dei Grandi Maestri*, Gabinetto Disegni e Stampe degli Uffizi, Florence.

Exhibition catalogue: *Paintings and Drawings from Christ Church, Oxford*, The Matthiesen Gallery, London.

1961 Berenson, B., *I Disegni dei Pittori Fiorentini*, 3 ed., 3 vols., Milan. *See also* Berenson 1903 and 1938.

Fenyö, I., "Sur Quelques Dessins Italiens du XVIe Siècle," *Bulletin du Musée National Hongrois des Beaux-Arts* 19, 59–75.

Freedberg, S. J., *Painting of the High Renaissance in Rome and Florence*, 2 vols., Cambridge, Mass.

Freedberg, S. J., and J. C. Rearick, "Pontormo's Predella for the S. Michele Visdomini Altar," *Burlington Magazine* 103, 7–8.

Schlegel, U., "Ein Terrakotta-Modell des Frühmanierismus," *Pantheon*, 19, 28–38.

Thiem, C. and G., "Andrea di Cosimo Feltrini und die Groteskendekoration der Florentiner Hochrenaissance," *Zeitschrift für Kunstgeschichte* 24, 1–39.

Exhibition catalogue: *Bacchiacca and His Friends*, The Baltimore Museum of Art.

1962 Collobi, L., and Ragghianti, C., *Disegni dell' Accademia Carrara di Bergamo*, Florence.

Shearman, J., "Pontormo and Andrea del Sarto, 1513," *Burlington Magazine* 104, 478–483.

1963 Merritt, H. S., "The Legend of St. Achatius: Bachiacca, Perino, Pontormo," *Art Bulletin* 45, 258–263.

Sinibaldi, G., "Un Disegno del Pontormo," *Paragone* 14, no. 165, 41–42.

Tolnay, C., "Un disegno sconosciuto del Pontormo a Bergamo. Postilla a 'Gli affreschi del Pontormo nel coro di San Lorenzo a Firenze,' " *Critica d'Arte* 10, 43–45.

CONCORDANCE: DRAWINGS OF THE FLORENTINE PAINTERS

The Berenson catalogue numbers in this concordance are those of the 1938 edition as amended in 1961. When there are two numbers in the column on the right, the first refers to the recto of the drawing, the second to the verso.

BERENSON NO.	CATALOGUE NO.	BERENSON NO.	CATALOGUE NO.	BERENSON NO.	CATALOGUE NO.
55H	A20	1956	A15	1978	A42
110J	A27	1957	A16	1979	A43
117A	A28	1957A	254; 222	1980	289
121	A52	1957B	A378	1981	A44
129C	A205	1958A	328	1982	292
140A	A205	1959	3; 4	1983	104; 361
141C	A221	1959A	357	1990	A50
141D	A228	1959B	234	1991	A51
159A	A243	1959B–1	A22	1991A	A54
601A	A78	1959C	A46	1991B	A55
601B	A102	1959D	36; 73	2011	346; A56
601C	A113	1959E	A48	2012	175; 176
601D	A134	1959F	174	2013	308
604A	A175	1959G	74; 75	2014	101; A57
605A	A333	1960	A24	2015	A58
605D	A246	1961	A25	2016	355; 380
605E	A260	1962	103; 173	2016A	A59
905	A192	1963	15	2017	336
998B	A244	1964	A29	2017A	152
1754A	171; A4	1967	89	2017B	158
1754D	A5	1968	287; 295	2018	263; 237
1754E	A6	1969	A33	2019	146; 140
1754F	A12	1970	324; 345	2020	135; 147
1754G	A13	1970A	A34	2021	225; 226
1761D	37; 64	1971	A35	2022	A60
1763A	A215	1972	A36	2023	227
1766B	A369	1972A	210; 209	2024	264; 296
1766G	A369	1973	278	2025	33; 32
1954	A8	1974	236; 193	2026	A61
1954A	A3; 159	1974A	A37	2027	A62
1954B	13	1974B	28	2028	51; 76
1954C	A9	1975	223; 141	2029	A65
1955	172	1976	132	2030	A66
1955A	151; 139	1977	131	2031	377; 334
1955B	340	1977A	319	2032	198; 202

CONCORDANCE

BERENSON NO.	CATALOGUE NO.	BERENSON NO.	CATALOGUE NO.	BERENSON NO.	CATALOGUE NO.
2033	177;149	2080	A88	2126	A110
2034	149	2081	43; 1	2127	A111
2035	A67	2082	356	2128	A112
2036	11	2083	317	2129	320
2037	325	2084	316	2130	285; 302
2038	370	2085	368	2132	A114
2039	271	2086	329	2133	A115
2040	297	2086A	277	2134	A116
2041	A68	2087	294	2135	349; 197
2042	238; 339	2088	A89	2136	312
2043	A69	2089	266	2137	163
2044	178	2090	A90	2138	157
2045	12; 21	2091	337	2139	A117
2046	77; 78	2092	347; A91	2140	A118
2047	A70	2093	80; 81	2141	281; 282
2048	40	2094	162	2142	A119
2049	A71	2095	181	2143	160
2050	A72	2096	161	2144	211; 240
2051	200; 201	2097	A92	2145	279
2052	A73	2098	137; 182	2146	382
2053	58; 31	2099	A93	2147	217; 216
2054	A75	2100	20; 71	2148	208
2055	A76	2101	A94	2149	A121
2055A	34; 79	2102	A95	2150	A122
2056	A77	2103	298; 299	2151	150; 133
2057	22; 5	2104	318	2152	153
2058	144	2105	330	2153	61; 82
2059	228; 229	2106	A96	2154	286
2060	142; 156	2107	A97	2155	207
2061	381	2108	359	2156	269; 303
2062	283; 284	2109	300	2156A	241; A124
2064	A79	2110	A98	2157	242; 243
2065	6	2111	168	2158	244; 245
2066	A80	2112	265; 270	2159	65; 62
2067	A82	2113	A99	2159A	206
2068	367	2114	371; 362	2159B	130
2069	A83	2115	309; 310	2159C	145; 148
2070	327; 328	2116	A101	2159D	A125
2071	98; 179	2117	267	2160	224
2072	348	2118	323	2161	8; 2
2073	A84	2119	212	2162	83; 183
2074	A85	2120	A103	2163	246; 258
2075	A86	2121	169	2164	A126
2076	268; A87	2122	274	2165	335
2077	275	2123	343	2166	A127
2078	199	2124	A108	2167	196; 247
2079	138	2125	262; 239	2168	344

CONCORDANCE

BERENSON NO.	CATALOGUE NO.	BERENSON NO.	CATALOGUE NO.	BERENSON NO.	CATALOGUE NO.
2169	A128	2214	A154	2251	A204
2170	136; 134	2215	363	2252	195
2171	260; 259	2216	338	2252A	314; 333
2172	205	2217	90; 91	2252B	25; 45
2173	9; 10	2218	A155	2252C	252; 276
2174	67; 69	2219	A156	2253	A212
2175	26; 66	2220	311	2253A	A214
2175A	63; 57	2221	350	2254	A213
2176	19; 23	2222	A157; 166	2255	124
2177	70; 68	2223	185; 186	2255A	253; 215
2178	96	2224	305; 291	2255B	A233
2179	A129	2225	A158	2256	60; 38
2180	A130	2225A	48; 35	2256A	214
2181	280; 290	2226	A159	2256B	A221
2181A	331	2227	352	2256B–1	220; 218
2182	A131	2228	322	2256B–2	A223
2183	A132	2229	321	2256B–3	219; 221
2184	288; 304	2230	354	2256B–4	A222
2185	248; 213	2231	364	2256C	A224
2186	A133	2232	A160	2256D	A225
2188	A135	2233	373	2256E	52
2189	A136	2234	374	2256F	233
2190	A137	2235	375	2256G	A229
2191	A138	2236	A162	2256H	188; 189
2192	A139	2239	315	2256I	A1
2193	A140	2240	341; 332	2256J	A234
2194	A141	2240A	A165	2257	A236
2195	A142	2240B	39; 50	2258	A237
2196	A143	2240C	307	2259	A238
2197	A144	2241	A169	2260	A239
2198	358	2242	A170	2261	A240
2199	A145	2243	369	2265	A254
2200	A146	2244	353	2266	A258
2201	A147	2245	A171	2266A	A259
2202	16	2246	A172	2267	A261
2203	A148	2247	378; 379	2268	A265
2204	A149	2248	A173	2278	A266
2205	230; 231	2248A	A31	2279	A268
2206	A150	2248A–1	44; 49	2280	A269
2207	A151	2248A–2	A31	2281	A270
2208	A152	2248B	A32	2282	A271
2209	165; 184	2248C	84; 30	2283	A272
2210	143	2248D	261	2284	A276
2211	249; 250	2249	194	2284A–2325	A277–A318
2211A	192; 251	2250	187	2326	A324
2212	273	2250A	A203	2327	A322
2213	A153	2250B	253; 215	2328	A327

CONCORDANCE

BERENSON NO.	CATALOGUE NO.	BERENSON NO.	CATALOGUE NO.	BERENSON NO.	CATALOGUE NO.
2329	A328	2359	121; 56	2368C	A367
2330	A329	2360	54; 55	2369	A374
2331	A330	2361	128; 110	2369A	A378
2332	A331	2361A	59; 129	2369B	A341
2333	A332	2361B	111	2370A	A10
2334	97	2362	107; 126	2370B	A163
2335	A241	2362A	27	2370C	A164
2336	A242	2363	127; 109	2370D	A232
2336A	24; 72	2363A	42	2370E	A357
2336B	190	2363B	53	2377	A335
2336C	A338	2363C	105; 106	2398	A49
2336D	A339	2364	118; 119	2430A	A161
2336D–1	A341	2365	115; 116	2431	A166
2336E	191	2366	92; 108	2442B	A353
2336F	93; 94	2366A	113	2448D	A230
2336G	85; 86	2366B	167	2448E	A231
2337	A343	2366C	A349	2450	A256
2337A	114	2367	170	2458D–2	A353
2337B	29,120	2368	A348	2458D–3	A358
2337C	122	2368A	87; 88	2458H	A104
2338	112	2368A–1	14; 203	2460A	A360
2338A	41	2368A–2	255; 256	2460C	A360
2338B	123	2368A–3	A359	2556	A100
2338C	125; 46	2368B	376	2556	A123
2358	47; 117	2368B–1	257; 204	2750	A325

REGISTER OF PLACES FOR DRAWINGS IN THE CATALOGUE RAISONNÉ

The number on the left in each column is the museum or collection inventory number. (A dash indicates the lack of an inventory number.) The number on the right is the catalogue number in this book.

Amsterdam, Rijksmuseum
59:02 — A1

Bergamo, Accademia Carrara
2357 — 366

Berlin-Dahlem, Kupferstichkabinett
401 — A2
465*r* — A3
465*v* — 159
4195 — 13
4626*r* — 171
4626*v* — A4
5153 — A5
5716 — A6
7715 — A7

Berlin, ex-Beckerath Collection
—— A8

Besançon, Musée
D.1511 — A9

Bremen, Kunsthalle
1475 — A10

Brunswick (Me.), Bowdoin College, Walker Art Museum
204 — A11

Budapest, Szépmüvészeti Múzeum
—— 172

Cambridge (Eng.), Fitzwilliam Museum
—— A12

Cambridge (Mass.), Fogg Art Museum
1932.143 — A13
1932.144 — 340
1932.212 — A14
1932.342*r* — 151
1932.342*v* — 139

Chantilly, Musée Condé
103 — A15

Chapel Hill (N.C.), William Hayes Ackland Memorial Art Center
—— A235

Chatsworth, Duke of Devonshire Collection
—— A16
—— A17
—— A18
—— A19

Cleveland, Museum of Art
51.492 — A378

Dijon, Musée des Beaux-Arts
819 — A20

Dresden, Kupferstichkabinett
C65 — 357
C80*r* — 3
C80*v* — 4
—— A21

Edinburgh, National Gallery
D.1612*r* — 234
D.1612*v* — 235
2230 — A22

Empoli, Museo della Collegiata
—— 102

REGISTER OF PLACES

REGISTER OF PLACES

6520F*r*	33
6520F*v*	32
6521F	A61
6522F	A62
6523F	A63
6524F	A64
6525F*r*	51
6525F*v*	76
6526F	A65
6527F	A66
6528F*r*	377
6528F*v*	334
6529F*r*	198
6529F*v*	202
6530F*r*	177
6530F*v*	149
6531F	149
6532F	A67
6533F	11
6534F*r*	325
6534F*v*	326
6535F	370
6536F	271
6537F	297
6538F	A68
6539F*r*	238
6539F*v*	339
6540F	A69
6541F	178
6542F*r*	12
6542F*v*	21
6543F*r*	77
6543F*v*	78
6544F	A70
6545F	40
6546F	A71
6547F	A72
6548F*r*	200
6548F*v*	201
6549F	A73
6550F	A74
6551*Fr*	58
6551F*v*	31
6552F	A75
6553F	A76
6554F*r*	34
6554F*v*	79
6555F	A77
6556F*r*	22
6556F*v*	5
6557F	144
6558F*r*	228
6558F*v*	229
6559F*r*	142
6559F*v*	156
6560F	381
6561F*r*	283
6561F*v*	284
6562F	A78
6563F	A79
6564F*r*	6
6564F*v*	7
6565F	A80
6566F	A81
6567F	A82
6568F	367
6569F	A83
6570F*r*	327
6570F*v*	328
6571F*r*	98
6571F*v*	179
6572F	348
6573F	A84
6574F	A85
6575F	A86
6576F*r*	268
6576F*v*	A87
6577F	275
6578F	199
6579F*r*	138
6579F*v*	180
6580F	A88
6581F*r*	43
6581F*v*	1
6582F	356
6583F	317
6584F	316
6585F	368
6586F	329
6587F	277
6588F	294
6589F	A89
6590F	266
6591F	A90
6592F	337
6593F*r*	347

6593F*v*	A91	6632F*v*	239
6594F*r*	80	6633F	A109
6594F*v*	81	6634F	A110
6595F	162	6635F	A111
6596F	181	6636F	A112
6597F	161	6637F	320
6598F	A92	6638F*r*	285
6599F*r*	137	6638F*v*	302
6599F*v*	182	6639F	A113
6600F	A93	6640F	A114
6601F*r*	20	6641F	A115
6601F*v*	71	6642F	A116
6602F	A94	6643F*r*	349
6603F	A95	6643F*v*	197
6604F*r*	298	6644F	312
6604F*v*	299	6645F*r*	163
6605F	318	6645F*v*	164
6606F	330	6646F	157
6607F	A96	6647F	A117
6608F	A97	6648F	A118
6609F	359	6649F*r*	281
6610F	300	6649F*v*	282
6611F	A98	6650F	A119
6612F	168	6651F	160
6613F*r*	265	6652F*r*	211
6613F*v*	270	6652F*v*	240
6614F	A99	6653F	279
6615F*r*	371	6654F	382
6615F*v*	362	6655F	A120
6616F*r*	309	6656F*r*	217
6616F*v*	310	6656F*v*	216
6617F	A100	6657F	208
6618F	A101	6658F	A121
6619F	267	6659F	A122
6620F	323	6660F*r*	150
6621F	A102	6660F*v*	133
6622F	212	6661F	153
6623F	A103	6662F*r*	61
6624F	A104	6662F*v*	82
6625F	169	6663F	A123
6626F	A105	6664F	286
6627F*r*	274	6665F	207
6627F*v*	301	6666F*r*	269
6628F	A106	6666F*v*	303
6629F	A107	6667F*r*	241
6630F	343	6667F*v*	A124
6631F	A108	6668F*r*	242
6632F*r*	262	6668F*v*	243

REGISTER OF PLACES

INDEX

INDEX

INDEX

INDEX

INDEX

INDEX

INDEX

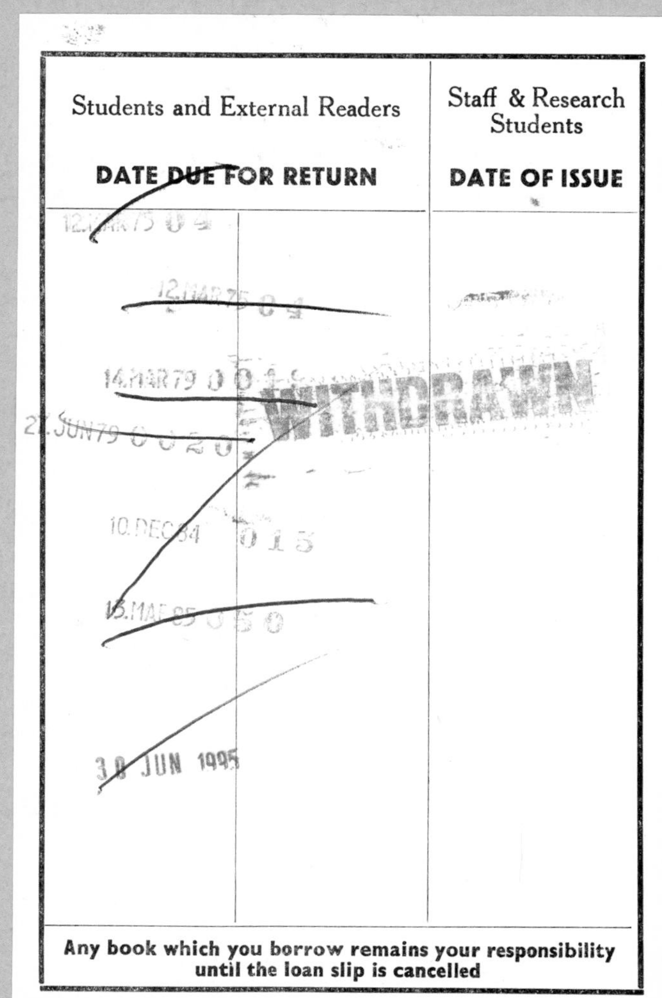